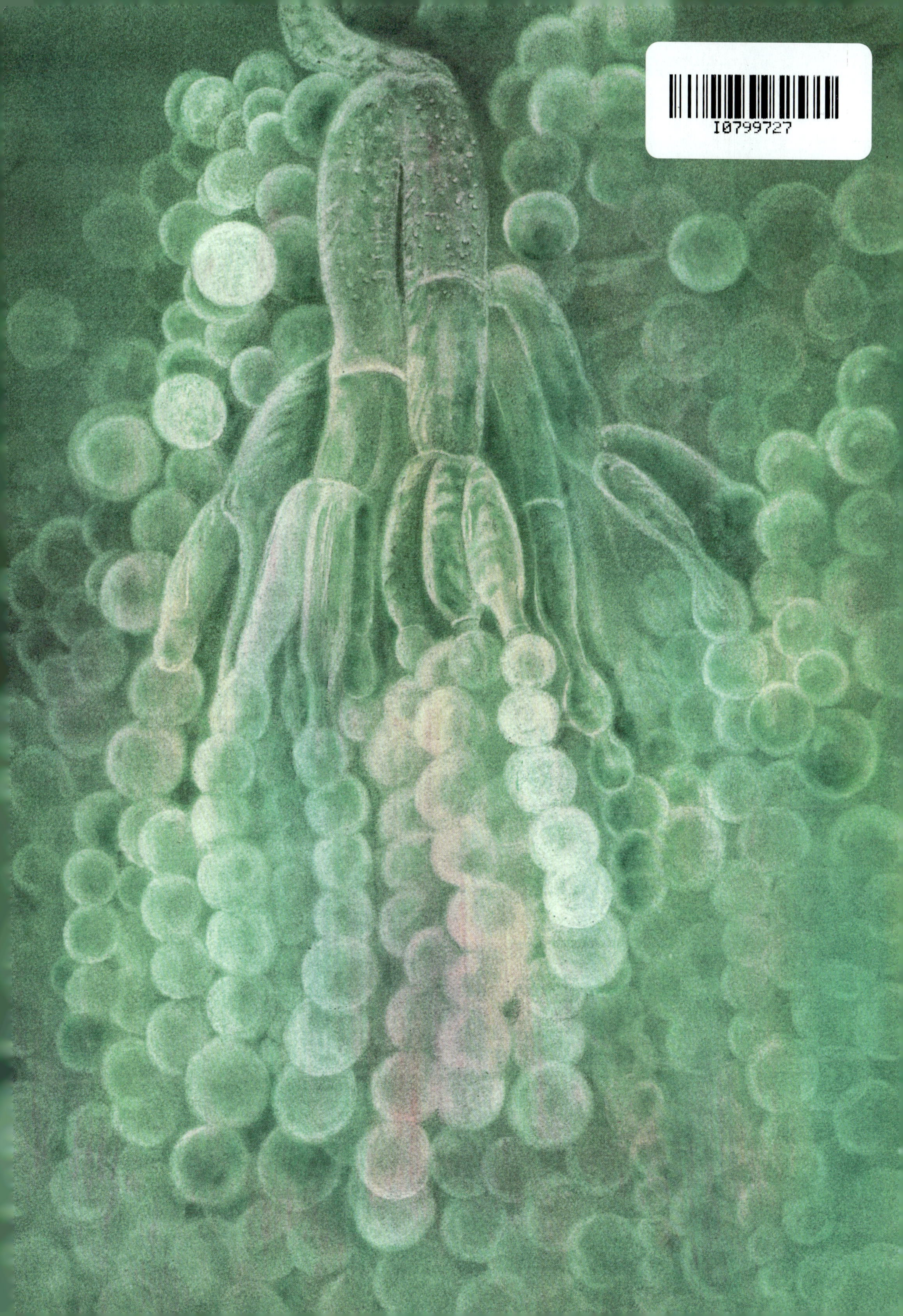

A ±
Z

Edition Angewandte – Book series of
the University of Applied Arts Vienna
Edited by Gerald Bast, Rector

Edition Angewandte – Buchreihe der
Universität für angewandte Kunst Wien
Herausgegeben von Gerald Bast, Rektor

edition:'ʌngewʌndtə
Universität für angewandte Kunst Wien
*University of Applied Arts Vienna*

Payer Gabriel

A±Z

# Payer Gabriel. Abwesenheit – Zufall / Absence – Accidental

DE GRUYTER

Pollenflug

Pollen

Pollen

Pollen

Pollen

Pollen

Pollen Pollen

Pollen

Mohn

Pilzspore

Orchidee

Stiefmütterchen

Tomate

Pfingstrose

Nelke

Meteorit

Ribisel

Warwick-Vase

Wurmfarn
Sporenbildung

Beere

Totenmaske
Dolly

welke Blätter

pollen drift

pollen

pollen

pollen

pollen

pollen

pollen pollen

pollen

poppy fungal spore

orchid

pansy

tomato

peony

carnation

meteorite

currant

Warwick vase

wood fern
spore production

death mask

berry

Dolly

withered leaves

Alphabet, Betagamm, Gammadelt

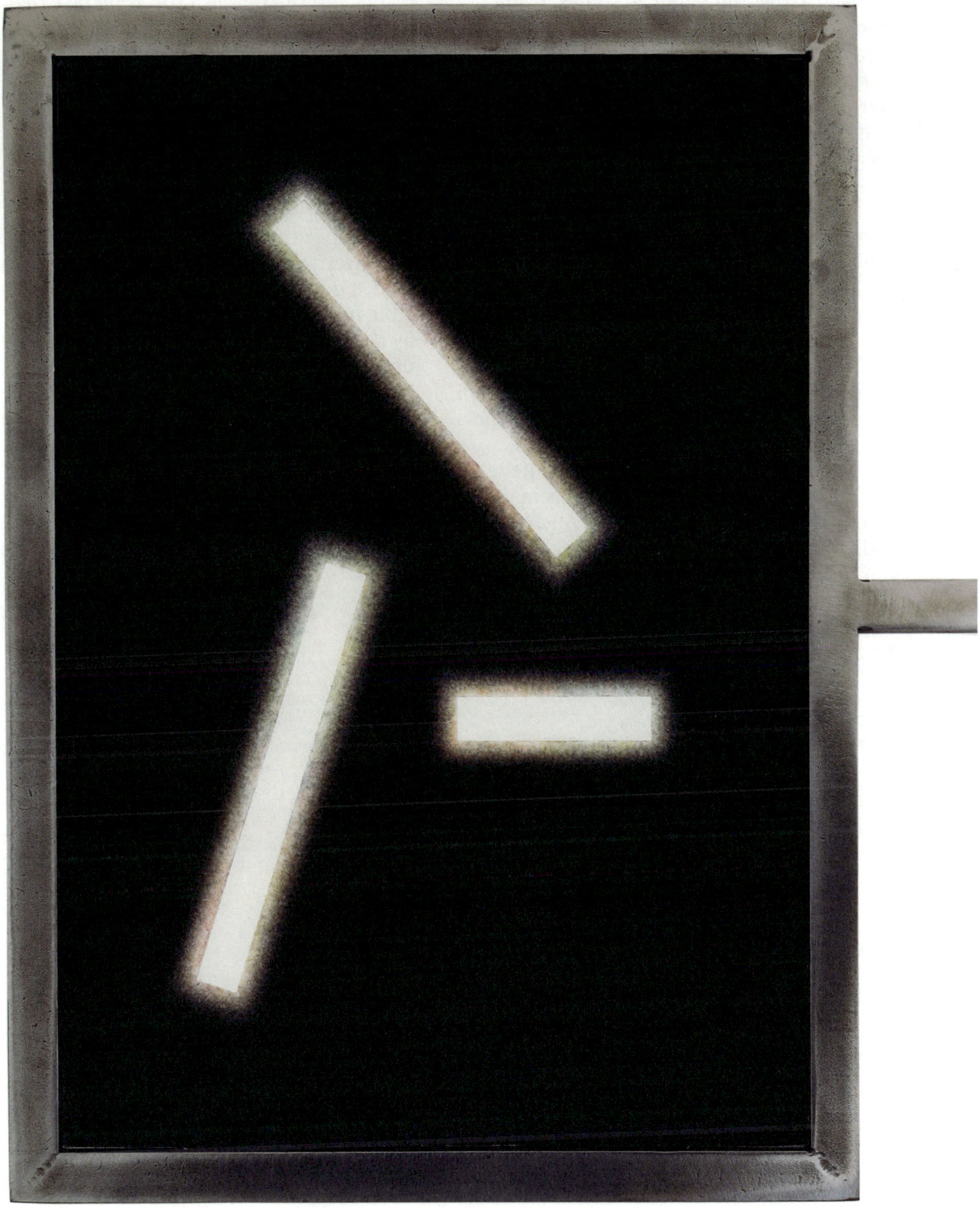

10

DE

„Am Anfang aller Erkenntnistheorie steht Angst – Angst, daß der Ariadnefaden der Vernunft zu kurz für die labyrinthische Welt ist; Angst, daß die Sinne zu schwach sind und der Verstand zu anfällig; Angst, daß das Gedächtnis schon zwischen zwei aufeinanderfolgenden mathematischen Beweisschritten versagt; Angst, daß Autorität und Konvention blind machen; Angst, daß Gott Geheimnisse für sich behält oder Dämonen uns täuschen. Objektivität ist ein Kapitel in dieser Geschichte intellektueller Ängste, sorgenvoll antizipierter Irrtümer und vorbeugender Gegenmaßnahmen. Aber Objektivität geht gegen eine Angst vor, die anders ist und tiefer sitzt als die anderen. Diese Bedrohung kommt nicht von außen – nicht aus einer komplexen Welt, von einem geheimnisvollen Gott oder einem trügerischen Dämon. Sie ist auch nicht die Sorge um die Schwäche der Sinne, die durch ein Teleskop oder Mikroskop behebbar ist, oder des Gedächtnisses, das man durch Merkzettel stützen kann. Auch individuelle Standfestigkeit gegenüber der herrschenden Meinung ist keine Hilfe gegen diese Angst, denn gerade das Individuum steht im Verdacht. Objektivität fürchtet Subjektivität, den Kern des Selbst.“

— Lorraine Daston und Peter Galison, *Objektivität*, übersetzt von Christa Krüger (Frankfurt am Main: Suhrkamp, 2017), 396.

EN

“All epistemology begins in fear—fear that the world is too labyrinthine to be threaded by reason; fear that the senses are too feeble and the intellect too frail; fear that memory fades, even between adjacent steps of mathematical demonstration; fear that authority and convention blind; fear that God may keep secrets or demons deceive. Objectivity is a chapter in this history of intellectual fear, of errors anxiously anticipated and precautions taken. But the fear objectivity addresses is different from and deeper than the others. The threat is not external—a complex world, a mysterious God, a devious demon. Nor is it the corrigible fear of senses that can be strengthened by a telescope or microscope or memory that can be buttressed by written aids. Individual steadfastness against prevailing opinion is no help against it, because it is the individual who is suspect. Objectivity fears subjectivity, the core self.”

— Lorraine Daston and Peter Galison, *Objectivity* (New York: Zone Books, 2007), 372–374.

11

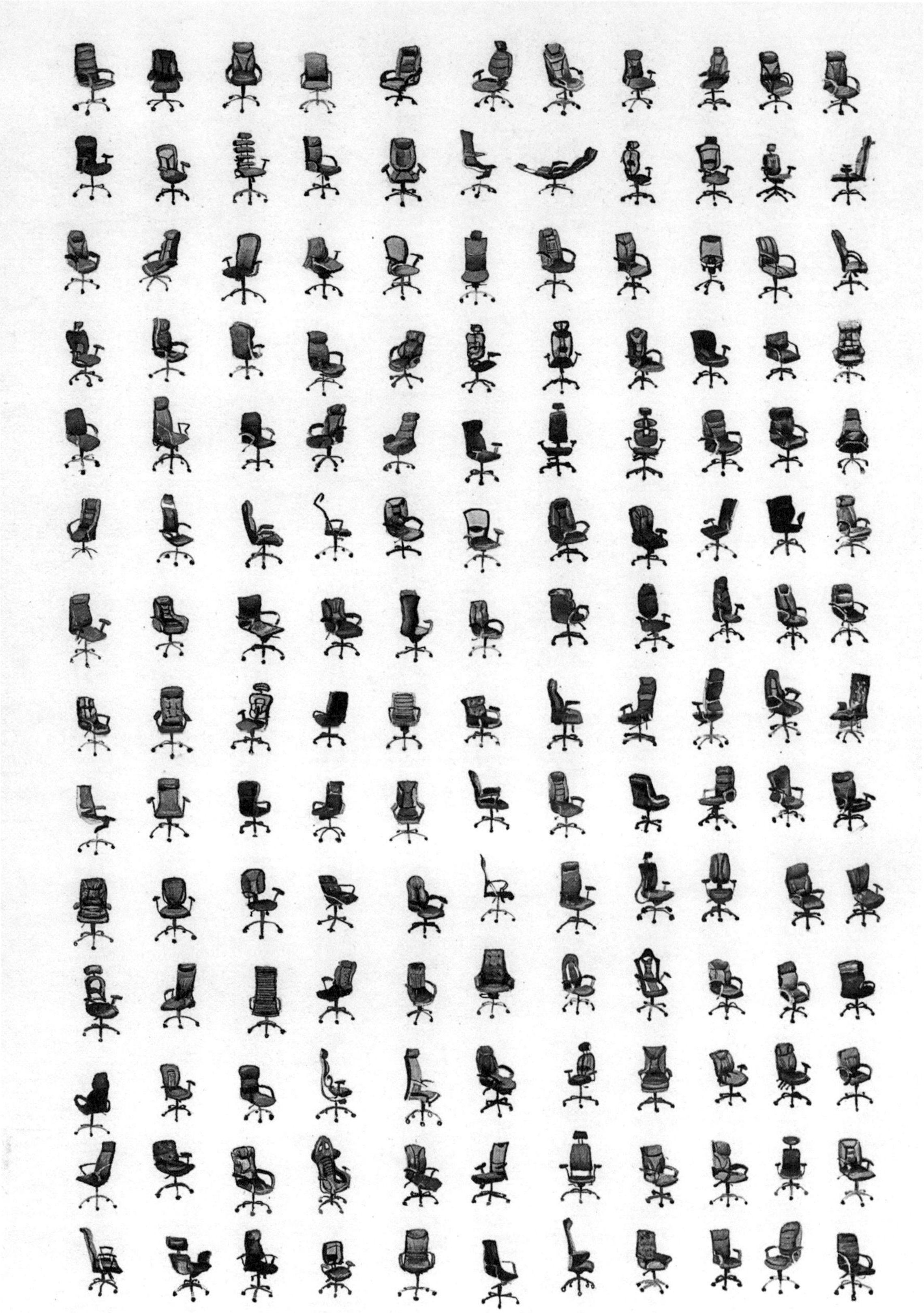

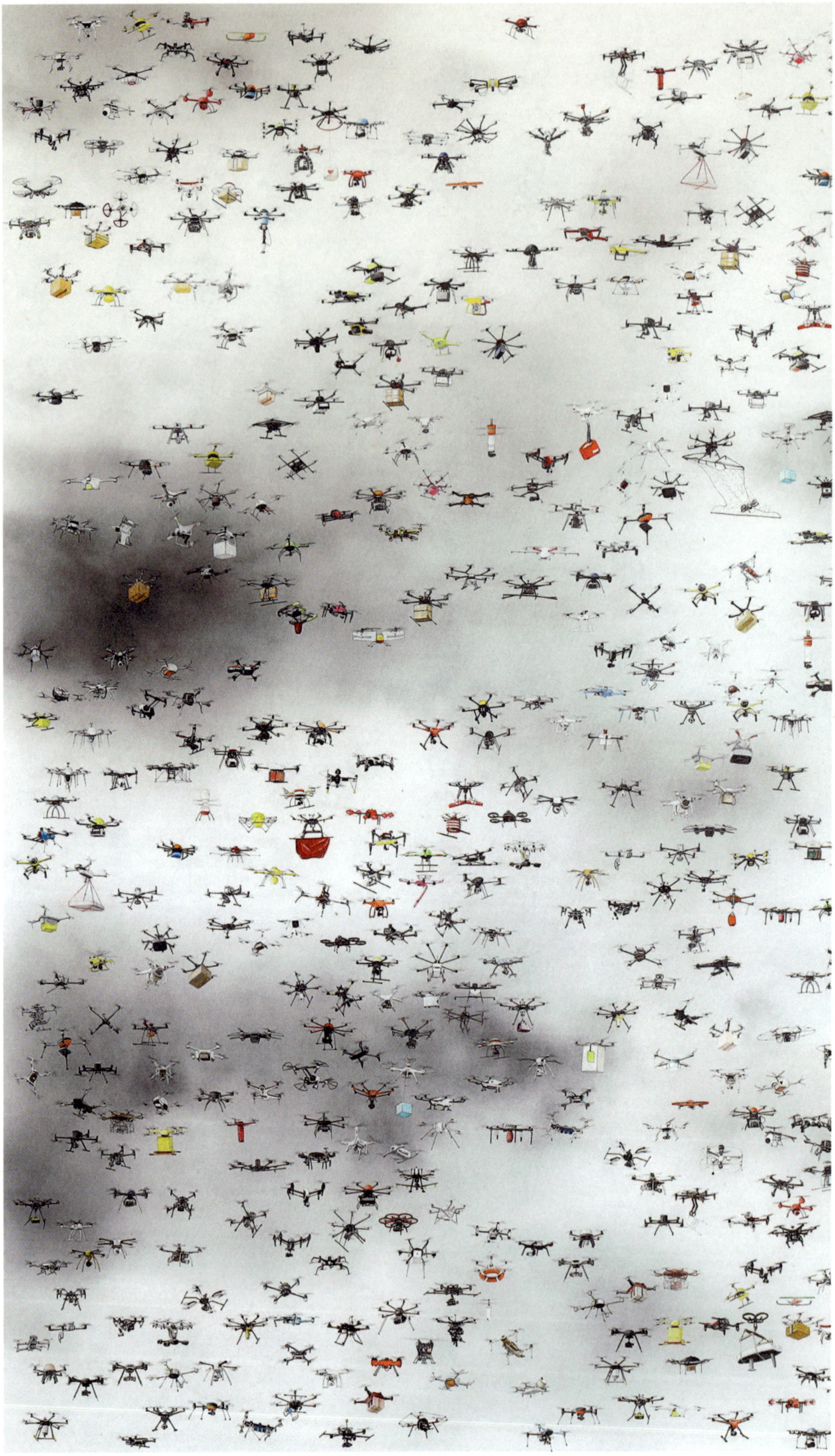

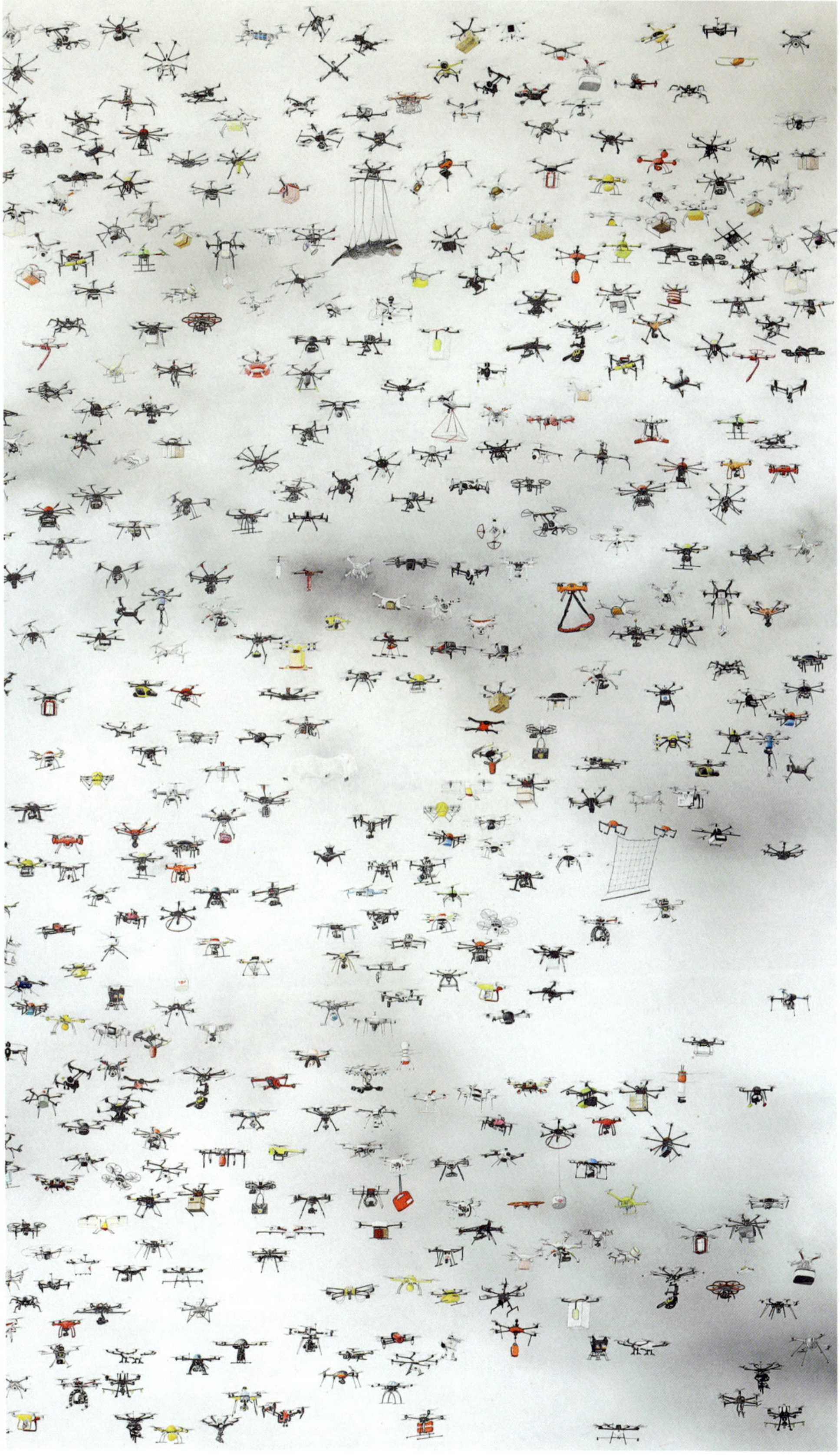

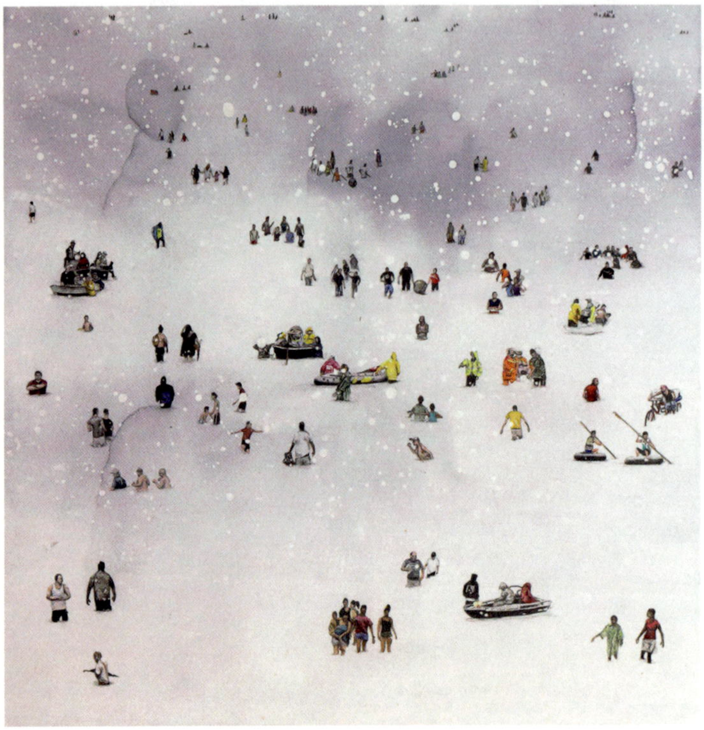

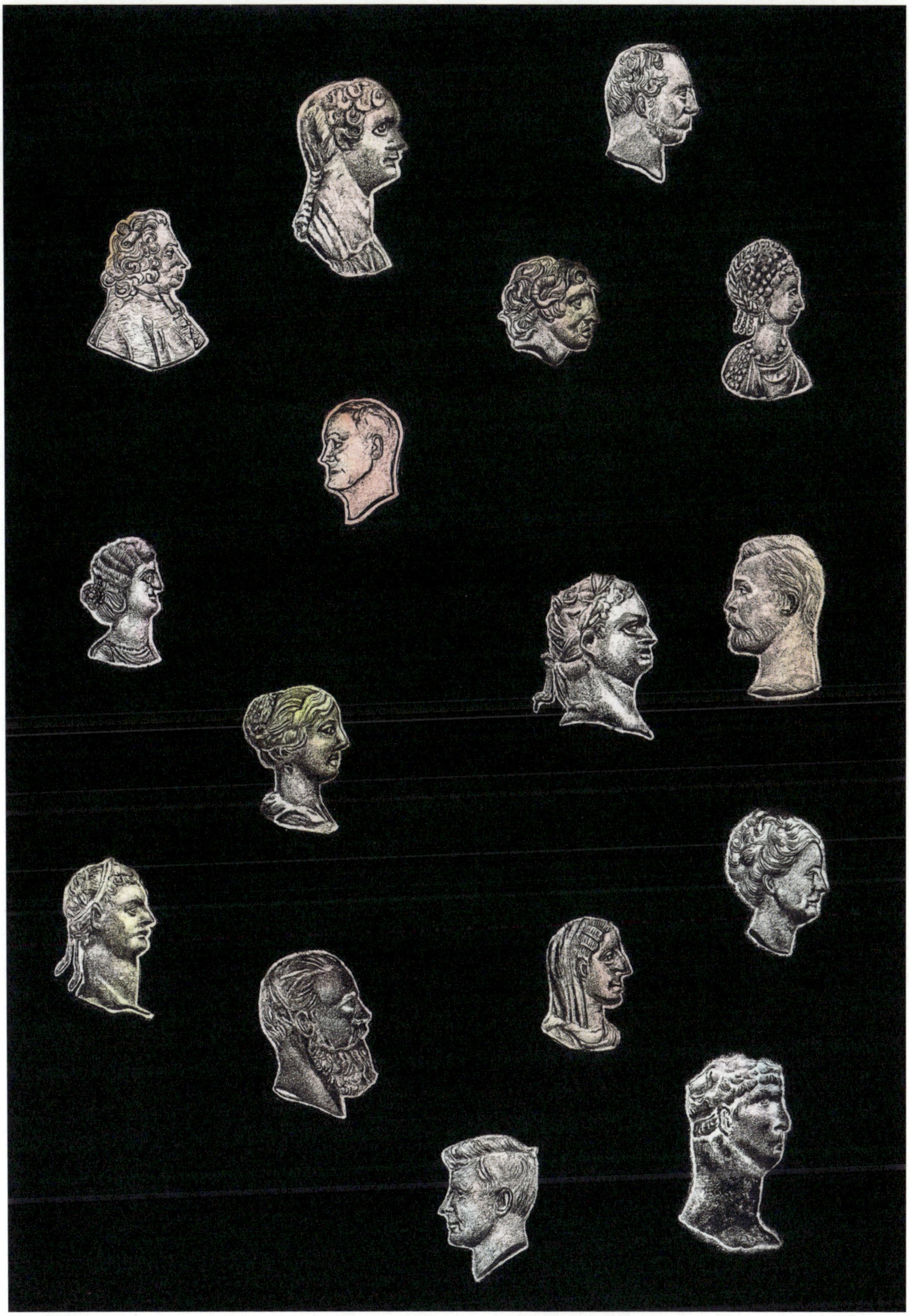

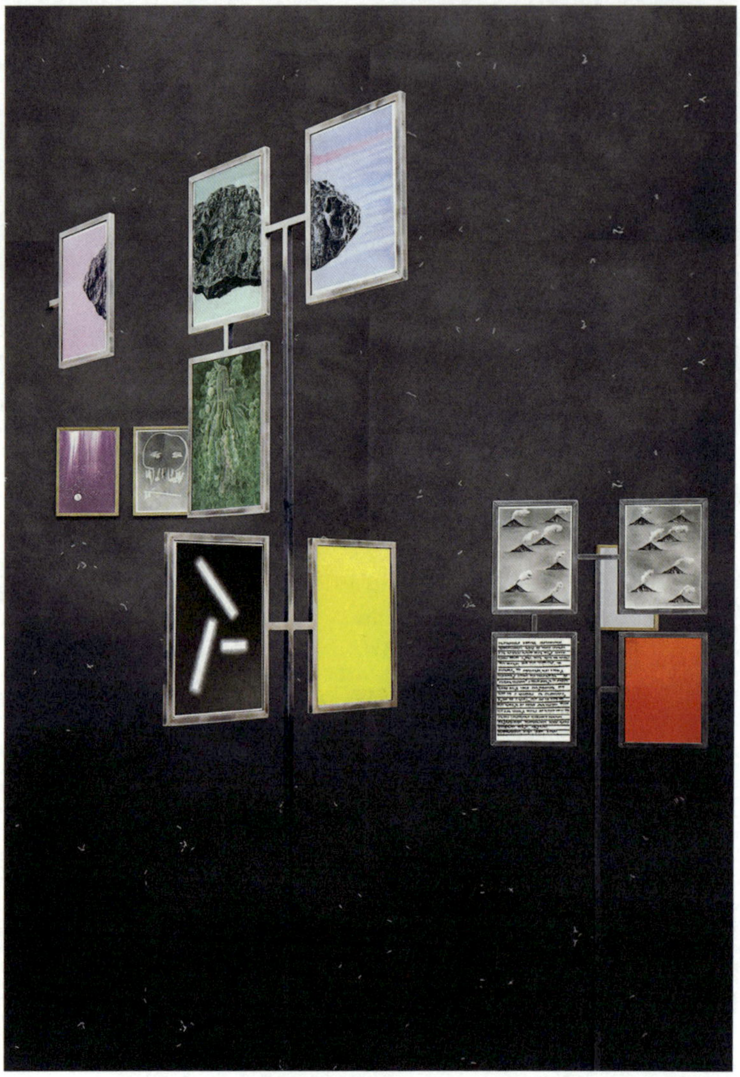

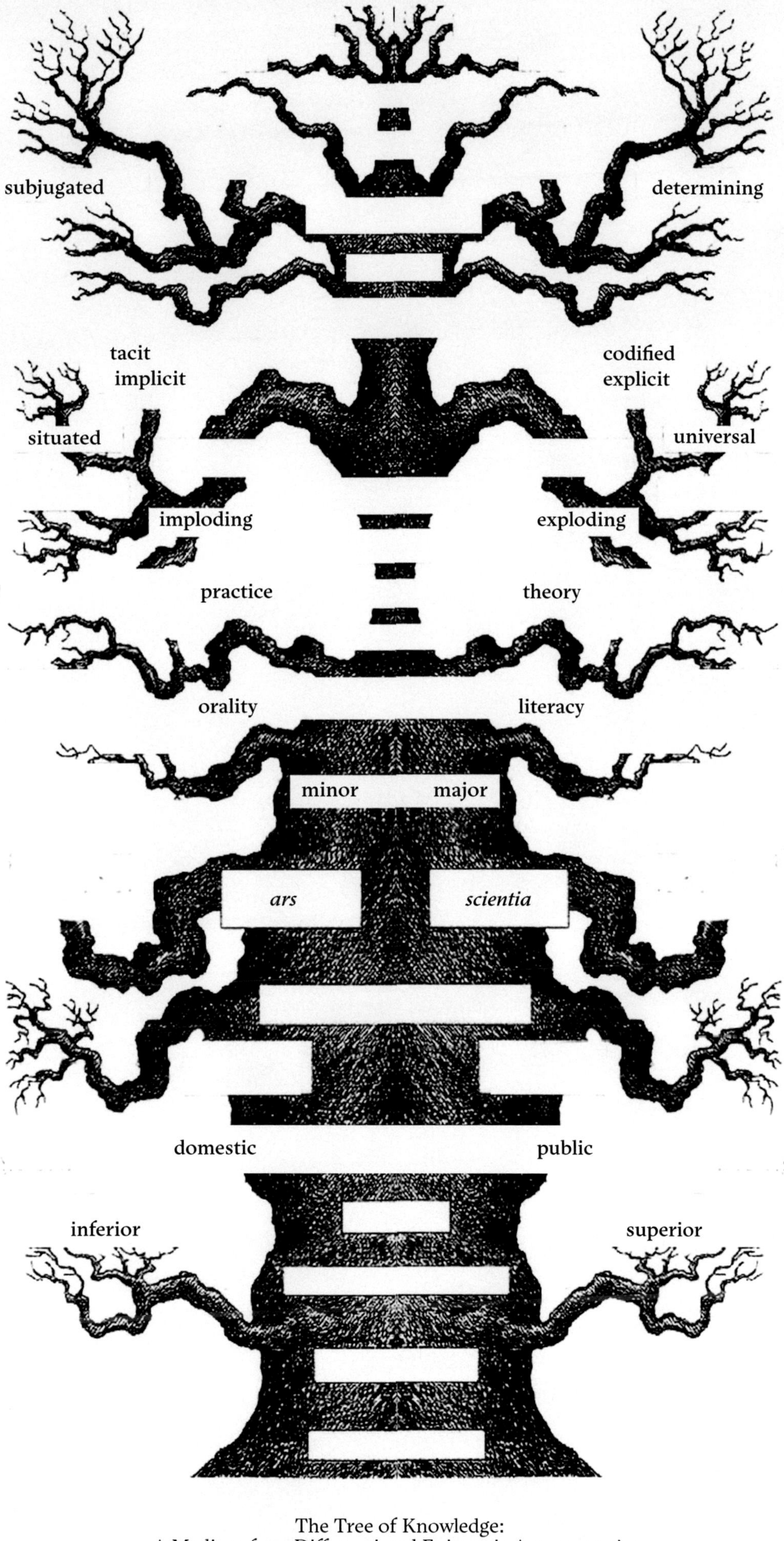


The Tree of Knowledge:
A Medium for a Differentiated Epistemic Argumentation

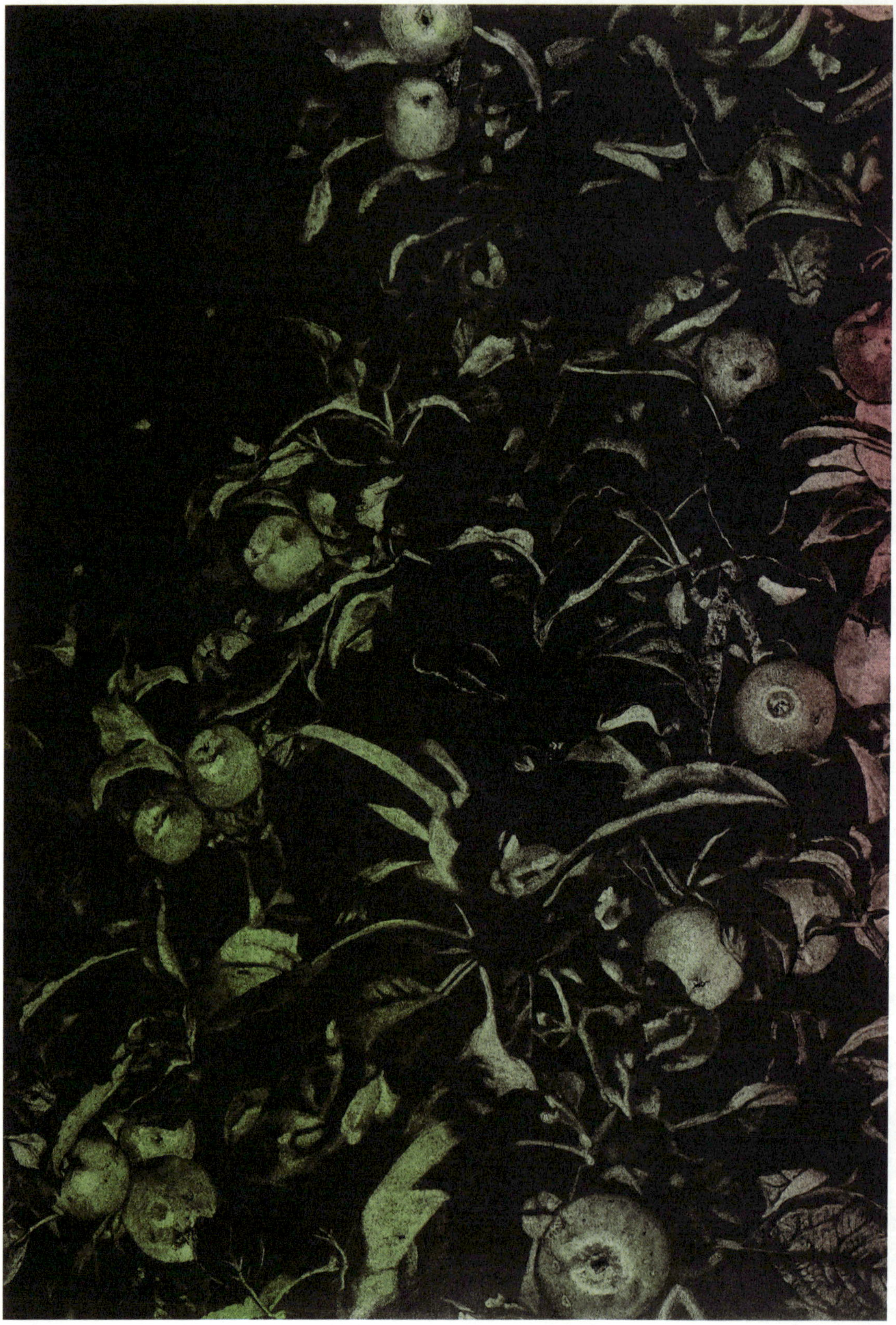

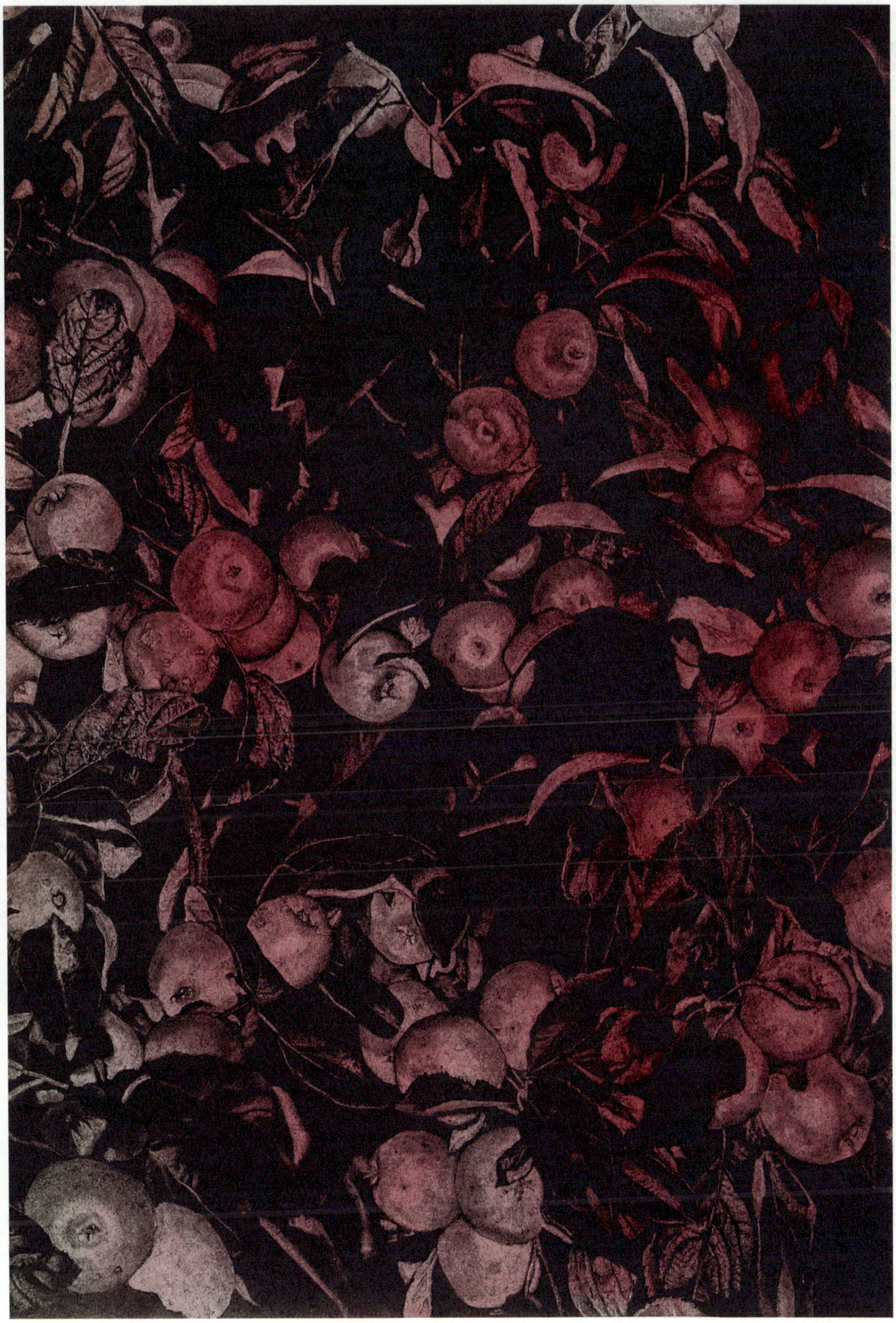

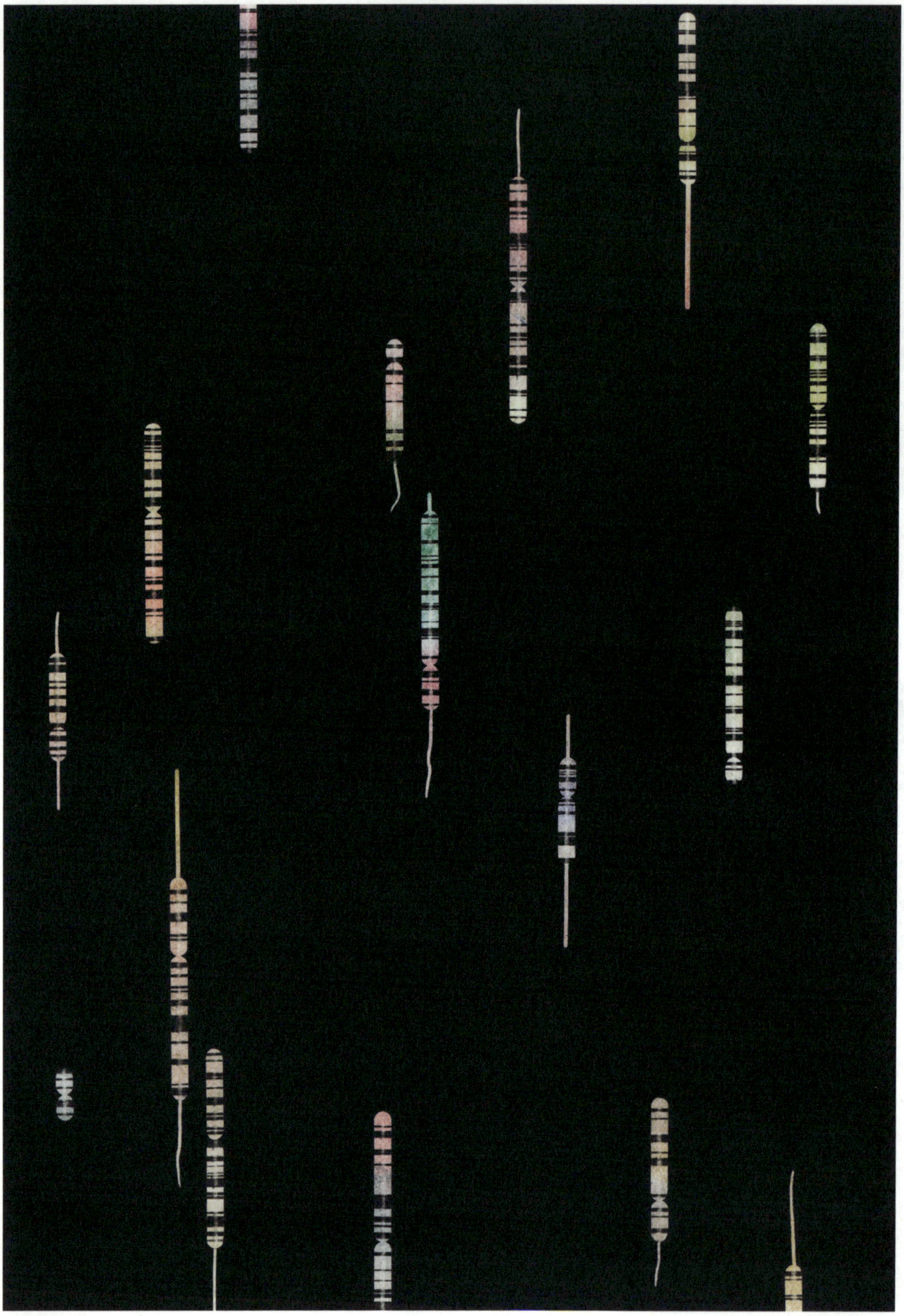

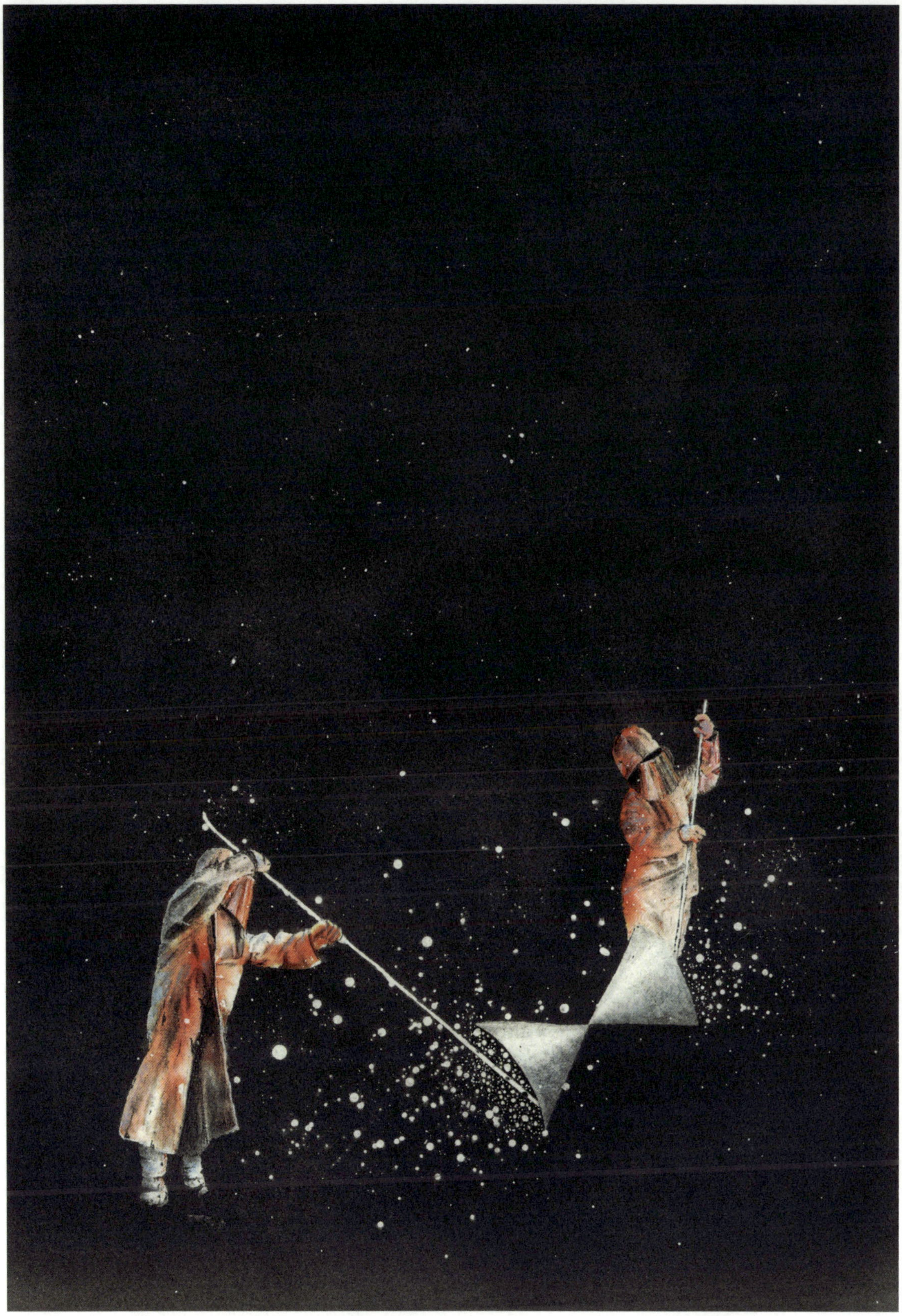

## B³

Begriff
Term



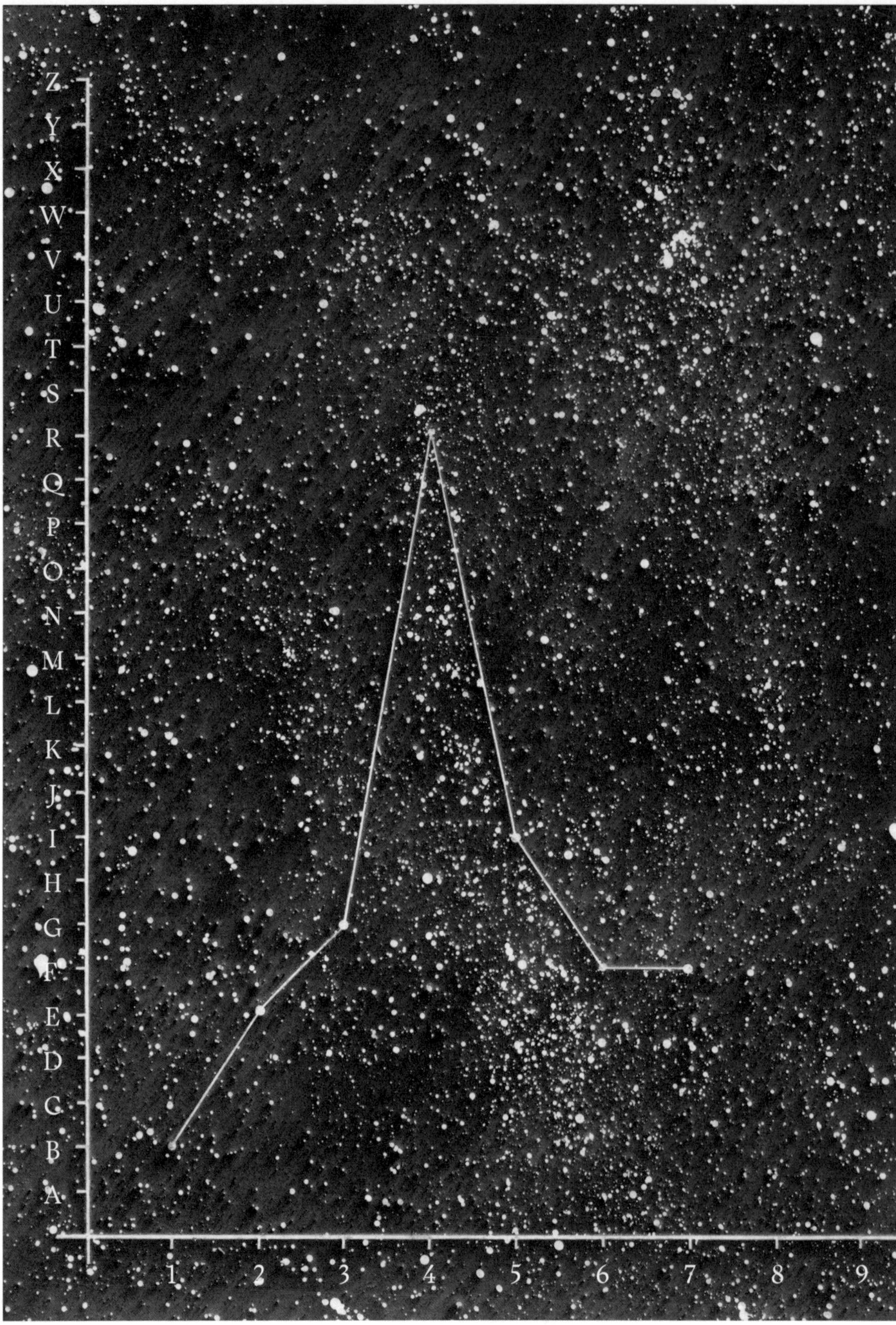

# B 4

Blättern
Browsing

25

DE

„Denken funktioniert wie eine Resonanzkammer, ein Schwingungsraum zwischen den vielschichtigen und vielsinnigen Plateaus unserer leiblichen, eingebetteten Position. [...] Denken ist nicht die Prädikation einer transzendentalen Wahrheit, sondern eine relationale Tätigkeit. [...] Insofern es relational ist, ist es eine Form des Weltbezugs. [...] Beim Denken gibt es keine Antinomie von Außen und Innen, kein Paradox, sondern ein ständiges Entfalten und Einfalten immanenter Kräfte (Deleuze [Gilles Deleuze, *Die Falte: Leibniz und der Barock*, Frankfurt am Main: Suhrkamp] 1995). Die Resonanz zwischen diesen vielfältigen Ebenen schlägt sich letztlich in der immanenten Struktur alles Lebendigen nieder."

— Rosi Braidotti, *Posthuman Knowledge* (Cambridge: Polity, 2019), 68 f.



EN

"Thinking functions like a chamber of resonance, a space of vibration, between the multi-layered and multi-directional plateaus of our embodied and embedded positions. [. . .] Thinking is not a predication of a transcendental truth, but it is a relational activity. [. . .] Being relational, thinking is a way of relating to the world. [. . .] In thinking there is no antinomy outside–inside, no paradox, but a constant unfolding and enfolding of immanent forces (Deleuze [Gilles Deleuze, *The Fold: Leibniz and the Baroque.* Minneapolis, MN: University of Minnesota Press], 1993). The resonance between these multiple levels shows conclusively the immanent structure of all living matter."

— Rosi Braidotti, *Posthuman Knowledge* (Cambridge: Polity, 2019 [ePub]), 68f.

# Differenz

In welcher Form lassen sich Differenzen denken, die bestehen, ohne Gegensätze zu erzeugen, ohne Hierarchien zu beschwören?

Der Text *Differenz und Wiederholung* des Philosophen Gilles Deleuze erscheint für philosophische Lai*innen als rätselhaft, schwer verständlich und äußerst umfangreich auf die Philosophiegeschichte referenzierend. Auch wenn man sich ihn daher nur fragmentarisch erschließen kann, so gibt es doch einige für künstlerische Fragestellungen reizvolle und zugängliche Anknüpfungspunkte gerade dort, wo die Sprache bildreich wird. Ein solcher Moment ist jener, wo Differenz als Begriff über zwei Szenarien ihrer Abwesenheit bzw. Unmöglichkeit diskutiert wird.

„Die Indifferenz hat zwei Aspekte: den undifferenzierten Abgrund, das schwarze Nichts, das unbestimmte Lebewesen, in dem alles aufgelöst ist – aber auch das weiße Nichts, die wieder ruhig gewordene Oberfläche, auf der unverbundene Bestimmungen wie vereinzelte Glieder treiben, Kopf ohne Hals, Arm ohne Schulter, Augen ohne Stirn.“[1]

Das Fürchterliche an diesen Bildern des Unbestimmten, die Assoziationen zu Hieronymus-Bosch-artigen Gemälden aufkommen lassen, ist, dass sich damit keine Sprache finden ließe, keine Wissenschaft, kein Denken möglich, keine Ordnung aufzustellen wäre. Wenn sich die Dinge nicht voneinander unterscheiden ließen, wenn alles, wie es Michel Foucault in *Die Ordnung der Dinge* ausdrückt, „absolute Verschiedenheit wäre, wäre das Denken der Einzähligkeit ausgesetzt, [...] wäre es der absoluten Verstreuung und der absoluten Monotonie ausgeliefert“.[2] Man kann sich eine begriffslose und relationslose Aufzählung ins Unendliche nicht vorstellen, weil das paradox und undenkbar wäre. Das Denken selbst wäre ohne Unterscheidung nicht möglich. Wenn einem Subjekt die Eigenschaften fehlen oder wenn es andererseits keine*n Träger*in, kein Subjekt für die Eigenschaften gibt, dann kann es kein Denken geben, weil kein Urteil ohne Subjekt und ihm zugeordneten Prädikat möglich ist und damit auch keine Repräsentation gegeben sein kann.[3] Deleuze beschreibt neben einer empirischen Differenz, die man macht, indem man Dinge voneinander unterscheidet, noch eine weitere Form der Differenz, wieder anhand eines Bildes, und zwar jene, die sich selbst macht:[4]

# Difference

How might differences that exist be conceived without creating antagonisms, without establishing hierarchies?

For philosophical laypeople the text *Difference and Repetition*, by the philosopher Gilles Deleuze, appears enigmatic and difficult to understand, and it makes extensive references to the history of philosophy. Though for this reason it yields only in fragments, it offers some highly interesting and accessible starting points for artistic questions in those passages where its language is rich in imagery. One such moment is when Deleuze discusses the concept of difference by means of two scenarios of its absence or impossibility.

“Indifference has two aspects: the undifferentiated abyss, the black nothingness, the indeterminate animal in which everything is dissolved—but also the white nothingness, the once more calm surface upon which float unconnected determinations like scattered members: a head without a neck, an arm without a shoulder, eyes without brows.”[1]

The fearsome thing about these images of indeterminacy, which evoke associations of Hieronymus-Bosch-like paintings, is that they are inconducive to language, knowledge, thought, or order. If things can’t be distinguished from one another, “if everything,” as Michel Foucault expresses it, “were absolute diversity, thought would be doomed to singularity, [...] it would be doomed also to absolute dispersion and absolute monotony.”[2] It is impossible to imagine a non-conceptual and non-relational infinite enumeration because that would be paradoxical and unthinkable. Thinking itself would be impossible without differentiation. If a subject lacks attributes, or if on the other hand there is no subject to carry the attributes, then there can be no thinking, because there is no judgment without a subject and its associated predicate, and therefore there can also be no representation.[3] Along with an empirical differentiation made when distinguishing between things, Deleuze describes another form of difference, once again using an image, namely the one that creates itself:

“Lightning, for example, distinguishes itself from the black sky but must also trail it behind, as though it were distinguishing itself from that which does not distinguish itself from it. It is as if the ground rose to

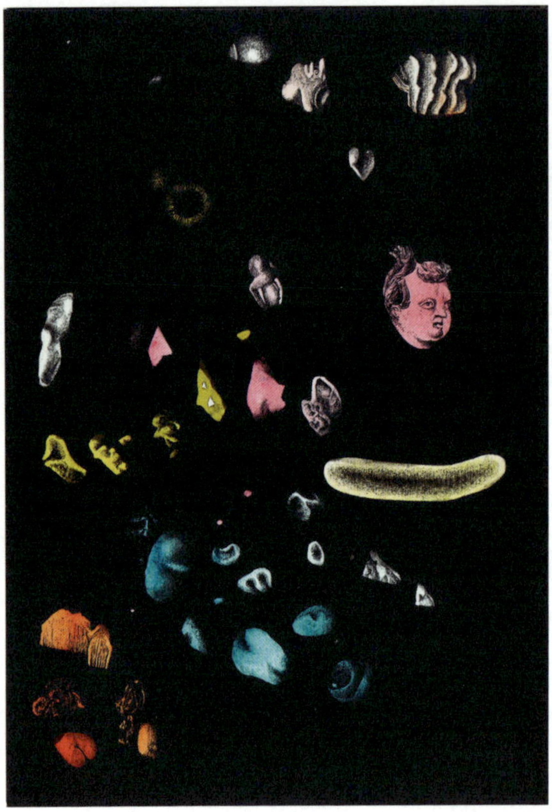

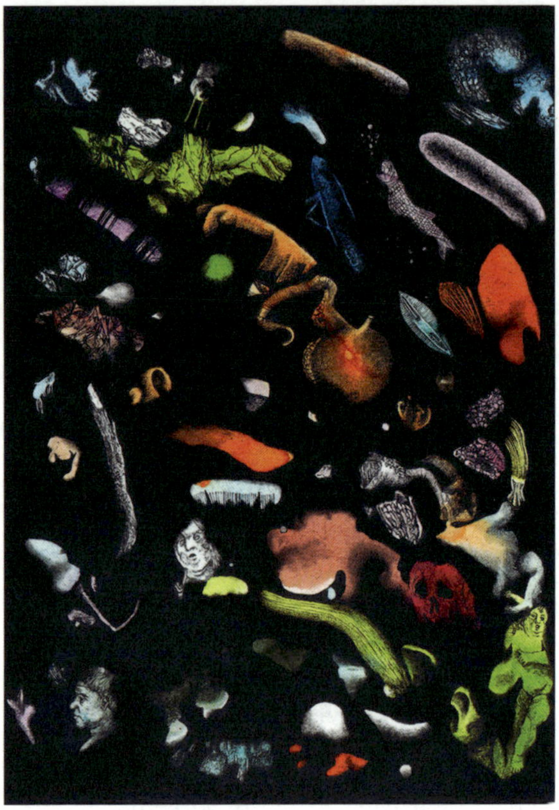

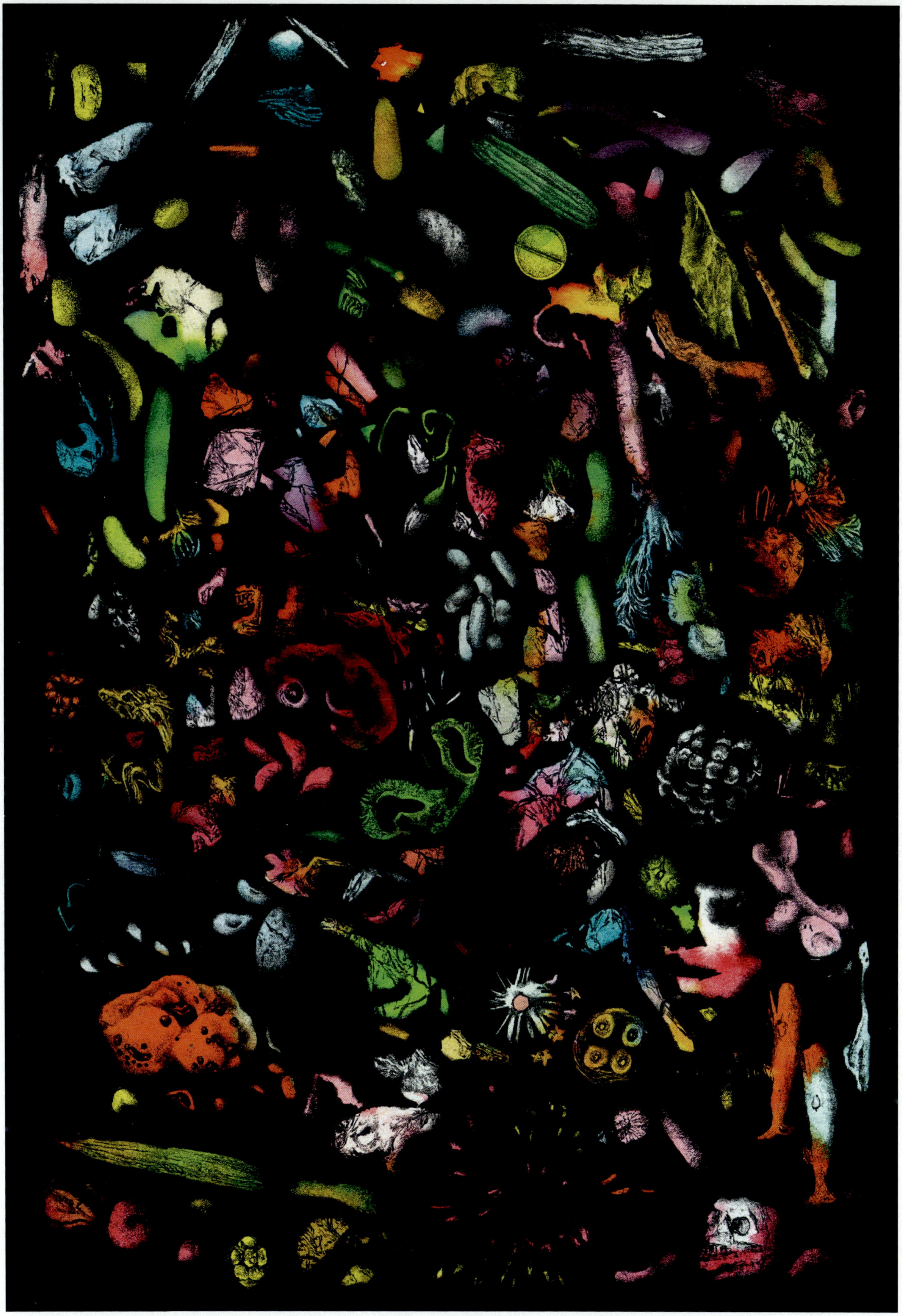

„Der Blitz zum Beispiel unterscheidet sich vom schwarzen Himmel, kann ihn aber nicht loswerden, als ob er sich von dem unterschiede, was sich selbst nicht unterscheidet. Man könnte sagen, der Untergrund steige zur Oberfläche auf, bleibe aber weiterhin Untergrund. Es liegt auf beiden Seiten etwas Grausames, ja Ungeheuerliches in diesem Kampf gegen einen unfaßbaren Gegner, in dem sich das Unterschiedene einer Sache entgegensetzt, die sich nicht von ihm unterscheiden kann und immer weiter mit dem vereinigt, was sich von ihr absetzt. Die Differenz ist diese Fassung der Bestimmung als einseitiger Unterscheidung."[5]

Diese Differenz nennt Deleuze „DIE Bestimmung" – etwas unterscheidet sich von etwas anderem, das im Umkehrschluss nicht davon unterschieden werden kann.[6] Anhand dieses Bildes wird die Problemstellung skizziert: Eine Form schält sich aus einem formlosen Grund, der selbst zur Oberfläche wird, aber primär formlos und undefinierbar ist.[7] Hier kommt der Begriff der Repräsentation ins Spiel. Für die Philosophie bedeutet Repräsentieren, die Wirklichkeit durch Denken oder durch Sprechen abzubilden, ein Unterfangen, das sowohl erkenntnistheoretisch als auch sprachphilosophisch problematisch ist.[8] Der Ort, von dem aus die Form zur Oberfläche aufsteigt und in den Moment der Bestimmung tritt, dieser undifferenzierte Abgrund, wie Deleuze ihn beschreibt und benennt, ist nicht repräsentierbar, also weder denkbar noch sprachlich vermittelbar. Die Differenz muss in das Raster der Repräsentation fallen, und zwar durch die Strukturen „der Identität des Begriffs, de[s] Gegensatz[es] der Prädikate, der Analogie des Urteils [und] der Ähnlichkeit der Wahrnehmung".[9] Dieses von Deleuze beschriebene aristotelische Erbe ist die Weise, wie wir die Dinge, ahnend, dass weder sie noch wir selbst in sich und in uns wirklich ident sind, in Repräsentationen einfassen. Wir schaffen uns Kategorien, Ordnungen und Hierarchien, weil das Chaos der Einzelfälle – der reinen Differenzen – schwer zu ertragen wäre. Uns mit dem Ähnlichen zu umgeben, das Ähnliche zu suchen, hilft uns dabei, einen Zustand zu erhalten, der uns beruhigt, Homöostase. Eigentlich aber ist die Frage der Differenzen die einer Setzung. Liegt am Grunde der Differenzen ein in sich Identes als eine Art Grundbedingung ihrer Setzung? Ist die Ähnlichkeit Bedingung für die Differenz? Wenn wir in Gegensätzen denken,

the surface, without ceasing to be ground. There is cruelty, even monstrosity, on both sides of this struggle against an elusive adversary, in which the distinguished opposes something which cannot distinguish itself from it but continues to espouse that which divorces it. Difference is this state in which determination takes the form of unilateral distinction."[4]

Deleuze calls this difference "determination *as such*"—something distinguishes itself from something else, from which, conversely, it cannot be distinguished.[5] The image he uses outlines the problem: a form separates out from a formless ground, which itself becomes a surface but is primarily nebulous and indefinable.[6] This brings the concept of representation into play. Representation, for philosophy, means depicting reality through thinking or speaking, a problematic endeavor, both epistemologically and in terms of language philosophy.[7] The place from which form rises to the surface and enters the moment of determination, that undifferentiated abyss described and named by Deleuze, is not representable, that is, neither thinkable nor communicable in language. Difference must fall into the pattern of representation, "subject to the identity of the concept, the opposition of predicates, the analogy of judgement and the resemblance of perception."[8] The legacy of Aristotle that Deleuze describes is the way in which we enclose things in representation, suspecting that neither they are really identical with themselves nor we with ourselves. We create categories, systems, and hierarchies because the chaos of isolated cases—of pure differences—would be difficult to endure. Surrounding ourselves with similarity, seeking similarity, helps us to preserve a reassuring state of homeostasis. But the question of difference is actually one of positing. Isn't there something identical with itself at the root of difference, a kind of basic condition of its positing? Isn't similarity the prerequisite of difference? If we think in terms of the opposites that feed on a negative, then difference—and "it is the same with every space: geometrical, physical, biophysical, social and linguistic"—should be understood as none other than a "flattened and inverted image" of the negative.[9] "The one not to be the other" is the basic process of differentiation that the mind carries out in regard to our ideas, as declared under the heading of "Knowledge" even in an early encyclopedic work of the eighteenth century,

die sich aus einem Negativum speisen, dann ist unter Differenzen – und das gilt im „geometrischen, physikalischen, biopsychischen, sozialen und sprachlichen Raum" – nichts anderes zu verstehen als ein „flachgedrücktes und verkehrtes Bild" des Negativen.[10] Das eine ist, was das andere nicht ist: „the one not to be the other" ist der grundlegende Differenzierungsprozess, den der Geist hinsichtlich unserer Ideen vollzieht, erfahren wir schon im enzyklopädischen Eintrag „Knowledge" in Ephraim Chambers' frühenzyklopädischem Werk des 18. Jahrhunderts, *Cyclopædia*.[11] Aber nur über die Identität wird die Differenz zum Negativen, nur über die Repräsentation wird sie starr und unbeweglich, monoperspektivisch.[12]

Wie also könnte eine versöhnliche Form von Differenz gefunden werden?

Die Differenz lässt sich anders denken, wenn sie als Bewegung gedacht wird, und der Grund, von dem aus die Differenz sich bildet, lässt sich anders denken, wenn wir ihn zu einem „Hier und Jetzt einer differentiellen Realität, die immer schon aus Singularitäten besteht", umdenken.[13] Die Differenz wäre demnach in einem Dazwischen verortet, eine Art beweglicher Übergang, aus dem heraus Veränderung wirksam wird und der den Fluss der vielen Einzelnen, die sich aktualisieren, in Bewegung hält. Dies würde einer „Dialektik negativer Differenz" entgegenwirken, die den Anthropos, der sich an die Spitze aller Spezies imaginiert, und jenen Humanisten, der sich als überlegenes, weil rationales Vernunftwesen denkt, so gewalttätig macht.[14] Es sind die Differenzen, die mit so einer Selbstverständlichkeit gedacht werden – in der Hautfarbe, im Geschlecht, in der Spezies, in der sozialen Klasse, in der (an)organischen Verfasstheit, in der ökonomischen Potenz –, die eine Unzahl an irrationalen Hierarchien und Machtverhältnissen erzeugen. Allerdings weist die Philosophin Rosi Braidotti auf eine wesentliche Verschiebung hinsichtlich der Differenz innerhalb eines „wissenschaftlichen Begriffs von ‚Materie'" hin, der sich im postanthropozentrischen Spektrum ergibt.[15] Die Differenz wird „von Binarismen zur Rhizomatik verlagert – vom Sex/Gender- oder Natur/Kultur-Gegensatz zu Sexualisierungs- und Naturalisierungsprozessen, die vor allem das Leben selbst oder die Lebenskraft der Materie zum Gegenstand machen", innerhalb deren die Machtdifferenzen jedoch nicht verschwinden.[16] Worauf die Philosophin damit hinauswill, ist, dass Unterscheidun-

Ephraim Chambers' *Cyclopædia*.[10] But difference only becomes negative through identity; only through representation does it become rigid and mono-perspectival.[11]

How, therefore, might a reconciliatory form of difference be found?

Difference may be conceived in another way if it is thought of as movement, and the ground from which it forms may likewise be reconceived as a "here-now of a differential reality always made up of singularities."[12] Difference would accordingly be located in an interstice, a kind of mobile transition from which change becomes effective and which maintains the flow of the many transpiring individual cases. This would counter "the dialectics of negative difference" that make the *anthropos*, which imagines itself at the apex of all species, and those humanists who think of themselves as rational beings and therefore superior, so dangerous.[13] It is the differences conceived as a matter of course—of skin color, gender, species, social class, (in)organic condition, economic clout—that generate a myriad of irrational hierarchies and power relations. Nevertheless, the philosopher Rosi Braidotti points to a crucial "scientific redefinition of 'matter'" in the postanthropocentric landscape.[14] There is a "dislocation of difference from binaries to rhizomatics; from sex/gender or nature/culture to processes of sexualization/racialization/naturalization that take Life itself, or the vitality of matter as the main target," but within which power differences are not resolved.[15] Braidotti's p oint here is that differentiation is no less powerful for being anatomical, morphologically visible, or binary-oppositional, and made on the cellular-molecular level or in the genetic code, for example.[16] She is concerned here with an impact on the so-called *zoe*, a dynamic, self-organizing, and vital life force subject to a political economy.[17] Braidotti looks for a way of conceiving difference without becoming entangled in a value-driven ideology of domination and hierarchy, and she points to "the principle of not-One": "This ethical principle breaks up the fantasy of unity, totality and one-ness, but also the master narratives of primordial loss, incommensurable lack and irreparable separation. What I want to emphasize instead, in a more affirmative vein, is the priority of the relation and the awareness that one is the effect of irrepressible flows of encounters, interactions, affectivity and desire, which one is not in charge of.

gen nicht zwingend anatomisch, morphologisch sichtbar oder binär-oppositionell sein müssen, aber deswegen nicht weniger mächtig sind, wenn sie etwa auf zellulär-molekularer Ebene oder im genetischen Code vollzogen werden.[17] Es geht hierbei um ein Einwirken auf die sogenannte „Zoé", eine dynamische, selbstorganisierende und vitale Lebenskraft, die einer politischen Ökonomie unterworfen wird.[18] Braidotti bemüht sich um eine Lösung darum, wie wir Differenzen denken können, ohne uns dabei in einem wertgetriebenen Herrschafts- und Hierarchiedenken zu verfangen, indem sie auf „das Prinzip des Nicht-Einen" verweist:

„Dieses ethische Prinzip sprengt die Illusion von Einheit, Totalität und Ein–heit, aber auch die Herrennarrative von ursprünglichem Verlust, unermesslichem Mangel und irreparabler Trennung. Was ich stattdessen, in stärker affirmativem Geiste, betonen will, ist die Vorrangigkeit der Beziehung und das Bewusstsein, dass man (*one*) der Effekt uneindämmbarer Ströme von Begegnungen, Interaktionen, Gefühlen und Begierden ist, die man nicht kontrollieren kann.

Diese zur Bescheidenheit zwingende Erfahrung der Nicht-Einheit, die grundlegend ist für das nicht-einheitliche Subjekt, verankert das Subjekt in einer ethischen Bindung an die Alterität, an die vielfältigen äußeren Anderen, die konstitutiv sind für jene Entität, die wir aus Bequemlichkeit und Gewohnheit das ‚Ich' nennen."[19]

Die Differenz muss sich also begrifflich emanzipieren von einem aufgebauschten, schablonenhaft individualismusgetriebenen und letztendlich doch wieder auf Ähnlichkeiten hinauslaufenden Identitätsdenken. Die Differenz ist notwendig, weil sie sich dem Indifferenten, das das Undenkbare ist, entgegenstellt. Die unendliche Vielheit und Wendigkeit in der Weise, wie sich das Lebendige aktualisiert, und die Komplexität und Verflochtenheit, die sich aus der Relationalität eines kontinuierlichen Aufeinandereinwirkens des Lebendigen ergeben, sind der Raum, in dem die Differenz sich entfalten kann.

This humbling experience of not-Oneness, which is constitutive of the non-unitary subject, anchors the subject in an ethical bond to alterity, to the multiple and external others that are constitutive of that entity which, out of laziness and habit, we call the 'self.'"[18]

So difference has to be conceptually liberated from an overinflated, schematic idea of identity that is driven by individualism but ultimately comes back down to similarity. Difference is necessary because it counters the indifference of the inconceivable. The infinite variety and agility in the occurrence of life, and the complexity and interlacement of its continual interaction, are the space in which difference can unfold.

1 Gilles Deleuze, *Differenz und Wiederholung*, übers. von Joseph Vogl (München: Wilhelm Fink, 2007), 49.
2 Michel Foucault, „Die Ordnung der Dinge. Eine Archäologie der Humanwissenschaften", in: ders., *Die Hauptwerke*, übers. von Ulrich Köppen (Frankfurt am Main: Suhrkamp, 2016), 167.
3 Vgl. Henry Somers-Hall, *Deleuze's Difference and Repetition* (Edinburgh: Edinburgh University Press, 2013), 22.
4 Vgl. Gilles Deleuze, *Differenz und Wiederholung*, 49.
5 Ebd., 49.
6 Ebd., 49.
7 Vgl. ebd., 50.
8 Vgl. Peter Prechtl und Franz-Peter Burkard, Hrsg., *Metzler Philosophie Lexikon: Begriffe und Definitionen* (Stuttgart, Weimar: Metzler, 1999), 512.
9 Gilles Deleuze, *Differenz und Wiederholung*, 58.
10 Ebd., 77.
11 „As to the identity, or diversity of our ideas, we may observe, that it is the first act of the mind to perceive its own ideas; and so far as it perceives them, to *know* each what it is, and thereby to perceive their difference; that is, the one not to be the other: by this the mind clearly perceives each idea to agree with itself, and to be what it is; and all distinct ideas to disagree." Ephraim Chambers, *Cyclopædia: or, An Universal Dictionary of Arts and Sciences* (London, 1741) 420, https://artflsrv03.uchicago.edu/philologic4/chambers_new/navigate/1/11858/, abgerufen am 30.3.2022.
12 Deleuze, *Differenz und Wiederholung*, 78, 83.
13 Deleuze, *Differenz und Wiederholung*, 78.
14 Rosi Braidotti, *Posthumanismus: Leben jenseits des Menschen* (Frankfurt: Campus Verlag, 2014), 73. Zu Anthropozän und Humanismus als problematischen Grundannahmen und zu Posthumanismus siehe ebd. und Rosi Braidotti, *Posthuman Knowledge* (Cambridge: Polity, 2019).
15 Ebd., 100.
16 Ebd., 100.
17 Vgl. ebd., 101. Rosi Braidotti bezieht sich hierbei auf viele Mechanismen der „Vermarktung des Lebens durch den modernen biotechnologischen Kapitalismus", vgl. ebd., 65.
18 Vgl. ebd., 65, 66, 101.
19 Vgl. ebd., 104.

1 Gilles Deleuze, *Difference and Repetition*, trans. Paul Patton (London: Continuum, 2001), 28.
2 Michel Foucault, *The Order of Things. An Archaeology of the Human Sciences* (New York: Pantheon Books, 1971 [ePub]), 346.
3 See Henry Somers-Hall, *Deleuze's Difference and Repetition* (Edinburgh: Edinburgh University Press, 2013), 22.
4 Gilles Deleuze, *Difference and Repetition*, 28.
5 Ibid.
6 See ibid., 29.
7 See the *Internet Encyclopedia of Philosophy*: https://iep.utm.edu/epistemo/ for epistemology; https://iep.utm.edu/lang-phi/ for the philosophy of language.
8 Gilles Deleuze, *Difference and Repetition*, 34.
9 Ibid., 51.
10 "As to the identity, or diversity of our ideas, we may observe, that it is the first act of the mind to perceive its own ideas; and so far as it perceives them, to *know* each what it is, and thereby to perceive their difference; that is, the one not to be the other: by this the mind clearly perceives each idea to agree with itself, and to be what it is; and all distinct ideas to disagree." Ephraim Chambers, *Cyclopædia: or, An Universal Dictionary of Arts and Sciences* (London, 1741), 420, https://artflsrv03.uchicago.edu/philologic4/chambers_new/navigate/1/11858/, (March 30, 2022).
11 Deleuze, *Difference and Repetition*, 5f, 54–56.
12 Ibid., 52.
13 Rosi Braidotti, *The Posthuman* (Cambridge: Polity, 2013), 68. For the Anthropocene and humanism as problematic basic assumptions, and for posthumanism, see ibid. and Rosi Braidotti, *Posthuman Knowledge* (Cambridge: Polity, 2019).
14 Ibid., 96.
15 Ibid.
16 See ibid., 97. Rosi Braidotti refers here to the "opportunistic trans-species commodification of Life that is the logic of advanced capitalism," ibid. 60.
17 See ibid. 60f, 96.
18 Ibid., 100.

Doppelgänger

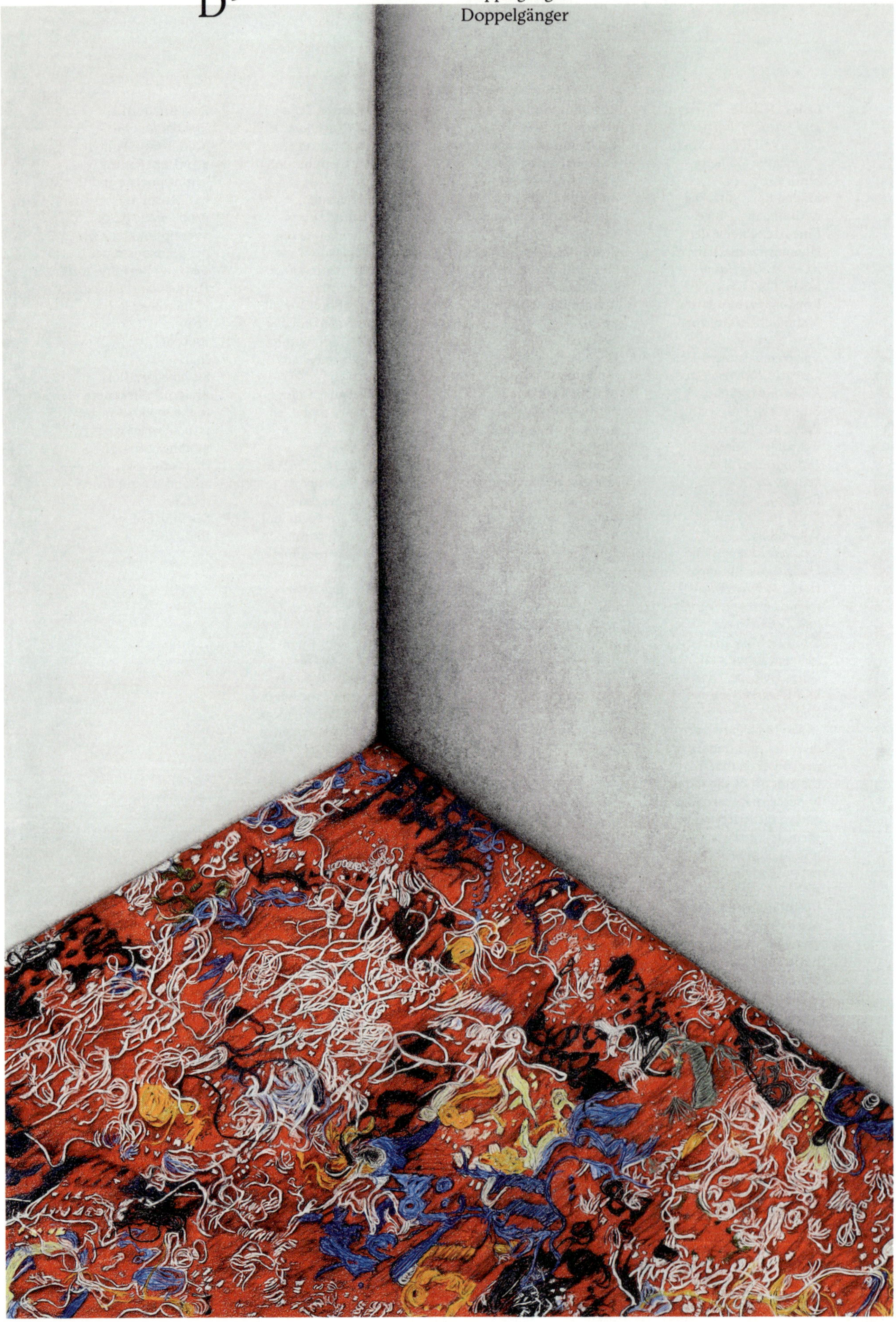

Doppelgänger

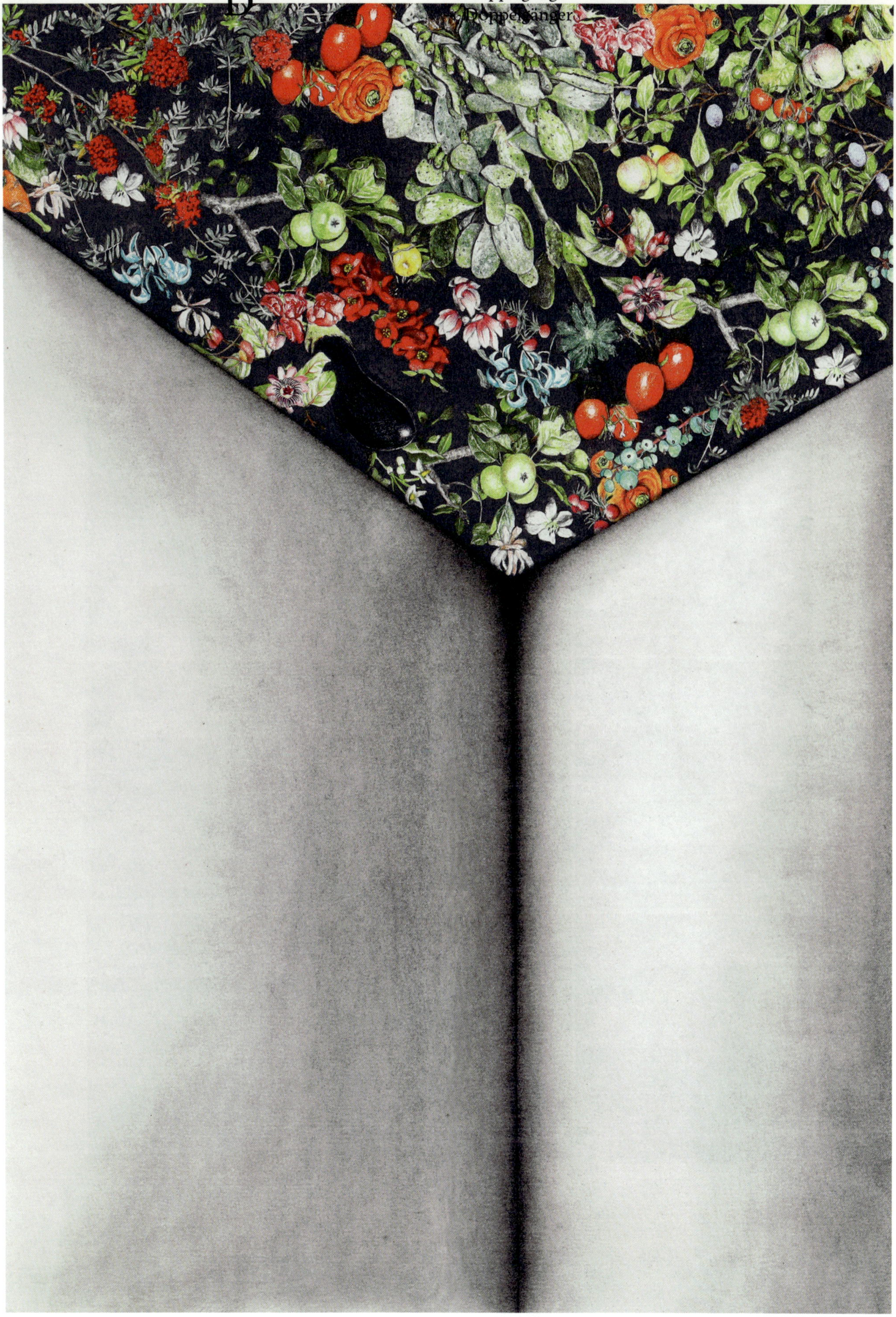

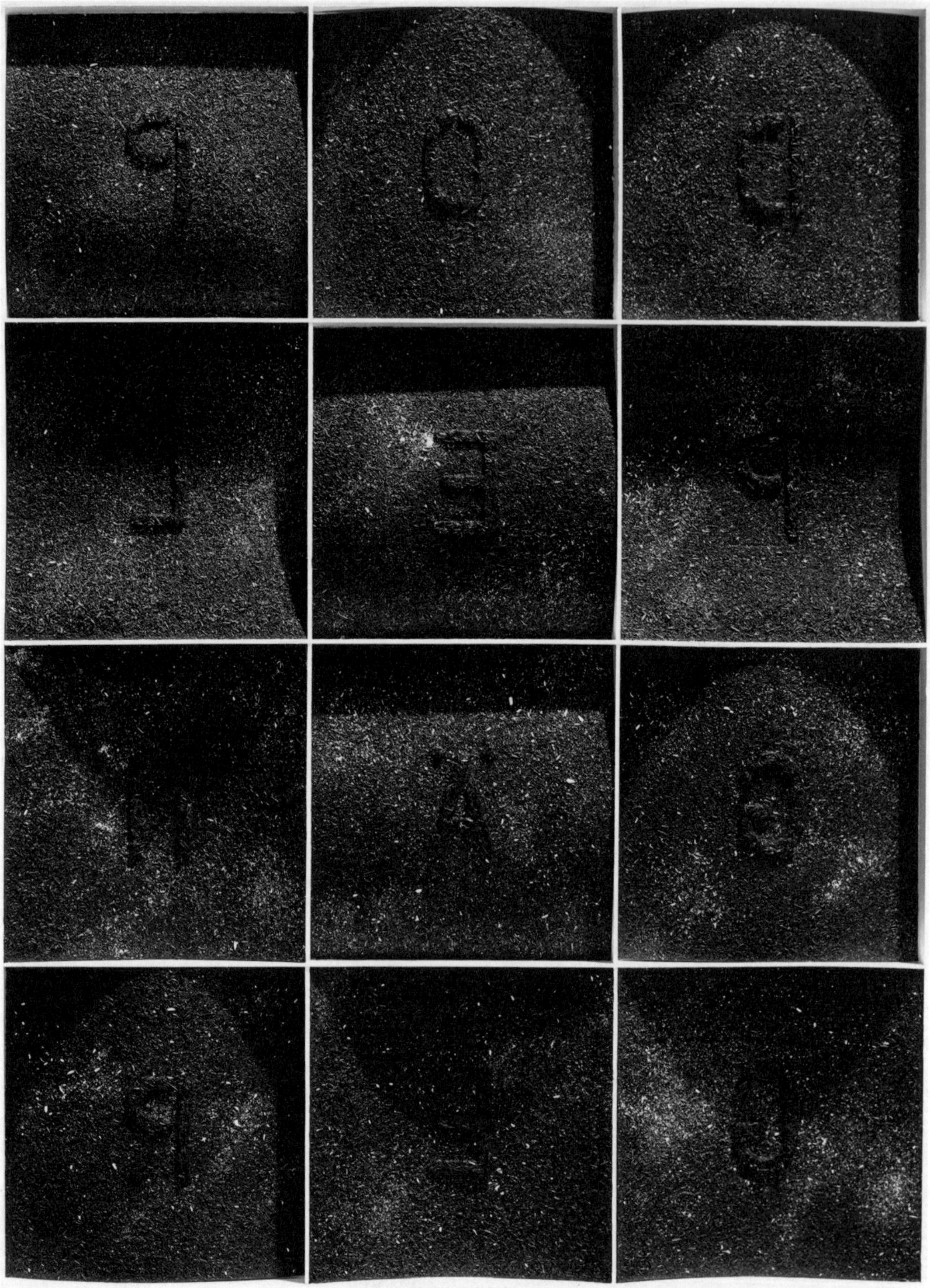

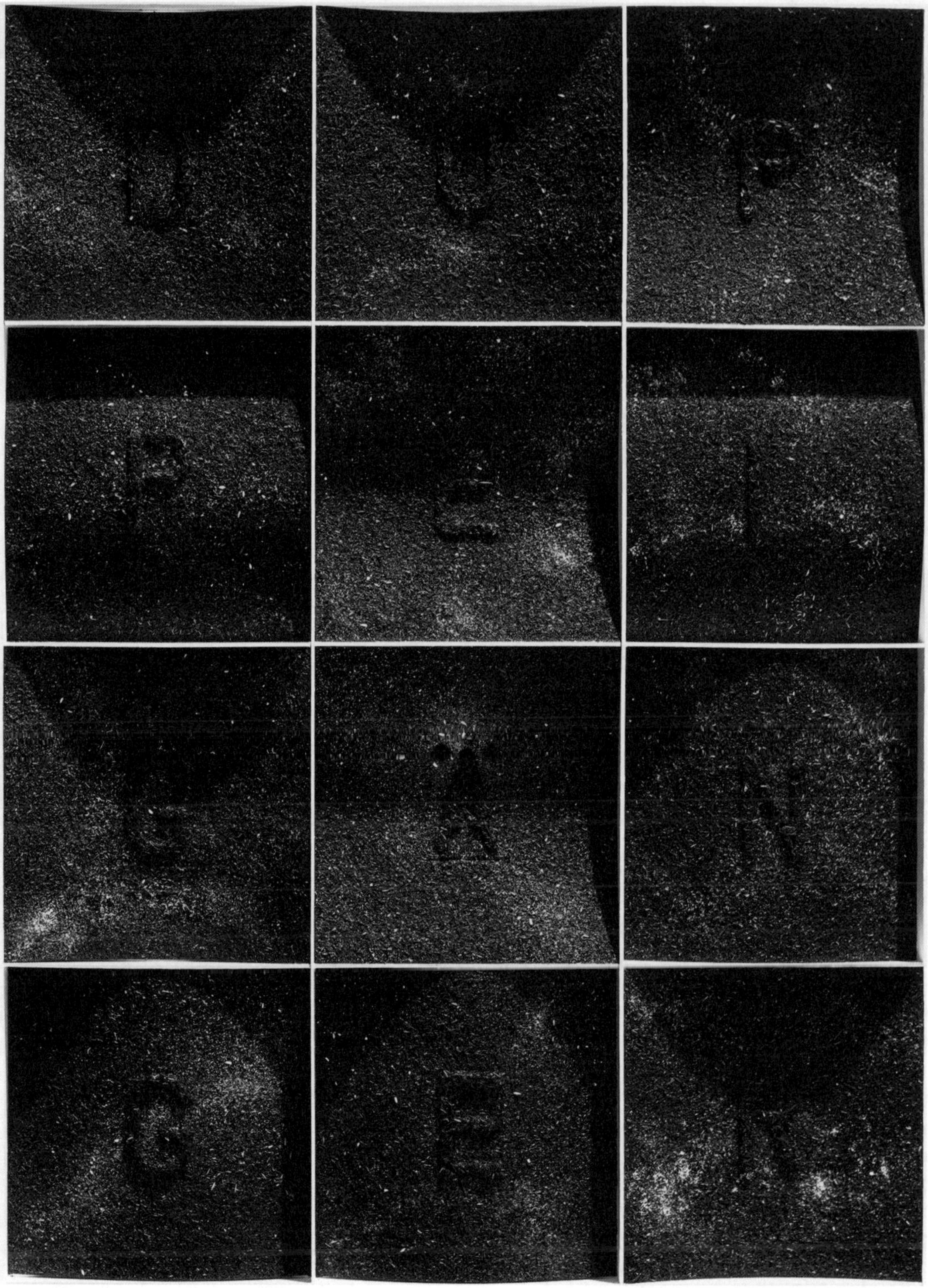

# Enzyklopädie

Die Enzyklopädie, das ist ein Kreisen zwischen Wissen und Unwissen, Aktualität und Vergangenem, Fülle und Lücke, Neugier und Zwang, Ordnung und Zufall.

Das Wort „Allgemeinbildung" trifft die Herkunftsbedeutung für „Enzyklopädie" (εγκυκλοπαίδεια, enkýklios paideía, Zyklus der Bildung) am präzisesten. In der griechischen Antike und im frühen Mittelalter beschränkte sich dieser Begriff auf das Curriculum an den Lehranstalten und Universitäten – die Artes liberales.[1] Bis ins 18. Jahrhundert war „Enzyklopädie" kein gängiger Begriff, vielmehr gab es eine Vielzahl an Begrifflichkeiten, die man der Praxis enzyklopädischen Schreibens in allen möglichen disziplinären Ausrichtungen zuordnen konnte: Bibliothek, Blütenlesen (*Florilegia*), kostbare Steine (*Gemma gemmarum*), Museum, Raritäten-, Schau-, Schatz- und Wunderkammer, Historia, Theatrum, Dictionarium, Lexikon und Wörterbuch.[2] All diese Begriffe vereint der Geist des enzyklopädischen Denkens: Wissen möglichst umfassend zu versammeln und systematisch zu ordnen.

Gerade in der alphabetischen Ordnung des Allumfassenden liegt ein immenses absichtslos poetisches Potenzial: *Sofa, sofort, Software, sogar, Sohle, Sohn*

# Encyclopedia

The encyclopedia is a circling around knowing and not knowing, present and past, abundance and void, curiosity and compulsion, order and coincidence.

The term "general knowledge" might be the most precise correspondence to the original meaning of "encyclopedia" (εγκυκλοπαίδεια, *enkýklios paideía*, all-round education). In Greek antiquity and the early Middle Ages the word was restricted to the curriculum of the schools and universities—the *artes liberales*.[1] "Encyclopedia" didn't come into currency until the early eighteenth century; it was preceded by a variety of terms under which the practice of encyclopedic writing in all manner of disciplines could be classified: library, anthology (*florilegium*), treasure trove (*gemma gemmarum*), museum, cabinet of curiosities, *historia*, *theatrum*, lexicon, glossary, and dictionary.[2] All these terms unite the spirit of encyclopedic thinking: to collect knowledge as comprehensively as possible and to order it systematically.

Alphabetical ordering in particular contains an immense, all-embracing, unintentionally poetic potential: *world, worm, worship, would, wound, woven*

Diese einem Herkunftswörterbuch entnommene melodische Wortfolge führt vor, was sowohl für das Sprachliche als auch für die Bildwelten der Enzyklopädie gilt. Ein Ordnungssystem etabliert sich zur Überwindung des Arbiträren und erzeugt als Nebeneffekt Zufälligkeit. Wie in einem Spiegelkabinett der Bedeutungen erhält man über den Zufall Zutritt zu einer Parallelwelt, in der die Bedeutung verschoben, die Wahrheit aufgesplittert und dennoch eine – wenn auch andere – Form von Erkenntnis gegeben ist. Die alphabetische Anordnung der Lemmata erzeugt über den Zufall eigentümliche Zusammenstellungen unterschiedlicher Wissensgebiete. Aber auch die Themenbereiche selbst, zu denen man Enzyklopädien bei einer Recherche im Internet findet, sind erstaunlich vielfältig und ergeben exemplarisch nebeneinandergestellt eine eigenwillige, multiperspektivische Sicht auf die Welt: So gibt es etwa eine Enzyklopädie der Geheimlehren, des strategischen Managements, der Feen, des Suizids, der Finanzen, des Wassers, der Sterne, der statistischen Wissenschaften, der Globalität, der Naturheilkunde, der psychoaktiven Pflanzen, der Säugetiere, der Rassehunde, der Serienmörder, des Holocaust, der technischen Indikatoren, der Cannabiszucht, der Toxikologie, der Science-Fiction, des Krebses, der Erfindungen, der Waffen des Zweiten Weltkrieges, der Signalpistolen, der Faulheit, der Komödientheorie, des modernen Bodybuildings, der Militäruniformen des 19. Jahrhunderts, der Möbel vom Barock bis zur Gegenwart, der Mythologie, der Anatomie, der Gartengehölze, der Steinheilkunde, der Pilze, der Neuzeit usw.[3]

Was einst Universalgelehrte der Renaissance und Enzyklopädisten der Aufklärung anstrebten und was im zeitgenössischen Begriff der Allgemeinbildung seinen Ausdruck findet, ist der Wunsch nach einer umfassenden, möglichst lückenlosen Bildung. Wenn man sich die exemplarische Liste der oben aufgezählten wissenschaftlichen und populärwissenschaftlichen Themenfelder vor Augen hält, erscheint so etwas wie ein „Universalwissen“ vollkommen aussichtslos, utopisch und unmöglich. Zu spezifisch, zu umfangreich ist, was es zu wissen gibt.

Nun werfen das Erstellen einer Enzyklopädie und das mit ihr einhergehende Konzept des Universalwissens zwei Fragen auf: Was *muss* man wissen und was *will* man wissen?

This melodious sequence taken from a dictionary demonstrates something common to both the linguistic and the visual worlds of the encyclopedia. An ordering system is established to overcome arbitrariness, and as a side effect it generates coincidence. As in a hall of mirrors, chance permits entry into a parallel world in which meanings are shifted and the truth fragmented, and yet there is a form of knowledge—though different. The coincidence of alphabetical order produces curious combinations of different areas of knowledge. But the thematic areas—on which encyclopedias can be found via Internet searches—are themselves astonishingly varied, and exemplarily juxtaposed they result in an idiosyncratic, multi-perspectival view of the world. There is an encyclopedia of esoteric doctrine, for example, of strategic management, of fairies, suicide, finances, water, stars, statistical sciences, globality, natural medicine, psychoactive plants, mammals, pedigree dogs, serial killers, the Holocaust, technical indicators, cannabis cultivation, toxicology, science fiction, cancer, inventions, World War II weapons, flare guns, laziness, theory of comedy, modern bodybuilding, nineteenth-century military uniforms, furniture from the Baroque to the present, mythology, anatomy, garden shrubs, lapidary medicine, mushrooms, modernity, and so on.[3]

What was once the aspiration of Renaissance polymaths and Enlightenment encyclopedists, and is expressed in the contemporary idea of an all-round education, is the desire for universal, gapless knowledge. But in casting our eyes over the above example list, something like “universal knowledge” seems futile, utopian, and impossible. What there is to know is too specific and to extensive.

The compilation of an encyclopedia, along with the associated concept of universal knowledge, now raises two questions: what does one *have to* know, and what does one *want* to know?

The first question alludes to the social function of knowledge.[4] In this light, general knowledge should be understood as an assurance of social belonging guaranteed by a comparison of respective levels of knowledge. A search for an object to best symbolize this social fact might yield the popular encyclopedia or “conversations lexicon,” as such books were originally known. These decorative prestige objects with

Die erste Frage spielt auf die gesellschaftliche Funktion des Wissens an.[4] Allgemeinbildung ist unter diesem Blickwinkel als Versicherung der sozialen Zugehörigkeit zu verstehen, die über den Abgleich des jeweiligen Kenntnisstandes garantiert ist. Suchte man nach einem Gegenstand, der diese soziale Tatsache bestmöglich symbolisiert, dann würde sich das Konversationslexikon anbieten. Konversationslexika – dekorative Repräsentationsobjekte mit aufwendig goldornamentierten Buchrücken – waren vor allem im 18. und 19. Jahrhundert im Bürgertum sehr beliebt und erinnern an den Ehrgeiz, ja Zwang des Bürgertums, alles zur Konversation dienliche Wissen, wenn nicht im Kopf, dann zumindest zum Nachschlagen in Buchform, zur Verfügung zu haben. Die Brockhaus-Online-Enzyklopädie bezeichnet sich selbst als „Konversationslexikon im digitalen Zeitalter [...] für den gebildeten Diskurs".[5] Der Begriff „Konversationslexikon" ist, so scheint es, aktueller, als man erwarten würde.

Welche Felder sind es, über die wir Bescheid wissen müssen? 1999 erscheint das selbstbewusst betitelte Buch *Bildung. Alles, was man wissen muß* von Dietrich Schwanitz.[6] Es verhandelt die Geschichte Europas aus kultureller Sicht und versammelt prägende Ereignisse und Personen der Geschichte, Literatur, Kunst und Musik sowie philosophische und wissenschaftliche Weltbilder, die mit einer europäischen Identität verbunden sind. 2003 antwortet Ernst Peter Fischer mit dem Buch *Die andere Bildung. Was man von den Naturwissenschaften wissen sollte* – das „muß" hier schon relativiert auf ein „sollte". Wie der Titel schon besagt, beabsichtigt der Autor, das kulturell-geisteswissenschaftliche Wissen um naturwissenschaftliches Wissen, Grundwissen zu unserer biologischen und physikalischen Beschaffenheit, zu ergänzen. Interessant ist hier die Frage der Gewichtung von Kultur- und Naturwissenschaften innerhalb eines Gesamtsystems Allgemeinbildung. Die Naturwissenschaften haben eine lange Tradition der Wissensvermittlung an ein interessiertes Publikum, das nicht vom Fach ist. Es sind die fünf Bände *Kosmos – Entwurf einer physischen Weltbeschreibung* von Alexander von Humboldt, die zu den meistgelesenen Büchern des 19. Jahrhunderts gehörten.[7] Die Begeisterung für populärwissenschaftliche Literatur, die die Naturwissenschaften in Buch- und

elaborate gold-decorated covers were very popular with the bourgeoisie of the eighteenth and nineteenth centuries, and they recall the desire, even compulsion, of that class to have all the knowledge conducive to conversation at one's disposal, if not in one's head then at least in book form for reference. The Brockhaus online encyclopedia describes itself as a "conversations lexicon in the digital age [...] for educated discourse."[5] The term appears to be more contemporary than we might expect.

What are the fields we need to know about? The self-confidently titled *Bildung. Alles, was man wissen muß* [Education. Everything You Have to Know], by Dietrich Schwanitz, appeared in 1999.[6] The book deals with the history of Europe from a cultural point of view, and brings together defining events and protagonists from history, literature, art, and music, as well as philosophical and scientific epistemes associated with European identity. In 2003 Ernst Peter Fischer responded with *Die andere Bildung. Was man von den Naturwissenschaften wissen sollte* [The Other Education. What You Should Know about the Natural Sciences]—"have to" already relativized here by "should." As the title conveys, the author's intention is to complement the humanities with scientific knowledge, with the basics of our biological and physical nature. The weighting of the cultural and natural sciences within the system of all-round education is interesting here. The sciences have a long tradition of conveying knowledge to an amateur interested public. The five volumes of Alexander von Humboldt's *Cosmos: A Sketch of a Physical Description of the Universe* was one of the most widely read books of the nineteenth century.[7] The enthusiasm for popular scientific literature in book and later in magazine form has continued until today.[8] The quality of these formats isn't always up to standard, so that a desire for a "science criticism" (in the sense of serious scientific journalism) similar to "art criticism," "theater criticism," or "music criticism" has been expressed.[9]

The question of what should be known soon turns general knowledge into a distinguishing mark of social class, as is the case with cultural preferences or the choice of clothing, place of residence, leisure activities, diet, and interior design—the habitus, all told, as determined by the sociologist Pierre Bourdieu. In an extensive empirical study

später Magazinform vermitteln, hält bis in die Gegenwart an.[8] Nicht immer ist die Qualität dieser Formate gewährleistet, sodass ein Wunsch nach einer „Wissenschaftskritik“ (im Sinne eines seriösen Wissenschaftsjournalismus) ähnlich einer „Kunstkritik“, „Theaterkritik“ oder „Musikkritik“ geäußert wird.[9]

Wenn es um die Frage geht, was man wissen muss, wird Allgemeinbildung sehr schnell zum Distinktionsmerkmal sozialer Klassen, genauso wie kulturelle Vorlieben oder die Auswahl der Kleidung, des Wohnortes, der Freizeitaktivitäten, der Ernährung und der Einrichtung – alles in allem der Habitus, wie der Soziologe Pierre Bourdieu feststellt. Er hat in einer umfangreichen empirischen Studie und einer theoretischen Analyse des Geschmacks „die feinen Unterschiede“ ausfindig gemacht, die eine Gesellschaft klassifizieren.[10] Bildung hat dabei selbstverständlich eine wesentliche Bedeutung. „Bildungseifer“, so nennt Bourdieu ein Prinzip, das sich je nach sozialer Klasse unterschiedlich manifestiert, hier beschrieben anhand des Kleinbürgertums (der 1970er-Jahre in Frankreich): „Der Bildungseifer zeigt sich unter anderem in einer besonderen Häufung von Zeugnissen bedingungsloser kultureller Beflissenheit (Vorliebe für ‚wohlerzogene‘ Freunde und für ‚bildende‘ oder ‚lehrreiche‘ Aufführungen), oft von einem Gefühl eigenen Unwerts begleitet (‚Malerei ist schön, aber schwierig‘, usw.), das genauso groß ist wie der Respekt, den man der Sache entgegenbringt.“[11] Aus dieser Perspektive ist die Aneignung von Wissen als Steigerung des kulturellen Kapitals zu verstehen und mit einem angestrengten Streben nach einer immer weiter zu verbessernden Position innerhalb eines sozioökonomischen Spektrums verbunden.[12] Die Aneignung von Wissen bedeutet die Erfüllung einer Pflicht, aber – das darf nicht unerwähnt bleiben – auch eine Stärkung des Selbstbewusstseins. Ein wissendes und selbstbewusstes Bürgertum, das wendig im Denken und damit politisch urteilsfähig ist, zu stärken, das war Intention der Enzyklopädien der Aufklärung – ein Sinnbild dafür ist die *Encyclopédie ou Dictionnaire raisonné des sciences, des arts et des métiers*, erstmals 1751 von Jean Le Rond d'Alembert und Denis Diderot herausgegeben. Der Freiheits- und Selbstbestimmungsgedanke, der diesen Wissenssammlungen inhärent ist und auch die Vorstellung von Allgemeinbildung formt, ist zweifelsfrei Bestandteil

and theoretical analysis of taste, Bourdieu has identified the “distinctions” by which a society is classified.[10] Education of course has a crucial significance. “Cultural goodwill” [*la bonne volunté culturelle*], as Bourdieu calls a principle that manifests differently according to social class, is here described with reference to the (1970s French) petit-bourgeoisie: “Cultural goodwill is expressed, inter alia, in a particularly frequent choice of the most unconditional testimonies of cultural docility (the choice of ‘well-bred’ friends, a taste for ‘educational’ or ‘instructive’ entertainments), often combined with a sense of unworthiness (‘paintings are nice but difficult’) commensurate with the respect that is accorded.”[11] From this perspective the acquisition of knowledge can be understood as an increase in cultural capital, linked with the aspiration to continual enhancement of one's position within a socio-economic spectrum.[12] The acquisition of knowledge represents the fulfillment of a duty, but also—it must be said—a strengthening of self-confidence. The consolidation of a knowledgeable and confident civil society, flexible in thinking and therefore capable of political judgement, was the intention of the Enlightenment encyclopedias—emblematic in this is the *Encyclopédie ou Dictionnaire raisonné des sciences, des arts et des métiers*, first published in 1751 by Jean Le Rond d'Alembert and Denis Diderot. The idea of freedom and self-determination inherent in these anthologies of knowledge is unequivocally an aspect of contemporary European identity. (See “Epistemic Violence” for the fact that many knowledge groups and forms are disregarded, and that knowledge is associated with exclusivity and exclusion.)

What does one *want* to know? This is a different, subjective question. Everyone is his or her own knowledge cosmos. What one wants to know depends on curiosity, and on an aspiration to knowledge, an enjoyment of learning. Research belongs in the category of wanting to know, and the dinosaurs in the pursuit of knowledge are the polymaths.[13] We may suppose that they were driven more by cultural goodwill than by a thirst for knowledge. The frequently announced extinction of this species is founded in the vast and insurmountable volume of thoroughly specialized knowledge that has accumulated over the generations.[14] Doubt as to the demise of this figure is expressed by

einer zeitgenössischen europäischen Identität. (Dass dabei jedoch viele Wissensgruppen und -formen ausgeklammert bleiben und Wissen mit Exklusivität und Exklusion verbunden ist, das ist unter „Epistemische Gewalt" nachzulesen).

Was will man wissen? Das ist eine andere Frage von subjektivem Charakter. Jedes Subjekt ist sein eigener Wissenskosmos. Was man wissen will, das ist mit Neugierde verbunden, auch mit einem Streben nach Erkenntnis, eine lustvolle Lernerfahrung. Die Forschung gehört in die Kategorie des Wissenwollens. Zu forschen bedeutet in seinem Ursprung zu fragen.[13] Ein besonderes Exemplar unter Forschenden sind Dinosaurier des Wissensbetriebes – Universalgelehrte. Es lässt sich vermuten, dass diese eher von einem Wissensdurst als einem Bildungseifer angetrieben werden. Im über die Generationen angehäuften unüberschaubar und unbewältigbar gewordenen Volumen an Wissen, das durch und durch spezialisiert ist, ist das oft angekündigte Aussterben dieser Spezies begründet.[14] Zweifel an der Auslöschung dieses Wissenstypus formuliert der Historiker Peter Burke, Verfasser von *The Polymath: A Cultural History from Leonardo da Vinci to Susan Sontag*. Seine Studie ist vom Interesse motiviert, das Fortbestehen der Universalgelehrten in einer Kultur wachsender Spezialisierung zu untersuchen und zu belegen.[15] Er konzentriert sich dabei auf Gelehrte mit „enzyklopädischen" Interessen und akademischen Karrieren.[16] Das Buch beinhaltet eine Liste von 500 vorwiegend westlichen Universalgelehrten vom 14. Jahrhundert bis in die Gegenwart (der erste in der Liste, Filippo Brunelleschi, 1377 geboren und 1446 verstorben, der letzte, Stephen J. Gould, 1941 geboren und 2002 verstorben), natürlich mit dem Vorbehalt von Auslassungen.[17]

Die Überzahl derer, die den Titel der Universalgelehrten tragen, ist männlich, weiß und europäisch. Ihre Wissensgebiete liegen in der Hierarchie der wissenschaftlichen Disziplinen weit vorne. Unter dem Blickwinkel der epistemischen Gewalt, die aus einer globalen Dominanz andro- und eurozentrischen Wissens im Zuge von Kolonialisierung und Christianisierung als wissenschaftliche Vorbedingungen resultiert, erscheint das Konzept der Universalgelehrten in einem anderen Licht. An dieser Stelle wäre nun ein gedanklicher Schnitt interessant, der sich assoziativ aus dem Wort universal ergibt:

the historian Peter Burke, author of *The Polymath: A Cultural History from Leonardo da Vinci to Susan Sontag*. His study is motivated by an interest in examining and documenting the continued existence of the polymath in a culture of increasing specialization.[15] He concentrates on scholars with "encyclopedic" interests and academic careers.[16] The book contains a list of 500 mostly Western polymaths from the fourteenth century to the present (the first on the list is Filippo Brunelleschi, born 1377, died 1446; the last is Stephen J. Gould, born 1941, died 2002), naturally with the proviso of omissions.[17]

The majority of those considered polymaths are male, white, and European. Their areas of knowledge dominate the hierarchy of scientific disciplines. From the perspective of epistemic violence, which results from a global hegemony of andro- and Eurocentric knowledge through colonization and Christianization as scientific preconditions, the polymath appears in a different light. And here the referential word given to the concept by the German language—*Universalgelehrter*, or "universal scholar"—prompts an associative cut to the meanings of "universal":

"**universal** } adjective of, affecting, or done by all people or things in the world or in a particular group; applicable to all cases [...]
ORIGIN Late Middle English: from Old French, or from Latin *universalis*, from *universus* (see universe). [...]
**universe** } noun (the universe) all existing matter and space considered as a whole; the cosmos. [...]
ORIGIN Late Middle English: from Old French *univers* or Latin *universum*, neuter of *universus* "combined into one, whole," from *uni-* "one" + *versus* "turned" (past participle of *vertere*)."[18]

The *uni*verse is the place that encompasses everything and can be nothing more. This denotation of completeness is also implicit in the word "universal." Purely on the level of meaning, theoretical physics can assist with a conceptual transfer here, as it postulates a "multiverse," the existence of parallel worlds. "What's at the heart of the subject," says the physicist Brian Greene, "is whether there exist realms that challenge convention by suggesting that what we've long thought to be the universe is only one component

**universal** „allgemein, gesamt, umfassend; weltweit": Das Adjektiv wurde im 16. Jh. aus spätlat. *universalis* „zur Gesamtheit gehörig, allgemein" entlehnt. Dies ist eine Bildung zu lat. *universus* „in eins gekehrt, zu einer Einheit zusammengefasst; ganz, sämtlich; allgemein; umfassend", eigener Zusammensetzung aus lat. *unus* „einer, ein Einziger" [...] und lat. *versus* „gewendet" [...].

**Universum** „Weltall": Das Fremdwort wurde im 17. Jh. aus lat. *universum* „das Ganze als Inbegriff aller Teile; die ganze Welt, das Weltall" entlehnt. Dies ist das substantivierte Neutrum von lat. *universus* „ganz, gesamt, allgemein" (vgl. *universal*).[18]

Das Welt*all* ist der Ort, der alles umfasst und nicht mehr sein kann. Diese auf Vollständigkeit beruhende Begrenzung ist auch der Bedeutung „universal" eingeschrieben. Hier kann, ganz auf der Bedeutungsebene, die theoretische Physik bei einem Gedankentransfer aushelfen. Diese nämlich postuliert, rein theoretisch, ein Multiversum, die Existenz von Parallelwelten. „Wird unsere konventionelle Vorstellung durch die Existenz von Bereichen in Frage gestellt, die nahelegen, dass das, was wir lange Zeit für *das* Universum gehalten haben, letztlich nur ein Bestandteil einer viel größeren, vielleicht auch viel seltsameren und größtenteils verborgenen Wirklichkeit ist?", fragt der Physiker Brian Greene.[19] Diese Frage, auf die die theoretische Physik mit unterschiedlichen Denkansätzen – Doppelgänger, inflationäre Expansion, Branwelt-Szenarien, Stringlandschaften[20] – antwortet, kann jedoch auch irdisch-semantisch, posthumanistisch und postkolonial Sinn ergeben: Gerade wenn es um das geht, was wir „Wissen" nennen, hier und jetzt, wäre es doch interessant, dieses Ideal eines „Universalwissens" multiversal umzudenken.

**Multiversum:** nicht im Sinne eines „noch mehr" oder „viel größer", sondern im Sinne eines „parallel", „nebeneinander", und „gleichwertig". Wenn sich, hier und jetzt, der Lichtkegel auf das Universale zu einem diffusen Licht auf das Multiversale zerstreut, in dem nicht alles lösbar und endgültig verstehbar erscheint und Lücken magische Löcher sind.

of a far grander, perhaps far stranger, and mostly hidden, reality."[19] This question, which theoretical physics takes various approaches to answer—doppelgänger, inflationary expansion, *braneworld* scenarios, string landscapes[20]—can also make sense in mundane, semantic, posthuman, postcolonial ways: particularly in relation to what we call "knowledge," here and now, it would be interesting to rethink the ideal of "universal knowledge" multiversally.

**Multiverse**: not in the sense of "even more" or "much larger," but in the sense of "parallel," "co-existing," and "equal." When, here and now, the ray of light focused on the universal disperses into a diffuse illumination of the multiversal, in which not everything seems resolvable and definitively comprehensible, and all gaps are magic holes.

## A±Z

"A–Z" is the subtitle often given to encyclopedias. The book's ordering system is thus explained in its title, but that isn't all. "A–Z" presumably also suggests a guarantee of completeness and a record of everything that can possibly be recorded. A and Z are the beginning and the end within which everything on the respective subject is dealt with, be it psychotropic drugs, periodontology, English manners, vegan cookery, industrial design, worker protection, meat, shop-council practice, dinosaur parades, medical terms, healing stones, snacks and starters, intervention in relationship and family therapy, trees, positive thinking, horseback-riding, self-sufficiency, fish diseases, or modern architecture.[21]

*A±Z* here means adding the numerical to the alphabetical. *A±Z* rethinks A–Z as a subtraction—the "to" sign is read as a minus. The ± (plus-minus sign) indicates the possibility of adding in or taking away; it points to an area of deviation, an existing uncertainty, or to a spectrum between negative and positive. It is a simultaneous double sign that includes an idea of "or" and has been used for almost 400 years.[22] *A±Z* denotes the space we are in here: a numerocentric, logocentric, native-language, anglicized, inherited, visualized, visualizing, metaphorical, metonymic, fragmentary, ordered, chance-generated, chance-affirmative, enumerative, and-so-on world view from A to Z.

## A±Z

„A–Z", das ist der Untertitel, der Enzyklopädien oftmals beigefügt wird. Damit wird das Ordnungssystem unmittelbar im Buchtitel geklärt, aber das dürfte nicht alles sein: Vermutlich suggeriert „A–Z" zudem, dass eine umfassende Fülle gewährleistet und alles festgehalten wurde, was festzuhalten möglich ist. A und Z sind der Anfang und das Ende, innerhalb deren alles zum jeweiligen Thema abgehandelt wird, seien es nun Psychopharmaka, Parodontologie, die feine englische Art, veganes Kochen, Industriedesign, Arbeitsschutz, Fleisch, Betriebsratspraxis, Dino-Parade, medizinische Fachwörter, Heilsteine, Snacks und Vorspeisen, Interventionen in der Paar- und Familientherapie, Bäume, positives Denken, Reiten, Selbstversorger, Fischkrankheiten oder moderne Architektur.[21]

*A±Z*, das bedeutet hier die Addition des Numerischen zum Alphabetischen. Durch *A±Z* wird das A–Z zu einer Subtraktion umgedacht – das Bis-Zeichen wird als Minus gelesen. Das ± (Plusminuszeichen) zeigt die Möglichkeit des Hinzufügens und des Wegnehmens, es verweist auf einen möglichen Bereich der Abweichung, auf eine gegebene Unsicherheit oder auf ein Spektrum zwischen Negativem und Positivem. Es ist ein simultanes Doppelzeichen, das ein gedankliches „oder" einschließt und seit beinahe 400 Jahren verwendet wird.[22] *A±Z* bezeichnet den Raum, in dem wir uns hier befinden: in einem numerozentrischen, einem logozentrischen, einem muttersprachlichen, einem anglizistischen, einem geerbten, einem verbildlichten, einem verbildlichenden, einem metaphorischen, einem metonymischen, einem lückenhaften, einem geordneten, einem zufallsgenerierten, einem zufallsaffirmativen, einem aufzählenden, einem Und-so-weiter-Weltbild von A bis Z.

1 Dazu zählen Trivium (Grammatik, Logik und Rhetorik) und Quadrivium (Arithmetik, Geometrie, Astronomie und Musiktheorie). Vgl. Peter Burke, *Papier und Marktgeschrei. Die Geburt der Wissensgesellschaft* (Berlin: Wagenbach, 2001), 92.

2 Vgl. Ulrich Johannes Schneider, *Die Erfindung des allgemeinen Wissens. Enzyklopädisches Schreiben im Zeitalter der Aufklärung* (Berlin: Akademieverlag, 2013), 16 f.

3 Diese Auswahl an Enzyklopädien ist deutsch- oder englischsprachig und wurde über die Google-Suche nach „Enzyklopädie der" und „Encyclopedia of" gefunden.

4 Die Rede ist hier von einer westlichen, europäischen Gesellschaft des Wissens.

5 https://brockhaus.at/info/konversationslexikon, abgerufen am 15.11.2022.

6 *Bildung. Alles, was man wissen muß* von Dietrich Schwanitz, Originalausgabe 1999, Eichborn Verlag, Frankfurt am Main, wurde bis heute mehr als 30-mal neu aufgelegt. Ob der Titel vom Autor selbst oder vom Verlag gewünscht wurde, kann hier nicht beantwortet werden.

7 Der Autor bezieht sich auf den deutschsprachigen Raum. Vgl. Klaus Taschwer, „Vom Kosmos zur Wunderwelt – Über Populärwissenschaftliche Magazine einst und jetzt" in: *Öffentliche Wissenschaft. Neue Perspektiven der Vermittlung in der wissenschaftlichen Weiterbildung*, hrsg. von Peter Faulstich (Bielefeld: Transcript Verlag, 2006), 74.

8 Ebd., 73 f.

9 Ebd., 82–84.

10 *Die feinen Unterschiede*, so lautet auch der deutschsprachige Titel dieses Schlüsselwerks der Sozialwissenschaften, das 1979 erstmalig unter dem Titel *La Distinction. Critique sociale du jugement* publiziert wurde.

11 Pierre Bourdieu, *Die feinen Unterschiede. Kritik der gesellschaftlichen Urteilskraft* (Frankfurt am Main: Suhrkamp, 2001), 503.

12 Vgl. dazu ebd., 212 f., das Diagramm zum Raum der sozialen Positionen und der Lebensstile.

13 „[F]orschen: Das ursprünglich nur im hochd. Sprachgebiet gebräuchliche Verb mhd. *vorschen*, ahd. *forscon* ‚fragen, [aus]forschen' geht wie lat. *proscere* ‚fordern, verlangen' (^postulieren) und aind. *prcchāti* ‚er fragt' auf die idg. Wurzel **per[e]k-* ‚fragen, bitten' zurück [...]. Heute wird ‚forschen' außer in der Bedeutung ‚zu finden, zu ermitteln suchen' besonders im Sinne von ‚sich um wissenschaftliche Erkenntnis bemühen, mit wissenschaftlichen Methoden ergründen' verwendet." In *Das Herkunftswörterbuch. Etymologie der deutschen Sprache* (Mannheim, Leipzig, Wien, Zürich: 2007), 232.

14 Eine Internetrecherche zeigt, dass in unterschiedlichen deutsch- und englischsprachigen Medien wiederholt von Gottfried Wilhelm Leibniz, aber auch von Hermann von Helmholtz als „letztem Universalgelehrten" gesprochen wird.

15 Peter Burke, *Polymath: A Cultural History from Leonardo da Vinci to Susan Sontag*, (New Haven und London: Yale University Press, 2020), 5.

16 Ebd., 2.

17 Ebd., 247.

18 *Das Herkunftswörterbuch. Etymologie der deutschen Sprache,* 881 f.
19 Brian Greene, *Die verborgene Wirklichkeit. Paralleluniversen und die Gesetze des Kosmos* (München: Siedler Verlag, 2012), 14.
20 Vgl. ebd., 17 f.
21 Diese Aufzählung besteht aus englisch- und deutschsprachigen Büchern, die im Buchtitel „A–Z" tragen und über eine Internetrecherche gefunden wurden.
22 Es taucht erstmalig 1626 im Tafelwerk von Albert Girard und 1631 in den *Clavis mathematicae* von William Oughtred auf, vgl. Florian Cajori, *A History of Mathematical Notations,* (New York: Dover Publications, 1993), 245.



1 They included the *trivium* (grammar, logic and rhetoric) and the *quadrivium* (arithmetic, geometry, astronomy and music theory). See Peter Burke, *Papier und Marktgeschrei. Die Geburt der Wissensgesellschaft* (Berlin: Wagenbach, 2001), 92.
2 See Ulrich Johannes Schneider, *Die Erfindung des allgemeinen Wissens. Enzyklopädisches Schreiben im Zeitalter der Aufklärung* (Berlin: Akademieverlag, 2013), 16f.
3 This selection of encyclopedias is German or English, and was found through a Google search for "Enzyklopädie" and "Encyclopedia of."
4 Speaking here of an occidental, European knowledge society.
5 Translated from https://brockhaus.at/info/konversationslexikon, (November 15, 2022).
6 Dietrich Schwanitz, *Bildung. Alles, was man wissen muß* (Frankfurt am Main: Eichborn Verlag, 1999), has been republished 30 times to date. Whether the title was given by the author or his publisher can't be ascertained here.
7 The author refers to the German-speaking world. See Klaus Taschwer, "Vom Kosmos zur Wunderwelt – Über Populärwissenschaftliche Magazine einst und jetzt," in *Öffentliche Wissenschaft. Neue Perspektiven der Vermittlung in der wissenschaftlichen Weiterbildung,* ed. Peter Faulstich (Bielefeld: Transcript Verlag, 2006), 74.
8 Ibid., 73f.
9 Ibid., 82–84.
10 This key work in the social sciences was first published in 1979 under the title of *La Distinction. Critique sociale du jugement.*
11 Pierre Bourdieu, *Distinction: A Social Critique of Judgement and Taste,* trans. Richard Nice (Cambridge: Harvard University Press, 1984), 321.
12 See ibid., 128f, diagrams of "The space of social position" and "The space of life-styles."
13 "From Greek *polymathēs* 'having learned much,' from *polyu-* 'much' + *manthanein* 'learn,'" in *The New Oxford Dictionary of English* (Oxford: Oxford University Press, 1998), 1437.
14 An Internet search shows that Gottfried Wilhelm Leibniz is frequently referred to as the "last polymath" in various German and English media, with Hermann von Helmholtz as a close second.
15 Peter Burke, *Polymath: A Cultural History from Leonardo da Vinci to Susan Sontag,* (New Haven and London: Yale University Press, 2020), 5.
16 Ibid., 2.
17 Ibid., 247.
18 *The New Oxford Dictionary of English* (Oxford: Oxford University Press, 1998), 2024.
19 Brian Greene, *The Hidden Reality* (New York: Alfred A. Knopf, 2011, epub), 17.
20 See ibid, 22ff.
21 List of books in English or German with A–Z in the title, found through an Internet search.
22 It first appears in 1626 in a volume of plates by Albert Girard, and in 1631 in William Oughtred's *Clavis mathematicae.* See Florian Cajori, *A History of Mathematical Notations,* (New York: Dover Publications, 1993), 245.

# Enzyklopädie

Ein Kommentar von Khadija von Zinnenburg Carroll

Wenn ich das Wort Enzyklopädie höre, kommt mir unwillkürlich Wilhelm Blandowski in den Sinn, der im 19. Jahrhundert eine Enzyklopädie des australischen Kontinents schaffen wollte. Das Ganze geschah im Gefolge Alexander von Humboldts und natürlich des französisch-revolutionären Strebens, vollständige Karten der Welt zu erstellen. Überdies träumt vielleicht nur der unglückliche Mensch davon, ein derartiges Buch zu machen. Ich denke, ich war ein unglücklicher Mensch, als ich meine Thesen in ein Buch zu packen versuchte und mich gern mit Blandowski identifizierte, der so spektakulär an der Darstellung des Kontinents gescheitert war, über den auch ich schreiben wollte: Terra Australis. Die Verflochtenheit aller Dinge an einem Ort und die Unvereinbarkeit vieler geheimer und geheiligter Landstriche in Australien lässt

# Encyclopedia

A Comment by Khadija von Zinnenburg Carroll

When I hear the word encyclopedia, I can't help but remember the figure of Wilhelm Blandowski, who was aspiring to make an encyclopedia of the Australian continent in the nineteenth century. This was a moment following Alexander von Humboldt, and of course the French Revolutionary aspiration to make complete maps of the world. Also, the hapless individual would dream of creating such a book. I think that was a moment in my own life when I was a hapless individual trying to create a book out of my thesis, and was readily identifying with Blandowski, who failed so spectacularly to represent the continent that I was also trying to write about: Terra Australis. The interrelation of everything in a place and the incommensurability of many secret and sacred parts in Australia makes the idea of the encyclopedia appealing to a critter

eine Enzyklopädie für eine arme Kreatur, die auf der Suche nach Heimat ist, als attraktive Idee erscheinen. (Meine Dissertation folgte, gestützt auf mündlichen Erzählungen und Kolonialarchive, mehreren solcher Kreaturen in die Vergangenheit.) Deshalb frage ich mich, ob der Begriff Enzyklopädie nicht die Art von Begriff ist, der sich als Spiegel für verschiedenste Momente und Praktiken eignet. Die vollständige Welt, die jede Person und jeder Moment sind, wenn sie ihr vollstes Sein erkennen. Die Enzyklopädie ist demnach auch ein Buch, das diese Vollständigkeit zu erfassen versucht.

Das Enzyklopädisieren könnte überdies als Versuch betrachtet werden, alles auf einen Schlag mit Sinn zu erfüllen, so wie *A±Z* oder auch andere Versuche, vollständig zu sein und die Welt mit Sinn zu erfüllen. Daraus folgt, dass die Begriffe Enzyklopädie und epistemische Gewalt miteinander verbunden sind, in diesem Buch wie in diesem Essay. Denn der Versuch, alles zu verstehen, ist eine Art Aufklärungsprojekt, das Wissen, welches sich rationaler Erklärung entzieht, ausschließt und abwertet. Diese Auslöschung nichtkanonischer Praktiken und Wissensformen wird als ein Bestandteil der Gewalt des europäischen Expansionsprojekts erlebt, das dann Materielles wie Immaterielles kolonisiert hat.

Wie können wir uns nach diesem massiven Auslöschungsversuch wieder mit dem verbinden, was keinen Eingang in die Enzyklopädien der Aufklärung fand? Ganz offensichtlich müssen wir uns zunächst einmal anderer Methoden bedienen; eine davon ist z. B. die Improvisation in der Performance. Ich schlage vor, dem anhand einer Zulu-Enzyklopädie (ein Oxymoron – denn was könnten diese beiden Begriffe miteinander gemein haben?) näher nachzugehen: einem Beutel voller Zeichen während des kurzen Moments, in dem ich eine Sangoma konsultierte, der so vollständig war, wie es eine Enzyklopädie nur sein kann. Die Konsultation nahm ich gemeinsam mit einer anderen Künstlerin, Pélagie Gbaguidi, nach einer intensiven Theaterimprovisation in Anspruch. Wir liefen zusammen durch die Straßen Johannesburgs in die Gegend, in der die Sangoma praktizieren. Da Praktiken wie Voodoo bis zur Unverständlichkeit exotisiert wurden, scheint es, als wäre eine Voodoo-Enzyklopädie in Zulu schwer zu lesen oder schreiben. Zu viel ist über schriftlose Kulturen gesagt und zu wenig dafür getan worden. Kulturen, in denen

in search of place. (My PhD thesis followed several such critters through portals to the past, drawing from oral histories and colonial archives.) This makes me wonder whether encyclopedia is not also the kind of term that lends itself to being a mirror of different moments and practices. The complete world that every person and every moment is when they recognize their fullest being. So too the encyclopedia is a book that attempts to capture this completeness.

Encyclopediarizing might also be said to be a practice of trying to make sense of everything, all at once, just like *A±Z*, just like other ways of being complete and making sense of the world. So it comes that the word encyclopedia and epistemic violence dovetail each other, both in this book and in this essay. For the attempt to understand everything is a kind of Enlightenment project that excludes and devalues knowledge that evades rational explanation. The erasure of those practices and forms of knowledge outside of the canon is experienced as part of the violence of the European expansionist project that then colonized the material and immaterial.

After this vigorous attempt at erasure, how can we begin to reconnect with that which was not included in the Enlightenment encyclopedias? Obviously we have to use different methods to begin with; for example, the play of improvisation in performance is one way. To explore this question I want to propose something: a Zulu encyclopedia (an oxymoron—for what could these two terms have to do with each other?), a bag of signs based on just a moment in which I consulted sangoma, and which indeed was so complete as an encyclopedia can also be. This consultation was something another artist Pélagie Gbaguidi and I sought out after an intensive session of improvisation in a theatre. We walked out through the streets of Johannesburg together to a street where the sangoma oracles practice. Of course, because practices like voodoo have been exoticized to obscurity, it feels like a voodoo encyclopedia in Zulu would be something hard to read or write. Too much has been said and too little has been done about cultures without a practice of writing. Cultures in which the lines drawn in flour are the material of most serious exegesis for the scholars.

If an encyclopedia is an aspiration to catalogue the world, it is a kind of oracle of the past, when one reads it against the grain

mit Mehl gezogene Linien das Material für äußerst ernsthafte Exegesen der Gelehrten sind.

Wenn eine Enzyklopädie das Bestreben ist, die Welt zu katalogisieren, so ist sie eine Art Orakel der Vergangenheit, wenn man sie gegen den Strich liest. Der Zeichenbestand, auf den sich andere Kulturen zum Verständnis ihrer Gegenwart und Zukunft stützen, ist ebenfalls ein solcher Index, der aber in eine andere zeitliche Richtung führen kann. Schließlich könnte die Enzyklopädie als Index einer bestimmten Kultur gesehen werden. Insofern ist auch *A±Z* von Payer Gabriel ein Index ihres Universums und ein Spiegel mitteleuropäischer, insbesondere Wiener Praktiken, selbstverständlich mit Einflüssen von überall her. Lassen Sie mich demgegenüber das extreme Beispiel durchspielen, nur um zu sehen, ob es aufgeht. Im Voodoo wird die Enzyklopädie vom Priester oder der Priesterin interpretiert. Sie oder er deutet die Zeichen und teilt mit, was sie bedeuten.

## Die Tragödie der Übersetzung

*A±Z* ist mehr als eine Enzyklopädie, weil die Einträge assoziativ zwischen Bildern stehen und textlich in die Tiefe gehen. Sie kommt mir darum eher wie ein hybrides Manifest für jeden Buchstaben vor.

Die Tragödie der Übersetzung besteht in der Unmöglichkeit, einen Text in eine andere Sprache zu übertragen, aber im Grunde ist das auch die Tragödie der Sprache an sich. Jede sinnliche Erfahrung wird als schwacher Abklatsch in Worte übersetzt. So wie jedes Bild die Welt unvollständig wiedergibt, zeigt die Enzyklopädie *A±Z*, dass wissenschaftliche Bilder subjektiv sind.

Sie erscheint verriegelt und verschlossen, selbst das umfassendste aller Bücher zwischen Deckel gepresst. Worte für alles. Ein Buch für alles. Warum können wir nicht zugeben, dass wir in Individualsprachen, Dialekten, Mundarten sprechen, die vielleicht einzig und allein die unseren sind? Auch wenn bei Ihnen etwas ankommt, fühlen sich das von mir Gemeinte und das von Ihnen Gehörte wie zwei Paar Schuhe an.

Die Absurdität des Übersetzens zeigt sich auch in Jorge Luis Borges' Geschichte von dem Reich, in dem die Verfertigung immer genauerer Landkarten schließlich zu einer Karte im Maßstab 1:1 führt, einer

in which it was intended. The range of signs that other cultures draw on to understand their present and future is also this kind of index, which may lead in another temporal direction. After all, the encyclopedia could be read as an index of a certain culture. So *A±Z* by Payer Gabriel is an index of their universe and a mirror of central European and Viennese practice in particular, with influences of course from all around. Let me take an extreme example in contrast, just to see if this idea plays out. In voodoo the encyclopedia is interpreted by the priest. This priest interprets the signs and gives their interpretation.

## The tragedy of translation

The *A±Z* is more than an encyclopedia because the entries are associative between visuals and with depth in their textual length. It appears to me therefore as a hybrid manifesto for each letter.

The tragedy of translation is the impossibility of ever rendering one text into another language, but then this is actually also the tragedy of language itself. Every sensorial experience is rendered as a poor translation into words. Just as each image translates the world in a partial way, the *A±Z* encyclopedia shows us how scientific images are subjective.

As if it were blocked and bottled up, like putting covers on even the most expansive of books: the encyclopedia. Words for everything. A book for everything. Why can we not acknowledge that we speak in idiosyncrasies, in dialects and vernaculars that are possibly our own, alone. While this might resonate for you, what I meant and you heard feel like two different things.

The absurdity of translating is also captured by Jorge Luis Borges in a story he wrote about an empire, proud of its accurate maps. Drawing ever more accurate maps, its cartographers end up with a 1:1 scale map, a map the size of the whole empire. I imagine this map of Borges's as a printed transparency that could be overlaid onto our world, and if aligned it would be invisible, but if it slipped a bit this 1:1 map would also distort our view of the actual terrain under it. But what is the actual terrain? What is actual and what of that can we see in the terrain?

This is a funny metaphor for the idea of an encyclopedia of research-led practices.

Landkarte von der Größe des ganzen Reiches. Ich stelle mir diese Karte als ein bedrucktes Transparentpapier vor, das sich über die Welt legen lässt und – ordentlich ausgerichtet – unsichtbar ist, leicht verschoben jedoch auch unseren Blick auf das eigentliche Land darunter verzerrt. Aber was ist das eigentliche Land? Was ist eigentlich und was davon erkennen wir an dem Land?

Das ist eine seltsame Metapher für eine Enzyklopädie forschungsgeleiteter Praktiken. Denn so wie sich eine Taxonomie schaffen lässt, so lässt sich jede Regel bei genauerer Betrachtung individuell auslegen, und offensichtlich geht es in der Wissenschaft üblicherweise um das Zerlegen, Generalisieren, Zusammenfassen von Dingen, das Schaffen von Regeln und Verallgemeinerungen, und einer Sprache, die natürlich die größte Abstraktion der Welt ist. Da wir nicht für jedes Atom im Universum über ein eigenes Wort verfügen, obwohl sich das Universum eigentlich aus diesen unzähligen Atomen zusammensetzt, müssen wir eben in groben Begriffen wahrnehmen. Jede Taxonomie stellt eine grobe Generalisierung dar und ist damit auch eine Form von Epistemizid, eine strategische Auslöschung von Bedeutung mit dem Ziel, die Dinge zu kontrollieren und zu ordnen. Diesen Willen zur Kontrolle und Ordnung der Dinge legen Menschen nicht nur in Bezug auf ihre künstlerischen Praktiken an den Tag. Ist das langsame Verfertigen einer Enzyklopädie eine Möglichkeit, sich dem Zwang zur Produktion ständig neuer Produkte für den Kunstmarkt zu entziehen?

### Eine Zulu-Enzyklopädie

In den Tagen vor der Konsultation der Zulu-Medizinfrau in Johannesburg, arbeitete ich an einer Performance über diese Art der Auslegung von Zukunftszeichen.

Ihre Materialien waren wirklich schön. Dominosteine, die, wenn sie verkehrt herum lagen, bedeuteten, dass ich meine Träume vergesse. Keine Ahnung, wie sie mein gebrochenes Herz erkannte oder den Ozean, der die Lieder meiner Vorfahren singt, aber irgendwo zwischen meinem Namen und diesem Beutel schaffte sie es.

Wenn uns die Zukunft vorhergesagt wird, erfasst uns ein gewisses Unbehagen, und die Zeichen bedürfen der Interpretation.

Wir benötigen eine Übersetzerin, sagt sie uns auf Englisch, denn ihre Arbeit wird in Zulu verrichtet. Ein junges Mädchen wird

Because as one could create a taxonomy, at the same time, when one looks closely, there are almost always individual takes to each rule, and of course science is traditionally about splitting things, generalizing them, clumping, creating rules and generalizations, and creating a language, which is of course the largest abstraction of the world. Because just as we don't have a word for every atom that exists in the universe, although the universe is actually made up of all these countless atoms, we have to perceive in more rudimentary terms. This is to say that any kind of taxonomy is a rudimentary generalization and therefore a form of epistemicide, a destruction of meaning, enacted strategically to control and organize things. This will to control and organize things is not something humans only have in relationship to their art practices. Is the slow making of an encyclopedia one way of escaping the need to constantly produce new products for the art market?

### A Zulu encyclopedia

The days before consulting the Zulu medicine woman in Johannesburg I was making a performance about this kind of reading of signs of the future.

Her materials were so beautiful, dominos whose face down meant I keep forgetting my dreams. Not sure how she saw my broken heart or the ocean that sings my ancestors' songs, but somewhere between my name and this bag she did.

When our future is foretold we feel some apprehension, and the signs need interpretation.

We need a translator, she tells us in English, for the work is done in Zulu. A young girl is summoned to translate for us, and sits down on the threshold of a tiny space in which the Zulu doctor and I face each other on the ground. I am enchanted and unaware that she is about to do a kind of analogue X-ray of my entrails. All these things I can't see and have forgotten, they are coming in these little voudon charms. The metallic monkey sits in curious openness. Soon my future is scattered faster than I can keep up with.

geholt, um für uns zu übersetzen, und setzt sich an die Schwelle des winzigen Raums, in dem die Zulu-Medizinfrau und ich einander auf dem Erdboden gegenübersitzen. Ich bin bezaubert und merke nicht, dass sie im Begriff ist, eine Art analoge Durchleuchtung meiner Eingeweide vorzunehmen. All die Dinge, die ich nicht sehen kann und vergessen habe, sie kommen in diesen kleinen magischen Vodun-Objekten zum Vorschein. Der Affe aus Metall sitzt in neugieriger Offenheit da. Bald ist meine Zukunft schneller ausgestreut, als ich ihr zu folgen vermag.

## Eine Woche im Centre for the Less Good Idea

Eine Einrichtung, gegründet von William Kentridge, um sich das Scheitern als möglichen Ausgangspunkt zu eigen zu machen; das ist nicht das Gleiche wie „This idea must die", aber doch verbunden mit der Aufwertung des Scheiterns, der Blockierung, was John Brockman in Form übersehener, verschollener und zu wenig gewürdigter wissenschaftlicher Ideen sammelt, die eigentlich verfolgt werden sollten.[1] Die Epistemiken kollidieren heftig miteinander, wie wir das Theater des Centre for the Less Good Idea aus verschiedenen Richtungen betreten, einige eindeutig aus dem Centre kommend, in dem die Aufführungen intuitiv aus einem Repertoire von Gesten und Bühnentechniken entwickelt werden, die der ungeheuer produktive William Kentridge und sein Team erarbeitet haben. Seitlich aus den Kulissen treten andere wie ich selbst auf, die, epistemisch gesehen, einen weiten Weg zurückgelegt haben um mitzuarbeiten. Zu einem gewissen Grad müssen wir das Materialarchiv, mit dem wir gekommen sind, furchtlos zerstören, um etwas Neues zu schaffen. Aber der Mangel an Ehrfurcht könnte auch dazu führen, dass wir an der Oberfläche der Dinge bleiben. Also schneide ich tagelang eine Szene mit einer Filmemacherin aus Benin, Adewole Falade. Die Szene ist Teil einer längeren Kurzfilmserie, an der ich arbeite – über Repatriierungsprozesse in verschiedenen Ländern, darüber, was passiert, wenn Ahnenartefakte in die Gemeinschaft zurückkehren, der sie während der Kolonisierung entwendet wurden.

Die Szene mit dem Fa-Priester ist eine, die Ade oft erlebt hat, in die ich aber erst durch das Betrachten des Films eintrete, was seine eigene Wirkung entfaltet, wenn man ihn immer neu schneidet, als Medium behandelt.

## A week in the Centre for the Less Good Idea

A place William Kentridge established to embrace the idea of failure as a possible departure point; apparently different from "This idea must die," but then again related to the valorization of the failure, the blockage where John Brockman collects overlooked, lost, and underappreciated scientific ideas that should actually be followed.[1] Epistemics are in thick contrast as we enter the Centre for the Less Good Idea's theatre from many different sides, some coming clearly from within the Centre, where performances are intuitively developed through a repertoire of gestures and stage techniques that the hugely prolific artist Kentridge and his team have developed. Walking in from the wings are others, like myself, who have come from very far, epistemically, to collaborate. To some extent we have to irreverently destroy the archive of material we come with in order to make something new. But irreverence could also leave us swimming on the surface of things. So, for days I am editing one scene with a filmmaker from Benin, Adewole Falade. This is part of a larger series of short films that I'm working on about repatriation processes in different countries, looking at what happens when ancestral artifacts return to communities from which they were taken during colonization.

The scene of the Fa priest is one Ade has witnessed many times, but one I enter through witnessing the film, which has its own effect when cut over and over again, when treated as a medium. I guess our epistemics have to do with mediums. I think of the materials of films that I sit with. I even write a short script that goes something like this (or rather I write this and then Ade chooses the Fa):

*Scene 2:*

The screen on which the future is foretold by the Fa priest

Our screen on which we show you the past of the future. Pixels for grains of flour

Shake. Throw. Read. Mark the flour screen with the sign. Repeat

Shake. Throw. Read. Mark the flour screen with the sign. Repeat

Where the pixels flour on our screen, we take the film, watch it, stop it, rewind it, pause it, screenshot, project it, talk about it, and then we set out in earnest to cut it, to pick the best bits out of it, to arrange it, move it, watch it, structure it, shift this part

Ich denke, unsere Epistemik hat mit Medien zu tun. Ich denke an die Materialien der Filme, an denen ich sitze. Ich schreibe sogar ein kleines Skript, das ungefähr so geht (eigentlich schreibe ich dies hier, und Ade wählt daraufhin den Fa):

*Szene 2:*

Der Bildschirm, auf dem vom Fa-Priester die Zukunft vorhergesagt wird.

Unser Bildschirm, auf dem wir die Vergangenheit der Zukunft zeigen. Pixel statt Mehlkörner.

Schüttle. Wirf. Lies. Markiere den Mehlschirm mit dem Zeichen. Wiederhole.

Schüttle. Wirf. Lies. Markiere den Mehlschirm mit dem Zeichen. Wiederhole.

Wo sich die Mehlpixel auf unserem Bildschirm verdichten, packen wir den Film, betrachten ihn, halten ihn an, spulen ihn zurück, halten ihn an, machen einen Screenshot, projizieren ihn, reden darüber, und fangen dann ernsthaft an zu schneiden, die besten Teile auszuwählen, sie zu arrangieren, herumzubewegen, zu betrachten, zu strukturieren, einen Teil zu verschieben, an den Anfang, in die Mitte, eine Geschichte entsteht, wir finden einige Lücken, also gehen wir zurück, um neu zu drehen, drehen, drehen, Drehorte, Hände, Performer, Tonaufnahmen zu machen, Interviews zu führen, eine Perspektive nachzudrehen. Dann ihn immer und immer wieder anschauen, bis diese Sekunde hierhin verschoben und dort noch ein wenig weggeschnitten werden könnte.

Am letzten Tag schließlich lesen und übersetzen wir zu dritt, überlassen uns aber auch gewissen Worten. Wir lesen nicht nur den Text, wir lesen auch uns gegenseitig und reagieren auf dieses Material. Wir arbeiten mit kleinen Steinen, sie laden zu bestimmten Gesten ein, sind etwas, das geworfen und im Verhältnis zueinander als komplexes Zeichen gelesen werden kann. Ein Beutel voller Zeichen, so wie diese Seite ein aufgereihter Zeichenhaufen ist, der in diesem Augenblick gelesen wird.

In diesem Beutel voller Dinge stecken auch Epistemiken. Wir fragen uns: Wohnen sie den Dingen inne oder der Person, die sie wirft? Es ist nicht ganz klar.

Der Chor liest und hört dann zu lesen auf, um miteinander zu reden, und mündet schließlich in ein Schöpfungsritual, in das Pélagie Gbaguidi einen weiteren Performer aus dem Centre, Vuzi Mdoyi, einbezieht.

of it, the front of it, to the middle of it, a story comes from it, and then we have some gaps in it, so we go back to film, film, film, locations, film hands, film performers, record sound, record interviews, catch that angle. Look at it again, and again, and again, till that little second could go here, and a bit more is cut there.

Finally on the last day, together three of us read and translate, but also abandon ourselves to certain words. We do not just read *it*, we also read each other and respond to these materials. We use small rocks, they invite certain gestures, small pieces that can be thrown and read as complex signs in relation to each other. A bag of signs, just like this page is a bunch of signs lined up, being read right now.

In this bag of things are also epistemologies. We wonder: are they in these objects or in the person who throws them? That is not entirely clear.

The chorus read and then stop reading to just speak together is wrapped up in a ritual of creation that Pélagie Gbaguidi draws another performer from the Centre, Vuzi Mdoyi, in too. They improvise a bathing in flour and the moment of conception. Pepper's ghost is a device in which the past and the future are divided by the screen of a kind of present projection. Therefore, behind the screen I could not see the front, only through voice and sound did we meet. In the intense repetition of "again" that became "gain" we "looked at it again and again."

With Noah Cohen, who filmed the performance, I was speaking about the language of "shooting" and capturing on film that has such strong hunting etymology. Why do we not speak of mirroring or absorbing when we use the camera to document?

I am digressing here from the entry on the epistemology of the encyclopedia because I have wandered in my own practice from the madness of trying to make encyclopedias to the consultation with this Zulu priestess. Somehow there is a link I have walked between the two. Here I am retracing my steps.

Sangoma—she is not sure how I talk to my ancestors, but can see that it is through water and especially the ocean. We are in a desert I have flown over for six hours marveling at the inhospitable dryness and the lush geometries and oasis. From my window in the plane I am mesmerized by

Sie improvisieren ein Mehlbad und den Augenblick der Empfängnis. Der Pepper's Ghost ist eine Vorrichtung, durch die Vergangenheit und Zukunft mithilfe des Bildschirms, auf dem eine Art Gegenwartsprojektion stattfindet, getrennt werden. So konnte ich hinter dem Schirm nicht sehen, was sich davor abspielte, und wir trafen uns nur stimmlich und akustisch. In der fortwährenden Wiederholung des Wortes „again" entstand ein „gain" (Gewinn) und „wir schauten ihn uns immer und immer wieder an".

Mit Noah Cohen, der die Performance filmte, sprach ich über die Jagdmetaphorik des Filmens mit seiner Rede vom „Schießen", „Bannen" und „Einfangen". Warum sprechen wir nicht von „Spiegeln" oder „Absorbieren", wenn wir mit der Kamera arbeiten?

Ich schweife hier von einem Eintrag zur Epistemologie der Enzyklopädie ab, weil ich in meiner eigenen Praxis vom Wahn, Enzyklopädien zu machen, abgekommen und bei der Konsultation dieser Zulu-Priesterin gelandet bin. Irgendwie besteht eine Verbindungslinie dazwischen. Hier zeichne ich meinen Weg vom einen zum anderen nach.

Die Sangoma – sie weiß nicht, wie ich mit meinen Ahnen spreche, aber sieht, dass es mittels Wasser, vor allem des Meeres geschieht. Wir befinden uns in einer Wüste, die ich sechs Stunden lang überflogen habe, der unwirtlichen Trockenheit und den reichen Geometrien und Oasen nachsinnend. Von meinem Fenster im Flugzeug aus folge ich gebannt den feinen Linien der Straßen durch die Sahara, dann die Kalahari, hinein nach Johannesburg.

Den ganzen Weg, um den Gemeinschaftsgeist zu spüren, der uns verbindet und der in Performances wie der, die wir auf der Bühne erschaffen, greifbar wird.[2] Wir begeben uns mit Worten in Trance, betreten eine Zukunft, die uns nicht loslässt, werden gehalten. Auf und ab bewegen sich die Steine und Thabos Stimme, der Ade und ich in Übersetzung folgen. Ich greife mit dem Schatten nach Thabos Schatten. Nicht wirklich, sondern in der Luft. Für eine Anthropologin im Publikum gelingt es dem Film nicht, die Voodoo-Zeremonie einzufangen, und diese Unmöglichkeit der Übersetzung ist tragisch. Andere sagen hinterher, es sei traumatisch gewesen und es sei ihnen übel geworden.

Pélagie ruft das Wasser an. Ich schwimme im Rhythmus der Worte.

the thin lines of roads through the Sahara, then Kalahari, and finally into Johannesburg.

All this way to sense the community of spirit that we have, and in performances like the one we create on stage can feel.[2] We go into a trance with words, we enter into a future that won't let us go, we are held. Up and down go the rocks and Thabo's voice, which Ade and I follow, in translation. I am reaching with the shadow to Thabo's shadow. I can't quite reach, but I am stroking the air. For an anthropologist in the audience the film cannot capture the voodoo ceremony, and this impossibility of translation is tragic. Afterwards others say it was traumatic and feel nauseated.

Pélagie is summoning the water. I am swimming in the rhythm of words.

I wonder about my practice of speaking, and what it means to be captured (on film) to be captivated (by a ritual) to be captured in life in a kind of drama and then within a theatre, within a dramatic ritual. Then to be stuck within language and unstuck from one's dreams.

If I am to translate the endeavor of encyclopedia-making, then making a film and the entries one follows on the way is a transgressive equivalent in lived experience. The concept of *A±Z* is a wholistic one in which the entries catalogue a life of art works 1:1, like Borges's map, the page and stage disappear, and we are on the same plane as the lived present.

Ich denke über meine Sprachgewohnheiten nach und was es heißt, (auf Film) gebannt und (von einem Ritual) gefesselt zu sein, im Leben in einer Art Drama, und in einem Theater in einem dramatischen Ritual, gefangen zu sein. Dann in der Sprache festzustecken und von seinen Träumen losgelöst zu sein.

Müsste ich den Versuch, Enzyklopädien zu machen, übersetzen, würde ich im Machen eines Films und der Einträge, denen man dabei folgt, ein transgressives Äquivalent in der gelebten Erfahrung sehen. Das Konzept von *A±Z* ist ganzheitlich; die Einträge darin katalogisieren ein Leben von Kunstwerken im Maßstab 1:1 wie Borges Landkarte; Buchseite und Bühne verschwinden, und wir befinden uns mit der gelebten Gegenwart auf derselben Ebene.

1 Eine Referenz auf Payer Gabriels enzyklopädischen Eintrag „Idee / Idea“, der sich auf eine von John Brockman herausgegebene Buchreihe mit den Titeln „This Idea Must Die: Scientific Theories That Are Blocking Progress“ und „This Idea Is Brilliant: Lost, Overlooked, and Underappreciated Scientific Concepts Everyone Should Know“ bezieht.

2 Ein kleiner Auszug daraus findet sich unter: https://vimeo.com/repatriates/again. Durchgeführt wurde diese Forschungsarbeit mit Mitteln des Europäischen Forschungsrats (ERC) im Rahmen des Forschungs- und Innovationsprogramms Horizont 2020 (Grant Agreement Nr. 101 001407 – REPATRIATES) und mit Unterstützung des Centre for the Less Good Idea, Johannesburg, und von Universität Paris 8.

1 A reference to Payer Gabriel's encylopedic entry "Idee / Idea", which refers to a series of books, edited by John Brockman with the titles "This Idea Must Die: Scientific Theories That Are Blocking Progress" and "This Idea Is Brilliant: Lost, Overlooked, and Underappreciated Scientific Concepts Everyone Should Know."

2 A short sample of this can be seen at https://vimeo.com/repatriates/again. This research has received funding from the European Research Council (ERC) under the European Union's Horizon 2020 research and innovation programme (grant agreement No. 101001407 – REPATRIATES) and the support of the Centre for the Less Good Idea Johannesburg and University of Paris 8.

Episteme

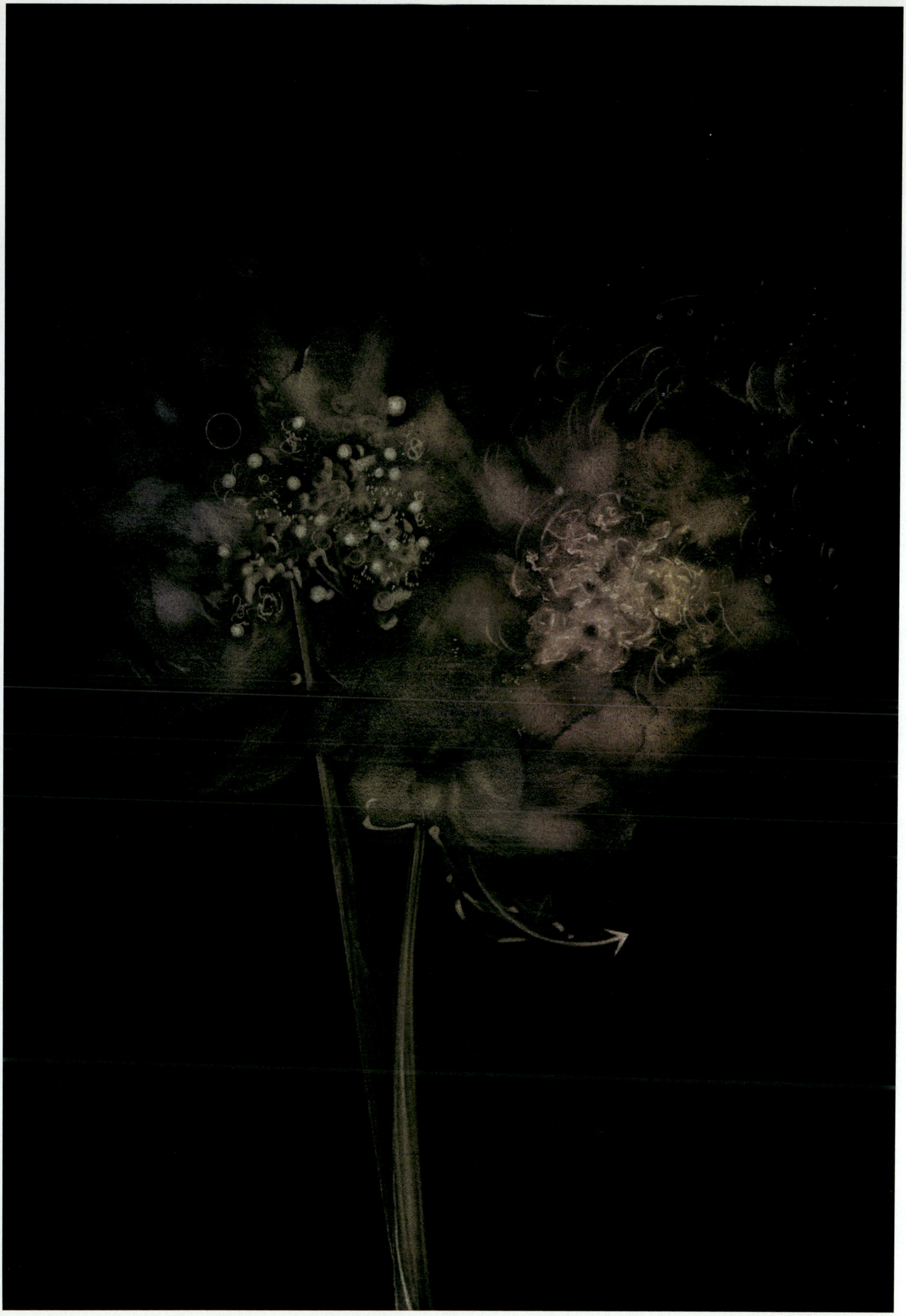

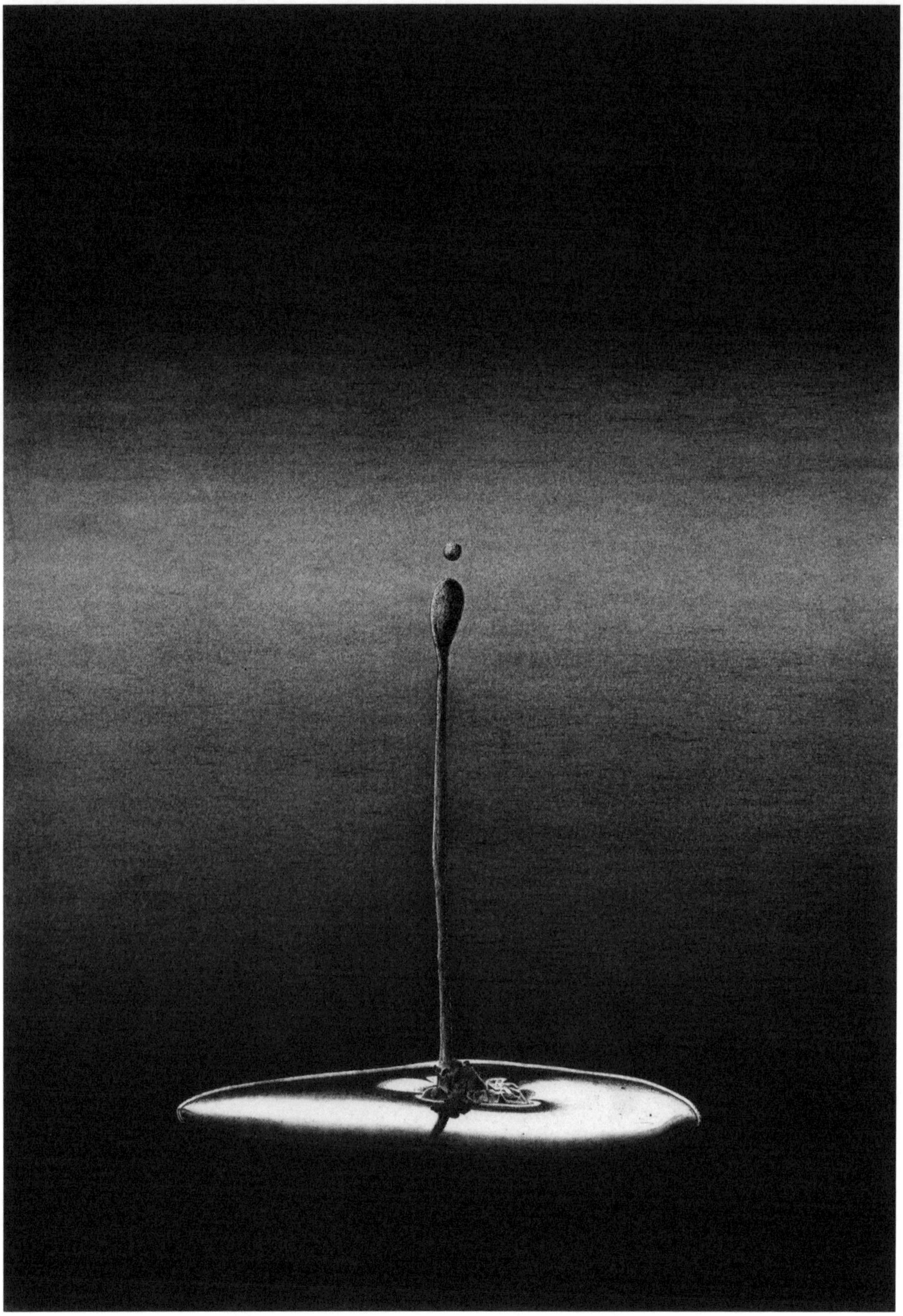

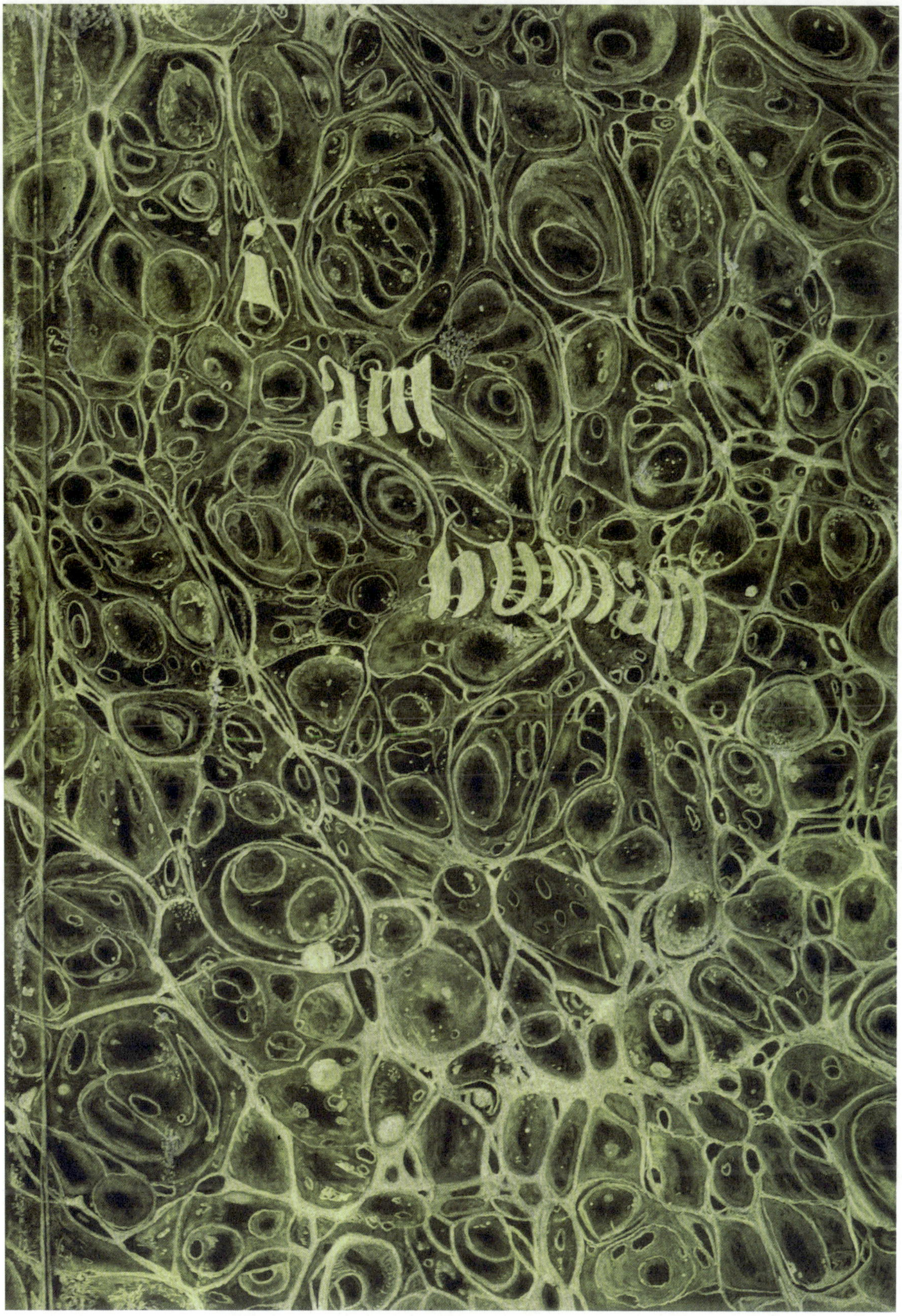
i
am
human

# Episteme
# Episteme

DE

58

*Episteme*, griechisch Wissen, Wissenschaft, wird in der griechischen Philosophie von „Meinen (doxa), Glauben (pistis) und Kunstfertigkeit (techne)“ unterschieden.[1] Platon zählt die *episteme* neben *doxa* (Meinung) und *agnoia* (Nichtwissen) zu den „dynameis, [das sind] Fähigkeiten, [...] die verschiedenen Seienden, Gegenständen, zugeordnet sind“.[2]

Die *episteme* ist die Fähigkeit, „das wahrhaft Seiende“ zu erkennen, „im Unterschied zum Nichtwissen, das dem Nichtseienden zugeordnet ist, und der doxa, die inmitten steht und das erkennt, was zwischen Sein und Nichtsein in der Mitte steht [...]“.[3] Bei Platon und Aristoteles ist die *episteme* eng mit Theorie (*theoria*) verknüpft.[4]

EN

In Greek philosophy *episteme*, knowledge, science, is distinguished from "thought (doxa), belief (pistis) and skill (techne)."[1] Plato classes *episteme* along with *doxa* (opinion) and *agnoia*, (not knowing) among the "dynameis, [which are] abilities [...] ascribed to various entities, objects."[2]

The *episteme* is the ability to recognize "true existence [...] as distinct from not knowing, which is classed with non-existence, and from doxa, which is in the middle and recognizes what comes between existence and non-existence."[3] Plato and Aristotle closely link *episteme* with theory (*theoria*).[4]

## Episteme bei Michel Foucault als Denkkonfigurationen und Denkbrüche im Wissenschaffen

Episteme sind für den Philosophen Michel Foucault erkenntnistheoretische Dispositionen, also Bedingungen für die Möglichkeiten Wissenschaft zu betreiben und Wissen zu produzieren. Diese haben sich im Laufe der Geschichte verändert und werden sich weiterhin verändern. Sie sind Grundbedingungen, die bestimmte Wissensformen erst möglich machen, gewissermaßen historische A-priori-Situationen also, auf denen menschliches Wissenschaffen fußt.[5]

„Dieses Apriori ist das, was in einer bestimmten Epoche in der Erfahrung ein mögliches Wissensfeld abtrennt, die Seinsweise der Gegenstände, die darin erscheinen, definiert, den alltäglichen Blick mit theoretischen Kräften ausstattet und die Bedingungen definiert, in denen man eine Rede über die Dinge halten kann, die als wahr anerkannt wird."[6]

Der wissenschaftliche Blick auf die Welt, die Weise, wie Wissen generiert wird, ist immer in ein Diskurssystem eingebettet, das die Möglichkeiten des Denkens bestimmt und begrenzt.

*Die Ordnung der Dinge* ist Foucaults viel beachtetes philosophisches Werk, in dem er über eine Analyse der drei Wissensgebiete Grammatik, Naturgeschichte und Ökonomie vom Mittelalter bis zum Ende des 20. Jahrhunderts auf drei Episteme schließt. Dabei ergeben sich die zentralen Fragen, wie das Denken immer wieder neu in die Welt kommt und wie sich Erkenntnisweisen und diskursive Praktiken qualitativ und methodisch verändert haben.[7] Es stellt sich aus heutiger Sicht im Weiteren die Frage, ob sich durch ein posthumanes Denken eine epistemische Neukonfiguration andeutet, die an das oft zitierte Bild vom Verschwinden des Menschen – „wie am Meeresufer ein Gesicht im Sand" – aus der „Disposition des Wissens" anschließt.[8]

Im Folgenden werden diese drei Episteme – das Zeitalter der Ähnlichkeit, der Repräsentation und der Geschichte – knapp zusammengefasst: Ausgehend vom Mittelalter bis etwa zum Beginn des 17. Jahrhunderts ist die Ähnlichkeit in Form von „aemulatio, convenientia, Analogie und Sympathie" das erkenntnisleitende Charakteristikum, welches das Denken strukturiert.[9] Die Ähnlichkeit findet sich in der Proportion, in der Magie, in der Spiegelung,

## Michel Foucault: epistemes as configurations and disruptions of thought in the creation of knowledge

For the philosopher Michel Foucault epistemes are categorical arrangements, that is, preconditions for the pursuance of science and the production of knowledge. They have changed in the course of history, and will continue to do so. They are the basic conditions that make certain forms of knowledge possible in the first place; a-priori historical situations, to a certain extent, on which the production of human knowledge rests.[5]

"This a priori is what, in a given period, delimits in the totality of experience a field of knowledge, defines the mode of being of the objects that appear in that field, provides man's everyday perception with theoretical powers, and defines the conditions in which he can sustain a discourse about things that is recognized to be true."[6]

The scientific view of the world, the way in which knowledge is generated, is always embedded within a discursive system that determines and delimits the possibilities of thought. *The Order of Things* is the much-acclaimed work in which Foucault extrapolates three epistemes from an analysis of the three scientific fields of grammar, natural history, and economics from the Middle Ages to the end of the twentieth century. This results in central questions about how thought continually comes into the world anew, and how the forms of knowledge and discursive practices have changed, both qualitatively and methodically.[7] A further question arises, from today's point of view, as to whether posthuman thought indicates a new epistemic configuration, which is connected to the often cited image of the disappearance of human beings—"like a face drawn in sand at the edge of the sea"—from the "arrangements of knowledge."[8]

These three epistemes—the eras of similarity, representation, and history—are summarized in the following: From the Middle Ages to around the early seventeenth century, similarity, in the form of aemulatio, convenientia, analogy, and sympathy, is the primary cognitive characteristic that structures thought.[9] Similarity is found in proportion, in magic, in reflection, in proximity, or in sympathy, and inspires a macrocosm-in-the-microcosm way of thinking at the center of which man "reproduces [...] the immense order of the heavens, the stars, the

in der örtlichen Nähe oder in der Sympathie und befeuert ein Macrocosmos-in-microcosmo-Denken, in dessen Zentrum der Mensch „die unmeßbare Ordnung des Himmels, der Gestirne, der Gebirge, der Flüsse und Gewitter reproduziert".[10] Der Erkenntnisprozess ist ein interpretativer Prozess, der darauf beruht, nach Zeichen zu suchen, Signaturen, die auf den Dingen niedergelegt sind, zu identifizieren und zu interpretieren.[11] Die Dinge müssen gelesen werden, damit sie erkannt werden können.[12] „Ein Tier oder eine Pflanze oder irgendeine Sache der Erde zu erkennen heißt die ganze dicke Schicht der Zeichen zusammenzusuchen, die in ihnen oder auf ihnen deponiert worden sein können."[13] Das Zeitalter der Ähnlichkeit ist das Zeitalter der Deutung der Zeichen, die von Gott in die Welt gelegt werden (Divinatio), und der Worte, die aus der Antike geerbt wurden (Eruditio).[14]

Am Anfang des 17. Jahrhunderts ändert sich etwas in der Beziehung zwischen dem Zeichen und dem Bezeichneten – „die Sachen und die Wörter werden sich trennen", und die Bedeutung der Zeichen findet sich in der Repräsentation wiedergegeben.[15] Foucault bezeichnet diese kulturelle Neuordnung als klassische Episteme, als das Zeitalter der Repräsentation, welche die „Seinsweise für die Sprache, die Einzelwesen, die Natur, die Gegenstände des Bedürfnisses und des Verlangens" bestimmt.[16] Die Ähnlichkeit verschwindet jedoch nicht aus dem Erkenntnisprozess, sondern wird, wie Foucault ausführt, „in Termini der Identität und des Unterschieds, des Maßes und der Ordnung" analysiert.[17] Erkennen bedeutet nun nicht mehr, die Dinge zu interpretieren, sondern zu unterscheiden und, darauf basierend, in eine Ordnung zu bringen. Daraus ergibt sich dann ein „Tableau der Zeichen" als „*Bild* der Dinge", welches für die allgemeine Grammatik, die Naturgeschichte und die Analyse der Reichtümer gilt.[18] Dieser Raum des Tableaus, der für das 17. und 18. Jahrhundert prägend ist, zeigt sich in der Etablierung von Taxonomien, Systematiken und Klassifikationen.[19] *Systema naturae,* Carl von Linnés taxonomische Ordnung der Lebewesen, Pflanzen und Mineralien, die 1735 zum ersten Mal erscheint, steht wohl exemplarisch für die von Foucault beschriebene Ordnung des Sichtbaren, in der jedes Lebewesen dadurch definiert ist, dass es durch einen Unterschied markiert wird, und gleichzeitig einen festen und unverrückbaren Platz in einem von Klasse, Ordnung, Familie, Gattung und Art

mountains, rivers, and storms."[10] The process of recognition is an interpretative one, and is based on looking for signs and identifying and interpreting the similitudes within things.[11] Things had to be read in order to be recognized.[12] "To know an animal or a plant, or any terrestrial thing whatever, is to gather together the whole dense layer of signs with which it or they may have been covered."[13] The era of similarity is that of the interpretation of the signs that God set into the world (*divinatio*) and the words inherited from antiquity (*eruditio*).[14]

In the early seventeenth century something changes in the relationship between the sign and the signified—"things and words were to be separated from one another"—and meaning and sign were conveyed through representation.[15] Foucault calls this cultural reordering the classical episteme, the era of representation, which "defines a certain mode of being for language, natural individuals, and the objects of need and desire."[16] But similarity doesn't disappear from the process of recognition; rather, as Foucault explains, it is analyzed "in terms of identity, difference, measurement, and order."[17] Recognition no longer means interpreting but distinguishing things and ordering them on this basis. It results in a *tableau*[18] of signs, an "image of the things" valid for a "general grammar, natural history, and the analysis of wealth."[19] The space of the tableau, which is characteristic of the seventeenth and eighteenth centuries, is one of taxonomies, systematics, and classifications.[20] *Systema Naturae*, Carl von Linné's taxonomic ordering of living creatures, plants, and minerals, first published in 1735, is exemplary of the ordering of the visible described by Foucault, in which every living thing is marked by a difference and at the same time has a fixed and unalterable place in a system structured by class, order, family, genus, and type.[21] The tableau is formed as an ordered synthesis of individual appearances based on differentiating observation. It is an arrangement of the visible; it is presentation, selection, enumeration, distinction, recollection, and idealization. In this pattern of thought, in which everything—both essence and expression—is defined through difference, the desire for an either-or outweighs the wish for a both-and. The tableau links here to the logic of binary opposition, which in various manifestations is also operative today: as the basis of computer technology (0, 1); in visualized infographics and decision

strukturierten System hat.[20] Das Tableau wird als geordnete Synthese einzelner Erscheinungen gebildet, die auf einem differenzierenden Blick beruht. Es ist eine Ordnung des Sichtbaren, es ist Präsentation, Auswahl, Aufzählung, Unterscheidung, Erinnerung und Idealisierung. In diesem Denkraster, in dem alles – Wesen wie Wort – über den Unterschied definiert ist, überwiegt der Wunsch nach einem Entweder-oder jenen nach einem Sowohl-als-auch. Hier verbindet sich das Tableau mit der Logik der binären Opposition, die auch in der Gegenwart in unterschiedlichen Ausprägungen wirksam ist: als Grundlage der Computertechnologie (0, 1); in visualisierten Informationsgrafiken und Entscheidungsbäumen; in Entscheidungsprozessen bei der Benützung von Interfaces; in binär oppositionellen Denkformen hinsichtlich des Geschlechts, der Herkunft, der sexuellen Orientierung, der kulturellen Prägung, der ökonomischen Kraft oder der Zugehörigkeit zu einer Spezies, die der Posthumanismus kritisch überdenken und überwinden möchte.

Nun weiter in der Folge der Episteme: Am Ende des 18. Jahrhunderts kommt es erneut zu einem Bruch in der Disposition des Wissens, der sich darin manifestiert, dass „die Dinge plötzlich nicht mehr auf die gleiche Weise perzipiert, beschrieben, genannt, charakterisiert, klassifiziert und gelernt werden".[21] An die Stelle der Ordnung tritt nun die Geschichte als „der Grund, von dem aus alle Wesen zu ihrer Existenz [...] gelangen".[22] Die neuen Wissensgebiete, die sich formieren – Biologie, Philologie und politische Ökonomie –, interessieren sich für innere Funktionszusammenhänge, die nicht auf der Oberfläche, sondern im Verborgenen stattfinden.[23] Wo *Ich* war, ist jetzt *Es*, im Verborgenen, als zu bearbeitendes Projekt mit dem Ziel der Ichfindung. Man könnte sagen, dass das Tableau sich zum Bild eines Displays wandelt, das zwar als geordnete Oberfläche erscheint, aber als Summe endlos überlagerter Fenster in seiner inneren Ordnung einer komplexen Programmierung, einer Serie von Fällen folgt. „Das Denken wird nicht mehr nach Art eines Tableaus konstituiert, sondern als eine Folge, als eine Verkettung oder ein Werden."[24]

Der Mensch selbst wird zum Untersuchungsgegenstand, ist gleichzeitig Subjekt und Objekt der Forschung – ein problematisches Verhältnis, in dem er als „empirisch-transzendentale Dublette" erscheint.[25] Das moderne Denken ermöglicht die Human-

trees; in decision-taking processes in the use of interfaces; in binary-opposite ways of thinking about gender, origin, sexual orientation, cultural influence, economic power, or membership of a species, which posthumanism aims to critically rethink and overcome.

To continue in epistemic sequence. In the late eighteenth century there is another break in the disposition of knowledge, in that "things are no longer perceived, described, expressed, characterized, classified, and known in the same way."[22] In place of order, history now becomes "the depths from which all beings emerge into their [...] existence."[23] The newly forming fields of knowledge—biology, philology, and political economy—are concerned with inner functional connections that don't take place on the surface but in obscurity.[24] Where once was *ego* there is now an invisible *id*, a project to be undertaken with the aim of finding the self. We could say that the system has transformed into the image of a display, which may look like an ordered surface but whose inner order, as a sum of endlessly superimposed windows, is subject to a complex programming, a series of traps. "Knowledge is no longer constituted in the form of a [tableau] but in that of a series, of sequential connection, and of development."[25]

The human being itself is now examined, is simultaneously subject and object of research—a problematic relationship in which it appears as an "empirico-transcendental doublet."[26] Modern thinking enables the humanities, in which the human being is central as a living, speaking, and working entity.[27]

"It is as a living being that he grows, that he has functions and needs, that he sees opening up a space whose movable coordinates meet in him; in a general fashion, his corporeal existence interlaces him through and through with the rest of the living world; since he produces objects and tools, exchanges the things he needs, organizes a whole network of circulation along which what he is able to consume flows, and in which he himself is defined as an intermediary stage, he appears in his existence immediately interwoven with others; lastly, because he has a language, he can constitute a whole symbolic universe for himself, within which he has a relation to his past, to things, to other men, and on the basis of which he is able equally to build something like a body of knowledge."[28]

wissenschaften, in deren Zentrum der Mensch als lebendiges, sprechendes und arbeitendes Wesen steht.[26]

„Als lebendiges Wesen wächst er, hat er Funktionen und Bedürfnisse, sieht er einen Raum sich öffnen, dessen bewegliche Koordinaten er in sich selbst verknüpft. Auf allgemeine Weise überschneidet seine körperliche Existenz sich teilweise mit dem Lebendigen. Als Produzent von Gegenständen und von Werkzeugen, im durch seine Bedürfnisse bestimmten Tausch und in der Organisation eines Zirkulationsnetzes, das das durchläuft, was er konsumieren kann und worin er sich als ein Relais definiert findet, erscheint er in seiner Existenz unmittelbar mit den anderen verflochten. Da er eine Sprache hat, kann er sich schließlich ein ganzes Universum aus Symbolen bilden, innerhalb dessen er Beziehung zu seiner Vergangenheit, zu den Dingen, zu anderen Menschen hat, mit Hilfe dessen er ebenfalls so etwas wie ein Wissen bilden kann [...].“[27]

Der Mensch, der also erst in dieser epistemischen Formation, erst nach dem Denken in Ähnlichkeiten und in Repräsentationen, ins Zentrum des Wissens gerückt und zum Kern der Forschung geworden ist, wird, so kündigt es Michel Foucault in seiner Abschlusspassage an, möglicherweise wieder aus der Disposition des Wissens verschwinden.[28] Wie ist diese Ankündigung des Endes des Menschen bei Foucault zu verstehen? Die Philosophin Rosi Braidotti sieht in Foucaults Werk *Die Ordnung der Dinge* eine Kritik am Humanismus, welcher sich epistemologisch wie moralisch in einer Krise befindet, die aus den Abgründen unserer europäischen Geschichte – Kolonialismus, Faschismus, Nationalsozialismus, Rassismus, Sexismus – resultiert und den Menschen als Vernunftwesen infrage stellt.[29] Was es bedeutet, ein Subjekt zu sein, in einer zugleich mehr als menschlichen, aber auch weniger als menschlichen Epoche, fragt Braidotti.[30] Als technologisch-vermittelte Gesellschaft sind wir mehr, als Gesellschaft sozialer Polarisierungen und als auf die Umwelt irreversibel schädlich einwirkende Kraft sind wir weniger als menschlich.[31] Zwangsläufig ist die Position des Humanen damit schwer lokalisierbar, dezentral. Der kritische Posthumanismus wurzelt in Foucaults Hinterfragung eines Humanismus, der nicht nur aufgrund der „Heterogenität seiner historischen Verschiedenheiten“ zu hinterfragen ist, sondern vielmehr, weil er sein eigenes dogmatisches und regelbe-

Therefore, Michel Foucault concludes, the human being—who only became the center of knowledge and the core of research in this epistemic formation, only after the thought forms of similarity and representation—will probably disappear once more from the disposition of knowledge.[29] How should this conclusion be understood? The philosopher Rosi Braidotti sees Foucault's *Order of Things* as a critique of humanism, which is in an epistemological and moral crisis that arises from the depths of our European history—colonialism, fascism, National Socialism, racism, sexism—and calls the human being as rational into question.[30] Braidotti asks what it means to be a subject in an era that is both more and less than human.[31] As a technologically conveyed society we are more human; as a society of social polarization and as a force causing irreversible harm to the environment we are less.[32] The human position is thus inevitably more peripheral and difficult to localize. Critical posthumanism is rooted in Foucault's questioning of a humanism that is thrown into doubt not only because of the "sheer heterogeneity of [its] historical varieties," but to a greater degree because of "its own dogma, replete with its own prejudices and assumptions [...] from which the Enlightenment sought to break free."[33] Cary Wolfe argues along with Foucault—who points out the conflict between humanism and the Enlightenment—that in order to overcome the political and scientific dogma of the human, the nature of thinking itself needs to be changed.[34] What epistemological disposition might this make apparent?

### Images that create knowledge: Lorraine Daston and Peter Galison's epistemic virtues

A particular class of images—scientific images that follow certain epistemological rules—are found in atlases, also called "dictionaries of the sciences of the eye."[35] On the basis of an extensive and meticulous analysis of these atlas images from various scientific disciplines, Lorraine Daston and Peter Galison have analyzed certain "practices of seeing"[36] from which conclusions can be drawn about three epistemic virtues. They call these virtues, which developed in "specific historical contexts" and "infused the making of images in scientific atlases from roughly the early eighteenth to the mid-twentieth century, in Europe and North

haftetes Denkkorsett bildet, dem der Geist der Aufklärung eigentlich entkommen wollte.[32] Mit Foucault, der auf das Spannungsfeld zwischen Humanismus und Aufklärung hinweist, argumentiert Cary Wolfe, dass, um das politische und wissenschaftliche Dogma des Humanen zu überwinden, die Natur des Denkens selbst verändert werden muss.[33] Welche epistemische Disposition könnte sich dadurch abzeichnen?

### Bilder, die Wissen erschaffen: epistemische Tugenden bei Lorraine Daston und Peter Galison

Eine besondere Art von Bildern – wissenschaftliche Bilder, die gewissen epistemischen Regeln folgen – findet man in Atlanten, auch „Wörterbücher der Augenwissenschaften".[34] Basierend auf einer umfangreichen, akribischen Analyse dieser Atlasbilder unterschiedlicher wissenschaftlicher Disziplinen, haben Lorraine Daston und Peter Galison bestimmte „Praktiken des Sehens" beschrieben, aus denen Folgerungen auf drei epistemische Tugenden gezogen werden können.[35] Naturwahrheit, mechanische Objektivität und geschultes Urteil nennen die beiden Forschenden diese Tugenden, die sich in „spezifischen historischen Kontexten" entwickelt haben, in der hier genannten Reihenfolge die jeweilige Vorbedingung für die folgende Tugend darstellen und in einem Zeitraum „ungefähr vom frühen achtzehnten Jahrhundert bis zur Mitte des zwanzigsten Jahrhunderts die Bildgebung der wissenschaftlichen Atlanten in Europa und Nordamerika prägten".[36]

Die epistemische Tugend der Naturwahrheit wird zunehmend mit dem Beginn des 18. Jahrhunderts gepflegt und zielt auf die Abbildung eines Idealexemplars ab, das zwar in der Natur selbst nicht vorkommt, dafür aber für alle in der Natur vorkommenden Einzelexemplare steht. Auf der Suche nach einer Allgemeinheit, nach den Regeln, nicht nach den Ausnahmen in der Natur hat „[d]as ‚ideale' Bild [...] den Anspruch, nicht nur das Typische, sondern das Vollkommene wiederzugeben, während das ‚Charakteristische' das Typische im Individuellen lokalisiert".[37] Die Zeichnung nach der Natur, die Radierung, der Kupferstich und die Lithografie sind die Techniken der Wahl für die Synthese von Bildern, die sich als „Destillat aus vielen, sorgfältig beobachteten Einzelbeispielen" zusammensetzen.[38]

America,"[37] truth-to-nature, mechanical objectivity, and trained judgement. In sequence they represent the necessary preconditions for each subsequent virtue.

The epistemic virtue of truth-to-nature is increasingly cultivated from the early eighteenth century, with the aim of depicting an ideal example that while not itself occurring in nature stands for all naturally occurring individual examples. In search of a generality, of rules not exceptions, "what the image represented, or ought to represent, was not the actual individual specimen [...] but an idealized, perfected, or at least characteristic exemplar of a species or other natural kind."[38] The drawing from nature, the etching, the copperplate, and the lithograph are the techniques of choice for synthesizing images that "would be the distillation of not one but many individuals carefully observed."[39] Truth-to-nature aims to create a "reasoned image," which results from a collaboration between scientists and artists, not infrequently women artists, and is thus a "four-eyed sight."[40] "In four-eyed sight, epistemology and ethos merged along with the vision of naturalist and artist."[41] For in aiming to create types and classes that would order nature so it could be recognized, the "scientific self" has to observe and select, and therefore to actively and decisively participate in the generation of the image. But this is inconsistent with the ethos of scientific objectivity, which then develops into the epistemic virtue of mechanical objectivity.[42]

Daston and Galison date the atlas images created in the spirit of mechanical objectivity to the nineteenth and early twentieth centuries, between around 1830 and 1930.[43] The production of scientific images occurs with the aid of apparatuses and instruments, and requires a certain self-discipline and abstinence from the image producer, whose authorship the image may in no way contain.[44] Photography is the preferred medium, and a "blind sight" the visual practice aimed at the creation of "automatic images."[45] The machine as image producer is both a "literal and guiding ideal" because it delivers reproducible and authentic images while working more efficiently and precisely.[46] "Objectivity enforced the irregularity of the world on minds set to believe in the ideal regularity of nature."[47] The flaws, distortions, and errors delivered by the mechanical image were willingly accepted. Initial doubts about mechanical objectivity arise in the early twentieth century. What if objective

Die Naturwahrheit zielt auf die Erzeugung eines „Vernunft-Bildes“, welches sich aus einer Zusammenarbeit von Naturforscher und Künstler, nicht selten Künstlerin ergibt, und damit ein „Sehen mit vier Augen“ ist.[39] „Beim Sehen mit vier Augen wurden nicht nur der Blick des Naturforschers und der des Künstlers zu einer Einheit, sondern auch Erkenntnistheorie und Ethik.“[40] Denn mit dem Ziel, Typen und Klassen zu erstellen, um die Natur zu ordnen, damit sie erkannt werden kann, muss „das wissenschaftliche Selbst“ beobachten und selektieren und folglich an der Bilderzeugung aktiv und entscheidend partizipieren. Das jedoch ist mit dem Ethos einer wissenschaftlichen Objektivität nicht vereinbar, welche sich darauffolgend mit der epistemischen Tugend der mechanischen Objektivität entwickeln wird.[41]

Atlasbilder, die im Geiste der mechanischen Objektivität entstehen, verorten Daston und Galison im 19. und frühen 20. Jahrhundert, etwa zwischen 1830 und 1930.[42] Die Produktion von wissenschaftlichen Bildern erfolgt mithilfe von Apparaturen und Instrumenten und erfordert eine gewisse Selbstdisziplin und Abstinenz der Bildproduzenten, deren Autorschaft keinesfalls im Bild enthalten sein darf.[43] Die Fotografie ist das bevorzugte Medium, und ein „Blindsehen“ ist die visuelle Praxis, die auf die Erzeugung „automatischer Bilder“ abzielt.[44] Die Maschine als Bilderzeuger ist zugleich „Modell und Leitidee“, weil sie reproduzierbare und authentische Bilder liefert und zudem viel leistungsfähiger und präziser arbeitet.[45] „Objektivität zwang dem Geist, der gewohnt war, an die ideale Regelmäßigkeit in der Natur zu glauben, die Unregelmäßigkeit der Welt auf.“[46] Dafür ist man gerne bereit, die Mängel, Verzerrungen und Fehler, die das mechanische Bild liefert, in Kauf zu nehmen. Zu Beginn des 20. Jahrhunderts regen sich erste Zweifel an einer Objektivität, die durch Mechanik erzeugt wird. Was, wenn sich objektive, mechanische Bilder zum Beispiel durch unterschiedliche Belichtungszeiten voneinander unterscheiden, wenn Strukturen dadurch anders aussehen oder Details verloren gehen?[47] „Wie kann ein Individuum ohne Idealisierung oder auch nur ohne Auswahl für eine Klasse stehen?“[48] Es erscheint fragwürdig, aus den Eigenarten eines Einzelobjekts allgemeine Schlüsse zu ziehen. Die „Selbstverleugnung“, die beim Umgang mit und der Erzeugung von wissenschaftlichen Bildern betrieben wird, wird zunehmend hinterfragt und um eine „neue Form epistemischer Ethik ergänzt“.[49]

mechanical images differed from one another because of varying exposure times, changing the appearance of structures or causing details to be lost?[48] "How could an individual stand for a class without idealization or even selection?[49] It seems questionable to draw general conclusions from the characteristics of an individual object. The "self-denial" practiced in the generation and use of scientific images is increasingly questioned and confronted by "a new form of epistemic ethic."[50] Interpretation becomes an important aspect in the engagement with images. And so in the early twentieth century a new, self-aware generation of scientists emerges who take a critical approach to purely mechanical image production and give credence to expertise based on experience and teaching in the generation of scientific images. The epistemic virtue of this time is trained judgement, a "supplementing of automatic procedures" that "extended deep into domains as diverse as geology, particle physics, and astronomy," as well as medicine, for example in the reading of encephalograms.[51] "Physiognomic sight" requires a "practiced eye" in order to recognize patterns and "family resemblances."[52]

Daston and Galison point out that these three different approaches to the image, which manifest in epistemic virtues, exist side by side and that "there is no 'programmatic,' 'paradigmatic,' or 'epistemic rupture' here."[53] The decisive thing is that different collective practices of seeing (four-eyed sight, blind sight, physiognomic sight) become "ways of knowing" and not only describe empirical phenomena but also "undeniably produce knowledge and therefore qualify as the stuff of epistemology."[54]

### Vision, presentation, recognition: images, thought charts, and epistemic objects

Michel Foucault's epistemes and Lorraine Daston and Peter Galison's epistemic virtues deal with images differently. What they share is the relevance of the function of the image to the process of recognition. The central significance of the image for Foucault becomes apparent in the first sentence of the first chapter of *The Order of Things*: "The painter is standing a little back from his canvas."[55] The painter is Diego Velázquez, who in *Las Meninas*, as well as depicting members of the royal family and court, portrays himself painting a picture that can

Die Interpretation wird zu einem wichtigen Aspekt im Umgang mit Bildern. So formiert sich zu Beginn des 20. Jahrhunderts eine neue, selbstbewusste Generation von Wissenschaftler*innen, die, kritisch gegenüber einer rein mechanistischen Bildproduktion, eine auf Erfahrung und Lehre beruhende Expertise für die Produktion wissenschaftlicher Bilder mitberücksichtigt. Die epistemische Tugend dieser Zeit ist das geschulte Urteil, das sich als „Ergänzung automatischer Verfahren in Fachgebieten wie der Geologie, Teilchenphysik oder Astronomie", aber auch in der Medizin, zum Beispiel beim Lesen von Enzephalogrammen, etabliert.[50] Das „physiognomische" Sehen bedarf eines „geübten Auges", um Muster zu erkennen und Familienähnlichkeiten herzustellen.[51]

Daston und Galison weisen darauf hin, dass diese drei unterschiedlichen Herangehensweisen an das Bild, die sich in epistemischen Tugenden manifestieren, nebeneinander existieren und nicht als „programmatische, paradigmatische oder epistemische Brüche" verstanden werden dürfen.[52] Entscheidend ist jedenfalls, dass unterschiedliche kollektive Praktiken des Sehens (Sehen mit vier Augen, Blindsehen, physiognomisches Sehen) zu „Erkenntnisweisen" werden und folglich empirische Erscheinungen nicht nur beschreiben, sondern auch Wissen erzeugen und damit zu einem „Thema der Epistemologie" werden.[53]

### Sehen, Zeigen und Erkennen: Bilder, Gedankentableaus und epistemische Objekte

Die Episteme bei Michel Foucault und die epistemischen Tugenden bei Lorraine Daston und Peter Galison behandeln Bilder auf unterschiedliche Weise; gemeinsam ist ihnen, dass die Funktion des Bildes für den Erkenntnisprozess relevant ist. Die zentrale Bedeutung des Bildes für Foucault zeigt sich bereits im ersten Satz des ersten Kapitels in *Die Ordnung der Dinge*: „Der Maler steht etwas vom Bild entfernt."[54] Gemeint ist Diego Velázquez, der sich im Gemälde *Las Meninas* beim Malen eines Bildes, das nur von seiner Rückseite zu sehen ist, gemeinsam mit Mitgliedern der königlichen Familie und Hofstaat „mitporträtiert". Nicht im kunsthistorischen Diskurs wird das Bild analysiert, sondern hinsichtlich einer Blickweise, die sich im Barock als epistemische Konfiguration abzeichnet, als Raum, in dem die Repräsentation als Wissensordnung

only be seen from the reverse. Foucault doesn't analyze the picture within an art-historical discourse, but in relation to a way of seeing that emerged as an epistemic configuration during the Baroque as a space in which representation begins to take effect as a system of knowledge. For the image theorist W. J. T. Mitchell "an encyclopedic labyrinth of pictorial self-reference, representing the interplay between the beholder, the producer, and the object or model of representation as a complex cycle of exchanges and substitutions"[56] is a "metapicture." The painting not only presents a kaleidoscope-like image of various forms of representation, but itself represents a configuration of knowledge—that of the above-described classical epistemes, characterized by tableau-like simultaneity. In Foucault's analysis of *Las Meninas* the notion of the tableau oscillates between its original meaning, painting, and an extended meaning as configuration of knowledge, episteme.

The tableau (→ Tableau) is an ordered image resulting from processes of comparison, separation, and distinction. It is an overview in which individual elements display their differences through the act of synopsis. It is a taxonomic image, and undoubtedly emerged from applied systematics.

It shows us how things are ordered and thought about, and should not be abandoned as a historical visual concept out of necessity. The nineteenth-century literary tableau, to which the literary scholar Annette Graczyk has devoted an extensive analysis, is a new and particularly important form characterized by a blending of the artistic and the scientific that no longer portrays "fixed structural frameworks but processual and interdependent correlations."[57] The tableau is more than a sum of well-ordered and systematized individual cases presented as a synoptic surface. There are possibilities here for a renewed consideration and further development of the concept.

The attitude to the image adopted in this book, and its artistic-scientific approach, should be seen as a circular process without beginning or end; the encyclopedia is understood here as the circulation of variable forms of knowledge, and the tableau as the ceremonial snapshot of a complex interaction. The book is based on a curiosity about the way in which these forms of knowledge—be they different kinds of text, quotations, photographs, or documented

wirksam wird. Als „enzyklopädisches Labyrinth pikturaler Selbstreferenz, welches das Wechselspiel zwischen dem Betrachter, dem Produzenten und dem Objekt oder Modell der Darstellung als einen komplexen Zyklus von Austauschvorgängen und Substitutionen zeigt", ist es für den Bildtheoretiker W. J. T. Mitchell ein „Meta-Metabild".[55] Das Gemälde zeigt nicht nur ein kaleidoskopartiges Bild von Repräsentationsweisen, sondern repräsentiert selbst eine Wissenskonfiguration – die der weiter oben beschriebenen klassischen Episteme, die von einer tableauartigen Gleichzeitigkeit geprägt ist. In Foucaults Analyse von *Las Meninas* oszilliert der Begriff des Tableaus zwischen seiner Herkunftsbedeutung, Gemälde, und einer erweiterten Bedeutung als Konfiguration des Wissens, Episteme.

Das Tableau (→ Tableau) ist ein Bild. Es ist ein geordnetes Bild, das sich aus Prozessen des Vergleichens, Trennens und Unterscheidens ergibt. Es ist ein Übersichtsbild, auf dem einzelne Elemente über den Akt der Zusammenschau ihre Unterschiede vorführen. Es ist ein taxonomisches Bild, entstanden ohne Zweifel an der angewandten Systematik.

Es zeigt uns, wie geordnet und gedacht wird. Nicht gezwungenermaßen sollte das wissensordnende Bildkonzept des Tableaus gänzlich als vergangen und historisch aufgegeben werden. Mit dem literarischen Tableau, dem die Literaturwissenschaftlerin Annette Graczyk eine ausführliche Analyse widmet, entwickelt sich eine neue Ausprägung des Tableaus, die im 19. Jahrhundert von besonderer Wichtigkeit ist. Kennzeichnend für das literarische Tableau, welches das künstlerische mit dem wissenschaftlichen Tableau verschmilzt, ist, dass nun „nicht mehr feststehende Ordnungsgefüge, sondern prozesshafte und interdependente Abhängigkeiten" dargestellt werden.[56] Das Tableau ist mehr als die Summe von wohl geordneten und systematisierten Einzelfällen, die es synoptisch als Oberfläche darbietet. Damit eröffnen sich Anknüpfungsmöglichkeiten für eine Neubetrachtung und Weiterentwicklung des Tableaubegriffs.

Die Haltung gegenüber dem Bild und die künstlerisch-wissenschaftliche Herangehensweise an dieses Buch sind als ein zirkulärer Prozess zu verstehen, der keinen Anfang und kein Ende hat: Die Enzyklopädie wird hier als Zirkulieren variabler Wissensformen verstanden und das Tableau als feierliche Momentaufnahme eines komplexen Auf-

drawings—can be ordered, how they fit together, whether they fall into line or produce contradictions. It was created with the awareness that any result, for example a printed book, a drawing, or a text, basically represents a captured, materialized moment—in fact a kind of tableau of juxtaposed thoughts, ideas, images, references, texts, and quotes, potentially alterable and developable, always re-thinkable.

Through the analysis of images, through experiencing and observing images, and also through theoretical discourse about images, knowledge can be gained that is reflected via the medium of the image in the process of image-making. How do we look at images? Under what premises and with what ideas and intentions are images produced? What are our expectations of an image? Paul Watzlawick's much quoted axiom that human beings can't not communicate also applies to the image, both in the way it is produced and how it is viewed. The "sage" guided by the epistemic virtue of truth-to-nature wishes to produce a "reasoned image"; the diligent "worker," believing in an objectivity obtained with the aid of automatism and apparatuses, delivers the "mechanical image"; a trained judgement, on the other hand, helps the "expert" to come up with an "interpreted image."[58] But how does the scientific image behave in comparison with the artistic image? While science and art were in close proximity during the Renaissance, the two worlds have become increasingly separate since the Enlightenment, and where artists have been required to celebrate their subjectivity since the nineteenth century, scientists must subdue theirs as best they can.[59] Stereotypes of analytical scientists and intuitive creative artists have become ingrained.[60] But it isn't merely polarizing and simplistic to keep the worlds of science and art apart, it's plainly impossible, as both "well up, in all their various forms, from the same inner necessities to gratify our systems of perception, cognition, and creation."[61] Our visual perception is oriented to the production of pattern and order; we follow an "aesthetic impulse."[62] For the art historian Martin Kemp, however, an examination of similarities in the production of artistic and scientific images is far more decisive than following the configurative logic and intuition resulting from the complex development of our sense of sight: "Observation, structured speculation, visualization, exploitation of analogy and

einandereinwirkens. Es fußt in einer Neugier danach, wie diese Wissensformen – seien es unterschiedliche Textsorten, Zitate, Fotografien oder dokumentierte Zeichnungen – miteinander geordnet werden können, wie sie zusammenpassen, ob sie sich fügen oder Widersprüche produzieren. Das Buch entstand im Bewusstsein, dass jedes Resultat, zum Beispiel ein gedrucktes Buch, eine Zeichnung oder ein Text, im Grunde einen festgehaltenen, materialisierten Moment darstellt – eben eine Art Tableau aus Nebeneinanderstellungen von Gedanken, Ideen, Bildern, Referenzen, Texten und Zitaten, potenziell veränderungs- und entwicklungsfähig, immer überdenkbar.

Über die Analyse von Bildern, über die Erfahrung mit und über die Betrachtung von Bildern, aber auch über bildtheoretische Diskurse können Erkenntnisse gewonnen werden, die über das Medium des Bildes im Prozess des Bildermachens selbst reflektiert werden. Wie betrachtet man ein Bild? Unter welchen Prämissen und mit welchen Vorstellungen und Absichten stellt man ein Bild her? Welche Erwartung setzt man in ein Bild? Das von Paul Watzlawick formulierte und viel zitierte kommunikative Schicksal des Menschen, nämlich dass er nicht nicht kommunizieren kann, trifft wohl auch auf das Bild zu. Das gilt sowohl für die Art seiner Herstellung als auch für die Weisen, wie es betrachtet wird. Der „weise Gelehrte", der von der epistemischen Tugend der Naturwahrheit geleitet wird, möchte ein „Vernunft-Bild" herstellen; der von Fleiß erfüllte „Arbeiter", der an eine mithilfe von Automatismen und Apparaturen erzeugte Objektivität glaubt, liefert das „mechanische Bild"; ein geschultes Urteil hingegen hilft dem „Experten" dabei, ein „interpretiertes Bild" zu erzeugen.[57] Wie aber verhält sich das wissenschaftliche Bild im Vergleich zum künstlerischen? Während in der Renaissance Wissenschaft und Kunst miteinander in enger Verbindung stehen, trennen sich die beiden Welten seit der Aufklärung in zunehmendem Maße, und wo der Künstler seit dem 19. Jahrhundert seine Subjektivität zelebrieren soll, muss der Wissenschaftler sie so gut er kann unter drücken.[58] Eingebrannt haben sich die Stereotype vom „leidenschaftslosen Wissenschaftler" und vom instinktgetriebenen, schöpferischen Künstler.[59] Doch ist es nicht nur polarisierend und vereinfachend, die Welten von Wissenschaft und Kunst voneinander getrennt zu halten, es ist schlicht nicht möglich, weil beide „in all ihren unterschied-

metaphor, experimental testing, and the presentation of a remade experience in particular styles" are procedures shared by art and science.[63] We shouldn't forget that both artistic and scientific images are abstractions that result from interpretation. Many scientific images are time-tested, historically rooted, and sometimes highly successful normative systems, such as maps, plans, or simulations. They construct something that doesn't exist in the world in this way, and in doing so they create reality.

Bruno Latour describes how scientific processes are ultimately rendered by visual inscriptions: "What is visible is only the freeze-frame of a process of transformation that remains extremely difficult to grasp, a proper form of invisibility."[64] There are parallels here to the artistic process of drawing, which is also based on invisibly resonating consideration, thought, research, decision, and rejection. The use of scientific "subject matter" in anti-disciplinary form is a reference to the many invisibilities that scientific images contain. A conflation, even a confusion, of the scientific with the artistic image could create a particular kind of epistemic object, one that relieves images of their discursive and functional context and reconsiders them in a non-disciplinary way. An ambiguous image of this kind would point to a different reality, or to the fact that images create more than one reality.

lichen Formen denselben inneren Bedürfnissen entspringen, unsere Systeme der Wahrnehmung, Kognition und Kreation zufrieden zu stellen".[60] Unsere visuelle Wahrnehmung ist darauf ausgelegt, Ordnungen und Muster herzustellen, wir folgen einem „ästhetischen Impuls".[61] Aber noch viel Entscheidenderes, als der Logik von Gestaltprinzipien und Intuitionen zu folgen, die sich aus der Komplexität und Entwicklung unseres Sehsinnes ergeben, liegt für den Kunsthistoriker Martin Kemp darin, die Ähnlichkeiten in der Hervorbringung von künstlerischen und wissenschaftlichen Bildern zu untersuchen: „Beobachtung, strukturierte Spekulation, Visualisierung, Nutzung von Analogie und Metapher, experimentelle Überprüfung und die Präsentation rekonstruierter oder simulierter Erfahrung unter Verwendung spezieller Stilmittel" sind Vorgangsweisen, die Kunst und Wissenschaft gemeinsam haben.[62] Wir dürfen nicht vergessen, dass nicht nur künstlerische, sondern auch wissenschaftliche Bilder aus interpretativen Handlungen resultieren und Abstraktionen sind. Viele wissenschaftliche Bilder sind lange erprobte, historisch verwurzelte und manchmal sehr erfolgreiche normative Systeme wie etwa Karten, Pläne, aber auch Simulationen. Sie konstruieren etwas, das es so in der Welt nicht gibt, und erzeugen damit Wirklichkeit.

Bruno Latour beschreibt, wie wissenschaftliche Prozesse letztlich über visuelle Inskriptionen sichtbar gemacht werden: „Was sichtbar ist, ist ein Standbild eines Prozesses von Transformationen, der schwer greifbar ist, eine angemessene Form von Unsichtbarkeit."[63] Hier ergeben sich Parallelen zum künstlerischen Prozess des Zeichnens. Auch die Zeichnung beruht auf unzähligen Prozessen des Abwägens, Nachdenkens, Recherchierens, Entscheidens und Verwerfens, die unsichtbar mitschwingen. Die Verwendung wissenschaftlicher „Sujets" in antidisziplinärer Form ist ein Verweis auf etwaige Unsichtbarkeiten, die wissenschaftliche Bilder mit sich tragen. Eine Verschmelzung, sogar Verwechslung des wissenschaftlichen mit dem künstlerischen Bild könnte eine besondere Art von epistemischen Objekten erzeugen, und zwar, indem Bilder aus ihrem diskursiven und funktionalen Kontext gehoben und damit einer Neubetrachtung unterzogen werden, die sich einer disziplinären Zuordnung entzieht. So ein Wechselbild würde auf eine andere Wirklichkeit verweisen oder auf die Tatsache, dass Bilder eben mehr als eine Wirklichkeit erzeugen.

1 Wulff D. Rehfus Hrsg., *Handwörterbuch Philosophie* (Göttingen: Vandenhoeck und Ruprecht, 2003), 684.
2 Peter Prechtl und Franz-Peter Burkard, Hrsg., *Metzler Philosophie Lexikon: Begriffe und Definitionen* (Stuttgart, Weimar: Verlag J. B. Metzler, 1999), 139.
3 Ebd., 139.
4 Rehfus, Hrsg., *Handwörterbuch Philosophie,* 684.
5 Vgl. Gérard Simon, „Knowledge, savoir, and epistêmê", in *Dictionary of Untranslatables: A Philosophical Lexicon,* hrsg. von Barbara Cassin, übers. von Steven Rendall, Christian Hubert, Jeffrey Mehlman, Nathanael Stein und Michael Syrotinski (Princeton und Oxford: Princeton University Press, 2004), 275.
6 Vgl. Michel Foucault, „Die Ordnung der Dinge: Eine Archäologie der Humanwissenschaften", in *Michel Foucault: Die Hauptwerke,* übers. von Ulrich Köppen (Frankfurt am Main: Suhrkamp, 2016), 208.
7 Vgl. ebd., 86 f.
8 Ebd., 463.
9 Ebd., 59.
10 Ebd., 65.
11 Vgl. ebd., 65.
12 Vgl. ebd., 75.
13 Ebd., 75.
14 Vgl. ebd., 68.
15 Ebd., 79.
16 Ebd., 264.
17 Ebd., 89.
18 Ebd., 105.
19 Vgl. ebd., 115.
20 Vgl. ebd., 175, 192.
21 Ebd., 270.
22 Ebd., 272 f.
23 Vgl. ebd., 271.
24 Ebd., 322.
25 Ebd., 389, 415.
26 Vgl. ebd., 422.
27 Ebd., 422.
28 Vgl. ebd., 463.
29 Vgl. Rosi Braidotti, *Posthumanismus: Leben jenseits des Menschen,* übers. von Thomas Laugstien (Frankfurt: Campus Verlag, 2014), 22–28.
30 Von der Autorin frei übersetzt, Rosi Braidotti, *Posthuman Knowledge* (Cambridge: Polity Press, 2020), 42. „What does it mean to be a subject in an era that claims to be simultaneously more-than-human and less-than-human?"
31 Von der Autorin frei übersetzt, ebd., 43.
32 Cary Wolfe, *What Is Posthumanism?* (Minneapolis, London: University of Minnesota Press, 2010), xiv.
33 Ebd., xvi.
34 Lorraine Daston, und Peter Galison, *Objektivität,* übers. von Christa Krüger (Frankfurt am Main: Suhrkamp, 2017), 22.
35 Ebd., 391.
36 Ebd., 18 f.
37 Ebd., 73 f.
38 Ebd., 84.
39 Ebd., 87 f.
40 Ebd., 103.
41 Ebd., 103.
42 Ebd., 128.
43 Ebd., 127.
44 Ebd., 132, 146.
45 Ebd., 146 f.
46 Ebd., 169.
47 Vgl. ebd., 199.
48 Ebd., 265.
49 Ebd., 338.
50 Ebd., 348 f.
51 Ebd., 332, 336, 356.
52 Ebd., 338.
53 Ebd., 390 f.
54 Michel Foucault, „Die Ordnung der Dinge", 33.
55 W. J. T. Mitchell, *Bildtheorie,* hrsg. von Gustav Frank, übers. von Jürgen Blasius (Frankfurt am Main: Suhrkamp, 2008), 201.

56 Damit widerspricht Graczyk der These, dass das Tableau im 19. Jahrhundert als Wissensordnung abgelöst wurde. In ihrer Analyse fokussiert sie auf das literarische Tableau zwischen 1750 und 1850, im Speziellen *Tableau de Paris* von Louis-Sébastien Mercier, das Naturgemälde bei Alexander von Humboldt und das Tableau zwischen Naturwissenschaft, Kunst, Literatur und Malerei bei Johann Wolfgang von Goethe. Annette Graczyk, *Das literarische Tableau zwischen Kunst und Wissenschaft* (München: Fink, 2004), 18, 20.

57 Daston, Galison, *Objektivität,* 394.

58 Ebd., 39.

59 Martin Kemp, *Bilderwissen: Die Anschaulichkeit naturwissenschaftlicher Phänomene,* übers. von Jürgen Blasius (Köln: DuMont, 2003), 14.

60 Ebd., 13.

61 Ebd., 13.

62 Ebd., 15.

63 „[…] what is visible is only the freeze-frame of a process of transformation that remains extremely difficult to grasp, a proper form of invisibility." Bruno Latour, „How to Be Iconophilic in Art, Science, and Religion?", in *Picturing Science. Producing Art,* hrsg. von Carrie Jones und Peter Galison (London: Routledge, 1998), 436.

1 Translated from Wulff D. Rehfus, ed., *Handwörterbuch Philosophie* (Göttingen: Vandenhoeck und Ruprecht, 2003), 684.

2 Translated from Peter Prechtl and Franz-Peter Burkard, eds., *Metzler Philosophie Lexikon: Begriffe und Definitionen* (Stuttgart, Weimar: Verlag J. B. Metzler, 1999), 139.

3 Ibid., 139.

4 See Rehfus, ed., *Handwörterbuch Philosophie,* 684.

5 See Gérard Simon, "Knowledge, savoir, and epistêmê," in *Dictionary of Untranslatables: A Philosophical Lexicon,* ed. Barbara Cassin, trans. Steven Rendall, Christian Hubert, Jeffrey Mehlman, Nathanael Stein and Michael Syrotinski (Princeton, Oxford: Princeton University Press, 2004), 275.

6 Michel Foucault, *The Order of Things. An Archaeology of the Human Sciences* (New York: Pantheon Books, 1971 [ePub]), 446.

7 See ibid., 170f.

8 Ibid., 1020f.

9 Ibid., 88.

10 Ibid., 118.

11 See ibid., 119f.

12 See ibid., 140.

13 Ibid., 140f.

14 See ibid., 124.

15 Ibid., 148.

16 Ibid., 148, 572.

17 Ibid., 174.

18 The French term is retained here for this special pictorial type, or epistemic configuration, rather than the "table" used by Foucault's English translator.

19 Ibid., 211, 188.

20 See ibid., 229f.

21 See ibid., 403f., 618.

22 Ibid., 592.

23 Ibid., 597.

24 See ibid., 594.

25 Ibid., 709.

26 Ibid., 853, 863.

27 See ibid., 422.

28 Ibid., 929.

29 See ibid., 1020f.

30 See Rosi Braidotti, *The Posthuman* (Cambridge: Polity Press, 2013), 15–25.

31 See Rosi Braidotti, *Posthuman Knowledge* (Cambridge: Polity Press, 2020 [ePub]), 42.

32 See ibid., 43.

33 Cary Wolfe, *What Is Posthumanism?* (Minneapolis, London: University of Minnesota Press, 2010), xiv.

34 Ibid., xvi.

35 Lorraine Daston and Peter Galison, *Objectivity* (New York: Zone Books, 2007), 22.

36 Ibid., 368.

37 Ibid., 113, 19.

38 Ibid., 42.

39 Ibid., 79.

40 Ibid., 84f. 86.

41 Ibid., 98.

42 Ibid., 35f. 105.

43 Ibid., 122.

44 See ibid.

45 Ibid., 125, 138.

46 Ibid., 138f.

47 Ibid., 160.

48 See ibid., 169.

49 Ibid., 250.

50 Ibid., 172, 319.

51 Ibid., 329f.

52 Ibid., 314, 324, 336.

53 Ibid., 319.

54 Ibid., 368f.

55 Michel Foucault, *The Order of Things,* 45.

56 W. J. T. Mitchell, "Metapictures," in ibid., *Picture Theory: Essays on Verbal and Visual Representation* (Chicago: University of Chicago Press, 1994), 58.

57 Graczyk thus disagrees with the proposition that the tableau was superseded as a system of knowledge in the nineteenth century. Her analysis focuses on the literary tableau between 1750 and 1850, particularly on the *Tableau de Paris,* by Louis-Sébastien Mercier, the nature painting by Alexander von Humboldt and the tableau between science, art, literature, and painting by Johann Wolfgang von Goethe.
See Annette Graczyk, *Das literarische Tableau zwischen Kunst und Wissenschaft* (Munich: Fink, 2004), 18, 20.

58 Daston, Galison, *Objectivity,* 357.

59 See ibid., 17.

60 See Martin Kemp, *Visualizations: The Nature Book of Art and Science* (Berkeley, Los Angeles: University of California Press, 2000), 2.

61 Ibid.

62 Ibid.

63 Ibid., 4.

64 Bruno Latour, "How to Be Iconophilic in Art, Science, and Religion," in *Picturing Science. Producing Art,* ed. Carrie Jones and Peter Galison (London: Routledge, 1998), 436.

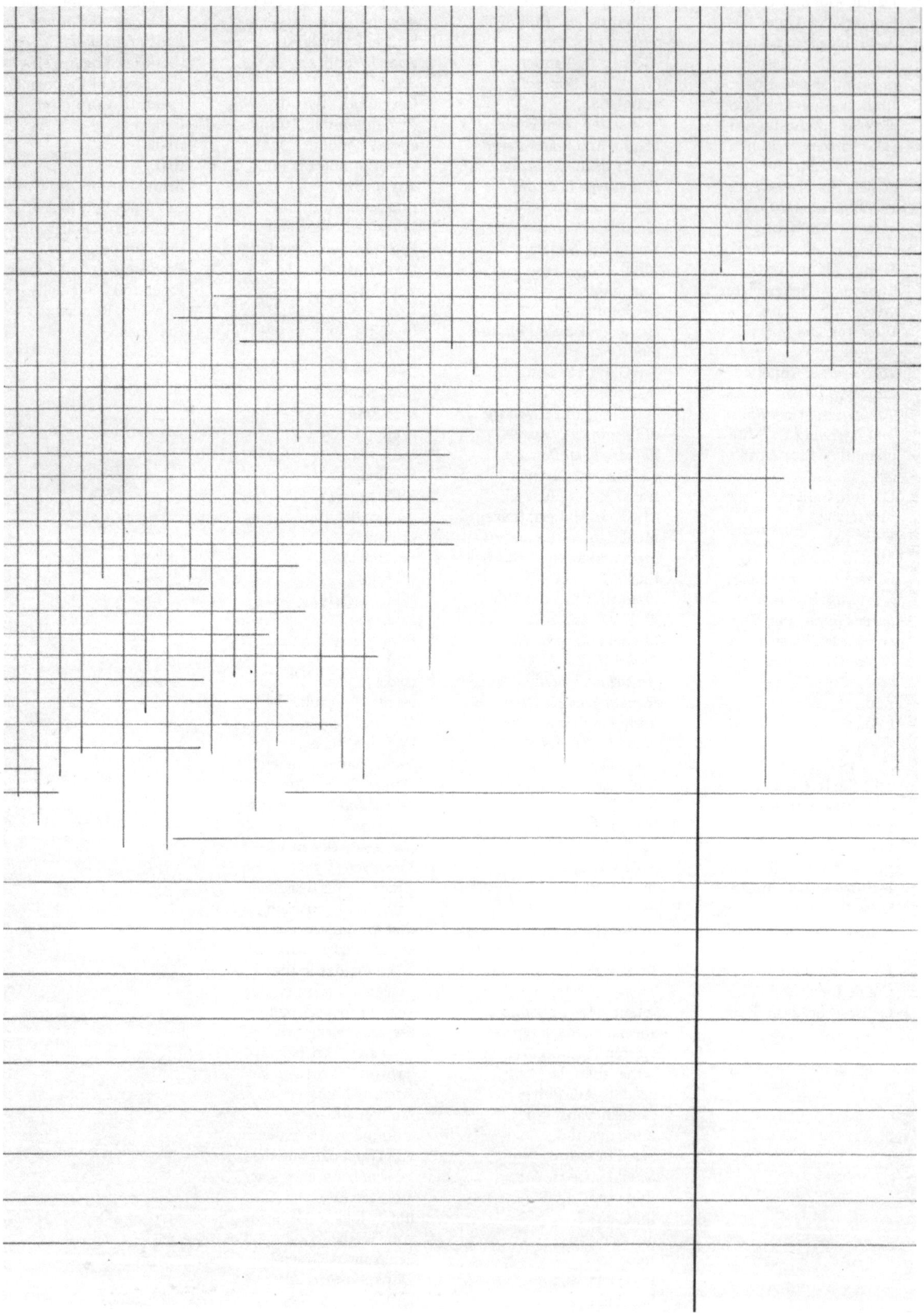

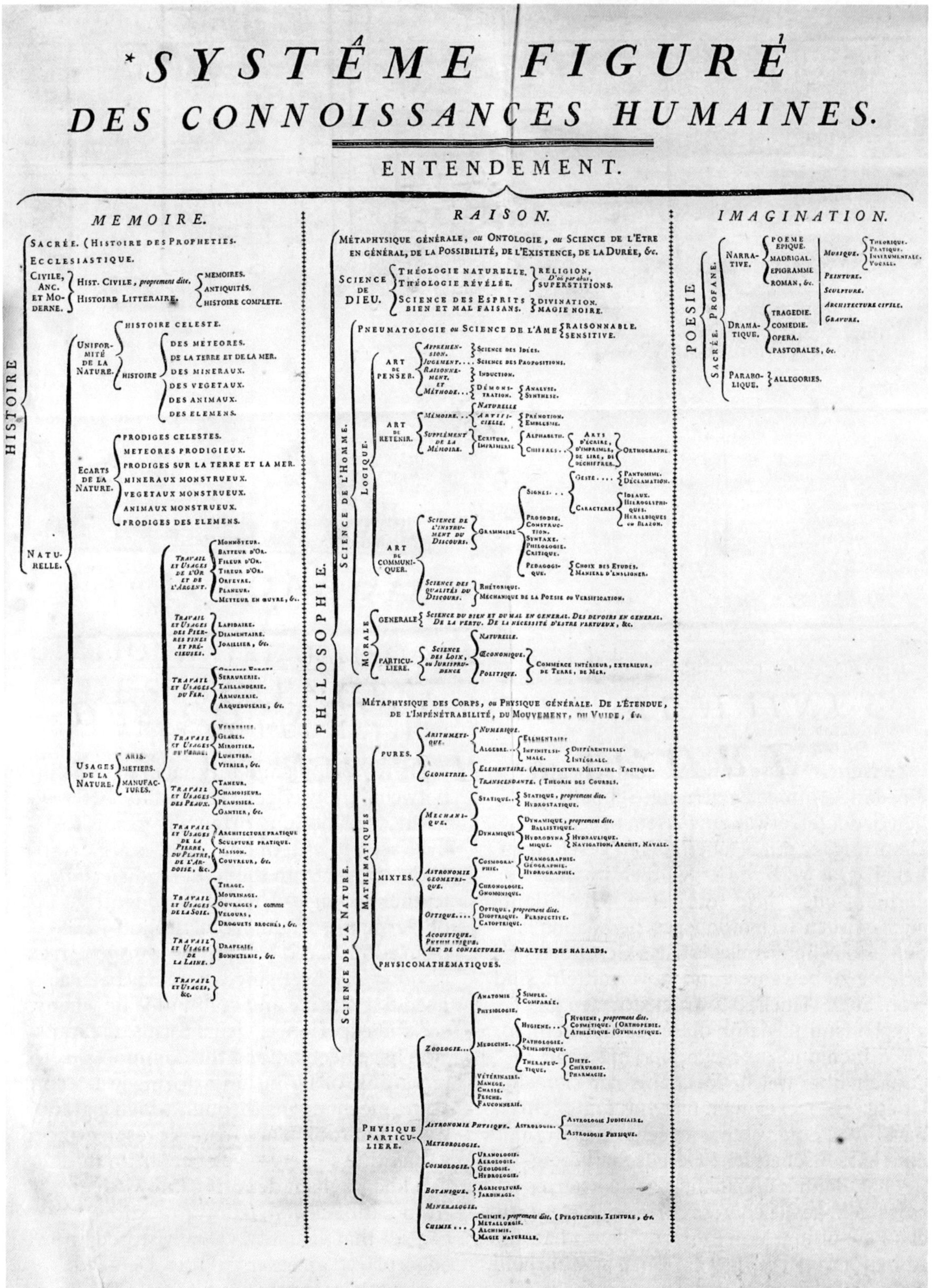
*SYSTÊME FIGURÉ
DES CONNOISSANCES HUMAINES.
ENTENDEMENT.
MEMOIRE.
RAISON.
IMAGINATION.
HISTOIRE
Sacrée. (Histoire des Prophéties.
Ecclesiastique.
Civile, Anc. et Moderne.
Hist. Civile, proprement dite.
Histoire Litteraire.
Memoires.
Antiquités.
Histoire complete.
Histoire celeste.
Uniformité de la Nature.
Histoire
Des meteores.
De la terre et de la mer.
Des mineraux.
Des vegetaux.
Des animaux.
Des elemens.
Ecarts de la Nature.
Prodiges celestes.
Meteores prodigieux.
Prodiges sur la terre et la mer.
Mineraux monstrueux.
Vegetaux monstrueux.
Animaux monstrueux.
Prodiges des elemens.
Naturelle.
Usages de la Nature.
Arts.
Metiers.
Manufactures.
PHILOSOPHIE.
Métaphysique générale, ou Ontologie, ou Science de l'Etre en général, de la Possibilité, de l'Existence, de la Durée, &c.
Science de Dieu.
Théologie naturelle.
Théologie révélée.
Religion, D'où par abus, Superstitions.
Science des Esprits bien et mal faisans.
Divination.
Magie noire.
Science de l'Homme.
Pneumatologie ou Science de l'Ame.
Raisonnable.
Sensitive.
Logique.
Art de penser.
Art de retenir.
Art de communiquer.
Morale.
Generale.
Particuliere.
Science de la Nature.
Métaphysique des Corps, ou Physique générale. De l'Etendue, de l'Impénétrabilité, du Mouvement, du Vuide, &c.
Mathematiques.
Pures.
Mixtes.
Physicomathematiques.
Physique particuliere.
Zoologie.
Astronomie Physique.
Meteorologie.
Cosmologie.
Botanique.
Mineralogie.
Chimie.
POESIE
Sacrée.
Profane.
Narrative.
Poeme epique.
Madrigal.
Epigramme.
Roman, &c.
Dramatique.
Tragedie.
Comedie.
Opera.
Pastorales, &c.
Parabolique.
Allegories.
Musique.
Peinture.
Sculpture.
Architecture civile.
Gravure.

# Visuelle Epistemologie

Zwischen Wissen und Visualität besteht eine lange, innige Beziehung. Schließlich bedeutet, etwas zu wissen, in seinem Ursprung, es mit eigenen Augen gesehen zu haben. Das Verb wissen wurzelt im indogermanischen „*ueid-* ‚erblicken, sehen', dann auch ‚wissen' (eigentlich ‚gesehen haben')".[1] Seit es das Bedürfnis gibt, das Gesehene und Erlebte zu bewahren und zu vermitteln, sind wohl auch visuelle Ausdrucksformen gängige Hilfsmittel dafür, dieses aufzuzeichnen, zu ordnen und zu speichern. Fragt man danach, über welche Mechanismen sich ein Übergang – sei er auch fließend und nicht hart – von einer vorwissenschaftlichen in eine wissenschaftliche Gesellschaft ereignet hat, dann hat Visualität, visualisiertes Wissen in gespeicherter Form, eine wesentliche Bedeutung. Man findet in Bruno Latours Abhandlung über Inskriptionen ausführliche Antworten dazu (→ Inskription).[2] Inskriptionen systematisieren das, was man gesehen hat und weiß. Dazu zählen auch zu Bildern gemachte oder grafisch strukturierte Einschreibungen vielfältiger Art – Karten, Pläne, Skizzen, Tabellen, Diagramme, Koordinaten u. v. m. Diese Inskriptionen können miteinander in Beziehung gesetzt und überlagert

# Visual Epistemology

There is a long and intimate relationship between knowledge and visuality. After all, to know something originally means to have seen it with one's own eyes. The verb *to know* comes from the "Old English *cnāwan* (earlier *gecnāwan*) 'recognize, identify', of Germanic origin; from an Indo-European root shared by Latin *(g)noscere*, Greek *gignōskein*."[1] Ever since there has been a need to preserve and communicate what we see and experience, visual forms of expression have been among the common aids to recording, ordering, and storing it. Looking at the mechanisms through which a gradual transition took place from a prescientific to a scientific society—"science" from the "Middle English (denoting knowledge) … from Latin *scientia*, from *scire* 'know'[2]—we can see that visuality, visually stored knowledge, played an essential role. Detailed explanations for this can be found in Bruno Latour's article on inscription below (→ Inscription).[3] Inscriptions systematize what we have seen and what we know. They include a variety of graphically structured media—maps, plans, sketches, tables, diagrams, coordinates, and so on. They can be correlated and superimposed. They enable

werden. Sie ermöglichen es, das Überdimensionierte und Komplexe in eine annehmbare Form zu bringen, die man in eine Tasche stecken kann: Man denke zum Beispiel an den Plan eines Gebäudes, der es möglich macht, dieses in jeden Ort der Welt zu kopieren, ohne es selbst versetzen zu müssen. Latour nennt dies *immutable mobiles*, sehr praktikable, unverrückbare, aber dennoch mobile Träger von Wissensinhalten.[3] Das Wissen lässt sich so leichter in der Welt zerstreuen, und die anderen, die Forschungsgemeinschaft kann man mit Inskriptionen leichter informieren, überzeugen oder sogar eines Besseren belehren.[4] So wirkmächtig, durchgängig und entscheidend visuelle Kodierungsformen des Wissens sein mögen, so erstaunlich ist es, dass es kein eindeutiges und abgegrenztes wissenschaftliches Feld gibt, das sich einer systematisierten Analyse widmet. Vielleicht ist das der Tatsache geschuldet, dass die akademischen Felder, die mit visuellen Wissensformen arbeiten, sich nicht unbedingt überschneiden: „Eine visuelle Epistemologie ist integraler Bestandteil vieler Bereiche, wie Technik, Architektur, Industriedesign, Kartografie, Textilien, wissenschaftliche Illustrationen und statistische Analysen", aber die Kunstgeschichte und die bildende Kunst legten keinen besonderen Fokus auf dieses Wissensfeld, obwohl grafisches Wissen eine lange Tradition und weit zurückreichende Geschichte hat.[5] Eine umfangreiche Zusammenschau über eine so historisch zerstreute wie disziplinär heterogene visuelle Produktion von Wissen ermöglichen die beiden Werke *Graphesis* und *Visualization and Interpretation* der Autorin, Künstlerin und Wissenschaftlerin Johanna Drucker. In diesen Werken beleuchtet sie das Feld der visuellen Epistemologie. Kodex, digitale Benutzeroberflächen, Bildschirme, virtuelle Renderings und Informationsvisualisierungen weisen in ihrer Medialität sehr unterschiedliche Qualitäten auf und teilen doch ihre Funktion als Medium für visuelle Wissensproduktionen.[6] Sie werden daher bei Johanna Drucker für eine Analyse herangezogen, die auf das Argumentative und Autonome an grafischen Strukturen fokussiert. Es geht also insbesondere um solche ungegenständlichen Bilder, die Wissen nicht repräsentieren, sondern vielmehr herstellen.[7]

Für die visuelle Epistemologie sind vor allem zwei wesentliche, in bildtheoretischen Diskursen rund um den *pictorial turn*

what is oversized and complex to be brought into a reasonable, even pocket-sized form: think for example of the plan of a building, which enables it to be transferred anywhere in the world without having to be moved. Latour calls these *immutable mobiles*, very useful, unalterable, but nevertheless mobile bearers of information.[4] Knowledge can thus be dispersed more easily, and the others—the research community—are more easily informed, convinced, or even disabused by inscriptions.[5] As potent, pervasive, and decisive as the visual coding of knowledge may be, it is all the more astonishing that there is no distinct field of science devoted to its systematic analysis. Perhaps this is due to the fact that the academic subjects that work with visual forms of knowledge don't necessarily overlap: "Visual epistemology may have been integral to engineering, architecture, industrial design, textiles, cartography, scientific illustration, and statistical analysis, but it failed to become a separate field among academic disciplines. [...] Though ignored by fine arts for most of its history, the systematic production of graphic knowledge has a very long tradition."[6] A comprehensive summary of such a historically dispersed and multidisciplinary visual production of knowledge is given in the two books *Graphesis* and *Visualization and Interpretation*, by the writer, artist, and scientist Johanna Drucker. In these works she illuminates the field of visual epistemology. The codex, digital user interfaces, monitors, virtual renderings, and visualized information exhibit very different properties in their mediality, yet they share a function in the visual production of knowledge.[7] Johanna Drucker therefore cites them in an analysis focused on the argumentative and autonomous aspects of graphic structures. She is particularly concerned with those images that don't represent knowledge but rather produce it.[8]

Two basic assumptions extensively discussed in theoretical discussions about the *pictorial turn* are primarily important to visual epistemology. They include philosophical problems historically presented by the image, such as its reduction to depiction and the failure to see its materiality.

1.

The occidental realm is characterized by a logocentric world view. The pictorial is seen as problematic to the cognitive process because an image's lack of sharpness can

umfangreich besprochene Grundannahmen von Bedeutung. Zu den beiden Problematiken, die das Bild philosophiegeschichtlich mit sich trägt, zählen die Reduktion seiner Funktion auf ein Abbild und das Übersehen seiner Materialität.

1.

Der westlich-europäische Raum ist durch ein logozentrisches Weltbild geprägt. Das Bildhafte wird für den Erkenntnisprozess problematisch erachtet, weil das Bild täuschen, verfälschen oder zu Fehldeutungen verführen kann, da es gewisse Unschärfen birgt.

Das Vorurteil des Trügerischen und Erkenntnisverzerrenden am sinnlich wahrgenommenen Bild besteht seit Platon und hält sich hartnäckig. Numerische und alphabetische Codierungen des Wissens sind stabil im Gegensatz zu Bildern, für die es kein Äquivalent zu diesen Codierungsweisen in Form einer festgeschriebenen Systematik gibt.[8] Dieses Dauerproblem des Bildes kann sich jedoch als vorteilhaft erweisen. Die Eigenschaft der Widerständigkeit, das Fehlen einer Systematik bei grafischen Formen (bei Drucker „graphicality" – Grafizität), ist eine epistemologische Eigenheit des Bildhaften, die wirksam wird, wenn wir den Wissensbegriff nicht statisch, sondern situiert und eingebettet in Interaktionen von Wissensakteur*innen denken.[9]

Ein gewisser Bildskeptizismus spiegelt sich auch im Bildungssystem. Es weist den Künsten – den auf sinnlicher Wahrnehmung beruhenden Fächern – eine untergeordnete Rolle zu, weil sinnliche Wahrnehmung, weil Sehen philosophiegeschichtlich nicht mit Denken in Verbindung gebracht wird.[10] Und dennoch hat die Psychologie gezeigt, dass in die visuelle Wahrnehmung etliche kognitive Prozesse involviert sind.[11] „Visuelle Wahrnehmung ist visuelles Denken", lautet die Gleichung bei Rudolf Arnheim, einem Pionier in Sachen Rehabilitierung des Bildes und unseres Sehsinnes hinsichtlich seiner erkenntnishaften Funktion.[12] Sehen bedeutet, in Relation zu setzen, abzuwägen, Nähe und Entfernung zu adaptieren, Lichtsituationen zu berücksichtigen, zu selektieren, zu fokussieren. Das alles passiert im Allgemeinen, ohne sich darüber bewusst zu sein, und im Rahmen einer Prägung, die sich aus evolutionären und persönlichen Ereignissen und Verkettungen zusammensetzt. Unser Sehen – Blicken, Schauen, Betrachten, Beobachten, Fixieren, Starren – befindet

deceive, distort, or invite misinterpretations. This prejudice about the deceptiveness and the distortive effect of the sensorially perceived image has persisted since Plato. The numerical and alphabetical coding of knowledge is stable in contrast to visualization, for which there is no established systematic equivalent.[9] But this ongoing problem of the image can have its advantages. The quality of resistance due to the lack of a systematics of graphic forms (which Drucker calls "graphicality") is an epistemological property of the pictorial that becomes effective if the concept of knowledge is not conceived statically but is situated and embedded in the interaction of those seeking it.[10]

The education system also reflects a degree of visual skepticism.It ascribes an inferior role to the arts—those subjects based on sensory perception—because historically and philosophically, seeing has not been linked with thinking.[11] And yet psychology has shown that a number of cognitive processes are involved in visual perception.[12] "Visual Perception is Visual Thinking" declares Rudolf Arnheim, a pioneer in the rehabilitation of the image and our sense of sight in regard to its cognitive function.[13] Seeing means correlation, consideration, adapting proximity and distance, taking the light into account, selecting, focusing. All this occurs in a general way, unconsciously, and as a result of a chain of evolutionary and personal events. Our seeing—looking, watching, regarding, observing, glaring, staring—is in a constant state of flux. Our sense of sight is to some extent an evolutionary, culturally and personally influenced, adaptive ordering function that enables us to navigate in a highly complex, flexible, constantly changing environment, but at the same time—necessarily due to our orientation in the world—involves conventional ways of seeing that imply oversight. And this too is a skill that can be highly useful for survival. In certain situations an absolute focus is vital, but even within the information glut of our everyday visual culture we are frequently called upon to make use of our ability to ignore.

2.

A second problem of interest to visual epistemology is the fact that images used by science to support its findings are often treated as transparent surfaces whose material properties are looked through like the glass in a picture frame. In the scientific

sich in einem permanenten Fließzustand. Unser Sehsinn ist gewissermaßen ein evolutionär, kulturell und persönlich geprägter, adaptiver Ordnungssinn, der uns ein Navigieren in einer hochkomplexen, beweglichen, sich ständig verändernden Umwelt ermöglicht, der aber gleichzeitig – unserer Orientierung in der Welt geschuldete, daher auch notwendige – Sehkonventionen mit sich bringen muss, die ein Übersehen implizieren. Und auch Übersehen ist eine Kompetenz, die überlebensstrategisch äußerst nützlich sein kann. Manche Situationen machen absolute Fokussierung lebensnotwendig, aber auch in der Informationsfülle unserer visuellen Alltagskultur sind wir häufig darauf angewiesen, unsere Kompetenzen des Ausblendens anzuwenden.

2.

Eine zweite Problemstellung, für die sich die visuelle Epistemologie interessiert, ist die Tatsache, dass jene Bilder, die in der Wissenschaft erkenntnisstützend herangezogen werden, oft wie transparente Oberflächen behandelt werden, durch deren bildhafte, materielle Eigenschaften hindurchgeblickt wird wie durch ein Glas in einem Bilderrahmen. In jenen Wissenschaften, in denen Bilder argumentativ verwendet werden, spricht man durch sie hindurch und ohne Berücksichtigung ihres Status als Bilder.[13] Die eigentümlichen Arten, über Bilder zu sprechen, ergeben sich aus dem Kontext ihrer Anwendung, aus ihrer diskursiven Zuordnung. Beim wissenschaftlichen Bild ist eine besondere Sprechweise erforderlich: „Man sagt [...], auf ein Bild blickend, ‚das ist ein Dreieck', und nicht ‚das erscheint mir als Darstellung einer triangulären Struktur'."[14] Die Haptik eines Röntgenbildes etwa und eine Reflexion über eine Durchleuchtung als Voraussetzung seiner Lesbarkeit sind für eine diagnostische Beurteilung irrelevant. Es wäre eine irrationale Unordnung, die Diskurse zu vertauschen. Aber dennoch muss man feststellen, dass die „den Bildern eigene evidentielle Kraft" oder „pikturale Evidenz" für viele wissenschaftliche Disziplinen in der Erarbeitung von Argumenten eine entscheidende Rolle spielt, ohne die Bedeutung der Bilder als Bildobjekte zu berücksichtigen.[15] Johanna Drucker betont, dass Technologien und Medien für die Produktion visuellen Wissens große Bedeutung haben: Bilder werden durch die Technologien ihrer Herstellung codiert und verkörpern somit die Qualitäten der Medien, über die sie

fields that use images as a means of argumentation, they are spoken through regardless of their status as images.[14] The strange ways of talking about images result from the context of their use, from their assignment within the discourse. A special type of speech is required for scientific images: "One says [...], looking at an image, 'That is a triangle,' and not 'That appears to me to be the portrayal of a triangular structure.'"[15] The hapticity of an X-ray image, for example, and a reflection on illumination as the precondition of its readability are irrelevant to a diagnostic judgement. It would be an irrational disorder to transpose the discourses. But it must be observed that in many scientific disciplines the "evidential power inherent in images" or "pictorial evidence" play a decisive role in the development of argumentation irrespective of the significance of the images as objects.[16]

Johanna Drucker emphasizes the importance of technology and media in the production of visual knowledge: "All images are encoded by their technologies of production and embody the qualities of the media in which they exist."[17] Digital codes too rely on a material basis, and the assumption of the code as "pure difference" is a fundamental misunderstanding based on ignorance of the complicated materiality of the digital media.[18]

Because of the complexity of images that convey knowledge, and naturally also because of our image-dominated environment, Drucker advocates "graphesis." Her neologism should be understood as a systematic study of the visual production of knowledge. The aim of such a study is the attainment of a critical understanding of how we process visual information.[19] Graphesis makes no distinction between the digital or analogue visual production of knowledge. Drucker traces a wide arc from the lines that structure an over 5,000-year-old Sumerian cuneiform tablet, for example, to those that model a virtual object as a three-dimensional network. The question is always how visual structures behave in relation to the production of knowledge. Don't they produce knowledge in a distinct way, like the line that underscores a word to give it emphasis, the knowledge tree that assigns an element to its unalterable, the arrow that indicates the dynamics of a thought process? Our visual history of knowledge contains numerous examples of this.[20] These visual structures, which

existieren.[16] Auch digitale Codes sind auf eine materielle Basis angewiesen, und die Betrachtung von „Code als purer Differenz" ist ein grundlegendes Missverständnis, das auf einer Ignoranz der komplizierten Materialität von digitalen Medien beruht.[17]

Aufgrund der Komplexität wissensvermittelnder Bilder und natürlich auch aufgrund unserer bildreichen, bilddominanten Umwelt plädiert Drucker für eine „Graphesis". Unter diesem von ihr geprägten Neologismus ist eine systematische Studie visueller Produktion von Wissen zu verstehen. Das Ziel dieser Analyse besteht darin, zu einem kritischen Verständnis darüber zu gelangen, wie wir visuelle Informationen verarbeiten.[18] Graphesis zieht keine Trennlinie durch die Bereiche digitaler und analoger visueller Wissensproduktion. Drucker spannt einen weiten Bogen von den Linien, die beispielsweise die Zeichen einer über 5000 Jahre alten sumerischen Keilschrifttafel strukturieren, bis zu den Linien, die, zu einem dreidimensionalen Netz gefügt, ein virtuelles Objekt modellieren. Immer geht es um die Frage: Wie verhalten sich visuelle Strukturen in Bezug zur Wissensproduktion? Stellen sie nicht Wissen auf eigenständige Art her – wie die Linie, die das Wort unterstreicht, ihm gleichzeitig Nachdruck verleiht, wie der Wissensbaum, der den Elementen einen unverrückbaren Platz zuordnet, wie der Pfeil, der die Dynamik eines Denkprozesses abbildet. Unzählige Beispiele dieser Art lassen sich in unserer visuellen Wissensgeschichte finden.[19] Diese visuellen Strukturen, die keine Zeichen, keine Buchstaben, keine Zahlen und keine Datensätze sind, haben die Funktion, eben diese Elemente in eine Form einzupassen, zu rahmen, zu gliedern und vorzuführen. Dabei darf aber die Form dieser Übersicht selbst, ihre Tabellierung, nicht übersehen werden, denn über diese werden Relationen hergestellt, Gewichtigkeiten zum Ausdruck gebracht und Zuordnungen fixiert.[20] Es wird ermöglicht und verunmöglicht: Ermöglicht werden ein Überblick, eine Lesbarkeit, Erfassbarkeit und Orientierung komplexer Sachverhalte; verunmöglicht wird, die Elemente anders zu sehen, anders zu verbinden und die Auswahl und Herkunft der Elemente selbst infrage zu stellen. Vorsichtig sollte man mit der Vorstellung sein, Daten wären bloß versammelte empirische Gegebenheiten, die man wie eine Probe der Natur entnimmt, sammelt und zu einem Bild visualisiert, anhand dessen Muster sichtbar gemacht

are not signs, letters, numbers, or sets of data, aim to fit these elements into a form, to frame, arrange and present them. But the form itself of this overview should not be overlooked, as it is through it that relations are produced, weight given, and attributions fixed.[21] Things are made both possible and impossible: overview, readability, ascertainment, and orientation become possible; seeing or connecting the elements differently and questioning the selection and origin of the elements themselves become impossible. We should be wary of the idea that data are merely collated empirical facts sampled from nature and visualized in an image that makes their pattern visible. Numerous decisions have to be taken from sample to pie chart.

Images that present something—Drucker refers here to nonrepresentational images for the purpose of argumentation—are particularly likely not to bring to light existing facts, but to create and structure knowledge.[22] Drucker gives one particularly clear example of the necessity for a differentiated view of visualized knowledge in the model of the atom, which has continually been readapted:

"The image of the atom as a small solar system of particles in orbit, for instance, is not based on observation, but on an idea of how to represent a model of a phenomenon. The creation of images, such as traces in a cloud chamber, may affirm or undermine a theoretical hypothesis. But conceptualization of phenomena is often as strongly influenced by the models made as by observation (think of gender categories as an example where changing models have changed perception)."[23]

The atom can't be observed; it can only be conceptualized in paraphrase. Yet the visualized concept looks like an observation. We are accustomed to visual models that concretize theoretical concepts and look to us like actual facts. What is presented as an image, we can see, and what we can see, we know. Under the heading of visual epistemology we could paraphrase "what can we see?" with "how can we see?" What happens when visualized models like these images that look like observations are smuggled into the artistic process? When they are given different signs and relieved of their epistemological function to enter a different semantic space. What happens when we examine the aesthetic decisions around scientific images?

werden. Unzählige Entscheidungen sind von der Stichprobe bis zum färbigen Tortendiagramm zu treffen.

Insbesondere Bilder, die etwas präsentieren – Drucker meint damit ungegenständliche, zur Argumentation dienliche Bilder –, fördern nicht etwas faktisch Vorhandenes zutage, sondern kreieren und strukturieren Wissen.[21] Ein besonders anschauliches Beispiel für die Notwendigkeit einer differenzierten Sicht auf visualisiertes Wissen liefert Drucker mit dem Atommodell, das als Modellvorstellung immer wieder neu adaptiert wurde:

„Das Bild eines Atoms als kleines Sonnensystem aus Partikeln in einem Orbit, zum Beispiel, basiert nicht auf einer Beobachtung, sondern auf einer Idee davon, wie man ein Modell eines Phänomens repräsentieren kann. Die Erzeugung von Bildern, wie die Spuren in einer Nebelkammer, mögen eine theoretische Hypothese bekräftigen oder unterstreichen. Aber die Konzeptualisierung von Phänomenen wird oft genauso sehr von den erzeugten Modellen wie von der Beobachtung beeinflusst (man denke an Geschlechterkategorien als ein Beispiel, wo die Veränderung von Modellen die Wahrnehmung verändert haben).“[22]

Das Atom kann nicht beobachtet werden, es kann nur umschrieben konzeptualisiert werden. Dennoch erscheint das visualisierte Konzept wie eine Beobachtung.

Wir sind also an visualisierte Modelle gewöhnt, die theoretische Konzepte greifbar machen und uns wie tatsächliche Gegebenheiten erscheinen. Was uns als Bild dargeboten wird, das können wir sehen, und was wir sehen können, das wissen wir. „Was können wir sehen?“, könnte man im Zeichen einer visuellen Epistemologie in: „Wie können wir sehen?“, umschreiben. Was passiert, wenn visualisierte Modelle, eben diese wie Beobachtungen erscheinenden Bilder, in den künstlerischen Prozess eingeschleust werden? Wenn sie unter andere Vorzeichen gesetzt werden und, ihrer epistemischen Funktion enthoben, in einen anderen visuellen Bedeutungsraum treten? Was, wenn die Machweise wissenschaftlicher Bilder auf ästhetische Entscheidungen hin befragt wird?

In der bildenden Kunst – einer Weise, mit der Welt visuell umzugehen – hat sich ein reicher Erfahrungsschatz an Reflexionen und Analysen über Zusammenstellungen, Ordnungen, Strukturen und Relationen einzelner Elemente in einem Gesamtsystem,

Visual art—one way of dealing with the world visually—has accrued a wealth of experience in reflecting on and analyzing the combination, arrangement, structure, and relationship of individual elements, whether abstract or figurative, within an overall system. Making images means thinking extensively about chance and necessity, and taking any number of decisions. How are these decisions taken in the visual configuration of scientific ideas? The methods of semantic permutation, a "transfer of meaning" into a different field of knowledge, could shed some light on this. In visual art, images question themselves without overlooking their own status, material, or style. So it would seem natural to propose that visual art might prove fruitful for a visual epistemology, at the point where the spectrum widens to an examination and comparative analysis of scientific images. Or where semantic permutation reveals the intention of images and discloses ideologies. Or where images chafe at the texts and texts at the images. Where contrast can be felt, where the ephemerality of looking meets the linearity of reading.

seien sie nun abstrakt oder gegenständlich, angesammelt. Bilder zu machen bedeutet, über Zufälle und Notwendigkeiten ausführlich nachzudenken und eine Unzahl an Entscheidungen zu treffen. Wie erfolgen diese Entscheidungen bei der Ausgestaltung wissenschaftlicher visueller Konzeptionen? Die Methode der Bedeutungsvertauschung, ein „Sinntransfer" in ein anderes Wissensfeld, könnte Aufschluss darüber geben.

In der bildenden Kunst sind Bilder Befragungen ihrer selbst, sie übergehen nicht ihren eigenen Status, ihr Material und ihre Machart. Es wäre daher eigentlich naheliegend zu behaupten, dass die bildende Kunst für eine visuelle Epistemologie ein fruchtbares Feld sein könnte, da, wo das Spektrum sich zur Befragung und vergleichenden Analyse zu wissenschaftlichen Bildern hin öffnet. Oder da, wo über Bedeutungsvertauschungen die Intentionen der Bilder aufgedeckt, die Ideologien sichtbar gemacht werden. Oder da, wo sich die Bilder an den Texten und die Texte an den Bildern reiben. Wo der Kontrast spürbar wird, wenn die Flüchtigkeit im Schauen und die Linearität im Lesen aufeinandertreffen.

1 Dudenredaktion, Hrsg., *Das Herkunftswörterbuch. Etymologie der deutschen Sprache* (Mannheim, Leipzig, Wien, Zürich: 2007), 931.

2 Vgl. Bruno Latour, „Visualisation and Cognition: Drawing Things Together". Siehe → „Inskription" in diesem Buch, wo der Text in voller Länge abgedruckt ist.

3 Vgl. ebd.

4 Vgl. ebd.

5 Johanna Drucker, *Graphesis: Visual Forms of Knowledge Production* (Cambridge, Massachusetts: Harvard University Press, 2014), 17 f. „Visual epistemology may have been integral to engineering, architecture, industrial design, textiles, cartography, scientific illustration, and statistical analysis, but it failed to become a separate field among academic disciplines." – „Though ignored by fine arts for most of its history, the systematic production of graphic knowledge has a very long tradition."

6 Vgl. ebd., 10. „But paradoxically, the primary effect of visual forms of knowledge production in any medium – the codex book, digital interface, information visualizations, virtual renderings, or screen displays – is to mask the very fact of their visuality, to render invisible the very means through which they function as argument."

7 Vgl. ebd., 10.

8 Vgl. Johanna Drucker, *Visualization and Interpretation: Humanistic Approaches to Display* (Cambridge, Massachusetts: MIT Press, 2020), 30. „But no equivalent to either alphabetic or numeric code exists in images."

9 Vgl. ebd., 30.: „The resistance of graphicality to systematicity is one of its fundamental (epistemological) properties, [...]."

10 Rudolf Arnheim, *Visual Thinking* (Berkeley, Los Angeles: University of California Press, 1979), 3.

11 Vgl. ebd., 13. „My contention is, that the cognitive operations called thinking are not the privilege of mental processes above and beyond perception but the essential ingredients of perception itself."

12 Ebd., 14. „Visual Perception is Visual Thinking."

13 Ludger Schwarte, *Pikturale Evidenz. Zur Wahrheitsfähigkeit der Bilder* (Paderborn: Wilhelm Fink, 2015), 185.

14 Ebd., 185.

15 Ebd., 185.

16 Johanna Drucker, *Graphesis,* 21, 22. „But of course, all images are encoded by their technologies of production and embody the qualities of the media in which they exist."

17 Reine Differenz meint den grundlegendsten aller Unterschiede zwischen Nichts (0) und Etwas (1). Reinheit wird immateriell – eine physische Verkörperung überschreitend – gedacht. Vgl. Johanna Drucker, *Visualization and Interpretation: Humanistic Approaches to Display* (Cambridge, Massachusetts: MIT Press, 2020), 23. „This idea of a ‚pure difference' [of code], one that was constituted without material instantiation, was completely false, but it found many eager advocates nonetheless." – „Ignorance of the complicated materiality of digital technology underpins this belief [...]."

18 Ebd., 3.

19 In *Graphesis* von Johanna Drucker findet man einen umfangreichen Überblick über die Spielarten visueller Ordnungsstrukturen des Wissens, siehe insbes. das Kapitel „Interpreting Visualization: Visualizing Interpretation", 64–137.

20 Dies können unterschiedliche visuelle Strukturen sein, wie Kreis-, Balken-, Fluss-, Linien-, Flächendiagramme, Tabellen, Piktogramme, Karten.

21 Vgl. Drucker, *Visualization and Interpretation,* 70.

22 Ebd., 18. „The image of the atom as a small solar system of particles in orbit, for instance, is not based on observation, but on an idea of how to represent a model of a phenomenon. The creation of images, such as traces in a cloud chamber, may affirm or undermine a theoretical hypothesis. But conceptualization of phenomena is often as strongly influenced by the models made as by observation (think of gender categories as an example where changing models have changed perception." Übersetzt von der Autorin.

1 *The New Oxford Dictionary of English,* ed. Judy Pearsall (Oxford: Oxford University Press, 1998), 1018.

2 Ibid., 1664.

3 See Bruno Latour, "Visualisation and Cognition: Drawing Things Together" under → "Inskription" in this book, where the text is reprinted in full.

4 See ibid.

5 See ibid.

6 Johanna Drucker, *Graphesis: Visual Forms of Knowledge Production* (Cambridge, Massachusetts: Harvard University Press, 2014), 17f.

7 See ibid., 10: "But paradoxically, the primary effect of visual forms of knowledge production in any medium—the codex book, digital interface, information visualizations, virtual renderings, or screen displays—is to mask the very fact of their visuality, to render invisible the very means through which they function as argument."

8 See ibid., 10.

9 See Johanna Drucker, *Visualization and Interpretation: Humanistic Approaches to Display* (Cambridge, Massachusetts: MIT Press, 2020), 30: "But no equivalent to either alphabetic or numeric code exists in images."

10 See ibid., 30: "The resistance of graphicality to systematicity is one of its fundamental (epistemological) properties."

11 See Rudolf Arnheim, *Visual Thinking* (Berkeley, Los Angeles: University of California Press, 1979), 3.

12 See ibid., 13: "My contention is, that the cognitive operations called thinking are not the privilege of mental processes above and beyond perception but the essential ingredients of perception itself."

13 Ibid., 14.

14 Ludger Schwarte, *Pikturale Evidenz. Zur Wahrheitsfähigkeit der Bilder* (Paderborn: Wilhelm Fink, 2015), 185.

15 Translated from ibid., 185.

16 Ibid., 185.

17 Johanna Drucker, *Graphesis,* 21f.

18 "Pure difference" means the most basic of all distinctions, namely between nothing (0) and something (1). Purity is conceived as immaterial—transcending physical embodiment. See Johanna Drucker, *Visualization and Interpretation: Humanistic Approaches to Display* (Cambridge, Massachusetts: MIT Press, 2020), 23: "This idea of a 'pure difference' [of code], one that was constituted without material instantiation, was completely false, but it found many eager advocates nonetheless. [...] Ignorance of the complicated materiality of digital technology underpins this belief."

19 Ibid., 3.

20 Johanna Drucker gives an extensive overview of the different ways to organize knowledge visually in *Graphesis,* particularly in the chapter "Interpreting Visualization: Visualizing Interpretation," 64–137.

21 It may vary considerably, and includes such visual structures as circle, bar, flow, line, and area diagrams, pictograms, and maps.

22 See Johanna Drucker, *Visualization and Interpretation,* 70.

23 Ibid., 18.

# F[1]

Fleck, blinder
Blind Spot

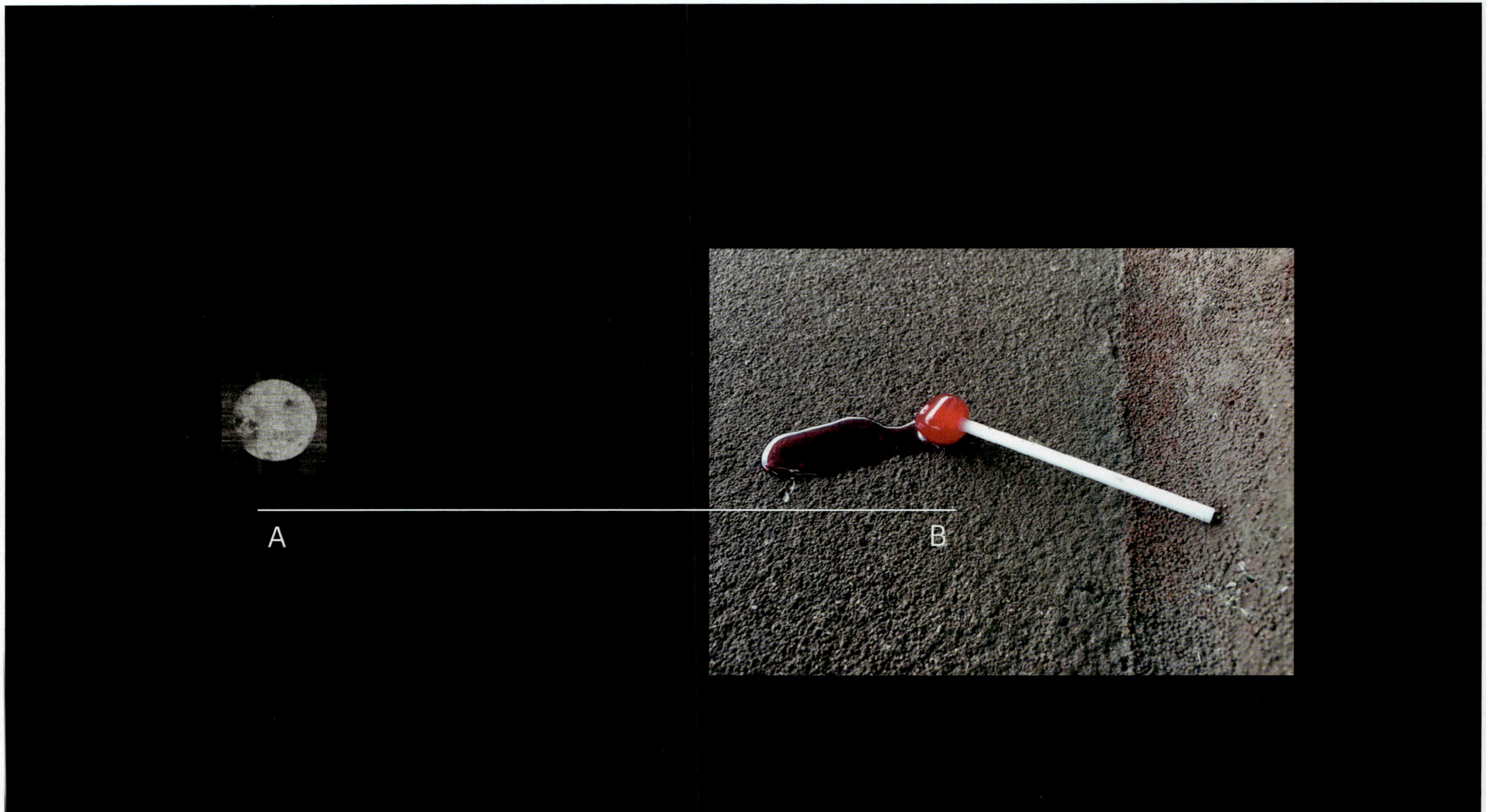


**Der „Blinde Fleck“ — eine Unvollkommenheit des menschlichen Auges**

Skizze zur Sichtbarmachung des „Blinden Fleckes“. Wenn man das rechte Auge mit der Hand verdeckt und nun in gewöhnlicher Leseentfernung (etwa 40—45 cm) den Punkt beim Buchstaben B mit dem linken Auge fixiert, so verschwindet die Scheibe bei A

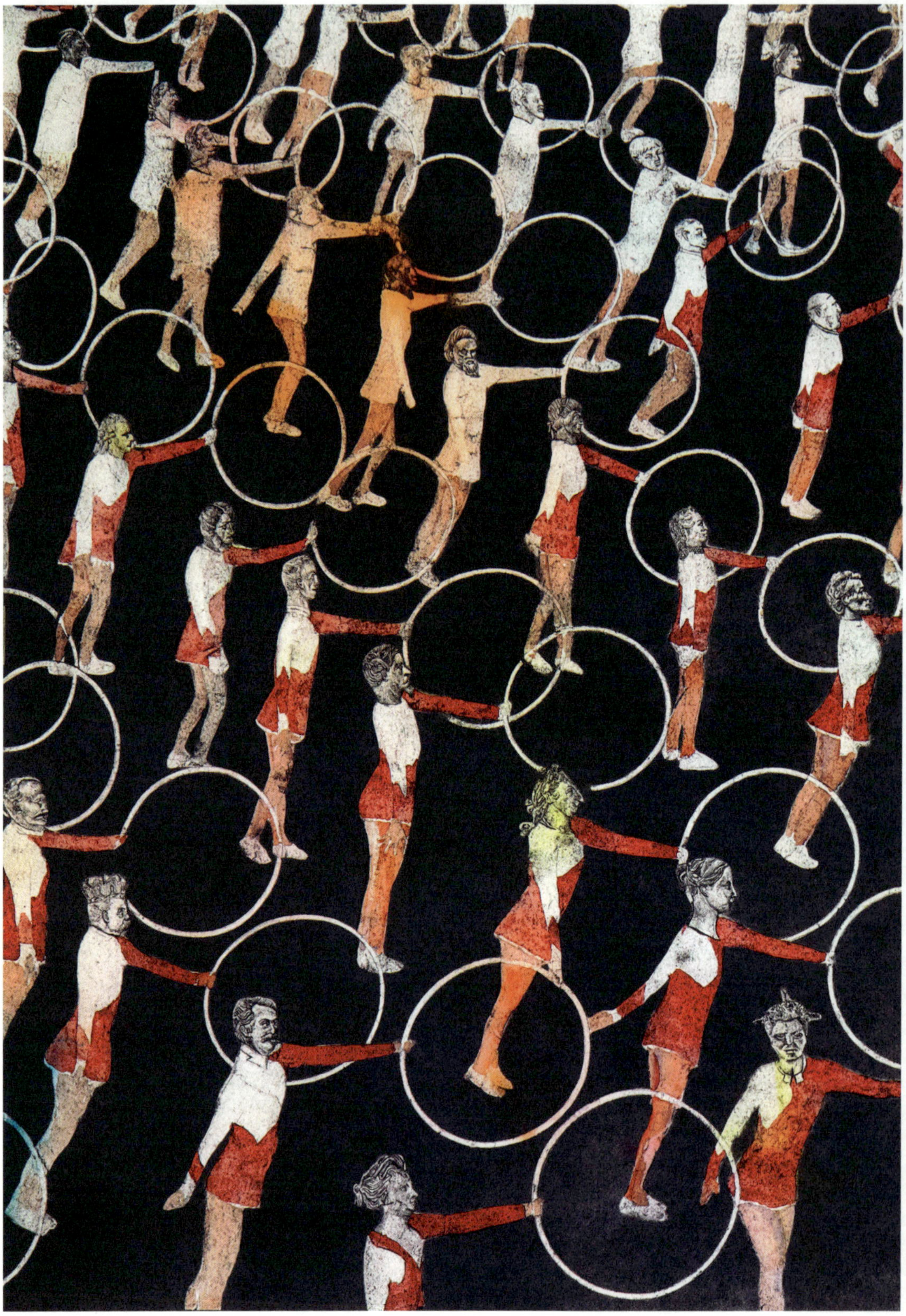

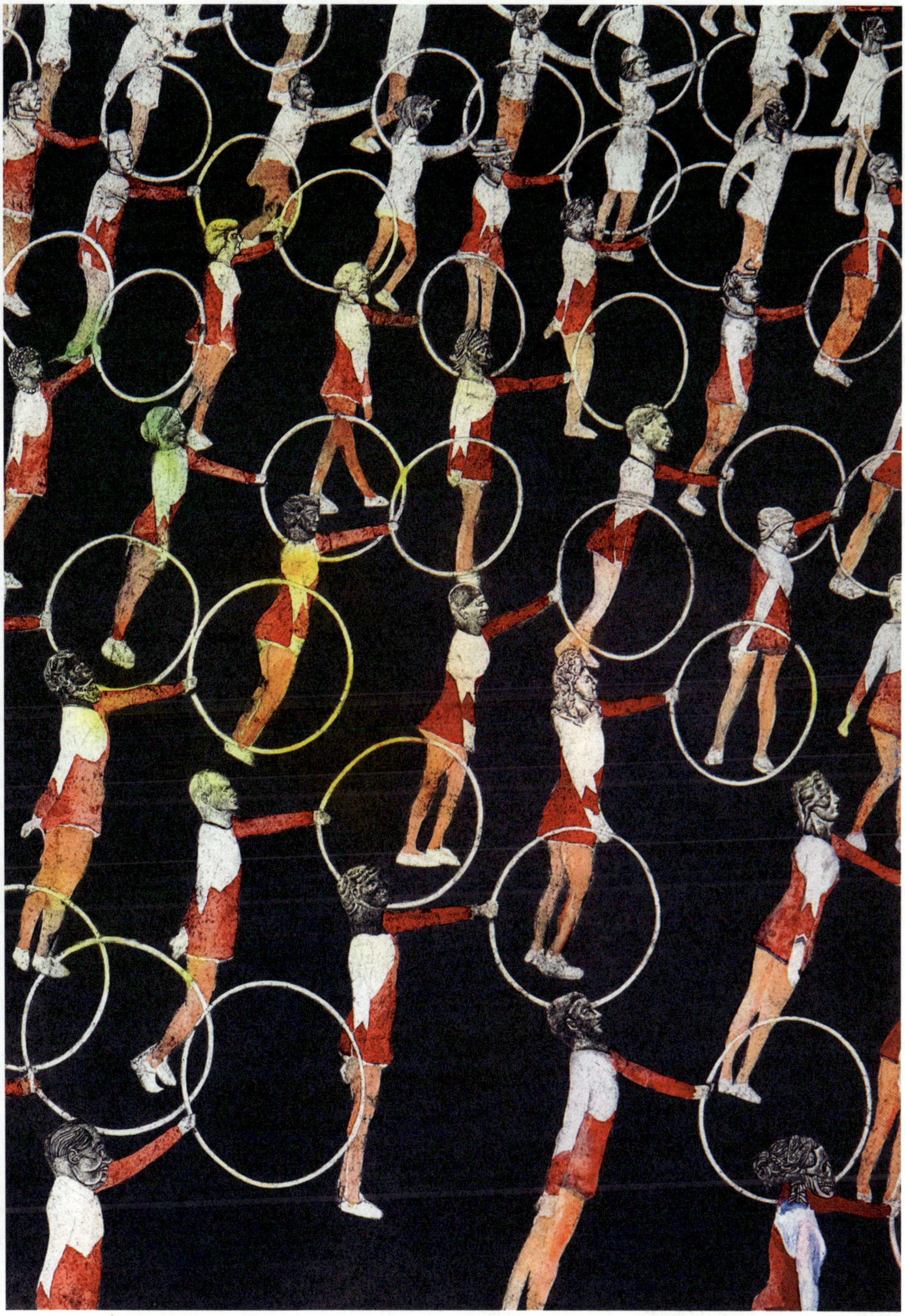

# Epistemische Gewalt

Epistemische Gewalt, diese unruhige Verbindung zweier erwartungsgemäß zueinander gegensätzlich erscheinender Begriffe, ist ein blinder Fleck der europäischen Wissensgeschichte. Wo die Aufklärung mit dem Vorantreiben der Wissenschaft und dem Etikett der Vernunft als Fundament von Freiheit und Selbstbestimmtheit verstanden wird, ist der Begriff der epistemischen Gewalt ein Irritationsmoment, welches das Narrativ einer kontinuierlichen Vernunftgeschichte infrage stellt. Wissen wird und wurde nicht nur hierarchisch strukturiert, sondern auch gewaltvoll angewandt. Die europäische Geschichte ist eine Kolonialgeschichte und damit eine Gewaltgeschichte, in der die Wissensformen der Mächtigen (ökonomisch und technologisch Bessergestellten) über die Wissensformen der Unterdrückten gesiegt haben. Wissen ist Bestandteil eines Kräftemessens. Der Begriff der epistemischen Gewalt kann als Instrument zur Analyse der Komplexität und Globalität dieser Kräfteverteilung des Wissens hilfreich sein.

Obwohl gerade die Wissenschaft – und das aus ihr hervorgehende Wissen – als Lösungsansatz gegen Gewalt gedacht wird, wurde längst erkannt, dass sie strukturell in die Erzeugung von Gewalt involviert ist. Den Begriff „epistemische Gewalt" verwendet die Literaturwissenschaftlerin, Theoretikerin und postkoloniale Intellektuelle Gayatri Chakravorty Spivak in ihrem 1988 erschienenen Essay „Can the Subaltern Speak?". Dabei stellt sie zunächst fest, dass der Philosoph Michel Foucault epistemische Gewalt in der epistemischen Neuausrichtung des psychiatrischen Diskurses am Ende des 18. Jahrhunderts, als der Wahnsinn zum Gegenbild der Vernunft erklärt wurde, ansiedelt.[1]

Genau so, wie Irre als Andere konstituiert werden, so wird auch das koloniale Subjekt als Anderes konstituiert.[2] Dahinter stecken dieselben Mechanismen, beides sind „Projekte einer epistemischen Überarbeitung", die „als dislozierte und uneingestandene Teile einer immensen zweiarmigen Maschine" arbeiten.[3] Für ihre kritische Auseinandersetzung mit der schwierigen Rolle der Intellektuellen hinsichtlich des Umgangs mit der Gruppe der Subalternen – jenen, die vom politischen System ausgeschlossen werden und ungehört bleiben – wählt Spivak einen Dialog zwischen den Intellektuellen Michel Foucault und Gilles Deleuze.[4] Beide sind sich einig, dass „Intellektuelle versuchen müssen, den Diskurs des/der Anderen der Gesellschaft zu enthüllen und zu erkennen", ignorieren aber ihre eigenen ideologischen, historischen, ökonomischen und intellektuellen Verstrickungen, so der Vorwurf Spivaks.[5]

Damit befreien sie sich von ihrer institutionellen Verantwortung als Kritiker*innen.[6] Sie überlassen es den Unterdrückten, von denen sie behaupten, dass sie „für sich selbst wissen und sprechen" könnten, sich selbst zu repräsentieren.[7] Auf die Frage, ob Subalterne sprechen könnten, gibt Spivak jedoch die eindeutige Antwort „Nein". Anhand des brutalen Rituals der Witwenverbrennung und dessen Verbots durch britische Kolonialherren zeigt Spivak, wie komplex und aussichtslos die Rolle der subalternen Frau der „sogenannten Dritten Welt" ist.[8] Sie wird als kolonialisiertes, vergeschlechtlichtes Subjekt zum stummen Spielball zweier konkurrierender Herrschaftsdiskurse.[9] Die britische Kolonialmacht stilisiert sich dabei zur rettenden Stimme der Vernunft und Humanität, mit dem Hintergedanken, ihre territoriale Präsenz zu legitimieren.[10] Mit einer analytischen Dekonstruktion des Satzes: „Weiße Männer retten braune Frauen vor braunen Männern", verdeutlicht Spivak nicht nur, wie stumm die Position der zum Objekt gemachten Frau zwischen Imperialismus und Patriarchat ist, sondern auch, welche ideologischen Gefahren damit einhergehen, wenn andere für sie sprechen.[11] Mit „Can the Subaltern Speak?" unternimmt Spivak, wie sie selbst sagt, den Versuch, das Schweigen zu vermessen.[12]

Eine Theoretisierung des Begriffes der epistemischen Gewalt ist ein wichtiges Forschungsanliegen der Friedens- und Konfliktforscherin Claudia Brunner.[13] Sie definiert epistemische Gewalt als „jenen Beitrag zu gewaltförmigen gesellschaftlichen Verhältnissen, die im Wissen selbst, in seiner Genese, Ausformung, Organisationsform und Wirkmächtigkeit angelegt sind".[14] Epistemische Gewalt hat ihre Wurzeln in Europa, ihre „spezifische Geschichte" im Kolonialismus und Kapitalismus, und sie funktioniert über Rassisierung und Sexualisierung „als Grundlage von globaler Arbeits- und Ressourcenteilung".[15]

Brunner differenziert drei Ebenen epistemischer Gewalt, die sich gegenseitig konstituieren: Mikro-, Meso- und Makroebene. Auf der Mikroebene geht es um das Individuum, um seine Leiblichkeit und

den damit einhergehenden Subjektstatus, der durch Kategorien wie Geschlecht, Sexualität, Herkunft oder ethnische Zugehörigkeit konstituiert wird.[16] Das Subjekt erfährt epistemische Gewalt über Ausgrenzungs- und Diskriminierungserfahrungen, über die Erfahrung, nicht gehört zu werden oder keine Stimme zu haben.[17] Den Subjekten, den Ungehörten und Subalternen stehen diejenigen gegenüber, die epistemische Gewalt ausüben. Diese wären sich jedoch ihrer Privilegien weder bewusst, noch würden sie diesen „Normalzustand" mit dem Begriff von Gewalt in Zusammenhang bringen, so Brunner.[18] Im universitären und wissenschaftlichen Kontext sind sie insofern an Epistemiziden – an der Auslöschung von Wissenskulturen – beteiligt, als sie eine „epistemische Monokultur in der wissenschaftlichen Praxis" forcieren.[19] Epistemische Gewalt wirkt auf der Mikroebene direkt und als persönliche Erfahrung auf das einzelne Subjekt, dennoch darf sie nicht als individuelle Problematik verstanden werden, weil damit ihre strukturelle, normative Einbettung übersehen wäre.

Auf der Mesoebene bezieht sich epistemische Gewalt vor allem auf die Rahmenbedingungen und Strukturen der Wissenschaft. Es geht jedoch nicht allein um die Analyse des Wissens als Resultat eines wissenschaftlichen Prozesses, sondern vielmehr um die Bedingungen seiner Entstehungsmöglichkeiten, um Diskurssysteme. Im Zentrum dieser Überlegungen steht hier die „Tatsache, dass [...] sich ein vormals religiös-theologisches christliches Wissenssystem im Prozess der kolonialen Expansion Europas säkularisiert und naturalisiert hat und zur Grundlage des aufgeklärt-modernen Wissenschaftsparadigmas geworden ist".[20] Selbstverständlich resultiert dies in einer Dominanz andro-, eurozentrischen und okzidentalistischen Wissens sowie einer Klassifizierung und Hierarchisierung von Wissen, die zur Etablierung wissenschaftlicher Disziplinen sowie zu einer Verhärtung von deren Abgrenzungen führte.[21]

Mit der Makroebene epistemischer Gewalt meint Brunner „nicht nur [den] geographischen und politischen, sondern auch [den] epistemischen Raum der kolonialen Moderne".[22] Innerhalb dieses globalen Raumes entwickelten sich Ordnungs- und Herrschaftsstrukturen, die sich historisch über religiöse zu säkularisierten und akademisierten Wissenssystemen transformierten, „mit denen es möglich wurde, die gewaltsamen Unterwerfungs-, Ausbeutungs- und Vernichtungsprozesse von Mensch und Natur in globalem Ausmaß zu rationalisieren und zu legitimieren".[23] Das Wissenschaftssystem ist damit Bestandteil für die Entstehung und Aufrechterhaltung einer Kolonialität der Macht, die global gesehen eine Asymmetrie in den Lebens- und Arbeitsbedingungen und in der Lebensqualität und Lebenszeit zur Folge hatte.[24]

### *Kopf oder Zahl*

Die Zeichnung *o. T. (Arirang)* entstand intuitiv und aus der Überlegung, dass es innerhalb der Positionen, die ein Subjekt einnehmen kann, eine grundlegende Gegensätzlichkeit gibt. Sie ist ein Versuch, deren äußerste Ränder zu erfassen: Disziplinierung und Individualisierung.[25]

Ob einem Subjekt epistemische Gewalt widerfährt, ist untrennbar mit seinen „Koordinaten" und „Eckdaten" innerhalb eines Spektrums möglicher Subjektpositionen verbunden. Dieses Spektrum ergibt sich aus globalen genauso wie aus nationalen, sozialen und kulturellen Prägungen und Normen, die eine Gesellschaft kontinuierlich verhandelt.

Die Ornamentierung des Leibes, der Versuch, den Körper in eine Choreografie der Gleichförmigkeit zu bringen, in der jede Individualität eliminiert wird, verkörpert einen äußersten Pol in diesem Spektrum. Die Arirang-Massenspiele, die jährlich in der nordkoreanischen Hauptstadt Pjöngjang stattfinden, sind ein Sinnbild für die Unterdrückung jeglicher Individualität des Subjekts. Die angestrebte Ästhetik verlangt nach einer lupenreinen Kollektivität, die sich aus der Distanz zu einem geometrischen Bild fügt. Siegfried Kracauer analysiert diese ornamenthafte Tanzformation bereits 1927 anhand des Beispiels der Tiller Girls in seinem Essay *Das Ornament der Masse*. Die Tiller Girls waren große, ausschließlich weibliche Tanzgruppen zu Beginn des 20. Jahrhunderts, deren Tänze in Revuen in synchronen Bewegungen vorgeführt wurden, die Kracauer als „mathematische Demonstrationen" bezeichnet.[26] „Den Beinen der Tillergirls entsprechen die Hände in der Fabrik", so Kracauer.[27] Das aus anonymen Tänzerinnen (deren Namen in den Programmheften unerwähnt blieben) bestehende Massenornament ist „der ästhetische Reflex der von dem herrschenden Wirtschaftssystem erstrebten Rationalität".[28] Der Tanz ergibt eine Abstraktion, die ein Abbild der

tayloristischen Arbeits- und Lebensbedingungen der Massen in den Fabriken und Büros zu jener Zeit ist. Die Uni-Formierungen der Körper bedeuten ihre Anonymisierung und die Ausklammerung des Menschen, seiner Persönlichkeit und Eigenheiten. Das Massenornament ist ein stummes Muster, denn im Gegensatz zu religiösen Kulten und Riten entbehrt es der Mächtigkeit der Symbolkraft – es ist eine „rationale Leerform des Kultes".[29] Der zu einer Einheit gewordene Volkskörper, der sich im Massenornament darbietet, ist eine Unterwerfungsform, die auf der Ausklammerung des Subjektiven und der Individualität der Einzelnen basiert.

Im Spektrum möglicher Subjektpositionen gibt es aber auch einen zweiten, entgegengesetzten Pol – das elitäre Individuum, das in politischer, kultureller, religiöser, ökonomischer oder wissenschaftlicher Hinsicht an der Spitze steht. In der Zeichnung *o. T. (Arirang)* wurden die Köpfe der Tänzerinnen von Münzporträts überlagert, die in der Überzahl männliche Figuren der europäischen Geschichte, beginnend mit der römischen Antike bis zur Gegenwart, aber auch Porträts asiatischer, amerikanischer und afrikanischer Volksrepräsentierender abbilden. Die porträtierten Eliten, deren Profile in die Münzen geprägt werden, sind eine verdoppelte Repräsentation. Sie repräsentieren nicht nur einen ökonomischen Wert, sondern auch das Individuum als jenes Subjekt, das sich in seiner führenden Funktion von den Anderen abhebt und unterscheidet. Die Eigenheiten jener Subjekte werden zu biografischen Besonderheiten stilisiert. Das Interesse gilt allen Aspekten ihrer Persönlichkeit. Biografie um Biografie wird das Individuum durch neue Erkenntnisse, durch noch differenziertere Betrachtungen aufgesplittert.

Es ist vorwiegend das „Schicksalszufällige" – so nennt es der Philosoph Odo Marquard (siehe → Zufall) –, das für die Subjektposition bestimmend ist, die wir in diesem Spektrum einnehmen, dessen entgegengesetzte Pole weiter oben beschrieben wurden. Wie viel Raum durch Selbstentfaltung, wie viel Eingrenzung durch Disziplinierung und Normativität erfahren wir? Die Wissensdiskurse, in die wir eingepasst werden, diktieren unsere sozialen und kulturellen Praktiken. Sie nehmen vorweg, welche Narrative wir bevorzugt zu hören bekommen. Epistemische Gewalt kann nur vermieden werden, wenn eine Selbstermächtigung und Selbstbestimmung im Prozess der Aneignung von Wissen gegeben sind. Welche Möglichkeiten und Räume ist eine Gesellschaft bereit zu schaffen, um sich einer Monokultur des Wissens zu widersetzen? Das Prinzip der Artenvielfalt ist in der Natur ein essenzieller Garant für die Aufrechterhaltung eines Ökosystems, und es stellt sich die Frage, ob dieses Prinzip der Vielfalt nicht auch für das von einer Gesellschaft hervorgebrachte Wissen gelten sollte.

1 Vgl. Michel Foucault *Wahnsinn und Gesellschaft: Eine Geschichte des Wahns im Zeitalter der Vernunft*, übers. von Ulrich Köppen (Frankfurt am Main: Suhrkamp, 2013), 391, und Gayatri Chakravorty Spivak, *Can the Subaltern Speak? Postkolonialität und Subalterne Artikulation*, übers. von Alexander Joskowicz und Stefan Nowotny (Wien, Berlin: Turia + Kant, 2020), 42.
2 Vgl. Foucault, *Wahnsinn und Gesellschaft*, 176, und Spivak, *Can the Subaltern Speak?*, 42.
3 Spivak, *Can the Subaltern Speak?*, 42.
4 Spivak bezieht sich dabei auf „Die Intellektuellen und die Macht: ein Gespräch zwischen Michel Foucault und Gilles Deleuze", in: Spivak, *Can the Subaltern Speak?*, 21.
5 Ebd., 22.
6 Ebd., 40.
7 Ebd., 38.
8 „Sogenannte Dritte Welt" ist ein Ausdruck, den Spivak häufig verwendet.
9 Spivak hat keineswegs die Absicht, das Witwenopfer zu verteidigen. Sie verwendet das historische Beispiel der britischen Abschaffung des Witwenopfers 1829, um auf die diskursive Gegensätzlichkeit zwischen „Ritual" und „Verbrechen" – „das eine durch Aberglauben fixiert, das andere durch die Rechtswissenschaft" – zu verweisen. Spivak, *Can the Subaltern Speak?*, 80, 83.
10 Vgl. ebd., 99.
11 Ebd., 78.
12 Ebd., 78.
13 Claudia Brunner, *Epistemische Gewalt: Wissen und Herrschaft in der kolonialen Moderne* (Bielefeld: transcript Verlag, 2020), 9.
14 Ebd., 274.
15 Ebd., 274 f.
16 Vgl. ebd., 278.
17 Vgl. ebd., 278.
18 Vgl. ebd., 279.
19 Ebd., 280.
20 Ebd., 284.
21 Ebd., 285.
22 Ebd., 292.
23 Ebd., 292 f.
24 Vgl. ebd., 292 f.
25 Das „Subjekt" wird hier im Sinne der Definition von Andreas Reckwitz verstanden als „eine *sozial-kulturelle Form* [...], als kontingentes Produkt symbolischer Ordnungen, welche auf sehr spezifische Weise modellieren, was ein Subjekt ist, als was es sich versteht, wie es zu handeln, zu reden, sich zu bewegen hat und was es wollen kann". Andreas Reckwitz, *Das hybride Subjekt. Eine Theorie der Subjektkulturen von der bürgerlichen Moderne zur Postmoderne* (Berlin: Suhrkamp, 2020), 47.
26 Siegfried Kracauer, *Das Ornament der Masse* (Frankfurt am Main: Suhrkamp, 1977), 50.
27 Ebd., 54.
28 Ebd., 54.
29 Ebd., 61.

# Epistemic Violence

Epistemic violence, this unquiet connection between two predictably contradictory concepts, is a blind spot in the European history of knowledge. Where the Enlightenment, with its advocacy of science and badge of reason, is understood as the foundation of freedom and self-determination, the concept of epistemic violence is an irritation that questions the narrative of a continual rationality. Science has not only been hierarchically structured but also violently applied. European history is a colonialist and therefore violent history in which the forms of knowledge belonging to the powerful (economically and technically better off) prevailed over those of the oppressed. Knowledge is part of a trial of strength. The concept of epistemic violence can be helpful in analyzing the complexity and globality of this deployment of knowledge.

Although science—and the knowledge it produces—is thought of as a solution to violence, it has long been recognized that it is structurally involved in the production of violence. The term "epistemic violence" is used by the literary scholar, theorist, and postcolonial intellectual Gayatri Chakravorty Spivak in her essay "Can the Subaltern Speak?" from 1988. Spivak initially observes that the philosopher Michel Foucault locates epistemic violence in the reframing of the psychiatric discourse at the end of the eighteenth century, when madness was declared the opposite of reason.[1]

Just as the mad are constituted as other, so too is the colonial subject.[2] The same mechanisms lie behind both; both are "projects of epistemic overhaul" that work as the "dislocated and unacknowledged parts of a vast two-handed engine."[3] For her critical examination of the difficult role of intellectuals in relation to subalterns—that group of people excluded from the political system and left unheard—Spivak chooses a dialogue between the intellectuals Michel Foucault and Gilles Deleuze.[4] Both agree that "intellectuals must attempt to disclose and know the discourse of society's other," but they ignore their own ideological, historical, economic, and intellectual entanglements, argues Spivak.[5]

In doing so they relieve themselves of their institutional responsibility as critics.[6] They leave it to the oppressed, of whom they claim that they "speak, act, and know *for themselves*," to represent themselves.[7] Spivak,

however, answers the question as to whether the subaltern can speak with a clear "no." In reference to the brutal ritual of widow-burning and its prohibition by the British colonial rulers, Spivak shows how complex and desperate the role of the subaltern woman in the Third World is. As a colonized, genderized subject she becomes a pawn in the hands of two competing hegemonic discourses.[8] British colonial power styled itself as the saving voice of rationality and humanity, with the ulterior motive of legitimizing its territorial presence.[9] In an analytical deconstruction of the sentence "White men are saving brown women from brown men," Spivak not only illustrates the muteness women's position objectified between imperialism and the patriarchy but also the dangers that arise when others speak for them.[10] "Can the Subaltern Speak?" is Spivak's attempt to measure such silences.[11]

A theorization of the concept of epistemic violence is an important focus of the peace and conflict researcher Claudia Brunner.[12] Brunner defines epistemic violence as "that contribution to the violent social conditions inherent in knowledge itself, in its generation, formation, organization, and effectiveness."[13] Epistemic violence has its roots in Europe, its "specific history" in colonialism and capitalism, and it functions through racism and sexualization "as the basis of the global division of labor and resources."[14]

Brunner differentiates three mutually constitutive levels of epistemic violence: micro, meso, and macro. The microlevel has to do with individuals, with their physicality and its associated subject status, which is constituted by categories such as gender, sexuality, origin, or ethnic affiliation.[15] Epistemic violence is experienced through exclusion and discrimination, through the lack of a voice and of not being heard.[16] Subalterns and the unheard are subject to those who exercise epistemic violence—who, however, are neither aware of their privileges nor would they associate this "normal situation" with violence, says Brunner.[17] In academic and scientific contexts they participate in epistemicide—the obliteration of cultures of knowledge—to the extent that they expediate "epistemic monoculture in scientific practice."[18] On the microlevel epistemic violence effects the individual subject directly as personal experience, but it should not be understood as an individual problem because this would overlook its normative structural embeddedness.

On the mesolevel epistemic violence primarily refers to the preconditions and structures of knowledge. But this doesn't have solely to do with the analysis of knowledge as the result of a scientific process, but more with its possible conditions for emergence and discursive systems. Central to these considerations is the "fact that [...] a previously religious-theological Christian system of knowledge was secularized and naturalized in the course of Europe's colonial expansion to become the basis of the enlightened modern scientific paradigm."[19] This naturally results in the dominance of androcentric, Eurocentric, occidental knowledge, and its classification and hierarchization leads to the establishment and exclusionary hardening of the academic disciplines.[20]

Brunner's macrolevel refers not only to "the geographical and political space of the colonial modern era but also to its epistemic realm."[21] Hegemonic and ordering structures develop within this global sphere, and transform historically from religious to secular and academic systems of knowledge "with which it became possible to rationalize and legitimize the violent and global subjugation, exploitation, and annihilation of human beings and the natural world."[22] The academic system is thus an element in the emergence and maintenance of a coloniality of power, with the global consequence of an asymmetry in living and working conditions, quality of life, and life expectancy.[23]

### *Heads or tails*

The drawing *Untitled (Arirang)* was made intuitively with the idea that there is a fundamental contradiction within the positions a subject can adopt. It is an attempt to capture the outer edges of this contradiction: disciplining and individualization.[24]

Whether someone experiences epistemic violence is inextricably linked with his or her "coordinates" and "key data" within a spectrum of subject positions. This spectrum results from the continual negotiation of global as well as national, social, and cultural influences and norms.

Ornamentation of the body, and the attempt to align the body with a choreography of uniformity in which all individuality is eliminated, is one extreme pole on this spectrum. The Arirang mass games, which take place every year in the North Korean capital, Pyongyang, are a symbol of the suppression of all individuality of the subject. The intended aesthetic requires a perfect

collectivity that from a distance results in a geometrical image. Siegfried Kracauer analyzed such ornamental dance formations using the example of the Tiller Girls in his 1927 essay *The Mass Ornament.* The Tiller Girls were large, exclusively female early twentieth-century dance groups whose movements consisted of synchronized movements that Kracauer called "demonstrations of mathematics."[25] "The hands in the factory correspond to the legs of the Tiller Girls," according to Kracauer.[26] The mass ornament, consisting of anonymous dancers (whose names do not appear in the program), is "the aesthetic reflex of the rationality to which the prevailing economic system aspires."[27] The dance is an abstraction of the Taylorist working and living conditions of the masses in the factories and offices of the time. The uni-formation of the bodies represents their anonymization and the exclusion of personhood. The mass ornament is a mute pattern, for in contrast to religious cults and rites it lacks symbolic power—it is "the *rational and empty form* of the cult."[28] The body of the people, as portrayed in the mass ornament, is a form of subjugation based on the elimination of subjectivity and individuality.

But there is also an opposite pole on the spectrum of possible subject positions—the elite individual at the political, cultural, religious, economic, or scientific forefront. In the drawing *Untitled (Arirang)* the heads of the female dancers are superimposed by coin portraits of mainly male European historical figures, from ancient Rome to the present, but also portraits of Asian, American, and African people's representatives. The elites portrayed on coins are a doubled representation, standing not only for an economic value but also for the individual as the subject that stands out and is distinguished from the others in its leading function. The characteristics of these subjects are stylized into biographical singularities. All aspects of the personality become a matter of interest. The individual is fragmented by new insight and increasingly differentiated reflection in biography after biography.

For the most part it is the "fateful accident"—as the philosopher Odo Marquard calls it (see → Accidental)—that determines the subject position we adopt on this spectrum, whose opposite poles have been described above. How much space for self-development or limitation through disciplining and normativity do we experience? The knowledge discourses we are fitted into dictate our social and cultural practices. They anticipate the narratives we are more likely to hear. Epistemic violence can only be avoided if self-empowerment and self-determination are inherent in the process of acquiring knowledge. What possibilities and spaces is a society prepared to create in order to resist a monoculture of knowledge? In nature the principle of biodiversity is an essential guarantee for the maintenance of an ecosystem, and the question arises as to whether this principle of pluralism shouldn't also apply to the knowledge a society produces.

1 See Michel Foucault *History of Madness,* trans. Jonathan Murphy, Jean Khalfa (New York: Routledge, 2006), 28ff, and Gayatri Chakravorty Spivak, *Can the Subaltern Speak? Reflections on the History of an Idea,* ed. Rosalind C. Morris (New York: Columbia University Press, 2010), 35.
2 See Foucault, *History* of *Madness,* 181, and Spivak, *Can the Subaltern Speak?* 36.
3 Spivak, *Can the Subaltern Speak?* 35.
4 Spivak refers here to "Intellectuals and Power: A Conversation between Michel Foucault and Gilles Deleuze," in Michel Foucault, *Language, Counter-Memory, Practice: Selected Essays and Interviews,* trans. Donald Bouchard and Sherry Simon (Ithaca: Cornell University Press, 1977), 205–217.
5 Spivak, *Can the Subaltern Speak? 23.*
6 See ibid., 34.
7 Ibid., 30.
8 Spivak in no way defends the practice of widow-burning. She uses the historical example of its abolition by the British in 1829 in order to discuss the discursive contrast between "ritual" and "crime"— "the one fixed by superstition, the other by legal science." Spivak, *Can the Subaltern Speak?* 51, 56.
9 See ibid., 61.
10 See ibid., 48.
11 Ibid.
12 Claudia Brunner, *Epistemische Gewalt: Wissen und Herrschaft in der kolonialen Moderne* (Bielefeld: transcript Verlag, 2020), 9.
13 Translated from ibid., 274.
14 Ibid.
15 See ibid., 278.
16 See ibid.
17 See ibid., 279.
18 Translated from ibid., 280.
19 Translated from ibid., 284.
20 See ibid., 285.
21 Translated from ibid., 292.
22 Translated from ibid., 292f.
23 See ibid., 292f.
24 The "subject" is understood here, after Andreas Reckwitz, as "a *socio-cultural form* […], as the contingent product of symbolic orders that in very specific ways model what a subject is, how it sees itself, how it is supposed to act, speak, and move, and what it can want." Translated from Andreas Reckwitz, *Das hybride Subjekt. Eine Theorie der Subjektkulturen von der bürgerlichen Moderne zur Postmoderne* (Berlin: Suhrkamp, 2020), 47.
25 Siegfried Kracauer, "The Mass Ornament," in ibid. *The Mass Ornament. Weimar Essays,* trans., ed. Thomas Y. Levin (Cambridge, Mass.: Harvard University Press, 1995), 76.
26 Ibid., 79.
27 Ibid.
28 Ibid., 84.

# I 1

Idee
Idea

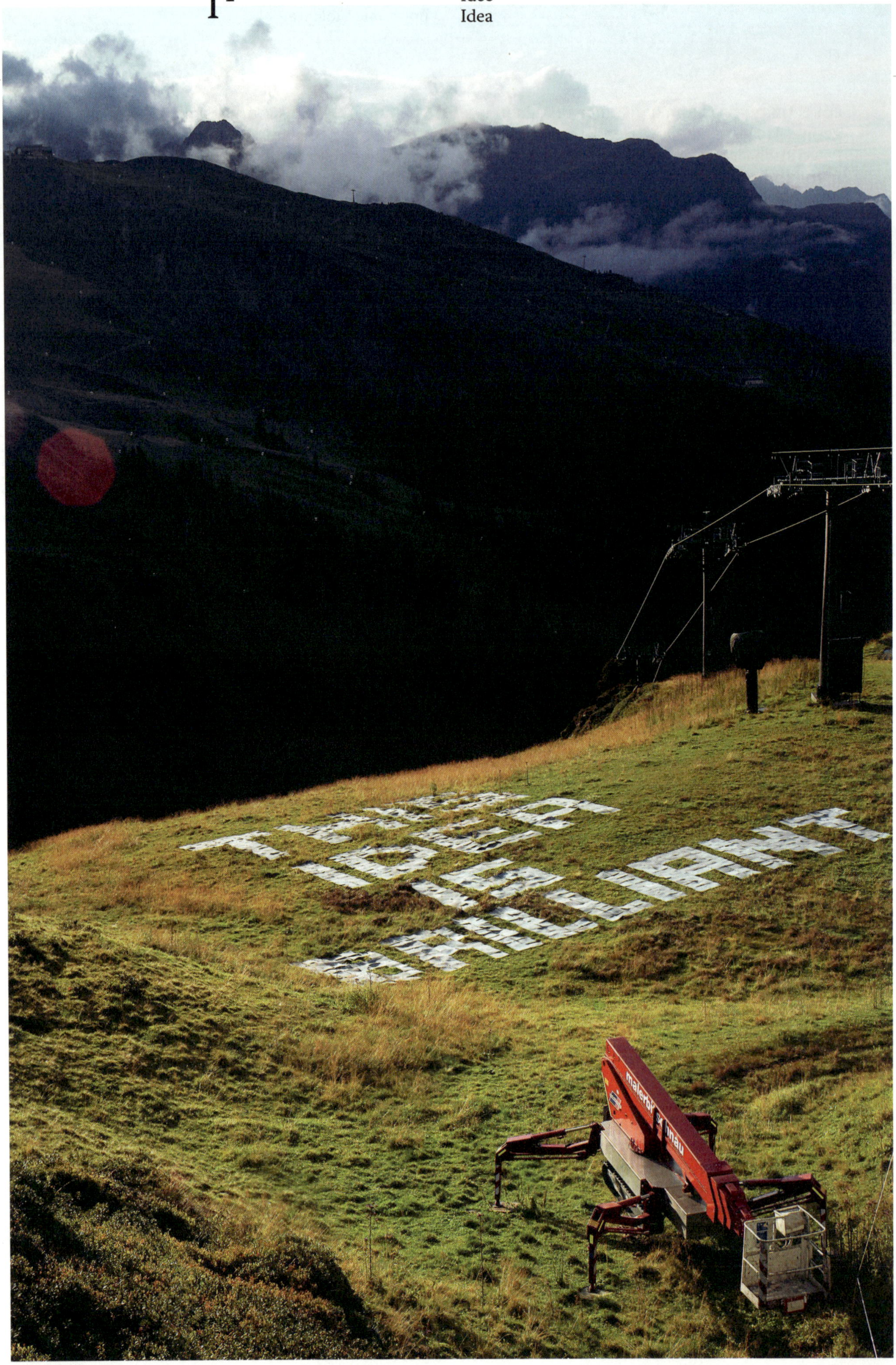

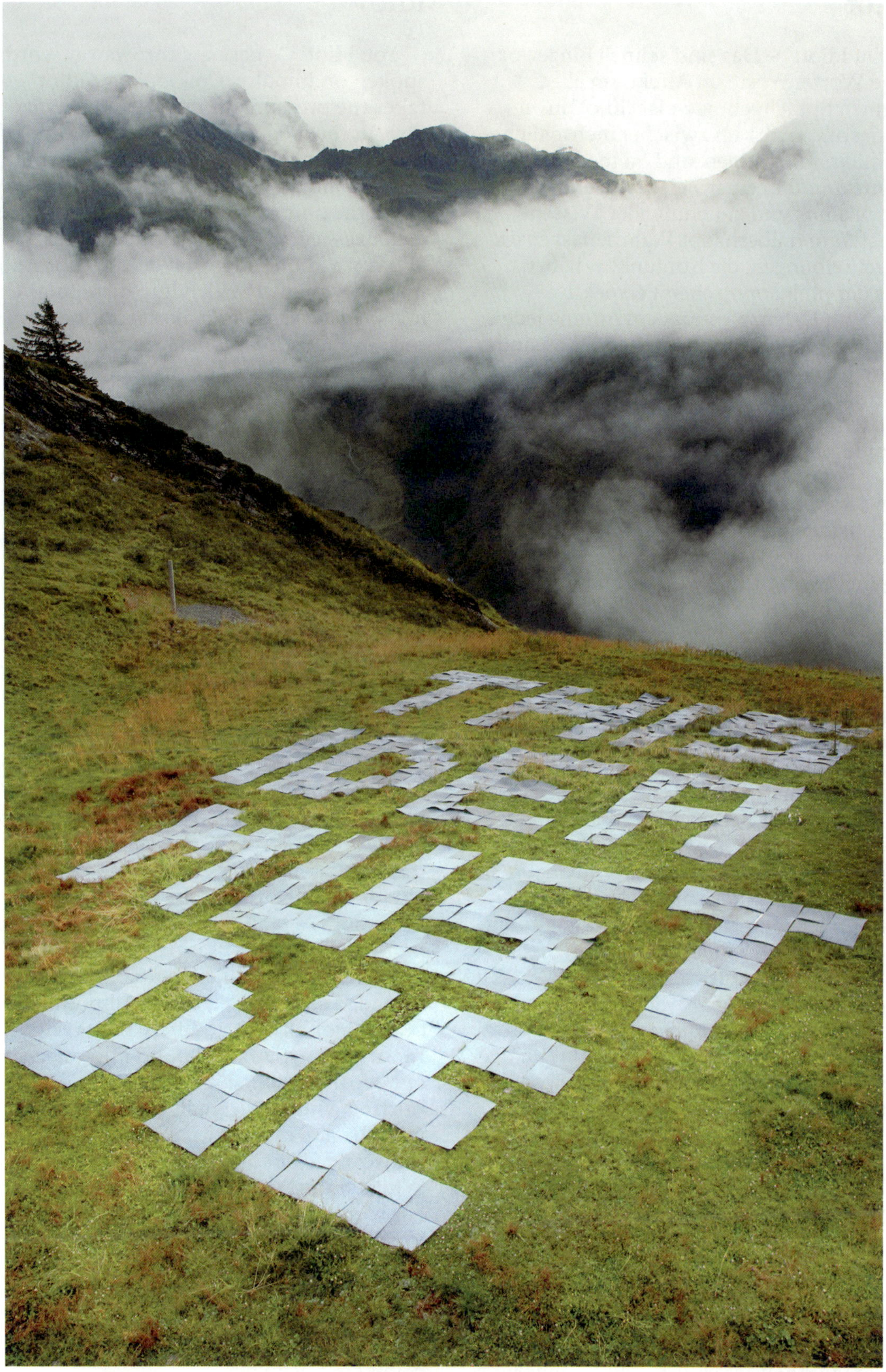
THIS
IDEA
MUST
DIE

# Idiot

„Du Idiot!" – Das sind schnell hingeworfene Worte, Worte im Affekt. Im allgemeinen Sprachgebrauch ist „Idiot*in" ein Entlastungswort im zwischenmenschlichen Konflikt. Idiot*innen sind im medialen Kontext und in einer Zeit wachsenden Populismus und zunehmender Wissenschafts- und überhaupt Wahrheitsskepsis Zuschreibungen, die Konjunktur haben. Aus der philosophischen Perspektive – rund um Deleuze – muss am Anfang jeden Denkens ein Idiotismus stehen.[1] Was sind Idiot*innen und was machen sie? Und sind sie zu Unrecht in Verruf geraten? Kann es auch sinnvoll sein, sich zur Idiotin oder zum Idioten zu machen? Antworten zu einer philosophischen Betrachtungsweise von Idiot*innen finden sich im Kapitel „Idiotismus" in *Psychopolitik: Neoliberalismus und die neuen Machttechniken* des Philosophen Byung-Chul Han, welches in *A±Z* ebenfalls zu lesen ist.

Auch dieses enzyklopädische Vorhaben, *A±Z*, kann nur unter der Voraussetzung der Idiotie entstehen. Ein Buch „Enzyklopädie" nennen zu wollen, in einer gänzlich und endgültig post-homo-universalistischen Ära, das ist empörend idiotisch. Aber idiotisch kann auch methodisch sein.

„Idiot", dieser Begriff ist doppel- und mehrdeutig zu verstehen, etymologisch beginnt er harmlos und pathosfrei: „lat. *idiota, idiotes* → griech. *idiotes* [ἰδιώτης] ‚Privatmann; gewöhnlicher einfacher Mensch; unkundiger Laie, Stümper'", lautet die Herkunftsbedeutung.[2] Der Idiot kultiviert das Eigene („griechisch *ídiota*, ‚eigen, privat, eigentümlich'").[3] Der Idiot, das ist „der gemeine Mann", „der Einflusslose", „der Privatmann", „Unkundige", „Banause", „Laie" und „Nichtkenner", der sich nicht um die Belange der *polis* kümmert.[4] Der Idiot ist ein Janus bifrons. Hart in der Abgrenzung (asozial, unpartizipativ), weich im Reich der Undenkbarkeiten (grenzenlos erweitert im Begriffedenken). Er ist unpolitisch, aber nonkonformistisch; teilnahmslos, aber kritisch. Im frühen Christentum bedeutet Idiot zu sein, sich dem Establishment, den Eliten entgegenzustellen – ein „Kokettieren mit intellektueller Beschränktheit", aber zum Zwecke einer höheren Erkenntnis, die jede Form von irdischer Erkenntnis transzendiert.[5] Während im Mittelalter dem Idioten noch ein absichtsvoller Erkenntnisverzicht zugestanden wird, ist die Verbindung von Idiotie und

# Idiot

"You idiot!"—these are throwaway words, spoken on impulse. Colloquially, "idiot" takes the pressure off interpersonal conflict. In the media context, and at a time of increasing populism and skepticism about science and even truth, idiots are all the rage. From the philosophical perspective—around Deleuze—every thought is initially idiotic.[1] What are idiots, and what do they do? And have they unjustly fallen into disrepute? Can it also make sense to make an idiot of yourself? A philosophical perspective on idiots can be found in the chapter "Idiotism" in *Psychopolitics: Neoliberalism and New Technologies of Power*, by Byung-Chul Han, which can also be read in this volume.

This encyclopedic endeavor, *A±Z*, likewise requires the precondition of idiotism. Calling a book an "encyclopedia" in an entirely and conclusively post-homo-universalist era is outrageously idiotic. But there may be method in idiocy.

The term "idiot" is ambiguous. Etymologically it begins innocuously enough: "Latin *idiota, idiotes* → Greek *idiotes* [ἰδιώτης], 'private citizen; ordinary person; ignorant layperson, bungler,'" reads the derivation.[2] The idiot cultivates what is his own ("Greek *ídiota*, 'own, private, specific'").[3] The idiot is "the common man," is "without influence," a "private person," an "ignoramus," a "layman," a "non-initiate," someone who pays no heed to the affairs of the *polis*.[4] The idiot is a Janus bifrons. Hard in differentiation (anti-social, non-participatory), soft in the realm of the inconceivable (endlessly extended conceptually). He is unpolitical but nonconformist, indifferent but critical. In early Christianity, to be an idiot meant to oppose the establishment and the elites—a "flirting with intellectual narrowness," but with the aim of a greater understanding that transcended all forms of earthly knowledge.[5] While in the Middle Ages a deliberate abandonment of knowledge was still ascribed to the idiot, the link between idiotism and madness is a latter-day phenomenon.[6] From the sixteenth century onwards—at the latest in the seventeenth—no one wanted to be called an idiot any more.[7] And now idiots belong in hospital.

There's something pathological and melodramatic about idiots. When melodramatic they are unsettling, in a productive form of refusal. For those keen on idiotism, being an idiot is a method. An idiot deliberately

Wahnsinn eine neuzeitliche Erscheinung.[6] Seit dem 16. und spätestens im 17. Jahrhundert möchte niemand mehr Idiot*in genannt werden.[7] Nun sind Idiot*innen ein Fall für die Nervenheilanstalt.

Idiot*innen haben etwas Pathologisches und etwas Pathetisches an sich. Das Pathetische an Idiot*innen ist ihre Irritationskraft, eine produktive Form der Verweigerung. Leidenschaftlich methodische Idiot*innen sind solche, die das Idiot*insein zur Methode machen. Sie wollen die Zeichen absichtlich verkennen und dieses Verkennen im Sinne einer Bedeutungsvertauschung als methodisch-künstlerisches Verfahren anwenden. Sie sind die „regellosen Spieler des Gleichen und des Anderen".[8] So beschreibt Michel Foucault Don Quichotte an der Schwelle zu einer neuen Episteme. Er verkennt die Welt, indem er die Zeichen falsch deutet. So ähnlich ergeht es auch dem Protagonisten im grimmschen Märchen vom gescheiten Hans. Was in diesem Märchen passiert, ist eine Kette an methodischen Fehlanwendungen bei der Brautwerbung. Es ist eine Geschichte von Verschiebungen: Der Rat der Mutter wird immer befolgt, jedoch zeitlich versetzt auf die darauffolgende Situation angewandt, wo er sich als unpassend erweist. Wie Zahnräder, deren Zähne nie ineinander einrasten können. Die Nadel landet im Heuhaufen, das Messer im Hemdsärmel, das Kalb am Kopf, und zuletzt werden den Stalltieren die Augen ausgerissen, um sie der Gretel entgegenzuwerfen. Es entsteht eine wundersam surreale Geschichte, an deren Ende der gescheiterte Hans steht.

Methodische Unseriosität ist aus künstlerischer Sicht sehr fruchtbar, ein durchaus gangbarer Weg, der eine gewisse Verweigerungshaltung impliziert, die wir von Idiot*innen kennen. Absichtliche, also bewusst angewandte Methodenverfehlung erinnert in diesem Sinne an die Mutation in der Natur – der Zufall, der sich als das Unvorhergesehene in die abgenützte Gewohnheit von festen, erwartbaren Abläufen einschiebt. In der Wissenschaft sind Regelverletzungen Notwendigkeiten, um Fortschritte zu erzielen.[9] Diese passieren jedoch in voller Absicht und nicht aus Unwissen oder Nachlässigkeit.[10] Die Wissenschaftsgeschichte beweist, dass „es keine einzige Regel gibt, so einleuchtend und erkenntnistheoretisch wohl verankert sie auch sein mag, die nicht zu irgendeiner Zeit verletzt worden wäre".[11] Und auch in der künstlerischen Arbeit muss man umsichtig sein, um sich nicht von den sich selbst

misreads the signs, using transposition of meaning as an artistic approach. "He is the disordered player of the Same and the Other,"[8] says Michel Foucault of Don Quixote at the threshold of a new episteme. He misjudges the world by falsely interpreting the signs. It's similar with Clever Hans in Grimms' fairy tale. What happens here is a methodical misapplication in courtship. It's a story of displacement: Hans always follows his mother's advice, but offset in time and applied to the subsequent situation, where it turns out to be inappropriate, like cogs whose notches fail to engage. The needle lands in a haystack, the knife in a sleeve, the calf on its head, and finally the eyes of the livestock are gouged out so as to be thrown at Gretel. It's a quaintly surreal story, and it ends in failure.

From an artistic point of view, methodical lack of seriousness is very fruitful, a practicable approach that implies a certain attitude of refusal familiar from idiots. The deliberate—that is, consciously applied—methodical lapse is reminiscent of natural mutation, of chance, which edges into the predictability of habitual orders of events. In science it's necessary to break the rules in order to make progress.[9] But this doesn't happen entirely intentionally, nor is it the result of ignorance or negligence.[10] The history of science proves that "there is not a single rule, however plausible, and however firmly grounded in epistemology, that is not violated at some time or other."[11] And artistic work, too, needs to avoid being trapped in self-imposed rules; they always need breaking, in some way or other—through idiotism, for example. But idiots don't necessarily insist on discovering something new. They're more interested in exchanging the usual with the usual. One form of development.

auferlegten Gesetzen verpflichten zu lassen. Immer muss man sie irgendwie brechen. Zum Beispiel im Idiotischsein. Idiot*innen beharren jedoch nicht unbedingt darauf, das Neue entdecken zu wollen. Es geht vielmehr darum, Gewohntes mit Gewohntem zu vertauschen. Eine Form der Entfaltung.

1 Mit Idiotie ist bei Deleuze ein voraussetzungsloser Anfang im Denken gemeint. „Die Philosophie schlägt sich auf die Seite des Idioten als eines Mannes ohne Voraussetzungen." In: Gilles Deleuze, *Differenz und Wiederholung*, übers. von Joseph Vogl (München: Wilhelm Fink, 2007), 170. Und vgl. „Idiotismus" von Byung-Chul Han in diesem Buch.

2 Dudenredaktion, Hrsg., *Das Herkunftswörterbuch: Etymologie der deutschen Sprache* (Mannheim, Leipzig, Wien, Zürich: 2007), 358.

3 Ebd., 358.

4 Andreas Urs Sommer, „Kurze Geistesgeschichte des Idioten", in *Zeitschrift für Ideengeschichte,* Heft IV/2, Sommer 2010, hrsg. von Warren Breckman, Jost Philipp Klenner, Wolfert von Rahden (München: C. H. Beck, 2010), 5.

5 Ebd., 7.

6 Ebd., 10.

7 Ebd., 11.

8 Michel Foucault, „Die Ordnung der Dinge. Eine Archäologie der Humanwissenschaften", in *Michel Foucault: Die Hauptwerke*, übers. von Ulrich Köppen (Frankfurt am Main: Suhrkamp, 2008), 85.

9 Vgl. Paul Feyerabend, *Wider den Methodenzwang* (Frankfurt am Main: Suhrkamp, 2018), 21.

10 Vgl. ebd., 21.

11 Vgl. ebd., 21.

1 For Deleuze, idiocy is a presuppositionless beginning of thought: "The philosopher takes the side of the idiot as though of a man without presuppositions." In Gilles Deleuze, *Difference and Repetition*, trans. Paul Patton (New York: Columbia University Press, 1994), 130. See also Byung-Chul Han, "Idiotism," in this book.

2 Translated from *Das Herkunftswörterbuch: Etymologie der deutschen Sprache* (Mannheim, Leipzig, Vienna, Zurich: 2007), 358.

3 Ibid.

4 Translated from Andreas Urs Sommer, "Kurze Geistesgeschichte des Idioten," in *Zeitschrift für Ideengeschichte*, no. IV/2, summer 2010, ed. Warren Breckman, Jost Philipp Klenner, Wolfert von Rahden (Munich: C. H. Beck, 2010), 5.

5 Ibid., 7.

6 Ibid., 10.

7 Ibid., 11.

8 Michel Foucault, *The Order of Things. An Archaeology of the Human Sciences* (1971) (New York: Vintage, 1994 [ePub]), 49.

9 See Paul Feyerabend, *Against Method* (1975/88) (London: Verso, 1993), 14.

10 Ibid.

11 Ibid.

# Idiotismus

Byung-Chul Han

[In: *Psychopolitik: Neoliberalismus und die neuen Machttechniken* (Frankfurt am Main: Fischer, 2016), 107–113.]

In der Spinoza-Vorlesung von 1980 bemerkt Deleuze: „A la lettre, je dirais: ils font les idiots. Faire l'idiot. Faire l'idiot ça a toujours été une fonction de la philosophie."[1] Es ist eine Funktion der Philosophie, den Idioten zu spielen. Die Philosophie ist von Anfang an eng mit dem Idiotismus verknüpft. Jeder Philosoph, der ein neues Idiom, eine neue Sprache, ein neues Denken hervorbringt, wird notwendig ein Idiot gewesen sein. Allein der Idiot hat Zugang zum *ganz Anderen.* Der Idiotismus erschließt dem Denken ein *Immanenzfeld aus Ereignissen und Singularitäten*, das sich jeder Subjektivierung und Psychologisierung entzieht.

Die Philosophiegeschichte ist eine Geschichte der Idiotismen. Sokrates, der nur weiß, dass er nicht weiß, ist ein Idiot. Ein Idiot ist ebenfalls Descartes, der alles in Zweifel zieht. *Cogito ergo sum* ist ein Idiotismus. Eine innere Kontraktion des Denkens macht einen anderen Anfang möglich. Descartes *denkt,* indem er *das Denken denkt.* Das Denken gewinnt den jungfräulichen Zustand zurück, indem es sich auf sich selbst bezieht. Deleuze lässt dem cartesianischen Idioten einen anderen Idioten entgegentreten: „Der alte Idiot wollte Evidenzen, zu denen er aus sich selbst gelangen würde: unterdessen würde er an allem zweifeln [...]. Der neue Idiot will überhaupt keine Evidenzen [...], er will das Absurde – das ist ein völlig anderes Bild vom Denken. Der alte Idiot wollte das Wahre, der neue aber will das Absurde zur höchsten Macht des Denkens erheben."[2]

Heute scheint der Typus des Außenseiters, des Narren oder des Idioten aus der Gesellschaft so gut wie verschwunden zu sein. Die digitale Totalvernetzung und Totalkommunikation erhöht den Konformitätszwang erheblich. Die Gewalt des Konsenses unterdrückt Idiotismen. Botho Strauß ist der Unterschied zwischen dem heutigen Konformismus und der bürgerlichen Konvention wohl bekannt: „Für ihn, den Idioten, ist es, als ob alle anderen fein aufeinander abgestimmt sprächen. Heruntergeregelt auf den verträglichsten Stimmungsgrad. [...] Eine viel unnachgiebigere Konvention als jede frühere, aus bürgerlicher Zeit bekannte."[3]

# Idiotism

Byung-Chul Han

[In *Psychopolitics: Neoliberalism and new Technologies of Power,* trans. Erik Butler (London, New York: Verso, 2017), 81–87. Reproduced with permission of the licensor through PLSclear.]

In his 1980 course on Spinoza, Deleuze observed: "To the letter, I'd say they play the fool [*ils font les idiots*]. Play the fool. Playing the fool, that's always been one function of philosophy."[1] One of the roles of philosophy is to play the fool, or idiot. From its inception, philosophy has been closely tied to idiotism. Every philosopher who has brought forth a new idiom—a new language, a new way of thinking—has necessarily been an idiot. Only the idiot has access to the *wholly Other.* Idiotism discloses a *field of immanence of events and singularities* for thought; this field eludes subjectivation and psychologization altogether.

The history of philosophy is a history of idiotisms. Socrates knows only that he does not know; he is an idiot. Likewise, Descartes—who casts doubt on everything—is an idiot. *Cogito ergo sum* is idiotic. It takes an inner contraction of thinking to make a new beginning possible. Descartes *thinks* by *thinking Thought* [*das Denken denkt*]. By relating (only) to itself, Thought regains a virginal state. Deleuze places the Cartesian idiot in opposition to an idiot of another kind: The old idiot wanted indubitable truths at which he could arrive by himself: in the meantime he would doubt everything ... The new idiot has no wish for indubitable truths; he ... wills the absurd—this is not the same image of thought. The old idiot wanted truth, but the new idiot wants to turn the absurd into the highest power of thought.[2]

Today, it seems, the type of the outsider—the idiot, the fool—has all but vanished from society. Thoroughgoing digital networking and communication have massively amplified the compulsion to conform. The attendant violence of consensus is suppressing idiotisms. Botho Strauss pinpoints the difference between contemporary conformism and bourgeois convention of old: "For him, the idiot, it's as if everyone else were speaking in subtle attunement with each other: brought down to the most agreeable level [*verträglichster Stimmungsgrad*] ... This is a far more implacable convention than any convention known before, in bourgeois times."[3]

Der Idiot ist ein Idiosynkrat. Die Idiosynkrasie bedeutet wörtlich eine eigentümliche Mischung der Körpersäfte und die daraus resultierende Überempfindlichkeit. Wo es gilt, die Kommunikation zu beschleunigen, stellt die Idiosynkrasie aufgrund ihrer immunologischen Abwehr des Anderen ein Hindernis dar. Sie blockiert den entgrenzten kommunikativen Austausch. Notwendig für die Beschleunigung der Kommunikation ist daher die Immunsuppression. Die Immunreaktion wird massiv unterdrückt, damit sich der Kreislauf von Information und Kapital beschleunigt. Die Kommunikation erreicht dort ihre maximale Geschwindigkeit, wo das Gleiche auf das Gleiche reagiert. Die Widerständigkeit und Widerspenstigkeit der Andersheit oder Fremdheit stört und verzögert dagegen die glatte Kommunikation des Gleichen. Gerade in der *Hölle des Gleichen* erreicht die Kommunikation ihre höchste Geschwindigkeit.

Angesichts des Kommunikations- und Konformitätszwanges stellt der Idiotismus eine Praxis der Freiheit dar. Der Idiot ist seinem Wesen nach der Unverbundene, der Nichtvernetzte, der Nichtinformierte. Er bewohnt das *unvordenkliche Draußen,* das sich jeder Kommunikation und Vernetzung entzieht: „Der Idiot dreht sich wie eine abgerissene Rose im Flussstrudel zielstrebiger Menschen – Menschen im Konsens. Eingemeindete, Zugehörige eines wundersamen Einvernehmens".[4]

Der Idiot ist ein moderner Häretiker. Häresie bedeutet ursprünglich *Wahl.* Der Häretiker ist also jemand, der über eine *freie Wahl* verfügt. Er hat den Mut zur Abweichung von der Orthodoxie. Mutig befreit er sich vom Konformitätszwang. Der Idiot als Häretiker ist eine Figur des Widerstandes gegen die Gewalt des Konsenses. Er rettet den Zauber des Außenseiters. Angesichts des zunehmenden Konformitätszwanges wäre es heute dringender denn je, das *häretische Bewusstsein* zu schärfen.

Der Idiotismus opponiert gegen die neoliberale Herrschaftsmacht, gegen deren Totalkommunikation und Totalüberwachung. Der Idiot ‚kommuniziert' nicht. Ja er kommuniziert mit dem Nicht-Kommunizierbaren. So hüllt er sich ins Schweigen. Der Idiotismus errichtet *Freiräume des Schweigens, der Stille und der Einsamkeit,* in denen es möglich ist, etwas zu sagen, das es wirklich verdient, gesagt zu werden. Schon 1995 kündigte Deleuze diese *Politik des Schweigens* an. Sie ist gegen jene neoliberale Psychopolitik

The idiot is idiosyncratic. Literally, idiosyncrasy refers to a specific and peculiar mixture of the body's humors and the oversensitivity this entails. When communication is to be accelerated, idiosyncrasy poses an obstacle inasmuch as it amounts to an immunological defense against the Other. Idosyncrasy stands in the way of unbounded communicative exchange. Accordingly, immunosuppression is necessary for acceleration to proceed. But now, immune responses are subjected to massive suppression so that information will circulate faster and capital will accelerate. Communication achieves maximum velocity when the Same reacts to the Same. In contrast, the resistance and recalcitrance of otherness, of foreignness, troubles and impedes the smooth communication of the Same. In the *Inferno of the Same,* communication attains its highest speed.

In light of compulsive and coercive communication and conformism, idiotism represents a practice of freedom. By nature, the idiot is unallied, un-networked, and uninformed. The idiot inhabits the *immemorial outside,* which escapes communication and networking altogether: "The idiot spins about like a plucked rose in the whirling river of single-minded people—people in consent, those who have been incorporated and belong to a wondrous, common understanding."[4]

The idiot is a modern-day heretic. Etymologically, *heresy* means "choice." Thus, the heretic is one who commands *free choice*: the courage to deviate from orthodoxy. As a heretic, the idiot represents a figure of resistance opposing the violence of consensus. The idiot preserves the magic of the outsider. Today, in light of increasingly coercive conformism, it is more urgent than ever to heighten *heretical consciousness.*

Idiotism stands opposed to the neoliberal power of domination: total communication and total surveillance. The idiot does not "communicate." Indeed, he communicates with the In-communicable. As such, the idiot veils himself in silence. Idiotism erects *spaces for guarding silence [Freiräume des Schweigens], quiet, and solitude,* where it is still possible to say what really deserves to be said. Deleuze already called for such a *politics of silence* in 1995. He directed it against neoliberal psychopolitics, which forces communication and disclosure:

"It's not a problem of getting people to express themselves but of providing little

97

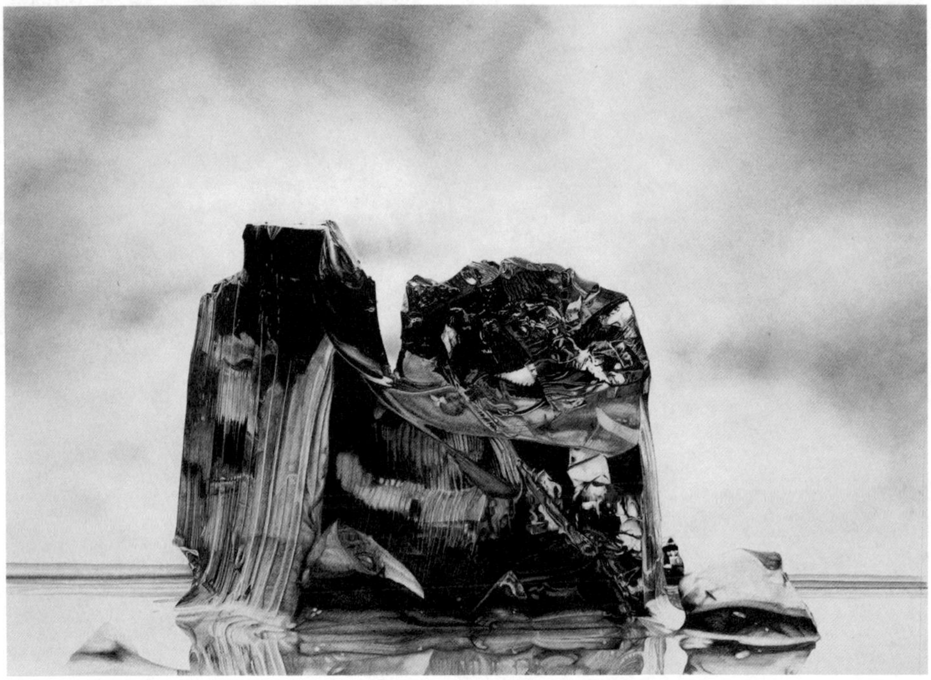

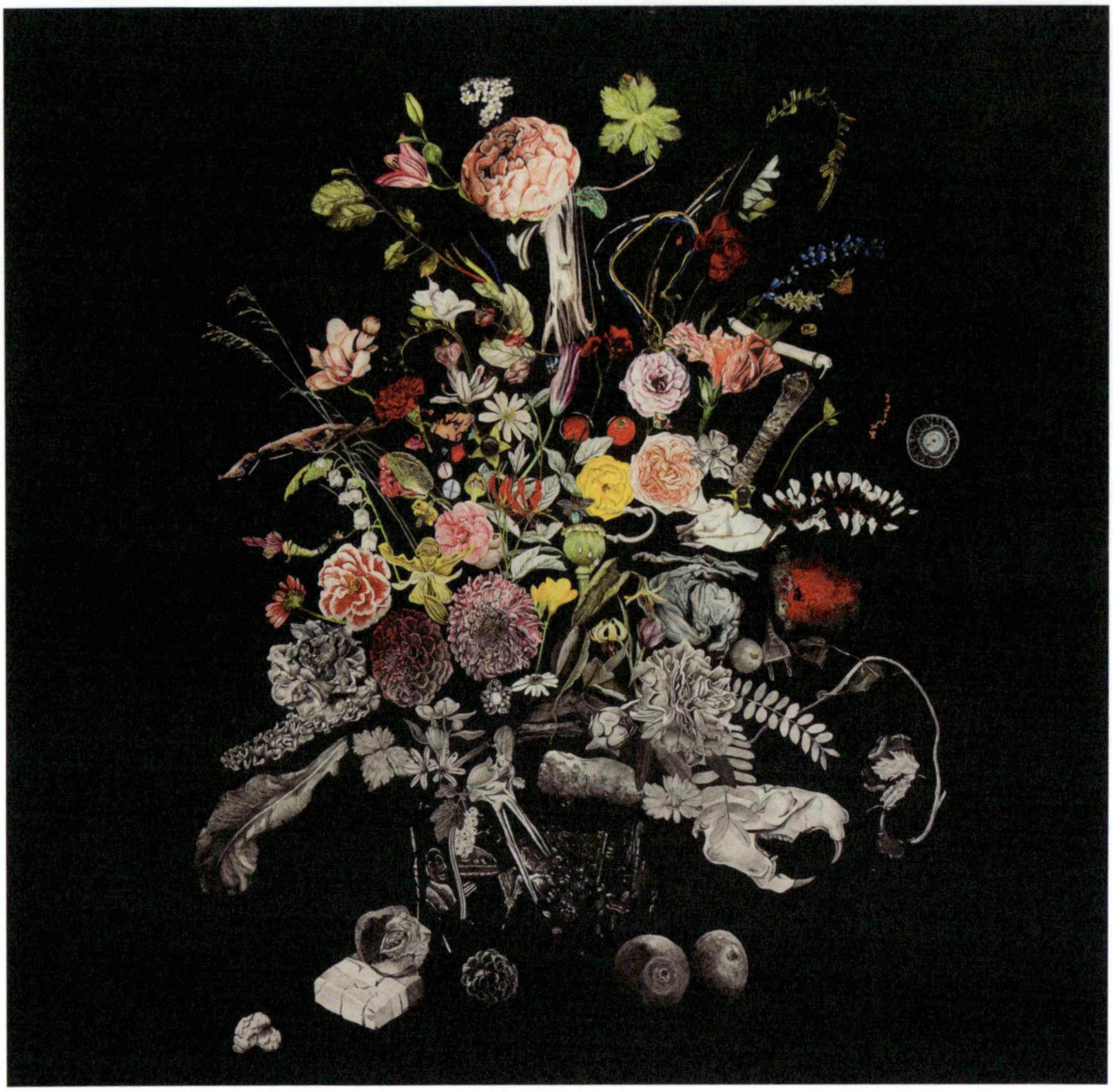

gerichtet, die zur Kommunikation und Mitteilung geradezu zwingt: „Die Schwierigkeit ist heute nicht mehr, dass wir unsere Meinung nicht frei äußern können, sondern Freiräume der Einsamkeit und des Schweigens zu schaffen, in denen wir etwas zu sagen finden. Repressive Kräfte hindern uns nicht mehr an der Meinungsäußerung. Im Gegenteil, sie zwingen uns sogar dazu. Welche Befreiung ist es, einmal nichts sagen zu müssen und schweigen zu können, denn nur dann haben wir die Möglichkeit, etwas zunehmend Seltenes zu schaffen: Etwas, das es tatsächlich wert ist, gesagt zu werden.“[5]

Der *idiot savant* hat den Zugang zu ganz anderem Wissen. Er erhebt sich über das Horizontale, über das *bloß Informiert- und Vernetztsein:* „Der idiot savant, wie man zuerst den Autisten nannte, wäre als Begriff zu entlasten und vielleicht verwendbar für jene Abenteurer, die anders verbunden sind als nur untereinander.“[6] Der Idiotismus eröffnet einen jungfräulichen Raum, die Ferne, die das Denken braucht, um zu einem ganz anderen Sprechen anzusetzen. Der *idiot savant* lebt von der Ferne wie der Stylit. Eine Vertikalspannung befähigt ihn zu einer *höheren Übereinstimmung,* die ihn empfänglich macht für *Ereignisse,* für *Sendungen aus der Zukunft:* „Stylit, Säulensteher, Antenne. Die Wellen der übermäßigen Sendung erzeugen im Mund des Heiligen das gleiche Rauschen wie die schwachen Signale, die der Idiot empfängt von der Welt.“[7]

Intelligenz bedeutet *wählen zwischen (interlegere).* Sie ist insofern nicht ganz frei, als sie in einem systembedingten *Zwischen* gefangen ist. Sie hat keinen Zugang zum *Draußen,* weil sie nur die Wahl zwischen Optionen innerhalb eines Systems hat. Sie hat also keine wirklich *freie Wahl,* sondern eine *Auswahl* von Angeboten, die das System bereithält. Die Intelligenz folgt der Logik eines Systems. Sie ist systemimmanent. Das jeweilige System definiert die jeweilige Intelligenz. So hat die Intelligenz keinen Zugang zu *ganz Anderem.* Sie bewohnt das Horizontale, während der Idiot das Vertikale berührt, indem er das vorherrschende System, das heißt die Intelligenz verlässt: „Das Innere der Dummheit ist zart und durchsichtig wie ein Libellenflügel, es schillert von überwundener Intelligenz.“[8]

In seinem letzten Text *Die Immanenz: ein Leben ...* erhebt Deleuze die Immanenz zu einer Formel der Glückseligkeit: „Man möchte sagen, die reine Immanenz sei Ein

gaps of solitude and silence in which they might eventually find something to say. Repressive forces don't stop people from expressing themselves but rather force them to express themselves. What a relief to have nothing to say, the right to say nothing, because only then is there a chance of framing the rare, and ever rarer, thing that might be worth saying."[5]

The *idiot savant* has access to knowledge of a different order. He raises himself above the horizontal plane—above *merely being informed and networked.* "The term *idiot savant,* as the autistic first were called, should perhaps be freed up and used for those adventurers who are not simply tied to one another, but to something else [*für jene Abenteurer, die anders verbunden sind als nur untereinander*]."[6] Idiotism opens up virginal space—forging the distance required by thought so that speaking may occur in an entirely different manner. The *idiot savant* lives from the faraway—like a stylite. Vertical tension enables him to find *higher agreement:* receptivity to *events, broadcasts* [*Sendungen*] *from the future:* "Stylite, pillar dweller, antenna. The waves of the overflowing message generate, in the mouth of the holy man, the same noise [*Rauschen*] as the faint signals the idiot receives from the world."[7] Intelligence means *choosing-between (interlegere).* It is not entirely free in so far as it is caught in a *between,* which depends on the system in operation. Intelligence has no access to *outside,* because it makes a choice between options in a system. Therefore, intelligence does not really exercise *free choice*: it can only *select* among the offerings the system affords. Intelligence follows the logic of a system. It is system-immanent. A given system defines a given intelligence. Accordingly, intelligence has no access to what is *wholly Other.* It inhabits a horizontal plane. In contrast, the idiot has contact with the vertical dimension inasmuch as he takes leave of the prevailing system—that is, abandons intelligence. "The inside of idiocy is delicate and transparent, like a dragonfly's wing—it glistens with intelligence that has been overcome."[8]

In his final work—*Pure Immanence: Essays on a Life*—Deleuze elevates immanence to a formula for beatitude: "We will say of pure immanence that it is A LIFE, and nothing else. It is not immanence to life, but the immanent that is in nothing is itself a life. A life is the immanence of immanence, absolute immanence: it is complete power,

Leben und nichts anderes. Sie ist nicht Immanenz im Leben, vielmehr ist sie als Immanentes, das in nichts ist, selbst ein Leben. Ein Leben ist die Immanenz der Immanenz, die absolute Immanenz: Es ist vollkommenes Vermögen, vollkommene Glückseligkeit."[9] Die Immanenz ist deshalb ein Immanentes, das „in nichts ist", weil sie nicht etwas anderem, sondern nur sich selbst immanent ist. So ist sie die „Immanenz der Immanenz". Sie ist nichts *unterworfen.* Vielmehr genügt sie sich selbst. Auf dieser Immanenzebene des Lebens lässt sich keine Herrschaftsordnung errichten. Das Kapital manifestiert sich als *Transzendenz,* die das Leben von sich selbst entfremdet. Die *Immanenz als Leben* hebt dieses Entfremdungsverhältnis auf.

Die reine Immanenz ist die *Leere,* die sich weder psychologisieren noch subjektivieren lässt. Das immanente Leben ist *um die Leere leichter, reicher, ja freier.*[10] Nicht die Individualität oder Subjektivität, sondern die Singularität zeichnet den Idioten aus. So ist er den Kindern wesensverwandt, die noch kein Individuum, keine Person sind. Nicht individuelle Eigenschaften, sondern unpersönliche *Ereignisse* machen ihr Dasein aus: „So ähneln einander etwa die Kinder im frühesten Alter und besitzen kaum Individualität; aber sie haben Singularitäten, ein Lächeln, eine Geste, eine Grimasse, Ereignisse, die keine subjektiven Merkmale sind. Die Kleinkinder werden von einem immanenten Leben durchdrungen, das reines Vermögen ist und sogar Glückseligkeit über die Leiden und Hinfälligkeiten hinweg."[11] Der Idiot gleicht jenem *„Homo tantum",* der „keinen Namen mehr hat, obwohl er sich mit keinem anderen verwechseln lässt".[12] Die Immanenzebene, zu der er Zugang hat, ist die Matrix der Ent-Subjektivierung und Ent-Psychologisierung. Sie ist die *Negativität,* die das Subjekt aus sich selbst herausreißt und es in jene „Unermesslichkeit der leeren Zeit"[13] befreit.

Der Idiot ist kein Subjekt: „Eher eine Blumenexistenz: einfache Öffnung zum Licht."[14]

complete bliss."[9] Immanence is something immanent that "is in nothing" because it does not occur in something else—it exists only in itself. As such, it is the "immanence of immanence." It is *subject* to nothing; rather, it is self-sufficient. No order of domination can be erected on this level of life's immanence [*Immanenzebene des Lebens*]. In contrast, Capital manifests itself as transcendence: it estranges life from itself. *Immanence as life* suspends this alienating relationship.

Pure immanence is the *void,* which can neither be psychologized nor subjectivized. Immanent life is *lighter and richer—indeed, freer*—for such emptiness.[10] The idiot is not defined by individuality or subjectivity, but by singularity. As such, the idiot is similar in nature to the child, who is not yet an individual, not yet a person. The child's existence is not determined by individual qualities so much as impersonal *events*:

"For example, very small children all resemble one another and have hardly any individuality, but they have singularities: a smile, a gesture, a funny face—not subjective qualities. Small children, through all their sufferings and weaknesses, are infused with an immanent life that is pure power and even bliss."[11]

The idiot is like Deleuze's *"homo tantum"*—one who "no longer has a name, though he can be mistaken for no other."[12] The sphere of immanence to which the idiot gains admittance is the matrix of de-subjectivation and de-psychologization. It is *negativity,* wresting the subject out of itself and liberating it into the "immensity of an empty time."[13] The idiot does not exist as a subject—he is "more like a flower: an existence simply open to light."[14]

1 www.univ-paris8.fr/deleuze/article.php3?id_article=131 und Philippe Mengue, *Faire l'idiot. La politique de Deleuze*, Éditions Germina 2013.

2 Gilles Deleuze, Félix Guattari, *Was ist Philosophie?*, Frankfurt a. M. 2000, 71.

3 Botho Strauß, *Lichter des Toren. Der Idiot und seine Zeit*, München 2013, 10.

4 Ebd., 11.

5 Gilles Deleuze, „Mediators", in: *Negotiations*, New York 1995, 121–134, hier: 129, zitiert in: M. Hardt, A. Negri, *Demokratie. Wofür wir kämpfen*, Frankfurt a. M. 2013, 21.

6 Strauß, *Lichter des Toren*, a. a. O., 11.

7 Ebd., 165.

8 Ebd., 7. In seinem *Traktat über die Idiotie* grenzt Clément Rosset die Dummheit ausdrücklich von der „Inintelligenz" als Gegenteil der Intelligenz ab. Damit spricht er der Dummheit ein kreatives Potential zu: „Im allgemeinen wird die Dummheit also mit der Inintelligenz gleichgesetzt, als das Gegenteil der Intelligenz angesehen. Auf diese Weise wird einer *aufnahmebereiten, flexiblen und umsichtigen* Intelligenz eine als *verschlafen, unempfindsam und mumifiziert* eingeordnete Dummheit entgegengesetzt. [...] Tatsächlich gibt es nichts so *aufnahmebereites, flexibles und umsichtiges* wie die Dummheit." (Clément Rosset, *Das Reale. Traktat über die Idiotie*, Frankfurt a. M. 1988, 183). Eine grenzenlose Offenheit und Empfänglichkeit zeichnet die Dummheit aus, während die Inintelligenz beschränkt ist. Die Inintelligenz ist *arm an Erfahrung.* So hat sie keinen Zugang zum *Ereignis*: „Die Inintelligenz verschließt hinter sich die Türen: sie signalisiert das Verbot bestimmter Zugänge zu diesem oder jenem Wissen und begrenzt auf diese Weise ihren Erfahrungshorizont." Die Dummheit ist dagegen „allem gegenüber aufgeschlossen, indem sie aus einem beliebigen Gegenstand ein Objekt der Aufmerksamkeit und des möglichen Engagements werden lässt". Sie ist eine „Berufung", ein „Priesteramt mit all seinen Idolen, seinen Priestern und seinen Anhängern" (ebd., 185).

9 Gilles Deleuze, „Die Immanenz: ein Leben ...", in: *Gilles Deleuze – Fluchtlinien der Philosophie*, hrsg. von F. Balke und J. Vogl, München 1996, 29–33, hier: 30.

10 Zum Begriff der Leere vgl. Byung-Chul Han, *Philosophie des Zen-Buddhismus*, Stuttgart 2002, und *Abwesen. Zur Kultur und Philosophie des Fernen Ostens*, Berlin 2007.

11 Deleuze, „Die Immanenz", a. a. O., 31 f.

12 Ebd., 31.

13 Ebd., 31.

14 Strauß, *Lichter des Toren*, a. a. O., 175.

1 Gilles Deleuze, *Spinoza cours du 02/12/80*, at www.univparis8.fr, and Philippe Mengue, *Faire l'idiot. La politique de Deleuze* (Paris: Germina, 2013).

2 Gilles Deleuze and Félix Guattari, *What Is Philosophy?*, trans. Hugh Tomlinson and Graham Burchell (New York: Columbia University Press, 1994), 62.

3 Botho Strauss, *Lichter des Toren. Der Idiot und seine Zeit* (Munich: Diederichs, 2013), 10.

4 Ibid., 11.

5 Gilles Deleuze, "Mediators," in *Negotiations* (New York: Columbia University Press, 1995), 121–34: 129.

6 Strauss, *Lichter des Toren*, 11.

7 Ibid., 165.

8 Ibid., 7. In his treatise on idiocy, Clément Rosset explicitly distinguishes stupidity (*sottise*) from unintelligence (*inintelligence*). In so doing, he ascribes a creative potential to stupidity: "Stupidity ... is generally assimilated to unintelligence, which is deemed the opposite of intelligence. This means opposing *attentive, nimble*, and *alert* intelligence to stupidity, which is understood as *sluggish, anesthetic*, and *mummified* ... In fact, there is nothing so *attentive, nimble*, and *alert* as stupidity" (*Le Réel. Traité de l'idiotie* [Paris: Minuit, 1977], 144). Boundless openness and receptivity distinguish stupidity, whereas lack of intelligence means limitation. Unintelligence is poor in experience. It has no access to the event: "Unintelligence closes doors: it signals that certain paths of approach to such or such knowledge are prohibited, thereby narrowing the field of experience." In contrast, "stupidity opens onto everything: it makes anything at all into an object of notice and possible engagement." It is a "calling, or better, a priesthood, with its idols, officiants, and faithful" (145).

9 Gilles Deleuze, *Pure Immanence: Essays on a Life*, trans. Anne Boyman (New York: Zone Books, 2001), 27.

10 On the concept of emptiness, see Byung-Chul Han, *Philosophie des Zen-Buddhimus* (Stuttgart: Reclam, 2002) and *Abwesen. Zur Kultur und Philosophie des Fernen Ostens* (Berlin: Merve, 2007).

11 Deleuze, *Pure Immanence*, 30.

12 Ibid., 28–29.

13 Ibid., 29.

14 Strauss, *Lichter des Toren*, 175.

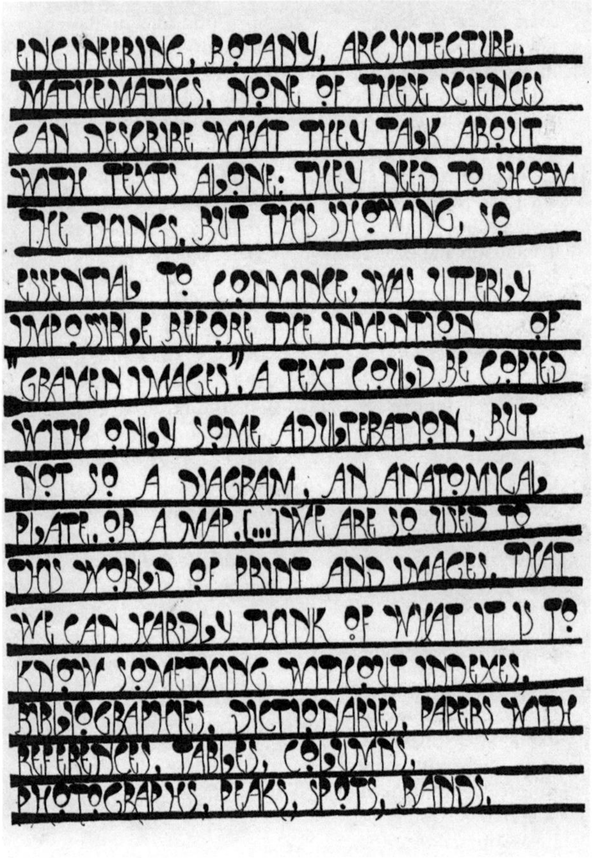


„Ingenieurwesen, Botanik, Architektur, Mathematik – keine dieser Wissenschaften kann das, worüber sie sprechen, nur durch Texte allein beschreiben; sie müssen die Dinge zeigen. Dieses Zeigen, das zur Überzeugung so wesentlich ist, war vor der Erfindung ‚eingravierter Bilder' vollkommen unmöglich. Ein Text konnte nur mit einigen Verfälschungen kopiert werden, nicht jedoch ein Diagramm, ein anatomischer Stich oder eine Karte. [...] Wir sind so an diese Welt von Formen und Bildern gewöhnt, dass wir kaum denken können, wie es ist, etwas ohne Index, Bibliographien, Wörterbücher, Papiere mit Referenzen, Tabellen, Spalten, Fotographien, Peaks, Punkte und Bänder zu wissen." Bruno Latour, „Drawing Things Together: Die Macht der unveränderlich mobilen Elemente", in *ANThology: Ein einführendes Handbuch zur Akteur-Netzwerk-Theorie,* hrsg. von Andréa Belliger und David J. Krieger (Bielefeld: Transcript Verlag, 2006), 274 f., 276.

# Drawing Things Together. Die Macht der unveränderlich mobilen Elemente[1]

Bruno Latour

[In: A. Belliger und D. J. Krieger (Herausgeber), *ANThology: Ein einführendes Handbuch zur Akteur-Netzwerk-Theorie* (Bielefeld: Transcript, 2006), 259–307, und in gekürzter Fassung in: A. Ziemann (Herausgeber), *Grundlagentexte der Medienkultur: Ein Reader* (Wiesbaden: Springer, 2019), 265–274.]

## I. Visualisierung und Kognition im Fokus

Es wäre schön, wenn man in der Lage wäre zu definieren, was für unsere moderne wissenschaftliche Kultur spezifisch ist. Es wäre sogar noch schöner, wenn man die ökonomischste Erklärung (die nicht die wirtschaftlichste sein muss) ihrer Ursprünge und besonderen Charakteristika finden könnte. Um bei einer sparsamen Erklärung anzukommen, ist es am besten, sich nicht auf universelle Charakterzüge der Natur zu beziehen. Hypothesen über Veränderungen im Geist oder im menschlichen Bewusstsein, in der Struktur des Gehirns, in sozialen Beziehungen, „mentalités" oder in der wirtschaftlichen Infrastruktur, die postuliert werden, um das Auftreten von Wissenschaft oder ihre momentanen Errungenschaften zu erklären, sind in den meisten Fällen einfach zu grandios – um nicht zu sagen hagiographisch –, in anderen Fällen offensichtlich rassistisch. Das Ockham'sche Rasiermesser sollte diese Erklärungen zurechtstutzen. Kein „neuer Mensch" trat irgendwann im 16. Jahrhundert plötzlich auf, genauso wenig arbeiten Mutanten mit größeren Gehirnen, die anders als der Rest von uns denken, in modernen Laboratorien. Die Idee eines rationaleren Geistes oder zwingender wissenschaftlicher Methoden, die aus Dunkelheit und Chaos auftauchten, stellt eine zu komplizierte Hypothese dar.

Der erste Schritt in Richtung auf eine überzeugende Erklärung scheint mir zu sein, eine A-priori-Position zu übernehmen. Sie reinigt das Forschungsfeld von allen Unterscheidungen zwischen vorwissenschaftlichen und wissenschaftlichen Kulturen, solchem Denken, solchen Methoden oder Gesellschaften. Wie Jack Goody (1977) herausstellt, sollte die „große Dichotomie" mit ihrer selbstgerechten Sicherheit durch viele *ungewisse und unerwartete* Trennungen ersetzt werden. Dieser negative erste Schritt befreit uns von positiven Antworten, die die Glaubwürdigkeit strapazieren. Alle solchen dichotomischen Unterscheidungen können nur solange überzeugend sein, wie sie von einer starken asymmetrischen einseitigen Sicht, die die beiden Seiten der Unterscheidung oder Grenze sehr unterschiedlich behandelt, durchgesetzt werden. Sobald dieses Vorurteil den Halt verliert, springen die kognitiven Fähigkeiten in alle Richtungen: Zauberer werden zu Popper'schen Falsifikationisten, Wissenschaftler zu naiven Gläubigen, Ingenieure zu herkömmlichen „bricoleurs"; die Bastler allerdings erscheinen als ganz vernünftig (Knorr 1981; Augé 1975). Diese schnellen Umschwünge beweisen, dass die Unterscheidung zwischen vorwissenschaftlicher und wissenschaftlicher Kultur lediglich eine Grenze darstellt – so wie die zwischen Tijuana und San Diego. Sie wird willkürlich von Polizei und Bürokraten durchgesetzt, repräsentiert jedoch keine natürliche Grenze. Obwohl sie für das Unterrichten, für Eröffnungsansprachen und Polemiken sehr nützlich sind, liefern diese „großen Trennungen" keine Erklärungen, sondern sind im Gegenteil das, was erklärt werden muss (Latour 1983).

Es gibt jedoch gute Gründe, weshalb diese Dichotomien – obwohl fortwährend widerlegt – hartnäckig aufrechterhalten werden oder weshalb die Kluft zwischen den beiden Seiten sich sogar noch vergrößert. Die relativistische Position, die dadurch erreicht wurde, den von mir vorgeschlagenen ersten Schritt vorzunehmen und große Dichotomien aufzugeben, wirkt wegen der enormen Konsequenzen der Wissenschaft lächerlich. Man kann nicht den von Goody beschriebenen „Intellektuellen" (1977: Kap. 2) und Galileo in seinen Studien gleichsetzen – genauso wenig wie das Volkswissen über medizinische Kräuter und die „National Institutes of Health", die sorgsamen Prozeduren an der Elfenbeinküste zur Leichenbefragung und die sorgsame Planung von DNA-Tests in einem kalifornischen Labor, das Erzählen von Ursprungsmythen irgendwo im südafrikanischen Busch und die Urknalltheorie, die zögernden Kalkulationen eines Vierjährigen in Piagets Labor und die Berechnung eines Gewinners der Field-Medaille, einen Abakus und einen Supercomputer. Die Unterschiede in den *Wirkungen* von Wissenschaft und Technik sind so enorm, dass es absurd erscheint, nicht nach enormen Ursachen zu suchen. Wenn Forschende mit diesen extravaganten Ursachen unzufrieden sind, sogar wenn sie zugeben, dass diese willkürlich definiert, durch tägliche Erfahrung falsifiziert und oft widersprüchlich sind, ziehen sie es vor, sie zu erhalten, um die absurden Konsequenzen des Relativismus zu umgehen. Partikelphysik muss sich auf radikale Weise von Volksbotanik unterscheiden; wir wissen nicht, auf welche Weise, aber als Verlegenheitslösung ist die Idee der Rationalität besser als nichts (Hollis/Lukes 1982).

Wir müssen einen Kurs steuern, der uns aus einem simplen Relativismus herausführt, und der, indem er einige einfache, empirisch verifizierbare Ursachen postuliert, die enormen Unterschiede in den Wirkungen, die jeder als real anerkennt, erklären kann. Wir müssen den Maßstab der Effekte beibehalten, jedoch nach schlichteren Erklärungen als der einer großen Trennung im menschlichen Bewusstsein suchen.

Hier werden wir jedoch mit einem anderen Problem konfrontiert. Wie schlicht ist schlicht? Wenn die Leute vor mentalen Ursachen zurückweichen, bedeutet das normalerweise, dass sie an materiellen Ursachen Vergnügen finden. Gigantische Veränderungen im kapitalistischen Produktionsmodus durch die Mittel vieler „Reflexionen", „Trübungen" und „Vermittlungen" beeinflussen die Arten von Beweisen, Argumentationen und Glauben. „Materialistische" Erklärungen beziehen sich oft auf tief verwurzelte Phänomene, zu deren Superstrukturen die Wissenschaft

gehört (Sohn-Rethel 1978). Das Endresultat dieser Strategie ist, dass nichts empirisch verifizierbar ist, da eine gähnende Kluft zwischen allgemeinen ökonomischen Trends und den feinen Details kognitiver Innovationen besteht. Am schlimmsten ist jedoch, dass wir zur Erklärung von Wissenschaft vor einer bestimmten Wissenschaft, der Ökonomie, niederknien müssen. Ironischerweise sind viele „materialistische" Darstellungen des Auftretens von Wissenschaft keineswegs materiell, da sie die präzise Praxis und Kunstfertigkeit des Wissens ignorieren und den allwissenden ökonomischen Historiker von genauerer Untersuchung abhalten.

Es scheint mir so zu sein, dass die einzige Möglichkeit, der simplizistischen, relativistischen Position zu entkommen, die ist, sowohl „materialistische" als auch „mentalistische" Erklärungen um jeden Preis zu vermeiden und stattdessen nach sparsameren Darstellungen zu suchen, die durch und durch empirisch und in der Lage sind, die großen Effekte von Wissenschaft und Technik zu erklären.

Es scheint, dass die besten Erklärungen – jene, die aus dem Wenigsten das Meiste machen – die sind, die die Handwerkskunst des Schreibens und der Visualisierung in Betracht ziehen. Sie sind sowohl materiell als auch schlicht, da sie so praktisch, so bescheiden, so durchdringend sind, so direkt vor Augen und Händen liegen, dass sie der Aufmerksamkeit entgehen. Jede von ihnen entleert grandiose Schemata und konzeptuelle Dichotomien und ersetzt sie durch einfache Modifikationen der Art, wie Personengruppen miteinander argumentieren und dabei Papier, Zeichen, Drucke und Diagramme verwenden. Trotz ihrer verschiedenen Methoden, Felder und Ziele verbindet diese Strategie der Deflation sehr verschiedene Forschungsansätze und stattet sie mit einem gleichermaßen ironischen wie erfrischenden Stil aus.[2]

Wie diese Forscher war auch ich während einer Studie über ein biologisches Laboratorium beeindruckt von der Art, wie viele Aspekte der Laborpraxis geordnet werden konnten, indem man sich weder die Gehirne der Wissenschaftler (zu denen mir der Zutritt verweigert wurde!) noch die kognitiven Strukturen (nichts Besonderes) oder die Paradigmen (seit 30 Jahren dieselben) ansah, sondern die Transformation von Ratten und Chemikalien in Papier (Latour/Woolgar 1979, 1986). Es war nicht, wie ich zuerst dachte, einfach meine subjektive Sicht, mich auf die Literatur sowie auf die Art, in der alles und jedes in Inskriptionen umgewandelt wurde, zu konzentrieren: das Labor war vielmehr genau dafür gemacht worden. Die Instrumente z. B. waren von verschiedener Art, verschiedenem Alter und unterschiedlichem Verfeinerungsgrad. Einige waren Möbelstücke, andere füllten große Räume, gaben vielen Technikern Arbeit und brauchten viele Wochen für ihren Betrieb. Ihr Endresultat jedoch, unabhängig vom Fachbereich, war immer ein kleines Fenster, durch das man einige wenige Zeichen eines ziemlich kärglichen Repertoires (Diagramme, Flecken, Bänder, Spalten) ablesen konnte. Alle diese Inskriptionen, wie ich sie nannte, waren kombinierbar, übereinander lagerbar und konnten – mit nur einem Mindestaufwand an Ordnen – als Darstellungen in den Text von Artikeln, die von Menschen geschrieben wurden, integriert werden. Viele der intellektuellen Glanzleistungen, die ich bewundern sollte, konnten neu formuliert werden, sobald diese Aktivität des Schreibens auf Papier und der Inskription in den Fokus der Analyse rückte. Statt hochtrabende Theorien oder Logikunterschiede zu bemühen, konnte ich mich so fest wie Goody an der Ebene einfacher Kunstfertigkeit festhalten. Die Domestizierung oder Disziplinierung des Geistes dauerte noch an, mit Instrumenten, die denen, auf die Goody sich bezog, sehr ähnlich waren. Fehlten diese Ressourcen, begannen dieselben Wissenschaftler zu stammeln, zu zögern und Unsinn zu reden und dabei jede Art politischer oder kultureller Vorurteile zur Schau zu stellen. Obwohl ihr Denken, ihre wissenschaftlichen Methoden, ihre Paradigmen, ihre Weltsichten und ihre Kulturen weiterhin galten, konnte ihre Konversation sie nicht am rechten Platz halten. Inskriptionen oder die Praxis des Inskribierens hätten das jedoch vermocht.

Die große Trennung kann in viele kleine, unerwartete und praktische Kompetenzen zerlegt werden, Bilder zu produzieren, über sie zu lesen und zu schreiben. Diese Strategie der Deflation hat jedoch einen gewichtigen Nachteil. Ihre Resultate scheinen gleichermaßen offensichtlich (an der Grenze zu einem wortwörtlichen Klischee) und zu schwach zu sein, um die gewaltigen Konsequenzen von Wissenschaft und Technik zu erklären, die nicht geleugnet werden können (wie wir oben einvernehmlich feststellten). Natürlich stimmt jeder zu, dass Schreiben, Drucken und Visualisieren wichtige Nebenprodukte der wissenschaftlichen Revolution oder der Psychogenese des wissenschaftlichen Denkens sind. Sie können notwendig sein, stellen jedoch keine zureichenden Gründe dar. Die Deflationsstrategie mag uns von einer mystischen großen Kluft befreien, wird uns jedoch allem Anschein nach in eine schlimmere Art von Mystizismus führen, wenn der Forscher, der sich mit Formen und Bildern beschäftigt, an die Macht von Zeichen und Symbolen glauben soll, die von allem anderen isoliert sind.

Dies ist ein starker Einwand. Wir müssen zugeben, dass es beim Sprechen über Bilder und Formen einfach ist, sich von der überzeugendsten hin zu einer trivialen Erklärung zu verschieben, die nur marginale Aspekte des Phänomens, das wir erklären möchten, enthüllt. Diagramme, Listen, Formeln, Archive, technische Zeichnungen, Akten, Gleichungen, Wörterbücher, Sammlungen und so weiter können abhängig von der Art, wie sie in den Fokus gerückt werden, nahezu alles oder nichts erklären. Es ist nur zu einfach, eine Reihe von Klischees – von der chinesischen Vorliebe für Ideogramme über die doppelte Buchführung (ohne die Bibel zu vergessen) bis hin zur Computerkultur – zusammenzuwerfen, um Havelocks Argumentation über das griechische Alphabet (1980) oder Walter Ongs Wiedergabe der Methode von Ramus (1971) zu erweitern. Jeder stimmt zu, dass Formen, Bilder und Schrift überall gegenwärtig sind. Aber wie viel Erklärungsbedarf können sie decken? Wie viele kognitive Fähigkeiten können durch sie nicht nur leichter, sondern erschöpfend erklärt werden? Während ich durch diese Literatur wate, habe ich das deprimierende Gefühl, dass wir uns abwechselnd auf festem, neuem Grund bewegen oder aber in einem alten Sumpf stecken geblieben sind. Ich möchte einen Weg finden, den Fokus beständig zu halten, sodass wir wissen, was wir von unserer Deflationsstrategie erwarten können.

Um diesen Fokus zu halten, müssen wir zuerst überlegen, wann wir erwarten können, dass Änderungen in den Schreib- und Visualisierungsprozeduren überhaupt einen Unterschied in der Art unseres Argumentierens, Beweisens oder Glaubens machen. Ohne diesen vorbereitenden Schritt wird den Inskriptionen – abhängig vom Kontext – entweder zu viel oder zu wenig Gewicht beigemessen.

Anders als Leroi-Gourhan (1964) wollen wir nicht die gesamte Geschichte des Schreibens und der visuellen Hilfsmittel vom primitiven Menschen bis zum Computer betrachten. Wir sind hier nur an ein paar spezifischen Erfindungen des Schreibens und der bildlichen Darstellung interessiert. Um diese Besonderheit zu definieren, müssen wir uns die Konstruktion härterer Fakten genauer ansehen.[3]

Wer gewinnt in einer agonistischen Begegnung zweier Autoren sowie zwischen ihnen und all jenen, die sie dazu brauchen, um eine Aussage A aufzubauen? Antwort: Derjenige, der in der Lage ist, *am schnellsten die größte*

*Anzahl gruppierter und treuer Alliierter aufzubieten*. Diese Definition von Sieg ist dem Krieg, der Politik, dem Recht und – wie ich jetzt zeigen werde – der Wissenschaft und der Technik gemeinsam. Ich behaupte, dass Schreiben und bildliche Darstellung nicht selbst die Veränderungen in unserer wissenschaftlichen Gesellschaft erklären können, sondern dazu *verhelfen, diese agonistische Situation* günstiger zu gestalten. Also ist es weder die gesamte Anthropologie des Schreibens noch die Geschichte der Visualisierung, die uns in diesem Kontext interessieren. Wir sollten uns lieber auf jene Aspekte konzentrieren, die beim Aufbieten, der Präsentation, der Zunahme, der effektiven Gruppierung oder der Rückversicherung der Treue neuer Verbündeter helfen. Wir müssen – in anderen Worten – die Art betrachten, in der jemand einen anderen davon überzeugt, eine Aussage aufzunehmen, sie weiterzugeben, sie wie eine Tatsache zu gestalten und die Autorschaft und Originalität des ersten Autors anzuerkennen. Das ist, was ich hinsichtlich Visualisierung und Kognition mit „den Fokus beständig halten" meine. Wenn wir nur auf der Ebene der visuellen Aspekte bleiben, fallen wir in eine Reihe schwacher Klischees zurück oder werden in alle nur denkbaren faszinierenden, akademischen Fragestellungen weit ab von unserem Problem geführt; wenn wir uns aber andererseits nur auf die agonistische Situation konzentrieren, entgleitet uns das Prinzip jedes Sieges, jeglicher Solidität in Wissenschaft und Technik für immer. Wir müssen die beiden Okulare zusammen halten, um sie in ein wirkliches *Bi*nokular zu verwandeln; es dauert eine Weile, sie zu fokussieren, aber das, was man am Ende sieht, lohnt hoffentlich das Warten.

Ein Beispiel zur Illustration: La Pérouse reist für Ludwig XVI. durch den Pazifik, mit der ausdrücklichen Mission, eine bessere Karte *zurück*zubringen. Eines Tages trifft er bei seiner Landung auf Sakhalin (wie er es nennt) auf Chinesen und versucht, von ihnen zu erfahren, ob Sakhalin eine Insel oder eine Halbinsel ist. Zu seiner großen Überraschung verstehen die Chinesen Geographie recht gut. Ein älterer Mann steht auf und zeichnet eine Karte der Insel in den Sand im Maßstab und mit den Details, die La Pérouse braucht. Ein Jüngerer sieht, dass die ansteigende Flut die Karte bald auslöschen wird und nimmt eines von La Pérouses Notizbüchern, um die Karte noch einmal mit einem Bleistift zu zeichnen.

Was sind die Unterschiede zwischen unzivilisierter und zivilisierter Geographie? Es ist weder notwendig, vorwissenschaftliches Denken ins Feld zu führen, noch zwischen einem geschlossenen und einem offenen Dilemma (Horton 1977) oder primären und sekundären Theorien (Horton 1982), implizit und explizit, konkreter und abstrakter Geographie zu unterscheiden. Die Chinesen sind sehr wohl in der Lage, in Begriffen einer Landkarte zu denken oder mit La Pérouse auf gleicher Augenhöhe über Navigation zu sprechen. Die Fähigkeit des Zeichnens und des Visualisierens macht, genauer gesagt, auch keinen wirklichen Unterschied, da sie alle Karten zeichnen, die mehr oder weniger auf demselben Projektionsprinzip basieren – zuerst auf Sand, dann auf Papier. Es gibt also vielleicht gar keinen Unterschied? Hat der Relativismus, da die Geographie gleich ist, Recht? Das kann nicht sein, weil La Pérouse etwas tut, das einen enormen Unterschied zwischen Chinesen und Europäern macht. Was für den einen eine unwichtige Zeichnung ist, die die Flut ruhig auslöschen kann, ist für den Letzteren *der einzige Gegenstand* seiner Mission. Was ins Bild gebracht werden muss, ist, wie das Bild zurückgebracht werden muss. Der Chinese braucht keine Aufzeichnungen zu machen, weil er so viele Landkarten erzeugen kann wie er will, da er auf dieser Insel geboren und dazu bestimmt ist, hier zu sterben. La Pérouse wird nicht länger als eine Nacht bleiben; er ist nicht dort geboren und wird weit entfernt sterben. Was macht er dann? Er durchquert alle diese Orte, um etwas nach Versailles *zurück*zunehmen, wo viele Leute erwarten, dass seine Karte bestimmt, wer in dem Punkt, ob Sakhalin eine Insel ist oder nicht, Recht hat und wer nicht; wem dieser oder jener Teil der Welt gehört und entlang welcher Routen das nächste Schiff segeln soll. Ohne diesen besonderen Trajektor wäre La Pérouses ausschließliches Interesse an Spuren und Inskriptionen unmöglich zu verstehen – dies ist der erste Aspekt; ohne Dutzende von Innovationen in der Inskription, Projektion, im Schreiben, Archivieren und Berechnen wäre seine Bewegung durch den Pazifik vollkommen vergeblich – und dies ist der zweite, ebenso entscheidende Aspekt. Wir müssen die beiden zusammen betrachten. Kommerzielle Interessen, kapitalistischer Geist, Imperialismus und Wissensdurst sind leere Begriffe, wenn man nicht Mercators Projektion, Schiffsuhren und ihre Hersteller, Kupfergravuren auf Karten, das Führen von „Logbüchern" und die vielen gedruckten Ausgaben von „Cooks Reisen", die La Pérouse bei sich trug, in Betracht zieht. An diesem Punkt ist die oben von mir skizzierte Deflationsstrategie stark. Andererseits würde keine Innovation in der Berechnung des Längen und Breitengrades, im Bau von Uhren, in der Zusammenstellung von Logbüchern, im Druck von Kupferplatten einen wie auch immer gearteten Unterschied machen, wenn sie nicht dazu beitragen würde, Alliierte aufzubieten, zu gruppieren und neue und unerwartete Verbündete weitab von Versailles zu gewinnen. Die Praktiken, an denen ich interessiert bin, wären sinnlos, wenn sie nicht auf bestimmte Kontroversen Einfluss hätten und Kritiker dazu bringen würden, neue Fakten zu glauben und sich auf neue Art zu verhalten. Hier versagt ein ausschließliches Interesse an Visualisierung – und Schrift und kann sogar kontraproduktiv sein. Nur den zweiten Argumentationsstrang zu verfolgen, würde eine mystische Sicht auf die von semiotischem Material gewährleisteten Mächte wie z. B. bei Derrida (1967) bedeuten; nur die erste zu erhalten würde bedeuten, eine idealistische Erklärung hochzuhalten (auch wenn diese einen materialistischen Anschein macht).

Ziel dieses Beitrags ist es, beide Argumentationsstränge gleichzeitig zu verfolgen. Wir finden, anders ausgedrückt, nicht alle Erklärungen betreffend Inskription gleichermaßen überzeugend, sondern nur die, die uns helfen zu verstehen, wie die Mobilisierung und Aufbietung neuer Ressourcen erreicht wird. Wir finden nicht alle Erklärungen hinsichtlich sozialer Gruppen, Interessen und ökonomischer Trends gleichermaßen überzeugend, sondern nur die, die einen spezifischen Mechanismus zur Zusammenfassung von „Gruppen", „Interessen", „Geld" und „Trends" anbieten: Mechanismen, von denen wir glauben, dass sie von der Manipulation von Papier, Formen, Bildern usw. abhängen. La Pérouse zeigt uns den Weg, da ohne neue Arten von Inskriptionen nichts Brauchbares von seiner langen, kostspieligen und schicksalsschweren Reise nach Versailles zurückgekommen wäre. Ohne seine seltsame Mission jedoch, die von ihm verlangte, fortzugehen und zurückzukehren, sodass andere in Frankreich überzeugt werden könnten, würde keine Modifikation der Inskription den auch nur kleinsten Unterschied gemacht haben.

Die wesentlichen Eigenschaften von Inskriptionen können nicht in Begriffen von Visualisierung, Form und Schrift definiert werden. Bei diesem Problem von Visualisierung und Kognition steht nicht *die Wahrnehmung* auf dem Spiel. Neue Inskriptionen und neue Arten, diese wahrzunehmen, sind vielmehr das Ergebnis von etwas, das tiefer liegt. Wenn man von *seinem* gewohnten Weg abweichen und schwer beladen zurückkehren möchte, um andere dazu zu zwingen, *ihre* gewohnten Wege zu verlassen, besteht das hauptsächlich zu lösende Problem in der *Mobilisierung*. Man muss fortgehen und mit den „Dingen" zurückkehren,

wenn die Bewegungen nicht vergeblich sein sollen; die „Dinge" müssen aber in der Lage sein, die Rückreise zu überstehen, ohne Schaden zu nehmen. Weitere Erfordernisse: Die gesammelten und verlagerten „Dinge" müssen alle gleichzeitig denen präsentierbar sein, die man überzeugen will und die nicht fortgegangen sind. Kurz: Man muss Objekte erfinden, die *mobil*, aber auch *unveränderlich*, *präsentierbar*, *lesbar* und miteinander *kombinierbar* sind.

## II. Über unveränderlich mobile Elemente

Es scheint mir, dass die meisten Forscher, die an den Beziehungen zwischen Inskriptionsprozeduren und Kognition gearbeitet haben, tatsächlich auf verschiedene Art und Weise über die Geschichte dieser unveränderlich mobilen Elemente geschrieben haben.

### *A. Optische Konsistenz*

Das erste Beispiel, das ich betrachten will, ist sehr bemerkenswert. Ivins schrieb vor Jahren darüber und fasste alles auf ein paar folgenreichen Seiten zusammen. Die Rationalisierung, die sich während der so genannten „wissenschaftlichen Revolution" ereignete, betrifft nicht den Geist, das Auge oder die Philosophie, sondern das *Sehen*. Wieso ist die Perspektive eine so wichtige Erfindung?

„Wegen ihres logischen Erkennens interner Invarianzen durch alle durch Veränderung der räumlichen Platzierung produzierten Transformationen." (Ivins 1973: 9)

In linearer Perspektive, ungeachtet aus welcher Entfernung und aus welchem Winkel ein Objekt gesehen wird, ist es immer möglich, dieses zu transferieren – zu übersetzen – und dasselbe Objekt in einer anderen Größe als der von einer anderen Position aus gesehenen zu erhalten. Im Verlauf dieser Übersetzung werden seine internen Eigenschaften nicht modifiziert. Diese Unveränderbarkeit der verlagerten Figur gestattet Ivins eine zweite wesentliche Feststellung: Da das Bild sich ohne Verzerrung bewegt, ist es im Rahmen linearer Perspektive möglich, eine von ihm so bezeichnete „Hin- und Rück"-Beziehung zwischen Objekt und Figur zu etablieren. Ivins zeigt uns, wie die Perspektive Bewegung durch den Raum sozusagen mit Rückfahrkarte ermöglicht. Man kann eine Kirche in Rom sehen, sie mit sich nach London nehmen, sodass man sie in London rekonstruieren kann oder nach Rom zurückkehren und das Bild verbessern. Durch die Perspektive werden genau wie durch La Pérouses Karte – und aus denselben Gründen – neue Bewegungen ermöglicht. Man kann seinen Weg verlassen und mit allen Orten, durch die man gegangen ist, zurückkehren; diese sind alle in derselben homogenen Sprache (Längengrad und Breitengrad, Geometrie) aufgeschrieben, die es erlaubt, den Maßstab zu wechseln, sie repräsentierbar zu machen und sie beliebig zu kombinieren.[4]

Für Ivins ist Perspektive eine wesentliche Determinante von Wissenschaft und Technik, weil sie „optische Konsistenz" oder, einfacher ausgedrückt, eine gerade Straße durch den Raum schafft. Ohne sie

„verändern sich mit der Verschiebung der Örtlichkeiten entweder die äußeren Beziehungen der Objekte wie etwa ihre Formen visueller Wahrnehmung oder dann ihre inneren Beziehungen." (Ebd.)

Die Verschiebung von den anderen Sinnen zum Sehen ist eine Konsequenz der agonistischen Situation. Man präsentiert abwesende Dinge. Niemand kann die Insel Sakhalin riechen, hören oder berühren, aber man kann auf die Karte schauen und bestimmen, auf welchem Kurs man das Land erreichen wird, wenn man die nächste Flotte schickt. Die Sprecher reden miteinander, fühlen, hören und berühren einander, *aber* sie sprechen jetzt *mittels* vieler abwesender Dinge, die alle gleichzeitig präsentiert werden. Diese Präsenz/Absenz ist durch die Hin- und Rück-Verbindung möglich, die von diesen Dingen etabliert wird – Perspektive, Projektion, Karte, Logbuch usw. – und die eine Übersetzung ohne Beeinträchtigung gestatten.

Auch Edgerton richtet unsere Aufmerksamkeit auf einen Vorteil linearer Perspektive (1976). Dieser unerwartete Vorteil zeigt sich, wenn religiöse oder mythologische Themen und Utopien mit der gleichen Perspektive dargestellt werden, die zur Wiedergabe von Natur verwendet wird (Edgerton 1980: 189).

„Sogar wenn der Inhalt des gedruckten Textes unwissenschaftlich wäre, präsentierte das gedruckte Bild im Westen immer ein rationales, auf den universellen Gesetzen der Geometrie basierendes Bild. In diesem Sinn verdankt die wissenschaftliche Revolution Albrecht Dürer mehr als Leonardo da Vinci." (Ebd.: 190)

Selbst die wildeste oder heiligste Fiktion und Dinge der Natur – sogar die niedrigsten – haben einen Versammlungsort, *einen gemeinsamen Platz*, weil sie alle von derselben „optischen Konsistenz" profitieren.[5] Man kann nicht nur Städte, Landschaften oder Ureinwohner verlagern und auf Straßen durch den Raum von ihnen weg und wieder zu ihnen hingehen, sondern man kann auch Heilige, Götter, Himmel, Paläste oder Träume mit denselben Hin- und Rück-Straßen erreichen und sie durch dieselbe „Fensterscheibe" auf derselben zweidimensionalen Oberfläche betrachten. Die doppelspurige Straße wird zu einer vierspurigen Autobahn! Unmögliche Paläste können realistisch gezeichnet werden, umgekehrt ist es aber auch möglich, mögliche Objekte so zu zeichnen, als seien sie utopisch. Wie Edgerton in seinem Kommentar zu Agricolas Drucken zeigt, können reale Objekte in getrennten Teilen oder explodierenden Ansichten gezeichnet oder in verschiedenen Maßstäben, Winkeln oder Perspektiven auf demselben Blatt Papier abgebildet werden. Es spielt keine Rolle, da die „optische Konsistenz" allen Teilen gestattet, sich miteinander zu mischen.

„Merkwürdigerweise erlauben lineare Perspektive und Chiaroscuro, die Bildern geometrische Stabilität verleihen, dem Betrachter ebenfalls eine momentane Aufhebung seiner Abhängigkeit vom Gesetz der Schwerkraft. Mit ein bisschen Übung kann sich der Betrachter solide Volumen vorstellen, die als abgetrennte Komponenten einer Vorrichtung frei im Raum treiben." (Ebd.: 193)

Wie Ferguson sagt, hat „der Geist" endlich „ein Auge".

In diesem Stadium, auf Papier, können Hybriden geschaffen werden, in denen sich Zeichnungen aus vielen Quellen vermischen. Perspektive ist nicht interessant, weil sie realistische Bilder bietet; andererseits ist sie doch von Interesse, weil sie vollständige Hybriden erschafft: Natur gesehen als Fiktion, Fiktion gesehen als Natur, mit allen Elementen, die im Raum so homogenisiert werden, dass es nun möglich ist, sie wie ein Kartenspiel zu mischen. In seinem Kommentar zum Gemälde „St. Jerome in seinem Studierzimmer" schreibt Edgerton:

„Antonellos Heiliger Jérome ist das perfekte Paradigma eines neuen Bewusstseins der physischen Welt, das von den westeuropäischen Intellektuellen im späten 15. Jahrhundert erlangt worden ist. Dieses Bewusstsein trat besonders bei Künstlern wie Leonardo da Vinci, Francesco di Giorgio Martini, Albrecht Dürer, Hans Holbein und einigen mehr zutage, die alle [...] eine verfeinerte Grammatik und Syntax zur Quantifizierung natürlicher Phänomene in Bildern entwickelt hatten. In ihren Händen wurde das Erschaffen von Bildern zu einer piktorialen Sprache, die mit etwas Übung mehr Informationen schneller und [sic] für ein potentiell größeres Publikum kommunizieren konnte als jede verbale Sprache in der menschlichen Geschichte." (Ebd.: 189)

Die Perspektive illustriert den doppelten Argumentationsstrang, den ich im vorangegangenen Abschnitt präsentiert habe. Innovationen in der graphischen Darstellung sind insofern wesentlich, als sie neue Hin-und Rückbeziehungen mit Objekten (aus der Natur oder aus der Fiktion) etablieren – und nur insofern sie Inskriptionen entweder erlauben, mobiler zu werden, oder durch alle Verlagerungen hindurch unveränderbar zu bleiben.

*B. Visuelle Kultur*

Noch bemerkenswerter als die italienische, von Ivans und Edgerton beschriebene Perspektive ist, wie Svetlana Alpers sehr schön aufzeigt (1983), die niederländische Perspektiven-Methode in der bildenden Kunst. Wie sie uns erzählt, malen die Holländer nicht grandiose historische Szenen, als würde man sie durch ein sorgfältig gerahmtes Fenster betrachten: sie verwenden die Oberfläche ihrer Gemälde (wie das Äquivalent einer Netzhaut), um die Welt direkt darauf zu malen. Wenn Bilder auf diese Weise eingefangen werden, gibt es für den Betrachter keinen privilegierten Standpunkt mehr. Die Tricks der Camera Obscura transformieren großformatige dreidimensionale Objekte in eine kleine zweidimensionale Oberfläche, um die sich der Betrachter nach Gutdünken bewegen kann.[6]

Für unsere Zwecke liegt das Hauptinteresse von Alpers Buch in der Art, in der sie die Veränderungen einer „visuellen Kultur" im Lauf der Zeit zeigt. Sie richtet ihr Hauptaugenmerk nicht auf die Inskriptionen oder Bilder, sondern auf die simultane Transformation von Wissenschaft, Kunst, Theorie des Sehens, Organisation der Handwerke und wirtschaftlichen Kräften. Die Leute sprechen oft von „Weltsichten", aber dieser kraftvolle Ausdruck wird metaphorisch verwendet. Alpers stattet diesen alten Begriff mit seiner materiellen Bedeutung aus: Wie eine Kultur die *Welt sieht* und sie sichtbar macht. Eine neue visuelle Kultur redefiniert sowohl, was Sehen bedeutet, als auch, was es zu sehen gibt. Ein Zitat von Comenius fasst auf passende Weise die neue Obsession, Objekte neu sichtbar zu machen, zusammen:

„Wir sprechen nun von der Art, in der Objekte den Sinnen präsentiert werden müssen, wenn der Eindruck deutlich sein soll. Dies ist einfach zu verstehen, wenn wir den Prozess des tatsächlichen Sehens betrachten. Wenn man das Objekt deutlich sehen will. ist es notwendig: (1) es vor unseren Augen zu platzieren, (2) das nicht weit entfernt, sondern in einem vernünftigen Abstand, (3) nicht von einer Seite, sondern genau vor unseren Augen, (4) sodass die Vorderseite des Objekts nicht vom Betrachter weg, sondern in Richtung auf den Betrachter gedreht ist, (5) dass die Augen zunächst das Objekt als Ganzes aufnehmen, (6) und dann fortfahren, die Teile zu unterscheiden, (7) diese dann der Reihe nach von Anfang bis Ende inspizieren, (8) die Aufmerksamkeit auf jedes einzelne Teil gerichtet wird, (9) bis sie alle anhand ihrer wesentlichen Attribute aufgenommen sind. Wenn alle diese Erfordernisse vollständig beachtet werden, findet das Sehen erfolgreich statt; wird nur eines vernachlässigt. gibt es nur einen Teilerfolg." (Zit. n. Alpers 1983: 95)

Diese neue Obsession, den Akt des Sehens zu definieren, kann in der Wissenschaft jener Zeit, aber auch in modernen Laboratorien gefunden werden. Comenius' Ratschlag ähnelt sowohl dem von Boyle, als er die Zeugen seines Luftpumpen-Experiments disziplinierte (Shapin 1984), als auch jenem von Lynch untersuchten Neurologen, als sie ihre Hirnzellen „disziplinierten" (Lynch 1985 a). Menschen in vorwissenschaftlicher Zeit und außerhalb von Laboratorien gebrauchen ihre Augen, aber nicht auf diese Weise. Sie schauen auf das Spektakel der Welt, aber nicht auf diesen neuen Typus von Bild, der dazu erdacht ist, die Objekte der Welt zu transportieren, sie in Holland zu akkumulieren, sie mit Unterschriften und Legenden zu versehen und nach eigenem Willen zu kombinieren. Alpers macht verständlich, was Foucault (1966) nur anriss: wie dieselben Augen plötzlich beginnen, „Repräsentationen" zu sehen. Das „Panoptikum", das sie beschreibt, ist ein *fait social total*, das alle Aspekte der Kultur neu definiert. Noch wichtiger ist, dass Alpers nicht eine neue Sicht erklärt, indem sie „soziale Interessen" oder die „ökonomische Infrastruktur" einbringt. Die neue präzise Szenographie, die in einer Weitsicht resultiert, definiert zugleich, was Wissenschaft oder Kunst ist und was es bedeutet, eine Weltwirtschaft zu haben. Wie ich es vorher schon formuliert habe, wird ein kleines flaches Land mächtig, indem es einige wesentliche Erfindungen macht, die es Menschen erlauben, ihre Mobilität zu beschleunigen und die Unveränderbarkeit der Inskriptionen zu verstärken: Auf diese Weise ist die Welt in diesem kleinen Land versammelt.

Alpers Beschreibung der niederländischen visuellen Kultur erreicht dasselbe Ergebnis wie Edgertons Studie der technischen Zeichnungen: Ein neuer Versammlungsplatz für Fakten und Fiktion, Wörter und Bilder ist entworfen. Die Karte selbst ist ein solches Ergebnis, umso mehr, als sie zur Inskribierung ethnographischer Inventare (Ende ihres Kapitels IV) oder Unterschriften (Kapitel V), Stadtumrisse usw. verwendet wird. Die Hauptqualität des neuen Raumes ist nicht die, „objektiv" zu sein, wie eine naive Realismusdefinition oftmals vorgibt, sondern: optische Konsistenz zu haben. Diese Konsistenz bringt die *Kunst*, alles *zu beschreiben*, und die Möglichkeit, von einem Typ von visueller Spur zu einer anderen zu gehen, mit sich. Folglich überrascht es uns nicht, dass Briefe, Spiegel, Linsen, gemalte Wörter, Perspektiven, Inventare, illustrierte Kinderbücher, Mikroskope und Teleskope in dieser visuellen Kultur zusammenkommen. Alle Innovationen werden ausgewählt, um „insgeheim und ohne Verdächtigung zu sehen, was weit entfernt an anderen Orten gemacht wird" (zit. in Alpers 1983: 201).

*C. Eine neue Art, Zeit und Raum zu akkumulieren*

Ein anderes Beispiel soll zeigen, dass Inskriptionen nicht per se interessant sind, sondern nur, weil sie entweder die Mobilität oder die Unveränderbarkeit von Spuren steigern. Die Erfindung des Buchdrucks und seine Auswirkungen auf Wissenschaft und Technik ist ein Klischee der Historiker; niemand hat jedoch diese Renaissance-Argumentation so vollständig erneuert wie Elizabeth Eisenstein (1979). Wieso? Weil sie die Druckerpresse als Mobilisierungsvorrichtung betrachtet oder, genauer, als Vorrichtung, die sowohl Mobilisierung als auch Unveränderbarkeit zur selben Zeit ermöglicht. Eisenstein sucht nicht nach einer einzigen Ursache der wissenschaftlichen Revolution, sondern nach einer Nebenursache, die alle Wirkursachen ins Verhältnis zueinander setzt. Die Druckerpresse ist offensichtlich eine machtvolle Ursache dieser Art. Unveränderbarkeit wird durch den Prozess des Druckens vieler identischer Kopien sichergestellt. Mobilität durch die Anzahl der Kopien, das Papier, die beweglichen Lettern. Die Verbindungen zwischen verschiedenen Orten in Zeit und Raum werden von dieser phantastischen Beschleunigung unveränderlich mobiler Elemente, die irgendwo in allen Richtungen Europas zirkulieren, vollständig modifiziert. Wie Ivins gezeigt hat, ist Perspektive plus Druckerpresse plus *Aqua Forte* die wirklich wichtige Kombination, da Bücher nun die realistischen Bilder dessen, worüber sie sprechen, bei sich tragen. Zum ersten Mal kann eine Örtlichkeit andere, in Raum und Zeit weit entfernte Orte akkumulieren und sie dem Auge synoptisch präsentieren; diese synoptische Präsentation kann, einmal überarbeitet, verbessert oder unterbrochen, noch besser ohne Modifikation an anderen Plätzen verbreitet und zu anderen Zeiten verfügbar gemacht werden.

Nachdem Eisenstein Historiker diskutiert hat, die viele widersprüchliche Einflüsse zur Erklärung des Aufstiegs der Astronomie vorschlugen, schreibt sie:

„Ob der Astronom des 16. Jahrhunderts mit Materialien aus dem vierten vorchristlichen Jahrhundert – oder im 14. Jahrhundert neu verfassten – konfrontiert war oder ob er empfänglicher gegenüber akademischen oder humanistischen Gedankenströmungen war, scheint in dieser bestimmten Verbindung von geringerer Bedeutung als die Tatsache, dass alle Arten diverser Materialien im Verlauf eines Lebens von einem Paar Augen gesehen wurden. Für Kopernikus wie für Tycho war das Ergebnis ein erhöhtes Bewusstsein und Unzufriedenheit mit den Diskrepanzen der inhärenten Daten." (Eisenstein 1979: 602)

Mit vernichtender Ironie verlagert die Autorin die Aufmerksamkeit vom Geist auf die Oberfläche der mobilisierten Ressourcen:

„‚Um die Wahrheit eines Satzes von Euklid zu entdecken', schrieb John Locke, ‚bedarf es kaum der Offenbarung: Gott hatte uns mit natürlicheren und sichereren Mitteln, Kenntnis über sie zu erlangen, ausgestattet'. Im elften Jahrhundert jedoch hatte Gott die westlichen Gelehrten nicht mit natürlicheren und sichereren Mitteln zum Erfassen eines Euklidschen Theorems ausgestattet. Stattdessen engagierten sich die gelehrtesten Männer der Christenheit in einer fruchtlosen Suche, um zu entdecken, was Euklid mit seinem Bezug auf innere Winkel gemeint hatte." (Ebd.: 649)

Für Eisenstein kann jede große Diskussion über die Reformation, die wissenschaftliche Revolution und die neue kapitalistische Wirtschaft umgeformt werden, indem man sich anschaut, was Verleger und die Druckerpresse ermöglichen. Der Grund, weshalb diese alte Erklärung in ihrer Behandlung neue Form annimmt, ist, dass Eisenstein sich nicht nur auf graphische Darstellung konzentriert, sondern auch auf deren Veränderungen, die mit dem Mobilisierungsprozess verbunden sind. Zum Beispiel erklärt sie (ebd.: 508 ff., nach Ivins 1953) das rätselhafte Phänomen eines Zeitabstandes zwischen der Einführung der Druckerpresse und der exakter realistischer Bilder. Zuerst wird die Presse nur zur Reproduktion von Herbarien, anatomischen Stichen, Karten und Kosmologien verwendet, die Jahrhunderte alt sind und die viel später als ungenau gelten werden. Wenn wir nur auf die semiotische Ebene schauen würden, wäre dieses Phänomen rätselhaft; wenn wir aber einmal die tiefere Struktur betrachten, ist es leicht zu erklären. Zuerst erfolgt die Verlagerung vieler unveränderbar mobiler Elemente; die alten Texte werden überall verbreitet und können billiger an einem Ort gesammelt werden. Aber dann wird der Widerspruch in ihnen schließlich auf wortwörtliche Weise *sichtbar*. Die vielen Orte, an denen diese Texte synoptisch gesammelt sind, bieten viele Gegenbeispiele (verschiedene Blumen, verschiedene Organe mit anderen Namen, verschiedene Formen der Küstenlinie, unterschiedliche Kurse verschiedener Währungen, verschiedene Gesetze). Diese Gegenbeispiele können den alten Texten hinzugefügt und in der gleichen Weise ohne Modifikation an all den Orten verbreitet werden, an denen dieser Prozess des Vergleichs wieder aufgenommen werden kann. In anderen Worten werden Fehler genau reproduziert und ohne Veränderung verbreitet. Korrekturen werden jedoch auch schnell, billig und ohne weitere Veränderungen reproduziert. Am Ende *verschiebt sich* also die Genauigkeit *vom Medium zur Botschaft*, vom gedruckten Buch zum Kontext, mit dem es eine Hin-und Rückverbindung eingeht. Ein neues Interesse an der „Wahrheit" kommt nicht von einer neuen Sichtweise, sondern von derselben alten, die sich selbst auf neue sichtbare Objekte anwendet, die Raum und Zeit unterschiedlich mobilisieren.[7]

Die Konsequenz von Eisensteins Argumentation besteht darin, dass mentalistische Erklärungen in die Geschichte unveränderlich mobiler Elemente transformiert werden. Wiederholt zeigt sie, dass vor dem Auftreten des Buchdrucks alle nur denkbaren intellektuellen Leistungen erbracht worden sind: organisierter Skeptizismus, wissenschaftliche Methode, Widerlegung, Datensammeln, Theoriebildung. Alles ist ausprobiert worden, in allen Disziplinen: Geographie, Kosmologie, Medizin, Bewegungslehre, Politik, Ökonomie usw. Aber jede Leistung blieb lokal und temporär, da es keine Möglichkeit gab, ihre Ergebnisse anderswohin zu bewegen und die anderer einzubringen, ohne neue Verfälschungen oder Fehler einzuführen. Zum Beispiel war jede sorgfältig verbesserte Version eines alten Autors nach ein paar Kopien wieder verfälscht. Keine irreversiblen Gewinne konnten erzielt werden; deshalb war auch keine groß angelegte langfristige Kapitalisierung möglich. Die Druckerpresse fügt aber nicht dem Denken, der wissenschaftlichen Methode oder dem Gehirn etwas hinzu. Sie konserviert und verbreitet alles – gleichgültig, wie falsch, seltsam oder wild es ist. Sie macht alles mobil, aber diese Mobilität wird nicht von Verfälschung entkräftet. Die neuen Wissenschaftler, die neuen Kleriker, die neuen Händler, die neuen Prinzen, die Eisenstein beschreibt, unterscheiden sich nicht von den alten, aber sie schauen sich nun neues Material an, das zahlreiche Orte und Zeiten verfolgt. Gleichgültig, wie ungenau diese Spuren auf den ersten Blick sein mögen, sie gewinnen alle an Genauigkeit *als Konsequenz* von mehr Mobilisierung und mehr Unveränderbarkeit. Ein Mechanismus, der irreversibel Genauigkeit einfangt, wurde erfunden. Der Buchdruck spielt dieselbe Rolle wie Maxwells Dämon. Keine neue Theorie, Weltsicht oder neuer Geist sind notwendig, um den Kapitalismus, die Reformation und die Wissenschaft zu erklären: Sie sind das Resultat eines ersten Schrittes in der langen Geschichte unveränderlich mobiler Elemente.

Indem sie Ivins Argumentation aufnehmen, konzentrieren sich sowohl Mukerji (1983) als auch Eisenstein wieder auf das *illustrierte* Buch. Für diese Autoren war McLuhans Revolution bereits geschehen, sobald Bilder gedruckt wurden. Ingenieurwesen, Botanik, Architektur, Mathematik – keine dieser Wissenschaften kann das, worüber sie sprechen, nur durch Texte allein beschreiben; sie müssen die Dinge zeigen. Dieses Zeigen, das zur Überzeugung so wesentlich ist, war vor der Erfindung „eingravierter Bilder" vollkommen unmöglich. Ein Text konnte nur mit einigen Verfälschungen kopiert werden, nicht jedoch ein Diagramm, ein anatomischer Stich oder eine Karte. Der Effekt auf die Konstruktion von Fakten ist beträchtlich, wenn ein Schreiber in der Lage ist, einen Leser mit einem Text, der eine große Anzahl von den Dingen, über die er spricht, an einem Ort präsentiert, zu versorgen. Wenn man annimmt, dass alle Leser und alle Schreiber dasselbe tun, wird ohne zusätzliche Ursache eine neue Welt aus der alten hervortreten. Wieso? Einfach weil der Kritisierte dasselbe tun muss wie sein Kritiker. Um sozusagen die „Kritik zu erwidern", wird er ein anderes Buch schreiben, es drucken lassen und mit Kupferplatten die Gegendarstellungen, die er ins Feld führen möchte, mobilisieren müssen. Die Kosten des Widersprechens werden ansteigen.[8]

Positive Rückmeldungen entstehen, sobald man in der Lage ist, eine große Zahl an mobilen, lesbaren, sichtbaren Ressourcen an einem Ort zusammenzubringen, um einen Punkt zu stützen. Nach Tycho Brahe (Eisenstein 1979) muss der Gegner entweder aufgeben und das, was Kosmologen sagen, als Tatsache akzeptieren, oder Gegenbeweise produzieren, indem er seinen Prinz dazu überredet, eine vergleichbare Geldsumme in Observatorien zu investieren. In diesem Punkt ist der „Wettlauf um Beweise" dem Rüstungswettlauf sehr ähnlich, weil der Feedbackmechanismus derselbe ist. Wenn einmal ein Konkurrent damit beginnt, harte Fakten aufzubauen, müssen die anderen dasselbe tun oder nachgeben.

Diese leichte Umformung von Eisensteins Argumentation in Begriffe unveränderbar mobiler Elemente erlaubt uns, eine Schwierigkeit in ihrer Argumentation zu überwinden. Obwohl sie die Wichtigkeit von Herausgeberstrategien betont, gibt sie keine Erklärung über technische Innovationen selbst. Die Druckerpresse platzt in ihre Darstellung hinein wie die exogenen Faktoren vieler Historiker, wenn sie über technische Innovationen sprechen. Sie richtet das Hauptaugenmerk ausgezeichnet auf den semiotischen Aspekt des Druckes und die Mobilisierung, die er erlaubt; die technischen Notwendigkeiten, um die Presse zu erfinden, sind jedoch alles andere als offensichtlich. Wenn wir die agonistische Situation betrachten, die ich als Referenzpunkt verwende, wird die Notwendigkeit, die so etwas wie die Druckerpresse begünstigt, klarer. *Alles*, was die Mobilität der Spuren, die eine Örtlichkeit über einen anderen Ort erhält, beschleunigt, oder *alles*, was diesen Spuren gestattet, sich ohne Transformation von einem Ort zu einem anderen zu bewegen, wird favorisiert: Geometrie, Projektion, Perspektive, Buchhaltung, Papierherstellung, *Aqua Forte*, Münzprägung, neue Schiffe (Law 1986). Das Privileg der Druckerpresse kommt von ihrer Fähigkeit, vielen Innovationen dazu zu verhelfen auf einmal zu agieren, aber sie selbst ist nur eine Innovation unter den vielen, die helfen, die einfachste aller Fragen zu beantworten: Wie ist Dominanz in großem Maßstab möglich? Diese Umformulierung ist nützlich, da sie uns zu sehen hilft, dass derselbe Mechanismus, dessen Wirkungen von Eisenstein beschrieben wurden, *heute noch funktioniert* – in einem stets zunehmenden Ausmaß an den Grenzen von Wissenschaft und Technik. Ein paar Tage in einem Labor enthüllen, dass dieselben Kräfte, die die Druckerpresse so notwendig machten, noch immer agieren, um neue Datenbanken, Raumteleskope, Chromatographien, Gleichungen, Scanner, Fragebögen usw. zu produzieren. Der Geist wird noch immer domestiziert.

## III.
## Über Inskriptionen

Was ist so wichtig an den Bildern und Inskriptionen, die Wissenschaftler und Ingenieure geschäftig gewinnen, zeichnen, inspizieren, berechnen und diskutieren? Zuallererst ist es der einzigartige Vorteil, den sie in rhetorischen oder polemischen Situationen verschaffen. „Sie zweifeln an dem, was ich sage? Ich werde es Ihnen zeigen." Und ohne mich mehr als ein paar Zentimeter zu bewegen, entfalte ich vor Ihren Augen Ziffern, Diagramme, Stiche, Texte, Umrisse und zeige hier und jetzt Dinge, die weit entfernt sind und mit denen nun eine Art von Hin-und Rückverbindung hergestellt worden ist. Ich glaube nicht, dass man die Wichtigkeit dieses simplen Mechanismus überbewerten kann. Eisenstein hat das für die Vergangenheit der Wissenschaft bewiesen, aber die Ethnographie von gegenwärtigen Laboratorien zeigt denselben Mechanismus (Lynch 1985 a, 1985 b; Star 1983; Law 1985). Wir sind so an diese Welt von Formen und Bildern gewöhnt, dass wir kaum denken können, wie es ist, etwas ohne Index, Bibliographien, Wörterbücher, Papiere mit Referenzen, Tabellen, Spalten, Fotographien, Peaks, Punkte und Bänder zu wissen.[9]

Eine einfache Art, die Wichtigkeit von Inskriptionen zu verdeutlichen, besteht darin, darüber nachzudenken, wie wenig wir zu überzeugen in der Lage sind, wenn man uns die graphische Darstellung nimmt, durch die Mobilität und Unveränderbarkeit erhöht werden. Wie Dagognet in zwei ausgezeichneten Büchern gezeigt hat (1969, 1973), existiert keine wissenschaftliche Disziplin, ohne zuerst einmal eine visuelle und geschriebene Sprache zu erfinden, die es ihr erlaubt, mit ihrer verwirrenden Vergangenheit zu brechen. Die Manipulation von Substanzen in Galipot und Alambik wird erst zur Chemie, wenn alle Substanzen in einer homogenen Sprache aufgeschrieben werden können, in der alles dem Auge simultan präsentiert wird. Das Aufschreiben von Wörtern innerhalb einer Klassifizierung ist nicht genug. Chemie wird erst dann mächtig, wenn ein visuelles Vokabular erfunden wird, das die Manipulationen durch Kalkulationen von Formeln ersetzt. Chemische Strukturen können auf dem Papier gezeichnet, komponiert, auseinander gebrochen werden, wie Musik oder Arithmetik, den ganzen Weg bis zu Mendeleievs Tabelle:

„Für die, die die periodische Tabelle zu betrachten und zu lesen wissen, entfalten sich die Eigenschaften der Elemente und die ihrer zahlreichen Kombinationen vollständig und direkt aus ihren Positionen in der Tabelle." (Dagognet 1969: 213)

Nachdem er die vielen Innovationen in chemischen Schriften und Zeichnungen analysiert hat, fügt er diesen kleinen Satz hinzu, der Goodys Sicht sehr nahe kommt:

„Es mag so scheinen, als ob wir triviale Details betrachten – eine leichte Modifikation in der Ebene, die zur Beschreibung eines Chlorins verwendet wird –, diese kleinen Details lösen jedoch paradoxerweise die Kräfte der modernen Welt aus." (Ebd.: 199)

In seiner bekannten Studie über klinische Medizin hat Foucault dieselbe Transformation von kleinformatiger Praxis zu einer Manipulation von Aufzeichnungen im großen Umfang (1963) gezeigt. Dasselbe medizinische Denken wird vollkommen unterschiedliches Wissen erzeugen, wenn man es auf Bäuche, Fieber, Hälse und Häute einiger weniger aufeinander folgender Patienten oder aber auf die gut geführten Berichte von Hunderten von beschriebenen Bäuchen, Fiebern, Hälsen und Häuten anwendet, die alle in derselben Weise kodiert und synoptisch präsent sind. Medizin wird nicht im Denken oder im Auge des Praktizierenden wissenschaftlich, sondern in der Anwendung alter Augen und alten Denkens auf neue Informationsblätter innerhalb neuer Institutionen, dem Krankenhaus. In „Überwachen und Strafen" (1976) kommt Foucaults diesbezügliche Darstellung der Forschung über Inskriptionen am nächsten. Das Hauptanliegen des Buches ist es, die Verschiebung von einer Macht, die von unsichtbaren Betrachtern gesehen wird, hin zu einer neuen unsichtbaren Macht, die alles über jeden sieht, zu illustrieren. Der Hauptvorteil von Foucaults Analyse liegt darin, sich nicht nur auf Akten, Buchhaltungsbücher, Zeitpläne und Drill zu konzentrieren, sondern auch auf die Art von Institutionen, in denen diese Inskriptionen aufhören, so bedeutend zu sein.[10] Die hauptsächliche Innovation ist die eines „Panoptikums", das der Kriminalstrafkunde, der Pädagogik, der Psychiatrie und der klinischen Medizin gestattet, als ausgewachsene Wissenschaften aus ihren sorgfältig geführten Akten hervorzutreten. Das Panoptikum ist eine andere Art die „optische Konsistenz", die für Macht im großen Maßstab notwendig ist, zu erhalten.

In einem berühmten Satz sagt Kant, dass wir der Vernunft einen Dienst leisten, wenn wir erfolgreich den Pfad entdecken, auf dem sie sich sicher bewegen kann. Der „sichere Pfad einer Wissenschaft" jedoch liegt zwangsläufig in der Konstruktion gut geführter Akten in Institutionen, die eine größere Anzahl von Ressourcen in einem größeren Maßstab mobilisieren wollen.

„Optische Konsistenz" wird – wie Rudwick gezeigt hat (1976) – in der Geologie erreicht, indem man eine neue visuelle Sprache erfindet. Ohne sie bleiben die Erdschichten versteckt, und gleichgültig, wie viele Reisende und Grabende sich dort auch bewegen, gibt es doch keine Möglichkeit, ihre Reisen, Visionen und Ansprüche zusammenzufassen. Die Kopernikanische Wende, die Kant sehr am Herzen lag, ist eine idealistische Darstellung eines sehr einfachen Mechanismus: Wenn wir nicht zur Erde gehen können, lass die Erde zu uns kommen, oder genauer, lasst uns alle zu vielen Plätzen auf der Erde gehen und mit

denselben, aber unterschiedlichen homogenen Bildern, die gesammelt, verglichen, überlagert und an ein paar Orten neu gezeichnet werden können, zusammen mit den sorgfältig etikettierten Proben von Gestein und Fossilien zurückkehren.

In einem anregenden Buch hat Fourquet (1980) dasselbe Sammeln von Inskriptionen durch die INSEE, die französische Institution, die die meisten ökonomischen Statistiken bereitstellt, illustriert. Es ist natürlich unmöglich, über die Ökonomie einer Nation zu sprechen, indem man „sie" sich anschaut. Dieses „sie" ist schlicht unsichtbar, solange nicht Kohorten von Forschenden und Inspektoren lange Fragebögen ausgefüllt haben, solange nicht die Antworten in Karten gestanzt, von Computern verarbeitet und in einem gigantischen Laboratorium analysiert worden sind. Erst am Ende kann die Wirtschaft in Stapeln von Karten und Listen sichtbar gemacht werden. Sogar das ist noch zu verwirrend, sodass neues Zeichnen und Extrahieren notwendig wird, um eine paar ordentliche Diagramme zu erstellen, die das Bruttosozialprodukt oder die Zahlungsbilanz zeigen. Das auf diese Weise erhaltene Panoptikum hat in der Struktur Ähnlichkeit mit einem riesenhaften wissenschaftlichen Instrument, das die unsichtbare Welt des Austausches in „die Wirtschaft" transformiert. Deshalb habe ich anfangs die materialistische Erklärung zurückgewiesen, die „Infrastruktur", „Märkte" oder „Verbraucherbedürfnisse" verwendet, um Wissenschaft oder Technik darzustellen. Die visuelle Konstruktion von etwas wie einem „Markt" oder einer „Ökonomie" ist das, was einer Erklärung bedarf, und dieses Endprodukt kann nicht verwendet werden, um Wissenschaft zu erklären.

In einem anderen anregenden Buch versucht Fabian, die Anthropologie zu erklären, indem er ihre Visualisierungskompetenz betrachtet (1983). Der Hauptunterschied zwischen uns und den Wilden, so argumentiert er, liegt nicht in der Kultur, im Geist, sondern in der Art, wie *wir sie* visualisieren. Es wird eine Asymmetrie geschaffen, weil wir einen Raum und eine Zeit kreieren, in die wir andere Kulturen platzieren, sie aber machen nicht dasselbe. Wir erfassen beispielsweise ihr Land auf Karten, sie aber haben weder Karten ihres noch unseres Landes; wir erfassen ihre Vergangenheit, sie nicht; wir schaffen schriftliche Kalender, sie nicht. Fabians Argumentation, die sowohl mit Goodys als auch mit Bourdieus Kritik der Ethnographie (1972) verbunden ist, lautet, dass, wenn diese erste Gewaltanwendung einmal verübt worden ist, wir diese Wilden nicht mehr verstehen können, ganz gleich, was wir tun. Fabian jedoch betrachtet diese Mobilisierung aller Wilden in einigen Ländern durch Sammlung, Karten- und Listenerstellung, Archive, Linguistik usw. als etwas Bösartiges. In aller Offenheit wünscht er, einen anderen Weg zu finden, um die Wilden zu „kennen". „Kennen" jedoch bedeutet keine desinteressierte kognitive Aktivität; härtere Fakten über die anderen Kulturen sind in unseren Gesellschaften produziert worden, in genau derselben Weise wie andere Fakten über Ballistik, Taxonomie oder Chirurgie. Ein Ort sammelt alle anderen und präsentiert sie dem Kritiker auf synoptische Weise, um das Ergebnis einer agonistischen Kontroverse zu modifizieren. Um eine große Anzahl von Konkurrenten und Landsleuten von ihren üblichen Wegen abzubringen, mussten viele Ethnographen sowohl weiter und länger von *ihren* üblichen Wegen abgehen als auch *zurückkommen*. Die Beschränkungen, die auferlegt werden, Menschen zum Weggehen und zur Wiederkehr zu überzeugen, sind so, dass dies nur erreicht werden kann, wenn alles über das Leben der Wilden in unveränderlich mobile Elemente transformiert wird, die einfach lesbar und präsentierbar sind. Trotz seines Wunsches kann es Fabian nicht besser machen. Entweder muss er das „Kennen" oder die Produktion harter Fakten aufgeben (Latour 1987).

Es gibt hinsichtlich der Besessenheit von graphischer Darstellung keinen messbaren Unterschied zwischen Natur- und Sozialwissenschaften. Wenn Wissenschaftler die Natur, die Wirtschaft, die Sterne oder die Organe betrachteten, würden sie nichts *sehen*. Dieser „Beweis" wird als klassische Widerlegung naiver Versionen des Empirizismus verwendet (Arnheim 1969). Wissenschaftler beginnen damit, etwas zu sehen, wenn sie einmal damit aufhören, die Natur anzuschauen und stattdessen ausschließlich und obsessiv auf Ausdrucke und flache Inskriptionen schauen.[11] Was in den Debatten über Wahrnehmung immer vergessen wird, ist diese einfache Verlagerung von einer Betrachtung verwirrender dreidimensionaler Objekte zu einer Inspektion zweidimensionaler Bilder, die *weniger verwirrend gemacht worden sind*. Wie alle Laborbeobachter war Lynch verblüfft von der außergewöhnlichen Besessenheit der Wissenschaftler von Papieren, Ausdrucken, Diagrammen, Archiven, Zusammenfassungen und Kurven auf Millimeterpapier. Gleichgültig, worüber sie sprechen, beginnen sie das Gespräch mit einem gewissen Grad an Zuversicht und Glauben, den ihnen ihre Kollegen entgegenbringen, wenn sie nur einmal auf einfache, geometrisierte, zweidimensionale Formen deuten. Die „Objekte" sind entfernt oder oft in den Labors nicht anwesend. Blutende und schreiende Ratten werden schnell entsorgt; was aus ihnen extrahiert wird, ist ein hübscher Satz von Ziffern. Diese Extraktion – wie die paar Längen- und Breitengrade, die La Pérouse von den Chinesen extrahierte – ist *alles, was zählt*. Man kann nichts über die Ratten sagen, aber eine ganze Menge über die Ziffern (Latour/Woolgar 1979). Knorr (1981) und Star (1983) haben ebenfalls die Vereinfachungsprozeduren, die am Werk sind, gezeigt, als seien die Bilder niemals einfach genug, um eine Kontroverse schnell beizulegen. Jedes Mal, wenn es einen Disput gibt, werden große Anstrengungen unternommen, um ein neues Instrument zur Visualisierung zu finden (oder manchmal sogar zu erfinden), das das Bild verstärkt, das Lesen beschleunigt und, wie Lynch gezeigt hat, sich mit den visuellen Charakteristika der Dinge, die sich zu Diagrammen auf Papier fügen (Küstenlinien, Sterne, die wie Punkte sind, schön gruppierte Zellen usw.), konspirativ zusammentun. Wiederum sollte der präzise Fokus sorgfältig gewählt werden, weil es nicht die Inskription selbst ist, die die Last tragen sollte, die Macht der Wissenschaft zu erklären; es ist die Inskription *als präziser Abschluss und letzte Stufe* eines ganzen Mobilisierungsprozesses, die die Größenordnung der Rhetorik modifiziert. Ohne die Verlagerung ist die Inskription wertlos; ohne die Inskription ist die Verlagerung umsonst. Deshalb ist Mobilisierung nicht auf das Papier beschränkt, sondern Papier erscheint immer am Ende, wenn die Größenordnung dieser Mobilisierung vergrößert werden soll. Sammlungen von Gestein, ausgestopfte Tiere, Proben, Fossilien, Artefakte, Genbanken sind die ersten, die bewegt werden (Star/Griesemer 1989). Was zählt, ist das Aufstellen und Aufbieten von Ressourcen (Biographien von Naturalisten, z. B. übervoll mit Anekdoten über Kisten, Archive und Musterexemplare), aber diese Aufstellung ist niemals einfach genug. Sammlungen sind wesentlich, jedoch nur, solange die Archive gut sortiert und die Etiketten an Ort und Stelle sind und die Musterexemplare nicht verderben. Sogar das ist nicht genug, da eine Museumssammlung noch zu viel zur Bewältigung für einen „Geist" ist. Also wird die Sammlung gezeichnet, niedergeschrieben, aufgezeichnet – und dieser Prozess wird sich so lange abspielen, bis nicht besser kombinierbare geometrische Formen von den Mustern abgeleitet worden sind (wobei der Prozess, durch den die Musterexemplare aus ihrem Kontext extrahiert werden, noch andauert).

Das Phänomen, das wir hier behandeln, ist also nicht die Inskription per se, sondern die *Kaskade* immer simplifizierterer Inskriptionen, die die Produktion harter Fakten zu größeren Kosten ermöglicht. Beispielsweise erfolgt

die Beschreibung menschlicher Fossilien, die gewöhnlich anhand von Zeichnungen vorgenommen wurde, heute durch Überlagerung einer Anzahl von mechanischen Diagrammen auf die Zeichnungen. Obwohl die Fotographien des Himmels säuberliche kleine Flecken produzieren, sind sie immer noch viel zu reichhaltig und verwirrend für das menschliche Auge; deshalb wurden ein Computer- und Laserauge erfunden, um die Fotographien zu lesen, sodass der Astronom weder in den Himmel (zu kostspielig) noch auf Fotographien schaut (zu verwirrend). Die gesamte Taxonomie der Pflanzen ist in einer berühmten Reihe von Büchern in Kew Gardens enthalten, aber die Manipulation dieses Buches ist so schwierig wie die alter Manuskripte, da es nur an einem Ort existiert; ein anderer Computer hat nun die Instruktion erhalten, zu versuchen, die verschiedenen Drucke dieses Buches zu lesen und so viele Kopien des taxonomischen Inventars wie möglich zu erstellen.

Pinch (1985) zeigt einen schönen Fall von Akkumulation solcher Spuren, wobei jede Schicht erst auf die vorherige aufgelegt wird, wenn die Sicherheit über ihre Bedeutung stabilisiert ist. „Sehen" die Astrophysiker die Neutrinos der Sonne oder irgendwelche der vermittelnden „Schleier", Spitzen" und „Flecken", die durch Akkumulation das sichtbare Phänomen bilden? Wieder können wir feststellen, dass die von Eisenstein für die Druckerpresse erforschten Mechanismen auch heute noch an jeder Wissenschaftsfront gegenwärtig sind. Die Ethologie der Paviane z. B. war gewöhnlicherweise ein Prosatext, in dem der Erzähler über Tiere sprach; der Erzähler musste in den Text einschließen, was er oder sie zuerst als Bilder und dann als statistische Darstellung der Ereignisse gesehen hatte. Jedoch: Mit zunehmender Konkurrenz um die Konstruktion härterer Fakten beinhalten die Artikel jetzt mehr und mehr Schichten graphischer Darstellungen, und die von Tabellen, Diagrammen und Gleichungen zusammengefasste Kaskade von Spalten entfaltet sich noch. In der Molekularbiologie wurde Chromatographie vor ein paar Jahren als Bänder verschiedener Graustufen gelesen; die Interpretation dieser Stufen wird nun von einem Computer vorgenommen – und direkt aus dem Computer erhält man schließlich einen Text: „ATGCGTTCGC". Obwohl mehr empirische Studien in vielen verschiedenen Feldern gemacht werden sollten, scheint ein Trend in diesen Kaskaden zu liegen. Sie bewegen sich immer in Richtung eines stärkeren Verschmelzens von Ziffern, Zahlen und Buchstaben, was durch ihre homogene Behandlung als binäre Einheiten in und durch Computer extrem erleichtert wird.

Dieser Trend zu immer einfacheren Inskriptionen, die immer größere Mengen von Ereignissen an einem Ort mobilisieren, kann nicht verstanden werden, wenn man ihn von dem agonistischen Modell trennt, das wir als unseren Referenzpunkt verwenden. Es ist so notwendig wie der Wettlauf, Gräben an der Front von 1914 zu graben. Derjenige, der schlecht visualisiert, verliert den Kampf; seine Fakten halten nicht stand. Knorr hat dieses Argument kritisiert, indem sie den ethnomethodologischen Standpunkt eingenommen hat (1981). Sie argumentiert zu Recht, dass ein Bild oder Diagramm niemanden überzeugen kann, sowohl, weil immer viele Interpretationen möglich sind, als auch und vor allem, weil ein Diagramm einen Zweifler nicht dazu zwingt, es anzusehen. Sie erachtet das Interesse an Inskriptionsmitteln als eine Übertreibung der Macht der Semiotik (und noch dazu als eine französische). Eine solche Position verfehlt jedoch den Punkt meiner Argumentation. Genau weil der Abtrünnige immer entkommen und eine andere Interpretation ausprobieren kann, wird ihm von den Wissenschaftlern so viel Energie und Zeit gewidmet, um ihn *in die Ecke zu treiben* und ihn mit immer dramatischeren visuellen Effekten zu umgeben. Obwohl im *Prinzip* jede Interpretation jedem Text und jedem Bild entgegengestellt werden kann, ist das *in der Praxis* bei Weitem nicht der Fall; die Kosten des Widerspruchs steigen mit jeder neuen Sammlung, mit jeder neuen Etikettierung, jeder Neuzeichnung. Das trifft besonders zu, wenn die Phänomene, die wir glauben sollen, mit bloßem Auge nicht sichtbar sind; Quasare, Chromosomen, Hirnpeptide, Leptonen, Bruttosozialprodukte, Klassen und Küstenlinien werden niemals anders als durch das „bewehrte" Auge der Inskriptionsmittel gesehen. Folglich können eine weitere Inskription, ein weiterer Kniff, um den Kontrast zu erhöhen, eine einfache Vorrichtung, um den Hintergrund zu vermindern oder eine weitere Kolorierungsprozedur *genügen*, wobei alle anderen Dinge gleich bleiben, um die *Machtbalance umschwingen zu lassen* und eine unglaubwürdige Aussage in eine glaubwürdige zu verwandeln, die dann ohne weitere Modifikation weitergegeben wird. Die Wichtigkeit dieser Kaskade von Inskriptionen mag ignoriert werden, wenn man Ereignisse des täglichen Lebens erforscht, aber sie kann bei der Analyse von Wissenschaft und Technik nicht hoch genug geschätzt werden.

Genauer gesagt ist es möglich, die Inskription überzubewerten, nicht jedoch das Setting, in dem die Kaskade von immer mehr geschriebenen und nummerierten Inskriptionen produziert wird. Womit wir wirklich umgehen, ist das Staging einer Szenographie, in der die Aufmerksamkeit auf einen bestimmten Satz dramatisierter Inskriptionen konzentriert wird. Das Setting wirkt wie eine gewaltige optische Vorrichtung, die ein neues Labor, eine neue Art von Sehen und ein neues Phänomen erschafft. Ich zeigte ein solches Setting, das ich als „Pasteurs Theater der Beweise" (Latour 1988 a) erzählte. Pasteur arbeitet genauso viel auf der Bühne wie in der Szenerie und der Handlung. Was am Ende zählt, ist eine einfache visuelle Wahrnehmung: tote ungeimpfte Schafe gegen lebende geimpfte Schafe. Je früher wir in die Geschichte der Wissenschaft zurückgehen, je mehr Aufmerksamkeit wird dem Setting gezollt und je weniger den Inskriptionen selbst. In seinem faszinierenden Bericht seines Vakuumpumpen-Experiments – beschrieben von Shapin (1984) – musste Boyle z.B. nicht nur das Phänomen erfinden, sondern auch das Instrument, um es sichtbar zu machen und die Anordnung, in der das Instrument aufgestellt wurde, die geschriebenen und gedruckten Berichte, durch die der stille Leser „über" das Experiment lesen konnte, die Art von Zeugen, die auf der Bühne zugelassen wurden, und sogar die Arten von Kommentaren, die die potentiellen Zeugen äußern durften. „Das Vakuum zu sehen" war nur möglich, nachdem alle diese Zeugen diszipliniert worden waren.

Das Staging solcher „optischer Mittel" ist das von Eisenstein beschriebene: Einige Personen im selben Raum sprechen miteinander und verweisen auf zweidimensionale Bilder; diese Bilder sind alles, was man von den Dingen, über die sie sprechen, sehen kann. Nur weil wir an ein solches Staging gewöhnt sind und es wie frische Luft atmen, heißt das nicht, dass wir nicht all die kleinen Innovationen beschreiben sollten, die es zum kraftvollsten Instrument machen, um Macht zu gewinnen. Tycho Brahe in Oranienburg hatte zum ersten Mal in der Geschichte alle Vorhersagen – wörtlich alle „Vorher-*Sehungen*" – der Planetenbewegungen – am selben Ort, geschrieben in *derselben* Sprache oder *demselben* Code, kann auch er *seine* eigenen Beobachtungen lesen. Das ist mehr als genug Begründung für Brahes neue „Einsichten".

„Nicht weil er in den Nachthimmel statt in alte Bücher schaute, unterschied sich Tycho Brahe von den Sternbeobachtern der Vergangenheit. Ich glaube auch nicht, dass es deshalb war, weil er sich mehr als die Alexandriner oder die Araber für ‚sture Fakten' und präzise Messungen interessierte. Aber ihm standen wie nur wenigen vor ihm zwei getrennte Reihen von Berechnungen zur Verfügung, die auf zwei verschiedenen Theorien basierten, die im

Abstand von einigen Jahrhunderten zusammengetragen worden waren und die er miteinander vergleichen konnte." (Eisenstein 1979: 624)

Historiker sagen, dass er der erste war, der die Planetenbewegung mit einem von den Vorurteilen des dunklen Zeitalters befreiten Geist sah. Nein, sagt Eisenstein, er ist der erste, der nicht in den Himmel schaute, sondern simultan auf alle vorhergehenden Vorhersagen und seine eigene, die zusammen in derselben Form niedergeschrieben worden waren.

„Der dänische Beobachter war nicht nur der letzte der großen Beobachter mit bloßem Auge; er war auch der erste sorgfältige Beobachter, der die neuen Mächte der Druckerpresse vollkommen ausnutzen konnte – Mächte, die Astronomen dazu befähigten, Anomalien in den alten Aufzeichnungen aufzuspüren, die Position jedes Sterns präziser festzulegen und in Katalogen zu registrieren. Mitarbeiter in vielen Regionen aufzulisten, jede neue Beobachtung in permanenter Form festzuhalten und notwendige Korrekturen in nachfolgenden Ausgaben vorzunehmen." (Ebd.: 625)

Die Diskrepanzen mehrten sich, nicht indem man in den Himmel schaute, sondern indem man sorgfältig Spalten von Winkeln und Azimut übereinander lagerte. Kein Widerspruch, keine gegenteiligen Vorhersagen hätten jemals sichtbar sein können. Widerspruch ist, wie Goody sagt, weder eine Eigenschaft des Geistes noch der wissenschaftlichen Methode, sondern eine Fähigkeit, Buchstaben und Zeichen innerhalb neuer Settings zu lesen, die die Aufmerksamkeit allein auf die Inskriptionen fokussieren.

Derselbe Mechanismus ist in Roger Guillemins Vision des Endorphins, eines Gehirnpeptides, sichtbar – um ein Beispiel aus einer anderen Zeit und von einem anderen Ort heranzuziehen. Das Gehirn ist so obskur und ungeordnet wie der Renaissancehimmel. Sogar die vielen erstgradigen Purifikationen von Gehirnextrakten sind eine „Suppe" von Substanzen. Die ganze Forschungsstrategie ist es, klar lesbare Peaks aus einem wirren Hintergrund zu erhalten. Jede der Proben, die einen ordentlicheren Peak gewährt, wird wiederum gereinigt, bis es im kleinen Fenster des Hochdruckflüssigkeitschromatographen nur noch einen Peak gibt. Dann wird die Substanz in kleinsten Mengen in den Darm eines Meerschweinchens injiziert. Die Kontraktionen des Darms werden mittels elektronischer Hardware an einen Physiographen übermittelt. Woran kann man hier das Objekt „Endorphin" sehen? Die Überlagerung des ersten Peaks mit der Kurve des Physiographen beginnt ein Objekt zu produzieren, dessen Grenzen die im Labor produzierten visuellen Inskriptionen sind. Das Objekt ist nicht mehr oder weniger ein reales Objekt als jedes andere, da viele solcher visuellen Schichten produziert werden können. Sein Widerstand als reales Faktum hängt nur von der Anzahl solcher visuellen Schichten ab, die Guillemins Labor auf einmal an einem Ort vor dem Kritiker mobilisieren kann. Für jeden „Einwand" gibt es eine Inskription, die den Dissens blockiert; bald ist der Zweifler gezwungen, das Spiel aufzugeben oder später mit anderem und besserem Anschauungsmaterial wiederzukommen. Durch die Mobilisierung von immer mehr treuen Verbündeten wird innerhalb der Wände des Laboratoriums langsam Objektivität errichtet.

## IV. Inskriptionen kapitalisieren, um Verbündete zu mobilisieren

Können wir zusammenfassen, weshalb es für Brahe, Boyle, Pasteur oder Guillemin so wichtig ist, an zweidimensionalen Inskriptionen statt am Himmel, an der Luft, der Gesundheit oder dem Gehirn zu arbeiten? Was können sie mit dem Ersten machen, was sie nicht mit dem Zweiten tun können? Lassen Sie mich ein paar Vorteile der „Schreibarbeit" auflisten.

1. Inskriptionen sind *mobil*, worauf ich in La Perouses Fall hingewiesen habe. Chinesen, Planeten, Mikroben – keines dieser Elemente kann sich bewegen; Landkarten, fotographische Stiche und Petrischalen jedoch können es.

2. Sie sind *unveränderlich*, wenn sie sich bewegen – oder zumindest wird alles getan, um dieses Ergebnis zu erhalten: Musterexemplare werden chloroformiert, Mikrobenkolonien in Gelatine eingelegt, sogar explodierende Sterne werden in jeder Phase ihrer Explosion auf Millimeterpapier aufgezeichnet.

3. Sie werden *flach* gemacht. Es gibt nichts, was so einfach zu dominieren ist wie eine flache Oberfläche auf ein paar Quadratmetern; nichts ist versteckt oder gewunden, keine Schatten, kein „double entendre". Wenn sowohl in der Politik als auch in der Wissenschaft von jemandem gesagt wird, er „meistere" eine Frage oder er „dominiere" einen Sachverhalt, sollte man normalerweise nach einer flachen Oberfläche suchen, die Beherrschung ermöglicht (eine Karte, eine Liste, eine Akte, ein Zensus, die Wand einer Galerie, ein Kartenindex, ein Repertoire), und man wird ihn finden.

4. Der *Maßstab* der Inskriptionen kann willentlich modifiziert werden, ohne irgendwelche Änderungen ihrer internen Proportionen. Beobachter bestehen niemals auf dieser einfachen Tatsache: Gleichgültig, welche (rekonstruierte) Größe die Phänomene haben, sie enden alle damit, nur mit derselben Durchschnittsgröße erforscht zu werden. Milliarden von Galaxien sind, wenn sie gezählt werden, niemals größer als nanometergroße Chromosomen; der internationale Handel ist niemals größer als Mesonen; Maßstabmodelle von Ölraffinerien haben am Ende dieselben Dimensionen wie Plastikmodelle von Atomen. Die Verwirrung beginnt wieder außerhalb von ein paar Quadratmetern. Diese triviale Veränderung des Maßstabs erscheint harmlos genug, ist jedoch der Grund für den größten Teil der „Überlegenheit" von Wissenschaftlern und Ingenieuren: Niemand sonst befasst sich mit Phänomenen, die mit den Augen dominiert und mit den Händen gefasst werden können; gleichgültig, aus welcher Zeit und woher sie kommen oder was ihre ursprüngliche Größe ist.

5. Sie können *reproduziert* und mit geringen Kosten verbreitet werden, sodass alle Momente in der Zeit und alle Orte im Raum in einem anderen Raum und einer anderen Zeit gesammelt werden können. Dies ist „Eisensteins Effekt".

6. Da diese Inskriptionen mobil, flach, reproduzierbar, still und von variierendem Maßstab sind, können sie neu gemischt und neu *kombiniert* werden. Das meiste, was wir Verbindungen im Geist zuschreiben, kann durch dieses erneute Mischen von Inskriptionen erklärt werden, die alle dieselbe „optische Konsistenz" haben. Dasselbe trifft auf das zu, was wir „Metapher" nennen (vgl. Latour/Woolgar 1979: Kap. 4; Goody 1977; Hughes 1979; Ong 1982).

7. Ein Aspekt dieser Neukombinationen ist die Möglichkeit, verschiedene Bilder von vollkommen unterschiedlichem Ursprung und Maßstab zu *überlagern*. Es scheint eine unmögliche Aufgabe zu sein, Geologie und Ökonomie zu verbinden. Die Überlagerung der geologischen Karte mit einem Ausdruck des Rohstoffmarktes an der New Yorker Börse erfordert gute Dokumentation und ein paar Zentimeter. Das Meiste, was wir „Struktur", „Muster", „Theorie" und „Abstraktion" nennen, sind Konsequenzen solcher Überlagerungen (Bertin 1973). „Denken ist Handarbeit", sagt Heidegger; was aber in den Händen ist, sind Inskriptionen. Lévi-Strauss' Theorien über die Wilden sind ein Artefakt der Kartenindexierung am Collège de France, genauso wie Rames Theorie für Ong ein Artefakt der in der Sorbonne gesammelten Drucke darstellt oder moderne

Taxonomie ein Ergebnis der Buchhaltung ist, die unter anderem in Kew Gardens unternommen wird.

8. Einer der wichtigsten Vorteile ist jedoch, dass die Inskription (nach etwas Reinigung) zum *Bestandteil eines geschriebenen Texts* gemacht werden kann. An anderer Stelle habe ich ausführlich diese allgemeine Grundlage erörtert, auf der Inskriptionen, die von Instrumenten kommen, sich mit bereits veröffentlichten Texten und neuen, im Entwurf befindlichen Texten vereinen. Dieses Charakteristikum wissenschaftlicher Texte ist für die Ver-gangenheit von Ivins und Eisenstein demonstriert worden. Ein heutiges Labor kann immer noch als einzigartiger Ort definiert werden, an dem ein Text gemacht wird, um Dinge zu kommentieren, die alle noch präsent sind. Weil der Kommentar, frühere Texte (durch Zitate und Referenzen) und „Dinge" dieselbe optische Konsistenz und dieselbe semiotische Homogenität haben, wird durch das Schreiben und Lesen dieser Artikel ein außerordentlicher Grad an Sicherheit erreicht (Latour/Bastide 1983; Lynch 1985 a; Law 1983). Der Text ist nicht einfach „illustriert", sondern er trägt alles, was es zu sehen gibt, in sich. Durch das Labor haben der Text und das Spektakel der Welt am Ende denselben Charakter.

9. Der letzte Vorteil ist jedoch der größte. Der zweidimensionale Charakter von Inskriptionen erlaubt ihnen, *mit der Geometrie zu verschmelzen*. Wie wir bei der Perspektive gesehen haben, kann zwischen Raum auf Papier und dreidimensionalem Raum eine Kontinuität hergestellt werden. Das Ergebnis ist, dass wir auf dem Papier mit Linealen und Zahlen arbeiten können, aber noch immer dreidimensionale Objekte „dort draußen" manipulieren (Ivins 1973). Besser noch: Aufgrund dieser optischen Konsistenz kann alles, gleichgültig, woher es kommt, in Diagramme und Zahlen umgewandelt werden; Kombinationen von Zahlen und Tafeln können verwendet werden, die noch einfacher zu handhaben sind als Wörter und Silhouetten (Dagognet 1973). Man kann die Sonne nicht messen, aber man kann eine Fotographie der Sonne mit einem Lineal messen. Dann kann die abgelesene Anzahl an Zentimetern einfach verschiedene Maßstäbe durchlaufen und die Solarmasse völlig verschiedener Objekte liefern. Dies nenne ich in Ermangelung eines besseren Begriffes den *zweitgradigen* Vorteil von Inskriptionen oder den Mehrwert, der durch ihre Kapitalisierung erzielt wird.

Diese neun Vorteile sollten nicht voneinander isoliert werden und immer in Verbindung mit dem Mobilisierungsprozess betrachtet werden, den sie beschleunigen und zusammenfassen. Jede mögliche Innovation, die irgendeinen dieser Vorteile bietet, wird in anderen Worten von eifrigen Wissenschaftlern und Ingenieuren ausgewählt: neue Fotographien; neue Farben, um mehr Zellkulturen einzufärben; neues reaktives Papier; ein empfindlicherer Physiograph; ein neues Indexsystem für Bibliothekare; eine neue Notation für algebraische Funktionen; ein neues Heizungssystem, um Proben länger zu halten. Die Wissenschaftsgeschichte ist die Geschichte dieser Innovationen. Die Rolle des Geistes wurde genau wie die der Wahrnehmung gewaltig übertrieben (Arnheim 1969). Ein durchschnittlicher Geist oder ein durchschnittlicher Mensch mit durchschnittlichen Wahrnehmungsfähigkeiten, innerhalb normaler sozialer Bedingungen, wird abhängig davon, ob er oder seine durchschnittlichen Fähigkeiten auf die verwirrende Welt oder auf Inskriptionen angewendet werden, vollkommen unterschiedliche Outputs erzeugen.

Es ist besonders interessant, sich auf den neunten Vorteil zu konzentrieren, weil er uns einen Weg eröffnet, „Formalismus" zu einer profaneren und materielleren Realität zu machen. Um sich von „empirisch" zu „theoretisch" zu bewegen, muss die Wissenschaft von langsameren zu schnelleren mobilen Elementen, von veränderlicheren zu weniger veränderlichen Inskriptionen gehen. Die Tendenzen, die wir oben studiert haben, brechen nicht zusammen, wenn wir den Formalismus betrachten, sondern nehmen im Gegenteil auf phantastische Weise zu. Tatsächlich ist, was wir Formalismus nennen, *die Beschleunigung der Verlagerung ohne Transformation*. Um diesen Punkt zu erfassen, müssen wir zurück zu Abschnitt 2 gehen. Die Mobilisierung vieler Ressourcen durch Raum und Zeit ist wesentlich für die Dominierung in großem Maßstab. Ich schlug vor, diese Objekte, die es erlauben, dass diese Mobilisierung stattfindet „unveränderlich mobile Elemente" zu nennen. Ich argumentierte ebenfalls, dass die besten dieser mobilen Elemente mit geschriebenen, nummerierten oder optisch konsistenten Papieroberflächen zu tun haben. Ich wies aber auch darauf hin – ohne jedoch eine Erklärung anzubieten –, dass wir mit Kaskaden von immer stärker vereinfachten und kostspieligeren Inskriptionen umgehen müssen. Diese Fähigkeit zur Kaskadenbildung muss nun erklärt werden, weil die Sammlung schriftlicher und bildlicher Ressourcen an einem Ort – auch mit Hin- und Rückverbindungen – demjenigen, der sie sammelt, allein noch *keine* Überlegenheit garantiert. Wieso? Weil der Sammler solcher Spuren sofort von ihnen überflutet wird. Ich habe ein solches Phänomen in Guillemins Labor beschrieben: Nach nur ein paar Tagen, in denen die Instrumente in Betrieb waren, gab es Stapel von Ausdrucken, genug, um den Verstand fassungslos zu machen (Latour/Woolgar 1979: Kap. 2). Dasselbe passierte Darwin nach ein paar Jahren des Sammelns von Musterexemplaren mit dem *Beagle*; es gab so viele Kisten, dass Darwin geradezu aus seinem Haus gedrückt wurde. Allein helfen die Inskriptionen also nicht, dass eine Örtlichkeit ein Zentrum wird, das den Rest der Welt dominiert. Etwas muss mit der Inskription gemacht werden, das dem ähnlich ist, was Inskriptionen mit „Dingen" tun, sodass am Ende einige Elemente alle anderen in großem Maßstab manipulieren können. Dieselbe Deflationsstrategie, die wir verwendeten, um zu zeigen, wie „Dinge" in Papier verwandelt werden, kann ebenfalls zeigen, wie Papier in *weniger* Papier umgewandelt werden kann. Nehmen wir als Beispiel „Die Effektivität der Arbeit Galileos", wie sie bei Drake betrachtet wird (1970). Drake verwendet tatsächlich das Wort Formalismus, um das zu kennzeichnen, wozu Galileo fähig war, seine Vorgänger jedoch nicht. Was beschrieben wird, ist jedoch interessanter als dies. Drake vergleicht die Diagramme und Kommentare Galileos mit denen von zwei älteren Gelehrten, Jordan und Stevin. Interessanterweise wird in Jordans Demonstration „das physikalische Element, wie man sieht, als ein Nachgedanke zur Geometrie eingebracht, gleichsam mit Gewalt" (1970: 103). Bei Stevins Diagramm ist es das Gegenteil: „Die vorherige Situation ist umgekehrt; Geometrie ist zugunsten reiner mechanischer Intuition eliminiert." (Ebd.) Was also scheinbar passiert, ist, dass Galileos zwei Vorgänger das Problem nicht visuell auf einer Papieroberfläche unterbringen und das Resultat gleichzeitig sowohl als Geometrie als auch als Physik betrachten konnten. Eine einfache Veränderung in der von Galileo verwendeten Geometrie gestattete ihm, viele verschiedene Probleme zu verbinden, während seine zwei Vorgänger an unverbundenen Formen arbeiteten, die sie nicht kontrollieren konnten:

„Galileos Art, Geometrie und Physik zu verschmelzen, wurde in seinem Beweis desselben Theorems in seinem frühen Traktat über Bewegung aus dem Jahr 1590 offensichtlich. Die Methode selbst legte ihm nicht nur viele logische Schlussfolgerungen nahe, sondern auch sukzessive Verbesserungen des Beweises selbst und dessen weitere physikalische Implikationen." (Ebd.: 104)

Diese Fähigkeit der Verbindung könnte in Galileos Geist lokalisiert werden. Was faktisch verbunden wird, sind drei verschiedene visuelle Horizonte, die synoptisch gehalten werden, weil die Papieroberfläche als geometrischer Raum betrachtet wird:

„Man sieht, wie die gesamte Demonstration eine *Reduktion* des Problems des Gleichgewichts auf geneigten Flächen zum Hebel konstituiert, die in sich selbst das Theorem aus der Isolation, in dem es zuvor stand, herausholt." (Ebd.: 106)

Dieser harmlose Begriff „aus der Isolation herausholen" wird fortwährend von denen gebraucht, die über Theorien sprechen. Kein Wunder. Wenn man Galileos Diagramm hält, hält man drei Domänen, wenn man die anderen hält, nur eine. Das von einer Theorie gestattete „Halten" ist nicht mysteriöser (und auch nicht weniger mysteriös) als das Halten von Armeen, von Aktien oder von Positionen im Raum. Es ist faszinierend zu sehen, dass Drake die Effizienz von Galileos Verbindung in Begriffen seiner Kreation eines geometrischen Mediums, in dem Geometrie und Physik verschmelzen, erklärt. Diese ist eine viel materiellere Erklärung als Koyrés idealistische, obwohl die „Sache" in Drakes Darstellung ein bestimmter Typ von Inskription auf Papier und eine bestimmte Betrachtungsweise dessen ist.

Ähnliche Taktiken, die Diagramme verwenden, um schnelle Verbindungen zwischen vielen unverbundenen Problemen herzustellen, werden von kognitiven Psychologen dokumentiert. Herbert Simon (1982) vergleicht die Taktiken von Experten und Anfängern im Zeichnen von Diagrammen, wenn sie über einfache physikalische Probleme befragt werden (Pumpen, Wasserfluss usw.). Der wesentliche Unterschied zwischen Experten und Anfängern ist genau derselbe, den Drake herausstellt:

„Das Wesentliche, das im Verhalten der Experten aufschien, war, dass die Formulierung der initialen und der finalen Bedingung auf eine Weise zusammengestellt wurde, dass die Beziehung zwischen ihnen und also die Antwort wesentlich von ihm [dem Diagramm] abgelesen werden konnte." (Ebd.: 169)

Mit dieser Frage vor Augen ist man beeindruckt von den Metaphern, die die „Theoretiker" verwenden, um Theorien zu feiern und ihnen Ränge zuzuteilen.[12] Die zwei Hauptarten von Metaphern bestehen in erhöhter Mobilität respektive erhöhter Unveränderbarkeit. Gute Theorien werden schlechten gegenübergestellt oder zu „bloßen Sammlungen empirischer Fakten", weil sie einen „leichten Zugang zu ihnen" gewähren. Hankel kritisiert z. B. Diophantus mit den Worten, die ein französischer Ingenieur verwenden würde, um das nigerianische Autobahnsystem zu verunglimpfen:

„Jede Frage erfordert eine ganz bestimmte Methode, die danach nicht einmal für ganz ähnliche Probleme dient. Es ist dementsprechend auch nach dem Studium von 100 Diophantischen Lösungen schwierig für einen modernen Mathematiker, das 100. Problem zu lösen; wenn wir den Versuch gemacht haben und nach einigen vergeblichen Unternehmungen Diophantus' eigene Lösung lesen, werden wir erstaunt sein zu sehen, wie er plötzlich die breite Hauptstraße verlässt, in einen Seitenweg rast und mit einer schnellen Drehung das Ziel erreicht." (Zitiert in Bloor 1976: 102)

Der sichere Pfad der Wissenschaft, wie Kant sagen würde, ist nicht derselbe für die Griechen, die Bororos und für uns; genauso wenig sind die Transportmittel identisch. Man könnte einwenden, dass diese nur Metaphern sind. Ja, aber die Etymologie des Begriffs *metaphoros* selbst ist erhellend. Genau bedeutet er Verlagerung, Transport, Transfer. Gleichgültig, ob sie bloße Bilder sind, *tragen* diese Metaphern treffend die Obsession der Theoretiker für einfachen Transport und schnelle Kommunikation. Eine kraftvollere Theorie, behaupten wir, ist die, die mit weniger Elementen und wenigeren und einfacheren Transformationen ermöglicht, an jede andere (vergangene und zukünftige) Theorie heranzukommen. Jedes Mal, wenn eine starke Theorie gefeiert wird, ist es möglich, diese Bewunderung in Begriffen des trivialsten Machtkampfes neu zu formulieren: Diesen Platz zu halten gestattet mir, alle anderen zu halten. Dies ist das Problem, dem wir durch diesen gesamten Artikel hindurch begegnet sind: wie man viele Verbündete an einem Ort versammelt (Latour 1988 b). Inskriptionen gestatten *Konskription*!

Eine ähnliche Verbindung zwischen der Fähigkeit zu abstrahieren und der praktischen Arbeit der Mobilisierung von Ressourcen, ohne sie zu transformieren, ist in weiten Teilen der kognitiven Wissenschaft erkennbar. In Piagets Tests wird beispielsweise viel Aufhebens um Wasser gemacht, das aus einem kleinen dünnen Becher in einen kurzen, flachen gegossen wird. Wenn die Kinder sagen, das Wasservolumen habe sich verändert, sind sie nicht konservativ. Wie aber jeder Laborbeobachter weiß, hängen die meisten Phänomene davon ab, welches Maß man abliest oder welchem man im Fall einer Diskrepanz glaubt. Die Verschiebung von nicht konservativ zu konservativ mag nicht eine Modifikation in der kognitiven Struktur sein, sondern eine Verschiebung der Indikatoren: Lies die Höhe des Wassers im ersten Becher ab und glaube ihm *mehr* als der Markierung des flachen Bechers. Die Idee des „Volumens" wird zwischen den kalibrierten Bechern genauso *gehalten* wie Guillemins Endorphin zwischen verschiedenen Peaks von mindestens fünf verschiedenen Instrumenten. Piaget bittet in anderen Worten seine Kinder, ein Laborexperiment auszuführen, das in der Schwierigkeit dem eines durchschnittlichen Nobelpreisträgers vergleichbar ist. Wenn irgendeine Verschiebung im Denken auftritt, hat das nichts mit dem Denken zu tun, sondern mit der Manipulation der Laboreinrichtung. Aus dieser Einrichtung kann keine Antwort über Volumen abgelesen werden. Der beste Beweis dafür ist, dass Piaget selbst ohne industriell kalibrierte Becher vollkommen unfähig wäre zu entscheiden, was konservativ ist (vgl. auch Cole/Scribner 1974: letztes Kap.). Wieder einmal mag das Meiste, dem wir a priori „höhere kognitive Funktionen" zugestehen, konkrete Aufgaben sein, die mit neu kalibrierten, graduierten und geschriebenen Objekten ausgeführt werden. Allgemeiner ausgedrückt ist Piaget von Konservation und Verlagerung durch den Raum ohne Veränderung besessen (Piaget/Garcia 1983). Denken ist gleichbedeutend mit der Fähigkeit, sich so schnell wie möglich zu bewegen, während man so viel wie möglich vom Muster konserviert. Was Piaget als die Logik der Psyche bezeichnet, ist die tatsächliche Logik der Mobilisierung und Unveränderbarkeit, die unseren wissenschaftlichen Gesellschaften so eigen ist, wenn sie harte Fakten zur Dominierung in einem großen Maßstab produzieren wollen. Kein Wunder, dass sich alle diese „Fähigkeiten", sich in solch einer Welt schnell zu bewegen, mit der Schulbildung verbessern![13]

Wir kommen nun näher an ein Verständnis jenes Sachverhalts, der Formalismus konstituiert. Der Ausgangspunkt ist, dass wir fortlaufend zwischen einer Vielzahl oft widersprüchlicher Indikationen unserer Sinne zögern. Das Meiste, was wir „Abstraktion" nennen, ist in der Praxis der Glaube, dass einer geschriebenen Inskription mehr Glauben geschenkt werden muss als jeglicher widersprüchlichen Indikation der Sinne.[14] Koyré z. B. hat gezeigt, dass Galileo an das Trägheitsprinzip aus mathematischen Gründen glaubte, sogar entgegen widersprüchlicher Beweise, die ihm nicht nur von den Schriften, sondern auch von seinen Sinnen geboten wurden. Koyré bemerkt, dass diese Zurückweisung der Sinne auf Galileos platonistische Philosophie zurückging. Dies mag so gewesen sein. Aber was bedeutet das in der Praxis? Es bedeutet, dass, wenn Galileo mit vielen gegensätzlichen Indikationen konfrontiert wurde, er in letzter Instanz dem Dreieckdiagramm für die Berechnung des Gesetzes fallender Körper mehr glaubte als jeder anderen Vision fallender Körper (Koyré 1966: 147): „Im Zweifel glaube den Inskriptionen, die in mathematischen

Begriffen ausgedrückt sind, *ungeachtet*, zu welchen Absurditäten dich das führt."[15]

Nach Eisensteins großartiger Überarbeitung der „Buch der Natur"-Argumentation und Alpers Neudefinition von „visueller Kultur" ist die Ethnographie der Abstraktion einfacher geworden: Was ist diese Gesellschaft, in der eine geschriebene, gedruckte, mathematische Form im Zweifelsfall größere Glaubwürdigkeit besitzt als alles andere: als gesunder Menschenverstand, andere Sinne als Sehen, politische Autorität, Tradition und sogar heilige Schriften? Es ist offensichtlich, dass dieser Wesenszug der Gesellschaft überdeterminiert ist, da er im geschriebenen Gesetz (Clanchy 1979), in der biblischen Exegese der heiligen Schriften und in der Geschichte der Geometrie (Husserl 1954; Derrida 1967; Serres 1980) gefunden werden kann. Ohne diese sonderbare Tendenz, das Geschriebene zu privilegieren, wäre die Macht der Inskriptionen vollkommen verloren, worauf Edgerton in seiner Diskussion chinesischer Diagramme hinweist. Gleichgültig, wie schön, reich, präzise oder realistisch Inskriptionen sein mögen, niemand würde glauben, was sie zeigten, wenn ihnen andere Beweise örtlichen, sinnlichen Ursprungs oder Erklärungen örtlicher Behörden widersprechen könnten. Ich glaube, dass wir einen beachtlichen Schritt vorwärts machen würden, wenn wir diesen besonderen Wesenszug unserer Kultur mit den Erfordernissen der Mobilisierung, die ich bereits mehrmals dargestellt habe, verbinden könnten. Ein Großteil der kognitiven Psychologie und Epistemologie existiert nicht, sondern ist mit diesem seltsamen anthropologischen Puzzle verbunden: mit einer Ausbildung (oft in Schulen), um geschriebene Inskriptionen zu manipulieren, sie in Kaskaden aufzustellen und der letzten in der Reihe mehr als jedem gegenteiligen Beweis zu glauben. In der Beschreibung dieser Ausbildung sollte die Anthropologie der Geometrie und der Mathematik stärker betont werden (Livingston 1986, Lave 1986, 1988; Serres 1982).

## V.
## Papierarbeit

Es gibt zwei Arten, den Visualisierungsprozess, an dem wir alle interessiert sind, zu ignorieren: erstens, dem wissenschaftlichen Denken das zuzuschreiben, was eigentlich Händen, Augen und Zeichen zusteht; zweitens, sich ausschließlich auf Zeichen *qua* Zeichen zu konzentrieren, ohne die Mobilisierung zu erwägen, deren feinen Rand sie lediglich darstellen. Ob die Wahl aller Innovationen im Erstellen von Bildern, in Gleichungen, Kommunikationen, Archiven, Dokumentationen, Instrumentationen und Argumentationen für oder gegen sie ausfällt, hängt davon ab, wie sie gleichzeitig entweder die Inskription oder die Mobilisierung beeinflussen. Dieses Bindeglied ist nicht nur in den empirischen Wissenschaften sichtbar, nicht nur im (früheren) Bereich von Formalismus, sondern ebenfalls in vielen „praktischen" Unternehmungen, von denen die Wissenschaft oft übermäßig getrennt wird.

In einem schönen Buch verfolgt Booker die Geschichte des technischen Zeichnens (1982). Lineare Perspektive (vgl. oben) „veränderte" progressiv „das Konzept des Bildes von der bloßen Repräsentation zur Projektion auf eine Ebene" (ebd.: 31). Aber die Perspektive hing noch von der Position des Beobachters ab, sodass die Objekte ohne Beeinträchtigung nicht wirklich überallhin bewegt werden konnten. Desargues und Monges Arbeiten

„halfen den ‚Blickpunkt', oder die Art der Betrachtung von Dingen seelisch zu verändern. Anstelle der imaginären Linien des Raumes, die man nur sehr schwierig klar wahrnehmen kann, die zu dieser Zeit die Basis der Perspektive waren, erlaubte die projektive Geometrie es, die Perspektive in Begriffen der soliden Geometrie zu sehen." (Booker 1982: 34)

Mit der deskriptiven Geometrie wird die Position des Beobachters irrelevant.

„Es kann von jedem Winkel betrachtet oder fotographiert oder auf jede Ebene projiziert – d.h. verzerrt – werden und das Resultat bleibt wahr." (Ebd.: 35)

Booker und sogar noch besser Baynes und Push (1981) zeigen in einem ausgezeichneten Buch (vgl. auch Deforges 1981), wie ein paar Ingenieure enorme Maschinen *meistern* konnten, die noch nicht einmal existierten. Diese Glanzleistungen sind ohne technische Zeichnungen nicht vorstellbar. Booker, der einen Ingenieur zitiert, beschreibt die Veränderung des Maßstabs, der den Wenigen erlaubt, die Vielen zu dominieren:

„Eine gezeichnete Maschine ist wie eine ideale Realisation davon, jedoch in einem Material, das wenig kostet und einfacher zu handhaben ist als Eisen oder Stahl. [...] Wenn alles zuerst gut ausgedacht ist und die wesentlichen Dimensionen durch Berechnungen oder Erfahrung bestimmt sind, kann der Plan einer Maschine oder die Installation schnell auf Papier gebracht und das Ganze genauso wie das Detail danach auf bequemste Weise der schärfsten Kritik ausgesetzt werden. Wenn es zuerst Zweifel gibt, welches der verschiedenen möglichen Arrangements das wünschenswerteste ist, werden sie alle aufgezeichnet, miteinander verglichen und das passendste auf einfache Weise gewählt." (Booker 1982: 187)

Eine industrielle Zeichnung erschafft nicht nur eine Papierwelt, die wie in drei Dimensionen manipuliert werden kann. Sie kreiert auch einen gemeinsamen Platz, an dem viele andere Inskriptionen zusammenkommen können. Toleranzgrenzen können auf der Zeichnung inskribiert, die Zeichnung für ökonomische Berechnungen, für eine Definition der zu erfüllenden Aufgabe oder zur Organisation der Reparaturen und Verkäufe verwendet werden.

„Zeichnungen sind jedoch nicht nur für die Planung, sondern auch für die Ausführung von äußerster Wichtigkeit, da durch sie von Anfang an die Bemessungen und Proportionen aller Teile so genau und endgültig festgelegt werden können, dass, wenn es zur Herstellung kommt, es nur noch notwendig ist, in den für die Konstruktion verwendeten Materialien genau das zu imitieren, was in der Zeichnung gezeigt wird. Jeder Teil der Maschine kann im Allgemeinen unabhängig von jedem anderen Teil hergestellt werden; deshalb ist es möglich, die gesamte Arbeit unter einer großen Anzahl von Arbeitern aufzuteilen. [...] Keine substantiellen Fehler können in der auf diese Weise organisierten Arbeit auftreten, und falls einmal ein Fehler gemacht wird, weiß man sofort, wer dafür verantwortlich ist." (Ebd.: 188)

Realitätssphären, die weit entfernt zu liegen scheinen (Mechanik, Ökonomie, Marketing, wissenschaftliche Organisationen), sind nur noch Zentimeter entfernt, wenn sie einmal auf derselben Oberfläche ausgebreitet werden. Die Ballung von Zeichnungen in einem optisch konsistenten Raum ist einmal mehr der „universelle Austauscher", der es erlaubt, Arbeit zu planen, prompt zu erledigen, zu erkennen und Verantwortlichkeit zuzuweisen.[16] Die verbindende Qualität geschriebener Spuren ist sogar noch sichtbarer im meistverachteten aller ethnographischen Objekte: in der Akte oder der Aufzeichnung. Die der Bürokratie seit Hegel und Weber gewährte „Rationalisierung" wurde versehentlich dem „Geist" (preußischer) Bürokraten zugeschrieben: Es liegt alles in den Akten selbst. Ein Büro ist – in vielen Hinsichten und mit jedem Jahr zunehmend – ein kleines Laboratorium, in dem viele Elemente miteinander verbunden werden können, weil ihr Maßstab und ihre Natur angeglichen wurden: juristische Texte, Spezifikationen, Standards, Gehaltslisten, Landkarten, Untersuchungen (seit der Eroberung durch die Normannen, wie aufgezeigt bei Clanchy 1979). Ökonomie, Politik, Soziologie

und harte Wissenschaften kommen nicht durch den grandiosen Zugang der „Interdisziplinarität" in Kontakt, sondern durch die Hintertür der *Akte*. Das „Kratie" im Wort „Bürokratie" ist mysteriös und schwer zu erforschen, aber das „Büro" ist etwas, das empirisch untersucht werden kann und das aufgrund seiner Struktur erklärt, weshalb etwas Macht an einen durchschnittlichen Geist abgegeben wird, einfach indem man Akten durchsieht: Weit entfernte Domänen rücken in unmittelbare Nähe, verschlungene und versteckte Domänen werden flach. Tausende von Vorkommnissen können synoptisch betrachtet werden. Noch wichtiger ist, dass, wenn Akten einmal überall zusammengetragen werden, um eine Hin- und Rückzirkulation unveränderlich mobiler Elemente sicherzustellen, sie in einer Kaskade aufgestellt werden können: Akten über Akten können erzeugt werden und man kann diesen Prozess fortsetzen, bis einige Menschen Millionen betrachten, als wären sie in ihrer Handfläche. Ironischerweise macht sich der gesunde Menschenverstand über diese „gratte-papiers" oder „Papiertiger" lustig und fragt sich, wozu dieser „Papierkrieg" notwendig ist; dieselbe Frage sollte jedoch bezüglich aller Themen von Wissenschaft und Technik gestellt werden. In unserer Kultur ist der Umgang mit Akten und Papier der Ursprung aller essentiellen Macht, was konstant der Aufmerksamkeit entgeht, da man deren Materialität ignoriert.

In seinem grundlegenden Buch „The Pursuit of Power" (1982) benutzt McNeill diese Fähigkeit, um chinesische Bürokratie von der des Okzidents zu unterscheiden. Die Akkumulation von Aufzeichnungen und Ideogrammen machten das chinesische Imperium möglich. Es gibt jedoch einen wesentlichen Nachteil bei Ideogrammen; wenn sie einmal gesammelt sind, kann man sie nicht zu einer Kaskade zusammenstellen, sodass Tausende von Aufzeichnungen – in eine verwandelt –, wortwörtlich durch geometrische oder mathematische Kompetenz „punktualisiert" werden können. Wenn wir sowohl die Qualität der Zeichen als auch den Mobilisierungsprozess im Fokus behalten, können wir verstehen, wieso dem Wachstum des chinesischen Imperiums in der Vergangenheit bestimmte Grenzen gesetzt worden sind und wieso diese Grenzen der Mobilisierung von Ressourcen in großem Maßstab in Europa durchbrochen worden sind. Die Macht, die durch die Konzentration von in einer homogenen und kombinierbaren Form verfassten Akten erlangt wird, kann man kaum hoch genug einschätzen (Wheeler 1969; Clanchy 1979).

Diese Rolle des Bürokraten, qua Wissenschaftler, qua Schreiber und Leser wird immer missverstanden, weil wir als selbstverständlich annehmen, dass irgendwo in der Gesellschaft Makro-Akteure existieren, die auf natürliche Weise die Szene dominieren: Korporationen, Staaten, Produktionskräfte, Kulturen, Imperialismus, „mentalités" usw. Wenn sie einmal akzeptiert sind, werden diese großen Entitäten verwendet, „kognitive" Aspekte der Wissenschaft und Technik zu erklären (oder nicht zu erklären). Das Problem ist, dass diese Einheiten ohne die Konstruktion eines langen Netzwerkes, in dem zahlreiche getreue Aufzeichnungen – Aufzeichnungen, die wiederum zusammengefasst und ausgestellt sind, um zu überzeugen – in beiden Richtungen zirkulieren, überhaupt nicht existieren könnten. Ein „Staat", eine „Korporation", eine „Kultur" oder eine „Ökonomie" sind das Ergebnis eines Punktualisierungsprozesses, der einige Indikatoren aus vielen Spuren herausholt. Um existieren zu können, müssen diese Entitäten irgendwo *zusammengefasst* sein (Chandler 1977; Beniger 1986). Weit davon entfernt, der Schlüssel zum Verständnis von Wissenschaft und Technik zu sein, sind diese Entitäten die tatsächlichen Dinge, die ein neues Verständnis von Wissenschaft und Technik erklären sollten. Die Akteure im großen Maßstab, denen Wissenschaftssoziologen gern „Interessen" beifügen, sind praktisch immateriell, solange keine präzisen Mechanismen vorgeschlagen werden, um ihren Ursprung oder ihre Extraktion und ihren Maßstabwechsel zu erklären.

Ein Mensch ist niemals viel mächtiger als ein anderer – sogar von einem Thron aus; von einem Mann jedoch, dessen Auge Aufzeichnungen dominiert, durch die gewisse Verbindungen mit Millionen anderer hergestellt werden können, kann man sagen, dass er dominiert. Diese Herrschaft ist jedoch kein gegebenes Faktum, sondern eine langsame Konstruktion, und sie kann korrodiert, unterbrochen oder zerstört werden, wenn die Aufzeichnungen, Akten und Zahlen immobilisiert, veränderbarer und weniger les- und kombinierbar oder bei ihrer Ausstellung undeutlich gemacht werden. Der *Maßstab* eines Akteurs ist mit anderen Worten kein absoluter, sondern ein relativer Begriff, der mit der Fähigkeit variiert, Information über andere Orte oder Zeiten zu produzieren, zu erfassen, zusammenzufassen und zu interpretieren (Callon/Latour 1981). Sogar die bloße Idee eines Maßstabs ist unmöglich zu verstehen, ohne eine Inskription oder Karte im Kopf zu haben. Der „große Mann" ist ein kleiner Mann, der auf eine gute Karte schaut. In Mercators Frontispiz wird Atlas von einem Gott, der die Welt trägt, in einen Wissenschaftler verwandelt, der sie in den Händen hält.

Seit dem Anfang der Darstellung darüber, wie man Dinge zusammenzieht, habe ich das einfache Problem von Macht umgeformt: Wie können die Wenigen die Vielen dominieren? Nach McNeills Hauptrekonzeptualisierung der Geschichte der Macht in Begriffen der Mobilisierung kann diese jahrhundertealte Frage der politischen Philosophie und Soziologie in einer anderen Weise umformuliert werden: Wie können entfernte oder fremde Orte und Zeiten an einem Ort versammelt werden in einer Form, die all den Orten und Zeiten gestattet, auf einmal präsentiert zu werden, und es ihnen zudem erlaubt, sich dorthin zurück zu bewegen, woher sie kommen? Über Macht zu sprechen ist eine endlose und mystische Aufgabe; von Distanz, Sammlung, Loyalität, Zusammenfassung, Transmission zu sprechen ist eine empirische Aufgabe, wie in einer neuen Studie von John Law über die portugiesische Gewürzroute nach Indien (1986) illustriert worden ist. Statt wie die meisten Wissenschaftler große Entitäten zu verwenden, um Wissenschaft und Technik zu erklären, sollten wir bei den Inskriptionen und ihren Mobilisierungen beginnen und sehen, wie sie kleinen Entitäten helfen, zu großen zu werden. In dieser Verschiebung von einem Forschungsprogramm zu einem anderen werden „Wissenschaft und Technik" aufhören, mysteriöse kognitive Objekte zu sein, die durch die soziale Welt erklärt werden müssen. Sie werden zu einer der Hauptquellen von Macht (McNeill 1982). Wenn man die Existenz von Makro-Akteuren als selbstverständlich annimmt, ohne das Material zu erforschen, das sie „makro" macht, macht man damit sowohl Wissenschaft als auch Gesellschaft mysteriös. Das Herstellen verschiedener Maßstäbe zu unserem Hauptinteresse zu machen bedeutet, die praktischen Mittel zur Erlangung von Macht auf eine feste Basis zu stellen (Cicourel 1981). Das Pentagon *sieht* nicht mehr von der Strategie der Russen als Guillemin von seinen Endorphinen. Es setzt einfach seinen Glauben in übereinander gelagerte Spuren verschiedener Qualität, stellt einige anderen gegenüber, geht den Schritten jener nach, die zweifelhaft sind, und gibt Milliarden dafür aus, neue Zweige von Wissenschaft und Technik zu schaffen, die die Mobilität von Spuren beschleunigen, ihre Unveränderbarkeit perfektionieren, die Lesbarkeit erhöhen, Kompatibilität sicherstellen, die Anzeige beschleunigen: Satelliten, Spionagenetzwerke, Computer, Bibliotheken, Radioimmunountersuchungen, Archive, Studien. Das Pentagon wird niemals mehr von diesen Phänomenen sehen als das, was

es durch diese unveränderlich mobilen Elemente aufbauen kann. Das ist *offensichtlich*, wird aber selten *gesehen*.

Wenn diese kleine Verschiebung von einer sozial/kognitiven Unterscheidung zum Studium von Inskriptionen akzeptiert wird, dann erscheint die Wichtigkeit der *Metrologie* im rechten Licht. Metrologie ist die wissenschaftliche Organisation stabiler Messungen und Standards. Ohne sie ist keine Messung stabil genug, um weder Homogenität der Inskriptionen noch ihre Umkehr zuzulassen. Es ist deshalb auch nicht überraschend, wenn man erfährt, dass die Metrologie bis zu dem Dreifachen des Budgets aller Forschungen und Entwicklungen kostet und dass sich diese Zahl nur auf die ersten Elemente der metrologischen Kette bezieht (Hunter 1980). Dank der metrologischen Organisation können die grundlegenden physikalischen Konstanten (Zeit, Raum, Gewicht, Wellenlänge) und viele biologische und chemische Standards „überallhin" ausgeweitet werden. (Zerubavel 1982; Landes 1983). Die Universalität von Wissenschaft und Technik ist ein Klischee der Epistemologie, aber Metrologie ist die praktische Durchsetzung dieser mystischen Universalität. In der Praxis ist sie kostspielig und voller Lücken (vgl. Cochrane 1966 für die Geschichte des Eichamts). Metrologie ist nur die offizielle und primäre Komponente einer stetig wachsenden Anzahl von Messaktivitäten, die wir alle in unserem täglichen Leben unternehmen müssen. Jedes Mal, wenn wir auf unsere Armbanduhr schauen oder eine Wurst bei einem Metzger wiegen lassen, jedes Mal, wenn Laboratorien die Bleibelastung oder die Reinheit des Wassers messen oder die Qualität von Industriegütern kontrollieren, erlauben wir mehr unveränderlich mobilen Elementen neue Orte zu erreichen. „Rationalisierung" hat sehr wenig mit der Vernunft der Büro- und Technokraten, aber eine Menge mit der Erhaltung metrologischer Ketten zu tun (Uselding 1981). Der Aufbau langer Netzwerke gewährleistet die Stabilität der physikalischen Hauptkonstanten, aber es gibt viele andere metrologische Aktivitäten für weniger „universelle" Messungen (Abstimmungen, Fragebögen, auszufüllende Formulare, Konten, Zählungen).

Es gibt noch eine weitere Domäne, in die diese Ethnographie der Inskription etwas „Licht" bringen könnte. Ich möchte darüber sprechen, weil ich am Anfang dieser Übersicht die Dichotomien zwischen „mentalistischen" und „materialistischen" Erklärungen zurückwies. Unter diesen interessanten, unveränderlich mobilen Elementen gibt es eines, das sowohl zu viel als auch zu wenig Aufmerksamkeit erhalten hat: das Geld. Die Anthropologie des Geldes ist so kompliziert und verwirrend wie die des Schreibens. Eines jedoch ist klar: Sobald Geld durch verschiedene Kulturen zu zirkulieren beginnt, entwickelt es einige deutlich ausgeprägte Charakteristika: Es ist mobil (in kleinen Teilen), unveränderlich (da es aus Metall besteht), zählbar (wenn es einmal gemünzt ist), kombinierbar und kann von den gewerteten Dingen zum bewertenden Zentrum zirkulieren und zurück. Geld hat zu viel Aufmerksamkeit erhalten, weil man es für etwas Besonderes gehalten hat, tief eingefügt in die Infrastrukturen von Ökonomien, während es einfach eines von vielen unveränderlich mobilen Elementen ist, die notwendig sind, wenn ein Ort über viele andere Orte, die in Raum und Zeit weit entfernt sind, Macht ausüben soll. Als ein Typ eines unveränderlich mobilen Elementes *unter anderen* hat es jedoch zu wenig Aufmerksamkeit erhalten. Geld wird verwendet, um alle Arten von Sachverhalten in genau derselben Weise zu kodieren, in der La Pérouse alle Orte mit Längengrad und Breitengrad kodierte. (Tatsächlich registrierte er in seinem Logbuch sowohl die Plätze auf der Karte als auch den Wert jedes Gutes, als sollte es an einem anderen Ort verkauft werden.) Auf diese Weise ist es möglich, alle diese Arten von Sachverhalten zu akkumulieren, zu zählen, zu zeigen und wieder zu verbinden. Geld ist weder mehr noch weniger „materiell" als Kartenzeichnen, technische Zeichnungen oder Statistiken.

Ist erst einmal sein gewöhnlicher Charakter erkannt, kann die „Abstraktion" des Geldes nicht länger das Objekt eines Fetischkults sein. Die Wichtigkeit der Kunst der Buchführung passt z. B. sowohl in der Ökonomie als auch in der Wissenschaft gut ins Bild. Geld als solches ist nicht interessant, sondern als eine Art unveränderlich mobiles Element, das Güter und Orte verbindet; es ist deshalb kein Wunder, dass es schnell mit anderen geschriebenen Inskriptionen wie Zahlen, Spalten und doppelter Buchführung verschmilzt (Roover 1963). Kein Wunder, dass es durch die Buchführung möglich ist, durch eine neue Kombination von Zahlen mehr zu verdienen (Braudel 1979: besonders Bd. 3; Chandler 1977). Hier sollte wieder nicht zu viel Betonung auf die Visualisierung von Zahlen per se gelegt werden; was man wirklich betonen sollte, ist die Kaskade mobiler Inskriptionen, die in einem Konto enden, was – buchstäblich – das Einzige ist, was *zählt*. Genau wie bei jeder wissenschaftlichen Inskription zieht der neue Buchhalter es im Zweifelsfalle vor, der Inskription zu glauben, gleichgültig, wie seltsam die Konsequenzen und kontraintuitiv das Phänomen erscheinen. Die Geschichte des Geldes ist also von denselben Trends ergriffen wie all die anderen unveränderlich mobilen Elemente; jede Innovation, die Geld beschleunigen kann, um seine Macht der Mobilisierung zu vergrößern, wird beibehalten: Schecks, Indossament, Papiergeld, elektronisches Geld. Dieser Trend hängt nicht von der Entwicklung des Kapitalismus ab. „Kapitalismus" ist im Gegenteil ein leeres Wort, solange nicht präzise materielle Instrumente vorgeschlagen werden, um Kapitalisierung überhaupt zu erklären, sei es die von Mustern, Büchern, Information oder Geld.

Folglich sollte der Kapitalismusbegriff nicht verwendet werden, um die Evolution von Wissenschaft und Technik zu erklären. Es scheint mir, als sollte es genau das Gegenteil sein. Wenn Wissenschaft und Technik in Begriffen von unveränderlich mobilen Elementen neu formuliert werden, wird es möglich, ökonomischen Kapitalismus als einen anderen Prozess von Mobilisierung und Konskription zu erklären. Die vielen Schwächen des Geldes weisen daraufhin; Geld ist ein hübsches, unveränderlich mobiles Element, das von einem Punkt zu einem anderen zirkuliert, jedoch sehr wenig bei sich trägt. Wenn das Ziel des Spiels darin besteht, genügend Verbündete an einem Ort zu akkumulieren, um den Glauben und das Verhalten aller anderen zu modifizieren, ist Geld eine schwache Ressource, solange es isoliert ist. Es wird nützlich, wenn es mit all den anderen Inskriptionsvorrichtungen verbunden wird; dann werden die verschiedenen Punkte der Welt tatsächlich in einer handhabbaren Form zu einem einzelnen Ort transportiert, der dann zu einem *Zentrum* wird. Genau wie bei Eisensteins Druckerpresse, die ein Faktor ist, der allen anderen erlaubt, miteinander zu verschmelzen, zählt nicht die Kapitalisierung des Geldes, sondern die Kapitalisierung aller kompatiblen Inskriptionen. Statt von Händlern, Prinzen, Wissenschaftlern, Astronomen und Ingenieuren zu sprechen, die eine Art von Beziehung zueinander haben, scheint es mir produktiver zu sein, über „Berechnungszentren" zu sprechen. Die Währung, in der sie rechnen, ist weniger wichtig als die Tatsache, dass sie nur mit Inskriptionen kalkulieren und in diese Kalkulationen Inskriptionen, die aus den verschiedenartigsten Disziplinen kommen, hineinmischen. Die Berechnungen selbst sind weniger wichtig als die Art, in der sie zu Kaskaden zusammengestellt werden, und die bizarre Situation, in der der letzten Inskription mehr geglaubt wird als allem anderen. Geld ist per se sicher nicht der universelle Standard, den Marx und andere Ökonomen suchten. Diese Qualifikation sollte Berechnungszentren und der Besonderheit geschriebener Spuren gewährt werden,

die schnelle Übersetzung zwischen einem Medium und einem anderen ermöglichen.

Viele Bemühungen wurden erbracht, um die Geschichte der Wissenschaft mit der Geschichte des Kapitalismus zu verbinden, und viele Bemühungen wurden erbracht, um den Wissenschaftler als Kapitalisten zu beschreiben. Alle diese Bemühungen (meine inbegriffen – Latour/Woolgar 1979: Kap. 5; Latour 1984 a) waren von Anfang an zum Scheitern verurteilt, da sie eine Unterscheidung zwischen mentalen und materiellen Faktoren als gegeben ansahen, ein Artefakt unserer Ignoranz bezüglich Inskriptionen.[17] Es gibt keine Geschichte der Ingenieure, dann der Kapitalisten, dann eine der Wissenschaftler, dann eine der Mathematiker, dann eine der Wirtschaftswissenschaftler. Es gibt vielmehr eine einzige Geschichte dieser Berechnungszentren. Es ist nicht nur, weil sie auf Karten, in Kontobüchern, Zeichnungen, Rechtstexten und Akten exklusiv aussehen, dass Kartographen, Händler, Ingenieure, Juristen und Bauingenieure den anderen überlegen sind. Es ist, weil alle diese Inskriptionen überlagert, neu gemischt, neu verbunden und zusammengefasst werden können und dass vollkommen neue Phänomene auftauchen, vor den anderen Leuten verborgen, von denen diese Inskriptionen erhoben worden waren.

Präziser ausgedrückt: Wir sollten mit dem Konzept und dem empirischen Wissen dieser Berechnungszentren in der Lage sein zu erklären, wie unbedeutende Menschen, die nur mit Papier und Zeichen arbeiten, die mächtigsten von allen werden. Papier und Zeichen sind unglaublich schwach und zerbrechlich. Deshalb erscheint es zuerst grotesk, irgendetwas mit ihnen erklären zu wollen. La Pérouses Karte ist nicht der Pazifik, genauso wenig wie Watts Zeichnungen und Patente die Maschinen sind oder die Wechselkurse der Bankiers die Ökonomien oder die Theoreme der Topologie die „echte Welt". Das ist genau das Paradoxon. Indem man nur auf Papier arbeitet, an zerbrechlichen Inskriptionen, die sehr viel weniger sind als die Dinge, aus denen sie extrahiert sind, ist es doch möglich, alle Dinge und alle Menschen zu dominieren. Was für alle anderen Kulturen unbedeutend ist, wird zum wichtigsten, zum einzig wichtigen Aspekt der Realität. Der Schwächste wird durch die obsessive und exklusive Manipulation aller möglichen Arten von Inskriptionen zum Stärksten. Dies ist das Verständnis von Macht, zu dem wir gelangen, wenn wir dem Thema von Visualisierung und Kognition in aller Konsequenz folgen. Wenn man verstehen möchte, was *Dinge* zusammenzieht, muss man sich anschauen, was Dinge *zusammen zeichnet*.

1 Der ursprüngliche Titel „Drawing Things Together" lässt sich in seiner doppelten Bedeutung von „Dinge an einem Ort zusammenziehen" und „visuell darstellen/zeichnen" nicht adäquat ins Deutsche übersetzen [Anm. d. Hg.].

2 Z. B. Lévi-Strauss' Unterscheidung zwischen Bastler und Ingenieur oder zwischen heißen und kalten Gesellschaften (1962); oder der von Garfinkel zwischen alltäglichen und wissenschaftlichen Gedankenmodi (1967); oder Bachelards vielen „coupures épistémologiques", die die Wissenschaft vom gesunden Menschenverstand, von der Intuition oder von ihrer eigenen Vergangenheit trennen (1934, 1967); oder Hortens differenzierte Unterscheidung zwischen der Akzeptanz von Monstern und ihrer Vermeidung (1977) oder primären und sekundären Theorien (1982).

3 Eine Tatsache ist härter oder weicher als eine Funktion dessen, was später in anderen Händen mit ihr geschieht. Jeder von uns agiert als ein Multikonduktor für die vielen Ansprüche, die uns begegnen: Wir mögen uninteressiert sein oder sie ignorieren oder interessiert sein – wir werden sie jedoch immer modifizieren und in etwas vollkommen anderes verwandeln. Manchmal agieren wir tatsächlich als Konduktor und geben den Anspruch ohne weitere Modifikation weiter (vgl. dazu Latour/Woolgar 1979; Latour 1984 b).

4 „Wissenschaft und Technik sind in mehr als direkter Proportion zur Fähigkeit des Menschen, Methoden zu entwickeln, durch die Phänomene, die andererseits nur durch die Sinne des Hörens, Schmeckens und Riechens erfahren werden könnten, vorangeschritten, in den Bereich des visuellen Erkennens und Messens gebracht worden und sind dann Gegenstand jener logischen Symbolisierung geworden, ohne die rationale Gedanken und Analyse unmöglich sind." (Ivins 1973: 13)

5 „Die bezeichnendsten Charakteristika der europäischen bildlichen Repräsentation seit dem 14. Jahrhundert waren einerseits ihr beständig zunehmender Naturalismus und andererseits ihre rein schematische und logische Ausdehnung. Es wird hier behauptet, dass beide in großen Teilen von der Entwicklung und Durchdringung von Methoden abhängen, die in invarianter Form wiederholbare Symbole bereitstellen, um das visuelle Bewusstsein und eine Grammatik der Perspektive zu repräsentieren, die es ermöglichten, logische Beziehungen nicht nur innerhalb des Symbolsystems, sondern auch zwischen dem System und den Formen und Örtlichkeiten der Objekte, die es symbolisiert, herzustellen." (Ivins 1973: 12)

6 „Charakteristischerweise versuchten nördliche Künstler, durch eine Transformation der Ausdehnung des Sehens auf ihre kleinen, flachen Arbeitsflächen alles zu repräsentieren [...]. Es ist die Kapazität der Bildoberfläche, eine Ähnlichkeit mit der Welt – ein Aggregat von Ansichten – zu beinhalten, die viele Bilder im Norden charakterisiert." (Ebd.: 51)

7 Der Beweis, dass die Bewegung zuerst kommt, liegt für Eisenstein in der Tatsache, dass sie den gegensätzlichen Effekt auf die heiligen Schriften mit sich bringt. Die Genauigkeit des Mediums enthüllt mehr und mehr die Ungenauigkeit in der Botschaft, die bald gefährdet ist. Die

Schönheit von Eisensteins Konstruktion liegt in der Art, in der sie zwei gegensätzliche Konsequenzen aus derselben Ursache erhält: Wissenschaft und Technik beschleunigen sich; das Evangelium wird zweifelhaft (Latour 1983).

8 Z. B. portraitiert Mukerji einen Geographen, der die neuen Geographiebücher hasst, seinem Hass jedoch in gedruckter Form Luft verschaffen muss. „Ironischerweise machte Davis seine Reise, weil er nicht darauf vertraute, dass gedruckte Information so komplett wie ein mündlicher Erfahrungsbericht ist; er beschloss jedoch, die Reise zu machen, nachdem er holländische Geographiebücher gelesen und aus seiner Reise einen anderen geographischen bzw. Navigationstext verfasst hatte." (Mukerji 1983: 114)

9 Aus diesem Grund schließe ich in die Diskussion die große Literatur über die Neurologie des Sehens oder über die Psychologie der Wahrnehmung nicht ein (vgl. z. B. Block 1981; de Mey 1982). Diese Disziplinen, wie wichtig sie auch sein mögen, verwenden den gleichen Prozess, den ich erforschen möchte, so ausgiebig, dass sie gegenüber einer Ethnographie der Kunstfertigkeit und den Tricks der Visualisierung so blind wie die anderen sind.

10 „Als wesentliches Element in den Räderwerken der Disziplin konstituiert sich eine ‚Schriftmacht', die sich zwar in vielen Punkten an die traditionellen Methoden der administrativen Dokumentation anlehnt, aber doch auch bedeutende Änderungen und Neuerungen einführt." (Foucault 1976: 244)

11 Diese einfachen Verschiebungen werden oft von Philosophen in vollkommene Trennungen vom gesunden Menschenverstand transformiert – etwa bei Bachelard in „coupures épistémologiques". Es ist nicht aufgrund der Naivität der Empiriker, dass man auf die Macht der Theorien zurückgreifen muss, um Daten einen Sinn zu geben. Der Fokus auf Inskriptionen und Manipulationen von Spuren liegt genau in der Mitte zwischen Empirie und Bachelards Argumentation über die Macht von Theorien.

12 Ein schönes Beispiel ist das von Carnots Thermodynamik, erforscht von Redondi (1980). Carnots Know-how bezieht sich nicht auf den Bau einer Maschine, sondern eher auf ein Diagramm. Dieses Diagramm ist so gezeichnet, dass es gestattet, von einer Maschine zu jeder weiteren zu gehen – und tatsächlich zu nichtexistenten Maschinen, die nur auf dem Papier gezeichnet waren. Wirkliche dreidimensionale Dampfmaschinen sind interessant, jedoch lokalisiert und schwerfällig. Für sie hat Thermodynamik dieselbe Bedeutung wie La Pérouses Karten für die pazifischen Inseln. Wenn man von einer Maschine zur Theorie geht oder von einer Insel zur Karte, geht man nicht vom Konkreten zum Abstrakten, vom Empirischen zum Theoretischen; man geht von einem Ort, der nichts dominiert, zu einem anderen Ort, der alle anderen dominiert. Wenn man Thermodynamik versteht, versteht man alle Maschinen (der Vergangenheit, der Gegenwart und der Zukunft – vgl. Diesel). Die Frage bei Theorien ist: Wer kontrolliert wen und zu welchem Ausmaß?

13 Einen schönen *a-contrario*-Beweis liefert Edgertons Studie zu chinesischen technischen Zeichnungen (1980). Er bemerkt, dass chinesische Künstler kein Interesse an Ziffern haben, oder genauer, dass sie Ziffern nicht in den perspektivischen Raum hineinnehmen, an dem ein Ingenieur arbeiten und Berechnungen und Vorhersagen machen kann, sondern sie als Illustrationen betrachten. Folglich werden alle Verbindungen zwischen den Teilen der Maschinen zu Dekorationen (ein komplexer Teil der Pumpe wird z.B. nach mehreren Kopien zu Wellen auf einem Teich!). Niemand würde behaupten, dass Chinesen nicht abstrahieren können; es wäre jedoch keineswegs absurd zu behaupten, dass sie nicht ihr volles Vertrauen in das Schreiben und in die graphische Darstellung setzen.

14 In einem schönen Artikel spricht Carlo Ginzburg von einem „Paradigma der Spuren", um diese besondere Obsession unserer Kultur zu bezeichnen, die er von der griechischen Medizin über Conan Doyles Detektivgeschichten, durch Freuds Interesse an Fehlleistungen bis zur Entdeckung von Kunstfälschungen (1980) aufspürt. Indem er jedoch auf ein klassisches Vorurteil zurückgreift, trennt Ginzburg Physik und harte Wissenschaften von einem solchen Paradigma, weil sie, wie er behauptet, sich nicht auf Spuren, sondern auf abstrakte, universelle Phänomene verlassen.

15 Ivins erklärt z. B., dass die meisten griechischen Parallelen in der Geometrie sich nicht treffen, weil sie mit den Händen berührt werden, während die Parallelen der Renaissance sich treffen, da sie nur auf Papier gesehen werden (1973: 7). Jean Lave zeigt in ihrer Studie kalifornischer Supermarkteinkäufer, dass Personen, die mit einer Schwierigkeit in ihren Berechnungen konfrontiert werden, selten beim Papier bleiben und niemals ihr Vertrauen in etwas Geschriebenes setzen (Lave et al. 1984). Es zu tun, gleichgültig, wie absurd die Konsequenzen sein mögen, erfordert eine zusätzliche Reihung sonderbarer Umstände, die mit der Laboreinrichtung verbunden sind, sogar wenn diese, wie Livingston (1986) sagt, „flache Laboratorien" sind. In einem seiner etwa zwölf Ursprünge der Geometrie argumentiert Serres, dass die Griechen, indem sie das Alphabet erfanden und damit jede Verbindung zwischen geschriebenen Formen und dem Bezeichneten abbrachen, die piktoriale Repräsentation bewältigen mussten. Er argumentiert, dass der von uns so genannte Formalismus ein Alphabettext ist, der versucht, visuelle Diagramme zu beschreiben. „Was ist diese Geometrie in der Praxis? Nicht >Idee<, sondern ein Tun, das sie voraussetzt. Sie ist in erster Linie eine Kunst des Zeichnens. Sie ist dann eine Sprache, die über die Zeichnung spricht, sei sie nun präsent oder abwesend." (Serres 1980: 176)

16 Die Verbindung zwischen technischem Denken und technischem Zeichnen ist so eng, dass Forscher sie sogar unwillentlich herstellen. Wenn z. B. Bertrand Gille die Schaffung eines neuen „système technique" in Alexandria während der hellenistischen Periode erklärt, ist er gezwungen, zu sagen, dass es die Verfügbarkeit einer guten Bibliothek und einer Sammlung von Maßstabsmodellen aller zuvor erfundenen Maschinen ist, die „bloße Praxis" in Techno-Logic

umwandelte (1980). Was das „système technique" zu einem System macht, ist die synoptische Vision aller vorherigen technischen Errungenschaften, die alle aus ihrer Isolation genommen werden. Die Verbindung ist am deutlichsten sichtbar, wenn eine Inskriptionsvorrichtung an eine arbeitende Maschine angeschlossen wird, um sie verständlich zu machen (Hills/Pacey 1981; Constant 1983). Eine schöne Darstellung der Papierwelt, die dazu notwendig ist, einen Computer real zu machen, findet sich in Kidder (1981). „Die Seele der Maschine" ist ein Stoß Papier.

17 Die Richtung, in die wir gehen, wenn wir solche Fragen stellen, ist sowohl von der der Wissenschaftssoziologie als auch von der der kognitiven Wissenschaften ziemlich verschieden (besonders wenn sie beide wie in Meys Synthese [1982] zu verschmelzen versuchen). Zwei jüngere Versuche wurden unternommen, um die feinen Strukturen der kognitiven Fähigkeiten mit der Sozialstruktur zu verbinden. Der erste verwendet Hesses Netzwerke und Kuhns Paradigmen (Barnes 1982), der zweite Wittgensteins „Sprachspiele" (Bloor 1983). Diese Versuche sind interessant, aber sie versuchen noch immer eine Frage zu beantworten, die der vorliegende Artikel zurückzuweisen wünscht: wie kognitive Fähigkeiten mit unseren Gesellschaften verbunden sind. Die Frage (und folglich die verschiedenen Antworten) geht von der Idee aus, dass der Stoff, aus dem Gesellschaft gemacht ist, irgendwie verschieden ist von dem unserer Wissenschaften, unserer Bilder und unserer Information. Das Phänomen, auf das ich mich konzentrieren möchte, unterscheidet sich etwas von jenen von Barnes und Bloor. Wir haben es mit einem einzelnen ethnographischen Rätsel zu tun: Einige Gesellschaften – tatsächlich sehr wenige – werden durch Kapitalisierung im großen Stil gebildet. Die Obsession mit schnellen Verlagerungen und stabilen Invarianzen, starken und sicheren Verbindungen, ist nicht Teil unserer Kultur oder durch soziale Interessen „beeinflusst"; sie ist unsere Kultur. Zu oft suchen Soziologen nach indirekten Beziehungen zwischen „Interessen" und „technischen" Details. Der Grund für ihre Blindheit ist einfach: Sie begrenzen die Bedeutung von „sozial" auf die Gesellschaft, ohne zu erkennen, dass die Mobilisierung von Verbündeten und im Allgemeinen die Transformation schwacher Assoziationen in starke auch die Bedeutung von „sozial" ist. Wieso nach weit hergeholten Verbindungen suchen, wenn technische Details der Wissenschaft direkt von Invarianz, Assoziation, Verlagerung, Unveränderbarkeit usw. sprechen (Law 1986; Latour 1984 b; Callon/Law/Rip 1986)?

LITERATUR

Alpers, S. (1983): *The Art of Describing: Dutch Art in the 17th Century*, Chicago: University of Chicago Press.

Arnheim, R. (1969): *Visual Thinking*, Berkeley: University of California Press.

Augé, M. (1975): *Theorie des pouvoirs et idéologie*, Paris: Hermann.

Bachelard, G. (1934): *Le nouvel esprit scientifique*, Paris: PUF.

Bachelard, G. (1967): *La formation de l'esprit scientifique*, Paris: Vrin.

Barnes, B. (1982): *T.S. Kuhn and Social Science*, London: Macmillan.

Baynes, K./Push, F. (1981): *The Art of the Engineer*, Guildford, Sussex: Lutherword Press.

Beniger, J. (1986): *The Control Revolution*, Cambridge, Mass.: Harvard University Press.

Bertin, J. (1973): *Sémiologie graphique*, Paris: Mouton.

Block, N. (Hg.) (1981): *Imagery*, Cambridge, Mass.: MIT Press.

Bloor, D. (1976): *Knowledge and Social Imagery*, London: Routledge.

Bloor, D. (1983): *Wittgenstein and the Social Theory of Knowledge*, London: Macmillan.

Booker, P.J. (1982): *A History of Engineering Drawing*, London: Northgate Publishing Co.

Bourdieu, P. (1972): *Esquisse d'une théorie de la pratique*, Genève: Droz.

Braudel, F. (1979): *Civilisation matérielle et capitalisme*, Paris: Armand Colin.

Callon, M./Latour, B. (1981): „Unscrewing the Big Leviathan". In: K. Knorr-Cetina/A.V. Cicourel (Hg.), *Toward an Integration of Micro- and Macro-Sociologies*, London: Routledge, 277–303.

Callon, M./Law, J./Rip, A. (Hg.) (1986): *Qualitative Scientometrics: Studies in the Dynamics of Science*, London: Macmillan.

Chandler, A. D. (1977): *The Visible Hand*, Cambridge, Mass.: Harvard University Press.

Cicourel, A. V. (1981): „Notes on the Integration of Micro and Macro Levels". In: K. Knorr-Cetina/A.V. Cicourel (Hg.), *Toward an Integration of Micro- and Macro-Sociologies*, London: Routledge, 51–80.

Clanchy, M. T. (1979): *From Memory to Written Records 1066–1300*, Cambridge, Mass.: Harvard University Press.

Cochrane, R. X. (1966): *Measure for Progress. A History of the National Bureau of Standards*, Washington, D.C.: U.S. Bureau of Commerce.

Cole, J./Scribner, S. (1974): *Culture and Thought. A Psychological Introduction*, New York: John Wiley and Sons.

Constant, E. W. (1983): „Scientific Theory and Technological Testability. Science, Dynamometer and Water Turbine in the 19th Century", In: *Technology and Culture 24/2*, 183–198.

Dagognet, F. (1969): *Tableau et langages de la chimie*, Paris: Le Seuil.

Dagognet, F. (1973): *Ecriture et iconographie*, Paris: Vrin.

Deforges, Y. (1981): *Le graphisme technique*, Le Creusot: Editions Champs-Vallon.

de Mey, M. (1982): *The Cognitive Paradigm*. Dordrecht: D. Reidel.

Derrida, J. (1967): *De la grammatologie*. Paris: Editions de Minuit.

Drake, (1970): *Galileo Studies*, Ann Arbor: University of Michigan Press.

Edgerton, S. (1976): *The Renaissance Discovery of Linear Perspective*, New York: Harper and Row.

Edgerton, S. (1980): „The Renaissance Artist as a Quantifier". In: M. A. Hagen (Hg.), *The Perception of Pictures, Bd. 1*, New York: Academic Press, 179–212.

Eisenstein, E. (1979): *The Printing Press as an Agent of Change*, Cambridge: Cambridge University Press.

Fabian, J. (1983): *Time and the Other: How Anthropology Makes its Object*, New York: Columbia University Press.

Ferguson, E. (1977): „The Mind's Eye. Nonverbal Thought in Technology". In: *Science 197*, 827 ff.

Ferguson, E. (1985): „La fondation des machines modernes: des dessins". In: B. Latour (Hg.), *Les „vues" de l'esprit*, Sonderausgabe von *Culture Technique*, 183–208.

Foucault, M. (1963): *Naissance de la clinique: une archéologie du regard médical*, Paris: PUF.

Foucault, M. (1966): *Les mots et les choses*, Paris: Gallimard.

Foucault, M. (1976): *Überwachen und Strafen. Die Geburt des Gefängnisses*, Frankfurt a. M.: Suhrkamp.

Fourquet, M. (1980): *Les comptes de la puissance*, Paris: Encres.

Garfinkel, H. (1967): *Studies in Ethnomethodology*, Englewood Cliffs, N.J.: Prentice-Hall.

Gille, B. (1980): *Les ingénieurs grecs*, Paris: Le Seuil.

Ginzburg, C. (1980): „Signes, traces, pistes". In: *Le Débat 6*, 2–44.

Goody, J. (1977): *The Domestication of the Savage Mind*, Cambridge: Cambridge University Press.

Hagen, M. A. (1980): *The Perception of Pictures*, Tome I und II, New York: Academic Press.

Hanson, N. R. (1962): *Perception and Discovery. An Introduction to Scientific Inquiry*, San Francisco: W. H. Freeman.

Havelock, E. B. (1980): *Aux origines de la civilisation écrite en occident*, Paris: Maspero.

Hills, R./A.J. Pacey (1982): „The Measurement of Power in Early Steam Dream Textile Mills". In: *Technology and Culture 13/1*, 25 ff.

Hollis, M./Lukes, S. (Hg.) (1982): *Rationality and Relativism*, Oxford: Blackwell.

Horton, R. (1977): „African Thought and Western Science". In: B. Wilson (Hg.), *Rationality*, Oxford: Blackwell, 153–187.

Horton, R. (1982): „Tradition and Modernity Revisited". In: M. Hollis/ S. Lukes (Hg.), *Rationality and Relativism*, Oxford: Blackwell, 201–260.

Hughes, T. (1979): „The System-Builders". In: *Technology and Culture 20/1*, 124–161.

Hunter, P. (1980): „The National System of Scientific Measurement". In: *Science 210*. 869–874.

Husserl, E. (1954/1962): *L'origine de la géométrie*, Paris: PUF.

Hutchins, E. (1980): *Culture and Inference: a Trobriand Case Study*, Cambridge, Mass.: Harvard University Press.

Ivins, W. M. (1953): *Prints and Visual Communications*, Cambridge, Mass.: Harvard University.

Ivins, W. M. (1973): *On the Rationalization of Sight*, New York: Plenem Press.

Kidder, T. (1981): *The Soul of a New Machine*, London: Allen Lane.

Koyré, A. (1966): *Etudes galiléennes*, Paris: Hermann.

Knorr, K. D. (1981): *The Manufacture of Knowledge*, Oxford: Pergamon Press.

Knorr, K. D./Ocourel, A.V. (Hg.) (1981): *Toward an Integration of Micro- and Macro-Sociologies*, London: Routledge.

Landes, D. (1983): *Revolution in Time: Clocks and the Making of the Modem World*, Cambridge, Mass.: Harvard University Press.

La Pérouse, J. F. de (o. J.): *Voyages autour du monde*, Paris: Michel de l'Ormeraie.

Latour, B. (1983): „Comment redistribuer le grand partage?". In: *Revue Internationale de Synthese 104/110*, 202–236.

Latour, B. (1984 a): „Le dernier des capitalistes sauvages, interview d'un biochimiste". In: *Fundamenta Scientiae 4 (3/4)*, 301–327.

Latour, B. (1984 b): *Les microbes: guerre et paix suivi des irréductions*, Paris: Métailié.

Latour, B. (1985): „Les ‚vue's de l'esprit", Sonderausgabe von *Culture Technique*.

Latour, B. (1987): *Science in Action*, Cambridge, Mass.: Harvard University Press.

Latour, B. (1988 a): *The Pasteurization of France*, Cambridge, Mass.: Harvard University Press.

Latour, B. (1988 b*): A Relativistic Account of Einstein's Relativity*, Cambridge Mass.: Harvard University Press.

Latour, B./Bastide, F. (1983): „Essai de Science-Fabrication". In: *Etudes Françaises 19*, numéro spécial sur la littérature scientifique, 11–132.

Latour, B./Woolgar, S. (1979/1986): *Laboratory Life: The Social Construction of Scientific Facts*, London: Sage. (1986, 2. Aufl., Princeton: Princeton University Press.)

Lave, J. (1986): „Tue Values of Quantification". In: J. Law (Hg.), *Power, Action and Belief: a New Sociology of Knowledge?*, London: Routledge and Kegan Paul, 88–111.

Lave, J. (1988): *Cognition in Practice*, Cambridge: Cambridge University Press.

Lave, J./Murtaugh, M./De La Rocha, O. (1984): „The Dialectic of Arithmetic in Grocery Shopping". In: B. Rogoff/J. Lave (Hg.), *Everyday Cognition: Its Development in Social Context*, Cambridge, Mass.: Harvard University Press, 9–40.

Law, J. (1983): „Enrôlement et contre-enrôlement. Les luttes pour la publication d'un article scientifique". In: *Social Science Information 22/2*, 237–251.

Law, J. (1985): „Les textes et leurs alliés". In: B. Latour (Hg.), „Les ‚vues' de l'esprit", Sonderausgabe von *Culture Technique*, 58–70.

Law, J. (1986): „On the Methods of Long-distance Control. Vessels, Navigations and the Portuguese Route to India". In: J. Law (Hg.), *Power, Action and Belief: a New Sociology of Knowledge?*, London: Routledge and Kegan Paul, 234–263.

Leroi-Gourhan, A. (1964): *Le geste et la parole*, Paris: Albin Michel.

Lévi-Strauss, C. (1962): *La pensée sauvage*, Paris: Plon.

Livingston, E. (1986): *An Ethnomethodological Investigation of the Foundations of Mathematics*, London: Routledge and Kegan Paul.

Lynch, M. (1985 a): „Discipline and the Material Form of Images. An Analysis of Scientific Visibility". In: *Social Studies of Science 15*, 37–66.

Lynch, M. (1985 b): *Art and Artefact in Laboratory Science*, London: Routledge and Kegan Paul.

McNeill, W. (1982): *The Pursuit of Power: Technology, Armed Forces and Society since A. D. 1000*, Chicago: University of Chicago Press.

Mukerji, S. (1983): *From Graven Images. Patterns of Modern Materialism*, New York: Columbia University Press.

Ong, W. (1971): *Rhetoric. Romance and the New Technology*, Ithaca, N.Y.: Cornell University Press.

Ong, W. (1982): *Orality and Literacy. The Technologizing of the World*, London: Methuen.

Perret-Clermont, A. N. (1979): *La construction de l'intelligence dans l'interaction sociale*, Berne: Peter Lang.

Piaget, J./Garcia. R. (1983): *Psychogenèse et histoire des sciences*, Paris: Flammarion.

Pinch, T. J. (1985): „Toward an Analysis of Scientific Observations. The Externality of Evidential Significance of Observational Reports in Physics". In: *Social Studies of Science 15*, 7–37.

Redondi, P. (1980): *L'accueil des idées de Sadi Carnot. De la légende à l'histoire*, Paris: Vrin.

Roover, R. de (1963): *The Rise and Decline of the Medici Bank*, Cambridge, Mass.: Harvard University Press.

Rudwick, M. (1976): „The Emergence of a Visual Language for Geological Sciences: 1760–1840". In: *History of Science 14*, 148–195.

Serres, M. (1980): *Le passage du Nord-Ouest*, Paris: Editions de Minuit.

Serres, M. (1982): *Hermes*, Baltimore: Johns Hopkins University Press.

Shapin, S. (1984): „Pump and Circumstance. Robert Boyle's Literary Technology". In: *Social Studies of Science 14*, 481–521.

Simon, H. (1982): „Cognitive Processes of Experts and Novices". In: *Cahier de la Fondation Archives Jean Piaget 2/3*, 154–178.

Sohn-Rethel, A. (1978): *Manual and Intellectual Labor. A Critique of Epistemology*, London: Macmillan.

Star, S. L. (1983): „Simplification in Scientific Work. An Example from Neuroscience Research". In: *Social Studies of Science 13*, 205–228.

Star, S. L/Griesemer, J. R. (1989): „Institutional Ecology, ‚Translations', and Boundary Objects. Amateurs and Professionals in Berkeley's Museum of Vertebrate Zoology, 1907-1939". In: *Social Studies of Science 19*, 387–420.

Uselding, P. (1981): „Measuring Techniques and Manufacturing Practice". In: O. Mayr/R. Post (Hg.), *Yankee Enterprise*, Washington, D.C.: Smithsonian Institute Press, 103–123.

Wheeler, J. (1969): *On Record Files and Dossiers in American Life*, New York: Russell Sage Foundation.

Zerubavel, E. (1982): „The Standardization of Time. A Sociohistorical Perspective". In: *American Sociological Review 88/1*, 1–29.

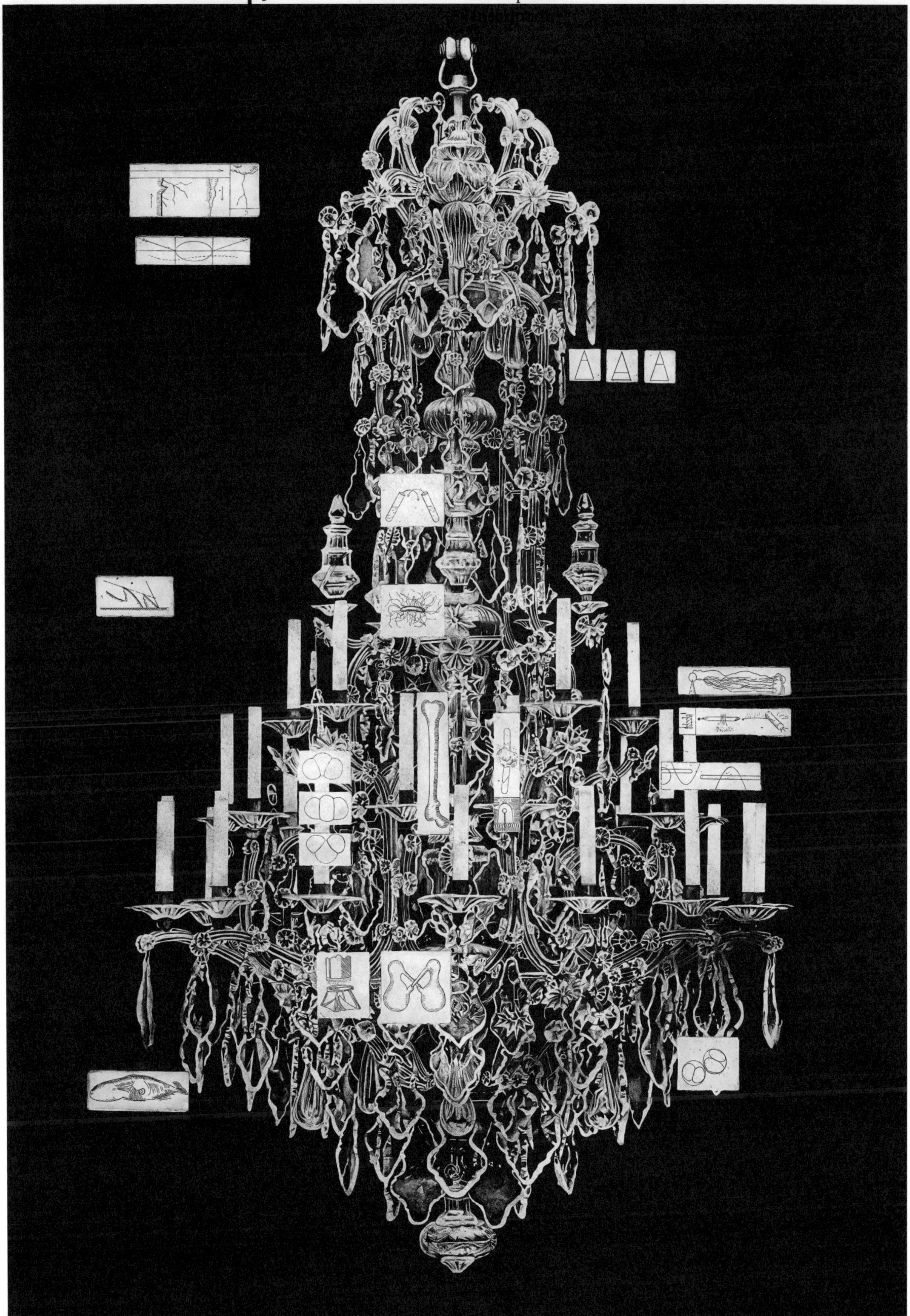

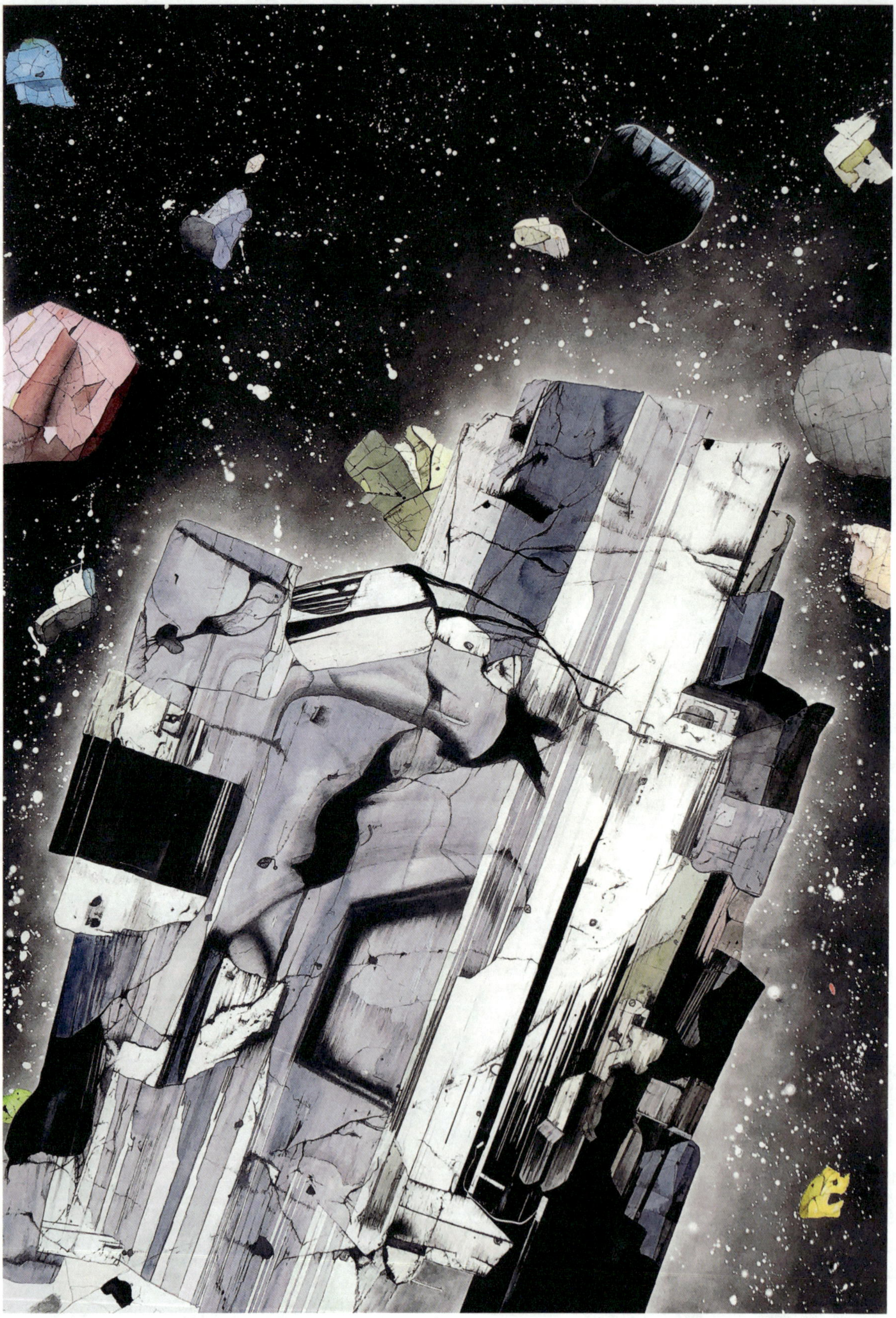

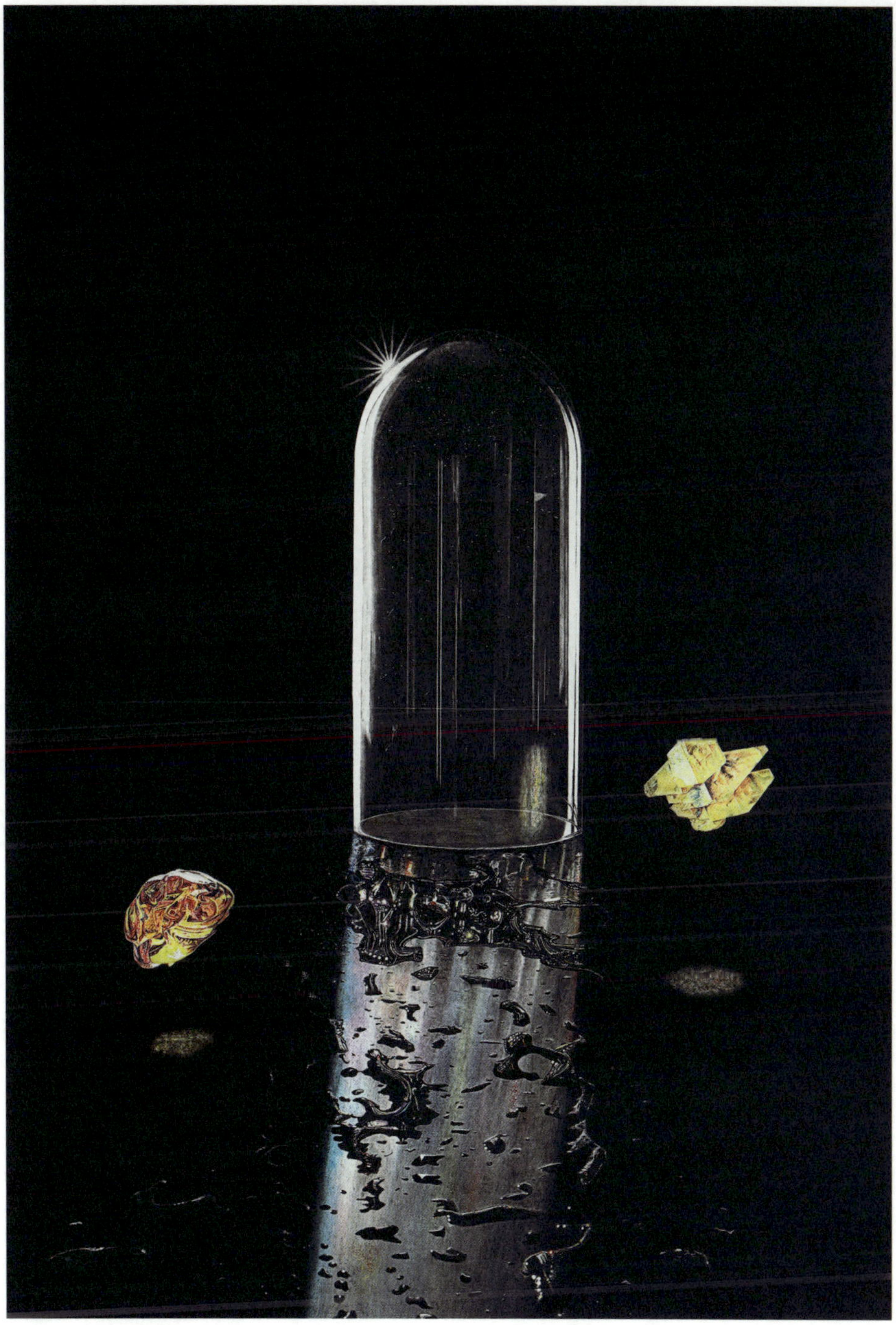

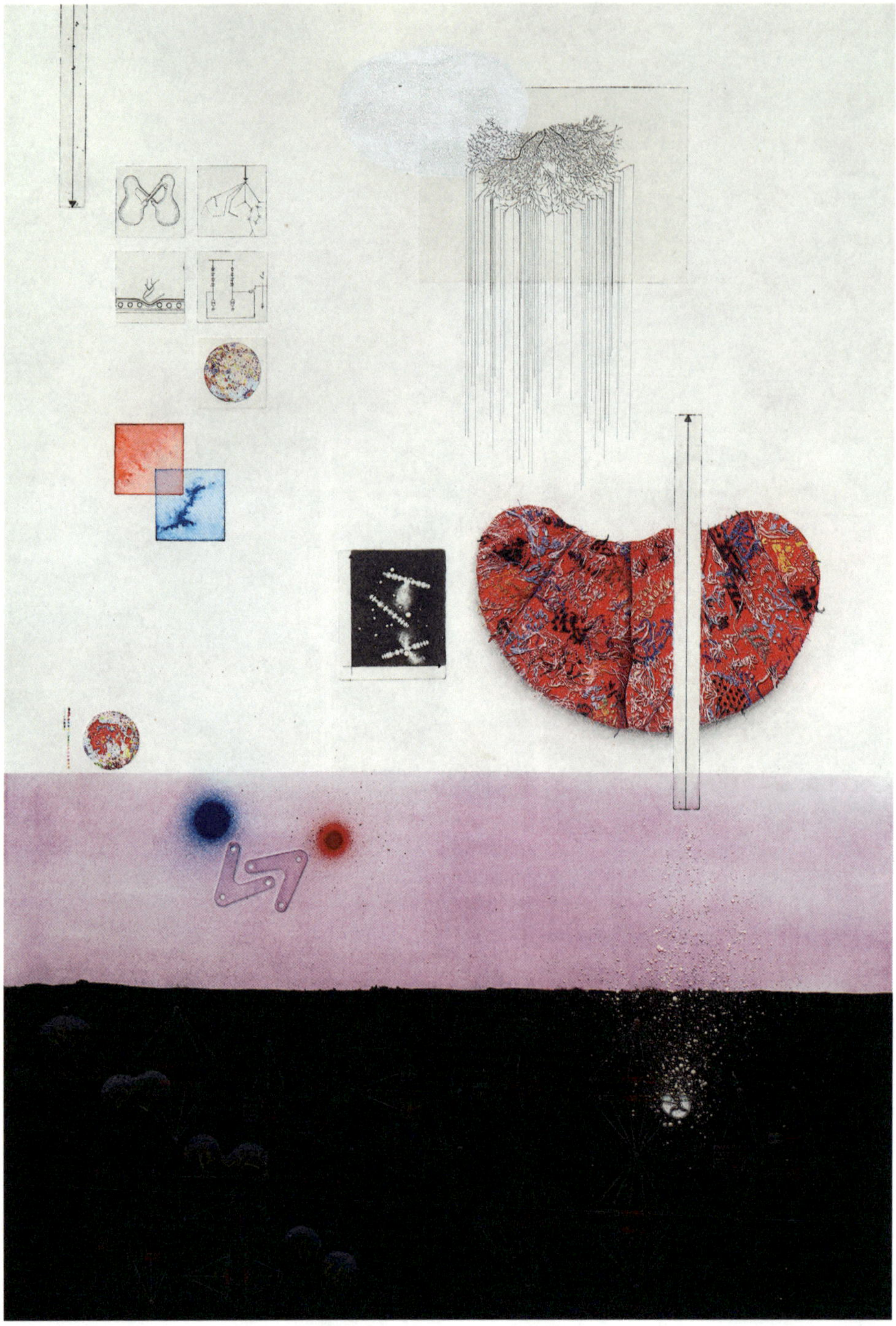

I[5]

Inskription
Inscription

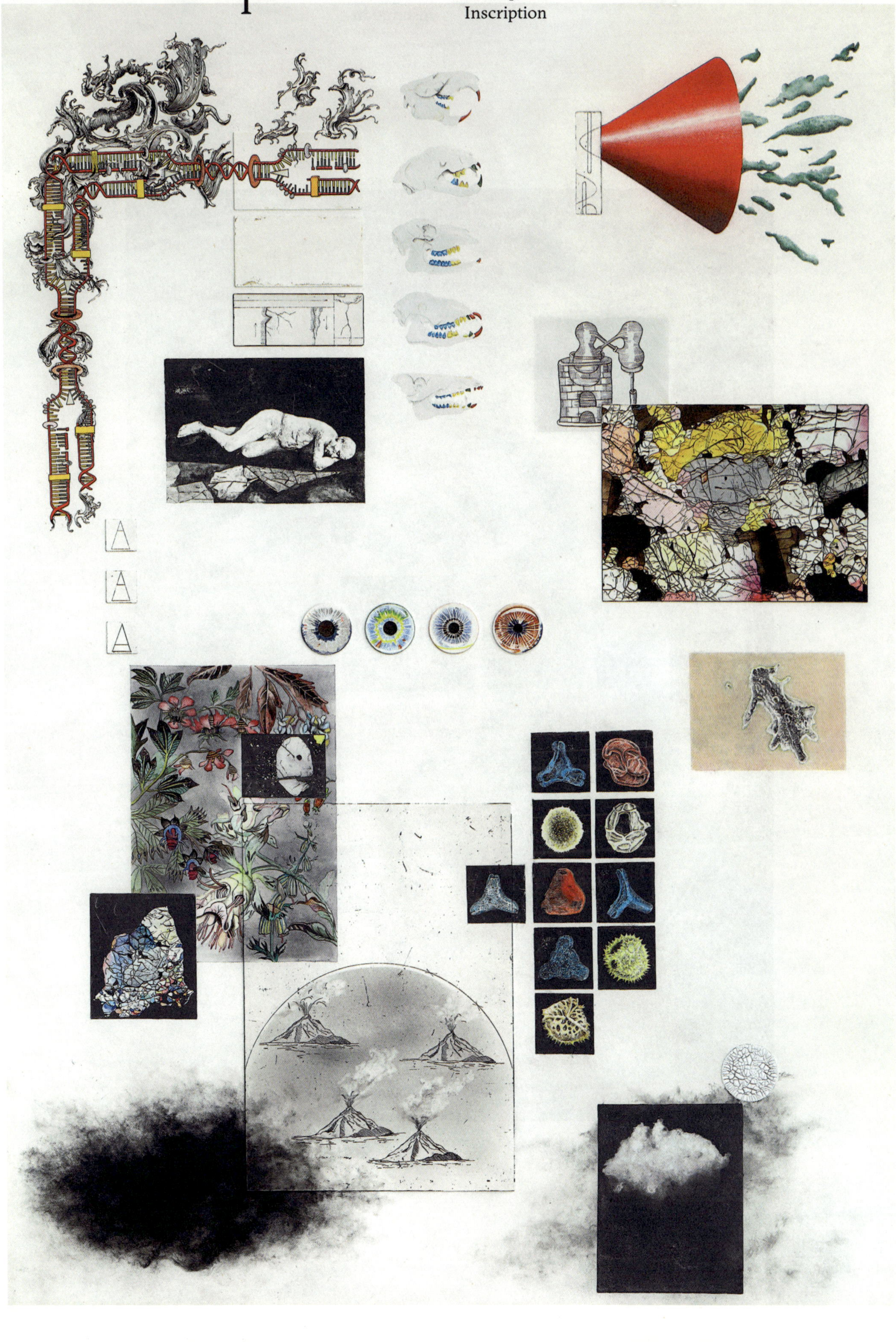

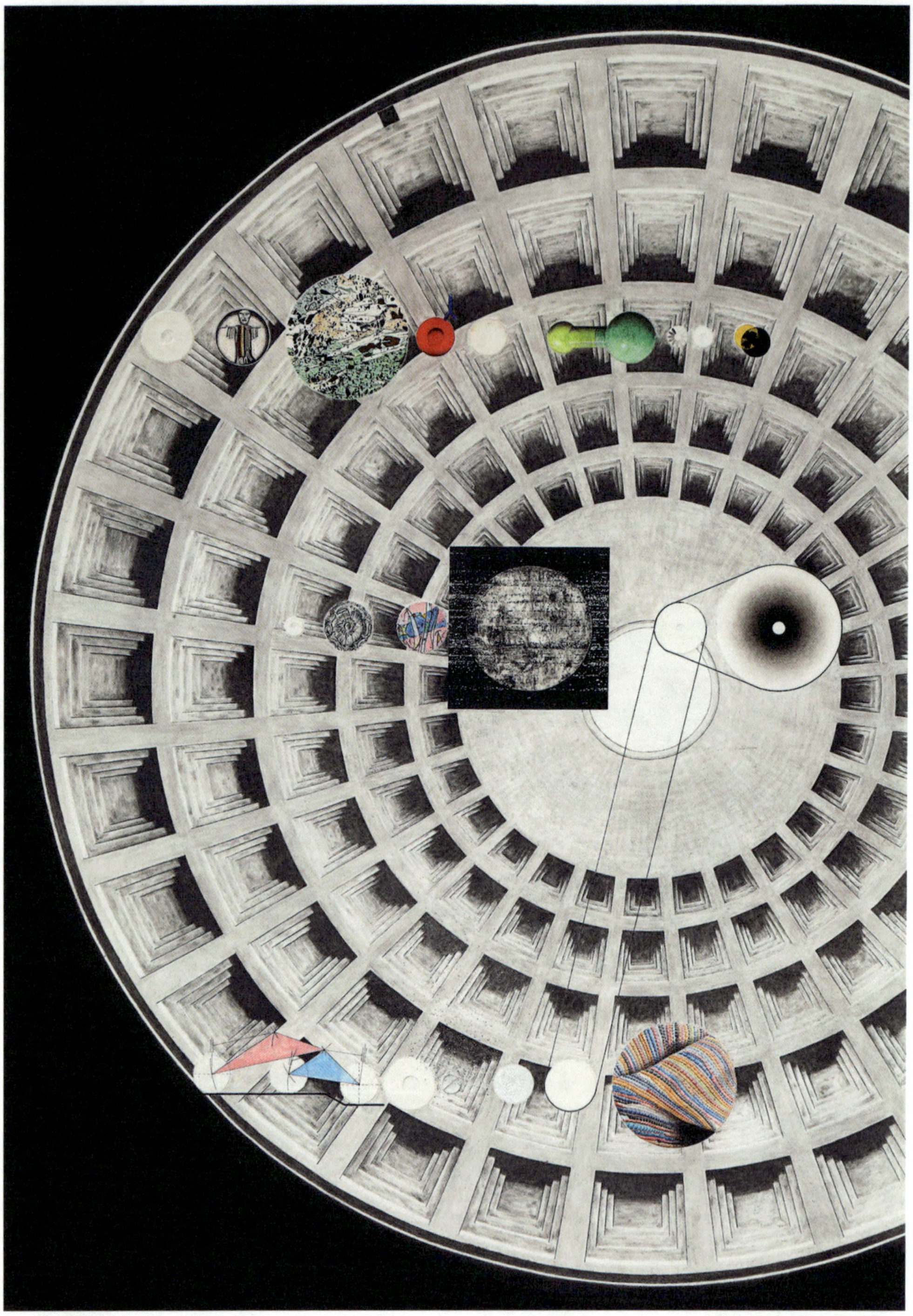

# Visualization and Cognition: Drawing Things Together

Bruno Latour

[In H. Kuklick (ed.) *Knowledge and Society: Studies in the Sociology of Culture Past and Present*, vol. 6, Stanford, Connecticut: Jai Press, 1986, 1–40.]

## I. Thinking with Eyes and Hands

It would be nice to be able to define what is specific to our modem scientific culture. It would be still nicer to find the most economical explanation (which might not be the most economic one) of its origins and special characteristics. To arrive at a parsimonious explanation it is best not to appeal to universal traits of nature. Hypotheses about changes in the mind or human consciousness, in the structure of the brain, in social relations, in "mentalités," or in the economic infrastructure which are posited to explain the emergence of science or its present achievements are simply too grandiose, not to say hagiographic in most cases and plainly racist in more than a few others. Occam's razor should cut these explanations short. No "new man" suddenly emerged sometime in the sixteenth century, and there are no mutants with larger brains working inside modern laboratories who can think differently from the rest of us. The idea that a more rational mind or a more constraining scientific method emerged from darkness and chaos is too complicated a hypothesis.

It seems to me that the first step towards a convincing explanation is to adopt this a priori position. It clears the field of study of any single distinction between prescientific and scientific cultures, minds, methods, or societies. As Jack Goody points out, the "grand dichotomy" with its self-righteous certainty should be replaced by many *uncertain* and *unexpected* divides (Goody, 1977). This negative first move frees us from positive answers that strain credulity.[1] All such dichotomous distinctions can be convincing only as long as they are enforced by a strong asymmetrical bias that treats the two sides of the divide or border very differently. As soon as this prejudice loses hold, cognitive abilities jump in all directions: sorcerers become Popperian falsificationists; scientists become naive believers; engineers become standard "bricoleurs"; as to the tinkerers, they may seem quite rational (Knorr, 1981; Augé, 1975). These quick reversals prove that the divide between prescientific and scientific culture is merely a border—like that between Tijuana and San Diego. It is enforced arbitrarily by police and bureaucrats, but it does not represent any natural boundary. Useful for teaching, polemics, commencement addresses, these "great divides" do not provide any explanation, but on the contrary are the things to be explained (Latour, 1983).

There are, however, good reasons why these dichotomies, though constantly disproved, are tenaciously maintained, or why the gap between the two terms, instead of narrowing, may even widen. The relativistic position reached by taking the first step I propose, and giving up grand dichotomies, looks ludicrous because of the enormous consequences of science. One cannot equate the "intellectual" described by Goody (1977, chap. 2) and Galileo in his study; the folk knowledge of medicinal herbs and the National Institute of Health; the careful procedure of corpse interrogation in Ivory Coast and the careful planning of DNA probes in a Californian laboratory; the story-telling of origin myths somewhere in the South African bush and the Big Bang theory; the hesitant calculations of a four-year-old in Piaget's laboratory and the calculation of a winner of the Field Medal; the abacus and the new super-computer Cray II. The differences in the *effects* of science and technology are so enormous that it seems absurd not to look for enormous causes. Thus even if scholars are dissatisfied with these extravagant causes, even if they admit they are arbitrarily defined, falsified by daily experience and often contradictory, they prefer to maintain them in order to avoid the absurd consequences of relativism. Particle physics must be radically different in some way from folk botany; we do not know how, but as a stop-gap solution the idea of rationality is better than nothing (Hollis and Lukes, 1982).

We have to steer a course that can lead us out of a simple relativism and, by positing a few, simple, empirically verifiable causes, can account for the enormous differences in effects that everyone knows are real. We need to keep the scale of the effects but seek more mundane explanations than that of a great divide in human consciousness.

But here we run into another preliminary problem. How mundane is mundane? When people back away from mental causes, it usually means they find their delight in material ones. Gigantic changes in the capitalist mode of production, by means of many "reflections," "distortions," and "mediations," influence the ways of proving, arguing, and believing. "Materialist" explanations often refer to deeply entrenched phenomena, of which science is a superstructure (Sohn-Rethel, 1978). The net result of this strategy is that nothing is empirically verifiable since there is a yawning gap between general economic trends and the fine details of cognitive innovations. Worst of all, in order to explain science we have to kneel before one specific science, that of economics. So, ironically, many "materialist" accounts of the emergence of science are in no way material since they ignore the precise practice and craftmanship of knowing and hide from scrutiny the omniscient economic historian.

It seems to me that the only way to escape the simplistic relativist position is to avoid both "materialist" and "mentalist" explanations at all costs and to look instead for more parsimonious accounts, which are empirical through and through, and yet able to explain the vast effects of science and technology.

It seems to me that the most powerful explanations, that is those that generate the most out of the least, are the ones that take writing and imaging craftmanship into account. They are both material and mundane, since they are so practical, so modest, so pervasive, so close to the hands and the eyes that they escape attention. Each of them deflates grandiose schemes and conceptual dichotomies

and replaces them by simple modifications in the way in which groups of people argue with one another using paper, signs, prints, and diagrams. Despite their different methods, fields and goals, this strategy of deflation links a range of very different studies and endows them with a style which is both ironic and refreshing.[2]

Like these scholars, I was struck, in a study of a biology laboratory, by the way in which many aspects of laboratory practice could be ordered by looking not at the scientists' brains (I was forbidden access!), at the cognitive structures (nothing special), nor at the paradigms (the same for thirty years), but at the transformation of rats and chemicals into paper (Latour and Woolgar, 1979). Focusing on the literature, and the way in which anything and everything was transformed into inscriptions was not my bias, as I first thought, but was what the laboratory was made for. Instruments, for instance, were of various types, ages, and degrees of sophistication. Some were pieces of furniture, others filled large rooms, employed many technicians and took many weeks to run. But their end result, no matter the field, was always a small window through which one could read a very few signs from a rather poor repertoire (diagrams, blots, bands, columns). All these inscriptions, as I called them, were combinable, superimposable and could, with only a minimum of cleaning up, be integrated as figures in the text of the articles people were writing. Many of the intellectual feats I was asked to admire could be rephrased as soon as this activity of paper-writing and inscription became the focus for analysis. Instead of jumping to explanations involving high theories or differences in logic, I could cling to the level of simple craftsmanship as firmly as Goody. The domestication or disciplining of the mind was still going on with instruments similar to those to which Goody refers. When these resources were lacking, the selfsame scientists stuttered, hesitated, talked nonsense, and displayed every kind of political or cultural bias. Although their minds, their scientific methods, their paradigms, their world-views, and their cultures were still present, their conversation could not keep them in their proper place. However, inscriptions or the practice of inscribing could.

The Great Divide can be broken down into many small, unexpected, and practical sets of skills to produce images, and to read and write about them. But there is a major drawback with this strategy of deflation. Its results seem both obvious—close to being a cliché—and too weak to account for the vast consequences of science and technology that cannot, we agreed above, be denied. Of course, everyone might happily agree that writing, printing, and visualizing are important *asides* of the scientific revolution or of the psychogenesis of scientific thought. They might be necessary, but they certainly cannot be sufficient causes. Certainly not. The deflating strategy may rid us of one mystical Great Divide, but it will, it seems, lead us into a worse kind of mysticism if the researcher who deals with prints and images has to believe in the power of signs and symbols isolated from anything else.

This is a strong objection. We must admit that when talking of images and print it is easy to shift from the most powerful explanation to one that is trivial and reveals only marginal aspects of the phenomena for which we want to account. Diagrams, lists, formulae, archives, engineering drawings, files, equations, dictionaries, collections, and so on, depending on the way they are put into focus, may explain almost everything or almost nothing. It is all too easy to throw a set of clichés together extending Havelock's argument about the Greek alphabet (1980), or Walter Ong's rendering of the Ramist method (1971), all the way to computer culture, passing through the Chinese obsession with ideograms and double-entry book keeping, and without forgetting the Bible. Everyone agrees that print, images, and writing are everywhere present, but how much explanatory burden can they carry? How many cognitive abilities may not only be facilitated but thoroughly explained by them? When wading through this literature, I have a sinking feeling that we are alternately on firm new ground and bogged down in an old marsh. I want to find a way to hold the focus firmly so that we know what to expect from our deflating strategy.

To get this focus, first we must consider the situations in which we might expect changes in writing and imaging procedures to make any difference at all to the way we argue, prove, and believe. Without this preliminary step, inscriptions will, depending on the context, be granted either too much or too little weight. Unlike Leroi-Gourhan (1964) we do not wish to consider all the history on writing and visual aids starting with primitive man and ending up with modem computers. From now on we will be interested only in a few specific inventions in writing and imaging. To define this specificity we have to look more closely at the construction of harder facts.[3]

Who will win in an agonistic encounter between two authors, and between them and all the others they need to build up a statement? Answer: *the one able to muster on the spot the largest number of well aligned and faithful allies.* This definition of victory is common to war, politics, law, and—I shall now show—to science and technology. My contention is that writing and imaging cannot by themselves explain the changes in our scientific societies, except in so far as *they help to make this agonistic situation more favorable.* Thus it is not all the anthropology of writing, nor all the history of visualization that interests us in this context. Rather, we should concentrate on those aspects that help in the mustering, the presentation, the increase, the effective alignment or ensuring the fidelity of new allies. We need, in other words, to look at the way in which someone convinces someone else to take up a statement, to pass it along, to make it more of a fact, and to recognize the first author's ownership and originality. This is what I call "holding the focus steady" on visualization and cognition. If we remain at the level of the visual aspects only, we fallback into a series of weak clichés or are led into all sorts of fascinating problems of scholarship far away from our problem; but, on the other hand, if we concentrate on the agonistic situation alone, the principle of any victory, any solidity in science and technology escapes us forever. We have to hold the two eyepieces together so that we turn it into a real *bi*nocular; it takes time to focus, but the spectacle, I hope, is worth the waiting.

One example will illustrate what I mean. La Pérouse travels through the Pacific for Louis XVI with the explicit mission of bringing *back* a better map. One day, landing on what he calls Sakhalin he meets with Chinese and tries to learn from them whether Sakhalin is an island or a peninsula. To his great surprise the Chinese understand geography quite well. An older man stands up and draws a map of his island on the sand with the scale and the details needed by La Pérouse. Another, who is younger, sees that the rising tide will soon erase the map and picks up one of La Pérouse's notebooks to draw the map again with a pencil . . .

What are the differences between the savage geography and the civilized one? There is no need to bring a prescientific mind into the picture, nor any distinction between the close and open predicaments (Horton, 1977), nor primary and secondary theories (Horton, 1982), nor divisions between implicit and explicit, or concrete and abstract geography. The Chinese are quite able to think in terms of a map but also to talk about navigation on an equal footing with La Pérouse. Strictly speaking, the ability to draw and to visualize does not really make a difference either, since they all draw maps more or less based on the same principle of projection, first on sand, then on paper. So perhaps

there is no difference after all and, geographies being equal, relativism is right? This, however, cannot be, because La Pérouse does something that is going to create an enormous difference between the Chinese and the European. What is, for the former, a drawing of no importance that the tide may erase, is for the latter the *single object* of his mission. What should be brought into the picture is how the picture is brought back. The Chinese does not have to keep track, since he can generate many maps at will, being born on this island and fated to die on it. La Pérouse is not going to stay for more than a night; he is not born here and will die far away. What is he doing, then? He is passing through all these places, in order to take something *back* to Versailles where many people expect his map to determine who was right and wrong about whether Sakhalin was an island, who will own this and that part of the world, and along which routes the next ships should sail. Without this peculiar trajectory, La Pérouse's exclusive interest in traces and inscriptions will be impossible to understand—this is the first aspect, but without dozens of innovations in inscription, in projection, in writing, archiving, and computing, his displacement through the Pacific would be totally wasted—and this is the second aspect, as crucial as the first. We have to hold the two together. Commercial interests, capitalist spirit, imperialism, thirst for knowledge, are empty terms as long as one does not take into account Mercator's projection, marine clocks and their markers, copper engraving of maps, rutters, the keeping of "log books," and the many printed editions of Cook's voyages that La Pérouse carries with him. This is where the deflating strategy I outlined above is so powerful. But, on the other hand, no innovation in the way longitude and latitudes are calculated, clocks are built, log books are compiled, copperplates are printed, would make any difference whatsoever if they did not help to muster, align, and win over new and unexpected allies, far away, in Versailles. The practices I am interested in would be pointless if they did not bear on certain controversies and force dissenters into believing new facts and behaving in new ways. This is where an exclusive interest in visualization and writing falls short, and can even be counterproductive. To maintain only the second line of argument would offer a mystical view of the powers provided by semiotic material—as did Derrida (1967); to maintain only the first would be to offer an idealist explanation (even if clad in materialist clothes).

The aim of this paper is to pursue the two lines of argument at once. To say it in yet other words, we do not find all explanations in terms of inscription equally convincing, but only those that help us to understand how the mobilization and mustering of new resources is achieved. We do not find all explanations in terms of social groups, interests, or economic trends equally convincing, but only those that offer a specific mechanism to sum up "groups," "interests," "money," and "trends": mechanisms which, we believe, depend upon the manipulation of paper, print, images, and so on. La Pérouse shows us the way since without new types of inscriptions nothing usable would have come back to Versailles from his long, costly, and fateful voyage; but without this strange mission that required him to go away and to come back so that others in France might be convinced, no modification in inscription would have made a bit of difference. The essential characteristics of inscriptions cannot be defined in terms of visualization, print, and writing. In other words, it is not perception which is at stake in this problem of visualization and cognition. New inscriptions, and new ways of perceiving them, are the results of something deeper. If you wish to go out of *your* way and come back heavily equipped so as to force others to go out of *their* ways, the main problem to solve is that of *mobilization*. You have to go and to come back *with* the "things" if your moves are not to be wasted. But the "things" have to be able to withstand the return trip without withering away. Further requirements: the "things" you gathered and displaced have to be presentable all at once to those you want to convince and who did not go there. In sum, you have to invent objects which have the properties of being *mobile* but also *immutable, presentable, readable,* and *combinable* with one another.

## II.
## On Immutable Mobiles

It seems to me that most scholars who have worked on the relations between inscription procedures and cognition have, in fact, in their various ways, been writing about the history of these immutable mobiles.

### *A. Optical Consistency*

The first example I will review is one of the most striking, since Ivins wrote about it years ago and saw it all in a few seminal pages. The rationalization that took place during the so-called "scientific revolution" is not of the mind, of the eye, of philosophy, but of the *sight.* Why is perspective such an important invention? "Because of its logical recognition of internal invariances through all the transformations produced by changes in spatial location" (Ivins, 1973: 9). In a linear perspective, no matter from what distance and angle an object is seen, it is always possible to transfer it—to translate it—and to obtain the same object at a different size as seen from another position. In the course of this translation, its internal properties have not been modified. This immutability of the displaced figure allows Ivins to make a second crucial point: since the picture moves without distortion it is possible to establish, in the linear perspective framework, what he calls a "two way" relationship between object and figure. Ivins shows us how perspective allows movement through space with, so to speak, a return ticket. You can see a church in Rome and carry it with you in London in such a way as to reconstruct it in London, or you can go back to Rome and amend the picture. With perspective exactly as with La Pérouse's map—and for the same reasons—a new set of movements are made possible: you can go out of your way and come back with all the places you passed; these are all written in the same homogeneous language (longitude and latitude, geometry) that allows you to change scale, to make them presentable and to combine them at will.[4]

Perspective, for Ivins, is an essential determinant of science and technology because it creates "optical consistency," or, in simpler terms, a regular avenue through space. Without it "either the exterior relations of objects such as their forms for visual awareness, change with their shifts in locations, or else their interior relations do" (1973: 9). The shift from the other senses to vision is a consequence of the agonistic situation. You present absent things. No one can smell or hear or touch Sakhalin island, but you can look at the map and determine at which bearing you will see the land when you send the next fleet. The speakers are talking to one another, feeling, hearing, and touching each other, *but* they are now talking *with* many absent things presented all at once. This presence/absence is possible through the two-way connection established by these many contrivances—perspective, projection, map, log book, and so on—that allow translation without corruption.

There is another advantage of linear perspective to which Ivins and Edgerton attract our attention (1976). This unexpected advantage is revealed as soon as religious or mythological themes and utopias are drawn with the same perspective as that which is used for rendering nature (Edgerton, 1980: 189).

"In the West, even if the subject of the printed text were unscientific, the printed picture always presented

a rational image based on the universal laws of geometry. In this sense the Scientific Revolution probably owes more to Albrecht Dürer than to Leonardo da Vinci." (p. 190)

Fiction—even the wildest or the most sacred—and things of nature—even the lowliest—have a meeting ground, *a common place*, because they all benefit from the same "optical consistency."[5] Not only can you displace cities, landscapes, or natives, and go back and forth to and from them along avenues through space, but you can also reach saints, gods, heavens, palaces, or dreams with the same two-way avenues and look at them through the same "windowpane" on the same two-dimensional surface. The two ways become a four-lane freeway! Impossible palaces can be drawn realistically, but it is also possible to draw possible objects as if they were utopian ones. For instance, as Edgerton shows when he comments on Agricola's prints, real objects can be drawn in separated pieces, or in exploded views, or added to the same sheet of paper at different scales, angles, and perspectives. It does not matter since the "optical consistency" allows all the pieces to mix with one another. As Ferguson says, the "mind" has at last "an eye":

"Oddly enough, linear perspective and chiaroscuro, which supply geometric stability to pictures, also allow the viewer a momentary suspension of his dependence on the law of gravity. With a little practice, the viewer can imagine solid volumes floating freely in space as detached components of a device." (Edgerton, 1980: 193)

At this stage, on paper, hybrids can be created that mix drawings from many sources. Perspective is not interesting because it provides realistic pictures; on the other hand, it is interesting because it creates complete hybrids: nature seen as fiction, and fiction seen as nature, with all the elements made so homogeneous in space that it is now possible to reshuffle them like a pack of cards. Commenting on the painting *St. Jérome in His Study*, Edgerton says:

"Antonello's St. Jérome is the perfect paradigm of a new consciousness of the physical world attained by Western European intellectuals by the late fifteenth century. This consciousness was shown especially by artists such as Leonardo da Vinci, Francesco di Giorgio Martini, Albrecht Dürer, Hans Holbein and more, all of whom ... had even developed a sophisticated grammar and syntax for quantifying natural phenomena in pictures. In their hands, picture making was becoming a pictorial language that, with practice, could communicate more information, more quickly and by (sic) a potentially wider audience than any verbal language in human history." (1980: 189)

Perspective illustrates the double line of argument I presented in the previous section. Innovations in graphism are crucial, but only insofar as they allow new two-way relations to be established with objects (from nature or from fiction) and only insofar as they allow inscriptions either to become more mobile or to stay immutable through all their displacements.

*B. Visual Culture*

Still more striking than the Italian perspective described by Ivins and Edgerton is the Dutch "distance point" method for drawing pictures, as it has been beautifully explained by Svetlana Alpers (1983). The Dutch, she tells us, do not paint grandiose historical scenes as observed by someone through a carefully framed windowpane. They use the very surface of their paintings (taken as the equivalent of a retina) to let the world be painted straight on it. When images are captured in this way there is no privileged site for the onlooker any more. The tricks of the "camera obscura" transform large-scale three-dimensional objects into a small two-dimensional surface around which the onlooker may turn at will.[6]

The main interest of Alpers' book for our purpose is the way she shows a "visual culture" changing over time. She does not focus on the inscriptions or the pictures but on the simultaneous transformation of science, art, theory of vision, organization of crafts, and economic powers. People often talk of "worldviews," but this powerful expression is taken metaphorically. Alpers provides this old expression with its material meaning: how a culture *sees* the *world* and makes it visible. A new visual culture redefines both what it is to see and what there is to see. A citation of Comenius aptly summarizes a new obsession for making new objects visible anew:

"We will now speak of the mode in which objects must be presented to the senses, if the impression is to be distinct. This can be readily understood if we consider the process of actual vision. If the object is to be clearly seen it is necessary: (1) that it be placed before the eyes; (2) not far off, but at a reasonable distance; (3) not on one side, but straight before the eyes; and (4) so that the front of the objects be not turned away from, but directed towards the observer; (5) that the eyes first take in the object as a whole; (6) and then proceed to distinguish the part; (7) inspecting these in order from the beginning to the end; (9) that attention be paid to each and every part; (9) until they are all grasped by means of their essential attributes. If these requisites be properly observed, vision takes place successfully; but if one be neglected its success is only partial." (cited in Alpers, 1983: 95)

This new obsession for defining the act of seeing is to be found both in the science of the period and in modern laboratories. Comenius's advice is similar to both that of Boyle when he disciplined the witnesses of his air-pump experiment (Shapin, 1984) and that of the neurologists studied by Lynch when they "disciplined" their brain cells (Lynch, 1985). People before science and outside laboratories certainly use their eyes, but not in this way. They look at the spectacle of the world, but not at this new type of image designed to transport the objects of the world, to accumulate them in Holland, to label them with captions and legends, to combine them at will. Alpers makes understandable what Foucault (1966) only suggested: how the same eyes suddenly began to look at "representations." The "panopticon" she describes is a *"fait social total"* that redefines all aspects of the culture. More importantly, Alpers does not explain a new vision by bringing in "social interests" or the "economic infrastructure." The new precise scenography that results in a world view defines at once what is science, what is art, and what it is to have a world economy. To use my terms, a little lowland country becomes powerful by making a few crucial inventions which allow people to accelerate the mobility and to enhance the immutability of inscriptions: the world is thus gathered up in this tiny country.

Alpers' description of Dutch visual culture reaches the same result as Edgerton's study of technical drawings: a new meeting place is designed for fact and fiction, words and images. The map itself is such a result, but the more so when it is used to inscribe ethnographic inventories (end of her chapter 4) or captions (chapter 5), skylines of cities and so on. The main quality of the new space is not to be "objective" as a naïve definition of realism often claims, but rather to have optical consistency. This consistency entails the *"art of describing"* everything and the possibility of going from one type of visual trace to another. Thus we are not surprised that letters, mirrors, lenses, painted words, perspectives, inventories, illustrated child books, microscope, and telescope come together in this visual culture. All innovations are selected "to secretly see and without suspicion what is done far off in other places" (cited in Alpers, 1983: 201).

*C. A New Way of Accumulating Time and Space*

Another example will demonstrate that inscriptions are not interesting per se, but only because they increase either the mobility or the immutability of traces. The invention of print and its effects on science and technology is a cliché of historians. But no one has renewed this Renaissance argument as completely as Elizabeth Eisenstein (1979). Why? Because she considers the printing press to be a mobilization device, or, more exactly, a device that makes both mobilization and immutability possible at the same time. Eisenstein does not look for one cause of the scientific revolution, but for a secondary cause that would put all the efficient causes in relation with one another. The printing press is obviously a powerful cause of that sort. Immutability is ensured by the process of printing many identical copies; mobility by the number of copies, the paper, and the movable type. The links between different places in time and space are completely modified by this fantastic acceleration of immutable mobiles which circulate everywhere and in all directions in Europe. As Ivins has shown, perspective *plus* the printing press *plus* aqua forte is the really important combination, since books can now carry with them the realistic images of what they talk about. For the first time a location can accumulate other places far away in space and time, and present them synoptically to the eye; better still, this synoptic presentation, once reworked, amended, or disrupted, can be spread with no modification to other places and made available at other times.

After discussing historians who propose many contradictory influences to explain the take-off of astronomy, Eisenstein writes:

"Whether the sixteenth century astronomer confronted materials derived from the fourth century b.c. or freshly composed in the fourteenth century a.d., or whether he was more receptive to scholastic or humanist currents of thoughts, seems of less significance in this particular connection than the fact that all manners of diverse materials were being seen in the course of one life time by one pair of eyes. For Copernicus as for Tycho, the result was heightened awareness and dissatisfaction with discrepancies in the inherent data." (1979: 602)

The author constantly shifts attention with devastating irony from the mind to the surface of the mobilized resources:

"To discover the truth of a proposition in Euclid," wrote John Locke "there is little need or use of revelation, God having furnished us with a natural and surer means to arrive at knowledge of them." In the eleventh century, however, God had not furnished Western scholars with a natural and sure means of grasping a Euclidean theorem. Instead the most learned men in Christendom engaged in a fruitless search to discover what Euclid meant when referring to interior angles." (1979: 649)

For Eisenstein every grand question about the Reformation, the scientific revolution, and the new capitalist economy can be recast by looking at what the publisher and the printing press make possible. The reason why this old explanation takes on new life in her treatment is that Eisenstein not only focuses on graphism but also on changes in the graphism that are linked to the mobilization process. For instance, she explains (p. 508ff, following Ivins, 1953) the puzzling phenomenon of a lag time between the introduction of the printing press and the beginning of exact realistic pictures. At first the press is used simply to reproduce herbaries, anatomical plates, maps, cosmologies which are centuries old and which will be deemed inaccurate much later. If we were looking only at the semiotic level, this phenomenon would seem puzzling, but once we consider the deeper structure this is easily explained. The displacement of many immutable mobiles comes first; the old texts are spread everywhere and can be gathered more cheaply in one place. But then the contradiction between them at last becomes *visible* in the most literal sense. The many places where these texts are synoptically assembled offer many counterexamples (different flowers, different organs with different names, different shapes for the coastline, the various rates of different currencies, different laws). These counterexamples can be added to the old texts and, in turn, are spread without modification to all the other settings where this process of comparison may be resumed. In other words, errors are accurately reproduced and spread with no changes. But corrections are also reproduced fast, cheaply and with no further changes. So, in the end, the accuracy *shifts from the medium to the message,* from the printed book to the context with which it establishes a two-way connection. A new interest in "Truth" does not come from a new vision, but from the same old vision applying itself to new visible objects that mobilize space and time differently[7].

The effect of Eisenstein's argument is to transform mentalist explanations into the history of immutable mobiles. Again and again she shows that before the advent of print every possible intellectual feat had been achieved—organized skepticism, scientific method, refutation, data collection, theory making—everything had been tried, and in all disciplines: geography, cosmology, medicine, dynamics, politics, economics, and so on. But each achievement stayed local and temporary just because there was no way to move their results elsewhere and to bring in those of others without new corruptions or errors being introduced. For instance, each carefully amended version of an old author was, after a few copies, again adulterated. No irreversible gains could be made, and so no large-scale long-term capitalization was possible. The printing press does not add anything to the mind, to the scientific method, to the brain. It simply conserves and spreads everything no matter how wrong, strange, or wild. It makes everything mobile but this mobility is not offset by adulteration. The new scientists, the new clerics, the new merchants, and the new princes described by Eisenstein are no different from the old ones, but they now look at new material that keeps track of numerous places and times. No matter how inaccurate these traces might be at first, they will all become accurate just *as a consequence* of more mobilization and more immutability. A mechanism is invented to irreversibly capture accuracy. Print plays the same role as Maxwell's demon. No new theory, world view, or spirit is necessary to explain capitalism, the Reformation and science: they are the result of a new step in the long history of immutable mobiles.

Taking up Ivins' argument, both Mukerji (1983) and Eisenstein focus again on the *illustrated* book. For these authors, MacLuhan's revolution had already happened as soon as images were printed. Engineering, botany, architecture, mathematics, none of these sciences can describe what they talk about with texts alone; they need to show the things. But this showing, so essential to convince, was utterly impossible before the invention of "graven images." A text could be copied with only some adulteration, but not so a diagram, an anatomical plate, or a map. The effect on the construction of facts is sizeable if a writer is able to provide a reader with a text which presents a large number of the things it is talking about in one place. If you suppose that all the readers, and all the writers, are doing the same, a new world will emerge from the old one without any additional cause. Why? Simply because the dissenter will have to do the same thing as his opponent. In order to "doubt back," so to speak, he will have to write another book, have it printed, and mobilize with copper plates the counterexamples he wants to oppose. The cost of disagreeing will increase[8].

Positive feedback will get under way as soon as one is able to muster a large number of mobile, readable, visible resources at one spot to support a point. After Tycho Brahe's achievement (Eisenstein, 1979) the dissenter either has to quit and accept what cosmologists say as a hard fact, or to produce counterproofs by persuading his prince to invest a comparable amount of money in observatories. In this the "proof race" is similar to the arms race because the feedback mechanism is the same. Once one competitor starts building up harder facts, the others have to do the same or else submit.

This slight recasting of Eisenstein's argument in terms of immutable mobiles may allow us to overcome a difficulty in her argument. Although she stresses the importance of publishers' strategies, she does not account for the technical innovations themselves. The printing press barges into her account like the exogeneous factors of many historians when they talk about technical innovations. She puts the semiotic aspect of print and the mobilization it allows into excellent focus, but the technical necessities for inventing the press are far from obvious. If we consider the agonistic situation I use as reference point, the pressure that favors something like the printing press is clearer. *Anything* that will accelerate the mobility of the traces that a location may obtain about another place, or *anything* that will allow these traces to move without transformation from one place to another, will be favored: geometry, projection, perspective, bookkeeping, paper making, aqua forte, coinage, new ships (Law, 1984). The privilege of the printing press comes from its ability to help many innovations to act at once, but it is only one innovation among the many that help to answer this simplest of all questions: how to dominate on a large scale? This recasting is useful since it helps us to see that the same mechanism, the effects of which are described by Eisenstein, *is still at work today*, on an ever increasing scale at the frontiers of science and technology. A few days in a laboratory reveal that the same trends that made the printing press so necessary still act to produce new data bases, new space telescopes, new chromatographies, new equations, new scanners, new questionnaires, and so on. The mind is still being domesticated.

## III.
## On Inscriptions

What is so important in the images and in the inscriptions scientists and engineers are busy obtaining, drawing, inspecting, calculating, and discussing? It is, first of all, the unique advantage they give in the rhetorical or polemical situation. "You doubt what I say? I'll show you." And, without moving more than a few inches, I unfold in front of your eyes figures, diagrams, plates, texts, silhouettes, and then and there present things that are far away and with which some sort of two-way connection has now been established. I do not think the importance of this simple mechanism can be overestimated. Eisenstein has shown it for the past of science, but the ethnography of present laboratories shows the same mechanism (Lynch, 1985a, 1985b; Star, 1983; Law, 1985). We are so used to this world of print and images that we can hardly think of what it is to know something without indexes, bibliographies, dictionaries, papers with references, tables, columns, photographs, peaks, spots, bands.[9]

One simple way to make the importance of inscriptions clearer is to consider how little we are able to convince when deprived of these graphisms through which mobility and immutability are increased. As Dagognet has shown in two excellent books, no scientific discipline exists without first inventing a visual and written language which allows it to break with its confusing past (1969, 1973). The manipulation of substances in gallipots and alembics becomes chemistry only when all the substances can be written in a homogeneous language where everything is simultaneously presented to the eye. The writing of words inside a classification are not enough. Chemistry becomes powerful only when a visual vocabulary is invented that replaces the manipulations by calculation of formulas. Chemical structure can be drawn, composed, broken apart on paper, like music or arithmetic, all the way to Mendeleev's table: "For those who know to observe and read the final periodic table, the properties of the element and that of their various combinations unfold completely and directly from their positions in the table" (1969: p. 213). After having carefully analyzed the many innovations in chemical writing and drawings, he adds this little sentence so close to Goody's outlook:

"It might seem that we consider trivial details—a slight modification in the plane used to write a chlorine—but, paradoxically, these little details trigger the forces of the modem world." (1969: p. 199)

Michel Foucault, in his well-known study of clinical medicine, has shown the same transformation from small-scale practice to a large-scale manipulation of records (1963). The same medical mind will generate totally different knowledge if applied to the bellies, fevers, throats, and skins of a few successive patients, or if applied to well-kept records of hundreds of written bellies, fevers, throats, and skins, all coded in the same way and all synoptically present. Medicine does not become scientific in the mind, or in the eye of its practitioners, but in the application of old eyes and old minds to new fact sheets inside a new institution, the hospital. But it is in *Discipline and Punish* (1975) that Foucault's demonstration is closest to the study of inscriptions. The main purpose of the book is to illustrate the shift from a power which is seen by invisible onlookers to a new invisible power that sees everything about everyone. The main advantage of Foucault's analysis is not to focus only on files, accounting books, time tables, and drill but also on the sort of institutions in which these inscriptions end up being so essential.[10] The main innovation is that of a "panopticon" which allows penology, pedagogy, psychiatry, and clinical medicine to emerge as fully fledged sciences from their carefully kept files. The "panopticon" is another way of obtaining the "optical consistency" necessary for power on a large scale.

In a famous sentence Kant asserts that "we shall be rendering a service to reason should we succeed in discovering the path upon which it can securely travel." The "sure path of a science", however, is, inevitably, in the construction of well-kept files in institutions that want to mobilize a larger number of resources on a larger scale.

"Optical consistency" is obtained in geology, as Rudwick has shown (1976), by inventing a new visual language. Without it the layers of the earth stay hidden and no matter how many travelers and diggers move around there is no way to sum up their travels, visions, and claims. The Copernican revolution, dear to Kant's heart, is an idealist rendering of a very simple mechanism: if we cannot go to the earth, let the earth come to us, or, more accurately, let us all go to many places on the earth, and come back with the same but different homogenous pictures that can be gathered, compared, superimposed, and redrawn in a few places, together with the carefully labeled specimens of rocks and fossils.

In a suggestive book, Fourquet (1980) has illustrated the same inscription-gathering for INSEE, the French institution that provides most economic statistics. It is of course impossible to talk about the economy of a nation by looking at "it." The "it" is plainly invisible, as long as cohorts of enquirers and inspectors have not filled in long questionnaires, as long as the answers have not been punched onto cards, treated by computers, analyzed in this gigantic

laboratory. Only at the end can the economy be made visible inside piles of charts and lists. Even this is still too confusing, so that redrawing and extracting is necessary to provide a few neat diagrams that show the Gross National Product or the Balance of Payments. The panopticon thus achieved is similar in structure to a gigantic scientific instrument transforming the invisible world of exchanges into "the economy." This is why, at the beginning, I rejected the materialist explanation that uses "infrastructures" or "markets" or "consumer needs" to account for science and technology. The visual construction of something like a "market" or an "economy" is what begs explanation, and this end-product cannot be used to account for science.

In another suggestive book Fabian tries to account for anthropology by looking at its craftsmanship of visualization (1983). The main difference between us and the savages, he argues, is not in the culture, in the mind, or in the brain, but in the way *we* visualize *them*. An asymmetry is created because we create a space and a time in which we place the other cultures, but they do not do the same. For instance, we map their land, but they have no maps either of their land or of ours; we list their past, but they do not; we build written calendars, but they do not. Fabian's argument, related to Goody's and also to Bourdieu's critique of ethnography (1972), is that once this first violence has been committed, no matter what we do we will not understand the savages any more. Fabian, however, sees this mobilization of all savages in a few lands through collection, mapping, list making, archives, linguistics, and so on as something evil. Candidly, he wishes to find another way to "know" the savages. But "knowing" is not a disinterested cognitive activity; harder facts about the other cultures have been produced in our societies, in exactly the same way as other facts about ballistics, taxonomy, or surgery. One place gathers in all the others and presents them synoptically to the dissenter so as to modify the outcome of an agonistic encounter. To make a large number of competitors and compatriots depart from their usual ways, many ethnographers both had to go further out of *their* usual ways, and then come *back*. The constraints imposed by convincing people, going out and coming back, are such that this can be achieved only if everything about the savage life is transformed into immutable mobiles that are easily readable and presentable. In spite of his wishes, Fabian cannot do better. Otherwise he would either have to give up "knowing" or give up making hard facts.

There is no detectable difference between natural and social science, as far as the obsession for graphism is concerned. If scientists were looking at nature, at economies, at stars, at organs, they would not *see* anything. This "evidence," so to speak, is used as a classic rebuttal to naïve versions of empiricism (Arnheim, 1969). Scientists start seeing something once they stop looking at nature and look exclusively and obsessively at prints and flat inscriptions.[11] In the debates around perception, what is always forgotten is this simple drift from watching confusing three-dimensional objects to inspecting two-dimensional images which have been *made less confusing*. Lynch, like all laboratory observers, has been struck by the extraordinary obsession of scientists with papers, prints, diagrams, archives, abstracts, and curves on graph paper. No matter what they talk about, they start talking with some degree of confidence and being believed by colleagues only once they point to simple geometrized two-dimensional shapes. The "objects" are discarded or often absent from laboratories. Bleeding and screaming rats are quickly dispatched. What is extracted from them is a tiny set of figures. This extraction, like the few longitudes and latitudes extracted from the Chinese by La Pérouse, is *all that counts*. Nothing can be said about the rats, but a great deal can be said about the figures (Latour and Woolgar, 1979). Knorr (1981) and Star (1983) have also shown the simplification procedures at work, as if the images were never simple enough for the controversy to be settled quickly. Every time there is a dispute, great pains are taken to find, or sometimes to invent, a new instrument of visualization, which will enhance the image, accelerate the readings, and, as Lynch has shown, conspire with the visual characteristics of the things that lend themselves to diagrams on paper (coast lines, stars which are like points, well-aligned cells, and so on).

Again, the precise focus should be carefully set, because it is not the inscription by itself that should carry the burden of explaining the power of science; it is the inscription as *the fine edge* and *the final stage* of a whole process of mobilization that modifies the scale of the rhetoric. Without the displacement, the inscription is worthless; without the inscription, the displacement is wasted. This is why mobilization is not restricted to paper, but paper always appears at the end when the scale of this mobilization is to be increased. Collections of rocks, stuffed animals, samples, fossils, artifacts, gene banks, are the first to be moved around. What counts is the arraying and mustering of resources (biographies of naturalists, for instance, are replete with anecdotes about crates, archives and specimens), but this arraying is never simple enough. Collections are essential but only while the archives are well kept, the labels are in place, and the specimens do not decay. Even this is not enough, since a museum collection is still too much for one "mind" to handle. So the collection will be drawn, written, recoded, and this process will take place as long as more combinable geometrized forms have not been obtained from the specimens (continuing the process through which the specimens had been extracted from their contexts).

So the phenomenon we are tackling is *not* inscription per se but the *cascade* of ever simplified inscriptions that allow harder facts to be produced at greater cost. For example, the description of human fossils, which used to be through drawings, is now made by superimposing a number of mechanical diagrams on the drawings. The photographs of the skies, although they produce neat little spots, are still much too rich and confusing for a human eye to look at; so a computer and a laser eye have been invented to read the photographs, so that the astronomer never looks at the sky (too costly), nor even at the photographs (too confusing). The taxonomy of plants is all contained in a famous series of books at Kew Garden, but the manipulation of this book is as difficult as that of the old manuscripts since it exists in only one location; another computer is now being instructed to try to read the many different prints of this book and provide as many copied versions as possible of the taxonomic inventory.

In a recent article Pinch (1985) shows a nice case of the accumulation of such traces, each layer being deposited on the former only when confidence about its meaning is stabilized. Do the astrophysicists "see" the neutrinos from the sun or any of the intermediary "blurs," "peaks," and "spots" which compose, by accumulation, the phenomenon to be seen? Again, we see that the mechanisms studied by Eisenstein for the printing press are still with us today at any of the frontiers of science. For instance, baboon ethology used to be a text in prose in which the narrator talked about animals; then the narrator had to include what he or she had seen in the text, as first pictures, then a statistical rendering of the events; but with an increasing competition for the construction of harder facts, the articles now include more and more layers of graphic display, and the cascade of columns summarized by tables, diagrams, and equations is still unfolding. In molecular biology, chromatography was read, a few years ago, by bands of different shades of grey; the interpretation of

these shades is now done by computer, and a text is eventually obtained straight out of the computer: "ATGC-GTTCGC ..." Although more empirical studies should be made in many different fields, there seems to be a trend in these cascades. They always move in the direction of the greater merging of figures, numbers, and letters, greatly facilitated by their homogeneous treatment as binary units in and by computers.

This trend toward simpler and simpler inscriptions that mobilize larger and larger numbers of events in one spot cannot be understood if separated from the agonistic model that we use as our point of reference. It is as necessary as the race for digging trenches on the front in 1914. He who visualizes badly loses the encounter; his fact does not hold. Knorr has criticized this argument by taking an ethnomethodological standpoint (1981). She argues, and rightly so, that an image, a diagram, cannot convince anyone, both because there are always many interpretations possible and, above all, because the diagram does not force the dissenter to look at it. She sees the interest in inscription devices as an exaggeration of the power of semiotics—(and a French one at that!) But such a position misses the point of my argument. It is precisely because the dissenter can always escape and try out another interpretation that so much energy and time is devoted by scientists to *corner* him and surround him with ever more dramatic visual effects. Although *in principle* any interpretation can be opposed to any text and image, *in practice* this is far from being the case; the cost of dissenting increases with each new collection, each new labelling, each new redrawing. This is especially true if the phenomena we are asked to believe are invisible to the naked eye; quasars, chromosomes, brain peptides, leptons, gross national products, classes, coast lines are never seen but through the "clothed" eye of inscription devices. Thus one *more* inscription, one more trick to enhance contrast, one simple device to decrease background, one coloring procedure, might be *enough*, all things being equal, *to swing the balance* of power and turn an incredible statement into a credible one which would then be passed along without further modification. The importance of this cascade of inscriptions may be ignored when studying events in daily life, but it cannot be overestimated when analyzing science and technology.

More exactly, it is possible to overestimate the inscription, but not the setting in which the cascade of ever more written and numbered inscriptions is produced. What we are really dealing with is the *staging* of a scenography in which attention is focused on one set of dramatized inscriptions. The setting works like a giant "optical device" that creates a new laboratory, a new type of vision, and a new phenomenon to look at. I have shown one such setting, which I called "Pasteur's theater of proofs" (Latour, 1984). Pasteur works as much on the stage as on the scene and the plot. What counts in the end is a simple visual perception: dead unvaccinated sheep versus live vaccinated sheep. The earlier we go back in history of science, the more attention we see being paid to the setting and the less to inscriptions themselves. Boyle, for instance, in the fascinating account of his vacuum pump experiment described by Shapin (1984), had to invent not only the phenomenon but the instrument to make it visible, the set-up in which the instrument was displayed, the written and printed accounts through which the silent reader could read "about" the experiment, the type of witnesses admitted onto the stage, and even the types of commentaries the potential witnesses were allowed to utter. "Seeing the vacuum" was possible only once all these witnesses had been disciplined.

The staging of such "optical devices" is the one Eisenstein describes: a few persons in the same room talk to one another and point to two-dimensional pictures; these pictures are all there is to see of the things about which they talk. Just because we are used to this setting, and breathe it like fresh air, does not mean that we should not describe all the little innovations that make it the most powerful device to achieve power. Tycho Brahe, in Uraniborg, had before his eyes, for the first time in history, all the predictions—that is literally the "*previsions*"—of the planetary movements; at the *same* place, written in the *same* language or code, he can read *his* own observations. This is more than enough to account for Brahe's new "insight."

"It was not because he gazed at night skies instead of at old books that Tycho Brahe differed from stargazers of the past. Nor do I think it was because he cared more for "stubborn facts" and precise measurement than had the Alexandrians or the Arabs. But he did have at his disposal, as few had before him, two separate sets of computations based on two different theories, compiled several centuries apart which he could compare with each other." (Eisenstein, 1979: 624)

The hagiographers say that he is the first to look at planetary motion, with a mind freed of the prejudices of the darker ages. No, says Eisenstein, he is the first *not* to look at the sky, but to look simultaneously to all the former predictions and his own, written down together in the same form.

"The Danish observer was not only the last of the great naked eye observers; he was also the first careful observer who took full advantage of the new powers of the press—powers which enabled astronomers to detect anomalies in old records, to pinpoint more precisely and register in catalogs the location of each star, to enlist collaborators in many regions, fix each fresh observation in permanent form and make necessary corrections in successive editions." (1979: 625)

The discrepancies proliferate, not by looking at the sky, but by carefully superimposing columns of angles and azimuths. No contradiction, or counterpredictions, could ever have been visible. Contradiction, as Goody says, is neither a property of the mind nor of the scientific method, but is a property of reading letters and signs inside new settings that focus attention on inscriptions alone.

The same mechanism is visible, to draw an example from a different time and place, in Roger Guillemin's vision of endorphin, a brain peptide. The brain is as obscure and as messy as the Renaissance sky. Even the many first-level purifications of brain extracts provide a "soup" of substances. The whole research strategy is to gel peaks that are clearly readable out of a confused background. Each of the samples which provides a neater peak is in turn purified until there is only one peak on the little window of a high pressure liquid chromatograph. Then the substance is injected in minute quantities into guinea-pig gut. The contractions of the gut are hooked up, through electronic hardware, to a physiograph. What is there at hand to see the object "endorphine"? The superimposition of the first peak with the slope in the physiograph starts to produce an object whose limits are the visual inscriptions produced in the lab. The object is a real object no more and no less than any other, since many such visual layers can be produced. Its resistance as a real fact depends only on the number of such visual layers that Guillemin's lab can mobilize all at once in one spot, in front of the dissenter. For each "objection" there is an inscription that blocks the dissent; soon the dissenter is forced to quit the game or to come back later with other and better visual displays. Objectivity is slowly erected inside the laboratory walls by mobilizing more faithful allies.

## IV. Capitalizing Inscriptions to Mobilize Allies

Can we summarize why it is so important for Brahe, Boyle, Pasteur, or Guillemin to work on two-dimensional inscriptions instead of the sky, the air, health, or the brain? What can they do with the first that you cannot do with the second? Let me list a few of the advantages of the "paper-work."

1. Inscriptions are *mobile*, as I indicated for La Pérouse's case. Chinese, planets, microbes—none of these can move; however, maps, photographic plates, and Petri dishes can.

2. They are *immutable* when they move, or at least everything is done to obtain this result: specimens are chloroformed, microbe colonies are stuck into gelatin, even exploding stars are kept on graph papers in each phase of their explosion.

3. They are made *flat*. There is nothing you can dominate as easily as a flat surface of a few square meters; there is nothing hidden or convoluted, no shadows, no "double entendre." In politics as in science, when someone is said to "master" a question or to "dominate" a subject, you should normally look for the flat surface that enables mastery (a map, a list, a file, a census, the wall of a gallery, a card-index, a repertory); and you will find it.

4. The *scale* of the inscriptions may be *modified* at will, without any change in their internal proportions. Observers never insist on this simple fact: no matter what the (reconstructed) size of the phenomena, they all end up being studied only when they reach the same average size. Billions of galaxies are never bigger, when they are counted, than nanometer-sized chromosomes; international trade is never much bigger than mesons; scale models of oil refineries end up having the same dimensions as plastic models of atoms. Confusion resumes outside a few square meters. This trivial change of scale seems innocuous enough, but it is the cause of most of the "superiority" of scientists and engineers: no one else deals only with phenomena that can be dominated with the eyes and held by hands, no matter when and where they come from or what their original size.

5. They can be *reproduced* and spread at little cost, so that all the instants of time and all the places in space can be gathered in another time and place. This is "Eisenstein's effect."

6. Since these inscriptions are mobile, flat, reproducible, still, and of varying scales, they can be reshuffled and *recombined*. Most of what we impute to connections in the mind may be explained by this reshuffling of inscriptions that all have the same "optical consistency." The same is true of what we call "metaphor" (see a funny case in Woolf, 1975; see also Latour and Woolgar, 1979: chap. 4; Goody, 1977; Hughes, 1979; Ong, 1982).

7. One aspect of these recombinations is that it is possible to *superimpose* several images of totally different origins and scales. To link geology and economics seems an impossible task, but to superimpose a geological map with the printout of the commodity market at the New York Stock Exchange requires good documentation and takes a few inches. Most of what we call "structure," "pattern," "theory," and "abstraction" are consequences of these superimpositions (Bertin, 1973). "Thinking is hand-work," as Heidegger said, but what is in the hands are inscriptions. Levi-Strauss's theories of savages are an artifact of card-indexing at the Collège de France, exactly as Ramist's method, for Ong, is an artifact of the prints accumulated at the Sorbonne; or modern taxonomy a result of the book-keeping undertaken amongst other places at Kew Gardens.

8. But one of the most important advantages is that the inscription, after only little cleaning up, can be *made part of a written text*. I have considered elsewhere at length this common ground in which inscriptions coming from instruments merge with already published texts and with new texts in draft. This characteristic of scientific texts has been shown by Ivins and Eisenstein for the past. A present-day laboratory may still be defined as the unique place where a text is made to comment on things which are all present in it. Because the commentary, earlier texts (through citations and references), and "things" have the same optical consistency, and the same semiotic homogeneity, an extraordinary degree of certainty is achieved by writing and reading these articles (Latour and Bastide, 1985; Lynch, 1984; Law, 1983). The text is not simply "illustrated," it carries all there is to see in what it writes about. Through the laboratory, the text and the spectacle of the world end up having the same character.

9. But the last advantage is the greatest. The two-dimensional character of inscriptions allow them to merge *with geometry*. As we saw for perspective, space on paper can be made continuous with three-dimensional space. The result is that we can work on paper with rulers and numbers, but still manipulate three-dimensional objects "out there" (Ivins, 1973). Better still, because of this optical consistency, everything, no matter where it comes from, can be converted into diagrams and numbers, and combinations of numbers and tables can be used which are still easier to handle than words or silhouettes (Dagognet, 1973). You cannot measure the sun, but you can measure a photograph of the sun with a ruler. Then the number of centimeters read can easily migrate through different scales and provide solar masses for completely different objects. This is what I call, for want of a better term, the second-degree advantage of inscriptions, or the surplus value that is gained through their capitalization.

These nine advantages should not be isolated from one another and should always be seen in conjunction with the mobilization process they accelerate and summarize. In other words, every possible innovation that offers any of these advantages will be selected by eager scientists and engineers: new photographs, new dyes to color more cell cultures, new reactive paper, a more sensitive physiograph, a new indexing system for librarians, a new notation for algebraic function, a new heating system to keep specimens longer. History of science is the history of these innovations. The role of the mind has been vastly exaggerated, as has that of perception (Arnheim, 1969). An average mind or an average person, with the same perceptual abilities, within normal social conditions, will generate totally different output depending on whether his or her average skills apply to the confusing world or to inscriptions.

It is especially interesting to focus on the ninth advantage, because it gives us a way to make "formalism" a more mundane and a more material reality. To go from "empirical" to "theoretical" sciences is to go from slower to faster mobiles, from more mutable to less mutable inscriptions. The trends we studied above do not break down when we look at formalism but, on the contrary, increase fantastically. Indeed, what we call formalism is *the acceleration of displacement without transformation*. To grasp this point let us go back to section II. The mobilization of many resources through space and time is essential for domination on a grand scale. I proposed to call immutable mobiles these objects that allow this mobilization to take place. I also argued that the best of these mobiles had to do with written, numbered, or optically consistent paper surfaces. But I also indicated, though without offering an explanation, that we had to deal with *cascades* of ever more simplified and costlier inscriptions. This ability to form a cascade must now be explained, because gathering written and imaged resources in one place, even with two-way connections, does *not* by itself guarantee any superiority for the one who gathers them. Why? Because the gatherer

of such traces is immediately swamped in them. I showed such a phenomenon at work in Guillemin's laboratory; after only a few days of letting the instruments run, the piles of printout were enough to boggle the mind (Latour and Woolgar, 1979: chap. 2). The same thing happened to Darwin after a few years of collecting specimens on the *Beagle*, there were so many crates that Darwin was almost squeezed out of his house. So by themselves the inscriptions do *not* help a location to become a center that dominates the rest of the world. Something has to be done to the inscriptions which is similar to what the inscriptions do to the "things," so that in the end a few elements can manipulate all the others on a vast scale. The same deflating strategy we used to show how "things" were turned into paper can show how paper is turned into *less* paper.

Let us take as an example "the effectiveness of Galileo's work," as seen by Drake (1970). Drake does indeed use the word formalism to designate what Galileo is able to do that his predecessors could not. But what is described is more interesting than that. Drake compares the diagrams and commentaries of Galileo with those two older scholars, Jordan and Stevin. Interestingly, in Jordan's demonstration "the physical element is, as you see, brought in as an afterthought to the geometry, by main force as it were" (1970: 103). With Simon Stevin's diagram this is the opposite: "The previous situation is reversed; geometry is eliminated in favor of pure mechanical intuition" (1970: 103). So what seems to happen is that Galileo's two predecessors could not visually *accommodate* the problem on a paper surface and see the result simultaneously as both geometry and physics. A simple change in the geometry used by Galileo allows him to connect many different problems, whereas his two predecessors worked on disconnected shapes over which they had no control:

"Galileo's way of merging geometry and physics became apparent in his proof of the same theorem in his early treatise on motion dating from 1590. The method itself suggested to him not only many corollaries but successive improvements of the proof itself and further physical implications of it." (Drake, 1970: 104).

This ability to connect might be located in Galileo's mind. In fact, what gets connected are three different visual horizons held synoptically because the surface of paper is considered as geometrical space:

"You see how the entire demonstration constitutes a reduction of the problem of equilibrium on inclined planes to the lever, which in itself removes the theorem from the isolation in which it stood before." (Drake,1970: 106)

This innocuous term "removing from isolation" is constantly used by those who talk of theories. No wonder. If you just hold Galileo's diagram, you hold three domains; when you hold the others, only one. The holding allowed by a "theory" is no more mysterious (and no less) than the holding of armies, or of stocks, or of positions in space. It is fascinating to see that Drake explains the efficiency of Galileo's connection in terms of his creation of a geometrical medium in which geometry and physics merge. This is a much more material explanation than Koyré's idealist one, although the "matter" in Drake's rendering is a certain type of inscription on papers, and certain ways of looking at it.

Similar tactics that use diagrams in order to establish rapid links between many unrelated problems are documented by cognitive psychologists. In a recent review Herbert Simon (1982) compares the tactics of experts and novices in drawing diagrams when they are questioned about simple physical problems (pumps, water flows, and so on). The crucial difference between experts and novices is exactly the same as that pointed out by Drake:

"The crucial thing that appeared in the expert behaviour was that the formulation from the initial and the final condition was assembled in such a way that the relations between them and hence the answer could essentially be read off from it (the diagram)." (Simon, 1982: 169)

With this question in mind, one is struck by the metaphors "theoreticians" use to celebrate and rank theories.[12] The two main sets of metaphors insist respectively upon increased mobility and increased immutability. Good theories are opposed to bad ones or to "mere collections of empirical facts" because they provide "easy access to them." Hankel, for instance, criticizes Diophantes in the words that a French civil engineer would use to denigrate the Nigerian highway system:

"Any question requires a quite special method, which after will not serve even for the most closely allied problems. It is on that accord difficult for a modern mathematician even after studying one hundred Diophantine solutions, to solve the 101st problem; and if we have made the attempt, and after some vain endeavours read Diophantus' own solution, we shall be astonished to see how suddenly he leaves the broad highroad, dashes into a side path and with a quick turn reaches the goal ... " (cited in Bloor, 1976: 102)

The safe path of science, as Kant would say, is not the same for the Greeks, for the Bororos, and for us; but neither are the systems of transportation identical. One could object that these are only metaphors. Yes, but the etymology of *metaphoros* is itself enlightening. It means precisely displacement, transportation, transfer. No matter if they are mere images, these metaphors aptly *carry* the obsession of theoreticians for easy transportation and rapid communication. A more powerful theory, we submit, is one that with fewer elements and fewer and simpler transformations makes it possible to get at every other theory (past and future). Every time a powerful theory is celebrated it is always possible to rephrase this admiration in terms of the most trivial struggle for power: holding this place allows me to hold all the others (Latour, 1984b: part 2). This is the problem we have encountered right through this paper: how to assemble many allies in one place.

A similar link between ability to abstract and the practical work of mobilizing resources without transforming them is seen in much of cognitive science. In Piaget's tests, for instance, much fuss is made of water poured from a tall thin beaker into a short flat one. If the children say the water volume has changed, they are non-conserving. But as any laboratory observer knows, most of the phenomena depend upon which measure to read, or which to believe in case of discrepancy. The shift from non-conserving to conserving might not be a modification in cognitive structure but a shift in indicators: read the height of the water in the first beaker and believe it *more* than the reading from the flat beaker. The notion of "volume" is held between the calibrated beakers exactly like Guillemin's endorphin is *held* between several peaks from at least five different instruments. In other words, Piaget is asking his children to do a laboratory experiment comparable in difficulty to that of the average Nobel Prize winner. If any shift in thinking occurs, it has nothing to do with the mind, but with the manipulation of the laboratory setting. Out of this setting no answer can be offered on volume. The best proof of this is that without industrially calibrated beakers Piaget himself would be totally unable to decide what is conserved (see also Cole and Scribner, 1974: last chapter). So again, most of what we grant a priori to "higher cognitive functions" might be concrete tasks done with new calibrated, graduated, and written objects. More generally, Piaget is obsessed with conservation and displacement through space without alteration (Piaget and Garcia, 1983). Thinking is tantamount to acquiring the ability to move as fast as possible while conserving as much of the pattern as possible. What Piaget takes as

the logic of the psyche is this very logic of mobilization and immutability so peculiar to our scientific societies when they want to produce hard facts to dominate on a large scale. No wonder that all these "abilities" to move fast in such a world get better with schooling![13]

We now come closer to an understanding of the matter that constitutes formalism. The point of departure is that we are constantly hesitating between several often contradictory indications from our senses. Most of what we call "abstraction" is in practice the belief that a written inscription must be believed more than any contrary indications from the senses.[14] Koyré, for instance, has shown that Galileo believed in the inertia principle on mathematical grounds even against the contrary evidences offered to him not only by the Scriptures but also by the senses. Koyré claims that this rejection of the senses was due to Galileo's Platonist philosophy. This might be so. But what does it mean practically? It means that faced with many contrary indications, Galileo, in the last instance, believed *more* in the triangular diagram for calculating the law of falling bodies then any *other* vision of falling bodies (Koyré, 1966: 147). When in doubt, believe the inscriptions, written in mathematical terms, *no matter* to what absurdities this might lead you.[15]

After Eisenstein's magisterial reworking of the Book of Nature argument, and Alper's redefinition of "visual culture," the ethnography of abstraction might be easier: What is this society in which a written, printed, mathematical form has greater credence, in case of doubt, than anything else: common sense, the senses other than vision, political authority, tradition, and even the Scriptures? It is obvious that this feature of society is overdetermined since it can be found in the written law (Clanchy, 1979); in the biblical exegesis of the Holy Scriptures and in the history of geometry (Husserl, 1954; Derrida, 1967; Serres, 1980). Without this peculiar tendency to privilege what is written, the power of inscription would be entirely lost, as Edgerton hints in his discussion of Chinese diagrams. No matter how beautiful, rich, precise, or realistic inscriptions may be, no one would believe what they showed, if they could be contradicted by other evidence of local, sensory origin or pronouncements of the local authorities. I feel that we would make a giant step forward if we could relate this peculiar feature of our culture to the requirement of mobilization I have outlined several times. Most of the "domain" of cognitive psychology and epistemology does not exist, but is related to this strange anthropological puzzle: a training (often in schools) to manipulate written inscriptions, to array them in cascades, and to believe the last one on the series more than any evidence to the contrary. It is in the description of this training that the anthropology of geometry and mathematics should be decisive (Livingston, 1983; Lave, 1985, 1986; Serres, 1982).

## V.
## Paperwork

There are two ways in which the visualization processes we are all interested in may be ignored; one is to grant to the scientific mind what should be granted to the hands, to the eyes, and to the signs; the other is to focus exclusively on the signs *qua* signs, without considering the mobilization of which they are but the fine edge. All innovations in picture making, equations, communications, archives, documentation, instrumentation, argumentation, will be selected for or against depending on how they simultaneously affect either inscription or mobilization. This link is visible not only in the empirical sciences, not only in the (former) realm of formalism but also in many "practical" endeavors from which science is often unduly severed.

In a beautiful book (1982), Booker retraces the history of engineering drawings. Linear perspective (see above) progressively "changed the concept of pictures from being just representation to that of their being projections onto planes" (p. 31). But perspective still depended on the observer's position, so the objects could not really be moved everywhere without corruption. Desargues's and Monge's works "helped to change the 'point of view' or way of looking at things mentally. In place of the imaginary fines of space—so difficult to conceive clearly—which were the basis of perspective at that time, projective geometry allowed perspective to be seen in terms of solid geometry." (Booker, 1982: 34)

With descriptive geometry, the observer's position becomes irrelevant. "It can be viewed and photographed from any angle or projected onto any plane—that is, distorted—and the result remains true" (p. 35). Booker and still better Baynes and Push (1981) in a splendid book (see also Deforges, 1981) show how *a few* engineers could *master* enormous machines that did not yet exist. These feats cannot be imagined without industrial drawings. Booker, quoting an engineer, describes the change of scale that allows the few to dominate the many:

"A machine that has been drawn is like an ideal realisation of it, but in a material that costs little and is easier to handle than iron or steel … If everything is first well thought out, and the essential dimensions determined by calculations or experience, the plan of a machine or installation of machines can be quickly put on paper and the whole thing as well as the detail can then most conveniently be submitted to the severest criticism … If at first there is doubt as to which of various possible arrangements is the most desirable then they are all sketched, compared with one another and the most suitable can easily be chosen." (Booker, 1982: 187)

Industrial drawing not only creates a paper world that can be manipulated as if in three dimensions. It also creates a common place for many other inscriptions to come together. Margins of tolerance can be inscribed on the drawing; the drawing can be used for economic calculation, or for defining the tasks to be made, or for organizing the repairs and the sales.

"But drawings are of the utmost importance not only for planning but also for execution since by means of them the measurements and proportions of all the parts can be so sharply and definitely determined from the beginning that when it comes to manufacture it is only necessary to imitate in the materials used for construction exactly what is shown in the drawing.

"Every part of the machine can in general be manufactured independently of every other part; it is therefore possible to distribute the entire work among a great number of workers … No substantial errors can arise in work organised in this manner and if it does happen that on a rare occasion a mistake has been made it is immediately known with whom the blame lies." (Booker, 1982: 198)

Realms of reality that seem far apart (mechanics, economics, marketing, scientific organization of work) are inches apart, once flattened out onto the same surface. The accumulation of drawings in an optically consistent space is, once again, the "universal exchanger" that allows work to be planned, dispatched, realized, and responsibility to be attributed.[16]

The connective quality of written traces is still more visible in the most despised of all ethnographic objects: the file or the record. The "rationalization" granted to bureaucracy since Hegel and Weber has been attributed by mistake to the "mind" of (Prussian) bureaucrats. It is all in the files themselves. In many ways, and more and more every year, a bureau is a small laboratory in which many elements can be connected together just because their scale

and nature has been averaged out: legal texts, specifications, standards, payrolls, maps, surveys (ever since the Norman Conquest, as shown by Clanchy, 1979). Economics, politics, sociology, hard sciences, do not come into contact through the grandiose entrance of "interdisciplinarity" but through the back door of the *file*. The "cracy" of bureaucracy is mysterious and hard to study, but the "bureau" is something that can be empirically studied, and which explains, because of its structure, why some power is given to an average mind just by looking at files: domains which are far apart become literally inches apart; domains which are convoluted and hidden become flat; thousands of occurrences can be looked at synoptically. More importantly, once files start being gathered everywhere to insure some two-way circulation of immutable mobiles, they can be arrayed in cascades: files of files can be generated and this process can be continued until a few men consider millions as if they were in the palms of their hands. Common sense ironically makes fun of these "gratte papiers" and "paper shufflers," and often wonders what all this "red tape" is for; but the same question should be asked of the rest of science and technology. In our cultures "paper shuffling" is the source of an essential power that constantly escapes attention since its materiality is ignored.

McNeill, in his fundamental book *The Pursuit of Power* (1982), uses this ability to distinguish Chinese bureaucracy from that of the Occident. Accumulation of records and ideograms make the Chinese Empire possible. But there is a major drawback with ideograms; once gathered you cannot array them in a cascade in such a way that thousands of records can be turned in one, that is, literally "punctualized" through geometrical or mathematical skills. So here again, if we keep both the quality of the signs and the mobilization process in focus, we may understand why careful limits have been put in the past to the growth of the Chinese imperium, and why these limits to the mobilization of resources on a grand scale have been broken in Europe. It is hard to overestimate the power that is gained by concentrating files written in a homogeneous and combinable form (Wheeler, 1969; Clanchy, 1979).

This role of the bureaucrat *qua* scientist *qua* writer and reader, is always misunderstood because we take for granted that there exist, somewhere in society, macro-actors that naturally dominate the scene: Corporation, State, Productive Forces, Cultures, Imperialisms, "Mentalités," and so on. Once accepted, these large entities are then used to explain (or to not explain) "cognitive" aspects of science and technology. The problem is that these entities could not exist at all without the construction of long networks in which numerous faithful records circulate in both directions, records which are, in turn, summarized and displayed to convince. A "state," a "corporation," a "culture," an "economy" are the result of a punctualization process that obtains a few indicators out of many traces. In order to exist these entities have to be *summed up* somewhere. Far from being the key to the understanding of science and technology, these entities are the very things a new understanding of science and technology should explain. The large-scale actors to which sociologists of science are keen to attach "interests" are immaterial in practice as long as precise mechanisms to explain their origin or extraction and their changes of scale have not been proposed.

A man is never much more powerful than any other—even from a throne; but a man whose eye dominates records through which some sort of connections are established with millions of others may be said to *dominate*. This domination, however, is not a given but a slow construction, and it can be corroded, interrupted, or destroyed if the records, files, and figures are immobilized, made more mutable, less readable, less combinable, or unclear when displayed. In other words, the *scale* of an actor is not an absolute term but a relative one that varies with the ability to produce, capture, sum up, and interpret information about other places and times (Callon and Latour, 1981). Even the very notion of scale is impossible to understand without an inscription or a map in mind. The "great man" is a little man looking at a good map. In Mercator's frontispiece Atlas is transformed from a god who carries the world into a scientist who holds it in his hand (Mukerji, 1985)!

Since the beginning of this presentation on visualization and cognition, I have been recasting the simple question of power: how the few may dominate the many. After McNeill's major reconceptualization of the history of power in terms of mobilization, this age-old question of political philosophy and sociology can be rephrased in another way: how can distant or foreign places and times be gathered in one place in a form that allows all the places and times to be presented at once, and which allows orders to move back to where they came from? Talking of power is an endless and mystical task; talking of distance, gathering, fidelity, summing up, transmission, and so on is an empirical one, as has been illustrated in a recent study by John Law of the Portuguese spice road to India (1986). Instead of using large-scale entities to explain science and technology, as most sociologists of science do, we should start from the inscriptions and their mobilization and see how they help small entities to become large ones. In this shift from one research program to another, "science and technology" will cease to be the mysterious cognitive object to be explained by the social world. It will become one of the main sources of power (McNeill, 1982). To take the existence of macro-actors for granted without studying the material that makes them "macro" is to make both science and society mysterious. To take the fabrication of various scales as our main center of interest is to place the practical means of achieving power on a firm foundation (Cicourel, 1981). The Pentagon does not *see* more of the Russians' strategy than Guillemin does his endorphin. They simply put faith in superimposed traces of various quality, opposing some to others, retracing the steps of those that are dubious, and spending billions to create new branches of science and technology that can accelerate the mobility of traces, perfect their immutability, enhance readability, insure their compatibility, quicken their display: satellites, networks of espionage, computers, libraries, radioimmunoassays, archives, surveys. They will never see more of the phenomena than what they can build through these many immutable mobiles. This is *obvious*, but rarely *seen*.

If this little shift from a social/cognitive divide to the study of inscriptions is accepted, then the importance of *metrology* appears in proper light. Metrology is the scientific organization of stable measurement and standards. Without it no measurement is stable enough to allow either the homogeneity of the inscriptions or their return. It is not surprising then to learn that metrology costs up to three times the budget of all Research and Development, and that this figure is for only the first elements of the metrological chain (Hunter, 1980). Thanks to metrological organization the basic physical constants (time, space, weight, wave-length) and many biological and chemical standards may be extended "every-where" (Zerubavel, 1982; Landes, 1983). The universality of science and technology is a cliché of epistemology, but metrology is the practical achievement of this mystical universality. In practice it is costly and full of holes (see Cochrane, 1966 for the history of the Bureau of Standards). Metrology is only the official and primary component of an ever increasing number of measuring activities we all have to undertake in daily life. Every time we look at our wristwatch or weigh

a sausage at the butchers shop; every time applied laboratories measure lead pollution or water purity, or control the quality of industrial goods, we allow more immutable mobiles to reach new places. "Rationalization" has very little to do with the reason of bureau and technocrats, but has a lot to do with the maintenance of metrological chains (Uselding, 1981). This building of long networks provides the stability of the main physical constants, but there are many other metrological activities for less "universal" measures (polls, questionnaires, forms to fill in, accounts, tallies).

There is one more domain into which this ethnography of inscription could bring some "light." I want to talk about it, since at the beginning of this overview, I rejected dichotomies between "mentalist" and "materialist" explanations. Among the interesting immutable mobiles there is one that has received both too little and too much attention: money. The anthropology of money is as complicated and entangled as that of writing, but one thing is clear. As soon as money starts to circulate through different cultures, it develops a few clear-cut characteristics: it is mobile (once in small pieces), it is immutable (once in metal), it is countable (once it is coined), combinable, and can circulate from the things valued to the center that evaluates and back. Money has received too much attention because it has been thought of as something special, deeply inserted in the infrastructure of economies, whereas it is just one of the many immutable mobiles necessary if one place is to exercise power over many other places far apart in space and time. As a type of immutable mobile *amongst others*, it has received too little attention, however. Money is used to code all states of affairs in exactly the way that La Pérouse coded all places by longitude and latitude (actually, in his log book La Pérouse registered both the places on the map and the values of each good as if it were to be sold in some other place). In this way it is possible to accumulate, to count, to display, and to recombine all the states of affairs. Money is neither more nor less "material" than map making, engineering drawings, or statistics.

Once its ordinary character is recognized, the "abstraction" of money can no longer be the object of a fetish cult. For instance, the importance of the art of accounting both in economies and science falls nicely into place. Money is not interesting as such but as one type of immutable mobile that links goods and places; so it is no wonder if it quickly merges with other written inscriptions: figures, columns, double-entry bookkeeping (Roover, 1963). No wonder if, through accounting, it is possible to gain more just by recombining numbers (Braudel, 1979, especially vol. 3). Here again, too much emphasis should not be placed on the visualization of numbers per se; what should really be stressed is the cascade of mobile inscriptions that end up in an account, which is, literally, the only thing that *counts*. Exactly as with any scientific inscription, in case of doubt the new accountant prefers to believe inscription, no matter how strange the consequences and counterintuitive the phenomena. The history of money is thus seized by the same trend as all the other immutable mobiles; any innovations that can accelerate money to enlarge its power of mobilization are kept: checks, endorsement, paper money, electronic money. This trend is not due to the development of capitalism. On the contrary, "capitalism" is an empty word as long as precise material instruments are not proposed to explain any capitalization at all, be it of specimens, books, information, or money.

Thus capitalism should not be used to explain the evolution of science and technology. It seems to me that it should be quite the contrary. Once science and technology are rephrased in terms of immutable mobiles it might be possible to explain economic capitalism as another process of mobilization. What indicates this are the many weaknesses of money; money is a nice immutable mobile that circulates from one point to another, but it carries very little with it. If the name of the game is to accumulate enough allies in one place to modify the belief and behavior of all the others, money is a poor resource as long as it is isolated. It becomes useful when it is combined with all the other inscription devices; then the different points of the world become really transported in a manageable form to a single place which then becomes a *center*. As with Eisenstein's printing press, which is one factor that allows all the others to merge with one another, what counts is not the capitalization of money but the capitalization of all compatible inscriptions. Instead of talking of merchants, princes, scientists, astronomers, and engineers as having some sort of relation with one another, it seems to me it would be more productive to talk about *"centers of calculation."* The currency in which they calculate is less important than the fact that they calculate only with inscriptions and mix together in these calculations inscriptions coming from the most diverse disciplines. The calculations themselves are less important than the way they are arrayed in cascades, and the bizarre situation in which the last inscription is believed more than anything else. Money per se is certainly not the universal standard looked for by Marx and other economists. This qualification should be granted to centers of calculation and to the peculiarity of written traces that makes rapid translation between one medium and another possible.

Many efforts have been made to link the history of science with the history of capitalism, and many efforts have been made to describe the scientist as a capitalist. All these efforts (including mine—Latour and Woolgar, 1979: chap. 5; Latour 1984a) were doomed from the start, since they took for granted a division between mental and material factors, an artifact of our ignorance of inscriptions.[17] There is not a history of engineers, then a history of capitalists, then one of scientists, then one of mathematicians, then one of economists. Rather, there is a single history of these centers of calculation. It is not only because they look exclusively at maps, account books, drawings, legal texts, and files that cartographers, merchants, engineers, jurists, and civil servants get the edge on all the others. It is because all these inscriptions can be superimposed, reshuffled, recombined, and summarized, and that totally new phenomena emerge, hidden from the other people from whom all these inscriptions have been exacted.

More precisely we should be able to explain, with the concept and empirical knowledge of these centers of calculation, how insignificant people working only with papers and signs become the most powerful of all. Papers and signs are incredibly weak and fragile. This is why explaining anything with them seemed so ludicrous at first. La Pérouse's map is not the Pacific, anymore than Watt's drawings and patents are the engines, or the bankers' exchange rates are the economies, or the theorems of topology are "the real world." This is precisely the paradox. By working on papers alone, on fragile inscriptions which are immensely less than the things from which they are extracted, it is still possible to dominate all things, and all people. What is insignificant for all other cultures becomes the most significant, the only significant aspect of reality. The weakest, by manipulating inscriptions of all sorts obsessively and exclusively, become the strongest. This is the view of power we get at by following this theme of visualization and cognition in all its consequences.

1 For instance, Levi-Strauss's divide between bricoleur and engineer or between hot and cold societies (1962); or Garfinkel's distinctions between everyday and scientific modes of thought (1967); or Bachelard's many "coupures épistémologiques" that divide science from common sense, from intuition or from its own past (1934, 1967); or even Horton's careful distinction between monster acceptance and monster avoidance (1977) or primary theories and secondary theories (1982).

2 Goody (1977) points to the importance of practical tasks in handling graphics (lists, dictionaries, inventories), and concludes his fascinating book by saying that "if we wish to speak of a 'savage mind' these are some of the instruments of its domestication" (182). Cole and Scribner (1974) shift the focus from intellectual tasks to schooling practice; the ability to draw syllogisms is taken out of the mind and put into the manipulation of diagrams on papers. Hutchins (1980) does the opposite in transforming the "illogical" reasoning of the Trobriand islanders into a quite straightforward logic simply by adding to it the land-use systems that give meaning to hitherto abrupt shifts in continuity. Eisenstein switches the enquiry from mental states and the philosophical tradition to the power of print (1979). Perret-Clermont (1979), at first one of Piaget's students, focuses her attention on the social context of the many test situations. She shows how "non-conserving" kids become conserving in a matter of minutes simply because other variables (social or pictorial) are taken into account. Lave has explored in pioneering studies how mathematical skills may be totally modified depending on whether or not you let people use paper and pencil (Lave, 1985, 1986; Lave, Murtaugh and De La Rocha, 1983). Ferguson has tried to relate engineering imagination to the abilities to draw pictures according to perspective rules and codes of shades and colors (1977): "It has been non-verbal thinking by and large that has fixed the outlines and filled in the details of our material surroundings ... Pyramids, cathedrals, and rockets exist not because of geometry, theory of structures, or thermodynamics, but because they were first a picture—literally a vision—in the minds of those who built them" (835) (see also Ferguson, 1985). These are some of the studies that put the deflating strategy I try to review here into practice.

3 A fact is harder or softer as a function of what happens to it in other hands later on. Each of us acts as a multi-conductor for the many claims that we come across: we may be uninterested, or ignore them, or be interested but modify them and turn them into something entirely different. Sometimes indeed we act as conductor and pass the claim along without further modification (see Latour and Woolgar, 1979; Latour, 1984b).

4 "Science and technology have advanced in more than direct ratio to the ability of men to contrive methods by which the phenomena which otherwise could be known only through the senses of touch, hearing, taste and smell, have been brought within the range of visual recognition and measurements and then become subject to that logical symbolization without which rational thought and analysis are impossible" (Ivins, 1973: 13).

5 "The most marked characteristics of European pictorial representation since the fourteenth century, have been on the one hand its steadily increasing naturalism and on the other its purely schematic and logical extension. It is submitted that both are due in largest part to the development and pervasion of methods which have provided symbols, repeatable in invariant forms, for representation of visual awareness and a grammar of perspective which made it possible to establish logical relations not only within the system of symbols but between that system and the forms and locations of the objects that it symbolizes" (Ivins, 1973: 12).

6 "Northern artists characteristically sought to represent by transforming the extent of vision onto their small, flat working surface ... It is the capacity of the picture surface to contain such a semblance of the world—an aggregate of views—that characterizes many pictures in the North" (Alpers, 1983: 51).

7 The proof that the *movement* comes first, for Eisenstein, lies in the fact that it entails exactly the opposite effects on the Scriptures. The accuracy of the medium reveals more and more inaccuracies in the message, which is soon jeopardized. The beauty of Eisenstein's construction resides in the way it obtains two opposite consequences from the same cause: science and technology accelerates; the Gospel becomes doubtful (Latour, 1983).

8 For instance, Mukerji portrays a geographer who hates the new geography books but has to cry his hate in print: "Ironically, Davis took his trip because he did not trust printed information to be as complete as oral accounts of experiences; but he decided to make the voyage after reading Dutch books on geography and produced from his travel another geographical/navigational text" (Mukerji, 1983: 114).

9 This is why I do not include in the discussion the broad literature on the neurology of vision or the psychology of perception (see for instance Block, 1981; de Mey, 1992). These disciplines, however important, make so much use of the very process I wish to study that they are as blind as the others to an ethnography of the crafts and tricks of the visualization.

10 "Un 'pouvoir d'écriture' se constitue comme une pièce essentielle dans les rouages de la discipline. Sur bien des points, il se modèle sur les méthodes traditionnelles de la documentation administrative mais avec des techniques particulières et des innovations importantes" (Foucault, 1975: 191).

11 These simple shifts are often transformed by philosophers into complete ruptures from common sense, into "coupures épistémologiques," as in Bachelard. It is not because of the empiricists' naïveté that one has to fall back on the power of theories to make sense of data. The focus on inscriptions and manipulation of traces is exactly mid-way between empiricism and Bachelard's argument on the power of theories.

12 A nice example is that of Carnot's thermodynamics studied by Redondi (1980). Carnot's know-how is not about building a machine but rather a diagram. This diagram is drawn in such a way that it allows one to move from one engine to any other, and indeed to nonexistent engines simply *drawn* on paper. Real three-dimensional steam engines are

interesting but localized and cumbersome. Thermodynamics is to them what La Pérouse's map is to the islands of the Pacific. When going from one engine to the theory or from one island to the map, you do not go from concrete to abstract, from empirical to theoretical, you go from one place that dominates no one, to another place that dominates all the others. If you grasp thermodynamics, you grasp all engines (past, present, and future—see Diesel). The question about theories is who controls whom and on what scale.

13 A nice *a contrario* proof is provided by Edgerton's study of Chinese technical drawings (1980). He claims that Chinese artists have no interest in the figures, or, more exactly, that they take figures not inside the perspective space on which an engineer can work and make calculations and previsions, but as *illustration*. In consequence all the links between parts of the machines become decorations (a complex part of the pump becomes, for instance, waves on a pond after a few copies!). No one would say that Chinese are unable to abstract, but it would not be absurd to say that they do not put their full confidence into writing and imaging.

14 In a beautiful article Carlo Ginzburg speaks of a "paradigm of the trace" to designate this peculiar obsession of our culture that he traces – precisely! from Greek medicine to Conan Doyle's detective story, through Freud's interest in lapsus and the detection of art forgeries (1980). Falling back, however, on a classical prejudice, Ginzburg puts physics and hard sciences aside from such a paradigm because, he contends, they do not rely on traces but on abstract, universal phenomena!

15 Ivins explains, for instance, that most Greek parallels in geometry do not meet because they are touched by the hands, whereas Renaissance parallels do meet since they are only seen on paper (1973: 7). Jean Lave, in her studies of Californian grocery shoppers, shows that people confronted with a difficulty in their computation rarely stick to the paper and never put their confidence in what is written (Lave et al., 1983). *To do so* no matter how absurd the consequences requires still another set of peculiar circumstances related to laboratory settings, even if these are, as Livingston says (1993), "flat laboratories." In one of his twelve or so origins of geometry, Serres argues that having invented the alphabet and thus broken any connection between written shapes and the signified, the Greeks had to cope with pictorial representation. He argues that what we came to call formalism is an alphabetic text trying to describe visual diagrams: "Qu'est-ce que cette géométrie dans la pratique? Non point dans les "idées" qu'elle suppose mais dans l'activité qui la pose. Elle est d'abord un art du dessin. Elle est ensuite un langage qui parle du dessin tracé que celui-ci soit présent ou absent" (Serres. 1990: 176).

16 The link between technical thinking and technical drawing is so close that scholars establish it even unwillingly. For instance, Bertrand Gille, when accounting for the creation of a new "système technique" in Alexandria during the Hellenistic period, is obliged to say that it is the availability of a good library and the gathering of a collection of scale models of all the machines previously invented that transformed "mere practice" into techno-*logy* (1990). What makes the "système technique" a *system* is the synoptic vision of all the former technical achievements which are all taken out of their isolation. This link is most clearly visible when an inscription device is hooked up to a working machine to make it comprehensible (Hills and Pacey, 1981; Constant, 1983). A nice rendering of the paper-world necessary to make a computer real is to be found in Kidder (1981). "The *soul* of the machine" is a pile of paper ...

17 The *direction* we go to by asking such questions is quite different from those of either the sociology of science or the cognitive sciences (especially when they both try to merge, as in de Mey's synthesis [1982]). Two recent attempts have been made to relate the fine structure of cognitive abilities to social structure. The first one uses Hesse's networks and Kuhn's paradigms (Barnes, 1982), the second Wittgenstein's "language games" (Bloor, 1983). These attempts are interesting, but they still try to answer a question which the present review wishes to reject: how cognitive abilities are *related* to our societies. The question (and thus the various answers) accept the idea that the stuff society is made of is somehow different from that of our sciences, our images, and our information. The phenomenon I wish to focus on is slightly different from those revealed by Barnes and Bloor. We are dealing with a single ethnographic puzzle: some societies—very few indeed—are made by capitalizing on a larger scale. The obsession with rapid displacement and stable invariance, for powerful and safe linkages, is not a part of our culture, or "influenced" by social interests: *it is our culture*. Too often sociologists look for *indirect* relations between "interests" and "technical" details. The reason for their blindness is simple: they limit the meaning of "social" to society without realizing that the mobilizing of allies, and in general the transformation of weak into strong associations, is what "social" also means. Why look for farfetched relations when technical details of science talk directly of invariance, association, displacement, immutability, and so on? (Law, 1986, Latour, 1984b; Callon, Law, and Rip, 1986)

ACKNOWLEDGMENTS

This paper was prepared as an introduction for the international seminar organized at the Ecole des Mines for the CNRS December 12, 13, and 14, 1983, and entitled "Visualization and Cognition." The proceedings of this seminar are published in French in the journal *Culture Technique*, no. 14, June 1985, under the title "Les 'vues' de l'esprit." I thank the CNRS and all the participants of the seminar for help in shaping my ideas. I especially thank John Law, who painstakingly reviewed the English version. I also thank Elihu Gerson, Howard Becker, and Steve Shapin.
I extend my thanks to all my colleagues who steadfastly refused to share my passion for "inscription devices" and forced me to read all the literature mobilized in this article in order to try to convince them.

REFERENCES

Alpers, S. 1983. The Art of Describing: Dutch Art in the 17th Century. Chicago: University of Chicago Press.
Arnheim, R. 1969. Visual Thinking. Berkeley: University of California Press.
Augé, M. 1975. Théorie des Pouvoirs et Idéologie. Paris: Hermann.
Bachelard, G. 1934. Le Nouvel Esprit Scientifique. Paris: PUF.
— 1967. La Formation de l'Esprit Scientifique. Paris: Vrin.
Barnes, B. and T. S. Kuhn 1992. Social Science. London: Macmillan.
Baynes, K. and F. Push 1981. The Art of the Engineer. Guildford, Sussex: Lutherword Press.
Bertin, P. 1973. Sémiologie Graphique. Paris: Mouton.
Block, N., ed. 1981. Imagery. Cambridge, MA: The MIT Press.
Bloor, D. 1976. Knowledge and Social Imagery. London: Routledge.
— 1983. Wittgenstein and the Social Theory of Knowledge. London: Macmillan.
Booker, P. J. 1982. A History of Engineering Drawing. London: Northgate Publishing Co.
Bourdieu, P. 1972. Esquisse d'une Théorie de la Pratique. Genève: Droz.
Braudel, L. 1979. Civilisation Matérielle et Capitalisme. Paris: Armand Colin.
Callon, M. and B. Latour 1981. "Unscrewing the big Leviathan." In K. Knorr and A. Cicourel, eds. Toward an Integration of Micro and Macro Sociologies, 277–303. London: Routledge.
Callon. M., J. Law, and A. Rip, eds. 1986. Qualitative Scientometrics: Studies in the Dynamic of Science. London: Macmillan.
Cicourel, A. 1981. "Notes on the integration of micro and macro levels." In K. Knorr and A. Cicourel, eds. Toward an Integration of Micro and Macro Sociologies, 51–80. London: Routledge.
Clanchy, M. T. 1979. From Memory to Written Records 1066–1300. Cambridge, MA: Harvard University Press.
Cochrane, R. X. 1966. Measure for Progress: A History of the National Bureau of Standards. Washington, D.C.: U.S. Bureau of Commerce.
Cole, J. and S. Scribner 1974. Culture and Thought: A Psychological Introduction. New York: John Wiley and Sons.
Constant, E. W. 1983. "Scientific theory and technological testability: science, dynamometer and water turbine in the 19th century." In Technology and Culture 24 (2), 183–199.
Dagognet, F. 1969. Tableaux et Langages de la Chimie. Paris: Le Seuil.
— 1973. Ecriture et Iconographie. Paris: Vrin.
Deforges, Y. 1991. Le Graphisme Technique. Le Creusot: Editions Champs-Vallon.
de Mey, M. 1982. The Cognitive Paradigm. Dordrecht: Reidel.
Derrida, J. 1967. De la Grammatologie. Paris: Minuit.
Drake, S. 1970. Galileo Studies. Ann Arbor: University of Michigan Press.
Edgerton, S. 1976. The Renaissance Discovery of Linear Perspective. New York: Harper and Row.
— 1980. "The Renaissance artist as a quantifier." In M, A. Hagen, ed. The Perception of Pictures. Vol. I. New York: Academic Press.
Eisenstein, E. 1979. The Printing Press as an Agent of Change. Cambridge: Cambridge University Press.
Fabian, J. 1983. Time and the Other: How Anthropology Makes Its Object. New York: Columbia University Press.
Ferguson, E. 1977. "The mind's eye: nonverbal thought in technology." In Science 197, 927ff.
— 1985. "La Fondation des machines modernes: des dessins." In B. Latour, ed. Les 'Vues' de l'Esprit, special issue of Culture Technique, 207–213.
Foucault, M. 1963. Naissance de la Clinique: Une Archéologie du Regard Médical. Paris: PUF.
— 1966. Les Mots et Les Choses. Paris: Gallimard.
— 1975. Surveiller et Punir. Paris: Gallimard.
Fourquet, M. 1980. Le Comptes de la Puissance. Paris: Encres.
Garfinkel, H. 1967. Studies in Ethnomethodology. Englewood Cliffs, NJ: Prentice-Hall.
Gille, B. 1980. Les Ingénieurs Grecs. Paris: Le Seuil.
Ginzburg, C. 1980. "Signes, traces, pistes." In Le Débat 6, 2–44.
Goody, J. 1977. The Domestication of the Savage Mind. Cambridge: Cambridge University Press.
Hagen, M. A. 1990. The Perception of Pictures. Vols. I and II. New York: Academic Press.
Hanson, N. R. 1962. Perception and Discovery: An Introduction to Scientific Inquiry. San Francisco: W. H. Freeman.
Havelock, E. B. 1980. Aux Origines de la Civilisation Écrite en Occident. Paris: Maspero.
Hills, R. and A. J. Pacey 1982. "The measurement of power in early steam driven textile mills." In Technology and Culture 13 (l), 25ff.
Hollis, M. and S. Lukes, eds. 1992. Rationality and Relativism. Oxford: Blackwell.
Horton, R. 1977. "African thought and western science." In B. Wilson. ed. Rationality, 131–171. Oxford: Blackwell.
— 1982. "Tradition and modernity revisited." In M. Hollis and S. Lukes, eds. Rationality and Relativism, 201–260. Oxford: Blackwell.
Hughes, T. 1979 "The system-builders." Technology and Culture 20(l), 124–161.
Hunter, P. 1980. "The national system of scientific measurement." In Science 210, 869–874.
Husserl, E. 1954. L'Origine de la Géométrie. Paris: PUF.
Hutchins, E. 1980. Culture and Inference: A Trobriand Case Study. Cambridge, MA: Harvard University Press.
Ivins, W. M. 1953. Prints and Visual Communications. Cambridge, MA: Harvard University Press.
— 1973. On the Rationalization of Sight. New York: Plenem Press.
Kidder, T. 1981. The Soul of a New Machine. London: Allen Lane.

Koyré, A. 1966. Etudes Galiléennes. Paris: Hermann.

Knorr, K. 1981. The Manufacture of Knowledge. Oxford: Pergamon Press.

Knorr, K. and A. Cicourel, eds. 1981. Toward an Integration of Micro and Macro Sociologies. London: Routledge.

Landes, D. 1983. Revolution in Time: Clock and the Making of the Modern World. Cambridge, MA: Harvard University Press.

La Pérouse, J. F. de n. d. (no date). Voyages Autour du Monde. Paris: Michel de l'Ormeraie.

Latour, B. 1983. "Comment redistribuer le grand partage?" In Revue Internationale de Synthèse 104 (110), 202–236.

— 1984a. "Le dernier des capitalistes sauvages, interview d'un biochimiste." In Fundamenta Scientiae 4 (3/4), 301–327.

— 1984b. Les Microbes: Guerre et Paix suivi de Irréductions. Paris: A.M. Métallié.

— 1985. Les 'Vues' de l'Esprit, special issue of Culture Technique.

— 1988. The Pasteurization of France. Trans. A. Sheridan, J. Law. Cambridge MA: Harvard University Press (paperback edition 1993).

— 1987. Science in Action, How to Follow Scientists and Engineers through Society. Cambridge MA: Harvard University Press.

— and F. Bastide 1985. "Science-fabrication." Chap. 4 in M. Callon, J. Law and A. Rip. eds. Qualitative Scientometrics: Studies in the Dynamic of Science. London: Macmillan.

— and S. Woolgar 1979. Laboratory Life: The Social Construction of Scientific Facts. London: Sage. (2nd edition 1986. Princeton: Princeton University Press.)

Lave, J. 1985. "Arithmetic Practice and Cognitive Theory: An Ethnographic Enquiry." Unpublished MS, University of California.

— 1986. "The values of quantification." In J. Law, ed. Power, Action and Belief, 88–111. London: Routledge.

Lave, J., M. Murtaugh and O. De La Rocha 1983. "The dialectic constitution of arithmetic practice." In B. Rogoff and J. Lave (eds.), Everyday Cognition: Its Development in Social Context, 230–270. Cambridge, MA: Harvard University Press.

Law, J. 1983. "Enrôlement et contre-enrôlement: les luttes pour la publication d'un article scientifique." In Social Science Information 22 (2), 237–251.

— 1985. "Les textes et leurs alliés." In B. Latour, ed. Les 'Vues' de l'Esprit, special issue of Culture Technique, 58–69.

— 1986. "On the methods of long-distance control: vessels, navigations and the Portuguese route to India." In J. Law, ed. Power, Action and Belief, 236–263. London: Routledge.

Leroi-Gourhan, A. 1964. Le Geste et la Parole. Paris: Albin Michel.

Levi-Strauss, C. 1962. La Pensée Sauvage. Paris: Plon.

Livingston, E. 1993. "An Ethnomethodological Investigation of the Foundations of Mathematics." Ph.D. thesis, University of California, Los Angeles.

Lynch, M. 1985a. "Discipline and the material form of images: an analysis of scientific visibility." In Social Studies of Science 15, 37–66.

— 1995b. "La rétine extériorisée." In B. Latour, ed. Les 'Vues' de l'Esprit, special issue of Culture Technique, 108–123.

McNeill, W. 1992. The Pursuit of Power, Technology, Armed Forces and Society Since a.d. 1000. Chicago: University of Chicago Press.

Mukerji, S. 1983. From Graven Images: Patterns of Modern Materialism. New York: Columbia University Press.

— 1995. "Voir le pouvoir." In B. Latour, ed. Les 'Vues' de l'Esprit, special issue of Culture Technique, 208–223.

Ong, W. 1971. Rhetoric, Romance and the New Technology. Ithaca, NY: Cornell University Press.

— 1982. Orality and Literacy: The Technologizing of the Word. London: Methuen.

Perret-Clermont, A. N. 1979. La Construction de l'Intelligence dans l'Intéraction Sociale. Berne: Peter Lang.

Piaget, J. and R. Garcia 1993. Psychogenèse et Histoire des Sciences. Paris: Flammarion.

Pinch, T. 1995. "Toward an analysis of scientific observations: the externality of evidential significance of observational reports in physics." Social Studies of Science 15, 3–37.

Redondi, P. 1980. L'accueil des Idées de Sadi Carnot: de la Légende à l'Histoire. Paris: Vrin.

Roover, R. de 1963. The Rise and Decline of the Medici Bank. Cambridge, MA: Harvard University Press.

Rudwick, M. 1976. "The emergence of a visual language for geological science: 1760–1940." In History of Science 14. 148–195.

Serres, M. 1980. Le Passage du Nord-Ouest. Paris: Minuit.

— 1982. Hermes. Baltimore, MD: Johns Hopkins University Press.

Shapin, S. 1984. "Pump and circumstance: Robert Boyle's literary technology." In Social Studies of Science 14, 481–521.

Simon, H. 1982. "Cognitive processes of experts and novices." In Cahiers de la Fondation Archives Jean Piaget 2 (3), 154–178.

Sohn-Rethel, A. 1978. Manual and Intellectual Labor: A Critique of Epistemology. London: Macmillan.

Star, S. L. 1983. "Simplification in scientific work: an example from neuroscience research." In Social Studies of Science 13, 205–228.

Uselding, P. 1981. "Measuring techniques and manufacturing practice." In O. Mayr and R. Post, eds. Yankee Enterprise, 103–126. Washington, D.C.: Smithsonian Institute Press.

Wheeler, J. 1969. On Records Files and Dossiers in American Life. New York: Russell Sage Foundation.

Woolf, P. 1975. "The second messenger, information communication in cyclic AMP research." In Minerva 13 (3), 349–373.

Zerubavel, E. 1982. "The standardization of time: a sociohistorical perspective." In American Sociological Review 88 (l), 1–29.

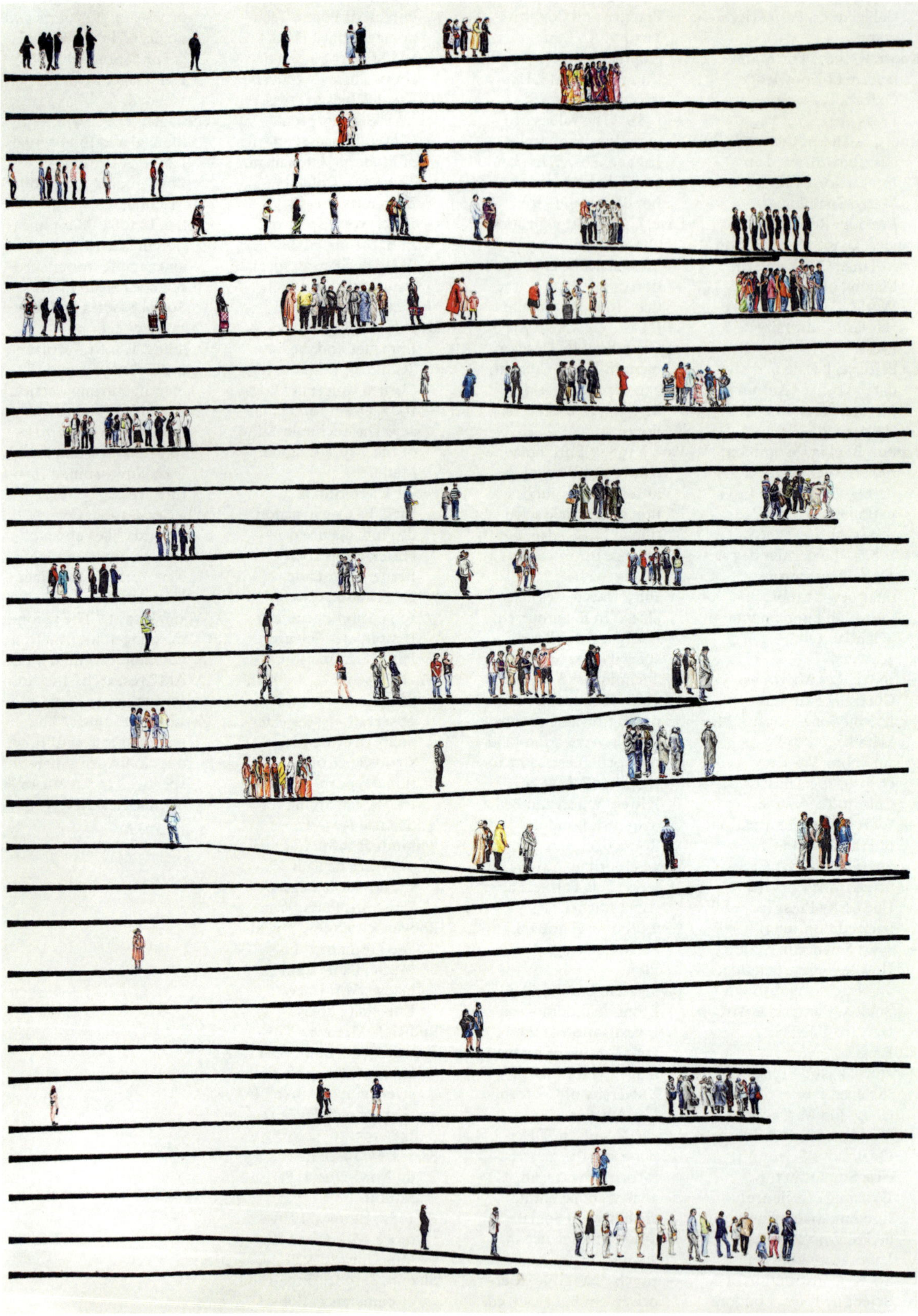

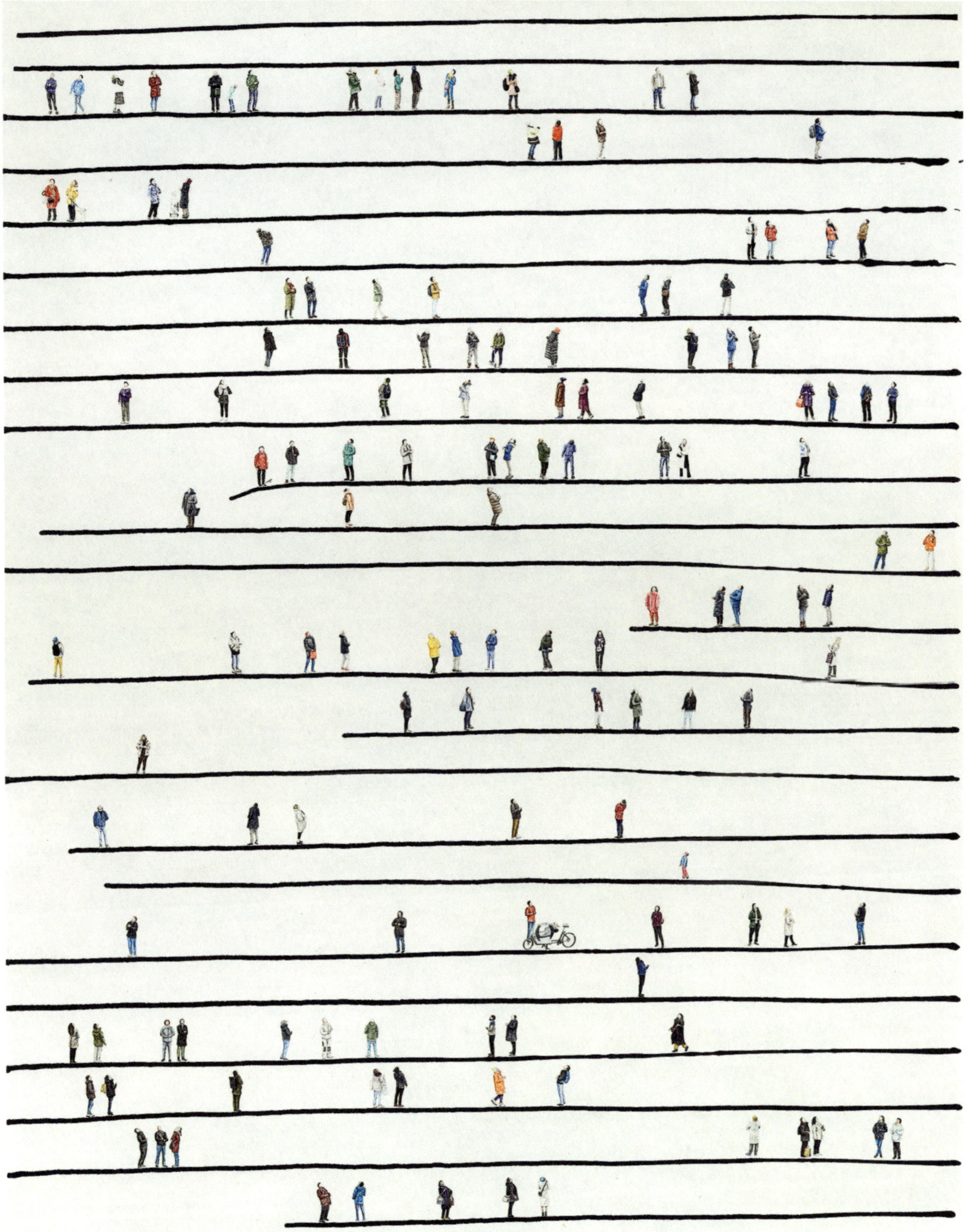

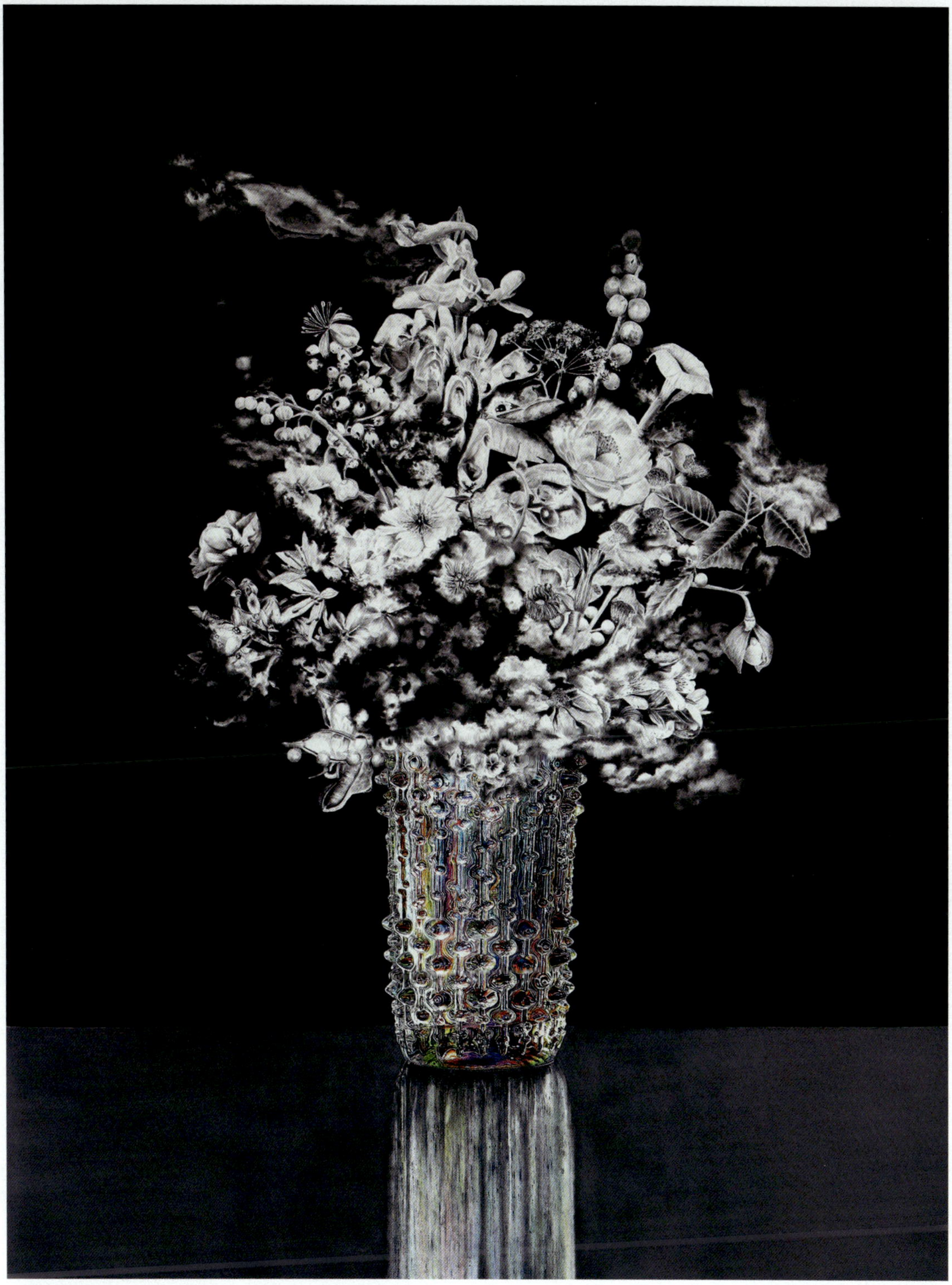

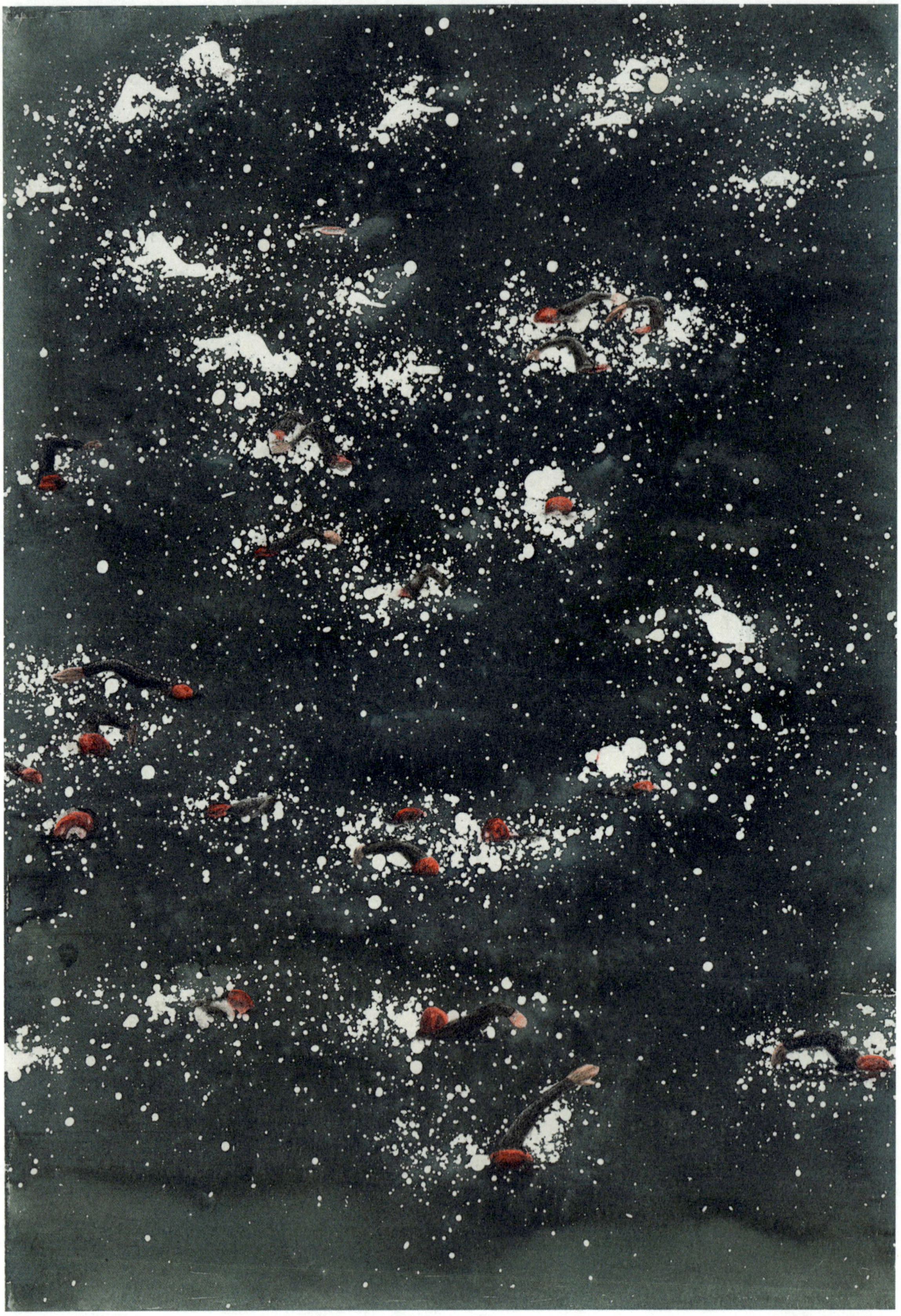

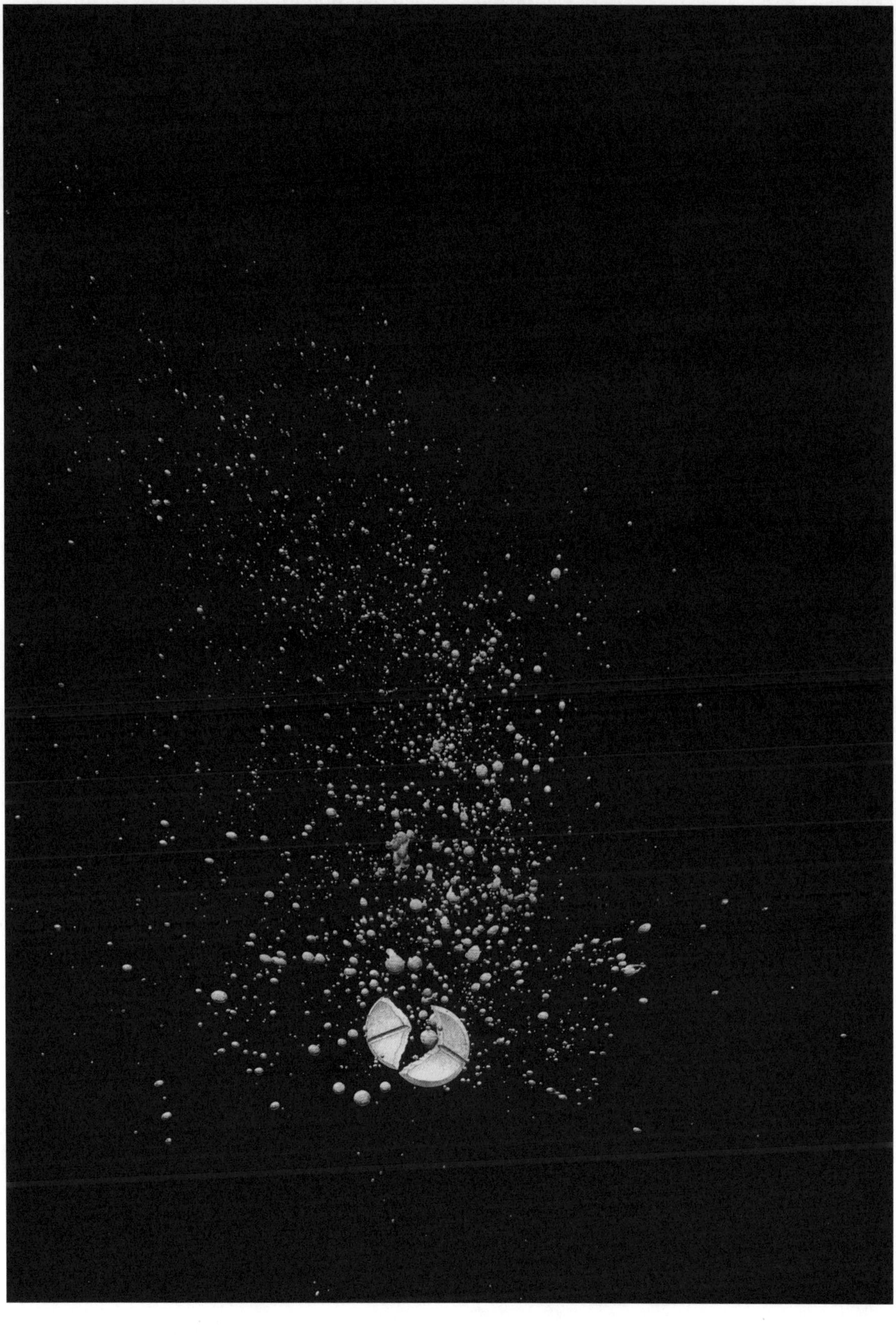

„Flüssigkeiten bewegen sich mit Leichtigkeit. Sie ‚fließen', werden ‚verschüttet', sie ‚laufen aus', sie ‚spritzen' und ‚fließen über', sie ‚tropfen' und ‚überfluten', sie ‚versickern' und ‚rinnen'. Sie sind im Gegensatz zu Festkörpern nicht leicht aufzuhalten – manche Widerstände umfließen sie, andere lösen sie auf oder werden von ihnen aufgesogen oder sickern durch sie hindurch. Das Zusammentreffen mit Festkörpern kann ihnen nichts anhaben, diese jedoch verändern sie, werden feucht oder durchnäßt.
Die außerordentliche Mobilität von Flüssigkeiten legt die Assoziation der ‚Leichtigkeit' nahe. [...] Bei ‚Leichtigkeit' und ‚Schwerelosigkeit' denken wir an Beweglichkeit und Ungebundenheit. Wir kennen das aus der eigenen Erfahrung – mit leichtem Gepäck kommt man schneller voran. Aus diesen Gründen bieten sich ‚Flüchtigkeit' und ‚Flüssigkeit' als passende Metaphern an, wenn man das Spezifische unserer Gegenwart, jener in vieler Hinsicht *neurartigen* Phase der Geschichte der Moderne, erfassen will."

— Zygmunt Bauman, *Flüchtige Moderne*, übersetzt von Reinhard Kreissl (Frankfurt am Main, Suhrkamp, 2006), 8.

„Mit der ‚flüchtigen'" Moderne beginnt die Epoche der Auflösung, des Ausweichens, der leichten Fluchten und hoffnungslosen Jagden. In der ‚flüchtigen' Moderne sind es diejenigen, die am besten ausweichen, die ohne Ankündigung verschwinden, sich in Luft auflösen können, die die Herrschaft übernehmen. [...] Die körperlose Arbeit des Softwarezeitalters bindet das Kapital nicht mehr: Es ist extraterritorial, flüchtig und wandelbar. Mit der körperlosen Arbeit bricht das Zeitalter des schwerelosen Kapitals an. Die gegenseitige Abhängigkeit ist einseitig aufgekündigt worden; während die Arbeitskraft für sich immer noch unvollständig und auf das Kapital angewiesen ist, gilt dies im umgekehrten Fall nicht mehr. Das Kapital ist unterwegs und guter Dinge, auf der Suche nach kurzen Abenteuern und voller Gewißheit, daß es immer wieder Abenteuer geben wird und Partner, mit denen man sie teilen kann. Das Kapital ist mit leichtem Marschgepäck unterwegs, und diese Leichtigkeit ist die Ursache zunehmender Unsicherheit, für alle anderen Beteiligten."

— Ebd., 144 f.

„Man könnte den historischen Abschnitt, der sich heute seinem Ende nähert, mangels einer besseren Bezeichnung die Ära der *Werkzeuge* oder die *schwere* Moderne nennen – die ‚volumen-verrückte Moderne', die ‚Je-größer-desto-besser-Moderne'.
Das war die Ära der Werkzeuge, der Hardware, die Epoche der immer größeren und undhandlicheren Maschinen, der immer größer werdenden Fabriken, mit immer größeren Mengen an Arbeitskräften, der wuchtigen Eisenbahnen und gigantischen Ozeandampfer. Das Hauptziel war die Eroberung des Raums – soviel man kriegen und halten konnte, eingezäunt und mit Schildern versehen: ‚Durchgang verboten'. Raum, Grund und Boden waren zentrale Obsessionen der Moderne, das Streben nach ihrem Erwerb geradezu zwanghaft – und die Bewachung der Grenzen entwickelte sich zur allgegenwärtigen, sich immer weiter verbreitenden Sucht."

— Ebd., 136.

„Während in der ‚festen' Moderne ewige Dauer Motiv und Prinzip des Handelns darstellten, ist in der ‚flüchtigen' Moderne diese Orientierung funktionslos. Das ‚Kurzfristige' hat das ‚Langfristige' abgelöst, und Unmittelbarkeit ist zum ultimativen Ideal avanciert. Zeit wurde zum Behältnis ohne Limit, zum Faß ohne Boden erklärt und ihre Dauer abgeschafft."

— Ebd., 149.

"Fluids travel easily. They 'flow,' 'spill,' 'run out,' 'splash,' 'pour over,' 'leak,' 'flood,' 'spray,' 'drip,' 'seep,' 'ooze,'; unlike solids, they are not easily stopped—they pass around some obstacles, dissolve some others and bore or soak their way through others still. From the meeting with solids they emerge unscathed, while the solids they have met, if they stay solid, are changed—get moist or drenched. The extraordinary mobility of fluids is what associates them with the idea of 'lightness.' [...] We associate 'lightness' or 'weightlessness' with mobility and inconstancy: we know from practice that the lighter we travel the easier and faster we move. These are reasons to consider 'fluidity' or 'liquidity' as fitting metaphors when we wish to grasp the nature of the present, in many ways novel, phase in the history of modernity."

— Zygmunt Bauman, *Liquid Modernity* (Cambridge: Polity Press, 2006), 2.

"If 'solid' modernity posited eternal duration as the main motive and principle of action, 'fluid' modernity has no function for the eternal duration to play. The 'short term' has replaced the 'long term' and made of instantaneity its ultimate ideal. While promoting time to the rank of an infinitely capacious container, fluid modernity dissolves—denigrates and devalues—its duration."

— Ibid., 125.

"That part of history, now coming to its close, could be dubbed, for the lack of a better name, the era of hardware, or heavy modernity—the bulk-obsessed modernity, 'the larger the better' kind of modernity, of 'the size is power, the volume is success' sort. That was the hardware era; the epoch of weighty and ever more cumbersome machines, of the ever longer factory walls enclosing ever wider factory floors and ingesting ever more populous factory crews, of ponderous rail engines and gigantic ocean liners. To conquer space was the supreme goal—to grasp as much of it as one could hold, and to hold to it, marking it all over with the tangible tokens of possession and 'No trespassing' boards. Territory was among the most acute of modern obsessions, its acquisition among the most compulsive of modern urges—while guarding the boundaries figured high among the most ubiquitous, resilient and relentlessly growing modern addictions."

— Ibid., 113f.

"'Fluid' modernity is the epoch of disengagement, elusiveness, facile escape and hopeless chase. In 'liquid' modernity, it is the most elusive, those free to move without notice, who rule."

— Ibid., 120.

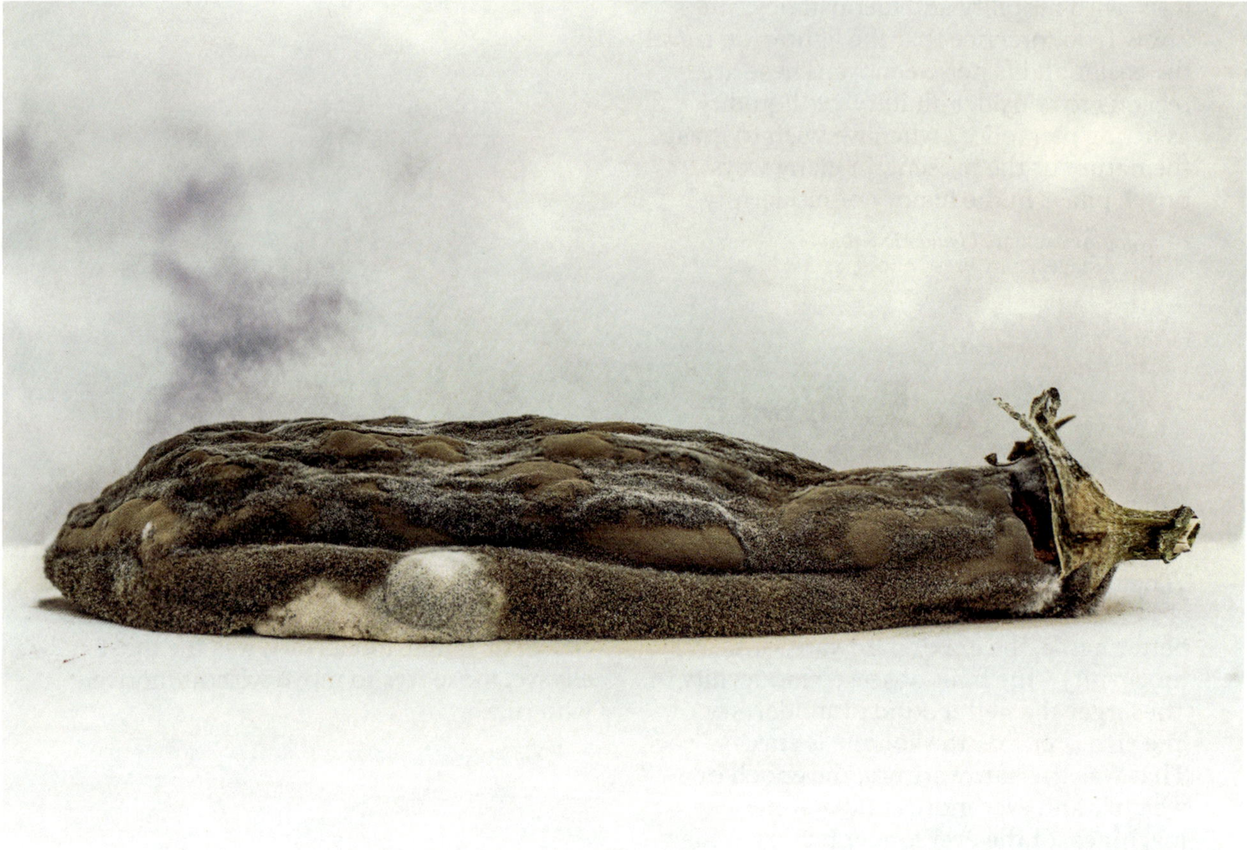

Der kritische Posthumanismus bringt eine Menge „gewagter Neologismen“ hervor, die das Begriffsschöpferische des posthumanen Denkens und die Notwendigkeit neuer Terminologien zum Verständnis der komplexen Verflechtungen von menschlichen und nichtmenschlichen Aktanten zeigen.[1] Da Worte unser Denken und unsere Informationsverarbeitung fundamental strukturieren und mitbestimmen, versetzen uns Neologismen sprachlogisch in die Lage, Dinge anders zu denken. Was einige, je nach ihrer Position im „akademisch-politischen Spektrum“, als „ziemlich innovativ“ ansehen, beschreiben andere als „offenkundig abwegig“.[2] „Abwegigkeit ist ein generativer Begriff mit einer ausgeprägten literarischen und wissenschaftlichen Genealogie. Als Figuren einer abgewerteten Differenz wurden Monstrosität und Nicht-Menschen oder auch entmenschte Menschen häufig miteinander verbunden (Braidotti, *Metamorphoses: Towards a Materialist Theory of Becoming.* Cambridge: Polity 2002).“[3] Die anhaltende Leidenschaft für das Monströse in Film, Literatur und Kunst hat zweifellos mit einer Furcht zu tun, den „Menschenstatus“ zu verlieren.[4]

„Humanimal“:[5] Bewohner eines „Chaosmos“,[6] verortet in einem Spektrum eines „Medien-Natur-Kultur-Kontinuums“;[7] Schöpfer einer „Post-Natur, [die] definiert [werden kann] als jene Organismen, die durch Methoden wie Zuchtwahl oder Gentechnologie erblich verändert wurden“;[8] das dreifaltige *Systema naturæ* überschreitend; „ein Subjekt, das zu geomorphischen Handlungen fähig ist; ein Wesen, das die Geologie nicht nur beeinflusst, sondern als eine ungezügelte Kraft innerhalb dieses Systems wirkt“;[9] ein Subjekt, das verzweifelt versucht, den humanistischen Überlegenheitskomplex bezüglich seines Erd-Status zu überwinden – ein kulturelles Erbe von Generationen „hyperalphabetisierter, zentral-perspektivisch durchtrainierter Post-Renaissance-Menschen“,[10] die dem ungerechtfertigten Glauben anhängen, Teil einer erhabenen, aufgeklärten Rationalität zu sein, gründend auf einem Denken, das auf binären Gegensätzen beruht und Ordnung als Hierarchie begreift.

1 Rosi Braidotti, *Posthuman Knowledge*, Cambridge: Polity, 2019, 75.
2 Ebd.
3 Ebd.
4 Ebd., 76.
5 Ein ebenda gefundener Neologismus, 78.
6 Ein von Félix Guattari geprägter Neologismus, vgl. ebd., 50.
7 Ebd., 76.
8 Ebd., 80.
9 Kathrin Yusoff, „Geologic life: prehistory, climate, futures in the Anthropocene“, in: *Environment and Planning D: Society and Space* 31, 2013, 780; doi:10.1086/d11512.
10 Ein Ausdruck von Klaus Theweleit in *Warum Cortés wirklich siegte: Technologiegeschichte der eurasisch-amerikanischen Kolonialismen*, Berlin: Matthes & Seitz, 2020, 271.

Critical posthuman scholarship produces quite a lot of “daring neologisms,” that reflect the conceptual creativity of posthuman thinking and the need for new terminologies to understand the complex entanglement of human and non-human agents.[1] As words are basic elements to structure and define the way we think and process information, in the realm of verbal reasoning neologisms enable us to rethink things in different ways. What some, depending on the position in the “academic political spectrum,” consider “quite innovative,” others describe as “distinctively weird.”[2] “Weirdness is a generative notion, with a rich literary and scientific genealogy. Monstrosity and non-humans as well as de-humanized humans have often been interconnected as figures of devalorized difference (Braidotti, *Metamorphoses: Towards a Materialist Theory of Becoming.* Cambridge: Polity, 2002).”[3] The continuing passion for monstrosity in film, literature and art can certainly be related to a fear of loosing the “status of the human.”[4]

“Humanimal”:[5] dweller of a “chaosmos”[6] located in a spectrum of a “media-nature-culture continuum,”[7] creator of the “post-natural [which can be] defined as the organisms that have been heritably altered by means including selective breeding or genetic engineering”;[8] transgressing a threefold *systema naturæ*; “a subject capable of geomorphic acts; a being that not only effects geology but is also an intemperate force within it”;[9] a subject that desperately tries to overcome a humanist superiority complex concerning its earth status—a cultural heritage from “hyperliterate, European post-Renaissance [generations] thoroughly trained in central perspective,”[10] with an unjustified belief in being part of a sublime, enlightened rationality that is grounded in a binary-oppositional, order-as-hierarchy way of thinking.

1 Rosi Braidotti, *Posthuman Knowledge* (Cambridge: Polity, 2019 [ePub]), 75.
2 Ibid.
3 Ibid.
4 Ibid., 76.
5 A neologism found in ibid., 78.
6 A neologism coined by Felix Guattari, see ibid., 50.
7 Ibid., 76.
8 Ibid., 80.
9 Kathrin Yusoff, “Geologic life: prehistory, climate, futures in the Anthropocene,” *Environment and Planning D: Society and Space*, vol. 31, 2013, 780; doi:10.1086/d11512.
10 “Hyperalphabetisierter, zentralperspektivisch durchtrainierter europäischer Post-Renaissance-Mensch” is an expression of Klaus Theweleit's in *Warum Cortés wirklich siegte: Technologiegeschichte der eurasisch-amerikanischen Kolonialismen* (Berlin: Matthes & Seitz, 2020), 271.

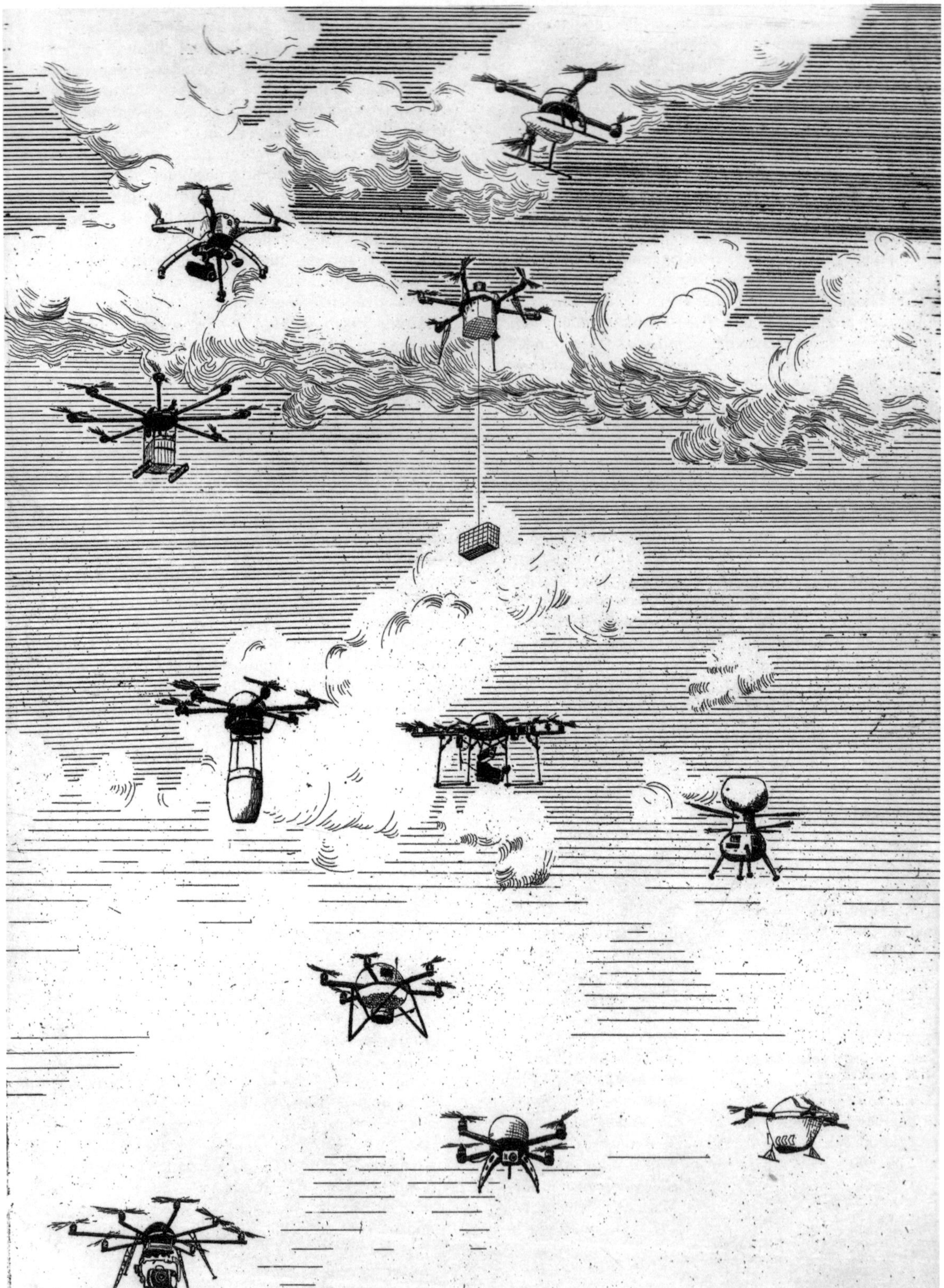

## 157

**Carolus Linnaeus, Systema Naturæ, 1st edition (1735)**

LAT HYDRA corpore anguino, pedibus duobus, collis septem, & totidem capitibus, alarum expers, asservatur Hamburgi, similitudinem referens Hydræ Apocalyptiae a S. Joanne Cap. XII. & XIII. descriptae. Eaque tanquam veri animalis speciem plurimis praebuit, sed falso. Natura sibi semper similis plura capita in uno corpore nunquam produxit naturaliter. Fraudem & artificium, cum Ipsi vidimus, dentes Ferino-mustelini, ab Amphibiorum dentibus diversi, facillime detexerunt.

DE Eine Hydra [Wasserschlange] mit dem Körper einer Schlange, zwei Beinen, sieben Hälsen und derselben Anzahl von Köpfen, ohne Flügel, wird in Hamburg konserviert und ähnelt der Beschreibung der Hydra in der Offenbarung des Johannes in den Kapiteln 12 und 13. Von den meisten wird sie als echte Tierart bezeichnet, aber fälschlicherweise. Die Natur, die immer auf gleiche Art und Weise wirkt, hat niemals auf natürliche Art mehrere Köpfe auf einem Körper hervorgebracht. Wie wir selbst gesehen haben, haben die Zähne eines fleischfressenden Wiesels, die sich von den Zähnen der Amphibien unterscheiden, leicht Täuschung und Trick offenbart.

EN A hydra [water snake] with the body of a snake, two legs, seven necks, and the same number of heads, without wings, is preserved in Hamburg and is similar to the description of the hydra in the Book of Revelation chap. 12 and 13. It is generally but falsely held to be a genuine species of animal. Nature, which always works in the same way, has never naturally brought forth several heads on a single body. As we have seen for ourselves, the fraud is revealed in the teeth of a flesh-eating weasel, which differ from those of an amphibian.

LAT RANA-PISCIS seu RANAE IN PISCEM METAMORPHOSIS valde paradoxa est, quum Natura mutationem Generis unius in aliam diversae Classis non admittat. Ranae, ut Amphibia omnia, pulmonibus gaudent & ossibus spinosis. Pisces spinosi, loco pulmonum, branchiis instruuntur. Ergo legi Naturae contraria foret haec mutatio. Si enim piscis hic instructus est branchiis, erit diversus a Rana & Amphibiis. Si vero pulmones, erit Lacerta: nam toto caelo a Chondropterygiis & Plagiuris differt.

DE Der Frosch-Fisch oder der Frosch, der sich in einen Fisch verwandelt, ist sehr unwahrscheinlich, da die Natur den Wechsel von einer Gattung in eine andere einer unterschiedlichen Klasse nicht erlaubt. Frösche besitzen wie alle Amphibien Lungen und stachelige Knochen. Stachelfische sind mit Kiemen anstelle von Lungen ausgestattet. Daher widerspricht eine solche Veränderung den Gesetzen der Natur. Denn wenn ein Fisch mit Kiemen ausgestattet ist, muss er sich von Fröschen und Amphibien unterscheiden. Wenn er aber wahrlich Lungen hat, dann ist er eine Echse: denn unter dem gesamten Himmel unterscheidet er sich von Knorpelfischen und Plagiuri.

EN The frog-fish, or frog that turns into a fish, is most improbable, as nature does not allow the transformation of one species into another. Like all amphibia, frogs have lungs and spinous bones. Quillfish are equipped with gills instead of lungs. Therefore such a mutation contradicts the laws of nature. For if a fish is equipped with gills, it must differ from frogs and amphibia. But if it truly has lungs, then it is a lizard. For in all creation it differs from the cartilaginous fishes and the Plagiuri.

LAT MONOCEROS *Veterum* corpore equino, pedibus ferinis; cornu recto, longo, spiraliter intorto, Pictorum figmentum est: MONODON *Artedi* ejusmodi cornu gerit, caeteris vero partibus multum differt.

DE Das Einhorn der Vorfahren mit dem Körper eines Pferdes, den Füßen eines wilden Tieres und einem geraden, spiralförmig gedrehten Horn ist eine Erfindung der Maler. Der Narwal des [Peter] Artedi hat ein solches Horn, unterscheidet sich aber in den übrigen Körperteilen.

EN The unicorn *of the ancestors*, with the body of a horse, the feet of a wild animal, and a straight, spiraling horn is an invention of the painters. The narwhale of [Peter] *Artedi* has such a horn, but it differs in its other parts.

LAT PELECANUS rostro vulnus infligens femori suo, ut emanante sanguine sitim pullorum levet, fabulose ab Iisdem traditur. Ansam fabulae dedit saccus sub gula pendulus.

DE Der Pelikan, der mit seinem Schnabel seinem Oberschenkel eine Wunde zufügt, um mit dem herausfließenden Blut den Durst der Brut zu stillen, wurde von denselben [Leuten] fabelhaft überliefert. Den Anhaltspunkt der Fabel gibt der Sack, der unter seiner Kehle hängt.

EN The pelican, which wounds itself in the thigh with its beak so as to quench the thirst of its brood, was fabulously passed down by the same [persons]. The fable's point of reference is the sack hanging from its throat.

**Carolus Linnaeus, Systema Naturæ, 1st edition (1735)**

LAT SATYRUS caudatus, hirsutus, barbatus, humanum referens corpus, gesticulationibus valde deditus, salacissimus, *Simiae* species est, si unquam aliquis visus fuit. *Homines* quoque *Caudati*, de quibus recentiores peregrinatores multa narrant, ejusdem generis sunt.

DE Der Satyr mit Schwanz, behaart, bärtig, mit einem menschlichen Körper, der viel gestikuliert, sehr trügerisch, ist eine Affenart, [wenn es wahr ist,] dass jemals einer gesehen wurde. Auch die Menschen mit Schwanz, von denen zeitgenössische Reisende viel erzählen, sind von derselben Gattung.

EN The tailed satyr, hairy, bearded with a very gesticulating human body, very elusive, is a type of ape, if one has indeed ever been seen. The tailed people much told of by travelers are of the same species.

LAT BOROMETZ seu AGNUS SCYTHICUS plantis accensetur, & agno adsimilatur; cui caulis alterius plantae e terra crumpens umbilicum intrat; idemque sanguine praeditus a feris devorari temere dicitur. Est autem artificiose ex radicibus Filicinis Americanis compositus. Naturaliter autem est *Embryo Ovis* allegorice descriptus, qui omnia data habet attributa.

DE Das Borometz [Barametz] oder Skythische Lamm zählt zu den Pflanzen und ist einem Lamm ähnlich. Der Stängel spießt den „Umbilicus" [= Nabel] einer anderen Pflanze auf, wenn er aus der Erde herausssprießt. Man sagt auch, dass es von wilden Tieren aufgefressen wird, weil es Blut enthält. Es ist aber künstlich aus Wurzeln amerikanischer Farne zusammengesetzt. Natürlich ist hingegen der Embryo des Schafs, der allegorisch beschrieben wurde, der alle Eigenschaften hat, die ihm zugeschrieben werden.

EN The barometz, or Scythian lamb, is one of the plants and is similar to the lamb. The stem spears the navel of another plant when it sprouts from the earth. It is also said to be eaten by wild animals because it contains blood. But it is artificially combined from the roots of American ferns. Whereas the allegorically described embryo of the sheep is natural, and has all the qualities ascribed to it.

LAT PHOENIX, Avis species, cujus unicum in mundo individuum, & quae decrepita ex ferali busto, quod sibi ex aromatibus struxerat, repuerascere fabulose fertur, felicem subitura prioris vitae periodum. Est vero PALMA DACTYLIFERA, vid. *Kaempf.*

DE Der Phoenix, eine Vogelart, von der es jedes Mal auf der Welt nur ein einziges Exemplar geben soll, erhebt sich aus dem Scheiterhaufen, den er sich selbst aus Gewürzen gebaut hat, und soll sagenhaft wieder jung werden, um glücklich frühere Lebensperioden wieder zu erleben. In Wahrheit ist er die Dattelpalme, siehe Kaempf [Amoenitates Exoticas p. 664].

EN The phoenix, a bird of which there is only ever one of its kind in the world, arises from the fire it has itself built from spices, and is fabulously said to rejuvenate, so as to experience earlier periods of life once again. In reality it is a date palm, see *Kaempf* [Amoenitates Exoticas p. 664].

LAT BERNICLA seu ANSER SCOTICUS & CONCHA ANATIFERA e lignis putridis in mare abjectis nasci a Veteribus creditur. Sed fucum imposuit *Lepas* interaneis suis penniformibus, & modo adhaerendi, quasi verus ille anser *Bernicla* inde oriretur.

DE Die Ringelgans oder Schottische Gans und Concha Anatifera wird, wie die Alten glauben, aus faulen Hölzern, die ins Meer geworfen wurden, geboren. Aber die *Lepas* legt Seegras auf ihre federartigen inneren Teile, und durch die Art, wie sie sich anhängt, [wirkt es,] als ob tatsächlich die Ringelgans sich von dort aus erhebt.

EN The ancients believe that the brant or Scottish goose and Concha anatifera is born from rotten wood thrown into the sea. But the *Lepas* lays seaweed about its feather-like inner parts and the way it is attached gives the appearance of the goose arising.

LAT DRACO corpore anguino, duobus pedibus, duabus alis, Vespertilionis instar, est *Lacerta alata*, vel *Raja* per artem monitrose ficta, & siccata.

DE Der Drache mit dem Körper einer Schlange, zwei Beinen und zwei Flügeln gleich einer Fledermaus ist eine geflügelte Eidechse oder ein Rochen, der künstlich wie ein Monster geformt und getrocknet wurde.

EN The dragon with the body of a snake, two legs, and two wings like a bat is a winged lizard or a ray artificially shaped like a monster and dried.

LAT AUTOMA MORTIS Horologii minimi sonitum edens in parietibus, est *Pediculus pulsatorius* dictus, qui ligna perforat, eaque inhabitat.

DE Die Todesuhr macht das Geräusch einer sehr kleinen Uhr in der Wand und wird *Pediculus pulsatorius* genannt, die Holz durchbohrt und darin wohnt.

EN The deathwatch makes a noise like a very small clock in the wall. It is called *Pediculus pulsatorius,* and bores through wood, in which it lives.

**159**

**Carolus Linnaeus, Systema Naturæ, 2nd edition (1740), 3rd edition (1740), 4th edition (1744), 5th edition (1747)**

LAT MANTICORA. Facie senis decrepiti, corpore Leonis, cauda apice aculeis stellata.
DE Der Mantikor mit dem Gesicht eines schwachen Greises, dem Körper eines Löwen und einem Schwanz, der mit scharfen Spitzen gestirnt ist
EN The manticore, with the face of very old person, the body of a lion, and a tail tipped with sharp spines.

LAT ANTILOPE. Facie Ferae, pedibus Pecoris, cornibus Caprae ferratis.
DE Die Antilope mit dem Gesicht eines wilden Tieres, Beinen eines Schafes und Hörnern einer Ziege.
EN The antilope, with the face of a wild animal, the legs of a sheep, and the horns of a goat.

LAT LAMIA. Facie Hominis; mammis virginis; corpore Quadrupedis squamato, pedibus anterioribus Ferae, posterioribus Pecoris.
DE Die Lamia mit dem Gesicht eines Mannes, den Brüsten einer Jungfrau, dem geschuppten Körper eines vierbeinigen Tieres, die Vorderbeine wie ein wildes Tier, die Hinterbeine wie ein Schaf.
EN The lamia, with the face of a man, the breasts of a virgin, the scaled body of a four-legged animal, the forelegs like a wild animal, the hind legs like a sheep.

LAT SIREN *Art. Gen.* 81. Syrene *Bart.* Quamdiu nec vivus, nec mortuus vivus, nec fide & perfecte satis descriptus in dubium vocatur.
DE Die Sirene, siehe *Art. Gen.* 81 Syrene Bartholin. Solange sie weder lebend noch tot gesehen wird und weder zuverlässig und gut genug beschrieben wird, kann man nur skeptisch sein.
EN The siren, see *Art. Gen.* 81. Syrene *Bartholin*. As long as she has neither been seen alive nor dead, nor reliably and adequately described, one can only remain skeptical.

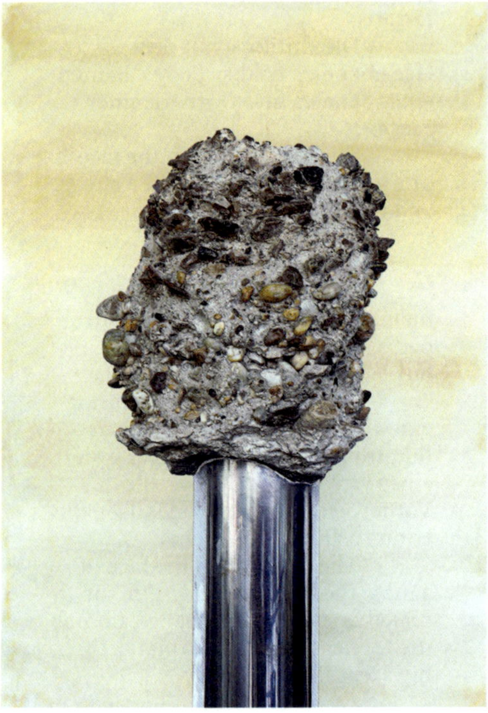

S[1]

Subjektposition
Subject Position

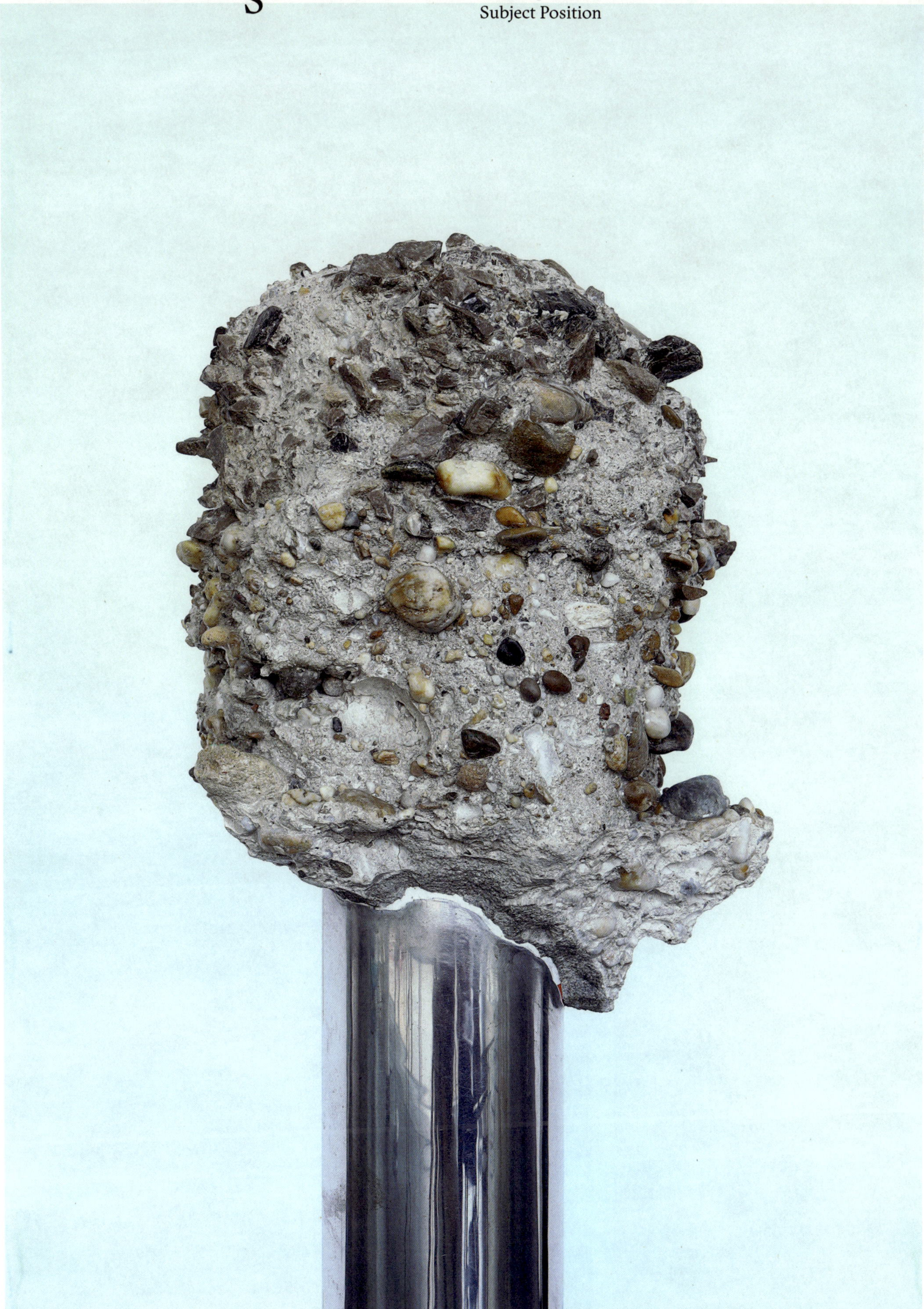

S[1]

Subjektposition
Subject Position

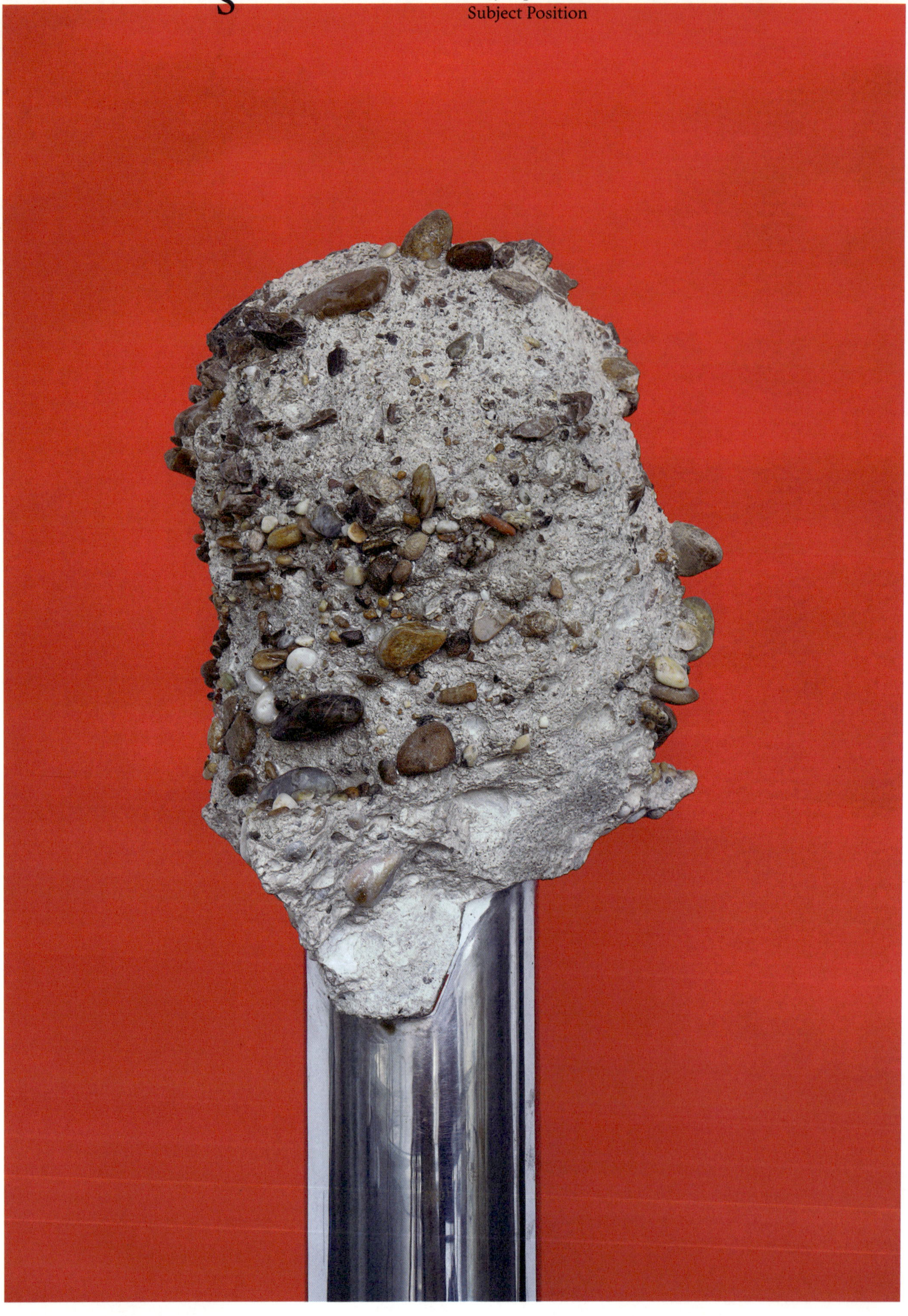

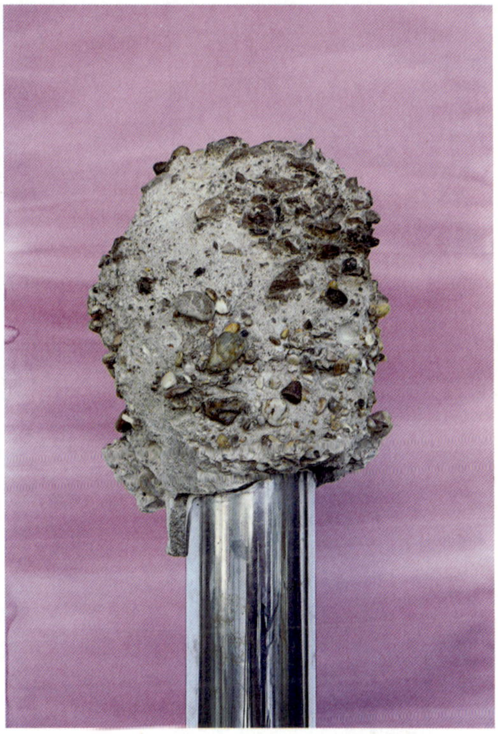

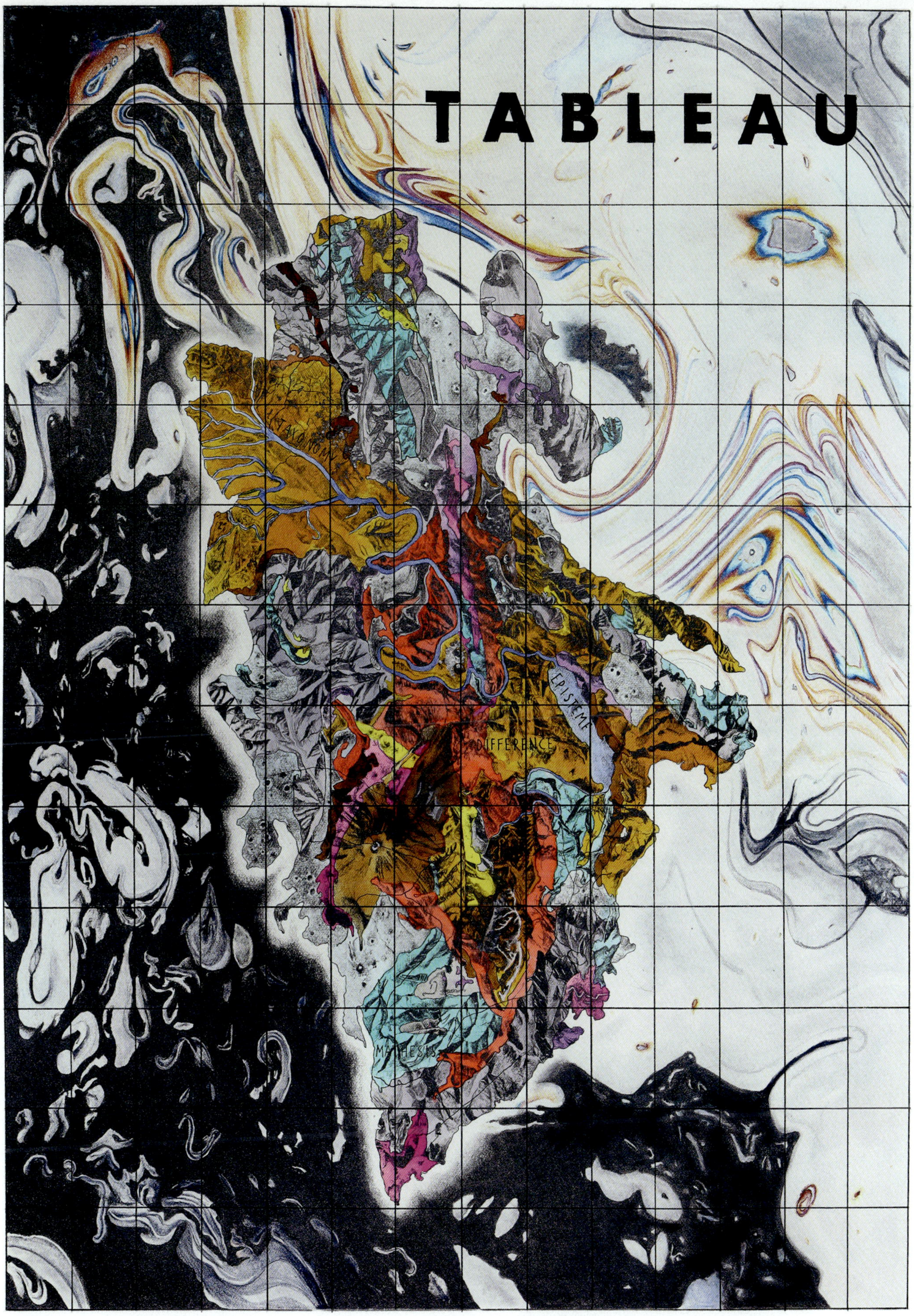
TABLEAU
TAXONOMY
EPISTEME
DIFFERENCE
MATHESIS

The word *tableau* describes the anticipation of a display in the form of a smooth ordering surface regulating our digitalized everyday life.

## References

1. Cf. Steffen Siegel, Tabula. Figuren der Ordnung um 1600 (Berlin: Akademie Verlag, 2009), 65: "Das semantische Spektrum der lateinischen Vokabel ‚tabula' erstreckt sich von ‚Brett' und ‚Tafel' über ‚Gemälde' und ‚Landkarte' bis hin zu ‚Urkunde', ‚Liste', ‚Verzeichnis' und ‚Register'."

2. Cf. Barbara Cassin, ed., Dictionary of Untranslatables. A Philosophical Lexicon (Princeton University Press, 2014), 1109.

3. Inscription is a term that Bruno Latour elaborates upon in "Visualisation and Cognition: Drawing Things Together," in Knowledge and Society. Studies in the Sociology of Cultures Past and Present, vol. 6, ed. Henrika Kuklick (Amsterdam: Elsevier Science, 1986), 1–40. See also the lemma inscription in the present book.

4. Cf. Siegel, Tabula, 47.

5. Siegel, Tabula, 160: "Mit der synoptischen Tabula entstand im Kontext des humanistischen Enzyklopädismus ein Medium, das zur Beglaubigung epistemischer Ordnungen die Vielfalt visuell wahrnehmbarer Form adaptierte." For detailed analyses of the term tableau also see Annette Graczuk, Das literarische Tableau zwischen Wissenschaft und Kunst (Munich: Fink, 2004), 11–28, 29–75.

6. Cf. Horst Bredekamp, Birgit Schneider, Vera Dünkel, eds., Das Technische Bild. Kompendium zu einer Stilgeschichte wissenschaftlicher Bilder (Berlin: Akademie Verlag, 2008), 116.

7. Cf. Michel Foucault, Die Ordnung der Dinge. Eine Archäologie der Humanwissenschaften, Michel Foucault, Die Hauptwerke (Frankfurt am Main: Suhrkamp, 2016), 419–412.

8. Cf. Graczuk, Das literarische Tableau, 15–17.

9. Graczuk explores several literary tableaus she considers exemplary such as Louis-Sébastian Mercier's Tableau de Paris, Johann Wolfgang von Goethe's systematization of physical experience, and Alexander von Humboldt's Tableau physique des régions équinoxiales; cf. Graczuk, Das literarische Tableau, 117–158, 159–252, 253–429.

10. "What is Tableau?", https://www.tableau.com/why-tableau/what-is-tableau; "A mission that matters," https://www.tableau.com/about/mission (accessed April 15, 2021).

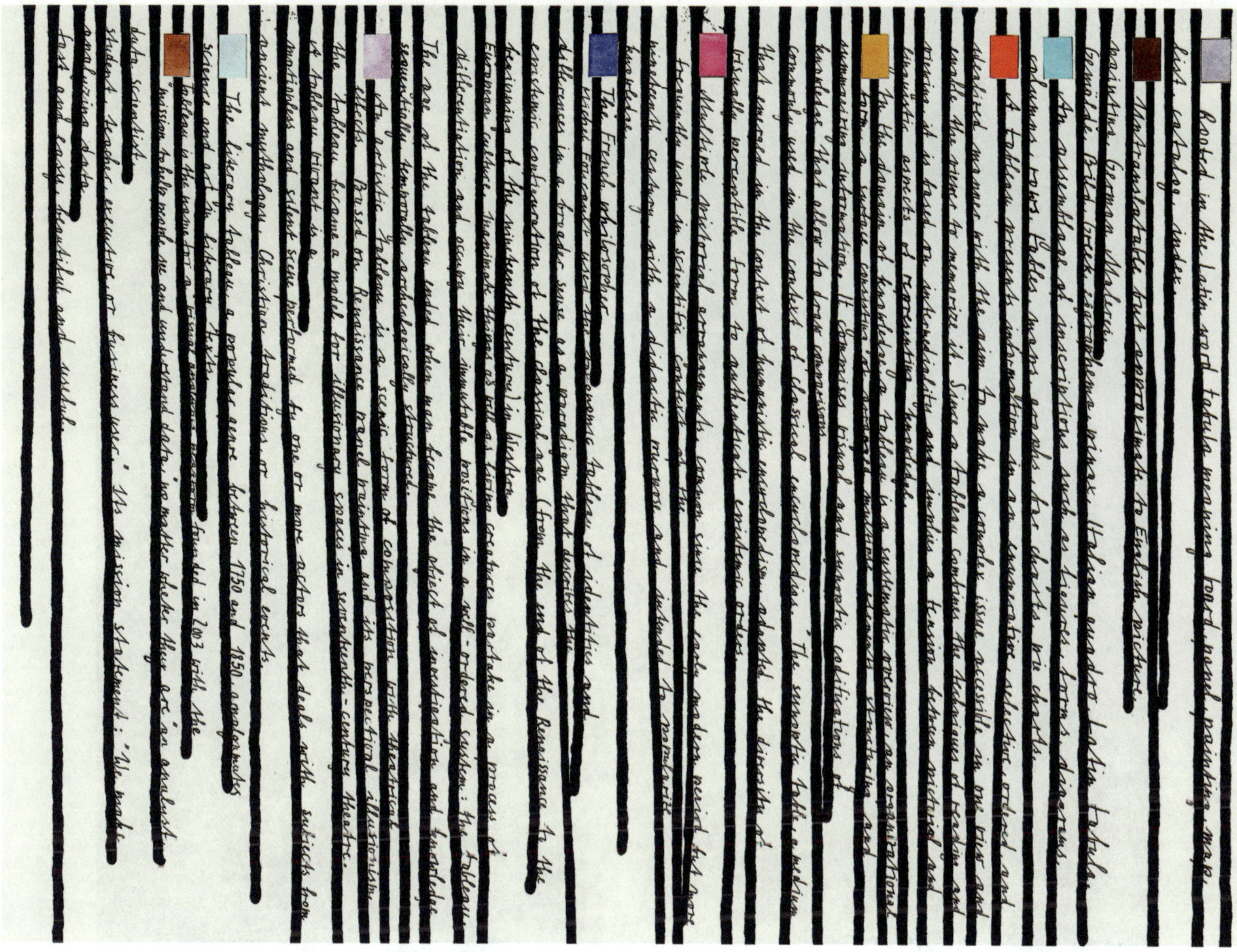

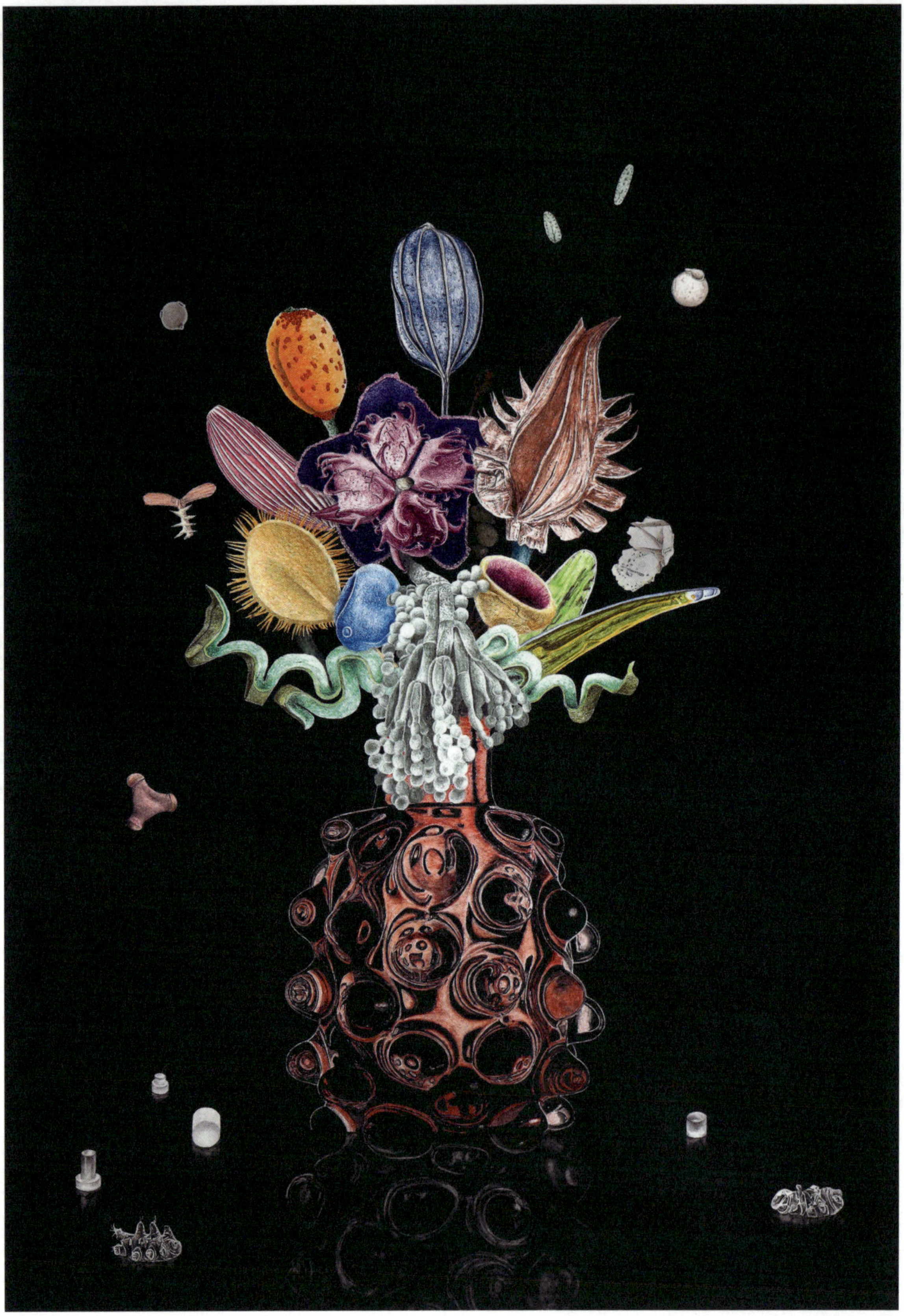

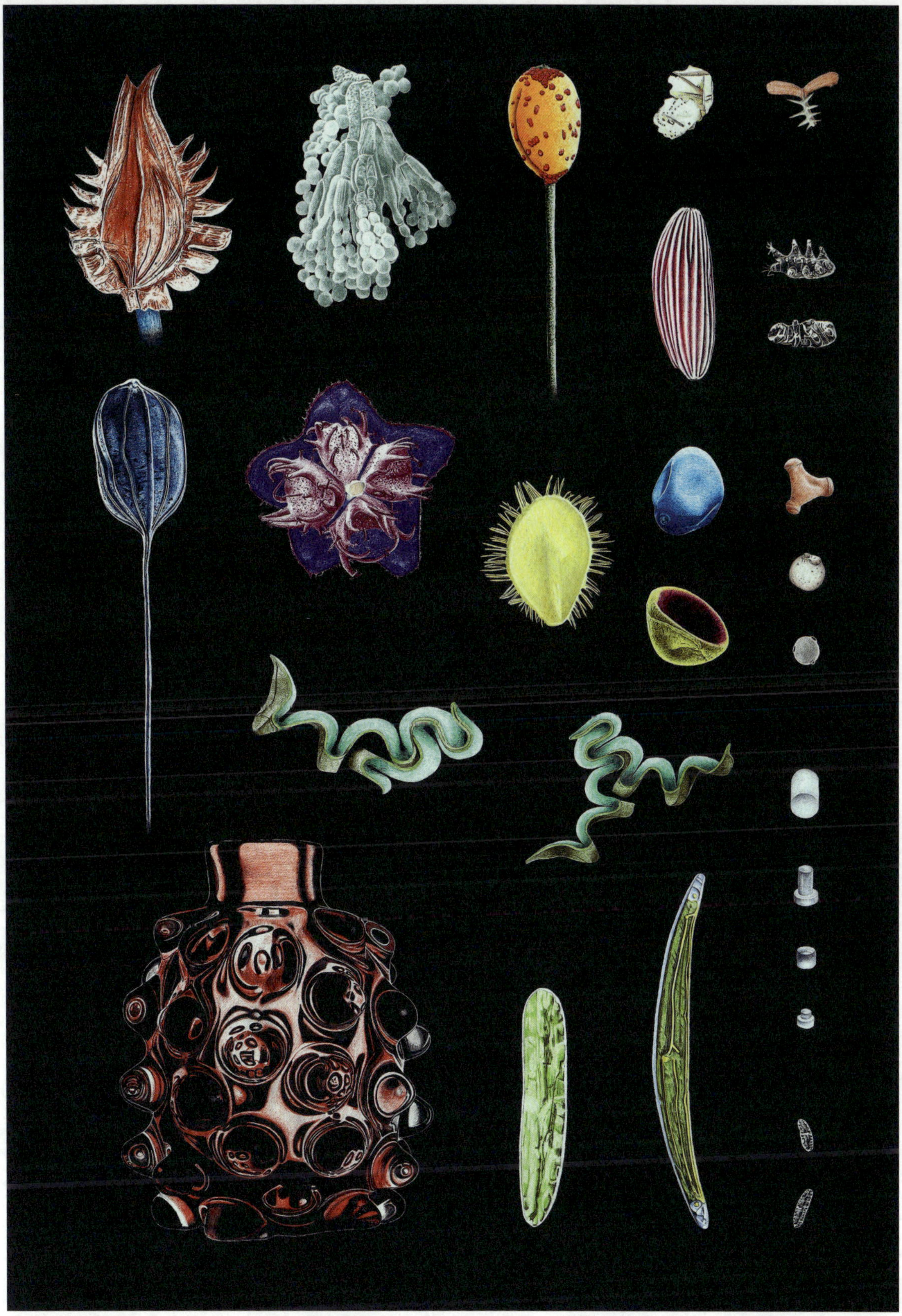

U[1] Unwissbares
The Unknowable

„Die posthumane Wissensproduktion profitiert von der methodologischen Praxis der Verfremdung, die in den letzten Jahrzehnten von der feministischen, subalternen und postkolonialen Theorie wiederbelebt wurde [Verfremdung wurde ursprünglich von Künstler*- und Schriftsteller*innen des 20. Jahrhunderts – insbesondere Bertolt Brecht, aber auch den Surrealist*innen – als künstlerisches Verfahren eingeführt. Diese Herkunft hat, speziell bei Foucault, unterschwellig einen starken Einfluss ausgeübt]. Sie fungiert als pädagogisches Mittel, um die Wissenssubjekte zu ermutigen, sich von der herrschenden normativen Vision des Selbst, an die sie sich gewöhnt haben, frei zu machen. Verfremdung ist eine Methode, die Verwicklung in die Machtverhältnisse zu entschlüsseln, das was Gayatri Spivak ‚das Verlernen der eigenen Privilegien' nennt [*The Post-Colonial Critic: Interviews, Strategies, Dialogues.* New York: Routledge 1999]. Heute gehören die eurozentrisch-humanistischen und anthropozentrischen Denkgewohnheiten sowie die durch sie gestützten Repräsentationsformen zu den zu verlernenden Privilegien, damit Platz für das Neue entsteht."

— Rosi Braidotti, *Posthuman Knowledge* (Cambridge: Polity Press, 2020), 139.

"The production of posthuman knowledge benefits from the methodological practice of defamiliarization, which has been revived by feminist, subaltern and post-colonial theory over the last decades [Defamiliarization—German *Verfremdung*—was originally proposed as an aesthetic approach by artists and writers in the twentieth century, notably Bertolt Brecht, but also the surrealists. This critical genealogy exercises a strong subterranean influence, especially in Foucault]. It functions as a pedagogical tool to encourage the knowing subjects to disengage themselves from the dominant normative vision of the self they had become accustomed to. Defamiliarization is a way of decoding one's implication in power relations, which Gayatri Spivak [*The Post-Colonial Critic: Interviews, Strategies, Dialogues.* New York: Routledge 1999] calls 'unlearning one's privileges.' Nowadays, these privileges include one's Eurocentric humanist and anthropocentric habits of thought and the forms of representation they sustain, so as to make room for the new."

— Rosi Braidotti, *Posthuman Knowledge* (Cambridge: Polity Press, 2020 [ePub]), 139.

Vergilbung ist das Schicksal der Seiten eines Buches.

## DIN 6167 Beschreibung der Vergilbung von nahezu weißen oder farblosen Materialien

### 1 Allgemeines

Die Einflüsse von Strahlung, Temperatur, Feuchtigkeit, chemischen Reaktionen usw. lassen ursprünglich nahezu weiße oder farblose Materialien, z. B. Papiere, Kunststoffe oder Anstriche, vergilben. Die Vergilbungszahl gibt die Änderung des Gelbwertes einer Probe durch einen oder mehrere der oben genannten Einflüsse während einer bestimmten Zeitspanne an.

Bei deutlichen Unterschieden der Proben im Buntton (röter-grüner) oder in der Helligkeit können Gelbwert und Vergilbungszahl nach dieser Norm und eine visuelle Bewertung zu unterschiedlichen Ergebnissen führen. In solchen Fällen ist eine volle farbmetrische Beschreibung der Proben erforderlich (siehe DIN 5033 Teil3, DIN 6174, DIN 55 980 und DIN 55 981).

Ein von dieser Norm abweichender Gelbwert kann durch Messung der spektralen Transmissions- oder Reflexionsgrade bei den Wellenlängen 450, 550 und 600 nm statt durch Messung der Normfarbwerte erhalten werden.

### 2 Gelbwert G

Der Gelbwert G einer Probe nach dieser Norm errechnet sich aus den Normfarbwerten X, Y, Z (siehe DIN 5033 Teil 2 und 7) nach Gleichung (1).

$$G = \frac{a \cdot X - b \cdot Z}{Y} \cdot 100 \qquad (1)$$

Die Faktoren a und b sind der Tabelle zu entnehmen;

| | | | |
|---|---|---|---|
| Normlichtart[1] | D 65 | D 65 | C |
| Normalbeobachter[2] | 10° | 2° | 2° |
| a | 1,301 | 1,298 | 1,277 |
| b | 1,149 | 1,133 | 1,059 |

Zu bevorzugen sind Werte für den 10°-Normalbeobachter und die Normlichtart D 65. Wenn eine Bewertung für den 10°-Normalbeobachter nicht möglich ist, darf ausnahmsweise auch der 2°-Normalbeobachter berücksichtigt werden.

### 3 Vergilbungszahl V

Die Vergilbungszahl V ist die Differenz der Gelbwerte der behandelten (*Index b*) und unbehandelten (*Index u*) Probe:

$$V = G_b - G_U \qquad (2)$$

### 4 Durchführung

Zur Messung des Gelbwertes einer Probe wird ein Farbmeßgerät verwendet, mit dem die Normfarbwerte X, Y und Z der Probe nach DIN 5033 Teil 2, Teil 3 und Teil 7 Aufsicht oder in Durchsicht ermittelt werden können. Bei der Messung lumineszierender Proben sind diese polychromatisch mit der entsprechenden Normlichtart zu beleuchten.

Da bei der Berechnung der Vergilbungszahl wegen der Differenzbildung gegen den Bezug keine besonders hohe Absolutgenauigkeit der Normfarbwerte notwendig ist, dürfen handelsübliche Farbmeßgeräte nach dem Dreibereichsverfahren mit guter Langzeitstabilität eingesetztwerden.

### 5 Prüfbericht

Der Prüfbericht muß mindestens die folgenden Angaben enthalten:

a) die Art und Bezeichnung des geprüften Erzeugnisses;
b) einen Hinweis auf diese Norm;
c) die Art und Dauer der Behandlung, die zur Vergilbung der Proben führte;
d) die Vergilbungszahl und/oder die Gelbwerte;
e) die bei der Messung angewandte Meßgeometrie und Art der Beleuchtung (siehe DIN 5033 Teil 7);
f) die den Normfarbwerten X, Y und Z zugrunde gelegte Normlichtart und der zugehörige Normalbeobachter (siehe DIN 5033 Teil 2 und Teil 7);
g) das Prüfdatum.

*Erläuterungen*

Zur vollständigen Farbkennzeichnung nahezu weißer oder vergilbter Proben sind genauso wie für alle anderen Farben drei Farbmaßzahlen erforderlich. Zur Kennzeichnung der Vergilbung werden in der Praxis jedoch eindimensionale Skalen verwendet.
Die in dieser Norm gegebenen Definitionen für den Gelbwert und die Vergilbungszahl haben den Vorteil einfacher Messung und einfacher Berechnung. Der Gelbwert stimmt für Normlichtart C und den 2°-Normalbeobachter angenähert mit dem Yellowness Index YI nach ASTM D 1925–70 überein.

Yellowing is the fate that awaits the pages of a book.

# DIN 6167 Description of the yellowness of near-white or near-colorless materials

## 1 General

The effects of radiation, temperature, moisture, chemical reactions, etc. make materials such as paper, plastics, or paints that were originally almost white or colorless go yellow. The yellowness index indicates the change in the yellow value of a sample as a result of one or more of the above-mentioned effects over a given period of time.

If the samples differ considerably in hue (redder-greener) or brightness, the yellow value and the yellowness index in accordance with this standard and a visual assessment can produce different results. In such cases a full colorimetric description of the samples is required (see DIN 5033 Part 3, DIN 6174, DIN 55 980, and DIN 55 981).

A yellow value that departs from this standard can be obtained by measuring the spectral transmission or reflection ratio at wavelengths of 450, 550, and 600 nm instead of measuring the tristimulus values.

## 2 Yellow value G

The yellow value G of a sample according to this standard is calculated from the tristimulus values X, Y, and Z (see DIN 5033 Parts 2 and 7) according to equation (1).

$$G = \frac{a \cdot X - b \cdot Z}{Y} \cdot 100 \qquad (1)$$

Factors a and b are given in the table:

| Standard illuminant[1] | D 65 | D 65 | C |
|---|---|---|---|
| Standard observer[2] | 10° | 2° | 2° |
| a | 1,301 | 1,298 | 1,277 |
| b | 1,149 | 1,133 | 1,059 |

Values for the 70° standard observer and standard illuminant D 65 should be preferred. If an assessment for the 10° standard observer is not possible, the 2° standard observer may be taken into consideration also by way of exception.

## 3 Yellowness index V

The yellowness index V is the difference between the yellow values of the treated (Index b) and untreated (Index u) sample:

$$V = G_b - G_U \qquad (2)$$

## 4 Procedure

In order to measure the yellow value of a sample, a colorimeter with which the tristimulus values X, Y, and Z of the sample according to DIN 5033 Part 2, Part 3, and Part 7 can be obtained in reflected or transmitted light is used. When measuring luminescent samples, these should be illuminated polychromatically with the relevant standard illuminant.

Since when calculating the yellowness index there is no need for a particularly high degree of absolute accuracy for the tristimulus values, because of subtraction compared with the reference, commercially available colorimeters that operate by the tristimulus method and with good long-term stability may be used.

## 5 Test report

The test report shall contain the following information as a minimum:

a) The nature and designation of the product tested;
b) a reference to this standard;
c) The nature and duration of the treatment that caused the samples to yellow;
d) The yellowness index and/or yellow values;
e) The measurement geometry used in the measurement and the type of illumination (see DIN 5033 Part 7);
f) The standard illuminant on which the tristimulus values X, Y, and Z were based and the associated standard observer (see DIN 5033 Part 2 and Part 7);
g) The date of the test.

*Explanatory notes*

As for all other colors, three colormetric values are required in order fully to identify the color of near-white or yellowed samples, although in practice one-dimensional scales are used to identify yellowness.
The definitions of the yellow value and the yellowness index that are given in this standard have the advantage of being simple to measure and to calculate. For standard illuminant C and the 2° standard observer, the yellow value approximately coincides with Yellowness Index YI according to ASTM D 1925–70.

# W[1]

Wahrheit
Truth

EN

175

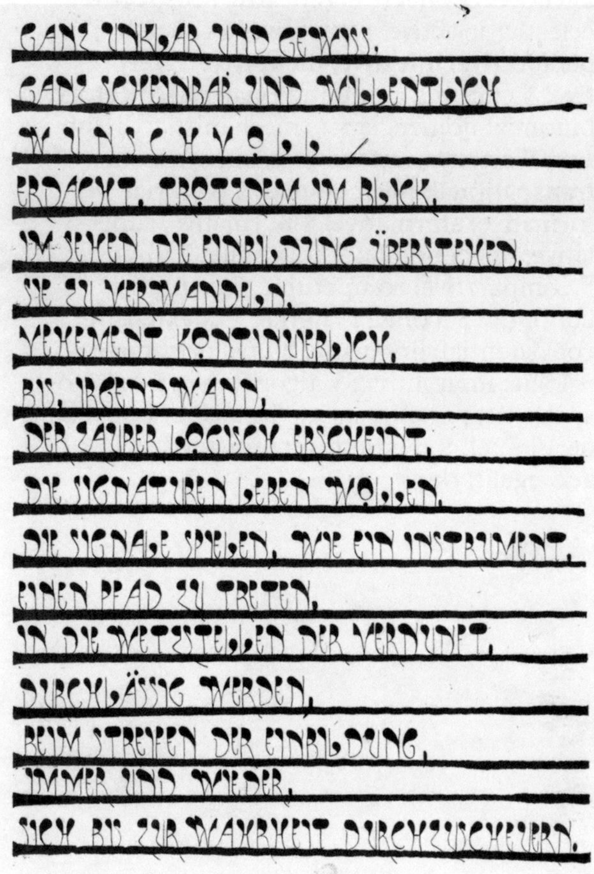

GANZ UNKLAR UND GEWISS,
GANZ SCHEINBAR UND WILLENTLICH
WUNSCHVOLL
ERDACHT, TROTZDEM IM BLICK,
IM SEHEN DIE EINBILDUNG ÜBERSTEHEN,
SIE ZU VERWANDELN,
VEHEMENT KONTINUIERLICH,
BIS, IRGENDWAND,
DER ZAUBER LOGISCH ERSCHEINT,
DIE SIGNATUREN LEBEN WOLLEN,
DIE SIGNALE SPIELEN, WIE EIN INSTRUMENT,
EINEN PFAD ZU TRETEN,
IN DIE WETZSTELLEN DER VERNUNFT,
DURCHLÄSSIG WERDEN,
BEIM STREIFEN DER EINBILDUNG,
IMMER UND WIEDER,
SICH BIS ZUR WAHRHEIT DURCHZUSCHEUERN.

Quite unclear and certain,
entirely apparent and knowingly
w i s h f u l l y
conceived, nonetheless in view.
Withstanding the imagination in seeing.
Transforming it,
with sustained vehemence.
Until, at some point,
the magic seems logical.
Willing to live the signatures.
Playing the signals like an instrument.
Treading a path
to where reason has thinned.
Becoming permeable.
Stroking and scraping
and scuffing
the imagination
to fray through to the truth.

affektive; konnektive; reflexive; prospektive; eklektische; selektive; protektive; ¶ kollektive; perspektivische; infektiöse; ineffektive; interpretative; ¶ kulturelle; komputative; klassifikatorische; binomialnomenklatorische; mechanistische; ¶ disruptive; elektrische; automobilistische; idiosynkratische; transnationale; postkoloniale; ¶ pikturale; performative; affirmative; ¶ normative; superlativische; unökonomische; ¶ epistemische; ¶ forensische; ¶ komparative; kompetitive; ¶ panoptische; banoptische; ¶ ikonische; materielle; ¶ ko-extensive; ko-existentielle; linguistische; ¶ meteorische; meteorologische; ¶ monolithische; algorithmische; ¶ organosynthetische; paradigmatische; pluralistische; ¶ räumliche; dekoloniale; ¶ methodische; proletarische; ¶ zoe-egalitäre;

affective; connective; reflexive; prospective; eclectic; selective; protective; ¶ collective; perspective; infective; ineffective; interpretive; ¶ cultural; computational; classificatory; binomial nomenclative; mechanistic; disruptive; ¶ electric; automotive; idiosyncratic; transnational; postcolonial; ¶ pictorial; performative; affirmative; ¶ normative; superlative; uneconomic; ¶ epistemic; ¶ forensic; ¶ comparative; competitive; ¶ panoptic; banoptic; ¶ iconic; material; ¶ coextensive; coexistential; linguistic; ¶ meteoric; meteorologic; monolithic; ¶ algorithmic; ¶ organosynthetic; paradigmatic; pluralistic; ¶ spatial; decolonial; ¶ methodical; proletarian; ¶ zoe-egalitarian;

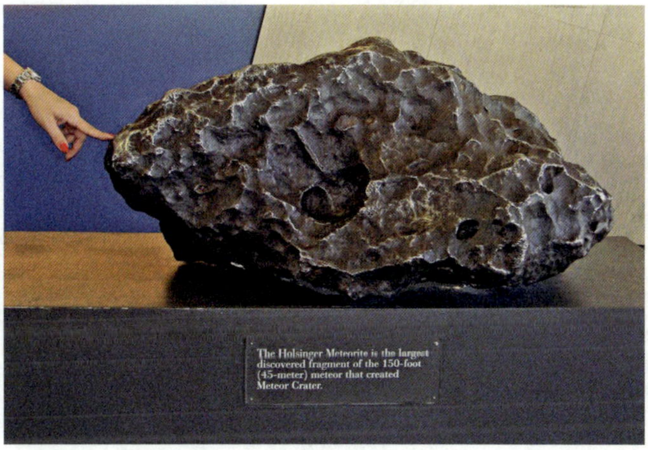
The Holsinger Meteorite is the largest
discovered fragment of the 150-foot
(45-meter) meteor that created
Meteor Crater.

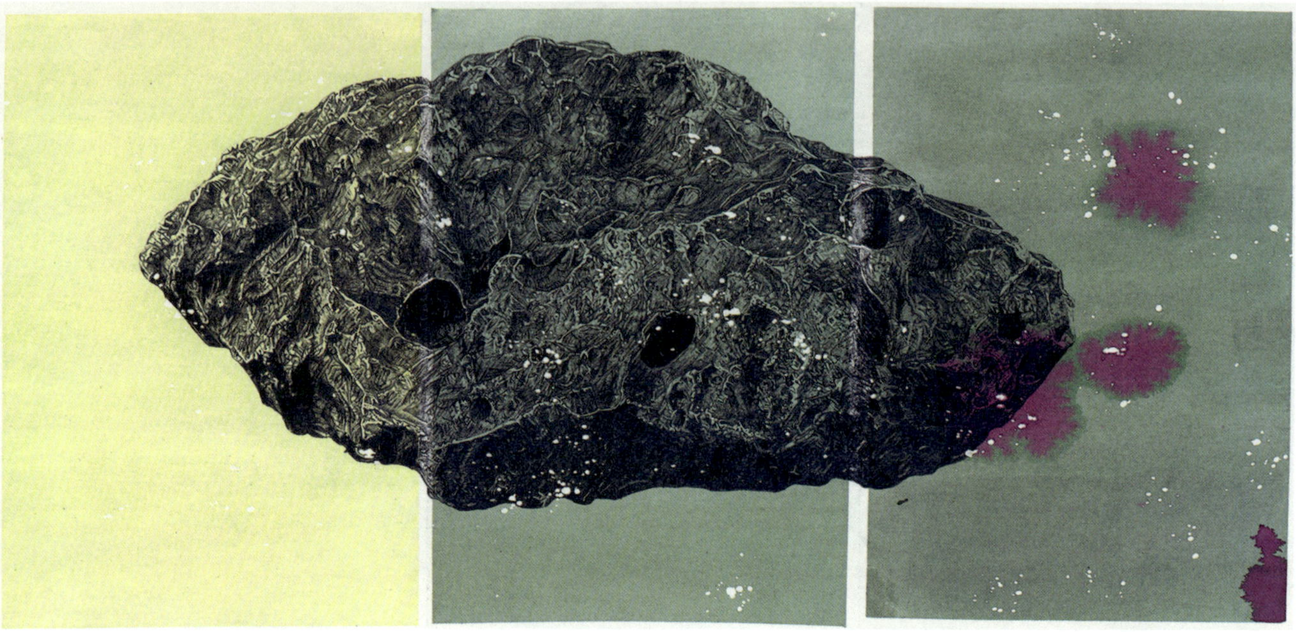

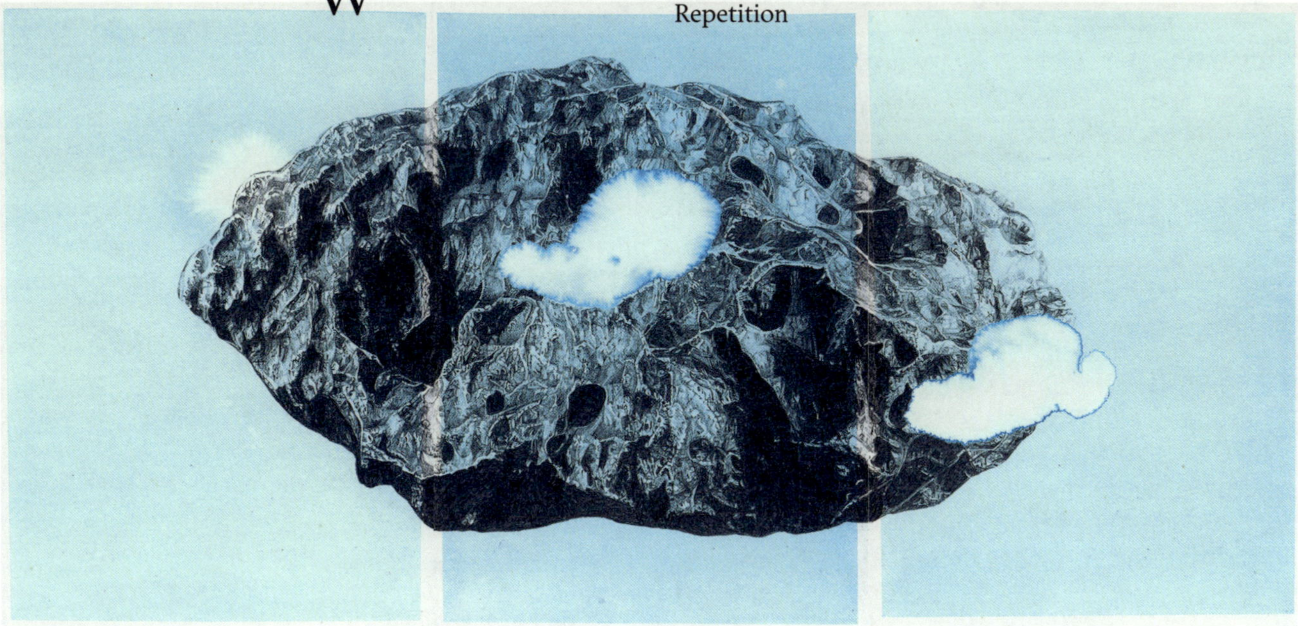

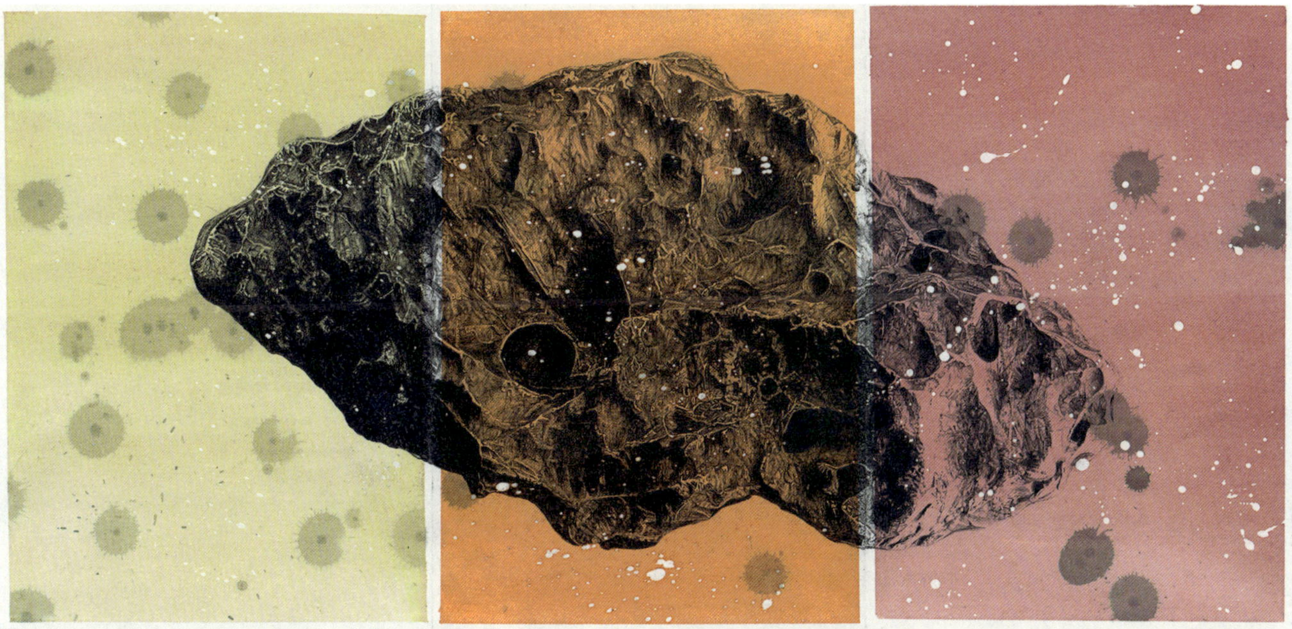

# W³

Wiederholung
Repetition

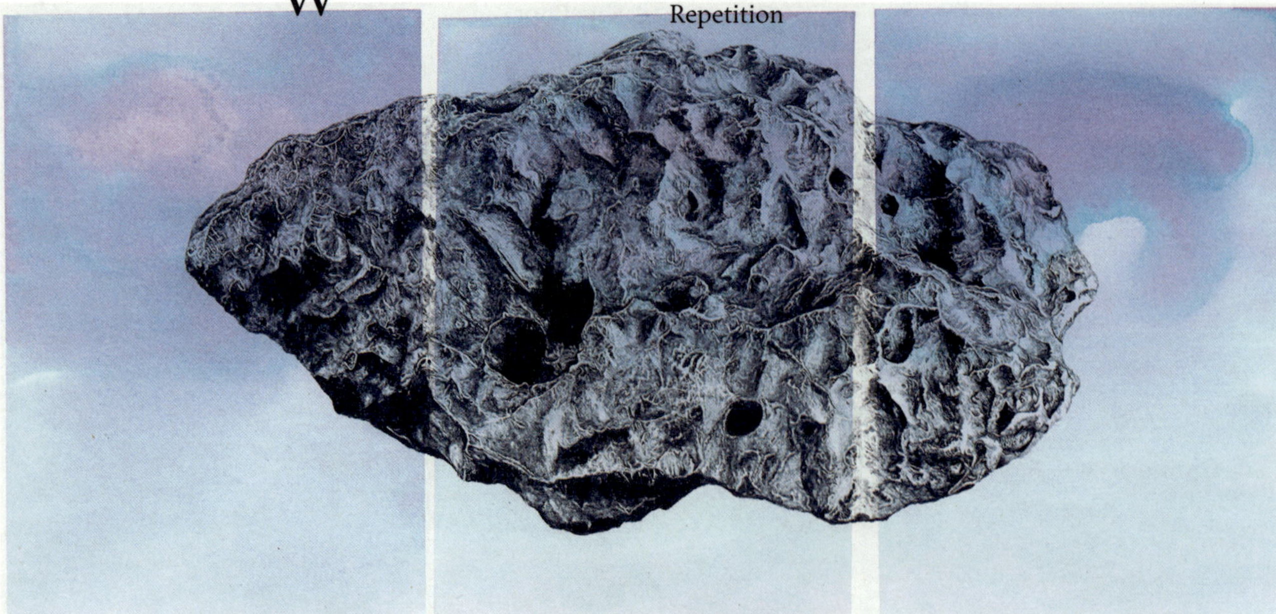

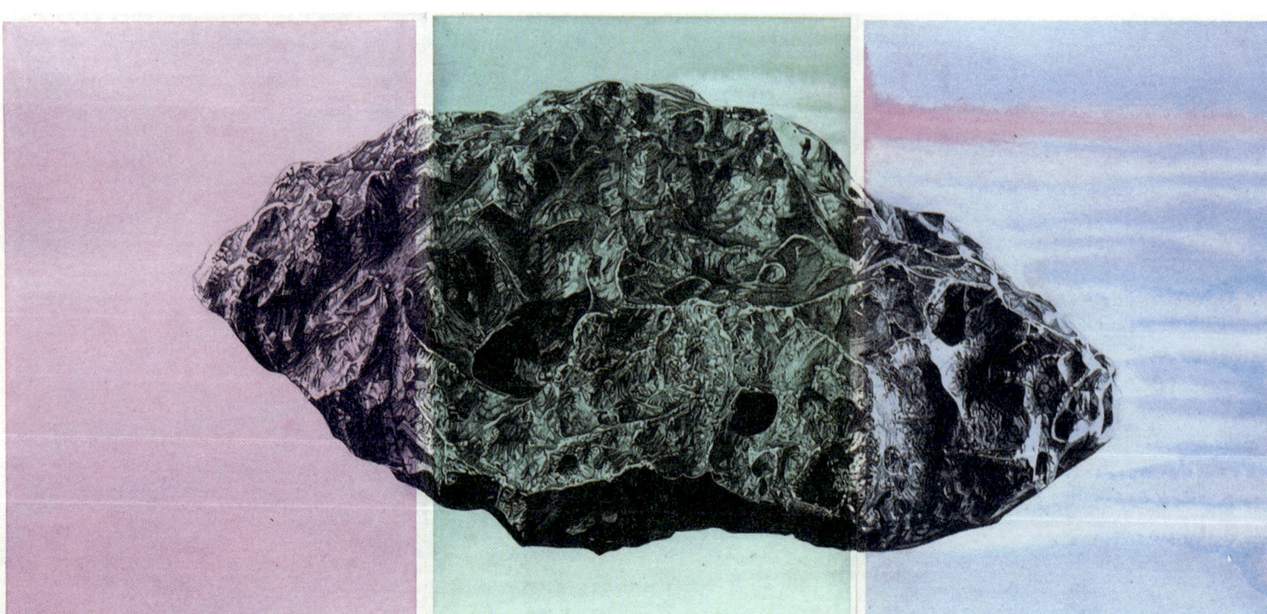

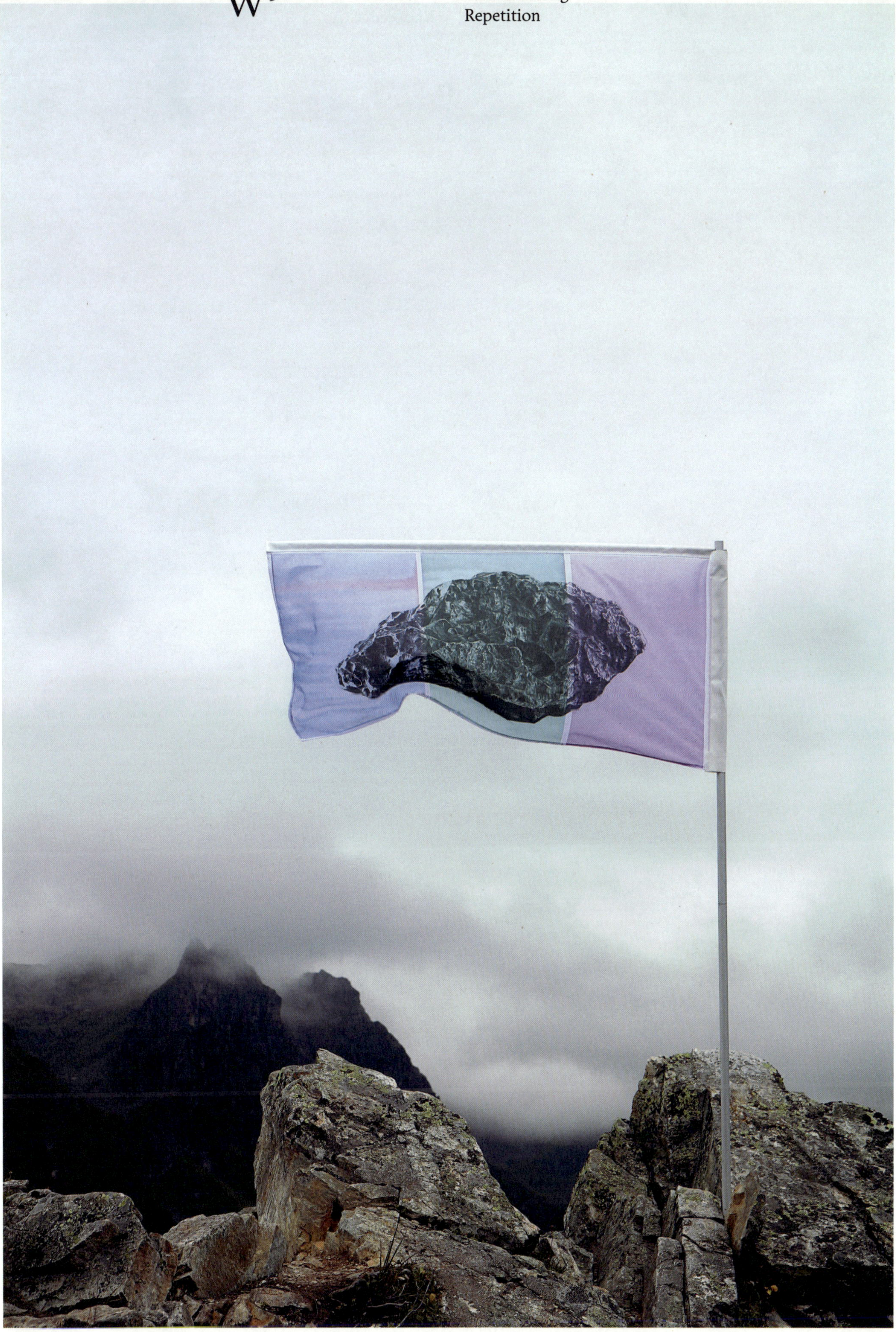

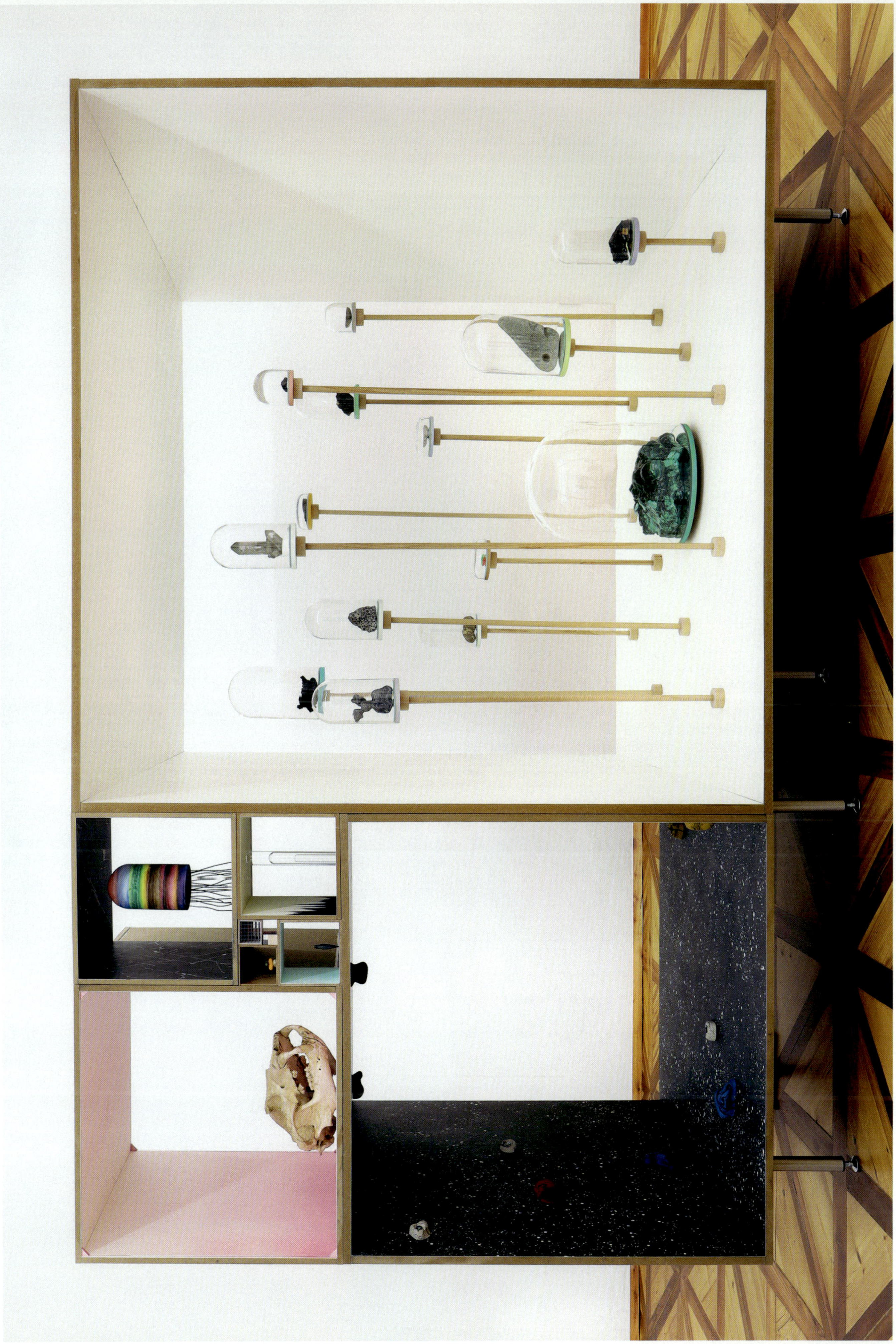

Was bedeutet Wissen für die künstlerische Praxis und die künstlerische Forschung? Wie verhalten sich künstlerische Arbeiten und Zeichnungen – wie etwa die Abbildungen in diesem Buch – zum Wissensbegriff? Wenn Wissen als philosophisch-epistemologischer Begriff aus der Analyse des Wissens definiert wird, wenn Wissen als historisch-soziologischer, sich aus der frühen Neuzeit einer europäisch-akademischen Wissensgeschichte der Universitäten und ihrer Disziplinierungen formierender Begriff gedacht wird, wenn Wissen sich in Form von geteilten Arbeitsprozessen innerhalb von Gesellschaftsordnungen manifestiert, dann stellt sich die Frage, auf welche Weise in den Künsten von Wissensproduktion gesprochen werden kann. Eine vergleichende Analyse des Wissensbegriffes aus künstlerischer und sozioökonomischer Perspektive setzt eine Klärung voraus, was Wissen in seiner „herkömmlichen" Form bedeutet. Erst über diesen theoretischen Aufwand ist es möglich, einen differenzierten Wissensbegriff der künstlerischen, in diesem Buch schwerpunktmäßig zeichnerischen Arbeit zu erschließen.

Unsere Gesellschaft wird über Wissen definiert: Wir nennen sie Wissensgesellschaft. Wissen ist ein eigentümliches Tauschgut, denn wir verlieren es nicht, wenn wir es weitergeben. Wissen ist ökonomisch relevant. Der Begriff der Wissensgesellschaft wird politisch gerne als Zeitdiagnose formuliert.[1] Welche Macht hat Wissen in einer ökonomisierten, kapitalisierten, funktional differenzierten und globalisierten Wissensgesellschaft? Wie eurozentrisch eingegrenzt wird dieser Begriff gedacht? Und welche Ohnmacht ergibt sich aus einer Überforderung angesichts der Masse an Wissen, die sich unaufhörlich akkumuliert und exponentiell vervielfältigt in Form einer täglich wachsenden Menge an Publikationen, Fachartikeln, Bucherscheinungen, aber auch Nachrichten und darüber hinaus in Form des Netzwissens, dieses ungeheuerlich gigantischen autopoietischen Wissens- und Unwissensapparates? Zweifellos bekommt Wissen im biotechnologischen, digitalen und globalisierten Zeitalter eine neue Bedeutung. Eine Verschiebung des Wissensbegriffes ergibt sich sicher auch durch eine technologisch ermöglichte Auslagerung von Wissensprozessen – immense Rechenleistungen, die außerhalb unserer Gehirne stattfinden. Das Unbehagen, das mit Informations- und Wissensflut einhergeht, ist ein affektiver Zustand der Sorge, für den sich etliche historische Belege finden lassen, die weit in unsere Wissensgeschichte zurückreichen. So etwa, wenn der Renaissancehumanist Francesco Petrarca im Jahr 1366 vor einem exzessiven Bücherkonsum warnt, mahnend, dieser würde den Leser in den Wahnsinn führen.[2] Auch einer der wohl prominentesten und bedeutsamsten Enzyklopädisten, Denis Diderot, hat diesen Zustand, etwa 400 Jahre später, sehr treffend und visionär beschrieben:

„Während die Jahrhunderte dahinfließen, wächst die Masse der Werke unaufhörlich, und man sieht einen Zeitpunkt voraus, in dem es fast ebenso schwierig sein wird, sich in einer Bibliothek zurechtzufinden wie im Weltall, und beinahe ebenso einfach, eine feststehende Wahrheit in der Natur zu suchen wie in einer Unmenge von Büchern."[3]

Enzyklopädien kann man als Ausdruck des Wunsches verstehen, in der unüberschaubaren Menge des Wissens Orientierung zu finden. Sie ermöglichen es, sich Spezialbereiche des Wissens überblicksartig zu erschließen oder eine Gesamtschau zu betreiben, um zu einem Allgemeinwissen über vielfältige Themen zu gelangen. Es gibt Spezialenzyklopädien zu den unterschiedlichsten Wissensbereichen in der Wissenschaft, aber auch zu populärwissenschaftlichen und populärkulturellen Themen. Man könnte die Enzyklopädie als Bewältigungsmechanismus verstehen. Ein Bewältigungsmechanismus für die Akkumulation von Wissen im Plural, das sich zwischen den Polen eines universellen unbewältigbaren Wissenskorpus und unzähliger aufgesplitterter Formen von Spezialwissen aufgespannt hat. Durch den von Donna Haraway geprägten Begriff eines situierten Wissens ergibt sich ein Perspektivwechsel auf die Welt des Enzyklopädischen. Universalität weicht dem Multiperspektivischen, dem Antidisziplinären. Die Wissensakteur*innen denken das Enzyklopädische spielerisch, begegnen dem Fragmentarischen sorglos, wenden Ordnungen irrational an, zelebrieren die Lücke und bauen Schränke, deren Fächer lustvoll spiralförmig das eigene Tun mit den diskursiv festgelegten Ordnungen der Welt verwickeln (siehe Fibonacci-Schrank im Text weiter unten).

### Genau dann, wenn: propositionales Wissen

Wie oft sagt man: „Ich weiß, dass …", ohne sich aber eigentlich der erforderlichen Bedingungen bewusst zu sein, die nötig sind, um behaupten zu können, dass man etwas weiß: eine davon ist Wahrheit. Wissen setzt Wahrheit voraus, denn etwas Unwahres kann nicht gewusst werden und verharrt im bloßen Glauben. Die klassische Analyse des Wissens definiert Wissen als wahre, gerechtfertigte Überzeugung.[4] Diese Definition geht auf Platon zurück, der im Dialog *Theaitetos* Wissen einer „mit einer Erklärung verbundenen, wahren Meinung" gleichsetzt.[5] Wann weiß man etwas? Man weiß etwas, wenn es wahr ist und wenn es gerechtfertigt ist, davon überzeugt zu sein. Es gilt also der Standardsatz:

Subjekt S weiß die Proposition P genau dann, wenn (gdw)
(i) P wahr ist,
(ii) S überzeugt ist, dass P,
(iii) S gerechtfertigt in der Überzeugung ist, dass P.[6]

Diese dreifaltige Begriffsdefinition von Wissen wurde mithilfe einiger Gedankenexperimente, auf die hier nicht näher eingegangen werden kann, in Zweifel gezogen, sodass seit einem 1963 publizierten Aufsatz von Edmund Gettier Wissen auf die Definition „wahre Überzeugung" eingegrenzt wurde.[7] Denn Gettier führt mehrere Fälle an, in denen zwar alle drei Bedingungen erfüllt werden, aber dennoch eine Rechtfertigung für die wahre Überzeugung auf falsch gezogenen Schlüssen beruht, die dem Zufall geschuldet sind. Man könnte auch von einem Mutationselement in einer Gedankenkette von logischen Schlüssen sprechen. In der Geschichte der Philosophie und „im Programm der Absolutmachung des Menschen" ist der Zufall ein störendes und ungern erlebtes Element, so der Philosoph Odo Marquard.[8] So unverträglich der Zufall mit Wissen ist, so bestimmend ist er in unserer Existenz, wo er in Form unserer Endlichkeit als „Schicksalszufall" eine geschichtliche Notwendigkeit darstellt.[9] Im Prozess der Erlangung von Wissen dulden wir den Zufall äußerst ungern, denn richtig zu raten kann kaum mit zu wissen gleichgesetzt werden. Was aber macht die Natur des Wissens aus? Was genau transformiert eine Überzeugung in Wissen? Wir wollen, so der Philosoph Ernest Sosa, dass unser Wissen in unserer intellektuellen Kompetenz begründet ist und nicht etwa daraus resultiert, dass wir zufälligerweise richtigliegen.[10] Wissen, um als solches gelten zu dürfen, ist mehr als eine wahre Überzeugung; es ist das Resultat einer kognitiven Leistung, ein Aneignungsprozess. Die Natur des Wissens, die auf eine Überzeugung abzielt, mit der man richtigliegt, definiert Sosa als treffende, epistemische Leistung, in der sich die Kompetenz der*des Überzeugten, die Wahrheit zu erlangen, manifestiert.[11]

### Diszipliniertes Wissen

Wissen ist ein Pluralbegriff, und wissensbasierte Gesellschaftsordnungen sind kein neuartiges Phänomen, sondern existieren schon seit der frühen Neuzeit.[12] Dennoch erhält der Begriff Wissensgesellschaft erst im 20. Jahrhundert seine festen Konturen. Wissen wird neben Kapital und Arbeit zu einer ökonomischen Ressource – bestimmend für das Wirtschaftswachstum einer Gesellschaft. Wissensarbeiter*innen, Forscher*innen, technologische Erneuer*innen sind wesentlicher, fachkenntnisreicher und innovativer Bestandteil von Organisationen, ohne aber selbst die Führung zu übernehmen.[13] Die Produktion von Wissen kann aber auch als soziale Handlung verstanden werden. „Wissen ist ein sozialer Prozess, der gesellschaftliche Machtverhältnisse bedingt und reproduziert, jedoch selbst wieder Bestandteil der kulturellen Reproduktion gesellschaftlicher Strukturen ist."[14]

Wenn man über die Beziehung von Wissen und Macht nachdenkt, drängt sich der Begriff der Disziplin auf, der in diesem System seine Doppeldeutigkeit entfaltet, und zwar als Strukturgeber sowohl für Wissens- als auch für Gesellschaftsordnungen. Der Begriff Disziplin, etymologisch von *discere*, lat. lernen, ist kein neutraler Ausdruck, er ist in der Antike militärisch und im Mittelalter klösterlich konnotiert und wurde im antiken Rom auf das Gesetz und die Künste angewandt.[15] In den Universitäten, den Schulen und der Kirche gab es eine Bewegung der Disziplinierung im 16. Jahrhundert, doch die Etablierung wissenschaftlicher Disziplinen fällt in die Zeit des späten 18. Jahrhunderts.[16] Die Etablierung von Disziplinen im universitären Bereich bedingt auch eine Territorialisierung von Wissenslandschaften sowie Kompetenzzuschreibungen und -beanspruchungen. Fachbegriffe sind die festen Parameter, die die Abgrenzungen von Wissensgebieten markieren und die Kluft

zwischen diesen begünstigen.[17] In der zweiten Hälfte des 19. Jahrhunderts kommt es zu institutionellen Differenzierungsprozessen an Universitäten, zur Herausbildung autonomer Disziplinen und zu einer funktionalen Veränderung der Universitäten von Lehranstalten zu Forschungszentren.[18]

„[D]ie Anwendung, die Produktion, die Akkumulation des Wissens [sind] nicht zu trennen von den Mechanismen der Macht, mit denen sie komplexe Beziehungen unterhalten, die analysiert werden müssen", so der Philosoph Michel Foucault, der den Begriff der Disziplinargesellschaft geprägt hat.[19] Die Ordnungsform des Wissens als Tableau der Identitäten und der Unterschiede, der Klassen und Taxonomien, wie Foucault sie für das klassische Zeitalter (Zeitalter der Repräsentation, etwa 1650 bis 1800) beschreibt, wiederholt auch eine soziale, auf Disziplin beruhende Ordnungsform von „lebenden Tableaus, die aus den unübersichtlichen, unnützen und gefährlichen Mengen geordnete Vielheiten machen".[20]

Das Verhältnis von Wissen und Macht kommt auch in der frühneuzeitlichen hierarchischen Differenzierung zwischen *scientia inferior* und *scientia superior* zum Ausdruck: Hier wird öffentliches, politisches und dem Männlichen zugeordnetes von weiblich besetztem und dem Häuslichen zugeordnetem Wissen unterschieden.[21] Eine Hierarchisierung des Wissens beschreibt auch die Philosophin Rosi Braidotti, wenn sie von qualitativ unterschiedlichen Denklinien spricht: Während eine profitgelenkte „Major Science" hierarchisch strukturiert und von einem kognitiven Kapitalismus angetrieben ist und ökonomisch nützliches Wissen favorisiert, meint „Minor Science" ein Wissen, das heterogen, nicht profitorientiert und von Neugier getrieben ist und dessen Akteur*innen inklusiv und neu gedacht werden als die Minderheiten, die Spezies und die Dinge.[22] Wissensproduktion sieht Braidotti in diesem Sinne als Prozess, der unterschiedlichen Subjektpositionen unterliegt, die geopolitisch, ökologisch, kulturell, historisch und genealogisch differieren.[23]

Wenn es sowohl im Prozess der Wissensgenerierung als auch in ihrer sozialen und ökonomischen Ordnung darum geht, einzelne Felder zu beackern, dann mündet diese Metapher buchstäblich in ihre Ursprungsbedeutung, wenn man die Wissensgeschichte aus Klaus Theweleits Perspektive betrachtet. Denn er beschreibt unsere westliche Kultur- und Zivilisationsgeschichte als kontinuierliche Folge zahlreicher Sequenzierungs- und Segmentierungsprozesse, als „Grundverfahren aller technischen Errungenschaften unserer Zivilisation", die mit dem Domestizieren und dem Sortieren von Samen und Zerteilen in Felder beginnt.[24] Die Vorgänge des Segmentierens und Sequenzierens definiert er als eine „Zerlegung der Welt in Einzelbestandteile und deren Neuverbindung zu künstlichen Ganzheiten".[25] Dazu zählen die unterschiedlichsten Technologien und Kulturtechniken einer eurasiatischen Kultur, etwa Säen, Züchten und Sortieren, Tradition und Religion, Domestizierung, Metallverarbeitung, Vokalalphabetisierung, Schiffsbau, Kartografierung und Statistik, Linearperspektive, Geometrisierung des Raumes und Koordinatensysteme, Bürokratie und Taylorismus, Zeitmessung, Geld, Schrift, Periodensysteme, Anatomie, Elementarteilchen und Quantentheorie, Grenzsicherung, Digitalisierung, Genomeditierung, Biotechnologie u. v. a. m.[26] Die Gemeinsamkeit all dieser sich auf den ersten Blick fremden Felder, auch „techno-soziale Prozesse", finden einerseits im Segment und in der Sequenz ihren gemeinsamen Nenner, andererseits aber auch in ihrer Eigenschaft, die Welt nicht nur zu strukturieren, sondern auch unser Denken selbst umzustrukturieren.[27] Den Forschungen des Neurowissenschaftlers António Damásio folgend, argumentiert Theweleit, dass sich im Zusammenhang mit soziokulturellen und technologischen Veränderungen auch die Genome von Menschen verändern und Gehirnsprünge erfolgen, die genetisch vererbbar sind.[28] Wissen wäre demnach nicht nur durch die Bedingungen seiner Möglichkeiten durch Diskurse (→ Episteme), sondern auch durch die Bedingungen seiner Möglichkeiten durch neurologische Struktur- und Veränderungsprozesse bestimmt.

### Who knows? Wissensakteur*innen im kritischen Posthumanismus

„Universitäten, Wissenschaftsakademien und spezialisierte Institute sind heute bei Weitem nicht alleinige Eigentümer der Kapazität von Wissensproduktion. Wenn der Kapitalismus tatsächlich eine kognitive Wende vollzogen hat, so wird kognitives Material auf vielzählige Wege und an unzähligen Orten erzeugt, die den Unternehmensbereich, die Kunstwelt, das Militär, den Aktivismus, die Blogosphäre und das Internet einschließen."[29]

Das Gefühl einer Überforderung durch ein stetiges, explosionsartiges Anwachsen von Wissen und damit auch von Nichtwissen ist nicht die einzige Problematik, mit der wir konfrontiert sind. Unsere Wissensgeschichte wird durch eine weitere, nicht weniger gefühlsbezogene Dimension ergänzt. Wir Subjekte des Posthumanismus und Postanthropozäns fühlen uns ohnmächtig angesichts der Menge an Information und Wissen, die außerhalb des „traditionellen Containers", der bisher immer der menschliche Geist war, produziert wird.[30] Algorithmisch ausgeführte Risikoeinschätzung, synthetisch herbeigeführte Zellbildungs- und Teilungsprozesse, künstlich hergestelltes Fleisch, die Adaptierung und Kopie neuraler und sensorischer Systeme anderer Spezies zählt die Philosophin Rosi Braidotti exemplarisch zu diesen „außermenschlich" erzeugten Wissensarten.[31] Sie spricht vom menschlichen Körper als altmodischer, anthropomorpher Maschine, die sich als ungeeignetes Gefäß für die wendige, schnelle Intelligenz unserer Technologien erweist.[32] In *Posthumanismus* beschreibt sie, wie der vitruvianische Mensch, bekannt durch Leonardo da Vincis einprägsame, geometrisierte Darstellung, zum Idealbild und normativen Modell eines europäischen Humanismus wird.[33] Dieser Humanismus, der von einem Glauben „an die einzigartigen, selbstregulierenden und im Kern moralischen Kräfte menschlicher Vernunft" geprägt wird, entwickelt sich zu einem universalistischen „Zivilisationsmodell", in dem Europa das Zentrum aller Vernunft darstellt.[34]

Das Bild einer normgebenden, männlichen, exklusiven und hierarchisch bessergestellten Idealfigur beschert der westlich-europäischen Gesellschaft einen chronischen Überlegenheitskomplex, der in den Fasern unserer europäisch-humanistischen Identität sitzt. Auch Klaus Theweleits Begriff eines „hyperalphabetisierten, zentralperspektivisch durchtrainierten europäischen Post-Renaissance-Menschen" weist Analogien zu dieser tradierten, Wissen verkörpernden Idealfigur auf.[35] Aus dieser Perspektive ist die europäische Geschichte vielmehr eine Gewalt- als eine Vernunftgeschichte:

„Die Europäer werden zu Mördern, eben *weil* sie zivilisiert sind. Ihr *zivilisierter* Blick auf die dritten und vierten Welten sagt: Wir sind Menschen; *ihr* nicht. Die Technologien von Perspektivismus, Geometrisierung, Mathematisierung, Projektion und Kartographierung sind spätestens im Verlauf des 16. Jahrhunderts so sehr in die Körper der über die Meere ausschweifenden Segment-Europäer hineingewachsen, dass Lebewesen, die nicht über diesen High-Tech-Körper verfügen, wenig (oder gar keine) Chancen hatten (haben), als ‚Gleiche' wahrgenommen zu werden; im Extremfall: nicht als ‚Menschen'."[36]

In einer hochtechnologischen und ökologisch höchst fragilen Zeit, in der das Humane „zu einer alles Leben beeinflussenden geologischen Kraft wird", muss das Konzept des Humanen und damit auch eine humane Wissensproduktion gezwungenermaßen überdacht werden.[37] Braidotti versteht posthumane Theorie als gestalterisches Instrument, um mit den Herausforderungen und Paradoxien unserer Zeit affirmativ umzugehen.[38] Posthumanismus und Postanthropozän meinen eine Abkehr von einem rein eurozentrisch geprägten Weltbild und eine Neupositionierung des Menschen im Sinne seiner Enthierarchisierung und einer Gleichstellung von anderen Akteur*innen, anderen Spezies dieses Planeten. In diesem Sinne wäre im Bezug auf Wissen also nicht nur zu fragen, welcher Art Wissen sein kann und welche Qualitäten und Formen es annehmen kann, sondern vielmehr, wer Wissen produziert. Es müsste sich ein fundamental anders strukturierter Wissensbegriff daraus ergeben, wenn wir Algorithmen, künstliche Intelligenzen, aber auch lebende Organismen, die nicht der Gattung Mensch angehören, als Wissensproduzent*innen verstehen und wenn wir das Humane, das als „normative Konvention" viel Potenzial für Ausgrenzung des Nichtnormalen, Nichtnormgerechten bietet sowie eine qualitative Differenzierung von „sexualisierten, rassisierten oder naturalisierten Anderen" vornimmt, als überholt erachten.[39] In einer posthumanen Produktion von Wissen geht es, basierend auf konzeptueller Kreativität, um ein Nachdenken, ein Neudenken des Wissensbegriffes: ein Wissen, das sich als Assemblage menschlicher und nichtmenschlicher Akteur*innen versteht und sich von Prinzipien der Multiplizität und Komplexität leiten lässt.[40] Das wissende Subjekt ist weder „homo universalis" noch „Anthropos" allein, so Braidotti, sondern ein komplexes Ensemble, welches unter anderem den Menschen beinhaltet.[41]

## Der Fibonacci-Schrank: eine Referenzspirale als enzyklopädischer Bewältigungsmechanismus

Der Fibonacci-Schrank versteht sich als eine situierte, temporäre Wissenssammlung. Er ist ein künstlerisch-wissenschaftliches und antidisziplinäres Tableau, das verschiedene Objekte, darunter museale Leihgaben einer erdwissenschaftlichen Sammlung, mit privaten Fundstücken, künstlerischen Objekten und Zeichnungen zu einer Gesamtschau vereint.[42] Die Dimensionen der Fächer des Fibonacci-Schrankes ergeben sich aus der Fibonacci-Zahlenfolge: Jede Zahl dieser Zahlenfolge ergibt sich aus der Summe ihrer beiden Vorgänger (0, 1, 0 + 1 = 1, 1 + 1 = 2, 1 + 2 = 3, 2 + 3 = 5, 3 + 5 = 8, 5 + 8 = 13, 8 + 13 = 21 usw.). Die Fibonacci-Zahlenfolge erzeugt, in Flächen übersetzt, eine Anordnung, die zu einer Spirale gedacht werden kann. Die Fibonacci-Spirale steht in Relation zum Goldenen Schnitt. In der Natur finden sich viele Beispiele für die Fibonacci-Folge, etwa in biologischen Systemen, bei spiralförmigen Ammoniten und in der Anordnung von Blättern und Fruchtständen vieler Pflanzen, Blüten und sogar bei Wetterphänomenen wie Tornados. In der Fibonacci-Suchtechnik wird die Zahlenfolge auf Algorithmen angewandt.

Die Fibonacci-Zahlenfolge bildet also das numerische System zur Erstellung einzelner Fächer, wobei die beiden kleinsten Fächer je 1 × 1 × 1 cm und das größte Fach 144 × 144 × 144 cm messen. Als künstlerisches Display ist der Fibonacci-Schrank als spiralförmig verschränktes Referenzsystem verschiedener Wissensformen zu verstehen. Die beiden kleinsten Fächer (mit je 1 × 1 × 1 cm) bestehen aus Würfeln, einmal aus einem Grafitstift zurechtgeschliffen und einmal aus Steinpapier verleimt. Die innerste und kleinste Einheit des Fibonacci-Schrankes ist somit ein Verweis auf die künstlerische Praxis des Zeichnens. Der Grafit taucht aber auch in Zeichnungen verarbeitet, als fiktives museales Objekt (Pfeilspitze) und als geologisches Schauobjekt unter einem Glassturz im größten Fach wieder auf.

Auf die beiden kleinsten Fächer folgen ein Holzkubus und ein Spiegelkubus, die ebenso Materialreferenzen sind. Sie verweisen auf das Repräsentative, Distanzierende: Rahmen und Verglasen. Im nächsten Fach wiederholt ein Gitter aus Grafitminen die Struktur eines Kristalls. Darauf folgt ein Fach mit drei zu einer Säule verklebten, lange Zeit verwahrten Vitaminpillen aus dem persönlichen Fundus, die in ihrer Oberflächenstruktur kleinen Kieselsteinen ähneln.

Abb. 1

Das darauf folgende Fach beinhaltet eine Pfeilspitze aus Grafit, ein künstlerisches „Beiprodukt“. Ein dicker Grafitstift wurde in eine Bohrmaschine eingespannt und gespitzt. Die dabei entstandenen Grafitspäne wurden für die Arbeit *Doppelgänger* verwendet (siehe → *Doppelgänger*). Die Grafitspitze erweckt Assoziationen zu prähistorischen Pfeilspitzen, die als museale Objekte in Vitrinen präsentiert werden. Wie kam der Pfeil von der Jagd in die Grafik, wo er die symbolische Funktion erfüllt, eine einseitige, gerichtete Dynamik zu beschreiben?

Abb. 2

In den beiden folgenden Fächern wird das Motiv des Glassturzes aufgegriffen, einmal durch seine verdreifachte Anwesenheit, einmal durch seine Abwesenheit. In einem Fach finden sich drei übereinandergestülpte Reagenzgläser. Sie spielen auf die vakuumgarantierenden Glasglocken an, unter denen das Pariser Urkilo lagert. Das Urkilo ist ein Zylinder aus einer Iridium-Platin-Verbindung und galt international als Referenznormal für die Maßeinheit des Kilogramms, bis es 2019 von einer Siliziumkugel abgelöst wurde, weil seine Masse messbar abnahm.

Im nächstgrößeren Fach ist ein Objekt zu sehen, das aus Steingussmasse und Tusche in vielen Schichten gegossen wurde. Als Negativform für den Guss diente genau so ein Glassturz wie diejenigen, die im größten Fach zum Einsatz kommen, um die Stein- und Kristallobjekte zu schützen. Der Bohrkern ist hier als Referenzmodell ideengebend. Bohrkerne kann man als zeitgeschichtliche Dokumente verstehen. Sie geben Aufschluss über geologische Ereignisse in der Erdgeschichte. Das geschichtete Objekt auf Drahtfüßen könnte ein Fossil sein.

Abb. 3

Animistisch gedacht ist auch das folgende Fach, in dem sich ein etwa 35.000 Jahre alter Höhlenbärenschädel befindet. Er wurde in den Zwanzigerjahren des letzten Jahrhunderts von Josef C. Groß bei Grabungen in der Uschowa-Höhle (zwischen Österreich und Slowenien) gefunden. Groß fertigte während der Grabungen tagebuchartig mehrere Protokolle an, darunter präzise Tuschezeichnungen mit zum Teil überraschenden Farbgebungen. Auf einem Grabungsprotokoll sind die Knochen des Höhlenbären von

einer rosa Tuschefläche umgeben – das Fach des Fibonacci-Schrankes wurde farblich darauf abgestimmt.

Abb. 4

Schließlich folgt das vorletzte Fach ohne Inhalt. Es ist ausgekleidet mit kosmischen Grafitzeichnungen, auf denen Klettergriffe angebracht wurden. Im letzten und größten Fach findet sich eine Sammlung von Kristallen, Fossilen, Steinen und Schlacke. Die Steine aus der persönlichen Sammlung wurden wegen ihrer spezifischen Formen ausgewählt (Nase, Hase, angesprayter Baustellenfundstein, „gefälschter" Meteorit vom Flohmarkt, verwitterter Stein). Zu den gezeigten musealen Objekten zählen ein großer Malachit, ein Grafit, ein Bergkristall und ein Ammonit.

Abb. 5

Das Herauslösen der Objekte aus den ihnen zugewiesenen oder eingeschriebenen Bedeutungszusammenhängen wird zur Methode, um ein System der Gleichwertigkeit zu erzeugen: ein Rearrangieren und eine Enthierarchisierung der Herkunftsobjekte, denen unterschiedliche ökonomische und ideelle Werte zugewiesen sind – zumindest innerhalb dieses symbolischen Raumes.

1 Eine ausführliche Klärung des Begriffs Wissensgesellschaft als Zeitdiagnose findet man bei Laura Kajetzke und Anina Engelhardt, „Leben wir in einer Wissensgesellschaft?", *Aus Politik und Zeitgeschichte* (April 2013), www.bpb.de/shop/zeitschriften/apuz/158659/leben-wir-in-einer-wissensgesell schaft, abgerufen am 14.2.2022.

2 Vgl. Steffen Siegel, *Tabula. Figuren der Ordnung um 1600* (Berlin: Akademie Verlag, 2009), 29.

3 Denis Diderot, „Enzyklopädie", in *Die Welt der Encyclopédie*, ediert von Anette Selg und Rainer Wieland, hrsg. von Hans Magnus Enzensberger (Frankfurt am Main: Eichborn, 2001), 82.

4 Vgl. Jonathan Jenkins Ichikawa und Matthias Steup, „The Analysis of Knowledge", *The Stanford Encyclopedia of Philosophy* (Summer 2018 Edition), hrsg. von Edward N. Zalta, https://plato.stanford.edu/archives/sum2018/entries/knowledge-analysis/, abgerufen am 8.7.2021.

5 Thomas Auinger, „Wissen, Anerkennung und implizite Normativität", *(Wie) entsteht Wissen?* (Nr. 3–4, 2005), hrsg. von Mitteilungen des Instituts für Wissenschaft und Kunst, 2.

6 „The Analysis of Knowledge".

7 Vgl. Edmund Gettier, „Is Justified True Belief Knowledge?", *Epistemology: An Anthology*, hrsg. von Ernest Sosa, Jaegwon Kim, Jeremy Fantl und Matthew McGrath (Oxford: Blackwell Publishing, 2009), 192.

8 Odo Marquard, *Apologie des Zufälligen. Philosophische Studien*, (Stuttgart: Reclam, 2013), 119.

9 Marquard, *Apologie des Zufälligen*, 129.

10 Vgl. Ernest Sosa, „The Place of Truth in Epistemology", in *Epistemology: An Anthology*, 478.

11 Von der Autorin frei übersetzt, vgl. Ernest Sosa, „Knowing Full Well: The Normativity of Beliefs as Performances", *Disputatio. Philosophical Research Bulletin*, 4:5, 2015, 87.

12 In dem zweibändigen Werk *A Social History of Knowledge* unternimmt der britische Historiker Peter Burke eine umfangreiche Untersuchung der Sozialgeschichte des Wissens von der frühen Neuzeit bis zur Gegenwart, in der unterschiedliche Differenzierungsprozesse des Wissens, welche zum Teil bis in die Gegenwart wirksam sind, beleuchtet werden. Peter Burke, *A Social History of Knowledge: From Gutenberg to Diderot* (Cambridge: Polity, 2008). Peter Burke, *A Social History of Knowledge: From the Encyclopédie to Wikipedia* (Cambridge: Polity, 2018).

13 Vgl. Jochen Steinbicker, „Peter Drucker: Wissensgesellschaft, wissensbasierte Organisation und Wissensarbeiter", in *Handbuch Wissensgesellschaft: Theorien, Themen und Probleme*, hrsg. von Anina Engelhardt und Laura Kajetzke (Bielefeld: Transcript, 2010), 22 f.

14 Marian Adolf, „Nico Stehr: Konzeption der Wissensgesellschaft", in ebd., 54.

15 Von der Autorin frei übersetzt, vgl. Burke, *A Social History of Knowledge: From Gutenberg to Diderot*, 90.

16 Ebd., 90 f.

17 Vgl. Peter Burke, *The Polymath: A Cultural History from Leonardo da Vinci to Susan Sontag* (London: Yale University Press, 2020), 134.

18 Von der Autorin frei übersetzt, vgl. Burke, *A Social History of Knowledge: From the Encyclopédie to Wikipedia*, 167.

19 Michel Foucault, „Michel Foucault, Gespräch mit Ducio Trombardi", in *Michel Foucault. Die Hauptwerke,* übers. von Ulrich Köppen (Frankfurt am Main: Suhrkamp, 2016), 1642.

20 Michel Foucault, „Überwachen und Strafen. Die Geburt des Gefängnisses", in *Michel Foucault. Die Hauptwerke,* übers. von Ulrich Köppen (Frankfurt am Main: Suhrkamp, 2016), 851. Vgl. Michel Foucault, „Die Ordnung der Dinge. Eine Archäologie der Humanwissenschaften", in ebd., 114

21 Burke, *A Social History of Knowledge: From Gutenberg to Diderot,* 84.

22 Von der Autorin frei übersetzt, vgl. Rosi Braidotti, *Posthuman Knowledge* (Cambridge: Polity Press, 2020), 153.

23 Von der Autorin frei übersetzt, vgl. Braidotti, *Posthuman Knowledge,* 49 f.

24 Klaus Theweleit, *Warum Cortés wirklich siegte: Technologiegeschichte der eurasisch-amerikanischen Kolonialismen* (Berlin: Matthes & Seitz, 2020), 15.

25 Ebd., 122.

26 Ebd., passim.

27 Ebd., 492.

28 Ebd., 247.

29 Übersetzt von der Autorin, Rosi Braidotti, *Posthuman Knowledge,* 91. „Universities, science academies and specialized institutes are by far not the sole owners of knowledge production capacity today. If capitalism has indeed taken a cognitive turn, then cognitive material is being produced in a myriad of ways and in multiple locations that include the corporate sector, the art world, the military, the activist sector, the blogosphere and the Internet."

30 Übersetzt von der Autorin, vgl. ebd., 14.

31 Übersetzt von der Autorin, vgl. ebd., 14.

32 Übersetzt von der Autorin, vgl. ebd., 14.

33 Vgl. Rosi Braidotti, *Posthumanismus: Leben jenseits des Menschen,* übers. von Thomas Laugstien (Frankfurt: Campus, 2014), 19.

34 Ebd., 19 f.

35 Theweleit, *Warum Cortés wirklich siegte,* 271.

36 Ebd., 269.

37 Braidotti, *Posthumanismus,* 11.

38 Vgl. ebd., 11.

39 Ebd., 31 f.

40 Vgl. Braidotti, *Posthuman Knowledge,* 18 f.

41 Vgl. ebd., 101.

42 Der Fibonacci-Schrank wurde im Zuge der Ausstellung *antispecies* 2021 in der Galerie 3, Klagenfurt, aufgebaut. Objekte der erdwissenschaftlichen Sammlung des Landesmuseums Kärnten waren Teil des gezeigten Inventars.

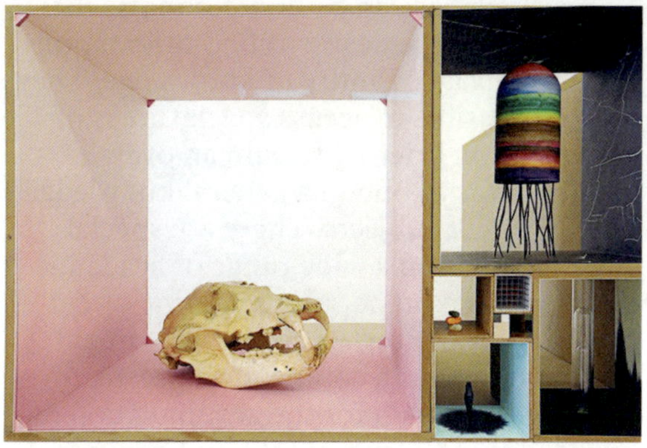

Abb. / Fig. 1

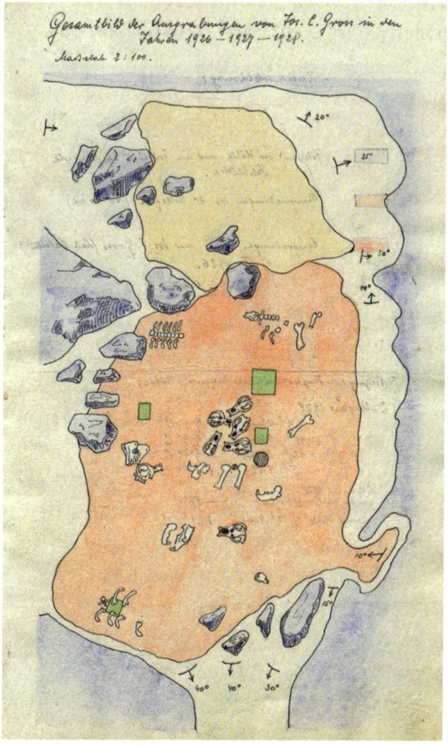



Abb. / Fig. 4
Josef C. Groß, Grabungsprotokoll / Excavation protocol, Sammlung Landesmuseum Kärnten

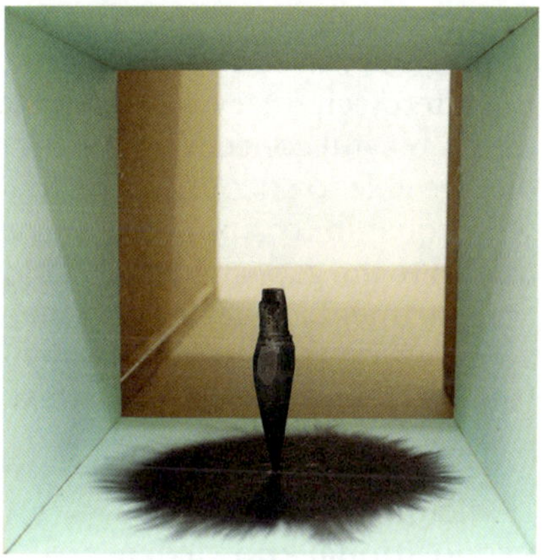

Abb. / Fig. 2

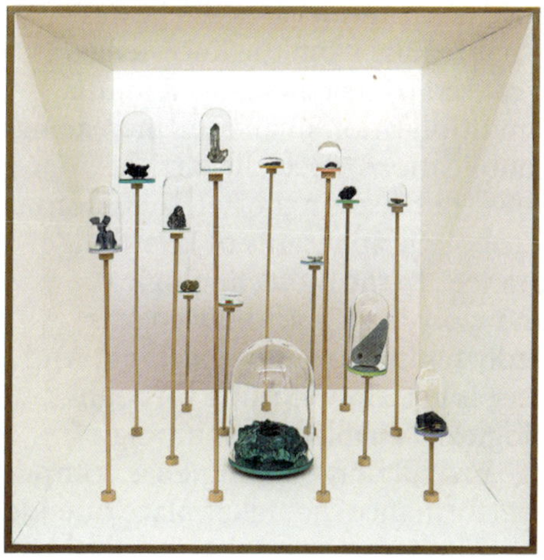

Abb. / Fig. 5

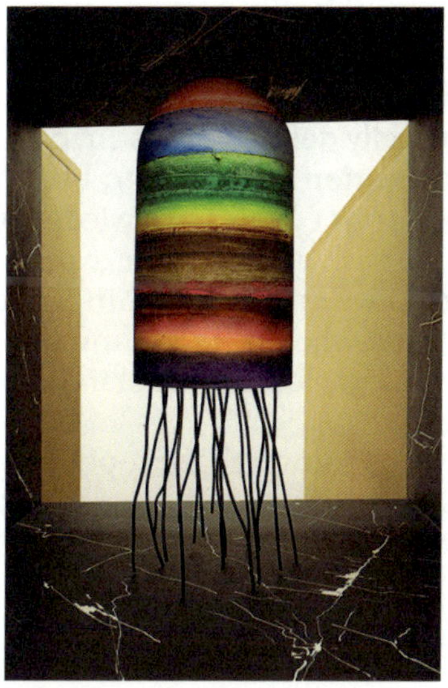

Abb. / Fig. 3

What does knowledge mean for artistic practice and artistic research? How do works of art—such as the images in this book—relate to the concept of knowledge? If knowledge is defined as a philosophical-epistemological term from knowledge analysis, if it is conceived as an early-modern sociological term from a European academic history of knowledge, if it is manifested as shared working processes within social systems, then the question arises as to how the production of knowledge can be discussed in the arts. A comparative analysis of the concept of knowledge from an artistic and socio-economic perspective requires a clarification of what knowledge means "conventionally." Only through this theoretical effort is it possible to extrapolate a differentiated concept of knowledge as represented by the drawings that predominate in this book.

Our society is defined by knowledge: we call it the knowledge society. Knowledge is a curious object of exchange, for we don't lose it if we pass it on. Knowledge is economically relevant. The term knowledge society is a ready political formulation to describe the present.[1] What power does knowledge have in a financialized, capitalized, functionally differentiated and globalized society? How Eurocentric is it? And what is the powerlessness that results from the knowledge overload caused by its constant accumulation and multiplication in an ever-increasing mass of publications, specialist articles, books, news, but also on the net, that monstrous autopoietic apparatus of knowledge and ignorance? In the biotechnological, digital, and globalized era, knowledge is undoubtedly taking on a new meaning. And the concept is certainly shifting through a technologically enabled outsourcing of knowledge production—an immense computational performance that takes place outside our brains. The unease associated with the flood of information and knowledge is an affective state of anxiety for which historical evidence can be found that goes far back in our history of knowledge. The Renaissance humanist Francesco Petrarca warned against the excessive consumption of books in 1366, saying that it could drive the reader to madness.[2] And around 400 years later one of the most prominent and significant encyclopedists, Denis Diderot, described this state with visionary aptness:

"As centuries pass by, the mass of works grows endlessly, and one can foresee a time when it will be almost as difficult to educate oneself in a library, as in the universe, and almost as fast to seek a truth subsisting in nature, as lost among an immense number of books."[3]

Encyclopedias can be understood as the expression of the desire to find orientation amidst the vast quantity of knowledge. They make it possible to access special areas of knowledge in brief, or to gain an overall picture, so as to obtain a general knowledge of a variety of subjects. There are special encyclopedias on a wide range of academic areas, but also on popular scientific or cultural subject matter. Encyclopedias might be understood as a coping mechanism. A coping mechanism for the accumulation of knowledge in the plural, situated between the poles of universal unmanageable corpus and myriad specialist learning. Donna Haraway's concept of "situated knowledge" results in a change of perspective: universality gives way to the multi-perspective, the interdisciplinary; seekers of knowledge have a playful concept of the encyclopedic, are able to encounter the fragmentary with equanimity, apply order irrationally, celebrate the gap, and build cabinets whose compartments helically entwine one's own activity with the discursively defined world (see Fibonacci cabinet in the text below).

## If and only if: propositional knowledge

How often do we say "I know that …" without actually being aware of the conditions required to make such a claim. One of these conditions is truth. Knowledge assumes truth, for something untrue can't be known and remains mere belief. Knowledge is classically defined as justified true belief.[4] This definition goes back to Plato, who in *Theaetetus* equates knowledge with "true opinion, with definition or explanation."[5] When do we know something? We know something when it is true and our belief in this is justified. So the standard formula applies:

Subject *S* knows that proposition *p*
if and only if (iff)
(i) *p* is true;
(ii) *S* believes that *p*;
(iii) *S* is justified in believing that *p*.[6]

This threefold definition of knowledge was called into doubt with the aid of a

thought experiment—which can't be elucidated here—so that since an article published by Edmund Gettier in 1963 knowledge has been limited to the definition of "true belief."[7] For Gettier instances several cases in which all conditions are fulfilled but the justification for true belief is nevertheless based on falsely drawn conclusions due to chance. One could also speak of a mutation in the logical chain. In the history of philosophy and the "program of making man absolute" the accidental is a disruptive and unwelcome element, according to the philosopher Odo Marquard.[8] Although incompatible with knowledge, the accidental determines our existence, in which our mortality represents a historical necessity in the form of the "fatefully accidental."[9] In gaining knowledge we are disinclined to tolerate chance, for guessing right can hardly be equated with science. But what constitutes the nature of knowledge? How exactly does belief transform into it? We want to found our knowledge in our intellectual competence, says the philosopher Ernest Sosa, not from happening to be right.[10] Knowledge, to count as such, is more than true belief; it is the result of a cognitive achievement, a learning process. Sosa defines the nature of knowledge aimed at belief, at being right, as an epistemic achievement that manifests the believer's competence to attain the truth.[11]

## Disciplined knowledge

Knowledge is a plural concept, and knowledge-based social systems are not a new phenomenon but have existed since the early modern period.[12] Nevertheless, the concept of the knowledge society only became fixed in the twentieth century. Knowledge became a resource along with capital and labor—and decisive to society's economic growth. Knowledge workers, researchers, technical innovators are an essential, expert, innovative—though not managerial—element of organizations.[13] But the production of knowledge can also be understood as a social activity. "Knowledge is a social process that determines and reproduces social power relationships, but that is itself an aspect of the cultural reproduction of social structures."[14]

Thinking about the relationship between knowledge and power brings to mind the concept of discipline, which takes on a double role in the provision of structure for both social systems and systems of knowledge. The term "discipline," derived from the Latin *discere*, to learn, is not a neutral concept; it was militarily connoted in antiquity, monastically in medieval times, and in ancient Rome it was applied to the law and to the arts.[15]

There was a movement of "disciplining" in universities, schools, and the church in the sixteenth century, but the establishment of academic "departments" occurs during the late eighteenth century.[16] The formulation of academic disciplines also leads to a territorialization of knowledge landscapes, together with ascriptions and claims of competence. Technical terms are the parameters that delimit areas of knowledge and encourage divisions between them.[17] In the second half of the nineteenth century, academic institutions are differentiated, autonomous disciplines develop, and universities undergo a functional change from teaching to research.[18]

"The exercise, production, and accumulation of this knowledge cannot be dissociated from the mechanisms of power; complex relations exist which must be analyzed,"[19] says the philosopher Michel Foucault, who coined the term "disciplinary society." Ordering knowledge as a tableau of identities and differences, classes and taxonomies, as Foucault describes the age for which this was typical (age of representation, around 1650 to 1800), repeats a discipline-based social system of "*tableaux vivants*, which transform the confused, useless or dangerous multitudes into ordered multiplicities."[20]

The relationship between knowledge and power is also expressed in the early modern hierarchical differentiation between *scientia inferior* and *scientia superior*. This is the distinction between public, political knowledge—ascribed to the male—and domestic knowledge—ascribed to the female.[21] The philosopher Rosi Braidotti describes a stratification of knowledge in terms of different lines of thought: while a profit-lead "major science" is hierarchically structured, driven by a cognitive capitalism, and favors knowledge with an economic benefit, curiosity-driven "minor science" seeks a heterogeneous knowledge that is not profit-oriented and whose components are inclusively reconceived as minorities, species, and things.[22] In this sense Braidotti sees the production of knowledge as a process

governed by different subject positions that vary geopolitically, ecologically, culturally, historically, and genealogically.[23]

When the aim is to plough individual fields in both the generation of knowledge and in its social and economic order, then this metaphor leads to its literal original meaning, if we consider the history of knowledge from Klaus Theweleit's perspective. Theweleit sees occidental culture as the continual result of numerous processes of sequencing and segmentation, for him "the basic procedures of all the technical achievements of our civilization," which begins with the domestication of animals, the sorting of seeds, and the division of land into fields.[24] He defines segmenting and sequencing as a "partitioning of the world into individual elements and their recombination into artificial wholes."[25] This includes the use of a wide range of Eurasian technologies and cultural techniques, such as sowing, cultivation and sorting, tradition and religion, domestication, metalwork, writing, ship-building, cartography and statistics, linear perspective, the geometrization of space, coordinate systems, bureaucracy and Taylorism, chronometry, money, periodic tables, anatomy, elementary particles and quantum theory, border security, digitalization, genome editing, biotechnology, and much else.[26] What these very different fields, which include "techno-social processes," have in common is segment and sequence on the one hand, and on the other the capacity to structure the world and to restructure our thinking.[27] Drawing on research by the neuroscientist António Damásio, Theweleit argues that sociocultural and technological changes affect the human genome, resulting in genetically inheritable changes to the brain.[28] Knowledge would thus not only be determined by its possible discursive preconditions but also by neurological structural alterations.

## Who knows? Knowledge operators in critical posthumanism

"Universities, science academies and specialized institutes are by far not the sole owners of knowledge production capacity today. If capitalism has indeed taken a cognitive turn, then cognitive material is being produced in a myriad of ways and in multiple locations that include the corporate sector, the art world, the military, the activist sector, the blogosphere and the Internet."[29]

The sense of mental overload due to a continual explosive increase in knowledge, and therefore also in non-knowledge, is not the only problem that confronts us. Our history of knowledge is complemented by another, no less affective dimension. We subjects of posthumanism and the post-Anthropocene feel powerless in face of the amount of information and knowledge produced outside the hitherto "traditional container" of the human mind.[30] Algorithmically executed risk assessment, synthetically induced cell formation and division, artificially produced meat, the adaption and copying of the neural and sensory systems of other species belong to what Rosi Braidotti includes among the types of knowledge produced outside the human being.[31] She speaks of the body as "a rather old-fashioned anthropomorphic engine not quite suited to contain the fast-moving intelligence of our technologies."[32] In *The Posthuman* she describes how Vitruvian Man, familiar from Leonardo da Vinci's memorable geometricized depiction, became the ideal image and normative model of European humanism.[33] Characterized by "faith in the unique, self-regulating and intrinsically moral powers of human reason," this humanism developed into a "civilizational model" that represented Europe as the center of all reason.[34]

The image of a normative, exclusively male, hierarchically better placed ideal figure has given occidental society a chronic superiority complex that is ingrained in our European humanist identity. Klaus Theweleit's concept of a "hyperliterate, European post-Renaissance person thoroughly trained in central perspective" is analogous to this traditional figure of knowledge.[35] European history, from this perspective, is more a history of violence than of reason:

"The Europeans become murders *because* they are civilized. Their *civilized* view of the third and fourth worlds says: We are human beings; *you* are not. In the course of the sixteenth century at the latest, the technologies of perspectivism, geometricization, mathematization, projection, and cartography became so much a part of the bodies of the ocean-crossing segment of Europeans that beings without these high-tech bodies had (have) little or no chance of being perceived as 'equals', or even, in extreme cases, as 'human' at all."[36]

In a highly technical and ecologically fragile time, in which "the Human has become a geological force capable of affecting all life on this planet," the concept of the human and thus of a human production of knowledge must of necessity be rethought.[37] Braidotti understands posthuman theory as a "generative tool" to deal with the challenges and paradoxes of our time.[38] Posthumanism and the post-Anthropocene mark the departure from a purely Eurocentric world view and a repositioning of the human being in the sense of its de-hierarchization and equalization with other protagonists, other species on this planet. So in regard to knowledge we should not only examine its types, qualities, and forms but to a greater degree who produces it. If we understand algorithms, artificial intelligences, and also living organisms that don't belong to the human species as producers of knowledge, and if we consider as obsolete the human sphere as a "normative convention" with much potential for the exclusion of the non-normal and non-standard and the differentiation of "sexualized, racialized, and naturalized others," this should result in a fundamentally differently structured concept of knowledge.[39] Based on conceptual creativity, posthuman knowledge production aims to rethink the concept of knowledge as an assemblage of human and non-human components that is guided by the principles of multiplicity and complexity.[40] The knowing subject is neither "homo universalis" nor "Anthropos" but a complex ensemble that includes the human being among others.[41]

## The Fibonacci cabinet: a referential spiral as an encyclopedic coping mechanism

The Fibonacci cabinet is a situated, temporary collection of knowledge. It's an artistic-scientific and anti-disciplinary tableau that combines various objects, including loans from a museum earth-sciences collection, with private found objects, artistic objects, and drawings into a whole.[42] The dimensions of its compartments result from the Fibonacci sequence: each number in this sequence results from the sum of two preceding it (0, 1, 0 + 1 = 1, 1 + 1 = 2, 1 + 2 = 3, 2 + 3 = 5, 3 + 5 = 8, 5 + 8 = 13, 8 + 13 = 21, etc.). Translated into surfaces, the Fibonacci sequence generates a configuration that can be thought of as a spiral. The Fibonacci spiral is related to the Golden Mean. Nature contains many examples of the Fibonacci sequence, for example in biological systems, in spiral-shaped ammonites, in the arrangement of the leaves and seed heads of numerous plants, in flowers, and even in weather phenomena such as tornados. The Fibonacci search technique applies the sequence to algorithms.

The Fibonacci sequence is used to produce the cabinet's individual compartments, the two smallest measuring 1 × 1 × 1 cm and the largest 144 × 144 × 144 cm. As an artistic display the Fibonacci cabinet should be understood as a spiral-shaped reference system of various forms of knowledge. The two smallest compartments consist of dice, one cut from a graphite chalk, the other glued together from stone paper. So the innermost units of the cabinet are a reference to the artistic practice of drawing, and graphite reappears in drawings, as a fictive museum object (arrowhead), and as a geological item beneath a glass cover in one of the larger compartments.

The two smallest compartments are followed by a wooden cube and a mirrored cube, which are also material references to presentation and distancing, framing and glazing. In the next compartment a grid of pencil leads repeats the structure of a crystal. Then comes a column of three specially kept vitamin pills that resemble small pebbles in their surface structure.

Fig. 1

The next compartment contains a graphite arrowhead, an artistic "by-product." A thick pencil was inserted into a drill and sharpened. The resulting graphite shavings were used for the work *Doppelgänger* (see → *Doppelgänger*). The pointed graphite awakens associations of prehistoric arrowheads in museum display cases. How did the arrow go from the hunt to the drawing, where it fulfills the symbolic function of describing a one-way, directional dynamic?

Fig. 2

The following compartments take up the motif of the glass cover, once in its threefold presence, once in its absence. One compartment contains a column of three test tubes, an allusion to the vacuum-guaranteeing glass cover over the international prototype of the kilogram (IPK). This is the cylinder of a platinum-iridium alloy that served as the international norm for the measuring unit

of the kilo until it was replaced in 2019 by a sphere of silicon because its mass had measurably decreased.

The next-largest compartment presents a many-layered object in cast stone and ink. A glass cover like the ones protecting the stone and crystal objects in the largest compartment served as a mold. Its reference model was the core sample. Core samples can be understood as historical documents, as they shed light on geological events in the earth's history. The layered object on wire feet could be a fossil.

Fig. 3

The following compartment is also an animist conception, as it contains the "around 35.000 years old skull" of a cave bear. This was found in the 1920s by Joseph C. Groß during excavations in the Uschowa cave (between Austria and Slovenia). Groß produced several diary-like protocols of his excavations, including precise, sometimes surprisingly toned watercolors. In one of these the bones of the cave bear appear in an area of pink—so this compartment was colored accordingly.

Fig. 4

The penultimate compartment is empty. It is lined with cosmic graphite drawings, on which climbing holds were mounted. The final and largest compartment contains a collection of crystals, fossils, stones, and slag. The stones from our personal collection were selected for their specific forms (nose, hare, sprayed construction-site remnant, phony flea-market meteorite, weathered stone). The museum objects include a large malachite, a graphite, a quartz, and an ammonite.

Fig. 5

Removing the objects from their assigned or implicit contexts becomes a method of creating a system of equivalence: a rearrangement and de-hierarchization of objects originally ascribed different economic and non-material value—at least within this symbolic space.

1 A detailed clarification of the term "knowledge society" can be found in Laura Kajetzke and Anina Engelhardt, "Leben wir in einer Wissensgesellschaft?" in *Aus Politik und Zeitgeschichte*, April 2013, www.bpb.de/shop/zeitschriften/apuz/158659/leben-wir-in-einer-wissensgesellschaft (February 14, 2022).

2 See Steffen Siegel, *Tabula. Figuren der Ordnung um 1600* (Berlin: Akademie Verlag, 2009), 29.

3 Denis Diderot, *Encyclopédie* (1755), quoted from Caspar Henderson, *The Book of Barely Imagined Beings* (Cambridge: Granta, 2012), i.

4 See Jonathan Jenkins Ichikawa and Matthias Steup, "The Analysis of Knowledge," in *The Stanford Encyclopedia of Philosophy*, ed. Edward N. Zalta, summer 2018, https://plato.stanford.edu/archives/sum2018/entries/knowledge-analysis/ (July 8, 2021).

5 Plato, "Theaetetus," in *The Dialogues of Plato*, vol. 4, trans. Benjamin Jowett (Oxford: Oxford University Press, 1892), https://en.wikisource.org/wiki/The_Dialogues_of_Plato (July 25, 2022).

6 Ichikawa and Steup "The Analysis of Knowledge."

7 See Edmund Gettier, "Is Justified True Belief Knowledge?" in *Epistemology: An Anthology*, ed. Ernest Sosa, Jaegwon Kim, Jeremy Fantl, and Matthew McGrath (Oxford: Blackwell Publishing, 2009), 192.

8 Odo Marquard, *In Defense of the Accidental. Philosophical Studies*, trans. Robert M. Wallace (Oxford: Oxford University Press, 1991), 113.

9 Marquard, *In Defense of the Accidental*, 119.

[10] See Ernest Sosa, "The Place of Truth in Epistemology," in *Epistemology: An Anthology*, 478.

[11] See Ernest Sosa, "Knowing Full Well: The Normativity of Beliefs as Performances," in *Disputatio. Philosophical Research Bulletin*, 4:5, 2015, 87.

[12] In his two-volume *A Social History of Knowledge*, the British historian Peter Burke undertakes an extensive examination of the social history of knowledge from the early modern period to the present day. He illuminates its various processes of knowledge differentiation, some of which remain operative today. Peter Burke, *A Social History of Knowledge: From Gutenberg to Diderot* (Cambridge: Polity, 2008 [ePub]); Peter Burke, *A Social History of Knowledge: From the Encyclopédie to Wikipedia* (Cambridge: Polity, 2018 [ePub])

[13] See Jochen Steinbicker, "Peter Drucker: Wissensgesellschaft, wissensbasierte Organisation und Wissensarbeiter," in *Handbuch Wissensgesellschaft: Theorien, Themen und Probleme*, ed. Anina Engelhardt and Laura Kajetzke (Bielefeld: Transcript, 2010), 22f.

[14] Translated from Marian Adolf, "Nico Stehr: Konzeption der Wissensgesellschaft," in ibid., 54.

[15] See Burke, *A Social History of Knowledge: From Gutenberg to Diderot*, 90f.

[16] Ibid., 90f.

[17] See Peter Burke, *The Polymath: A Cultural History from Leonardo da Vinci to Susan Sontag* (London: Yale University Press, 2020), 134.

[18] See Burke, *A Social History of Knowledge: From the Encyclopédie to Wikipedia*, 167.

[19] Michel Foucault, *Remarks on Marx. Conversations with Ducio Trombardi*, trans. R. James Goldstein and James Cascaito (New York: Semiotext(e), 1991), 165.

[20] Michel Foucault, *Discipline and Punish. The Birth of the Prison*, trans. Alan Sheridan (1977) (New York: Random House, 1995), 148. See also Michel Foucault, *The Order of Things. An Archaeology of the Human Sciences* (New York: Pantheon Books, 1971), 178.

[21] Burke, *A Social History of Knowledge: From Gutenberg to Diderot*, 84.

[22] See Rosi Braidotti, *Posthuman Knowledge* (Cambridge: Polity Press, 2020 [ePub]), 153.

[23] Ibid., 49f.

[24] Translated from Klaus Theweleit, *Warum Cortés wirklich siegte: Technologiegeschichte der eurasisch-amerikanischen Kolonialismen* (Berlin: Matthes & Seitz, 2020), 15.

[25] Ibid., 122.

[26] Ibid., passim.

[27] Ibid., 492.

[28] Ibid., 247.

[29] Braidotti, *Posthuman Knowledge*, 91.

[30] Ibid., 14.

[31] Ibid.

[32] Ibid.

[33] Rosi Braidotti, *The Posthuman* (Cambridge: Polity Press, 2013), 13f.

[34] Ibid.

[35] Translated from Theweleit, *Warum Cortés wirklich siegte*, 271.

[36] Ibid., 269.

[37] Braidotti, *The Posthuman*, 5.

[38] Ibid.

[39] Ibid., 15.

[40] See Braidotti, *Posthuman Knowledge*, 18f.

[41] Ibid., 101.

[42] The Fibonacci cabinet was assembled in 2021 in the exhibition *antispecies* at the Galerie 3, Klagenfurt. Its inventory included objects from the earth-sciences collection of the Landesmuseum Kärnten.

| DE | EN |
|---|---|
| gedacht, geflüstert, gesagt, gerufen; | thought, whispered, spoken, called; |
| gestammelt, gestottert; | stammered, stuttered; |
| gebärdet; | signed; |
| notiert; | noted; |
| geschrieben, korrigiert; | written, corrected; |
| durchgestrichen, ausradiert; | crossed out, erased; |
| getippt, vertippt, gespeichert; | typed, mistyped, saved; |
| gelöscht; | deleted; |
| ertastet; | felt; |
| gedruckt; gelesen; | printed; read; |
| buchstabiert, aufgezeichnet; | spelt, recorded; |
| übersetzt; | translated; |
| eingeprägt, vergessen; | memorized, forgotten; |
| gehört, nachgesprochen, wiederholt. | heard, repeated. |

# Apologie des Zufälligen. Philosophische Überlegungen zum Menschen

Odo Marquard

[In: *Apologie des Zufälligen: Philosophische Schriften* (Stuttgart: Reclam, 2013), 117–139.]

Einer der schlimmsten Feinde von Freiheit und Würde des Menschen scheint der Zufall zu sein. Indes, ich möchte hier ein gutes Wort einlegen für den Zufall: für das Zufällige. Spreche ich also gegen Freiheit und Würde des Menschen? Keineswegs. Ich meine nur: es wäre ein Zeichen mangelnder Freiheit, wenn der Mensch unwürdig über seine Verhältnisse lebte: über die Verhältnisse seiner Endlichkeit. Will er das nicht, so muß er das Zufällige anerkennen: durch Apologie des Zufälligen. Das ist hier meine These.[1]

Gegen diese These steht – scheint es – fast die gesamte philosophische Tradition. Ich zitiere: „Die philosophische Betrachtung hat keine andere Absicht, als das Zufällige zu entfernen." Das schrieb – diese Traditionsmeinung zusammenfassend – Hegel.[2] Ich widerspreche Hegel – dem großen Empiriker – selten und ungern. Hier aber tue ich es: notgedrungenerweise. Das Zufällige entfernen: das hieße, zum Beispiel, aus der Philosophie die Philosophen entfernen; es gibt aber keine Philosophie ohne Philosophen (ob es nun Amateure sind oder Profis): so würde man schließlich – im Namen der Philosophie – aus der Philosophie die Philosophie entfernen. Also muß – für die Philosophie – das Zufällige gerettet werden: denn nur dadurch hat sie Wirklichkeit. Oder: das Zufällige entfernen: das hieße, zum Beispiel, aus dem Menschen das Allzumenschliche entfernen; es gibt aber keinen Menschen ohne das Allzumenschliche: so würde man schließlich – im Namen des Menschen – aus dem Menschen den Menschen entfernen. Also muß – für den Menschen – das Zufällige gerettet werden: denn nur dadurch hat er Wirklichkeit.

Diese Fürsprache für das Zufällige kann ich im Folgenden keineswegs umfassend leisten; ich kann nur einige einschlägige – und, wie es sich im Falle des Zufälligen gehört, zufällige – Überlegungen beitragen und tue das in vier Abschnitten, die ich folgendermaßen überschreibe: 1. Das Programm der Absolutmachung des Menschen und seine moderne Zuspitzung; 2. Über die Unvermeidlichkeit von Üblichkeiten; 3. Wir Menschen sind stets mehr unsere Zufälle als unsere Wahl; 4. Menschliche Freiheit lebt von der Gewaltenteilung. Sogleich – ganz konventionell – zum Abschnitt

1. *Das Programm der Absolutmachung des Menschen und seine moderne Zuspitzung.* Wo – ich knüpfe an Hegels Formulierung an – „die philosophische Betrachtung [...] keine andere Absicht [hat], als das Zufällige zu entfernen", wird – je moderner, desto zugespitzter – dieses zu ihrem Programm: den Menschen absolut zu machen.

Im Gegenzug zu diesem Programm der Absolutmachung des Menschen – einem alten Programm, das eben modern nur zugespitzt wurde – kam es zu philosophischen Versuchen, den Zufall und das Zufällige in den Blick zu fassen, seit Aristoteles – alternativ zur megarischen Leugnung des Zufalls – das Zufällige gelten ließ als das, was weder unmöglich noch notwendig ist und darum auch nicht oder auch anders sein könnte.[3] Dieses Zufällige – Kontingente[4] – wurde in mindestens drei Richtungen zum

# In Defense of the Accidental: Philosophical Reflections on Man

Odo Marquard

[In *In Defense of the Accidental: Philosophical Studies*, trans. Robert M. Wallace (New York, Oxford: Oxford University Press, 1991), 109-129. Reproduced with permission of the licensor through PLSclear.]

Accident seems to be one of the worst enemies of man's freedom and dignity. Nevertheless, I would like to put in a good word here for accident, and for its results. Am I then speaking against man's freedom and dignity? By no means. It is just that I think that it would be a sign of deficiency of freedom if man were to live undignifiedly beyond his means: beyond the means, that is, of his finite nature. If he chooses not to do this, he has to acknowledge the results of accident, by a defense of the accidental. This is my thesis here.[1]

Almost the entire philosophical tradition seems to contradict this thesis. I quote: "Philosophical reflection has no other object than to get rid of what is accidental." This is Hegel's summing up of the traditional opinion.[2] It is seldom, and reluctantly, that I contradict that great empiricist, Hegel. But here I am doing it, by necessity. To get rid of what is accidental would mean, for example, to get rid of philosophers; but without philosophers (whether they are amateur or professional makes no difference) there would be no philosophy, so that in the end one would rid philosophy, in the name of philosophy, of philosophy. So the accidental has to be retrieved for philosophy; for it is only through it that philosophy has reality. To get rid of what is accidental would also mean, for example, to rid man of all his too-humanness; but without all-too-humanness, there is no man; so that one would finally rid man, in the name of man, of man. So the accidental has to be retrieved for man; for it is only through it that man has reality.

In what follows I cannot execute this plea for the accidental in a comprehensive manner; I can only contribute some relevant and (as is fitting in dealing with the accidental) accidental considerations, which I will do in four sections, under the following headings: 1. The program of making man absolute, and its modern pronounced form; 2. On the unavoidability of usual practices; 3. We human beings are always more our accidents than our choices; 4. And human freedom depends on the seperation of powers.

1. *The Program of Making Man Absolute, and Its Modern Pronounced Form.* When—to begin with Hegel's formulation—"philosophical reflection has no other object than to get rid of what is accidental," then philosophy's program becomes (and the more modern the circumstances, the more pronouncedly is this the case) the program of making man absolute.

As a countermove against this program of making man absolute—which is an old program, which only became more pronounced in modern times—philosophical attempts were made to arrive at an understanding of accident and its results, beginning with Aristotle's acceptance (in contrast to the Megarian school's denial) of the accidental as what is neither impossible nor necessary, and thus could also be different or not.[3] This realm of the accidental (or contingent)[4] became a problem in at least three ways: as an opponent of the necessary; as the foundation of the necessary; or in other ways as well. Here are three short remarks on these possibilites.

Problem: als Opponent des Notwendigen (a) oder als Grundlage des Notwendigen (b) oder noch anders (c). Dazu drei kurze Hinweise:

a) Si necessarium, unde contingens? Diese Frage – zugespitzt: Wenn es doch Gott gibt, warum dann das Endliche? – führt in der christlichen Tradition der Philosophie zum Kontingenzproblem der Schöpfung[5] und später dort, wo – seit Spinoza – in die Notwendigkeitsstelle Gottes die Natur eintritt, zusammen mit dem Freiheitsproblem zur Frage nach dem Undeterminierten. Der Zufall ist vielleicht die mißlungene Notwendigkeit.

b) Si contingens, unde necessarium? Diese Frage – die Motive der Deklinationslehre Epikurs und der Mutationslehre Darwins aufnimmt – wurde jüngsthin, etwa im Anschluß an Monod[6], radikalisiert und dadurch evolutionstheoretisch und synergetisch aktuell: wenn es das Chaos gibt, warum dann die Ordnung, und wenn es das Zufällige gibt, woher dann die Notwendigkeit? Die Notwendigkeit ist vielleicht der gelungene Zufall.

c) Zufälle – auch das hat zuerst Aristoteles gesehen – können dadurch entstehen, daß voneinander unabhängige Determinationsketten unvermutet aufeinandertreffen. Einer vergräbt einen Schatz, um ihn zu verstecken; ein anderer gräbt eine Grube, um einen Baum zu pflanzen: „Dies ist ein Zufall für jemanden, der eine Grube gräbt, nämlich dabei einen Schatz zu finden." Dabei ist der besondere – für den Menschen bedeutsame – Fall der, daß etwas anderes (das seinerseits determiniert ist) seiner Absicht dazwischenkommt: „Zufällig kam jemand nach Ägina, wenn er nicht deshalb hinkam, weil er wollte, sondern vom Sturm verschlagen oder von Räubern verschleppt."[7] Es widerfährt uns etwas, was wir nicht gewollt und gewählt haben. Denn wir Menschen sind nicht nur unsere – absichtsgeleiteten – Handlungen, sondern auch unsere Zufälle.

Das Programm der Absolutmachung des Menschen leugnet das: es will vor allem auch die Zufälle dieser letzten Art „entfernen", so daß – und ich verwende dabei Sartres Formel von der „Wahl, die wir sind"[8] – gelten soll: die Menschen sind durchgängig nicht ihre Zufälle, sondern sie sind ganz und gar nur ihre Wahl. Das bedeutet dann zweierlei:

1. Der Mensch ist – oder soll sein – ausschließlich das Resultat seiner Absichten. Er ist dann das handelnde Wesen, dem nichts mehr widerfährt. Nichts Menschliches darf unbeabsichtigt, nichts Menschliches darf ungewählt geschehen; nichts mehr darf dem Menschen zustoßen. Denn nur dann gilt: die Menschen sind nicht ihre Zufälle, sondern ganz und gar nur ihre Wahl.

2. Diese Wahl muß absolut sein: also keine zufällige Option, die auch anders sein könnte, durch andere Absichten ersetzbar. Darum müssen alle Menschen – wenn sie richtige, d. h. absolute Menschen sein wollen – die gleichen Absichten hegen. Denn nur dann gilt: die Menschen sind nicht ihre Zufälle, sondern ganz und gar nur ihre absolute Wahl.

Diese beiden Forderungen, philosophisch vertreten, nenne ich also das Programm der Absolutmachung des Menschen. Es dekretiert: die Menschen sind nicht ihre Zufälle, sondern ausschließlich ihre Wahl, und zwar ihre absolute Wahl. Man fragt mich zuweilen: Wer – genau – ist es denn nun, der dieses Programm der Absolutmachung des Menschen philosophisch vertreten hat oder vertritt?: Marquard, nennen Sie Roß und Reiter! Nun: vielleicht gehört der so Fragende selber zu den Rössern; und welche Tradition ihn dann reitet: das – wenn auch nur ultrakurz – schildere ich hier ja gerade. Außerdem gibt es gute Gründe für einschlägig sorgfältige Nachlässigkeit im Genauen: ein kurzer Vortrag kann sich nicht auf Fragen der Philologie – der Platon-Philologie, der Augustinus-Philologie, der Descartes-Philologie, der Fichte-Philologie, der Marx-, der Apel- und Habermas-Philologie – einlassen. Auch gebietet es der Takt, Philosophen – je moderner, je mehr – die

*Si necessarium, unde contingens?* [If there is something necessary, whence comes the contingent?] This question—whose pronounced form is: If God, after all, exists, why do finite things exist?—leads, in the Christian tradition in philosophy, to the problem of the contingency of the Creation,[5] and later (when, beginning with Spinoza, nature occupies the divine position of necessity), to the problem of freedom and the question of the undetermined. Perhaps accident is a necessity that miscarried.

*Si contingens, unde necessarium?* [If there is something contingent, whence comes the necessary?] This question, which picks up motives of Epicurus's doctrine of the declination of the atoms and Darwin's doctrine of mutation, has recently been radicalized (following, for example, Monod[6]) and thus given contemporary significance in the theory of evolution and synergy: If chaos exists, why is there order, and if accidental things exist, where do necessary ones come from? Perhaps necessity is successful accident.

To illustrate the third possibility, let us note that Aristotle was also the first to see that accidents can come about through the unexpected mutual encounter of chains of determining events that are independent of one another. One person buries a treasure in order to hide it; another person digs a hole in order to plant a tree: "It is an accident for a person who is digging a hole to find a treasure in doing so." A special case, and an important one for human beings, is when something else (which in its turn is determined) interferes with purposes that they have: "Going to Aegina was an accident for a man, if he went not in order to get there, but because he was carried out of his way by a storm or captured by pirates."[7] Something happens to us that we did not intend to choose. For we human beings are not only our (intention-guided) actions, but also our accidents.

The program of making man absolute denies this: It wants above all to "get rid of" the accidents of the last kind also, so that (and here I use Sartre's formula of the "choice, that we are"[8]) it will be the case that human beings are, without exception, not their accidents, but only and completely their choice. This means two things. First, man is, or should be, exclusively the outcome of his intentions. He is then the acting creature, to whom nothing happens any longer. Nothing human is allowed to be unintended; nothing human is allowed to happen without haven been chosen. Nothing is allowed to befall man any longer. For only then is it the case that human beings are not their accidents but only and completely their choice. Second, this choice has to be absolute: that is, not an accidental option that could also have been different, that could be replaced by other intentions. Consequently all human beings—if they want to be proper (that is, absolute) human beings—must cherish the same intentions. For only then is it the case that human beings are not their accidents, but only and completely their absolute choice.

I am sometimes asked, Who exactly is it, then, in philosophy, who advocated or advocates this program of making man absolute? Marquard, name the horse and the rider! Now, it may be that the person who asks this is himself among the horses, and the tradition that rides him is what I am describing right now (if only in ultrabrief form). Moreover, there are good reasons to take pains to neglect these details: A short lecture can not be involved with questions of philology—of Plato's philology, Augustine's philology, Descartes's philology, Fichte's philology, Marx's, Apel's, and Habermas's philology. Also, tactfulness enjoins us to allow philosophers (the more so, the more modern they are) the conviction that they are not the ones intended. In any case, we are not among poor people here; if need be, I will invent German Idealism (including Marxism and Neo-Marxism) myself. That is also the reason why I forbid no one the impression that the position that I have sketched here and

Überzeugung zu gestatten, sie seien nicht gemeint. Im übrigen ist man hier nicht bei armen Leuten: notfalls erfinde ich mir den deutschen Idealismus – einschließlich des Marxismus und Neomarxismus – selber. Darum auch verbiete ich niemandem den Eindruck, die von mir hier skizzierte und im folgenden angegriffene Position – das Programm der Absolutmachung des Menschen – sei von niemandem jemals vertreten worden. Denn wäre das schlimm? Ganz im Gegenteil: es wäre gerade gut für meine Apologie des Zufälligen, wenn sie weniger Gegner hat als angenommen. Kurzum: die Frage der Zurechnung des Programms der Absolutmachung des Menschen, sie ist ein weites Feld.

Man darf jedoch wohl sagen, was ich schon sagte: das Programm der Absolutmachung des Menschen – ein philosophisch und nicht nur philosophisch altes Programm – wird modern gesteigert und zugespitzt. Wo man sich – modern – nicht mehr darauf verlassen mag, daß die Teilhabe an Gott dem Menschen Absolutheit – zufallsfreies und absolut richtiges Leben – garantiert, muß die Absolutmachung des Menschen zunehmend auf den Menschen selber gegründet werden: auf seine Freiheit, seine eigene absolute Wahl. Daß dabei – im deutschen Idealismus, im Marxismus – vor allem die deutsche Philosophie der Vorreiter wurde, ist plausibel durch Plessners Thesen zur „verspäteten Nation"[9]: die verzögerte Liberalität im Realen wird kompensiert durch Absolutheit im Philosophischen. So kommt es – auch weil Gott als mäßigende Größe philosophisch zunehmend ausfällt – gerade modern – in Fortführung der von mir zitierten Sartre-Formel – im Sinne des Programms seiner Absolutmachung zur Definition des Menschen als der absoluten Wahl, die er ist. Die Menschen sollen also sein oder werden: absolut.

Indes: die Menschen sind nicht absolut, sondern sie sind endlich. Sie leben und wählen ihr Leben nicht – jedenfalls überwiegend nicht – absolut: denn sie müssen sterben; mit Heidegger zu reden: sie sind „zum Tode"[10]. Ihr Leben ist befristet: vita brevis. Für die absolute Wahl ist das Menschenleben zu kurz; ganz elementar: die Menschen haben einfach nicht genug Zeit, das, was sie – zufälligerweise – schon sind, absolut zu wählen oder abzuwählen und statt seiner etwas ganz anderes und Neues zu wählen oder gar absolut zu wählen: ihr Tod ist stets schneller als ihre absolute Wahl. Gegen das Programm der Absolutmachung des Menschen steht also seine – sterblichkeitsgeprägte – Wirklichkeit, und ich möchte im Folgenden dafür werben, daß man das philosophisch anerkennt: durch Apologie des Zufälligen.

2. *Über die Unvermeidlichkeit von Üblichkeiten.* Ich wiederhole: gegen das Programm der Absolutmachung des Menschen steht seine – sterblichkeitsgeprägte – Wirklichkeit. Darum gehört zum Programm der Absolutmachung des Menschen der Versuch, die Wirklichkeit des Menschen – die gegen dieses Programm steht – außer Kraft zu setzen: sie – griechisch-traditionell – zu veruneigentlichen oder sie – christlich-traditionell – zur schon gerichteten Wirklichkeit auf eschatologischen Abruf zu vervorläufigen oder sie – modern zugespitzt – vorsorglich methodisch einzuklammern.

Der repräsentative moderne Versuch einer solchen Wirklichkeitseinklammerung – der Aussetzung der menschlichen Wirklichkeit, solange sie nicht die absolute ist – ist der sogenannte „methodische Zweifel". Descartes – in seinen Meditationes[11] – hat ihn für den theoretischen Bereich entwickelt. Die Zweifelsregel von Descartes bestimmt: in dubio contra traditionem, anders gesagt: alles, was nicht absolut wahr ist und also falsch sein könnte (das sind alle vorhandenen Urteile unseres Wissens), ist so zu behandeln, als ob es wirklich falsch ist, und zwar so lange, bis es – durch scientia more certa methodo – „clare et distincte", d. h. absolut, als wahr erwiesen ist; solange dies nicht der Fall

which I attack in what follows—the program of making man absolute—has never been advocated by anyone. For would that be bad? Quite the contrary: It would be, precisely, good for my defense of the accidental if it had fewer opponents than I had assumed. In short: The question to whom to attribute the program of making man absolute leaves plenty of room for discussion.

However, one can certainly say what I already said: that the program of making man absolute, a program that is old in (and not only in) philosophy, is intensified, takes a more pronounced form, in modern times. When, in modern times, one no longer likes to rely on a participation in God which guarantees man's absoluteness (his accident-free and absolutely correct life), the process of making man absolute must increasingly be founded on man himself: on his freedom, his own absolute choice. The fact that it was above all German philosophy (in German Idealism and in Marxism) that played the leading role here can be understood with the help of Plessner's theses about the "delayed nation":[9] The retardation of liberal arrangements in the realm of reality is compensated for by absoluteness in the realm of philosophy. Thus it is precisely in modern times that (also because God, as a moderating quantity, increasingly drops out of philosophy) we arrive—following the program of making man absolute, and continuing with the Sartrean formula that I quoted—at the definition of man as the absolute choice that he is. Thus human beings are supposed to be, or to become, absolute.

However, human beings are not absolute; rather, they are finite. They live and they do not (at least not preponderantly) choose their life absolutely, and this is because they have to die. To use Heidegger's words, they are "toward death."[10] A limit is fixed to their lives: "vita brevis." Human life is too short for an absolute choice. On the most elementary level, human beings simply do not have enough time absolutely to choose, or to choose to reject, what they (accidentally) already are, and to choose (or even absolutely choose), instead of that, something entirely different and new. Their death is always swifter than their absolute choice. Thus the program of making man absolute is opposed by man's reality, which bears the stamp of mortality; and in what follows I would like—through a defense of the accidental—to promote a recognition of this fact by philosophy.

2. *On the Unavoidability of Usual Practices.* I repeat: The program of making man absolute is opposed by man's reality, which bears the stamp of mortality. Consequently part of the program of making man absolute is an attempt to abrogate the human reality that opposes it: in the Greek tradition, to declare that reality not genuine; or, in the Christian tradition, to declare that reality temporary, already judged, and subject to eschatological recall; or—in the program's modern, pronounced form—to bracket that reality out, precautionally and methodically.

The representative modern attempt at bracketing the reality out in that way—at suspending human reality, as long as it is not the absolute reality—is so-called methodical doubt. Descartes developed this attempt, for the realm of theory, in his *Meditationes.*[11] Descartes's rule of doubt lays down: *in dubio contra traditionem* [in case of doubt, reject tradition]. In other words: Everything that is not absolutely true, and could therefore be false (which is all of our present judgmental knowledge), is to be treated as though it were really false, and it is to be treated this way until it has been shown—through *scientia more certa methodo* [the sure method of science]—"clare et distincte," that is, absolutely, to be true. As long as this has not been done, all judgment has to be suspended. For all judgments are not, for example, permitted until they are forbidden as a result of their falsification; instead, they are prohibited until they are permitted as a result of their absolute verification. Knowledge remains

ist, muß alles Urteilen ausgesetzt werden: denn alle Urteile sind nicht etwa so lange erlaubt, bis sie durch Falsifikation verboten, sondern so lange verboten, bis sie durch absolute Verifikation erlaubt werden. Das Wissen bleibt suspendiert, solange es kein absolutes Wissen ist. Auf den praktischen Bereich haben diesen methodischen Zweifel die Diskursethiker – also etwa Apel und Habermas – übertragen: die Diskursethik ist der methodische Zweifel auch an Handlungsnormen.[12] Ihre Verdächtigungsregel bestimmt: in dubio contra traditionem (sive conventiones), anders gesagt: alles, was nicht (durch Konsens des herrschaftsfreien Diskurses) erwiesenermaßen, d. h. absolut, gut ist und also böse sein könnte (das sind alle vorhandenen Handlungsorientierungen), ist so zu behandeln, als ob es wirklich böse ist, und zwar so lange, bis es – durch den absoluten Diskurs – konsensual, d. h. absolut, als gut gerechtfertigt ist; solange dies nicht der Fall ist, muß alles konventionsgeleitete Handeln ausgesetzt, hilfsweise suspektiert werden: denn alle praktischen Lebensorientierungen sind nicht etwa so lange erlaubt, bis sie durch Malitätserweis verboten, sondern so lange verboten, bis sie durch diskursive Legitimierung absolut erlaubt werden. In beiden Fällen – bei Descartes und in der Diskursethik – wird also das Vorhandene vorsorglich negiert: das Übliche – das Wissen, das gilt, weil es schon galt; die Handlungsanweisungen, die gelten, weil sie schon galten – wird im Namen des Absoluten methodisch storniert. Insgesamt gilt – bei dieser negativen Seite des Programms der Absolutmachung des Menschen –, daß das Leben zu unterlassen (hilfsweise schlimm) ist, solange nicht – durch absolute Wahl: durch absolutes Wissen, durch absolute Handlungsrechtfertigung – absolut erwiesen ist, daß es das absolut richtige Leben ist. Das Programm der Absolutmachung des Menschen negiert vorsorglich das wirkliche Leben, soweit es das Ensemble der Üblichkeiten ist.

Freilich: das – gerade auch diese negative Seite des Programms der Absolutmachung des Menschen – kann nicht gelingen: auch sie scheitert an der menschlichen Endlichkeit, d. h. Sterblichkeit. Die Menschen müssen sterben, sie sind „zum Tode". Diese Aussage ist diesseits aller existenzialistischen Emphase philosophisch zentral und läßt sich auch ganz unemphatisch ausdrücken: in der menschlichen Gesamtpopulation beträgt die Mortalität hundert Prozent. Der Tod aber – wie lange er auch zögert – kommt immer allzubald: das Menschenleben ist zu kurz für die Durchführung des Programms der Absolutmachung des Menschen, denn der Tod läßt uns nicht die Zeit, auf das Ergebnis der absoluten Wahl aller lebensnötigen Orientierungen zu warten. Wenn aber zugleich die geschichtlich-faktisch vorhandenen Lebensorientierungen, die nicht absolut gewählt, sondern nur Üblichkeiten sind, so lange außer Kraft gesetzt sind, bis die absolute Wahl mit dem absoluten Wählen aller lebensnötigen absoluten Orientierungen fertig ist: dann läuft das für die Menschen im Effekt hinaus auf das Verbot, mit dem Leben anzufangen, bevor es zu Ende ist; denn – wie gesagt – unser Tod ist stets schneller als unsere absolute Wahl.

Darum kann man sagen: das Programm der Absolutmachung des Menschen ist für die Menschen die Philosophie für ihr Leben nach dem Tode, die die Frage einer Philosophie für ihr Leben vor dem Tode offenläßt. Doch gerade für ihr Leben vor dem Tode brauchen die Menschen die Philosophie. Wenn es also die absolute Philosophie – wegen der absoluten Dauer ihrer absoluten Wahl – noch nicht gibt und wenn es die Üblichkeiten – wegen ihrer absoluten methodischen Negation: ihrer Bezweifelung und Verdächtigung – nicht mehr gibt, muß offenbar ein interimistischer Lebensorientierungsersatz herbei, der in diese Zeitlücke – die unser Leben ist – einrückt. Bei Descartes wurde das – im dritten Teil seines *Discours* – zum Argument für die sogenannte „provisorische Moral"[13]. Sein Bild

suspended as long as it is not absolute knowledge. The rhetorists of discourse ethics—that is, for example, Apel and Habermas—have carried this methodical doubt over to the practical realm: Discourse ethics applies methodical doubt to norms of action, as well.[12] Its rule of suspicion lays down: *in dubio contra traditionem (sive conventiones)* [in case of doubt, reject tradition (or conventions)]. In other words: Everything that is not demonstrably (by the consensus of a dominance-free discourse)—that is, absolutely—good, and which could therefore be evil (which is to say, all of our present orientations for action), is to be treated as though it were really evil, and it is to be treated this way until it has been justified, through the absolute discourse, consensually—that is, absolutely—as good. As long as this has not been done, all convention-guided action must be suspended and, to help make this possible, suspected. It is not that practical orientations in life are permitted until they are forbidden as a result of their demonstrated badness; instead, they are prohibited until they are absolutely permitted as a result of their discursive legitimation. Thus in both cases—in Descartes and in discourse ethics—what is present is negated as a precaution: The "usual" (knowledge that is accepted because it was accepted in the past, and instructions for action that are accepted because they were accepted in the past) is methodically canceled out in the name of the absolute. Overall, the rule—in this negative side of the program of making man absolute—is that life should be discontinued (and, to help make this possible, seen as bad) as long as it has not been shown absolutely, by absolute choice (absolute knowledge, absolute justification of action), that it is the absolutely correct life. The program of making man absolute negates real life, precautionally, insofar as real life is the ensemble of usual practices.

Of course, this negative side of the program of making man absolute cannot succeed either. It, too, is frustrated by human finitude, by mortality. Human beings have to die, they are "toward death." Apart from any existentialist emphasis, this statement is philosophically central; and it can in fact be expressed quite unemphatically, as follows: In the total human population, the rate of mortality comes to 100 percent. But death, however long it may hesitate, always comes all too soon: Human life is too short for executing the program of making man absolute, because death does not allow us time to wait for the result of the absolute choice of all the orientations that are necessary for life. But if, at the same time, the orientations for life that are present, as a matter of historical fact, and that are not absolutely chosen but are only usual practices, are abrogated until absolute choice has finished absolutely choosing all the absolute orientations that are necessary for life—then this amounts, in effect, for human beings, to a prohibition of beginning life before it is over; because, as I said, our death is always swifter than our absolute choice.

Thus one can say that for human beings, the program of making man absolute is a philosophy for their life after death, and it leaves open the question of a philosophy for their life before death. But it is precisely for their life before death that human beings need philosophy. If then, the absolute philosophy does not yet exist (because of the absolute time required by its absolute choice), and if our usual practices no longer exist (because of their absolute methodical negation: their subjection to doubt and suspicion), then evidently a temporary substitute orientation in life is needed, which will step into this temporal gap that is our life. For Descartes, in the third part of his *Discours,* precisely that became the argument for the so-called "provisional ethic."[13] His image was that if one tears down a house in order to build a new one, one has to arrange for temporary lodgings. In my opinion, this is true not only (as Descartes thought) in regard to ethics, but also in regard to knowledge and to human orientations in life, in general. Consequently,

war: wenn man sein Haus abreißt, um ein neues zu bauen, muß man für eine Zwischenunterkunft sorgen. Das, meine ich, gilt nicht nur – wie Descartes meinte – für die Moral, sondern auch für das Wissen und die menschlichen Lebensorientierungen überhaupt. Darum muß – auch und gerade für das generelle Programm der Absolutmachung des Menschen – das generalisierte Pendant der provisorischen Moral aktuell werden: eine Philosophie der provisorischen Lebensorientierungen.

Freilich: sobald diese Philosophie – die des menschlichen Lebens nicht nach, sondern vor dem Tode – im Namen des Programms der Absolutmachung des Menschen auftritt (sozusagen als flankierende Maßnahme für die absolute Wahl), gerät sie in eine Aporie. Denn entweder sind die provisorischen Lebensorientierungen selber kein Produkt der absoluten Wahl: dann verfallen auch sie deren methodischer Negation der Üblichkeiten. Oder die provisorischen Lebensorientierungen sind doch selber Produkt der absoluten Wahl: dann lassen sie ihrerseits einigermaßen absolut auf sich warten und brauchen ihrerseits – als interimistischen Orientierungsersatz – wiederum weitere provisorische Lebensorientierungen, und so fort. Diese Aporie entsteht – abgeschwächt – auch dann, wenn das Orientierungsinterim eine andersartige umfassende Neuerfindung auch nur eines provisorischen Minimums aller lebensnötigen Orientierungen sein soll: auch dann reproduziert es das Problem, zu dessen Lösung es dienen sollte. Das ist nur dann nicht der Fall (und die genannte Aporie verschwindet), wenn die provisorischen Lebensorientierungen identisch sind mit den faktisch vorhandenen Lebensorientierungen: den vorhandenen Üblichkeiten[14], und wenn man diese vorhandenen Üblichkeiten gerade nicht methodisch negiert. Daraus folgere ich: die – gesuchte – Philosophie der provisorischen Lebensorientierungen ist keine andere als die Philosophie der vorhandenen Üblichkeiten, die geltend macht: ohne diese vorhandenen Üblichkeiten – Traditionen, Sitten, Usancen des Wissens und Handelns – können wir nicht leben; sie sind – mit oder ohne Programm der Absolutmachung des Menschen – nicht zu umgehen: unvermeidlich. Die Wahl, die wir sind, wird getragen durch sie als die Nichtwahl, die wir sind: Zukunft braucht Herkunft; Wahl braucht Üblichkeiten. Das bedeutet mitnichten, daß stets alle Traditionen unangetastet und alle Üblichkeiten unverändert bleiben müssen, denn im Gegenteil: Üblichkeiten sind durchaus änderbar, reformierbar. Es bedeutet nur: stets müssen mehr Üblichkeiten aufrechterhalten werden als verändert, sonst ruiniert man unser Leben; und die – durchaus immer wieder einmal erfolgreich zu tragende – Beweislast hat stets der Veränderer.[15] In diesem Sinn – nur in diesem – gilt für die Menschen die Unvermeidlichkeit der Üblichkeiten: wir Menschen sind stets mehr unsere Üblichkeiten als unsere Wahl, und erst recht sind wir stets mehr unsere Üblichkeiten als unsere absolute Wahl. Folglich muß die nichtabsolute, die menschliche Philosophie ebendieses sein: die Apologie der Üblichkeiten. Darum auch muß man die Üblichkeiten – das, was deswegen gilt, weil es (als das Usuelle) schon galt – gegen üble Nachrede schützen, auch wenn diese Nachrede philosophisch absolut einherkommt. Es trifft nicht zu, daß die Realität der modernen Welt – weil durch ihre Veränderungsbeschleunigung das Veraltungstempo wächst – alle Üblichkeiten dauernd in Frage stellt und verschleißt; denn es gibt, gerade in der modernen Welt, kompensierende Stabilitäten nicht zuletzt auch dadurch, daß in ihr – gerade wegen ihrer zunehmenden Veraltungsgeschwindigkeit – auch die Veraltungen immer schneller veralten. Im übrigen ist die Modernisierung selber längst zur Üblichkeit geworden: zur Usance Modernität. Zugleich scheint mir jenes Votum gegen die Üblichkeiten zunehmend dubios, das man das Eichmann-Argument nennen kann: wer aus den Üblichkeiten lebe, stehe in direkter Gefahr, zu einem Eichmann zu werden, der schließlich gerade nur

in the case (also) of the general program of making man absolute, and especially in that case, the generalized counterpart of the provisional ethic—namely, a philosophy of provisional orientations in life—must become a matter of present interest.

Of course, as soon as this philosophy (the philosophy of human life not after, but before death) makes its appearance in the name of the program of making man absolute—as, so to speak, a measure taken to protect the flank of absolute choice—it winds up in aporia. For either the provisional orientations in life are not themselves products of absolute choice, in which case they also are subject to the latter's methodical negation of usual practices, or else the provisional orientations in life are, after all, themselves products of absolute choice, in which case they, in their turn, will require us (more or less absolutely) to wait for them, and will once again need, as a temporary substitute orientation, further provisional orientations in life, and so on. A weaker form of this aporia also arises even if the temporary orientation is supposed to be a comprehensive new invention of a different kind, containing only a provisional minimum of all the orientations that are necessary in life: Then, too, it reproduces the problem that it was meant to solve. The only situation in which this is not the case, and in which the aporia that I have described disappears, is if the provisional orientations in life are identical with the orientations in life that are present in fact—that is, with the existing usual practices[14]—and if one does not methodically negate these existing usual practices. From which I conclude that the philosophy of provisional orientations in life, which we are seeking, is none other than the philosophy of the existing usual practices—which is a philosophy that asserts that we cannot live without these existing usual practices (traditions, mores, usages in knowledge and in action); that with or without a program of making man absolute, these practices cannot be bypassed: they are unavoidable. The choice that we are is supported by them as the nonchoice that we are: What is to come requires what we come from; choice requires usual practices. In no way does this mean that all traditions must always remain untouched and all usual practices unaltered, since, on the contrary, usual practices are quite capable of being changed and reformed. All that it means is that more usual practices must always be upheld than are changed, otherwise our life is ruined; and that the burden of proof (which can certainly be borne, successfully, again and again) is always on the advocate of change.[15] It is in this sense (and only in this sense) that usual practices are unavoidable for human beings: We human beings are always more our usual practices than our choice, and still more are we always more our usual practices than our *absolute* choice. Accordingly, a nonabsolute, human philosophy has to be just this: a defense of usual practices. That is why one also has to defend usual practices—the things that are accepted because (as the "usual") they were accepted in the past—against slanderous talk, even if this talk puts on philosophically absolute airs. It is not the case that the reality of the modern world—because its accelerating rate of change increases the tempo of obsolescence—continually puts all usual practices in question and wears them away; for precisely in the modern world there are compensating stabilities, not least of all in the fact that in it, just because of its increasing speed of obsolescence, the obsolescences themselves also become more and more rapidly obsolete. Besides, modernization itself has long since become a usual practice: the usage of modernity. At the same time, I find increasingly dubious the argument against usual practices that one can call the "Eichmann argument," and which says that someone whose life is guided by usual practices is in direct danger of becoming an Eichmann—Eichmann being a person who after all only wanted to do his usual duty.[16] It seems to me that here only the second aspect

seine übliche Pflicht habe tun wollen.[16] Mir scheint hier nur die zweite Hälfte der Untat in Rechnung gestellt, deren erste in der Verletzung einer Üblichkeit bestand: der Üblichkeit, seine Mitmenschen nicht umzubringen. Ich kann mich hier nicht differenziert zum „Fall Eichmann" und zur Debatte über die „Banalität des Bösen"[17] äußern, meine jedoch: diese primäre Abweichung vom Üblichen wurde vom Täter – schließlich auch vor sich selber – sekundär getarnt durch das Bewußtsein der Übererfüllung üblicher Pflicht. Dies spricht – meine ich – so wenig gegen die Üblichkeiten, wie es gegen die Wahrhaftigkeit spricht, daß die Lüge, um zum Erfolg zu kommen, sich – gegebenenfalls sogar gegenüber dem Lügner selber – als Wahrhaftigkeit geben und tarnen muß. Abusus non tollit usum: der Mißbrauch widerlegt nicht den Brauch. Eichmanns Schreibtischuntaten litten nicht an einem Zuviel, sondern an einem Zuwenig von Üblichkeiten: die Eichmann-Gefahr ist (meine ich) größer, wenn man alle Üblichkeiten – und sei es im Namen des Absoluten oder sonst einer guten Sache – zunächst einmal zur Disposition stellt, als wenn man sich weigert, es zu tun; man sollte sich daran erinnern, daß der Widerstand vor allem aus intakten Traditionen kam. Darum stimmt es auch nicht, daß die Schätzung der Üblichkeiten Kritik unmöglich mache, denn das Gegenteil ist der Fall: Kritik ist vor allem der Konflikt zwischen Üblichkeiten; um zu ihm fähig zu sein, muß man Üblichkeiten haben; und in unseren Zeiten und Gegenden ist dann schließlich Kritik selber eine Üblichkeit, die durch Üblichkeiten geregelt ist.

Man muß – ich wiederhole es – die Üblichkeiten vor übler Nachrede schützen und darum auch vor jenem bösen Blick auf die Üblichkeiten, der aus den perfektionistischen Sollforderungen des Programms der Absolutmachung des Menschen folgt. Hegel – ich formuliere es nicht ganz auf der Höhe Hegelscher Subtilität – Hegel (in seiner Sollenskritik) hat gezeigt: Sollenshypertrophie bewirkt Seinsvermiesung[18]; und wer nur die absolute Wahl des Absoluten gelten läßt, diskriminiert die vorhandenen Üblichkeiten. Doch darf man die Üblichkeiten gerade nicht verteufeln: nicht schon allein deswegen, weil sie nicht der Himmel auf Erden – das absolut Gute – sind, sind sie die Hölle auf Erden: das absolut Schlimme (als ob es dazwischen nichts gäbe, um das zu zittern und das zu verteidigen sich lohnte). Gerade weil die gegenwärtige Welt – unleugbar – schwierig ist, brauchen wir den geschärften Sinn für die Unterscheidung zwischen dem schlechthin Schlimmen und der vorhandenen Wirklichkeit: eine philosophische Apologie der Üblichkeiten.

3. *Wir Menschen sind stets mehr unsere Zufälle als unsere Wahl.* Das Programm der Absolutmachung des Menschen moniert: die Üblichkeiten sind – gemessen am Absoluten – zufällig. Ich meine: das trifft zwar zu, aber es ist kein Einwand. Zum Einwand wird es durch ein Mißverständnis: daß das Zufällige immer das Beliebige sei, beliebig wählbar und abwählbar. Gewiß ist Beliebigkeit keine zumutbare Verfassung für Lebensorientierungen, für solche des Handelns, des Wissens, des Lebens: wenn man Orientierungen ständig umtauschen kann, sind es keine; und wenn das Zufällige ausschließlich das Beliebige wäre, wäre dies – für die Üblichkeiten, die tatsächlich zufällig sind, und für das Menschenleben, für das Üblichkeiten unvermeidlich sind – in der Tat ruinös. Nur: daß das Zufällige ausschließlich das Beliebige sei, justament das stimmt nicht.

Der aus der christlichen Schöpfungstheologie kommende Endlichkeitsbegriff des Zufälligen (Kontingenten) – „contingens est, quod nec est impossibile nec necessarium" bzw. „contingens est, quod potest non esse"[19] – meint zwar das, was auch nicht sein könnte, bzw. das, was auch anders sein könnte: das aber ist, wenn man es nicht aus der Schöpferperspektive von Gott her, sondern – menschlicher aus der Lebensweltperspektive – vom Menschen her sieht,

of Eichmann's monstrous actions is taken into account, and that the first aspect consisted in his violation of a usual practice: the usual practice of not murdering one's fellow human beings. I cannot go into detail here on the Eichmann case and the debate about the "banality of evil,"[17] but in my view this primary deviation from the usual was secondarily camouflaged, by the perpetrator (camouflaged, in the end, from himself as well), by the consciousness that he was more than fulfilling his usual duty.

This does not, in my opinion, count as an argument against usual practices, any more than it counts as an argument against the kind of truthfulness that says that lying, in order to be succesful, must pretend to be, and camouflage itself as, truthfulness (and that the pretense and camouflage can extend, if need be, even to the liar). *Abusus non tollit usum:* Misuse does not refute use. Eichmann's bureaucratically perpetrated crimes suffered not from an excess but from a deficiency of usual practices: The "Eichmann" danger is, in my opinion, greater when one begins by putting all usual practices up for grabs (even if it is in the name of the absolute or of some other good cause), than when one refuses to do this. It is useful to remember that opposition came above all from groups with intact traditions.[a] That is why it is also not correct to say that setting store by usual practices makes critique impossible; because the opposite is the case. Critique is, above all, conflict between usual practices. To be capable of it, one must *have* usual practices; and in our times and our parts of the world critique is in fact itself a usual practice, which is regulated by usual practices.

We must (I repeat) defend usual practices against slander, and consequently we must also defend them against the jaundiced view of usual practices that is produced by the perfectionistic deontological demands of the program of making man absolute. In his critique of deontological thinking, Hegel showed that deontological hypertrophy has the effect of spoiling what exists.[18] Likewise, someone who grants validity only to the absolute's absolute choice treats the existing usual practices unfairly. But usual practices should not be demonized: The fact that they are not heaven on earth, the absolutely good, is not enough to make them hell on earth, the absolutely bad (as though there were nothing in between that it is worthwhile to be concerned about and to defend). Precisely because today's world is—undeniably—difficult, we need a sharpened appreciation of the difference between what is simply bad and the existing reality: We need, that is, a philosophical defense of usual practices.

3. *We Human Beings Are Always More Our Accidents Than Our Choice.* The program of making man absolute warns that, measured against the absolute, usual practices are accidental. As I see it, while that is true, it is not an objection. It becomes an objection as a result of a misconception, according to which what is accidental is always optional, something that can be arbitrarily chosen or rejected. It is certainly true that arbitrary optionalness is not a characteristic that can reasonably be imputed to orientations in life—in action, knowledge, and living. If one can continually exchange one orientation for another, the things being exchanged are not orientations; and if the accidental were only the arbitrarily optional, this would indeed have ruinous consequences, both for usual practices, which are indeed accidental, and for human life, for which usual practices are unavoidable. However, it is just not the case that the accidental is solely the arbitrarily optional.

The concept of the accidental—that is, the contingent—as finite, which derives from the Christian theology of creation and is summarized in the formulas "contingens est, quod nec est impossibile nec necessarium" [the contingent is what is neither impossible nor necessary], or "contingens est, quod potest non esse" [the contingent is what could not-be],[19] does indeed mean that which could also not be, or which

205

gerade doppelter Art.[20] Entweder nämlich ist das Zufällige „das, was auch anders sein könnte" und *durch uns änderbar ist* (z. B. kann man Wurst essen oder es lassen und statt dessen Käse essen, und dieser Vortrag könnte Ihnen auch Wurst sein, weil er Käse ist, oder er könnte auch gar nicht oder auch anders gehalten werden); dieses Zufällige als „das, was auch anders sein könnte" und durch uns änderbar ist, ist eine beliebig wählbare und abwählbare Beliebigkeit: ich möchte es das *Beliebigkeitszufällige* nennen, das Beliebige. Oder das Zufällige ist „das, was auch anders sein könnte" und gerade nicht durch uns änderbar ist (Schicksalsschläge: also Krankheiten, geboren zu sein und dgl.); dieses Zufällige als „das, was auch anders sein könnte" und gerade nicht – oder nur wenig – durch uns änderbar ist, ist Schicksal: in hohem Grade negationsresistent und nicht oder kaum entrinnbar; ich möchte es das *Schicksalszufällige* nennen, das Schicksalhafte. Es gibt also – das folgt aus dieser Unterscheidung – für die Menschen nicht nur eine Sorte des Zufälligen, sondern deren zwei: es gibt nicht nur das Beliebigkeitszufällige, sondern es gibt auch das Schicksalszufällige.

Es sind nun – meine ich – überwiegend Zufälle dieser zweiten Art (also Zufälle von der Art des Schicksalszufälligen), die, als natürliche und geschichtliche Gegebenheiten und Geschehnisse, welche uns zustoßen, unser Leben ausmachen. Das beginnt – um mit dem Anfang anzufangen – bei unserer Geburt: wir könnten auch nicht – oder zu anderer Zeit, in anderer Weltgegend, in anderer Kultur und Lebenslage – geboren sein; aber wenn wir es einmal sind, können wir das alles nicht mehr annullieren: selbst ein Suizid erfolgt ex suppositione nativitatis. Daß die Geburt ein Schicksalszufall ist, beleuchtet Alfred Polgars Kommentar zu Silen: „Das Beste ist es, nicht geboren zu sein: doch wem passiert das schon?" Das Schicksalszufällige ist die Wirklichkeit unseres Lebens, weil wir Menschen stets „in Geschichten verstrickt" sind (Wilhelm Schapp); denn – das hat vor allem Hermann Lübbe gezeigt – Handlungen werden dadurch zu Geschichten, daß ihnen etwas dazwischenkommt, passiert, widerfährt.[21] Eine Geschichte ist eine Wahl, in die etwas Zufälliges – etwas Schicksalszufälliges – einbricht: darum kann man Geschichten nicht planen, sondern muß sie erzählen. Unser Leben besteht aus diesen Handlungs-Widerfahrnis-Gemischen, die die Geschichten sind: ebendarum überwiegt in ihm das Schicksalszufällige. Zufällig – schicksalszufällig – ist es auch, daß wir jenen Naturgesetzen unterliegen, die die Naturwissenschaften entdecken: wir könnten auch anderen Determinationen unterworfen sein, doch wir unterliegen nun einmal – zufällig – diesen[22]; gerade diesen Zufall aber können wir nicht ändern: er ist ein Schicksalszufall für den Menschen. Der Zufall, der uns am schicksalhaftesten und – falls man ihn nicht als den Trost betrachtet, nicht endlos weiterturnen zu müssen – am härtesten trifft, ist unser Tod: wir sind – aus Schicksalszufall – durch Geburt zum Tode verurteilt, d. h. zu jener Lebenskürze, die uns nicht die Zeit läßt, uns aus dem, was wir zufällig schon sind, in beliebigem Umfang davonzumachen; unsere Sterblichkeit zwingt uns, jener Schicksalszufall, der für uns unsere Vergangenheit ist, zu „sein", d. h. überwiegend zu bleiben. Zu dieser Vergangenheit gehören – entscheidend und wesentlich – jene Zufälle, die unsere Üblichkeiten sind, die wir nicht erst wählen, sondern in denen wir stecken. Sie könnten ganz andere sein, aber wir – vita brevis – können sie überwiegend nicht ändern. Es ist ja nicht so, daß wir sie erst sozusagen aussuchen müßten, sondern wir haben sie stets schon und können sie – und brauchen sie – überwiegend nicht loswerden: sie sind Schicksalszufälle; und wer ihnen – wie die philosophisch normale absolute Argumentation – Beliebigkeit vorwirft, denkt und redet an ihnen vorbei, und sein Argument ist insofern nichts wert. Daß das Übliche das Zufällige ist, stimmt zwar; aber das ist – weil es nicht das Beliebige ist – kein Einwand. Denn wohl sind unsere Üblichkeiten

could also be different; but if one sees this not from the perspective of God, the Creator, but, more humanly, from the perspective of the life-world and man, it comes in two different forms.[20] *Either,* that is, the accidental is "that which could also be different" and which *we can change* (for example, one can drink tea, or refrain from drinking tea and instead eat bologna; and this lecture might also not be your cup of tea, because it is bologna, or it could also not be given at all, or be given in a different way). This kind of accidental thing, as "what could also be different" and which we could change, is an arbitrarily choosable or rejectable object of discretion, which I would like to call the "arbitrarily accidental," or the arbitrary. *Or,* on the other hand, the accidental is "that which could also be different" and is *precisely not changeable by us* (blows of fate, by which I mean illnesses, being born, and the like). This kind of accidental thing, as "what could also be different" and is precisely not (or only slightly) changeable by us, is fate. It is resistant, to a high degree, to negation, and is not (or is scarcely) escapable. I would like to call it the "fatefully accidental," or the fateful. It follows, then, from this distinction, that there exist, for human beings, not only one type of accidentalness, but two: We have not only the arbitrarily accidental but also the fatefully accidental.

Now it seems to me that it is overwhelmingly accidents of this second kind (accidents, that is, of the "fatefully accidental" type), the natural and historical facts and events that befall us, that make up our life. This starts, to begin at the beginning, at our birth: We could also not have been born, or we could have been born at a different time, in a different part of the world, a different culture, a different situation in life; but once we are born, we can no longer annul all of that. Even a suicide happens *ex suppositione nativiatatis* [from the supposition of birth). The fact that birth is a fateful accident is illuminated by Alfred Polgar's commentary on Silenus: "The best thing is not to be born—but who does that ever happen to?" Fateful accidents are the reality of our life, because as human beings we are always "entangled in stories" (Wilhelm Schapp); because, as Hermann Lübbe, above all, has shown, actions become stories when something interferes in them, happens to them, befalls them.[21] A story is a choice that is interrupted by something accidental, something fatefully accidental; this is why stories cannot be planned, but must be told. Our life is composed of these mixtures—which stories are—of our action and what befalls us; which is why the fatefully accidental element is predominant in it. It is also accidental, fatefully accidental, that we are subject to the natural laws that the natural sciences discover: We could also have been subject to other forms of determination, but we are in fact, accidentally, subject to these.[22] But just this is an accident that we cannot change: a fateful accident for man. The accident that affects us most fatefully and most severely—unless one regards it as the consolation of not having to go on performing our tricks forever—is our death. A fateful accident condemns us, by our birth, to death—that is, to the brevity of life that does not allow us the time to escape, as far as we might like, from what we accidentally already are. Our mortality forces us to "be"—that is, to remain, predominantly—the fateful accident that our past is for us. Part of this past is, decisively and essentially, the accidents that our usual practices are—practices that we do not choose, to begin with, but in which we are involved. They could be completely different, but, vita brevis, we cannot for the most part change them. It is not, after all, as though we first had to, as it were, seek them out; rather, we always already have them, and cannot (and do not need), for the most part, to get free of them. They are fateful accidents, and someone who accuses them (as in the absolute argumentation that is the norm in philosophy) of being arbitrarily optional, thinks and speaks right past them, and his argument is, to that extent, worthless. It is indeed true that the usual is accidental, but since it is

stets mehr unsere Zufälle als unsere Wahl: doch sie sind nicht beliebigkeitszufällig, sondern schicksalszufällig.

Ich übergehe – sie nur erwähnend – die Frage, wie die Menschen mit dem Zufälligen leben können und umgehen. Sicher gehört zum Umgang mit dem Beliebigkeitszufälligen die Kunst: die Beliebigkeitsersparung durch Form; und sicher gehört zum Umgang mit dem Schicksalszufälligen die Religion: die Verwandlung von Grenzsituationen in Routinen. Beide – Kunst und Religion – sind Kontingenzbewältigungsversuche; jene – die Kunst – bewältigt (vielleicht) Beliebigkeitskontingenz; diese – die Religion – bewältigt (vielleicht) Schicksalskontingenz.

In der Philosophie – meine ich also – hat man über dem Beliebigkeitszufälligen das Schicksalszufällige vergessen, um schnell mit dem Zufälligen fertig zu werden und es leicht „entfernen“ zu können. Das liegt nahe, wenn man beim Zufall – statt phänomenologisch auf der lebensweltlichen Binnensicht auch des Zufälligen zu bestehen – nur die absolute oder die Außensicht pflegt: z. B. kommt in der kreationstheologischen, stochastischen oder spieltheoretischen Diskussion des Zufälligen selten die Perspektive dessen vor, dem da durch Schöpfung und andere Zufälle mitgespielt wird. Auch gibt es eine Modifikation des Blicks auf das Zufällige, die mit der Alterslage zusammenhängt. In der modernen Welt – dem Zeitalter der tachogenen Weltfremdheit, in dem man zunehmend nicht mehr erwachsen wird – dominiert die Jugendsicht des Zufälligen. Die Angst vor der Beliebigkeit ist eine optische Täuschung der Jugend, die nur andauert, weil gilt: „daß es keinen Menschen gibt, der erwachsen wäre“.[23] Die Erfahrung des Überwiegens und der Lebensbedeutsamkeit jener Zufälle, die uns prägen, obwohl sie gerade nicht in unserem Belieben stehen (also nicht der Beliebigkeitszufälle, sondern der Schicksalszufälle), ist eine Alterserfahrung, die man schon früh im Leben machen kann, weil ebenso gilt: jeder – auch der jüngste – Mensch ist schon alt, d. h. so nah dem Tode, daß er jedenfalls nicht die Zeit hat, die Zufälligkeit der Zufälle, aus denen sein Leben besteht, in nennenswerter Weise zu löschen.

Es ist diese Alterserfahrung der Dominanz des Schicksalszufälligen, die – gegenüber dem Programm der Absolutmachung des Menschen – vor allem geltend gemacht werden muß. Nicht nur geben wir unserem Leben niemals – durch Wahl – überwiegend absolute Notwendigkeit, so daß es insofern im Sinne des Beliebigkeitszufälligen zufällig bleibt; sondern wir können unser Leben und seine Wirklichkeit auch niemals überhaupt in wesentlicher Weise wählen oder gar absolut wählen, so daß es auch und vor allem im Sinne des Schicksalszufälligen zufällig bleibt. Wir kommen mehr als durch Wahl – also über Pläne – durch Zufälle durchs Leben und zu uns selber; und das ist nicht – wie die Philosophie der absoluten Wahl und der Absolutmachung des Menschen uns weismachen will – ein Unglücksfall; denn der Zufall ist keine mißlungene Absolutheit, sondern – sterblichkeitsbedingt – unsere geschichtliche Normalität. Wir Menschen sind stets mehr unsere Zufälle als unsere Wahl. Ich sage, wohlgemerkt, nicht: wir Menschen sind nur unsere Zufälle; ich sage nur: wir Menschen sind nicht nur unsere Wahl; und ich sage außerdem nur noch: wir Menschen sind stets mehr unsere Zufälle als unsere Wahl. Und erst recht sind wir Menschen stets mehr unsere Zufälle als unsere absolute Wahl und haben das zu akzeptieren; denn wir sind nicht absolut, sondern endlich. Eine Philosophie, die – skeptisch – diese Untilgbarkeit des Zufälligen geltend macht, ist, insofern, die Apologie des Zufälligen.

4. *Menschliche Freiheit lebt von der Gewaltenteilung.* Das bisherige Fazit ist: zur Würde des Menschen gehört, daß er das Zufällige leiden kann; und zu seiner Freiheit gehört die Anerkennung des Zufälligen. Darin steckt positiv:

not arbitrarily optional, this is not an objection to it. For our usual practices are certainly always more our accidents than our choice, but they are not arbitrarily accidental, but fatefully accidental.

I will only mention in passing the question of how human beings can live and deal with the accidental. One of the ways of dealing with the arbitrarily accidental is certainly art: the use of form to reduce arbitrariness. And one of the ways of dealing with the fatefully accidental is certainly religion: the transformation of extreme situations into routines. Both of these, art and religion, attempt to master something; art (perhaps) masters arbitrary contingency, and religion (perhaps) masters fateful contingency.

In philosophy, then, it seems to me, people have focused on the arbitrarily accidental and forgotten the fatefully accidental, so as to deal quickly with the accidental and "get rid of" it easily. This is a natural thing to do if one cultivates only the absolute, or external, point of view in connection with accident, rather than insisting, phenomenologically, on the internal point of view—the view from the life-world—on the accidental, as well. For example, in the discussions of the accidental in the theology of creation, in stochastics, or in game theory, one seldom encounters the perspective of the person to whom the results of the creation or of other accidents are served up. There is also a modification of one's perspective on the accidental that is connected with one's position in terms of age. In the modern world—the age of tachogenic unworldliness, in which people increasingly do not grow up—the dominant perspective on the accidental is that of youth. Fear of arbitrariness is an optical illusion of youth, which only persists because of the rule that "there's no such thing as a grown-up person."[23] The experience of the preponderance and vital significance of the accidents that leave their imprint on us, although they are precisely not under our discretion (so that they are not arbitrary accidents, but fateful accidents), is an experience that is associated with age but which one can have early on in life, because it is also a rule thar every human being, even the youngest, is already old—that is, is so close to death that he or she does not, in any case, have time to efface (to any considerable extent) the accidental quality of the accidents of which his or her life is composed.

It is, above all, this experience (an experience associated with age), of the dominance of what is fatefully accidental that has to be asserted in opposition to the program of making man absolute. Not only do we never give our lives a predominantly absolute necessity, by our choice, so that to that extent they remain accidental in the sense of the arbitrarily accidental, but beyond that, we cannot, in general, essentially choose (not to speak of absolutely choosing) our life and its reality, so that it also (and above all) remains accidental in the sense of what is fatefully accidental. It is more through accidents than through our choice (that is, our plans) that we get through life and become ourselves. And that is not, as the philosophy of absolute choice and of making man absolute wants to make us believe, a misfortune—because accident is not a failure of absoluteness, but (under conditions of mortality) our historically normal state. We human beings are always more our accidents than our choice. Note that I do not say that we human beings are only our accidents; I only say that we are not only our choice, and that we human beings are always more our accidents than our choice. Still more are we human beings always more our accidents than our *absolute* choice, and we have to accept that; for we are not absolute, but finite. A philosophy that—skeptically—insists upon this ineradicability of the accidental is, to that extent, a defense of the accidental.

4. *Human Freedom Depends upon the Separation of Powers.* One could sum up our results, so far, in these propositions: Part of man's dignity is his ability to bear the accidental, and

die Respektierung menschlicher Würde ist vor allem das Mitleid; und die Respektierung menschlicher Freiheit ist vor allem die Toleranz. Darin steckt zugleich negativ: die Würde des Menschen ist nicht die einer absoluten Diva, die permanent beleidigt ist, nicht als Gott – oder als ausschließlicher Selbstzweck wenigstens halbwegs als Gott – behandelt zu werden; und die Freiheit des Menschen ist nicht (als die Macht der Vernunft) die absolute Wahl, für die es nichts Nichtgewähltes – nichts Zufälliges – gibt. Daß die menschliche Würde gleichwohl wirklich Würde und daß die menschliche Freiheit gleichwohl wirklich Freiheit ist oder sein kann, das folgt aus der folgenden – meiner abschließenden – Überlegung, die einschlägig die Gewaltenteilung ins Spiel bringt.

Des Menschen Wirklichkeit ist – wenn das bisher Gesagte stimmt – überwiegend das Zufällige. Zufällig ist das, was auch anders sein kann. Aber wenn es anders sein *kann*, dann – wenn auch zufälligerweise – *ist* es häufig auch anders: die zufällige Wirklichkeit – zufällig – ist vielfach so und auch anders; sie umfaßt Verschiedenes: sie ist vielgestaltig, bunt. Diese Buntheit – gerade sie – ist die menschliche Freiheitschance: es ist diejenige Freiheitsmöglichkeit, die die Lehre von der Gewaltenteilung zur Geltung bringt; denn die politische Freiheitswirkung der politischen Gewaltenteilung ist nur ein spezieller Fall der Freiheitswirkung der allgemeinen Buntheit der Wirklichkeit: daß die Zufälle, die dem Menschen als Schicksale zufallen, nicht uniform und monolithisch sind, sondern – zufällig – einander durchkreuzen und einander dadurch in gewissem Maße neutralisieren. Montesquieu – im berühmten Abschnitt über die englische Verfassung in *De l'esprit des lois*[24] – hat die Gewaltenteilung – als Teilung der drei politischen Gewalten Legislative, Exekutive und Jurisdiktion – zwar nur als Garantie der politischen Freiheit geltend gemacht; doch sollte man daran denken, daß Montesquieu – der im übrigen auch sonst die Buntheit der Bedingungen des menschlichen Lebens bis hin zum Klima ins Spiel brachte – in der Tradition der Moralistik[25] und die Moralistik in der Tradition der Skepsis stand.

Skepsis aber ist der Sinn für Gewaltenteilung: der Zweifel der Skepsis ist – wie das Wort Zweifel es sagt, das ja mit der „Zwei" die Vielheit enthält – justament jenes (in der Tradition der Skepsis „isosthenes diaphonia" genannte)[26] Verfahren, das zwei gegensätzliche Überzeugungen in solcher Art aufeinanderprallen läßt, daß beide dadurch so viel an Kraft einbüßen, daß der Einzelne – als lachender oder weinender Dritter – von ihnen freikommt; und was dieserart durch zwei Überzeugungen passiert, gilt erst recht von mehreren Überzeugungen: jede distanziert den Einzelnen von den jeweils anderen. Und was von Überzeugungen gilt, gilt ebenso von anderen Gewalten, Tendenzen, Größen der Realität: es ist – für die skeptisch geltend gemachte, d.h. endliche Freiheit – wesentlich, daß stets nicht nur eine, sondern – pluralistisch konkurrierend, einander durchkreuzend und dadurch wechselseitig einander balancierend – eine Mehrzahl solcher Potenzen wirkt. Jede – sozusagen – sichert dem Menschen, indem sie ihn mitdeterminiert, einen Spielraum (Distanz) gegenüber den jeweils anderen und rettet ihn vor dem determinatorischen Alleinzugriff einer einzigen Potenz, gegenüber der er aus Eigenem machtlos wäre: divide et fuge! Es ist also – als Freiheitswirkung – zuträglich für den Menschen, viele (mehrere) Überzeugungen zu haben: nicht gar keine und nicht nur eine, sondern viele; und zuträglich für ihn, viele (mehrere) Traditionen und Geschichten zu haben und auch viele Seelen – ach! – in der eigenen Brust: nicht gar keine und nicht nur eine, sondern viele; und vielleicht ist es auch zuträglich für ihn, viele (mehrere) Götter und Orientierungspunkte zu haben: nicht gar keinen und nicht nur einen, sondern mehrere oder sogar viele; es ist überhaupt zuträglich für den Menschen, viele Determinanten zu haben: nicht gar keine und nicht nur eine, sondern viele; denn die Menschen sind nicht dadurch frei,

part of his freedom is his acknowledgment of the accidental. This implies, positively, that respect for human diginity is, above all, compassion, and that respect for human freedom is, above all, tolerance. At the same time it also implies, negatively, that man's dignity is not the dignity of an absolute diva, who is permanently offended by not being treated as God or—as one who is solely an end in himself—at least to some degree as God; and it implies that man's freedom is not (as the power of reason) absolute choice, for which there is nothing unchosen, nothing accidental. That human dignity nevertheless really is or can be dignity, and human freedom really is or can be freedom, is a result of the following, concluding reflections, which bring the separation of powers into play in this connection.

If what has been said so far is correct, man's reality is predominantly accidental. That which is accidental can also be different. But if it *can* be different, it frequently, if only accidentally, also *is* different: Accidental reality is—accidentally—often thus and also different; it embraces various things; it is multiform, motley. This very motleyness is the human opportunity for freedom. It is the possibility of freedom that is put in the foreground by the doctrine of the separation of powers; for the effect of the political separation of powers, in terms of political freedom, is only a special case of the effect of the general motleyness of reality, in terms of freedom in general—a special case of the effect of the fact that the accidents that befall man, as fates, are not uniform and monolithic, but instead—accidentally—intersect and interfere with one another and thus, to a degree, neutralize one another. It is true that in the famous section on the English constitution in his *De l'esprit des lois*[24] Montesquieu put forward the separation of powers—as the division between the three political powers, the legislative, executive, and judicial—only as a guarantee of *political* freedom; but one should bear in mind that Montesquieu (who, incidentally, brought into play the motleyness of the conditions of human life in other areas as well, all the way to climate) belonged to the tradition of the moralists, and that they were part of the skeptical tradition.[25]

But skepticism is an appreciation of the separation of powers: Skepticism's doubt—as the word "Zweifel" [doubt] says (which, after all, contains the idea of multiplicity in its "zwei" [two])—is precisely the procedure, known in the skeptical tradition as "isosthenes diaphonia,"[26] of letting two opposed convictions collide with each other in such a way that both of them decline so much in power that the individual, as the laughing or crying third party, gets free of them. And what happens in this way with two convictions is still more the case with several convictions: Each of them distances the individual from the others. What is true of convictions is equally true of other forces, tendencies, magnitudes in reality: It is crucial, for the freedom that skepticism asserts (that is, for finite freedom), that there is never only one such power at work, but always a number of them, pluralistically competing, intersecting, and interfering with one another, and thus reciprocally balancing one another. By codetermining man, each of them—so to speak—guarantees him latitude (distance) in relation to the others, and protects him from the sole determining clutches of a single power, in the face of which he would be powerless, on his own. The principle is: "Divide et fuge!" [Divide and escape!]. Thus it is advantageous for man, because of the consequences in terms of freedom, to have many (several) convictions: not no convictions at all, and not only one, but many. And it is advantageous for him to have many (several) traditions and stories, and also many souls (alas!) in his own breast: not no tradition, story, or soul at all, and not only one, but many. And perhaps it is also advantageous for him to have many (several) gods and points of orientation: not none at all, and not only one, but several or even many. In general, it is advantageous for man to have

daß sie Gott kopieren: als quasi-allmächtige Chefs der Weltregie oder durch unbedingtes Vermögen; sondern sie sind frei durch Freiheiten im Plural, die ihnen zufallen, indem die Determinanten, die determinierend auf sie einstürmen, durch Determinantengedrängel einander wechselseitig beim Determinieren behindern: einzig dadurch, daß jede weitere Determinante den Determinationsdruck jeder anderen einschränkt, anhält, mildert, sind und haben Menschen ihre – bescheidene, durchaus endliche, begrenzte – je eigene (individuelle) Freiheit gegenüber dem Alleinzugriff einer jeden. Nicht die Nulldetermination – das Fehlen aller Determinanten – und nicht die Übermacht einer einzigen (gegebenenfalls besonders erhabenen) Determinante macht den Menschen frei, sondern die Überfülle an Determinanten tut es.[27]

Ich behaupte hier also – als meine These: als skeptisch-moralistisch generalisierte Gewaltenteilungsthese – die Freiheitswirkung der Überdetermination, mithin – wie ich schon sagte (und auf die Gefahr hin, daß Ihnen dies zu bunt wird) – den Freiheitseffekt der allgemeinen Buntheit der natürlichen und geschichtlichen Menschenwirklichkeit. Der Umstand, daß das Zufällige, das den Menschen zustößt, nicht ein einziger – ungeteilter – Zufall ist, sondern aus Zufällen im Plural besteht: dieser – selber schicksalszufällige – Umstand macht es, daß – in der Form von Freiheiten im Plural – den Menschen ihr Zufall Freiheit zufällt.

So muß der Mensch nicht die Determination fürchten, sondern die Ungeteiltheit ihrer Gewalt. Dabei darf seine Freiheit – bestehend aus Freiheiten im Plural – auf dasjenige an der Wirklichkeit bauen, das – durch Buntheit – Einheitszwänge kompensiert: so auch – neben den absoluten Universalisierungen und den modernen Uniformisierungen und Gleichschaltungen – jenen harten Einzigkeitszwang, dem wir alle unterliegen, weil wir nur ein einziges Leben haben; denn wir können ihm in die Kommunikation mit unseren Mitmenschen – die wir ebendeswegen brauchen – entkommen durch die Möglichkeit, ihre Leben – die ja viele sind – mitzuleben und dadurch unser eigenes Leben zu pluralisieren. Im übrigen ist es – auf daß ihr Arretierungspotential von Determinationsgewalten mit ins Spiel kommt – überhaupt wichtig, daß möglichst viele Determinanten in unser Leben einbezogen werden: also auch jene – schicksalszufälligen – Realitätsgrößen, die durch Bemerktwerden determinieren. So ist es zuträglich für Menschen, wenn Grenzen ihres Merkens kollabieren. Menschlichste oder gar allzumenschlichste Formen dieser „Grenzreaktionen" – die zu denen gehören, die, als So-ist-es-Reaktionen, die menschliche Vernunft bilden: den Verzicht auf die Anstrengung, dumm zu bleiben – sind, wie Helmuth Plessner und Joachim Ritter gezeigt haben, Lachen und Weinen[28]: also die leisen Formen der Anerkennung zuvor unbemerkter und verdrängter Schicksalszufälle, die – andere Determinanten balancierend – das Menschliche mitdeterminieren. Indem wir lachen oder weinen, akzeptieren wir – andeutungsweise – das, was – offiziell – ausgegrenzt blieb, aber – inoffiziell – mit im Spiel ist: jenes Zufällige, das dem offiziell Akzeptierten – zufällig – querkommt: durch es lachen oder weinen wir uns frei. So sind Lachbereitschaft und Weinbereitschaft – also Humor und Melancholie – Konkretionen von Toleranz und Mitleid: nicht nur menschlich, sondern auch allzumenschlich leistbare Respektierungen von Freiheit und Würde des Menschen. Frei – das gehört somit zu den Implikationen und Resultaten meiner Überlegung – frei ist, wer lachen und weinen kann; und Würde hat der, der lacht und weint, und – unter den Menschen – insbesondere der, der viel gelacht und geweint hat. Also auch diese Grenzreaktionen Lachen und Weinen sind Formen dessen, auf das ich hier aufmerksam machen wollte: Formen der Apologie des Zufälligen.

many determining factors: not none at all, and not only one, but many; because human beings are not free by virtue of the fact that they copy God (as quasi-omnipotent directors on the world stage, or by having unconditioned capability); rather, they are free through freedoms, in the plural, which fall to their lot because, in the crush of the determinants that bombard them, these determinants hinder each other, reciprocally, in their determining work. It is only by virtue of the fact that each further determinant curtails, impedes, and moderates the determining pressure of each of the others that each human being is and possesses his or her own (modest, entirely finite, limited ) individual freedom vis-à-vis the sole clutches of each determinant. What makes a human being free is not zero determination—the absence of all determinants—or the superior force of a single determinant, but a superabundance of determinants.[27] So the thesis about the separation of powers (generalized in the spirit of skeptical moralism) that I put forward here is that overdetermination promotes freedom and, consequently, as I said already (and at the risk that all of this may become too motley for you), that the general motleyness of the natural and historical human reality promotes freedom. The circumstance that what befalls human beings, in the way of accident, is not one unique and indivisible accident, but instead accidents in the plural—this (itself fatefully accidental) circumstance brings it about that the human lot turns out, accidentally, to be freedom (in the form of freedoms, in the plural).

Thus what man has to fear is not determination, but the undividedness of its power. In this connection, his freedom (which consists in freedoms, in the plural) can rely on the aspect of reality that compensates, through motleyness, for compulsions to unity, and which thus also compensates not only for absolute universalizations and for modern uniformities and streamlinings, but for the harsh compulsion to uniqueness to which we are all subject because we have only one, unique life. For we can escape from that one life into communication with our fellow human beings (whom we need, for just that reason) through the possibility of sharing their lives (which are, of course, many) and thus pluralizing our own lives. Furthermore, it is in general important—so that their capacity for arresting determining powers can come into play, too—that the greatest possible number of determinants should be incorporated into our lives, which means incorporating, as well, the fatefully accidental pieces of reality that exercise their determining effect by being noticed. Thus it is advantageous for human beings when the boundaries of what they notice collapse. The most human (or even all-too-human) of these "extreme reactions" [Grenzreaktionen]—which are among those that, as "That's the way it is" reactions, constitute human reason, or the abandonment of the effort to remain stupid—are, as Helmuth Plessner and Joachim Ritter have shown, laughing and crying:[28] that is, the gentle ways in which we acknowledge previously unnoticed and repressed fateful accidents, which—balancing other determinants—codetermine human reality. By laughing or crying, we intimate our acceptance of what remained, officially, excluded from consideration, but is, unofficially, part of the story: namely, the accidents that (accidentally) thwart what is officially accepted. Through them, we laugh or cry ourselves free. Thus a readiness to laugh and a readiness to cry—that is, humor and melancholy—are concrete forms taken by tolerance and compassion. They are ways of honoring, both humanly and all-too-humanly, the freedom and dignity of man. One of the implications and results of my reflections is, then, that someone who can laugh and cry is free; and that someone who laughs and cries, and especially—among human beings—someone who has laughed and cried a lot, has dignity. So these extreme reactions, laughing and crying, are forms of what I wanted to draw attention to here: forms of the defense of the accidental.

1 Als kurze Vorüberlegung zum Folgenden vgl. O. Marquard, „Einwilligung in das Zufällige", in: Neue Zürcher Zeitung, Nr. 30 vom 5./6. 2. 1983, 69 f., deren Hauptthese auf einen Text „Differenzierungen im Begriff Kontingenz" zurückgeht, den ich 1976 nicht habe zu Ende schreiben können. Eingegangen sind hier außerdem Überlegungen, die zuvor spezieller entwickelt wurden in: O. Marquard, „Das Über-Wir. Bemerkungen zur Diskursethik", in: K. Stierle / R. Warning (Hrsg.), Das Gespräch, München 1984 (*Poetik und Hermeneutik*, Bd. 11), 29–44.

2 G. W. F. Hegel, Die Vernunft in der Geschichte (1822/1828/1830), hrsg. von G. Lasson, Hamburg $^{5}$1955, 29.

3 Vgl. Aristoteles, Erste Analytik I 13: 32 a 18–20.

4 „Texte zum Problem der Kontingenz" habe ich im WS 1985/86 und im SS 1986 in meinem Seminar behandelt, dessen aktiven Teilnehmern ich für manche Anregung danke. Im Folgenden interessiert nur ein Ausschnitt aus der Gesamtproblematik. Was das Übrige betrifft, so verweise ich auf die Arbeit meines Kopiloten bei diesem Seminar, die im Entstehen begriffene Dissertation von F. J. Wetz, „Faktizität – ontologische Probleme von Zufall und Zeit" (Arbeitstitel); dort Literaturhinweise.

5 Vgl. H. Blumenberg, Artikel „Kontingenz", in: *Die Religion in Geschichte und Gegenwart*, Bd. 3, Tübingen 1959, 1793 f.

6 J. Monod, *Le Hasard et la Nécessité* (1970), dt.: *Zufall und Notwendigkeit. Philosophische Fragen der modernen Biologie*, übers. von F. Griese, München $^{7}$1985 (dtv 1069).

7 Aristoteles, *Metaphysik* Δ 30: 1025 a 14–34, bes. 16/17 und 25–27 (zufällig = symbebekos). Vgl. Aristoteles, *Physik* VI: 197 a 5–7. Dazu zugleich A. M. T. S. Boethius, *Philosophiae consolationis libri quinque* (524), bes. den Anfang des fünften Buches, dt.: *Trost der Philosophie*, übers. von Karl Büchner, Bremen [1955] (Sammlung Dieterich, Bd. 33), 134: „Man glaubt zwar, das sei zufällig geschehen, aber es ist nicht aus dem Nichts entstanden; denn es hat eigene Ursachen, deren plötzliches und unerwartetes Zusammentreffen einen Zufall bewirkt zu haben scheint. [...] Man kann also definieren: Zufall ist ein unvermutetes Geschehnis aus zusammenströmenden Ursachen in Dingen, die eines Bestimmten wegen unternommen werden."

8 J.-P. Sartre, *L'Être et le Néant*, Paris 1943, 638: „le choix que je suis".

9 Vgl. H. Plessner, „Die verspätete Nation. Über die politische Verführbarkeit bürgerlichen Geistes" (1935/1959), in: H. P., *Gesammelte Schriften*, Bd. 6, Frankfurt a. M. 1982, 7–223.

10 M. Heidegger, Sein und Zeit, Halle a. d. 1927, 235 ff.

11 R. Descartes, „Meditationes de prima philosophi"a (1641), in: *Œuvres de Descartes*, hrsg. von Ch. Adam und P. Tannery, Bd. 7, Nachdr. Paris 1957, 17 ff.

12 Vgl. insbes. K.-O. Apel, *Transformation der Philosophie*, Bd. 2, Frankfurt a. M. 1976, 221: „cartesische Radikalisierung der transzendentalen Fragestellung"; vor allem aber 392 f.: es „ist der methodische Ansatz des augustinisch-cartesischen Zweifels [...] auch für die Ethik [...] verbindlich", denn es „muß die Geltung moralischer Normen (also die Geltung der Sollensansprüche praktischer Sätze) prinzipiell ebenso eingeklammert und in Frage gestellt werden wie die Wahrheitsgeltung theoretischer Sätze über Tatsachen".

13 R. Descartes: „Discours de la méthode" (1637), in: *Œuvres de Descartes*, hrsg. von Ch. Adam und P. Tannery, Bd. 6, Nachdr. Paris 1956, 22 ff.: „morale par provision".

14 Vgl. O. Marquard, „Über die Unvermeidlichkeit von Üblichkeiten", in: W. Oelmüller (Hrsg.), *Normen und Geschichte*, Paderborn 1979 (Materialien zur Normendiskussion, Bd. 3), 332–342.

15 Vgl. M. Kriele, *Theorie der Rechtsgewinnung*, Berlin 1967. Ferner: O. Marquard, *Abschied vom Prinzipiellen*, Stuttgart 1981 [u. ö.] (Reclams Universal-Bibliothek, Nr. 7724[2]), bes. 16.

16 Vgl. D. Böhler, Diskussionsbemerkung in: K.-O. Apel / D. Böhler / G. Kadelbach (Hrsg.), *Praktische Philosophie / Ethik. Dialoge*, Bd. 1, Frankfurt a. M. 1984, 159.

17 Vgl. H. Arendt, *Eichmann in Jerusalem. Ein Bericht von der Banalität des Bösen*, Reinbek bei Hamburg 1978.

18 Vgl. O. Marquard, „Hegel und das Sollen" (1964), in: *O. M., Schwierigkeiten mit der Geschichtsphilosophie*, Frankfurt a. M. 1982 (stw 394), 37 ff.

19 Vgl. H. Schepers, „Zum Problem der Kontingenz bei Leibniz. Die beste der möglichen Welten", in: *Collegium Philosophicum. Studien, Joachim Ritter zum 60. Geburtstag*, hrsg. von H. Lübbe [u. a.], Basel/Stuttgart 1965, 326–350.

20 Die folgende Unterscheidung ist angeregt durch S. Kierkegaard, „Die Krankheit zum Tode" (1849), in: S. K., Gesammelte Werke, übers. von E. Hirsch, Abt. 24/25, Düsseldorf/Köln 1954, 32 ff.: Verzweiflung der Möglichkeit aus Mangel an Notwendigkeit, Verzweiflung der Notwendigkeit aus Mangel an Möglichkeit.

21 Vgl. W. Schapp, *In Geschichten verstrickt. Zum Sein von Mensch und Ding*, Hamburg 1953. Vor allem aber: H. Lübbe, *Geschichtsbegriff und Geschichtsinteresse. Analytik und Pragmatik der Historie*, Basel/Stuttgart 1977. Vgl. außerdem: R. Koselleck, „Der Zufall als Motivationsrest in der Geschichtsschreibung", in: H. R. Jauß (Hrsg.), *Die nicht mehr schönen Künste*, München 1968 (Poetik und Hermeneutik, Bd. 3), 129–141; dort ist 129 zit.: R. Aron, *Introduction à la philosophie de l'histoire*, Paris 1948, 20: „le hasard est le fondement de l'histoire".

22 Vgl. E. Boutroux, *De la contingence des lois de la nature* (1874), dt.: *Die Kontingenz der Naturgesetze*, Jena 1911.

23 A. Malraux, *Antimémoires* (1967), dt.: *Anti-Memoiren*, übers. von C. Schmid, Frankfurt a. M. 1968, 7.

24 Zit. nach: *Œuvres complètes*, hrsg. von R. Caillois, Bd. 2, Paris 1958 (Bibliothèque de la Pléiade, Bd. 86), 396 ff.

25 Vgl. F. Schalk (Hrsg.), Die französischen Moralisten, Bd. 1, München 1973 (dtv 6026), 203–257. Vgl. Die Einleitung des Herausgebers, bes. 32 ff.

26 Vgl. M. Hossenfelder, Einleitung zu: Sextus Empiricus, *Grundriß der pyrrhonischen Skepsis*, Frankfurt a. M. 1968, bes. 42 ff.

27 Diese hier nur angedeutete – keineswegs zureichend ausgearbeitete – Freiheitsthese versucht jenen Freiheitsgedanken, der aus der politischen Gewaltenteilungslehre kommt, mit jenem Freiheitsgedanken zu kreuzen und zu legieren, der aus der philosophischen Schichtenlehre kommt. Vgl. N. Hartmann, *Ethik* (1925), Berlin $^{3}$1949, 621–821, bes. 649 f.: „Der Kausalnexus und das Plus an Determination." Vgl. außerdem: N. H., *Der Aufbau der realen Welt* (1939), Berlin $^{3}$1964, 493 ff. und 510 ff., bes. 519: „Eine Welt, in der es Freiheit gibt, muß mindestens zweischichtig

sein. In einer vielschichtigen tritt kategoriale Freiheit von Schicht zu Schicht als Begleiterscheinung des Novums am höheren Determinationstypus auf; da gibt es dann so vielerlei Freiheit, als es Schichtendistanzen gibt. In einer einschichtigen Welt mit einem einzigen Determinationstypus ist sie ein Ding der Unmöglichkeit." Die schichtentheoretische Freiheitslehre ist hierarchisch, die gewaltenteilungstheoretische Freiheitslehre ist gerade nichthierarchisch. Die hier versuchte Kreuzung beider hat zur Folge: die Enthierarchisierung der schichtentheoretischen Lösung und die ontologische Ausweitung der gewaltenteilungstheoretischen Lösung. Heraus kommt – hoffe ich – eine determinationspluralistische Freiheitsthese.

28 J. Ritter, „Über das Lachen" (1940), in: J. R., *Subjektivität, Sechs Aufsätze*, Frankfurt a. M. 1974, 62–92. H. Plessner, „Lachen und Weinen. Eine Untersuchung der Grenzen menschlichen Verhaltens" (1941), in: H. P., *Gesammelte Schriften*, Bd. 7, Frankfurt a. M. 1982, 201–387. Vgl. O. Marquard, „Vernunft als Grenzreaktion", in: H. Poser (Hrsg.), *Wandel des Vernunftbegriffs*, Freiburg i. Br. / München 1981, 107–133. Außerdem: O. Marquard, „Loriot laureat. Laudatio auf Bernhard-Viktor von Bülow bei der Verleihung des Kasseler Literaturpreises für grotesken Humor 1985", in: *Wilhelm-Busch-Jahrbuch 1985*, Hannover 1986 (Mitteilungen der Wilhelm-Busch-Gesellschaft, Nr. 51), 81–85.



1 A short preliminary study on the same subject as what follows is O. Marquard, "Einwilligung in das Zufällige," *Neue Zürcher Zeitung*, no. 30, February 5–6, 1983, 69–70. The chief thesis of that piece goes back to a text on "Differentiations in the Concept of Contingency," which I was unable to complete in 1976. The present piece also reflects some thinking that was developed more specifically in O. Marquard, "Das Über-Wir. Anmerkungen zur Diskursethik," in K. Stierle, R. Warning, eds., *Poetik und Hermeneutik* 11 (Munich, 1984), 29–44.

2 G. W. F. Hegel, *Die Vernunft in der Geschichte* (1822, 1828, 1830), ed. G. Lasson (5th printing, Hamburg, 1955), 29.

3 See Aristotle, *Prior Analytics* I 13: 32 a 18–20.

4 I dealt with "Texts on the Problem of Contingency" in my seminar in the winter semester of 1985–86 and in the summer semester of 1986, and I thank the active participants in this seminar for many suggestions. In what follows, I am concerned with only one part of the overall problematic. For the rest of it, I refer the reader to the work of my copilot in this seminar: F. J. Wetz's dissertation in progress, whose working title is "Faktizität—Ontologische Probleme von Zufall und Zeit" [Facticity—Ontological Problems of Accident and Time]. References to the literature may be found there.

5 Cf. H. Blumenberg, "Kontingenz," in *Die Religion in Geschichte und Gesellschaft*, vol. 3 (3rd ed., Tübingen, 1959), cols. 793–94.

6 J. Monod, *Le hasard et la nécessité* (Paris, 1970); translated by A. Wainhouse as *Chance and Necessity* (New York, 1971).

7 Aristotle, *Metaphysics* IV 30: 1025 a 14–34, esp. 1617 and 25–27 (accidental= symbebēkos). Cf. Aristotle, *Physics* VI: 197 a 5–7. See also Boethius, *Philosophiae consolationis libri quinque* (524), esp. the beginning of the fifth book; in English, *The Consolations of Philosophy*, trans. W. J. Oates (NewYork, 1957), 50: "Such a thing is believed to have happened by chance, but not from nothing, for it has its own causes whose unforeseen and unexpected coincidence seems to have brought about a chance... Chance therefore may be defined as an unexpected result from the coincidence of certain causes in matters done for some other purpose."

8 J.-P. Sartre, *L'Être et le neant* (Paris, 1943), 638: "le choix que je suis."

9 Cf. H. Plessner, *Die verspätete Nation. Über die politische Verführbarkeit bürgerlichen Geistes* (1939, 1959), in Gesammelte Schriften, vol. 6 (Frankfurt, 1982), 7–223.

10 M. Heidegger, *Sein und Zeit* (Halle, 1927), 235ff.

11 R. Descartes, *Meditationes de prima philosophia* (1641), in *Oeuvres de Descartes*, ed. Ch. Adam and P. Tannery, vol. 7 (repr. Paris, 1957), 17ff.

12 Cf. especially K. O. Apel, *Transformation der Philosophie*, vol. 2. (Frankfurt, 1976), 221: "Cartesian radicalization of the transcendental point of view"; but above all 392–93: "the methodical approach of Augustinian/Cartesian doubt ... is obligatory ... for ethics as well," because "the validity of moral norms (that is, the validity of the deontological claims of practical propositions) must, in principle, be bracketed and placed in question just as much as the truth—validity of theoretical propositions about facts."

13 R. Descartes, *Discours de la méthode* (1637), in *Oeuvres de Descartes*, ed. Ch. Adam and

P. Tannery, vol. 6 (repr., Paris, 1956), 22ff: "morale par provision."

14 Cf. O. Marquard, "Über die Unvermeidlichkeit von Üblichkeiten," in W. Oelmüller, ed., *Normen und Geschichte,* Materialien zur Normendiskussion 3 (Paderborn, 1979), 332–42.

15 Cf. M. Kriele, *Theorie der Rechtsgewinnung* (Berlin, 1967), and also O. Marquard, *Farewell to Matters of Principle,* trans. Robert M. Wallace (Oxford, 1988) *(= Abschied vom Prinzipiellen* [Stuttgart, 1981]).

16 Cf. D. Böhler, discussion contribution, in K. O. Apel, D. Böhler, and G. Kadelbach, eds., *Praktische Philosophie/Ethik. Dialoge,* vol.1 (Frankfurt, 1984), 159.

17 Cf. Hannah Arendt, *Eichmann in Jerusalem: A Report on the Banality of Evil* (New York, 1963).

18 Cf. O. Marquard, "Hegel und das Sollen," *Philosophisches Jahrbuch 72.* (1964): 103–19; reprinted in O. Marquard, *Schwierigkeiten mit der der Geschichtsphilosophie,* 2nd ed. (Frankfurt, 1982), 37ff.

19 Cf. H. Schepers, "Zum Problem der Kotingenz bei Leibniz. Die beste der möglichen Welten," *Collegium Philosophicum. Studien, Joachim Ritter zum 60. Geburtstag,* ed. H. Lübbe et al. (Basel and Stuttgart, 1965), 326–50.

20 The distinction that follows is inspired by S. Kierkegaard, *The Sickness unto Death* (1849), trans. W. Lowrie (Princeton, 1941), 54ff: the despair of possibility that is due to the lack of necessity, and the despair of necessity that is due to the lack of possibility.

21 Cf. W. Schapp, *In Geschichten verstrickt. Zum Sein von Mensch und Ding* (Hamburg, 1953). But especially see H. Lübbe, *Geschichtsbegriff und Geschichtsinteresse. Analytik und Pragmatik der Historie* (Basel and Stuttgart, 1977). Cf. also R. Koselleck, "Der Zufall als Motivationsrest in der Geschichtsschreibung," in H. R. Jauss, ed., *Die nicht mehr schönen Künste,* Poetik und Hermeneutik 3 (Munich, 1968), 129–41. Koselleck (129) cites R. Aron, *Introduction à la philosophie de l'histoire.* (Paris, 1948), 20: "le hasard est le fondement de l'histoire."

22 Cf . E. Boutroux, *De la Contingence des lois de la nature* (1874), translated by F. Rothwell as *The Contingency of the Laws of Nature* (Chicago, 1916).

23 A. Malraux, *Anti-Memoirs,* trans. T Kilmartin (New York, 1968), 1.

24 For Montesquieu I follow *Oeuvres complètes,* ed. R. Caillois, vol. 2 (Paris, 1958), 396ff.

25 Cf. F. Schalk, ed., *Die französischen Moralisten,* vol. 1 (Munich, 1973), 203–57. Cf. the editor's introduction, esp. 32ff.

26 Cf. M. Hossenfelder, introduction to Sextus Empiricus, *Grundriss der pyrrhonischen Skepsis* (Frankfurt, 1968), esp. 42ff.

27 This thesis about freedom—a thesis that is only suggested here, and by no means adequately worked out—is an attempt to cross and to blend the idea of freedom that comes from the political doctrine of the separation of powers with the idea of freedom that comes from the philosophical doctrine of levels. Cf. N. Hartmann, *Ethik* (1925) (3rd printing, Berlin, 1949), 621–821, esp. 649–50: "The causal nexus and the surplus of determination." Cf. also N. Hartmann, *Der Aufbau der realen Welt* (1939) (3rd printing, Berlin, 1964), 493ff and 510ff, esp. 519: "A world in which there is freedom must have at least two levels. In a multileveled world, categorical freedom makes its appearance, between one level and the next, as a phenomenon accompanying the novelty in the higher type of determination. Then there are as many kinds of freedom as there are distances between levels. In a single-leveled world, wich one type of determination only, freedom is an impossibility." The doctrine of freedom that goes with the theory of levels is hierarchical, while the doctrine of freedom that goes with the separation of powers is, precisely, nonhierarchical. The cross between the two that is attempted here results in a dehierarchizing of the solution from the theory of levels and in an ontological broadening of the solution from the theory of the separation of powers. The outcome, I hope, is a doctrine of freedom as plurality of determination.

28 J. Ritter, "Über das Lachen" (1940), in J. Ritter, *Subjektivität, Sechs Aufsätze* (Frankfurt, 1974), 62–92. H. Plessner, "Lachen und Weinen. Eine Untersuchung der Grenzen menschlichen Verhaltens" (1941), in H. Plessner, *Gesammelte Schriften,* vol. 7 (Frankfurt, 1982), 201–387. Cf. O. Marquard, "Vernunft als Grenzreaktion," in H. Poser, ed., *Wandel des Vernunftbegriffs* (Freiburg and Munich, 1981), 107–33. See also O. Marquard, "Loriot lauréat. Laudatio auf Bernhard-Viktor von Bülow bei der Verleihung des Kasseler Literaturpreises für grotesken Humor 1985," in *Wilhelm-Busch-Jahrbuch 1985,* Mitteilungen der Wilhelm-Busch-Gesellschaft, no. 51 (Hannover, 1986), 81–85.

Translator's Note

a. The "opposition" Marquard refers to is, of course, opposition to the Nazi regime.

## A[1]

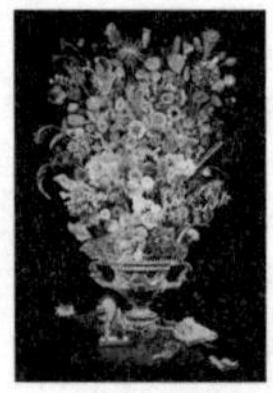

**The Absence of Nothingness**

2020
Bleistift, Buntstift und Grafitpaste auf Papier / Pencil, colored pencil, and graphite paste on paper
150 × 100 cm
Grafische Sammlung Albertina / Albertina Graphic Art Collection

## A[3]

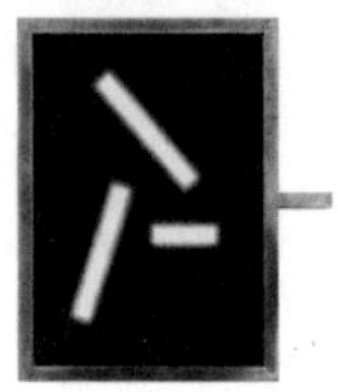

**Apologie des Zufälligen / Alphazerfall / In Defense of the Accidental / Alpha Decay**

2021
Pastell auf Papier / Pastel on paper
29,7 × 21 cm

## A[5]

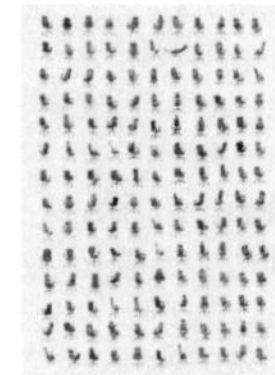

**Apologie des Zufälligen / But some are more equal / In Defense of the Accidental**

2020
Tusche und Bleistift auf Papier / Ink and pencil on paper
29,7 × 21 cm

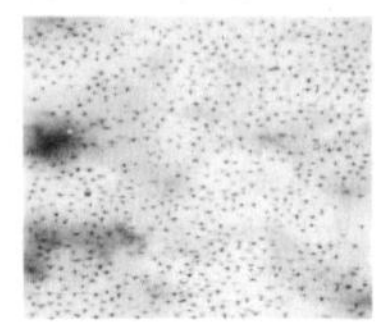

**O. T. / Drohnen No. 30 / Untitled / Drones No. 30**

2021/22
Bleistift, Buntstift und Grafitpulver auf Papier / Pencil, colored pencil, and graphite powder on paper
126 × 150 cm

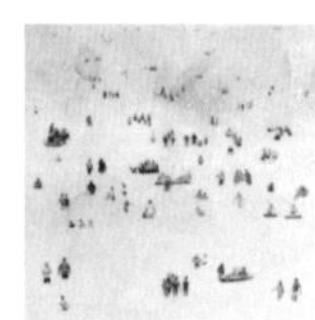

**wir schwimmen im wetter / we're swimming in weather**

2017
Tusche, Bleistift und Buntstift auf Papier / Ink, pencil, and colored pencil on paper
40 × 40 cm

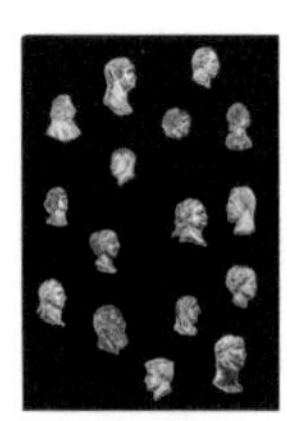

**Apologie des Zufälligen / Münzköpfe / In Defense of the Accidental / Coin Heads**

2018
Tusche und Bleistift auf Papier / Ink and pencil on paper
29,7 × 21 cm

## B[1]

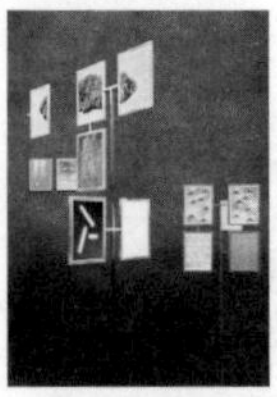

Zeichnungen der Serie *Apologie des Zufälligen*, installiert auf den *Trees of Knowledge* / Drawings from the series *In Defense of the Accidental*, installed on *Trees of Knowledge*
Installationsansicht / Installation view
Dimensionen variabel / Variable dimensions
© Edith Payer

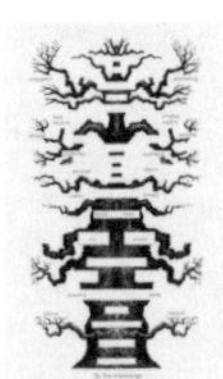

**Baum des Wissens / Collage, nach Ernst Haeckel, „Stammbaum des Menschen", 1874 / Tree of Knowledge / Collage, after Ernst Haeckel, "Genealogical Tree of the Human Being," 1874**
2022
Collage
29,7 × 21 cm

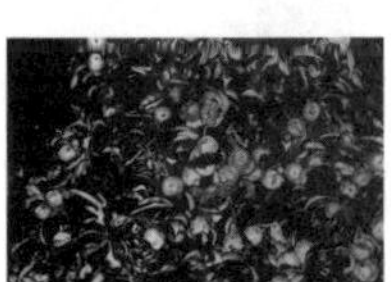

**Untitled / Tree of Knowledge**
2017/22
Bleistift, Grafitpulver und Tusche auf Papier / Pencil, graphite powder and ink on paper
50 × 70 cm

## B[2]

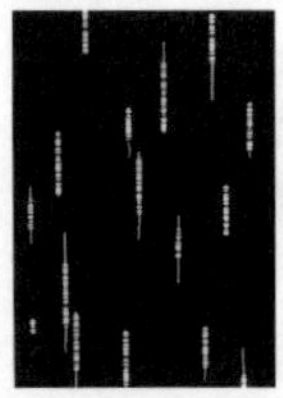

**Apologie des Zufälligen / Widerstand / In Defense of the Accidental / Resistance**
2022
Pastell auf Papier / Pastel on paper
29,7 × 21 cm

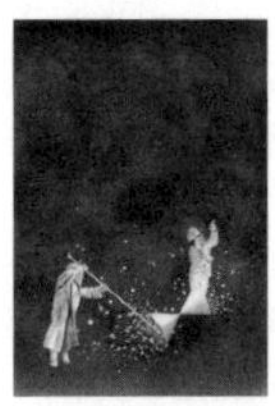

**Apologie des Zufälligen / Forscher No. 4 / In Defense of the Accidental / Explorers No. 4**
2021
Tusche, Bleistift, Buntstift und Grafitpulver auf Papier / Ink, pencil, colored pencil, and graphite powder on paper
29,7 × 21 cm

## B[3]

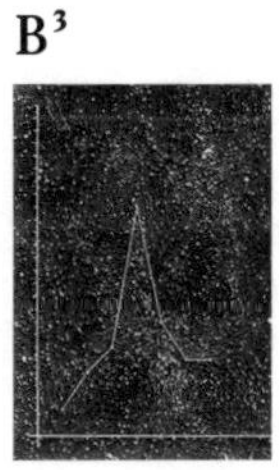

**Apologie des Zufälligen / Begriff / In Defense of the Accidental / Term**
2022
Pastell auf Papier / Pastel on paper
29,7 × 21 cm

## B[5]

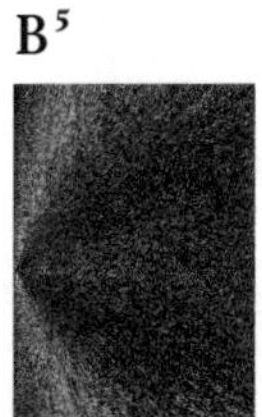

**O. T. / Untitled**
2022
Fotografie / Photograph
Dimensionen variabel / Variable dimensions

## D[2]

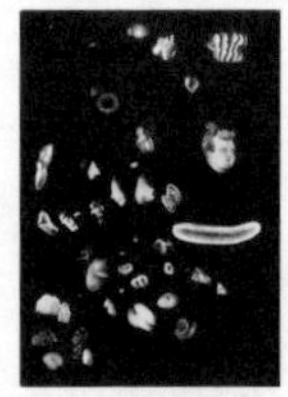

**Apologie des Zufälligen / Unverbundene Bestimmungen / In Defense of the Accidental / Unconnected Determinations**
2017
Tusche und Bleistift auf Papier / Ink and pencil on paper
29,7 × 21 cm

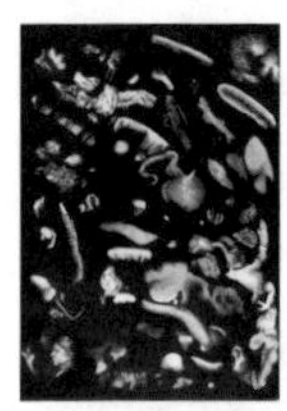

**Apologie des Zufälligen / Unverbundene Bestimmungen / In Defense of the Accidental / Unconnected Determinations**
2017
Tusche und Bleistift auf Papier / Ink and pencil on paper
29,7 × 21 cm

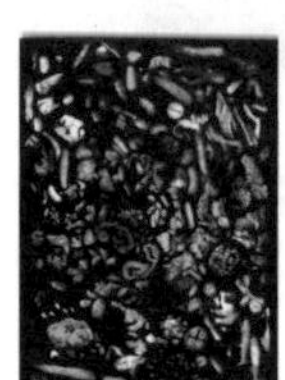

**Apologie des Zufälligen / Unverbundene Bestimmungen / In Defense of the Accidental / Unconnected Determinations**
2017
Tusche und Bleistift auf Papier / Ink and pencil on paper
29,7 × 21 cm

## D[3]

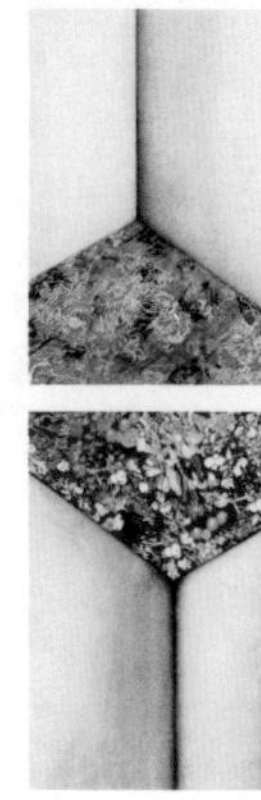

**O. T. / Untitled**
2018/22
Buntstift, Bleistift und Pastell auf Papier / Colored pencil, pencil, and pastel on paper
je 50 × 35 cm / 50 × 35 cm each

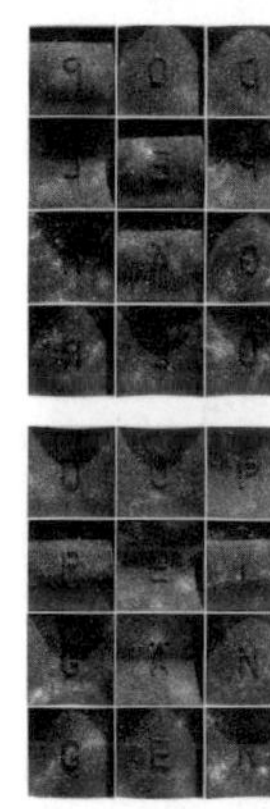

**Doppelgänger / Doppelgänger**
2018
Grafit- und Buntstiftspitzerreste auf Papier / Graphite- and colored-pencil granulate on paper
je 40 × 30 cm / 40 × 30 cm each

### E³

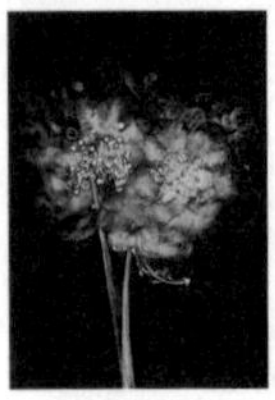

**Apologie des Zufälligen / botanische Studie / In Defense of the Accidental / Botanical study**

2022
Pastell und Bleistift auf Papier / Pastel and pencil on paper
29,7 × 21 cm

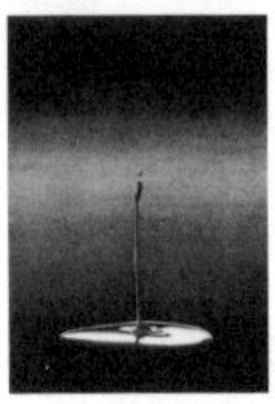

**Apologie des Zufälligen / Time after Contact / In Defense of the Accidental**

2022
Pastell und Bleistift auf Papier / Pastel and pencil on paper
29,7 × 21 cm

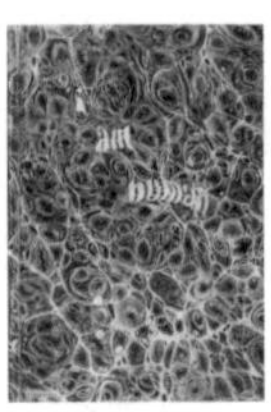

**Apologie des Zufälligen / Completely automated public Turing test to tell computers and humans apart / In Defense of the Accidental**

2022
Pastell und Bleistift auf Papier / Pastel and pencil on paper
29,7 × 21 cm

### E⁴



**Apologie des Zufälligen / Memoire, Raison, Imagination / In Defense of the Accidental**

2022
Tusche auf Papier / Ink on paper
29,7 × 21 cm

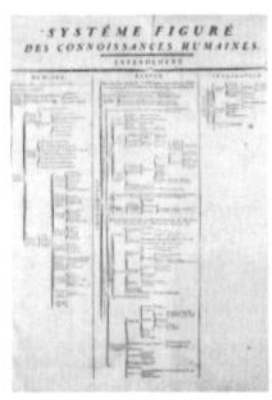

Jean d'Alembert, Denis Diderot, „Système figuré des connaissances humaines", in *Encyclopédie, ou dictionnaire raisonné des sciences, des arts et des métiers,* hrsg. / ed. Denis Diderot, Jean Le Rond d'Alembert gemeinfrei / Public domain

### F¹

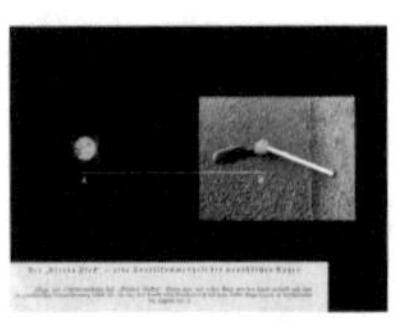

**O. T. / Untitled**

2021/22
Collage / Collage
Dimensionen variabel / Variable dimensions

### G¹

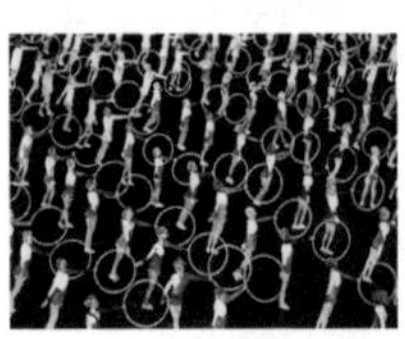

**O. T. / Arirang / Untitled**

2019/20
Tusche, Bleistift, Acrylfarbe und Grafitpulver auf Papier / Ink, pencil, acrylic paint, and graphite powder on paper
50 × 70 cm

### I¹

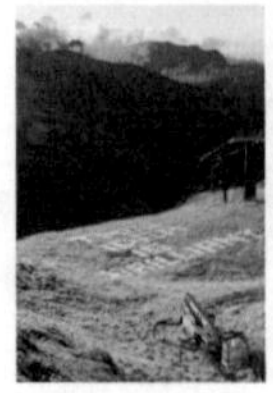

**This idea is brilliant**

2020
Fotografie / Photograph
Dimensionen variabel / Variable dimensions

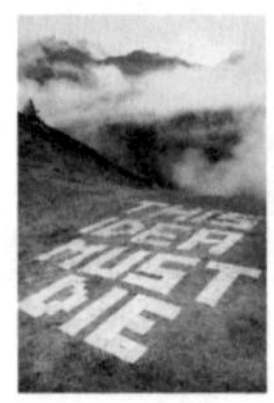

**This idea must die**

2020
Fotografie / Photograph
Dimensionen variabel / Variable dimensions

### I³

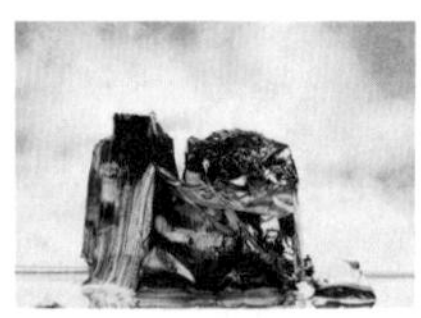

**Treibgut / No. 3 / Flotsam / No. 3**

2018
Bleistift und Grafitpulver auf Papier / Pencil and graphite powder on paper
59,4 × 84 cm

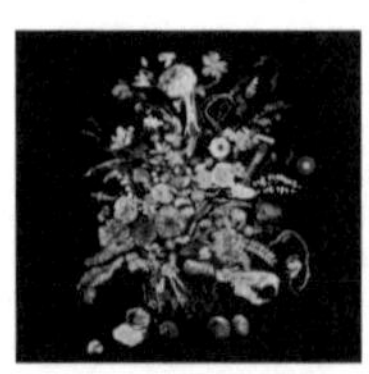

**O. T. / cAMP / Untitled**

2019
Bleistift, Buntstift und Grafitpaste auf Papier / Pencil, colored pencil, and graphite paste on paper
89,1 × 84 cm

### I⁴

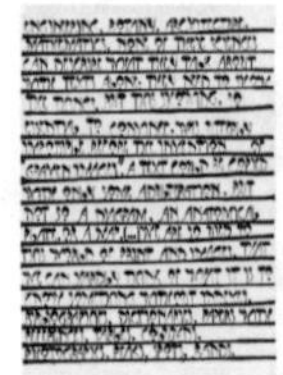

**Apologie des Zufälligen / Latour on Inscriptions / In Defense of the Accidental**

2020
Tusche auf Papier / Ink on paper
29,7 × 21 cm

### I⁵

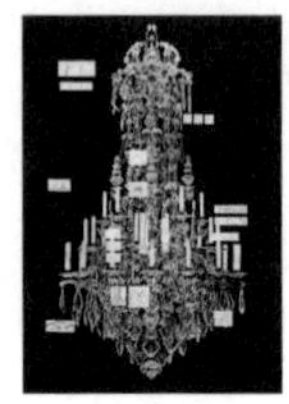

**On Inscriptions / Tableau No. 5**

2022
Radierung mit Grafitpaste und Bleistift auf Papier / Etching with graphite paste, and pencil on paper
100 × 70 cm

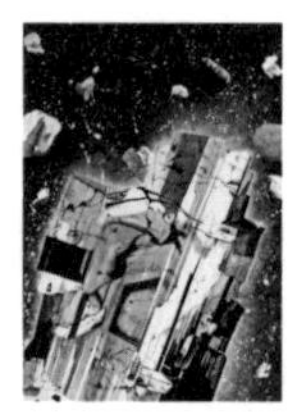

**On Inscriptions / Tableau No. 3**

2021
Tusche, Buntstift, Pastell und Bleistift auf Papier / Ink, colored pencil, pastel, and pencil on paper
100 × 70 cm

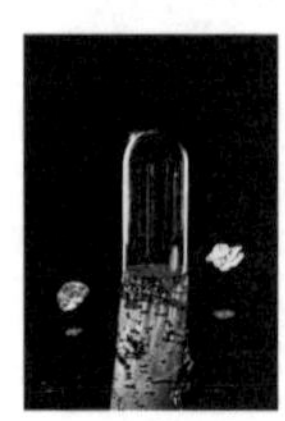

**On Inscriptions / Tableau No. 4**

2022
Pastell auf Papier / Pastel on paper
100 × 70 cm

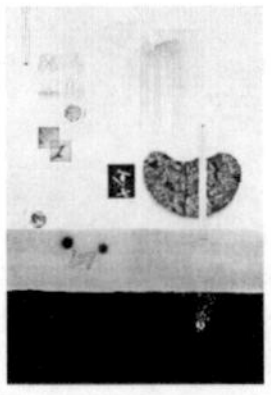

**On Inscriptions / Tableau No. 1**

2021
Radierung mit Tusche, Buntstift, Grafitpulver, Pastell, Bleistift und Fineliner auf Papier / Etching with ink, colored pencil, graphite powder, pastel, pencil, and fineliner on paper
100 × 70 cm

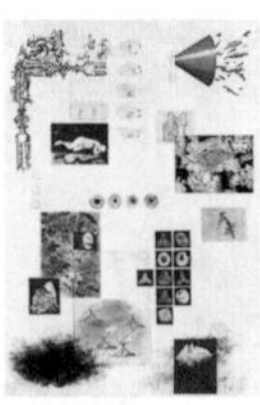

**On Inscriptions / Tableau No. 6**

2021/22
Radierung mit Tusche, Buntstift, Grafitpulver, Grafitpaste, Pastell und Bleistift auf Papier/ Etching with ink, pencil, graphite powder, graphite putty, pastel, and pencil on paper
100 × 70 cm

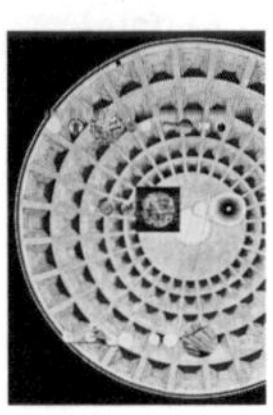

**On Inscriptions / Tableau No. 2**

2021
Prägungen mit Bleistift, Buntstift, Grafitpulver und Pastell auf Papier / Embossings with pencil, colored pencil, graphite powder, and pastel on paper
100 × 70 cm

## L[1]

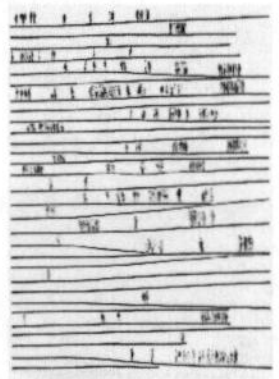

**Linearperspektive / The intimacy of waiting 1 / Linear Perspective**

2020
Tusche, Buntstift und Bleistift auf Papier /
Ink, colored pencil, and pencil on paper
80 × 60 cm

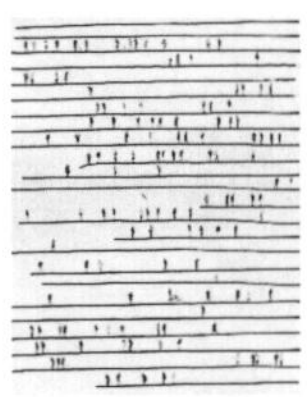

**Linearperspektive / The intimacy of waiting 2 / Linear Perspective**

2022
Tusche, Buntstift und Bleistift auf Papier /
Ink, colored pencil, and pencil on paper
90 × 70 cm

## M[1]

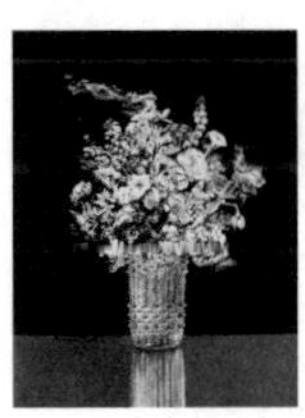

**O. T. / Stillleben / Untitled / Still Life**

2021
Pastell auf Papier /
Pastel on paper
140 × 100 cm
Lentos Kunstsammlung / Lentos Art Collectionm

## M[2]

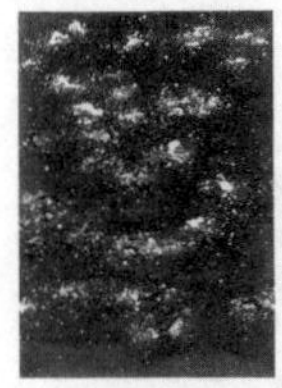

**Apologie des Zufälligen / Schwimmer / In Defense of the Accidental / Swimmer**

2017
Tusche, Buntstift und Bleistift auf Papier /
Ink, colored pencil, and pencil on paper
29,7 × 21 cm

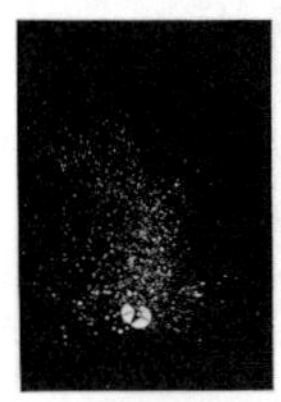

**Apologie des Zufälligen / +– / In Defense of the Accidental**

2017
Tusche und Bleistift auf Papier /
Ink and pencil on paper
29,7 × 21 cm

## N[1]

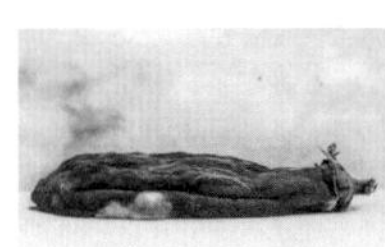

**O. T. / Melanzani / Untitled / Eggplant**

2017
Fotografie / Photograph
Dimensionen variabel /
Variable dimensions

## P[1]

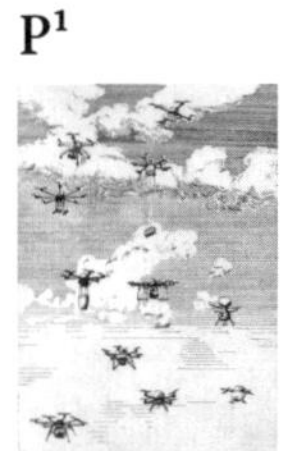

**Last things**

2020
Radierung / Etching
29,7 × 21 cm

## S[1]

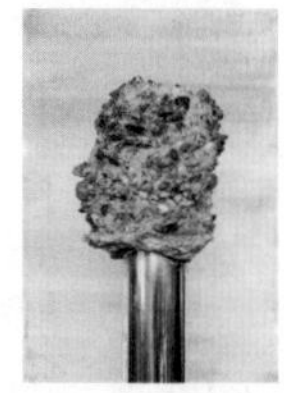

**O. T. / Subjektposition No. 5 / Untitled / Subject Position No. 5**

2022
Fotografie/ Photograph
Dimensionen variabel /
Variable dimensions

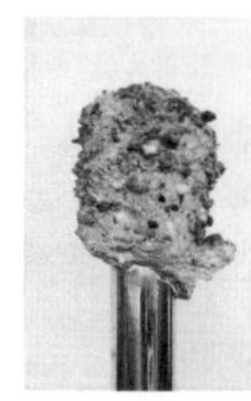

**O. T. / Subjektposition No. 2 / Untitled / Subject Position No. 2**

2022
Fotografie/ Photograph
Dimensionen variabel /
Variable dimensions

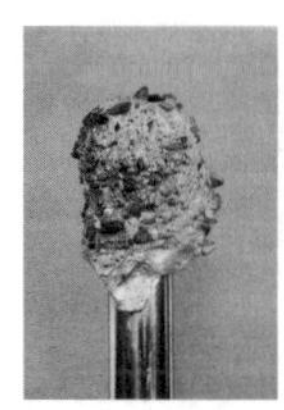

**O. T. / Subjektposition No. 1 / Untitled / Subject Position No. 1**

2022
Fotografie / Photograph
Dimensionen variabel /
Variable dimensions

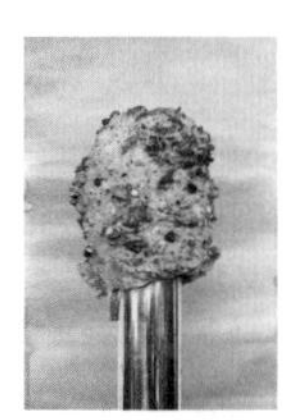

**O. T. / Subjektposition No. 3 / Untitled / Subject Position No. 3**

2022
Fotografie/ Photograph
Dimensionen variabel /
Variable dimensions

### T$^1$

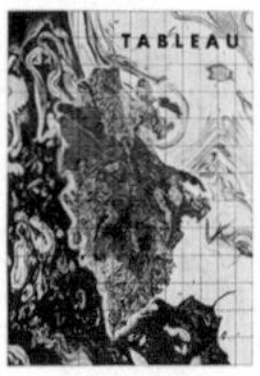


**O. T. / Tableau No. 1 / Untitled / Tableau No.1**

2022
Buntstift, Bleistift, Tusche und Pastell auf Papier / Colored pencil, pencil, ink, and pastel on paper
41 × 30 cm

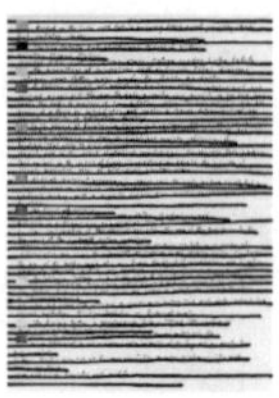

**O. T. / Tableau No. 2 Untitled / Tableau No. 2**

2022
Tusche auf Papier / Ink on paper
41 × 30 cm

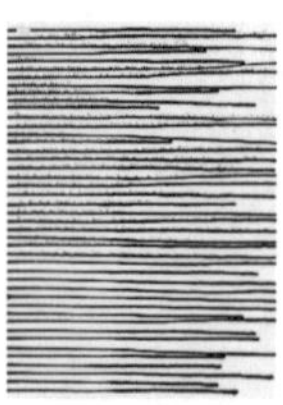

**O. T. / Tableau No. 3 / Untitled / Tableau No. 3**

2022
Tusche auf Papier / Ink on paper
41 × 30 cm

### T$^2$

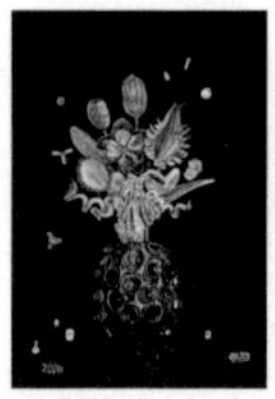

**The Absence of Nothingness / Still Life with Seeds**

2019
Bleistift, Buntstift und Grafitpaste auf Papier / Pencil, colored pencil, and graphite paste on paper
59,7 × 42 cm

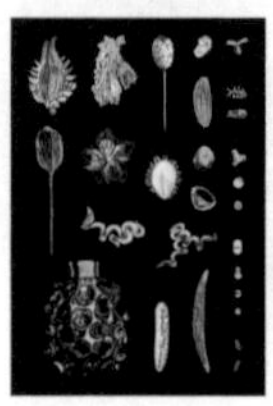

**The Absence of Nothingness subsp.**

2022
Bleistift, Buntstift und Grafitpaste auf Papier / Pencil, colored pencil, and graphite paste on paper
59,7 × 42 cm

### U$^1$

**Paralleluniversum No. 1 / Parallel Universe No. 1**

2018
Tusche auf Papier / Ink on paper
100 × 70 cm

### W$^1$

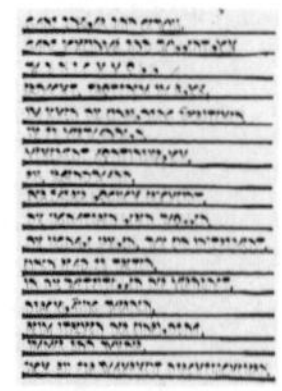

**Apologie des Zufälligen / Truth / In Defense of the Accidental**

2022
Tusche auf Papier / Ink on paper
29,7 × 21 cm

### W$^3$

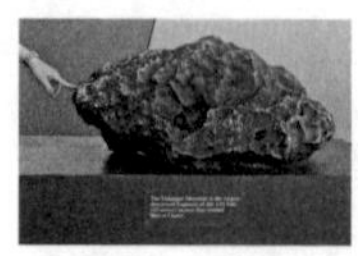

© Mario R. Duran Ortiz

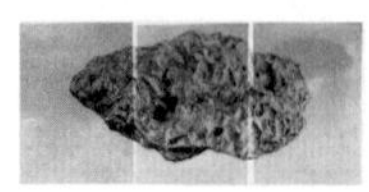

**Apologie des Zufälligen / Doppelgänger No. 1 / In Defense of the Accidental / Doppelgänger No. 1**

2017
Tusche und Bleistift auf Papier / Ink and pencil on paper

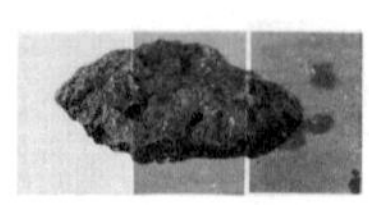

**Apologie des Zufälligen / Doppelgänger No. 4 / In Defense of the Accidental / Doppelgänger No. 4**

2017
Tusche und Bleistift auf Papier / Ink and pencil on paper
29, 7 × 63 cm
Sammlung ZF Kunst-stiftung

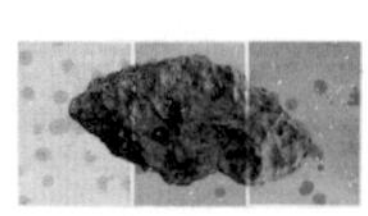

**Apologie des Zufälligen / Doppelgänger No. 3 / In Defense of the Accidental / Doppelgänger No. 3**

2017
Tusche und Bleistift auf Papier / Ink and pencil on paper
29, 7 × 63 cm

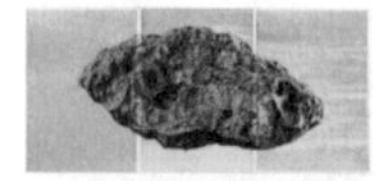

**Apologie des Zufälligen / Doppelgänger No. 5 / In Defense of the Accidental / Doppelgänger No. 5**

2017
Tusche und Bleistift auf Papier / Ink and pencil on paper
29, 7 × 63 cm

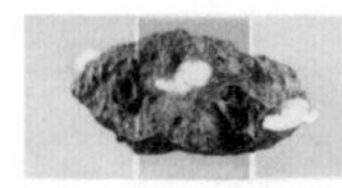

**Apologie des Zufälligen / Doppelgänger No. 6 / In Defense of the Accidental / Doppelgänger No. 6**

2017
Tusche und Bleistift auf Papier / Ink and pencil on paper
29, 7 × 63 cm
Sammlung ZF Kunst-stiftung

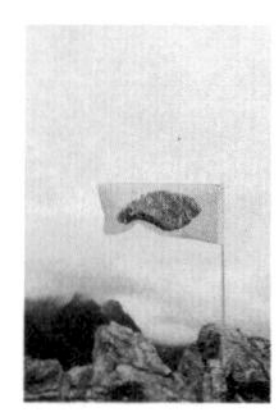

**O. T. / Untitled**

2020
Fotografie / Photograph
Dimensionen variabel / Variable dimensions

## W[4]

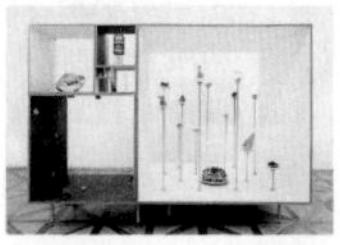
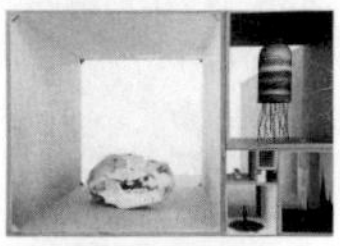
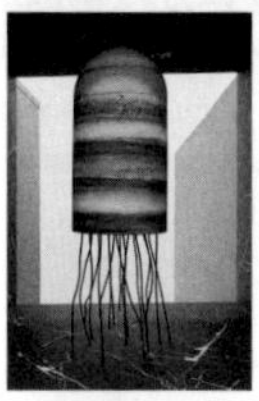
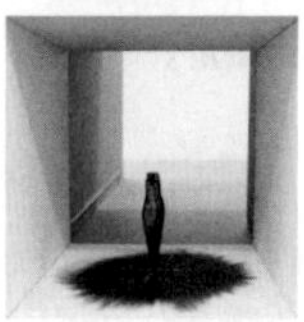
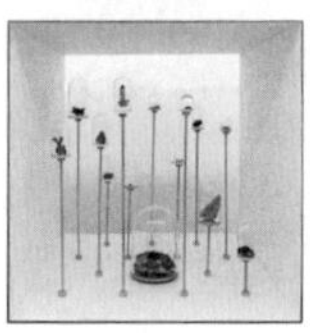

**Fibonacci-Schrank / Fibonacci Cabinet**

2020
Temporäre Installation mit Objekten und Zeichnungen von Payer Gabriel und Leihgaben der geologischen Sammlung des Landesmuseums Kärnten, Galerie 3, Klagenfurt / Temporary installation with objects and drawings by Payer Gabriel and loans from the geological collection of the State Museum of Carinthia
144 × 288 × 144 cm

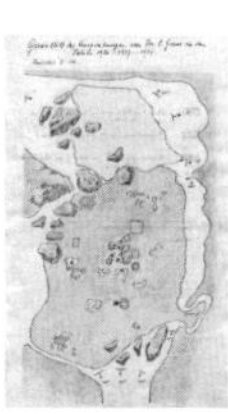

Josef C. Gross, Grabungsprotokoll Uschowa-Höhle, Slowenien, Zeichnung, 1926–28
© Geologische Sammlung des Landesmuseums Kärnten / Excavation protocol, Uschowa Cave, Slovenia, drawings, 1926–28, © Geological collection of the State Museum of Carinthia

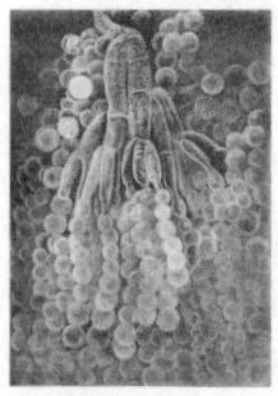

**Apologie des Zufälligen**

2022
Pastell auf Papier / Pastel on paper
29,7 × 21 cm

**Pillars of Creation**

2017
Grafitpulver und Bleistift auf Papier / Graphite powder and pencil on paper
100 × 70 cm

**Abwesenheit von Nichts**
Payer, Micha.
Wortbild. 2021.

**Angst, epistemische**
Daston, Lorraine, und Galison, Peter. *Objektivität.* Übersetzt von Christa Krüger. Frankfurt am Main: Suhrkamp, 2017.

**Denken**
Braidotti, Rosi. *Posthuman Knowledge.* Cambridge: Polity, 2019.
Übersetzt von Wilfried Prantner.

**Differenz**
Payer, Micha. 2022.

LITERATUR
Braidotti, Rosi. *Posthumanismus: Leben jenseits des Menschen.* Frankfur am Main: Campus Verlag, 2014.
Chambers, Ephraim. *Cyclopædia: or, An Universal Dictionary of Arts and Sciences.* London, 1741.
Deleuze, Gilles. *Differenz und Wiederholung.* Übersetzt von Joseph Vogl. München: Wilhelm Fink, 2007.
Foucault, Michel. „Die Ordnung der Dinge: Eine Archäologie der Humanwissenschaften". In *Michel Foucault: Die Hauptwerke.* Übers. von Ulrich Köppen. Frankfurt am Main: Suhrkamp, 2016.
Prechtl, Peter und Burkard, Franz-Peter, Herausgeber. *Metzler Philosophie Lexikon: Begriffe und Definitionen.* Stuttgart, Weimar: Metzler, 1999.
Somers-Hall, Henry. *Deleuze's Difference and Repetition.* Edinburgh: Edinburgh University Press, 2013

**Enzyklopädie**
Payer, Micha. 2022.

LITERATUR
Bourdieu, Pierre. *Die feinen Unterschiede: Kritik der gesellschaftlichen Urteilskraft.* Frankfurt am Main: Suhrkamp, 2001.
Burke, Peter. *Papier und Marktgeschrei: Die Geburt der Wissensgesellschaft.* Berlin: Wagenbach, 2001.
Burke, Peter. *Polymath: A Cultural History from Leonardo da Vinci to Susan Sontag.* New Haven und London: Yale University Press, 2020.
Cajori, Florian. *A History of Mathematical Notations.* New York: Dover Publications, 1993.
Dudenredaktion, Herausgeber. *Das Herkunftswörterbuch. Etymologie der deutschen Sprache.* Mannheim, Leipzig, Wien, Zürich: 2007.
Greene, Brian. *Die verborgene Wirklichkeit: Paralleluniversen und die Gesetze des Kosmos.* München: Siedler, 2012.
Schneider, Ulrich Johannes. *Die Erfindung des allgemeinen Wissens: Enzyklopädisches Schreiben im Zeitalter der Aufklärung.* Berlin: Akademieverlag, 2013.
Schwanitz, Dietrich. *Bildung: Alles, was man wissen muß.* Frankfurt am Main: Eichborn, 1999.
Taschwer, Klaus. "Vom Kosmos zur Wunderwelt – Über Populärwissenschaftliche Magazine einst und jetzt." In *Öffentliche Wissenschaft: Neue Perspektiven der Vermittlung in der wissenschaftlichen Weiterbildung.* Herausgegeben von Peter Faulstich. Bielefeld: Transcript, 2006.

**Enzyklopädie**
Ein Textbeitrag von Khadija von Zinnenburg Carroll, 2022.
Übersetzt von Wilfried Prantner.

**Episteme**
Payer, Micha. 2022.

LITERATUR
Cassin, Barbara, Herausgeber. *Dictionary of Untranslatables: A Philosophical Lexicon.* Übersetzt von Steven Rendall, Christian Hubert, Jeffrey Mehlman, Nathanael Stein und Michael Syrotinski. Übersetzung herausgegeben von Emily Apter, Jacques Lezra und Michael Wood. Princeton, Oxford: Princeton University Press, 2014.
Braidotti, Rosi. *Posthumanismus: Leben jenseits des Menschen.* Übersetzt von Thomas Laugstien. Frankfurt am Main: Campus Verlag, 2014.

**Absence of Nothingness**
Payer, Micha. Word Picture. 2021.
Translated by Michael Turnbull.

**Epistemic Fear**
Daston, Lorraine, and Peter Galison. Peter *Objectivity.* New York: Zone Books, 2007.

**Thinking**
Braidotti, Rosi. *Posthuman Knowledge.* Cambridge: Polity, 2019.

**Difference**
Payer, Micha. 2022.
Translated by Michael Turnbull.

LITERATURE
Braidotti, Rosi. *The Posthuman.* Cambridge: Polity, 2013.
Braidotti, Rosi. *Posthuman Knowledge.* Cambridge: Polity, 2019.
Chambers, Ephraim. *Cyclopædia: Or, An Universal Dictionary of Arts and Sciences.* London, 1741.
Deleuze, Gilles. *Difference and Repetition.* Translated by Paul Patton. London: Continuum, 2001.
Foucault, Michel. *The Order of Things: An Archaeology of the Human Sciences.* New York: Pantheon Books, 1971.
*Internet Encyclopedia of Philosophy*: https://iep.utm.edu.
Somers-Hall, Henry. *Deleuze's Difference and Repetition.* Edinburgh: Edinburgh University Press, 2013.

**Encyclopedia**
Payer, Micha. 2022.
Translated by Michael Turnbull.

LITERATURE
Bourdieu, Pierre. *Distinction: A Social Critique of Judgement and Taste.* Translated by Richard Nice. Cambridge: Harvard University Press, 1984.
Burke, Peter. *Papier und Marktgeschrei: Die Geburt der Wissensgesellschaft.* Berlin: Wagenbach, 2001.
Burke, Peter. *Polymath: A Cultural History from Leonardo da Vinci to Susan Sontag.* New Haven and London: Yale University Press, 2020.
Cajori, Florian. *A History of Mathematical Notations.* New York: Dover Publications, 1993.
Greene, Brian. *The Hidden Reality.* New York: Alfred A. Knopf, 2011.
*The New Oxford Dictionary of English.* Edited by Judy Pearsall. Oxford: Oxford University Press, 1998.
Schneider, Ulrich Johannes. *Die Erfindung des allgemeinen Wissens: Enzyklopädisches Schreiben im Zeitalter der Aufklärung.* Berlin: Akademieverlag, 2013.
Schwanitz, Dietrich. *Bildung: Alles, was man wissen muß.* Frankfurt am Main: Eichborn, 1999.
Taschwer, Klaus. "Vom Kosmos zur Wunderwelt – Über Populärwissenschaftliche Magazine einst und jetzt." In *Öffentliche Wissenschaft: Neue Perspektiven der Vermittlung in der wissenschaftlichen Weiterbildung.* Edited by Peter Faulstich. Bielefeld: Transcript, 2006.

**Encyclopedia**
A contribution by Khadija von Zinnenburg Carroll, 2022.

**Episteme**
Payer, Micha. 2022.
Translated by Michael Turnbull.

LITERATURE
Cassin, Barbara, editor. *Dictionary of Untranslatables: A Philosophical Lexicon.* Translated by Steven Rendall, Christian Hubert, Jeffrey Mehlman, Nathanael Stein, and Michael Syrotinski. Translation edited by Emily Apter, Jacques Lezra, and Michael Wood. Princeton, Oxford: Princeton University Press, 2014.
Braidotti, Rosi. *The Posthuman.* Cambridge: Polity Press, 2013.
Braidotti, Rosi. *Posthuman Knowledge.* Cambridge: Polity, 2019.

Braidotti, Rosi. *Posthuman Knowledge*. Cambridge: Polity, 2019.

Daston, Lorraine, und Galison, Peter. *Objektivität.* Übersetzt von Christa Krüger. Frankfurt am Main: Suhrkamp, 2017.

Foucault, Michel. „Die Ordnung der Dinge: Eine Archäologie der Humanwissenschaften." In *Michel Foucault: Die Hauptwerke.* Übersetzt von Ulrich Köppen. Frankfurt am Main: Suhrkamp, 2016.

Graczyk, Annette. *Das literarische Tableau zwischen Kunst und Wissenschaft.* München: Fink, 2004.

Kemp, Martin. *Bilderwissen: Die Anschaulichkeit naturwissenschaftlicher Phänomene.* Übersetzt von Jürgen Blasius. Köln: DuMont, 2003.

Latour, Bruno. „How to Be Iconophilic in Art, Science and Religion?" In *Picturing Science, Producing Art*, herausgegeben von Carrie Jones, und Peter Galison. London: Routledge, 1998.

Mitchell, W. J. T. *Bildtheorie*, herausgegeben von Gustav Frank. Übersetzt von Jürgen Blasius. Frankfurt am Main: Suhrkamp, 2008.

Prechtl, Peter und Burkard, Franz-Peter, Herausgeber. *Metzler Philosophie Lexikon: Begriffe und Definitionen*. Stuttgart, Weimar: Metzler, 1999.

Rehfus, Wulff D, Herausgeber. *Handwörterbuch Philosophie.* Göttingen: Vandenhoeck & Ruprecht, 2003.

Simon, Gérard. „Knowledge, savoir, and epistêmê.". In *Dictionary of Untranslatables: A Philosophical Lexicon*, herausgegeben von Barbara Cassin. Übersetzt von Steven Rendall, Christian Hubert, Jeffrey Mehlman, Nathanael Stein, und Michael Syrotinski. Übersetzung herausgegeben von Emily Apter, Jacques Lezra, und Michael Wood. Princeton, Oxford: Princeton University Press, 2014.

Wolfe, Cary. *What Is Posthumanism?* Minneapolis, London: University of Minnesota Press, 2010.

**Epistemologie, visuelle**

Payer, Micha. 2022.

LITERATUR

Arnheim, Rudolf. *Visual Thinking:* Berkeley, Los Angeles: University of California Press, 1979.

Dudenredaktion, Herausgeber. *Das Herkunftswörterbuch. Etymologie der deutschen Sprache.* Mannheim, Leipzig, Wien, Zürich: 2007.

Drucker, Johanna. *Graphesis: Visual Forms of Knowledge Production.* Cambridge, Massachusetts: Harvard University Press, 2014.

Drucker, Johanna. *Visualization and Interpretation: Humanistic Approaches to Display.* Cambridge, Massachusetts: MIT Press, 2020.

Latour, Bruno. „Visualisation and Cognition: Drawing Things Together." In *Knowledge and Society: Studies in the Sociology of Culture Past and Present*, herausgegeben von H. Kuklick. Jai Press, vol. 6.

Schwarte, Ludger. *Pikturale Evidenz: Zur Wahrheitsfähigkeit der Bilder.* Paderborn: Wilhelm Fink, 2015.

**Gewalt, epistemische**

Payer, Micha. 2022.

LITERATUR

Brunner, Claudia. *Epistemische Gewalt: Wissen und Herrschaft in der kolonialen Moderne.* Bielefeld: Transcript, 2020.

Foucault, Michel. *Wahnsinn und Gesellschaft: Eine Geschichte des Wahns im Zeitalter der Vernunft.* Übersetzt von Ulrich Köppen. Frankfurt am Main: Suhrkamp, 2013.

Kracauer, Siegfried. *Das Ornament der Masse.* Frankfurt am Main: Suhrkamp, 1977.

Reckwitz, Andreas. *Das hybride Subjekt: Eine Theorie der Subjektkulturen von der bürgerlichen Moderne zur Postmoderne.* Berlin: Suhrkamp, 2020.

Daston, Lorraine, and Peter Galison. *Objectivity.* New York: Zone Books, 2007.

Foucault, Michel. *The Order of Things: An Archaeology of the Human Sciences.* New York: Pantheon Books, 1971.

Graczyk, Annette. *Das literarische Tableau zwischen Kunst und Wissenschaft.* Munich: Fink, 2004.

Kemp, Martin. *Visualizations: The Nature Book of Art and Science.* Berkeley, Los Angeles: University of California Press, 2000.

Latour, Bruno. "How to Be Iconophilic in Art, Science and Religion?" In *Picturing Science, Producing Art.* Edited by Carrie Jones and Peter Galison. London: Routledge, 1998.

Mitchell, W. J. T. *Picture Theory: Essays on Verbal and Visual Representation.* Chicago: University of Chicago Press, 1994.

Prechtl, Peter, and Franz-Peter Burkard, editors. *Metzler Philosophie Lexikon: Begriffe und Definitionen.* Stuttgart, Weimar: Metzler, 1999.

Rehfus, Wulff D, editor. *Handwörterbuch Philosophie.* Göttingen: Vandenhoeck & Ruprecht, 2003.

Simon, Gérard. "Knowledge, savoir, and epistêmê." In *Dictionary of Untranslatables: A Philosophical Lexicon.* Edited by Barbara Cassin. Translated by Steven Rendall, Christian Hubert, Jeffrey Mehlman, Nathanael Stein, and Michael Syrotinski. Translation edited by Emily Apter, Jacques Lezra, and Michael Wood. Princeton, Oxford: Princeton University Press, 2014.

Wolfe, Cary. *What Is Posthumanism?* Minneapolis, London: University of Minnesota Press, 2010.

**Visual Epistemology**

Payer, Micha. 2022. Translated by Michael Turnbull.

LITERATURE

Arnheim, Rudolf. *Visual Thinking.* Berkeley, Los Angeles: University of California Press, 1979.

Drucker, Johanna. *Graphesis: Visual Forms of Knowledge Production.* Cambridge, Massachusetts: Harvard University Press, 2014.

Drucker, Johanna. *Visualization and Interpretation: Humanistic Approaches to Display.* Cambridge, Massachusetts: MIT Press, 2020.

Latour, Bruno. "Visualisation and Cognition: Drawing Things Together." In *Knowledge and Society: Studies in the Sociology of Culture Past and Present.* Vol. 6. Edited by H. Kuklick. Stanford, Connecticut: Jai Press, 1986.

*The New Oxford Dictionary of English*. Edited by Judy Pearsall. Oxford: Oxford University Press, 1998.

Schwarte, Ludger. *Pikturale Evidenz: Zur Wahrheitsfähigkeit der Bilder.* Paderborn: Wilhelm Fink, 2015.

**Epistemic Violence**

Payer, Micha. 2022. Translated by Michael Turnbull.

LITERATURE

Brunner, Claudia. *Epistemische Gewalt: Wissen und Herrschaft in der kolonialen Moderne.* Bielefeld: Transcript, 2020.

Foucault, Michel. *History of Madness.* Translated by Jonathan Murphy and Jean Khalfa. New York: Routledge, 2006.

Kracauer, Siegfried. *The Mass Ornament. Weimar Essays.* Translated and edited by Thomas Y. Levin. Cambridge, Massachusetts: Harvard University Press, 1995.

Spivak, Gayatri Chakravorty. *Can the Subaltern Speak? Postkolonialität und Subalterne Artikulation.* Übersetzt von Alexander Joskowicz und Stefan Nowotny. Wien, Berlin: Turia + Kant, 2020.

**Idiot**
Payer, Micha. 2022.

LITERATUR
Deleuze, Gilles. *Differenz und Wiederholung.* Übersetzt von Joseph Vogl. München: Wilhelm Fink, 2007.
Dudenredaktion, Herausgeber. *Das Herkunftswörterbuch: Etymologie der deutschen Sprache.* Mannheim, Leipzig, Wien, Zürich: 2007.
Feyerabend, Paul. *Wider den Methodenzwang.* Frankfurt am Main: Suhrkamp, 2018.
Foucault, Michel. „Die Ordnung der Dinge: Eine Archäologie der Humanwissenschaften." In *Michel Foucault: Die Hauptwerke.* Übersetzt von Ulrich Köppen. Frankfurt am Main: Suhrkamp, 2008.
Sommer, Andreas Urs. „Kurze Geistesgeschichte des Idioten." In *Zeitschrift für Ideengeschichte,* Heft IV/2, Sommer 2010, herausgegeben von Warren Breckman, Jost Philipp Klenner, Wolfert von Rahden. München: C. H. Beck, 2010.

**Idiot**
Kapitel „Idiotismus" in: Han, Byung-Chul. *Psychopolitik: Neoliberalismus und die neuen Machttechniken.* Frankfurt am Main: Fischer, 2016.

**Ikonografie des Beweises**
Latour, Bruno. „Drawing Things Together: Die Macht der unveränderlich mobilen Elemente." In *ANThology: Ein einführendes Handbuch zur Akteur-Netzwerk-Theorie,* herausgegeben von Andréa Belliger, und David J. Krieger. Bielefeld: Transcript, 2006.

**Inskription**
Latour, Bruno. „Drawing Things Together: Die Macht der unveränderlich mobilen Elemente." In *ANThology: Ein einführendes Handbuch zur Akteur-Netzwerk-Theorie,* herausgegeben von Andréa Belliger, und D. J. Krieger. Bielefeld: Transcript, 2006.
In gekürzter Fassung in *Grundlagentexte der Medienkultur: Ein Reader,* herausgeben von Andreas Ziemann. Wiesbaden: Springer, 2019.

**Moderne, flüchtige**
Bauman, Zygmunt. *Flüchtige Moderne.* Übersetzt von Reinhard Kreissl. Frankfurt am Main, Suhrkamp, 2006.

**Neologismus**
Payer, Micha. 2022.
Übersetzt von Wilfried Prantner.

LITERATUR
Braidotti, Rosi. *Posthuman Knowledge.* Cambridge: Polity, 2019.

**Paradoxa**
Carl von Linné. *Systema Naturæ.* Erste Ausgabe. Leyden: Theodor Haak. Ex typographia Joannis Wilhelm de Groot, 1735.
Carl von Linné. *Naturae Curiosorum.* Stockholm: Gottfried Kiesewetter, 1740.
Übersetzt vom Lateinischen ins Deutsche von Doris Vickers.

**Verfremdung**
Braidotti, Rosi. *Posthuman Knowledge.* Cambridge: Polity, 2019.
Übersetzt von Wilfried Prantner.

**Vergilbung**
Payer, Micha. 2021.

**Vergilbung**
*DIN 6167: Beschreibung der Vergilbung von nahezu weißen oder nahezu farblosen Materialien.* Berlin: Beuth, 1980.

**Wahrheit**
Payer, Micha. 2020.

**Wende**
Payer, Micha. 2022.
Übersetzt von Wilfried Prantner.

Reckwitz, Andreas. *Das hybride Subjekt: Eine Theorie der Subjektkulturen von der bürgerlichen Moderne zur Postmoderne.* Berlin: Suhrkamp, 2020.
Spivak, Gayatri Chakravorty. *Can the Subaltern Speak? Reflections on the History of an Idea.* Edited by Rosalind C. Morris. New York: Columbia University Press, 2010.

**Idiot**
Payer, Micha. 2022.
Translated by Michael Turnbull.

LITERATURE
Deleuze, Gilles. *Difference and Repetition.* Translated by Paul Patton. New York: Columbia University Press, 1994.
Feyerabend, Paul. *Against Method.* London: Verso, 1993.
Foucault, Michel. *The Order of Things: An Archaeology of the Human Sciences.* New York: Vintage, 1994.
*Das Herkunftswörterbuch: Etymologie der deutschen Sprache.* Mannheim, Leipzig, Vienna, Zurich: Duden Editors, 2007.
Sommer, Andreas Urs. "Kurze Geistesgeschichte des Idioten." In *Zeitschrift für Ideengeschichte.* No. IV/2, summer 2010. Edited by Warren Breckman, Jost Philipp Klenner, Wolfert von Rahden. Munich: C. H. Beck, 2010.

**Idiot**
Chapter "Idiotism." In Han, Byung-Chul. *Psychopolitics: Neoliberalism and new Technologies of Power.* Translated by Erik Butler. London, New York: Verso, 2017.

**Iconography of Proof**
Latour, Bruno. "Visualisation and Cognition: Drawing Things Together." In *Knowledge and Society: Studies in the Sociology of Culture Past and Present.* Vol. 6. Edited by H. Kuklick. Stanford, Connecticut: Jai Press, 1986.

**Inscription**
Latour, Bruno. "Visualisation and Cognition: Drawing Things Together." In *Knowledge and Society: Studies in the Sociology of Culture Past and Present.* Vol. 6. Edited by H. Kuklick. Stanford, Connecticut: Jai Press, 1986.

**Liquid Modernity**
Bauman, Zygmunt. *Liquid Modernity.* Cambridge: Polity Press, 2006.

**Neologism**
Payer, Micha. 2022.

LITERATURE
Braidotti, Rosi. *Posthuman Knowledge.* Cambridge: Polity, 2019.

**Paradoxes**
Carl von Linné. *Systema Naturæ.* 1st edition. Leyden: Theodor Haak. Ex typographia Joannis Wilhelm de Groot, 1735.
Carl von Linné. *Naturae Curiosorum.* Stockholm: Gottfried Kiesewetter, 1740.
Translated from German into English by Michael Turnbull.

**Defamiliarization**
Braidotti, Rosi. *Posthuman Knowledge.* Cambridge: Polity, 2019.

**Yellowing**
Payer, Micha. 2021.
Translated by Michael Turnbull.

**Yellowing**
*DIN 6167: Description of the yellowness of near-white or near-colorless materials.* Berlin: Beuth, 1980.

**Truth**
Payer, Micha. 2020.
Translated by Michael Turnbull.

**Turn**
Payer, Micha. 2022.

**Word**
Payer, Micha. 2022.
Translated by Michael Turnbull.

**Wort**

Payer, Micha. 2022.

**Wissen**

Payer, Micha. 2022.

LITERATUR


Auinger, Thomas. „Wissen, Anerkennung und implizite Normativität.“ In *Wie entsteht Wissen? Mitteilungen des Instituts für Wissenschaft und Kunst*, Nr. 3–4, Wien, 2005.

Braidotti, Rosi. *Posthuman Knowledge.* Cambridge: Polity Press, 2019.

Braidotti, Rosi. *Posthumanismus: Leben jenseits des Menschen.* Übersetzt von Thomas Laugstien. Frankfurt am Main: Campus, 2014.

Burke, Peter. *A Social History of Knowledge: From Gutenberg to Diderot.* Cambridge: Polity, 2008.

Burke, Peter. *A Social History of Knowledge: From the Encyclopédie to Wikipedia.* Cambridge: Polity, 2018.

Burke, Peter. *The Polymath: A Cultural History from Leonardo da Vinci to Susan Sontag.* London: Yale University Press, 2020.

Diderot, Denis. „Enzyklopädie.“ In *Die Welt der Encyclopédie*, ediert von Anette Selg und Rainer Wieland, herausgegeben von Hans Magnus Enzensberger. Frankfurt am Main: Eichborn, 2001.

Engelhardt, Anina, und Kajetzke, Laura, Herausgeber. *Handbuch Wissensgesellschaft: Theorien, Themen und Probleme.* Bielefeld: Transcript, 2010.

Foucault, Michel. „Die Ordnung der Dinge: Eine Archäologie der Humanwissenschaften.“ In *Michel Foucault: Die Hauptwerke.* Übersetzt von Ulrich Köppen. Frankfurt am Main: Suhrkamp, 2016.

Foucault, Michel. „Überwachen und Strafen: Die Geburt des Gefängnisses.“ In *Michel Foucault: Die Hauptwerke.* Übersetzt von Ulrich Köppen. Frankfurt am Main: Suhrkamp, 2016.

Foucault, Michel. „Michel Foucault, Gespräch mit Ducio Trombardi.“ In *Michel Foucault: Die Hauptwerke.* Übersetzt von Ulrich Köppen. Frankfurt am Main: Suhrkamp, 2016.

Gettier, Edmund. „Is Justified True Belief Knowledge?“ In *Epistemology: An Anthology,* herausgegeben von Ernest Sosa, Jaegwon Kim, Jeremy Fantl, und Matthew McGrath. Oxford: Blackwell Publishing, 2009.

Ichikawa, Jonathan Jenkins, und Steup, Matthias. „The Analysis of Knowledge.“ In *The Standford Encyclopedia of Philosophy* (Summer 2018 Edition), herausgegeben von Edward N. Zalta. https://plato.stanford.edu/archives/sum2018/entries/knowledge-analysis/

Marquard, Odo. *Apologie des Zufälligen: Philosophische Studien.* Stuttgart: Reclam, 2013.

Siegel, Steffen. *Tabula: Figuren der Ordnung um 1600.* Berlin: Akademie Verlag, 2009.

Sosa, Ernest. „Knowing Full Well: The Normativity of Beliefs as Performances.“ In *Disputatio: Philosophical Research Bulletin 4:5* (2015) http://gredos.usal.es/jspui/handle/10366/129333.

Sosa, Ernest. „The Place of Truth in Epistemology.“ In *Epistemology: An Anthology.* Oxford: Blackwell Publishing, 2009.

Theweleit, Klaus. *Warum Cortés wirklich siegte: Technologiegeschichte der eurasisch-amerikanischen Kolonialismen.* Berlin: Matthes & Seitz, 2020.


**Wort**

Payer, Micha. 2022.

**Zufall**


Marquard, Odo. *Apologie des Zufälligen: Philosophische Schriften.* Stuttgart: Reclam, 2013.


**Knowledge**

Payer, Micha. 2022. Translated by Michael Turnbull.

LITERATURE


Braidotti, Rosi. *The Posthuman.* Cambridge: Polity Press, 2013.

Braidotti, Rosi. *Posthuman Knowledge.* Cambridge: Polity Press, 2019.

Burke, Peter. *A Social History of Knowledge: From Gutenberg to Diderot.* Cambridge: Polity, 2008.

Burke, Peter. *A Social History of Knowledge: From the Encyclopédie to Wikipedia.* Cambridge: Polity, 2018.

Burke, Peter. *The Polymath: A Cultural History from Leonardo da Vinci to Susan Sontag.* London: Yale University Press, 2020.

Diderot, Denis. *Encyclopédie.* Quoted from Caspar Henderson. *The Book of Barely Imagined Beings.* Cambridge: Granta, 2012.

Engelhardt, Anina, and Laura Kajetzke, editors. *Handbuch Wissensgesellschaft: Theorien, Themen und Probleme.* Bielefeld: Transcript, 2010.

Engelhardt, Anina, and Laura Kajetzke. “Leben wir in einer Wissensgesellschaft?” In *Aus Politik und Zeitgeschichte,* April 2013. www.bpb.de/shop/zeitschriften/apuz/158659/leben-wir-in-einer-wissensgesellschaft/

Foucault, Michel. *Discipline and Punish: The Birth of the Prison.* Translated by Alan Sheridan, 1977. New York: Random House, 1995.

Foucault, Michel. *Remarks on Marx: Conversations with Ducio Trombardi.* Translated by R. James Goldstein and James Cascaito. New York: Semiotext(e), 1991.

Foucault, Michel. *The Order of Things: An Archaeology of the Human Sciences.* New York: Pantheon Books, 1971.

Gettier, Edmund. “Is Justified True Belief Knowledge?” In *Epistemology: An Anthology.* Edited by Ernest Sosa, Jaegwon Kim, Jeremy Fantl, and Matthew McGrath. Oxford: Blackwell Publishing, 2009.

Ichikawa, Jonathan Jenkins, and Matthias Steup. “The Analysis of Knowledge.” In *The Stanford Encyclopedia of Philosophy.* Edited by Edward N. Zalta, summer 2018. https://plato.stanford.edu//archives/sum2018/entries/knowledge analysis/

Marquard, Odo. *In Defense of the Accidental: Philosophical Studies.* Translated by Robert M. Wallace. Oxford: Oxford University Press, 1991.

Plato. “Theaetetus.” In *The Dialogues of Plato.* Vol. 4. Translated by Benjamin Jowett. Oxford: Oxford University Press, 1892.

Siegel, Steffen. *Tabula: Figuren der Ordnung um 1600.* Berlin: Akademie Verlag, 2009.

Sosa, Ernest. “Knowing Full Well: The Normativity of Beliefs as Performances.” In *Disputatio. Philosophical Research Bulletin,* 4:5, 2015. http://gredos.usal.es/jspui handle/103 66/129333.

Sosa, Ernest. “The Place of Truth in Epistemology.” In *Epistemology: An Anthology.* Oxford: Blackwell Publishing, 2009.

Theweleit, Klaus. *Warum Cortés wirklich siegte: Technologiegeschichte der eurasisch-amerikanischen Kolonialismen.* Berlin: Matthes & Seitz, 2020.


**Word**

Payer, Micha. 2022. Translated by Michael Turnbull.

**The Accidental**


Marquard, Odo. *In Defense of the Accidental: Philosophical Studies.* Translated by Robert M Wallace. Oxford: Oxford University Press, 1991.

# Impressum
# Imprint

Payer Gabriel
Micha Payer and Martin Gabriel, A-Vienna
www.payergabriel.com

With contributions by Khadija von Zinnenburg Carroll, Byung-Chul Han, Bruno Latour, Odo Marquard, and Micha Payer

Concept: Micha Payer

Project Management "Edition Angewandte" on behalf of the University of Applied Arts Vienna: Barbara Wimmer, A-Vienna

Content and Production Editor on behalf of the Publisher: Katharina Holas, A-Vienna

Translation from German into English: Michael Turnbull, DE-Berlin

Translation from English into German: Wilfried Prantner, A-Techelsberg

Translation from Latin into German: Doris Vickers, A-Vienna

Proofreading/copyediting German: Martin Gastl, A-Vienna

Proofreading/copyediting English: Michael Turnbull, DE-Berlin

Peer review: Ruth Anderwald, Leonhard Grond, Luciano Parodi, Edith Payer, Andreas Rumpfhuber, and Ferdinand Schmatz

Layout, cover design, and typography: Nik Thoenen, Hannah Sakai, A-Vienna

Image editing: Pascal Petignat, Nik Thoenen, A-Vienna

Printing: Holzhausen, the book-printing brand of Gerin Druck GmbH, A-Wolkersdorf

Paper: Arena Bulk 90 g/m², Uniset Supra 80 g/m², Colorplan 300 g/m²

Typeface: Lexik



Library of Congress Control Number: 2022948065

Bibliographic information published by the German National Library

The German National Library lists this publication in the Deutsche Nationalbibliografie; detailed bibliographic data are available on the Internet at http://dnb.dnb.de.



ISSN 1866-248X
ISBN 978-3-11-106624-0
e-ISBN (PDF) 978-3-11-106658-5



www.degruyter.com

Printed with the financial support of Bundesministerium für Kunst, Kultur, öffentlichen Dienst und Sport and Kulturabteilung der Stadt Wien

Bundesministerium
Kunst, Kultur,
öffentlicher Dienst und Sport

Stadt Wien | Kultur